Accession no.
36124751

KU-364-379

WITHDRAWN

Cognitive Sociolinguistics

Cognitive Linguistics Research
39

Editors
Dirk Geeraerts
René Dirven
John R. Taylor

Honorary editor
Ronald W. Langacker

Mouton de Gruyter
Berlin · New York

Cognitive Sociolinguistics

Language Variation, Cultural Models, Social Systems

Edited by
Gitte Kristiansen
René Dirven

LIS LIBRARY
Date 25/06/10 Fund la
Order No 2138785
University of Chester

Mouton de Gruyter
Berlin · New York

Mouton de Gruyter (formerly Mouton, The Hague)
is a Division of Walter de Gruyter GmbH & Co. KG, Berlin

♾ Printed on acid-free paper
which falls within
the guidelines of the ANSI
to ensure permanence and durability.

Library of Congress Cataloging-in-Publication Data

Cognitive sociolinguistics : language variation, cultural models, social systems / edited by Gitte Kristiansen and René Dirven.
p. cm. – (Cognitive linguistics research ; 39)
Includes bibliographical references and index.
ISBN 978-3-11-019625-2 (hardcover : alk. paper)
1. Sociolinguistics. 2. Cognitive grammar – Social aspects.
I. Kristiansen, Gitte, 1966– II. Dirven, René.
P40.C548 2008
306.44–dc22
2008040566

Bibliographic information published by the Deutsche Nationalbibliothek

The Deutsche Nationalbibliothek lists this publication in the Deutsche Nationalbibliografie; detailed bibliographic data are available in the Internet at http://dnb.d-nb.de.

ISBN 978-3-11-019625-2
ISSN 1861-4132

© Copyright 2008 by Walter de Gruyter GmbH & Co. KG, D-10785 Berlin

All rights reserved, including those of translation into foreign languages. No part of this book may be reproduced or transmitted in any form or by any means, electronic or mechanical, including photocopy, recording, or any information storage and retrieval system, without permission in writing from the publisher.

Typesetting: Meta Systems, Wustermark
Printed in Germany

Acknowledgments

The idea for this volume originated at the 30th International LAUD Symposium, at which some of the present contributions were originally presented. We would like to express our gratitude to all of the contributors for their comprehensive cooperation and for responding with professionalism to all the requests that have been made of them, including extensive reviewing and lengthy processes of refereeing.

Furthermore, our sincere thanks go to the staff at Mouton de Gruyter for handling the manuscript in a most efficient way. Warm thanks go specifically to Anke Beck for helpful advice and for her interest in this project, to Birgit Sievert for her professional expertise and support, and to Wolfgang Konwitschny who guided us through the production process in a very meticulous way.

Table of contents

Introduction
Cognitive Sociolinguistics: Rationale, methods and scope

Gitte Kristiansen and René Dirven

1. Why do we need a Cognitive Sociolinguistics?

Nine years ago Langacker (1999: 376) programmatically emphasised the necessity of extending Cognitive Linguistics to the areas of discourse and social interaction:

> Articulating the dynamic nature of conceptual and grammatical structure leads us inexorably to the dynamics of discourse and social interaction. While these too have been part of Cognitive Grammar from the very onset, they have certainly not received the emphasis they deserve.

In a similar vein, a series of scholars whose research likewise falls within the discipline of Cognitive Linguistics have in recent years repeatedly advocated the need for approaches which would bring the objects of study and the methodologies employed in sociolinguistics and Cognitive Linguistics closer together, and, more importantly, these researchers have taken important steps in the direction of an empirically validated investigation into the social dimensions of linguistic variation.

At the beginning of the new millenium, in other words, a heightened awareness regarding the social aspects of linguistic variation on the one hand, and the necessity of implementing – even developing – the right methodological tools on the other hand, match an already existing trend of research. For examples of descriptively and methodologically oriented studies, see many of the contributions in Dirven, Frank and Pütz (2003), Dirven (2005), Geeraerts (2005), the theme session on lectal categorization and lectal variation celebrated at ICLC9 in Seoul, and the theme session on Cognitive Sociolinguistics at ICLC10 in Kraków. On a more programmatic level, see Sinha (2007) on language as an epigenetic system, Zlatev (2005) on situated embodiment, Itkonen (2003) on the social nature of the linguistic system, Croft (forthcoming) on social interaction, Verhagen (2005) on the role of intersubjectivity, Harder (2003) and Bernárdez (2008) on typology, variation and cognition. We can thus now rightfully speak of a *Cognitive Sociolinguistics*. This volume testifies of such rich empirical and theoretical work and gives proof of an already vigorous cognitive-sociolinguistic strand inside the wider Cognitive Linguistics paradigm.

Four decades ago, William Labov objected to the term "sociolinguistics" on the grounds that there could surely be no way of doing linguistics which did not at the same time take social dimensions and social variables duly into account. Hence, the new term was thought to be redundant. Yet, from the perspective of Cognitive Linguistics – a model in which *usage-based* and *non-modularity* are key words and which thrives more than most other theories on interdisciplinary research – the inclusion of the term Cognitive Sociolinguistics is far from arbitrary. There are many good reasons why the type of studies included in the present volume should be brought together under the same descriptive heading. Let us mention just a few of them.

In the first place, as we just pointed out, the volume brings together various approaches from a burgeoning – but still fragmented – area of research. As such, it coins at the level of book title what is already a practice in several established schools and, in a less condensed and more scattered manner, in many other academic environments in many parts of the world. The volume will serve to show commonalities between these approaches and help those present and future scholars who embrace a socio-cognitive conception of language to better situate their reseach and to define their work in more precise terms.

In the second place, the volume – the first to bear the title *Cognitive Sociolinguistics* – contributes to establishing an interdisciplinary link between sociolinguists and practitioners of CL. In fact, we very much hope that the content will be equally appealing to sociolinguists and cognitive linguists. It is not uncommon to engage in conversation at a conference with scholars with a specific interest in cultural linguistics or sociolinguistics and discover that the term *cognitive linguistics* is still strongly associated with first generation (i.e. Chomskyan) cognitivism – and hard as one may try to explain the fact that the two disciplines share little more than the common denominator *cognitive*, these beliefs more often than not turn out to be very deep-rooted. Conversely, those scholars who are anxious to see how social variation is dealt with in grammatical theories that take an inherent interest in cognitive processes and contextualised meaning, and which cannot commit themselves to the Chomskyan belief in the homogeneity of language, have unfortunately so far not had access to a representative volume. This survey of current research and possible inroads will hopefully serve to bridge the gap.

In the third place, it is firmly believed that Cognitive Linguistics itself will unescapably benefit from turning its attention towards variational and interactionist linguistics. For a start, there is still a widespread tendency within Cognitive Linguistics towards studies based on the written production of standardised varieties, but a truly usage-based Cognitive Linguistics cannot ignore the qualitative and quantitative variation to be found within the standard and non-standard varieties of a language. It cannot afford, in other words, to work around language at the almost Chomskyan level of homogeneous speech communities. A usage-based linguistics takes language as it is actually used by real speakers in real situations in a specific historical moment as the basis of its enquiry. As a logical consequence of this fact, Cognitive Linguistics needs to employ empirical methods capable of dealing in adequate ways with social variation: methods that conform to the traditionally high standards of sociolinguistic research and which are capable of distinguishing between social and conceptual types of variability. As argued by Geeraerts (2005: 168–182), Cognitive Linguistics will not only have to come to terms with the fact that social variation systematically appears in the raw linguistic data brought under scrutiny, but also with the fact that the only way to systematically deal with variation which comprises a variety of different social dimensions inevitably involves a solid, empirical analysis. In short, social implies empirical, and empirical implies social.

Furthermore, it is very natural for a fundamentally usage-based discipline such as Cognitive Linguistics to opt for "context" as a key word. After all, just like sociolinguistics and pragmatics, in part it first saw the light as a recontextualising reaction towards a number of very predominant approaches which were reluctant to see language in terms of a social construct and consider cognition in terms of a capacity grounded in social dimensions. These approaches include generativism as a forceful exponent of such a decontextualising trend, and, in a less prominent but still harmful manner, structuralism. The *langue-parole* dichotomy left room for a certain social conception but not at the intermediate level of lectal variation, where the real variationist dance goes on: that part of the scenario where social identities are enacted and where linguistic variants relate to social variables. That part, in short, which ultimately leads to linguistic change. In structuralism, in broad terms, the leap is directly from individual variation to a societally shared code. It is safe to say that none of the opponents to such trends would object to the claim that studying real language in use implies a multivariate type of analysis, involving facets such as user-related variation, situationally determined variability and conceptual motivation. Research that endeavours to unravel, examine and compare social and cognitive dimensions can in a most natural way be subsumed under the cover term Cognitive Sociolinguistics.

2. Scope and organisation of the volume

This volume takes a broad and non-exclusive view on Cognitive Sociolinguistics. To that effect, the contributions included exemplify four different and well-defined areas. The main sections included in this volume cover four major areas: 1) theoretical work on fundamental aspects (in this case semantic and lectal variation), 2) usage-based and corpus-based research on language variation, 3) research on cultural models, and 4) ideology research on sociopolitical and socio-economic systems. Let us briefly spell out in full why these areas deserve special attention.

As a usage-based approach to language, Cognitive Linguistics is bound to be open to sociolinguistic problem areas such as regional and social language variation. Up till now in Cognitive Linguistics, grammatical and lexical studies have mainly focused on the conceptual and referential functions of linguistic symbolisation. Cognitive Sociolinguistics intends to extend the cognitive paradigm into the regional and social patterns involved in linguistic symbolisation, to be studied either as a topic in its own right or parallel to conceptual structure. This focus on the way in which language usage in different regional and social groups is characterised by different conceptualisations, by different grammatical and lexical preferences, and by differences in the salience of particular connotations adds a necessary social dimension to the Cognitive Linguistic enterprise. And as a usage-based approach, Cognitive Linguistics has a very natural basis for sharing concerns with Sociolinguistics. To begin with, far from investigating language form independent of context, cotext, topic and speakers, Cognitive Sociolinguistics naturally puts speakers in their socio-cognitive functioning in the centre of attention. The relationship between society and language has of course been widely examined in the fields of Sociolinguistics and the Social Psychology of Language, but neither discipline has made use of a Cognitive Linguistic explanatory framework. However, it is a working assumption within Cognitive Sociolinguistics that the theoretical framework of CL may serve to 'throw new light on old problems'.

Usage-based variation research is practised, among other centres in the world, by the Leuven school (which implements large corpora and advanced quantitative techniques) and by the group of scholars working around the tools developed by Stefan Th. Gries and Anatol Stefanowitsch (i.e. collostructional analysis).

Cognitive Sociolinguistics is also bound to look into the differentiated conceptual links between language and culture, as laid down in the concept of cognitive cultural models, already initiated in cognitive anthropology by Holland and Quinn (1987) with various linguistic contributions, a.o. by Lakoff/Kövecses, Sweetser, and Kay; further, see Palmer (1996). The present volume contributes to this research by focusing on models underlying language policies and their impact in expert analysis (i.e. analyses by linguists) and in folk perception, alike.

Further, the volume also covers the link between language and the sociopolitical and socio-economic ideologies which permeate the institutional systems that channel and dominate society. In this respect, the book continues the line of research initiated by Lakoff, who in an interview with Pires de Olivera (2000: 43–44) was asked about the existence of a Cognitive Sociolinguistics and answered: "There is a cognitive sociolinguistics in existence, in my *Moral Politics*, in Steven Winter's new book on law and CL, *A Clearing in the Forest*, in the dissertation by Pamela Morgan on political speeches, and in the dissertation by Nancy Urban on business metaphors being used to restructure education." The latter two researchers contribute to this volume with new research results.

As Lakoff's answer confirms, he largely identifies Cognitive Sociolinguistics with ideology research, but Cognitive Sociolinguistics comprises much more than that. This volume brings together various major Cognitive Linguistic inroads into the research areas of Sociolinguistics, and as such, it will not only give more substance and weight to Lakoff's claim, but also widen his view of Cognitive Sociolinguistics considerably.

Now, the broad perspective provided could also easily give the impression that everything that might possibly be included within the confines of Cognitive Sociolinguistics would have the same status within that category. To explain why this is not exactly the case, let us briefly envisage Cognitive Sociolinguistics in terms of a prototype category. As in any other non-classical category, some combinations of features and dimensions are bound to be more central and others more marginal. In this particular case and in the light of the considerations spelled out above, it is safe to say that Cognitive Sociolinguistic research can loosely be characterised as that which a) explores language-internal or cross-linguistic variation of a social origin in its own right or incorporates it into an investigation with other aims, b) draws on the theoretical framework developed in Cognitive Linguistics and c) arrives at its findings by implementing solid empirical methods. The most prototypical contributions will be those that possess all the features of such a combination. Contributions that to varying degrees fail to meet the latter requirement might still be considered as pertaining to the category, but it must not go without saying that they will be much more marginal than those which combine all three characteristics.

3. Overview of the various sections and contributions

3.1. Theoretical aspects: Semantic and lectal variation

The first section explores the necessity of a Cognitive Sociolinguistics from a predominantly theoretical perspective. The social dimensions of semantics and language-internal conceptualisation, it is argued, cannot be neglected in a usage-based model of grammar. Prototype theory, for instance, has been widely accepted and implemented in Cognitive Linguistics, but stereotypicality and normativity have remained as peripheral and ill-defined notions. In the same vein, a number of issues which have traditionally been studied from a sociolinguistic perspective, such as style-shifting and code-shifting, are eminently well-suited for a cognitively oriented type of analysis.

In “Prototypes, stereotypes, and semantic norms”, **Dirk Geeraerts** engages in a comparison of the notions of prototype (Eleanor Rosch) and stereotype (Hilary Putnam) with specific reference to the distribution of meaning within a linguistic community. Geeraerts first argues that prototype-theoretical research should abandon the idea of homogeneous linguistic communities. In the second place, it is observed that the rigid designation and division of linguistic labour associated with Putnam’s theory are logically independent. Hence, the socio-semantic model proposed by Putnam needs to be expanded. The alternative model proposed by Geeraerts involves three types of sociosemantic forces: a semantics of cooperation (underlying prototype-based extensions of meaning as described by Renate Bartsch), a semantics of authority (as in Putnam’s view on the division of linguistic labor), and a semantics of conflict and competition (as when semantic choices are implicitly questioned or explicitly debated).

In "Style-shifting and shifting styles: A socio-cognitive approach to lectal variation" **Gitte Kristiansen** combines variationist and interactionist sociolinguistics (relatively stable speaker-related factors vs. dynamic, situational phenomena) with a series of well-known notions from CL, such as prototype theory and reference point construction, so as to provide a socio-cognitive account of style-shifting. The paper analyses the possible processes and mechanisms by means of which speakers shift towards codes or styles that are different with respect to their own – or form part of their habitual repertoire. The paper progresses in two major steps. Part one centres on the human capacity for accent-based dialect identification and argues that our awareness of linguistic and social categories is experientially grounded and that these are systematically related by means of a metonymic link: LANGUAGE STANDS FOR SOCIAL IDENTITIES. The second part of the paper focuses on a more active type of competence: LANGUAGE IS A TOOL FOR EXPRESSING SOCIAL IDENTITIES.

3.2. Usage-based variation research

Cognitive Linguistics claims to be fundamentally usage-based, but it is often heavy on theory and surprisingly light on method. As Geeraerts (2005) argues, a usage-based linguistics necessarily involves not only a solid empirical method (because it aims at examining actual, non-elicited language behaviour), but also an investigation of the social variation that naturally manifests itself in actual language use, as attested in e.g. large textual corpora.

This section comprises a series of articles by scholars who all employ quantitative corpus analysis in their linguistic research, in accordance with the usually high empirical standards of sociolinguistics. While the first paper serves as a theoretical lead-in by spelling out the intricacies of investigating linguistic variables by means of corpus-based methods and by comparing different methodological approaches, the rest of the chapters are examples of actual case studies based on the use of large textual corpora

The chapter by **Kris Heylen**, **José Tummers** and **Dirk Geeraerts**, entitled "Methodological issues in corpus-based Cognitive Linguistics", contributes to an ongoing discussion about methodological innovation in Cognitive Linguistics. The authors critically review the methodologically most advanced quantitative case studies of syntactic variation and explore the issues that arise when methodological choices have to be made. The paper compares two schools that both endeavour to develop a methodology for empirical research in Cognitive Linguistics based on quantitative analysis of corpus data: the collostructional approach as adopted by Stefan Gries and Anatol Stefanowitsch vs. the methods developed by the research unit Quantitative Lexicology and Variational Linguistics at the University of Leuven, of which the authors form part.

In their chapter, "Channel and constructional meaning: A collostructional case study", **Anatol Stefanowitsch** and **Stefan Th. Gries** respond to the criticism voiced by Heylen at al. in the previous contribution and provide the reader with a number of case studies to exemplify the extent to which variational dimensions such as channel can be incorporated within a collostructional analysis. On the basis of their findings, they conclude that (i) constructions may display channel-specific associations to individual lexical items, (ii) constructions differ with respect to their channel sensitivity, and (iii) the meaning of a given construction does not vary across channels.

In the chapter "National variation in the use of *er* "there". Regional and diachronic constraints on cognitive explanations", **Stefan Grondelaers**, **Dirk Speelman** and **Dirk Geeraerts** question the assumption that there should invariably be a one-to-one relationship between linguistic variation and underlying conceptual mechanisms. By means of multivariate and regression analyses, the authors show that the different distribution of 'er' (there) in adjunct-initial sentences as manifested in the national varieties of Dutch cannot be attributed to functional differences – in both Belgian and Netherlandic Dutch the same human reference point ability govern the usage of 'er' – nor to differences in discursive or syntactic parameters. More plausibly, the authors argue, the cause is related to the delayed linguistic standardisation of Belgian Dutch.

In the last chapter in this section, entitled "Variation in the choice of adjectives in the two main national varieties of Dutch", **Dirk Speelman**, **Stefan Grondelaers** and **Dirk Geeraerts** exemplify the use of a word frequency list based method for comparing corpora, the *stable lexical marker analysis*, by means of a case study on the choice of adjectives in Netherlandic and Belgian Dutch. The findings reveal robust national differences across registers, and robust register differences across nations. The authors conclude that the method of stable lexical markers is a useful exploratory technique for detecting patterns of variation and for identifying different sources of variation.

3.3. Cultural models of language and language policy

Since Holland and Quinn's (1987) seminal publication, only very few publications have systematically pursued the topic of cognitive cultural models. This section limits itself to cultural models in language and language policies, but as the work represented shows, the heading is still quite broad. Scholars in this section explore cultural models underlying attitudes to global languages or towards the use and instruction of foreign languages, investigate how cultural conceptualisations often live on in a newly adopted language, and discuss the cultural adaptations of various instances of World English.

In their contribution, "Rationalist or Romantic models in globalisation", **Frank Polzenhagen** and **René Dirven** analyse views on global languages from a discourse-analytic and metatheoretical perspective. Leaning on Geeraerts (2003), the authors analyse the underlying politico-philosophical positions and conceptions of language in relation to two central competing cognitive cultural models in Western thinking, namely the rationalist model and the romantic model. Polzenhagen and Dirven relate the key arguments made in the debate on global languages to conceptualisations that are characteristic of these two models, in particular to specific metaphoric and metonymic conceptualisations of language, and critically discuss the ideologies inherent in the linguistic reflexes of two models in the current, heated debate on globalisation.

In "A nation is a territory with one culture and one language: The role of metaphorical folk models in language policy debates", **Raphael Berthele** in turn aims at better understanding of the folk cultural models that underlie attitudes towards particular languages. Berthele focuses on two instances of national language ideologies in the Western world: the debates around the use and instruction of foreign languages in the US and in Switzerland. While in the US the contentious issue is whether there is space for more than one official language (namely English), in Switzerland the currently most controversial issue is the space public schooling has to attribute to "non-native" languages, such as English, as opposed to the four national languages. Berthele concludes that the differences in language policy issues cannot simply be boiled down to two or more different choices in metaphors for language. Rather, it is the precise way in which the metaphors are being used which contributes to the opposing ideologies.

The chapter by **Farzad Sharifian**, entitled "Cultural models of Home in Aboriginal children's English" examines the extent to which cultural conceptualisations may vary across ethnic groups, even when the same language is spoken with hardly any difference in pronunciation. By means of the word-association method, Sharifian shows how the lexical item "home" has quite different meanings for Aboriginal and Anglo-Australian children. The results provide evidence for two distinct, but overlapping, conceptual systems among the two cultural groups studied. From a theoretical perspective, Sharifian views distributed, emergent cognition in terms of patterns which result from the interactions between the members of a cultural group but which are not reducible to what is stored in the mind of each individual. Instead, cultural cognition is heterogeneously distributed, constantly negotiated and renegotiated by the members of a cultural group and distributed in people across time and space.

Finally, the contribution by **Hans-Georg Wolf**, "A Cognitive Linguistic approach to the cultures of World Englishes: The emergence of a new model" addresses a similar problem: a common core of English grammar and lexis is used all over the world in the various World Englishes, but the symbolisations these systems express may strongly reflect variety-related conceptualisations. Wolf characterizes the main theoretical approaches and positions within the field of World Englishes and sketches recent developments in Cognitive Linguistics which pave the way for a partial theoretical merger of the two linguistic enterprises. Cognitive Sociolinguistics, Wolf argues, can explain culture-specific patterns like keywords, differences in prototypicality, and conceptualisations realised in these varieties, which descriptivists disregard due to their theoretical outlook or cannot explain because they lack the appropriate methodology.

3.4. Socio-political systems

The last section comprises publications by some of the scholars mentioned by Lakoff in the above-mentioned interview and by renowned researchers into social and political systems from a Cognitive Linguistics perspective.

In her chapter, entitled "Corporate brands as socio-cognitive representations", **Veronika Koller** examines corporate identities in business media discourse. To this end, the study compares earlier work by the author (Koller 2004) on the cognitive construction of corporate identities in business media discourse with a corpus of corporate mission statements as instances of companies' communicated identities (i.e. corporate brands) The methods employed by Koller in tracing these cognitive models include a computer-assisted quantitative analysis and a qualitative systemic-functional analysis. The author concludes that corporate discourse as instantiated in mission statements relies mostly on literalised concepts of partnership and emotion to convey the company's ideal self. Self representation thus entails a move from competitive to cooperative models of business.

In the chapter "Metaphorically speaking: Gender and classroom discourse", **Susan Fiksdal** analyses naturally ocurring discourse on seminar discussions by a group of North American college students. Upon examining the metaphors employed, the author tests Reddy's (1979) formulation of the conduit metaphor, showing in analytical ways how the framework was extended by describing the shape of the discussion metaphorically. 7 metaphor clusters were found that indicate distinct cultural schemas. When the metaphors were categorised by the speakers' gender, the metaphorical expressions used by male students were found to be grounded in the conceptual metaphor SEMINAR IS A GAME. The female students, in turn, predominantly employed expressions grounded in the mapping SEMINAR IS A COMMUNITY. The author concludes that the same goal of collaboration is present in the students' metaphors, regardless of gender, but that gender differences in the formulations highlight different alignments towards the discussion.

The next two chapters go further in the direction of metaphor studies in the Lakovian vein. In the chapter entitled "The business model of the university: Sources and consequences of its construal", **Nancy Urban** examines the models that underlie higher education in the United States. To that end the author elicits a series of metaphorical mappings from a selection of texts, and argues that university education is predominantly and increasingly conceptualised in terms of a business: a service bought and paid for like any other, subject to efficiency and productivity, and restricted to those who can afford it. The central metaphor for understanding the domain of business and the market, Urban explains, comes from a folk model of the Darwinian conception of the natural world and the mechanism of natural selection.

In "Competition, cooperation, and interconnection: 'Metaphor families' and social systems", **Pamela S. Morgan** in turn extracts a wide range of metaphorical mappings in order to examine the relationship of the source and target domains that characterize interactions and systems. Morgan concludes that social systems are conventionally characterized in one of three ways: as competitive, as cooperative, or as an interconnected system. For each of these "metaphor families", it is argued, we have a schematised model and a set of core domains whose stereotypes inherently fit the schema. Although we can logically speaking usually construe the domain into more than one metaphor family, there are nevertheless conventionalised choices: business is viewed competitively with respect to "rival" businesses, but cooperatively with respect to much of its internal structure. Politics is viewed competitively during elections, but cooperatively when forming alliances to achieve common goals. The interconnected systems view is less well developed in most domains.

Finally, in "How cognitive linguists can help to solve political problems" **Karol Janicki** discusses the problem of the use of definitions in the political domain. The author predicts that definitions of words play a significant role in political conflicts and that contemporary politicians are largely unaware of how a non-essentialist approach to language could solve some of their problems. These hypotheses are tested by analytically examining a series of press reports on three political events: the Clinton-Lewinsky scandal, the Florida vote conflict, and the stem cell research debate. When faced with the inadequacy of essentialist definitions, Janicki surprisingly opts for a solution according to which no attempt to define should be made. From the point of view of the editors of this volume, it would be more instructive and more helpful to engage in explanations involving a range of more or less prototypical and more or less peripheral senses – a pool of possibilites from which ideological and pragmatic choices can be made. In spite of this caveat, the case studies included in the present chapter still provide interesting evidence that a non-prototypical conception of categories is a problem in political discourse.

References

Achard, Michel and Suzanne Kemmer (eds.)
2004 *Language, Culture, and Mind.* Stanford, Calif.: CSLI.

Bartsch, Renate
1987 *Norms of Language.* London and New York: Longman.

Bernárdez, Enrique
2008 Collective cognition and individual activity: Variation, language and culture. In: Roslyn M. Frank, René Dirven, Tom Ziemke and Enrique Bernárdez (eds.) *Body, Language and Mind: Sociocultural Situatedness*, 137–166. Cognitive Linguistics Research 35.2. Berlin/ New York: Mouton de Gruyter.

Berthele, Raphael
2002 Static spatial relations in German and Romance. Towards a cognitive dialectology of posture verbs and locative adverbials. *Selected Proceedings of the Methods XI Conference*, Joensuu, Finland.

2003 The typology of motion and posture verbs: a variationist account. In: Bernd Kortmann (ed.), *Dialectology Meets Typology. Dialect Grammar from a Cross-Linguistic Perspective,* 93–126. Berlin/New York.

Croft, William
to appear Toward a social Cognitive Linguistics. In: Vyvyan Evans and Stéphanie Pourcel (eds.), *New Directions in Cognitive Linguistics.* Amsterdam/Philadelphia: Benjamins.

Delbecque, Nicole
2003 *Aproximaciones Cognoscitivo-funcionales al Español.* Foro Hispánico 23. Amsterdam: Rodopi.

Dirven, René
2005 Major strands in Cognitive Linguistics. In: Francisco J. Ruiz de Mendoza Ibáñez and M. Sandra Peña Cervel (eds.), *Cognitive Linguistics: Internal Dynamics and Interdisciplinary Interaction,* 17–68. Cognitive Linguistics Research 32. Berlin/New York: Mouton de Gruyter.

Dirven, René, Roslyn Frank and Martin Pütz (eds.)
2003 *Cognitive Models in Language and Thought. Ideology, Metaphors and Meanings.* Cognitive Linguistic Research 24. Berlin/New York: Mouton de Gruyter.

Dirven, René and Martin Pütz
2004 Der übergeordnete ideologische Rahmen der Sprachkonflikte weltweit. In: Katrin Bromber and Birgit Smieja (eds.), *Globalisation and African Languages: Risks and Benefits,* 9–30. Trends in Linguistics Studies and Monographs 156. Berlin/New York: Mouton de Gruyter.

Eckert, Penelope and John R. Rickford (eds.)
2001 *Style and Sociolinguistic Variation.* Cambridge: Cambridge University Press.

Geeraerts, Dirk
2003 Cultural models of linguistic standardization. In: René Dirven, Martin Pütz and Roslyn Frank (eds.), *Cognitive Models in Language and Thought,* 25–68. Cognitive Linguistics research 24. Berlin/New York: Mouton de Gruyter.

2005 Lectal variation and empirical data in Cognitive Linguistics. In: Francisco J. Ruiz de Mendoza Ibáñez and M. Sandra Peña Cervel (eds.), *Cognitive Linguistics: Internal Dynamics and Interdisciplinary Interaction,* 163–189. Cognitive Linguistics Research 32. Berlin/New York: Mouton de Gruyter.

2007 Cognitive sociolinguistics and the sociology of Cognitive Linguistics. *Annual Review of Cognitive Linguistics* 5: 289–305.

Geeraerts, Dirk and Stefan Grondelaers
1995 Looking back at anger: Cultural traditions and metaphorical patterns. In: John R. Taylor and Robert E. MacLaury (eds.), *Language and Cognitive Construal of the World,* 153–180. Trends in Linguis-

tics, Studies and Monographs 82. Berlin/New York: Mouton de Gruyter.

Geeraerts, Dirk, Stefan Grondelaers and Peter Bakema
1994 *The Structure of Lexical Variation. Meaning, and Context.* Berlin/New York: Mouton de Gruyter.

Gries, Stefan Th.
2003 Grammatical variation in English: A question of 'structure vs. function'? In: Günter Rohdenburg and Britta Mondorf (eds.), *Determinants of Grammatical Variation in English*, 155–173. Berlin/New York: Mouton de Gruyter.
2004 Isn't that fantabulous? How similarity motivates intentional morphological blends in English. In: Michel Achard and Suzanne Kemmer (eds.), *Language, Culture, and Mind,* 415–428. Stanford, CA: CSLI.

Gries, Stefan Th. and Anatol Stefanowitsch
2004a Extending collostructional analysis: A corpus-based perspective on 'alternations'. *International Journal of Corpus Linguistics* 9.1: 97–129.
2004b Co-varying collexemes in the *into*-causative. In: Michel Achard and Suzanne Kemmer (eds.), *Language, Culture, and Mind*, 225–236. Stanford, CA: CSLI.

Grondelaers, Stefan and Dirk Speelman
2001 Noord/Zuid-variatie in het gebruik van *er. Over Taal* 40/3: 51–55.

Grondelaers, Stefan, Marc Brysbaert, Dirk Speelman and Dirk Geeraerts
2002 "Er als accessibility marker: on- en offline evidentie voor een procedurele interpretatie van presentatieve zinnen." Gramma/TTT 9/1, 1–22.

Grondelaers, Stefan, Dirk Speelman and Dirk Geeraerts
2002 Regressing on *er.* Statistical analysis of texts and language variation. In: A. Morin & P. Sébillot (eds.) *6ièmes Journées internationales d'Analyse statistique des Données Textuelles – 6th International Conference on Textual Data Statistical Analysis*, 335–346. Rennes: Institut National de Recherche en Informatique et en Automatique.

Halliday, Michael. A. K.
1978 *Language as Social Semiotic.* London: Edward Arnold.

Harder, Peter
2003 The status of linguistics facts: Rethinking the relation between cognition, social institution and utterance from a functional point of view. *Mind and Language* 18: 52–76.

Hogg, Michael A. and Deborah J. Terry
2000 Social identity and self-categorization processes in organizational contexts. *Academy of Management Review* 25 (1): 121–140.

Holland, Dorothy and Naomi Quinn
1987 *Cultural Models in Language and Thought.* Cambridge: Cambridge University Press.

Itkonen, Esa
2003 *What is Language? A Study in the Philosophy of Linguistics*. Turku: Åbo Akademis tryckeri.
Janicki, Karol
1990 *Toward Non-Essentialist Sociolinguistics*. Berlin/New York: Mouton de Gruyter.
2006 *Language Misconceived. Arguing for Applied Cognitive Linguistics*. Mahwah, New Jersey: Lawrence Erlbaum.
Janssen, Theo and Gisela Redeker (eds.)
1999 *Cognitive Linguistics: Foundations, Scope, and Methodology*. Berlin: Mouton de Gruyter.
Koller, Veronika
2004 *Metaphor and Gender in Business Media Discourse: A Critical Cognitive Study*. Basingstoke: Palgrave Macmillan.
Kristiansen, Gitte
2001 Social and linguistic stereotyping: A cognitive approach to accents. *Estudios Ingleses de la Universidad Complutense*, 9: 129–145.
2003 How to do things with allophones: Linguistic stereotypes as cognitive reference points in social cognition. In: René Dirven, Martin Pütz and Roslyn Frank (eds.), *Cognitive Models in Language and Thought*. CLR 24, 69–120. Berlin/New York: Mouton de Gruyter.
2006 Towards a usage-based cognitive phonology. *International Journal of English Studies* 6 (2): 107–140.
Labov, William
1994 *Principles of Linguistic Change*. Volume I: Internal Factors. Oxford: Basil Blackwell.
2001 *Principles of Linguistic Change*. Volume 2: Social factors. Oxford: Blackwell.
Lakoff, George
1992 Metaphor and war: The metaphor system used to justify war in the Gulf. In: Martin Pütz (ed.), *Thirty Years of Linguistic Evolution: Studies in Honour of René Dirven*, 463–481. Amsterdam/Philadelphia: Benjamins.
1996a The metaphor system for morality. In: Adele E. Goldberg (ed.), *Conceptual Structure, Discourse and Language*, 249–266. Stanford, Calif.: CSLI Publications.
1996b Moral Politics: What Conservatives Know that Liberals Don't. Chicago, Ill.: University of Chicago Press.
2002 *Moral Politics: How Liberals and Conservatives Think* (2nd edition). Chicago: University of Chicago Press.
Lambert, Wallace E., Richard Hodgson, Robert C. Gardner and Samuel Fillenbaum
1960 Evaluational reactions to spoken languages. *Journal of Abnormal and Social Psychology* 60: 44–51.
Langacker, Ronald W.
1993 Reference point constructions. *Cognitive Linguistics* 4 (1), 1–38.

1999 *Grammar and Conceptualization*. Berlin/New York: Mouton de Gruyter.

Morgan, Pamela S.
1997 Self-presentation in a speech of Newt Gingrich. *Pragmatics* 7: 275–308.
2000 The semantics of an impeachment. In: René Dirven, Roslyn Frank and Cornelia Ilie (eds.), *Language and Ideology. Volume II: Descriptive Cognitive Approaches*, 77–106. Amsterdam/ Philadelphia: Benjamins.

Pires de Olivera, Roberta
2001 Language and ideology: An interview with George Lakoff. In: René Dirven, Bruce Hawkins and Esra Sandikcioglu (eds.), *Language and Ideology. Volume I: Theoretical Cognitive Approaches*, 23–47. Amsterdam/Philadelphia: Benjamins.

Preston, Dennis (ed.)
1999 *Handbook of Perceptual Dialectology*. Amsterdam/Philadelphia: Benjamins.

Palmer, Gary B.
1996 *Toward a Theory of Cultural Linguistics*. Austin: University of Texas Press.

Putnam, Hilary
1975 The Meaning of 'Meaning'. In: Keith Gunderson (ed.) *Language, Mind, and Knowledge*, 131–193. Minneapolis: Minnesota.

Sharifian, Farzad
2002 Conceptual-Associative System in Aboriginal English. Edith Cowan University, Perth, Western Australia: Unpublished Ph.D. dissertation.
2003 On cultural conceptualisations. *Journal of Cognition and Culture* (3) 3: 187–207.

Sinha, Chris
2007 Cognitive linguistics, psychology and cognitive science. In: Dirk Geeraerts and Hubert Cuyckens (eds.), *Handbook of Cognitive Linguistics*, 1266–1294. New York: Oxford University Press.

Soares da Silva, Augusto
2006 *O Mundo dos Sentidos em Português. Polissemia, Semântica e Cognição*. Coimbra: Edições Almedina.

Speelman, Dirk, Stefan Grondelaers and Dirk Geeraerts
2003 Profile-based linguistic uniformity as a generic method for comparing language varieties. *Computers and the Humanities* 37: 317–337.

Stefanowitsch, Anatol
2004 Happiness in English and German: A metaphorical-pattern analysis. In: Achard, Michel and Suzanne Kemmer (eds.), *Language, Culture, and Mind*, 137–150. Stanford: CSLI.

Trudgill, Peter
2002 *Sociolinguistic Variation and Change*. Washington D.C.: Georgetown University Press.

Urban, Nancy Y.
1999 The school business: Rethinking educational reform, Department of Linguistics, University of California at Berkeley: Ph.D. dissertation.

Verhagen, Arie
2005 *Constructions and Intersubjectivity: Discourse, Syntax, and Cognition.* Oxford: Oxford University Press.

Verhagen, Arie and Jeroen van de Weijer (eds.)
2003 *Usage-based Approaches to Dutch.* Utrecht: LOT.

Winter, Steven L.
2001 *A Clearing in the Forest: Law, Life, and Mind.* Chicago: University of Chicago Press.

Wolf, Hans-Georg and Frank Polzenhagen
2003 Conceptual metaphor as ideological stylistic means: An exemplary analysis. In: René Dirven, Roslyn Frank and Martin Pütz (eds.), *Cognitive Models in Language and Thought: Ideologies, Metaphors, and Meanings.* Berlin/New York: Mouton de Gruyter.

Zlatev, Jordan
2005 What's in a schema? Bodily Mimesis and the grounding of language. In: Beate Hampe (ed.), *From Perception to Meaning: Image Schemas in Cognitive Linguistics*, 313–342. Cognitive Linguistics Research 29. Berlin/New York: Mouton de Gruyter.

Part one

Theoretical aspects: Semantic and lectal variation

Prototypes, stereotypes, and semantic norms

Dirk Geeraerts

Abstract

The relationship between the concept of prototype as popularized by Eleanor Rosch and the concept of stereotype as defined by Hilary Putnam remains largely unexplored in the context of Cognitive Linguistics. The present paper is devoted to a comparison of both notions, with specific reference to the distribution of meaning in a linguistic community, i.e. to the notion of semantic norms. First, it is argued that prototype-theoretical research should abandon the naive idea of a completely homogeneous linguistic community. Second, it is shown that rigid designation and the division of linguistic labor (as associated with Putnam's approach) are logically independent, which means that Putnam's proposal for a sociosemantic theory needs to be amended. Third, an attempt is made to define a sociosemantic model that realistically expands Putnam's approach. The model takes into account three different types of sociosemantic forces: a semantics of cooperation (underlying prototype-based extensions of meaning as described by Renate Bartsch), a semantics of authority (as in Putnam's view on the division of linguistic labor), and a semantics of conflict and competition (as when semantic choices are implicitly questioned or explicitly debated).

Keywords: prototype, stereotype, semantic norm, sociosemantics, division of linguistic labor, cooperation, authority, semantic conflict, rigid designation.

1. Bill Clinton as a cognitive semantician

When Bill Clinton gave his testimony to the Grand Jury, arguing that he did not have sexual relations with Monica Lewinsky, his argumentation took a decidedly semantic turn. He admits that there were certain occasions in 1996 and 1997 when he was alone with Ms Lewinsky and engaged in "conduct that was wrong", but "these encounters did not consist of sexual intercourse. They did not constitute sexual relations as I understood that term to be defined at my January 17th, 1998 deposition". So what would that definition be? All through the testimony, Clinton uses a restrictive interpretation of *sexual relation*. A case in point is the following excerpt from the beginning of the testimony.

> CLINTON: I thought the definition included any activity by the person being deposed, where the person was the actor and came in contact with those parts of the bodies with the purpose or intent of gratification, and excluded any other activity. For example, kissing is not covered by that, I don't think.
> QUESTION: Did you understand the definition to be limited to sexual activity?
> CLINTON: Yes, I understood the definition to be limited to, to physical contact with those areas of the bodies with the specific intent to arouse or gratify. That's what I understood it to be.
> (This and following quotations are taken from the transcripts as found on the Washington Post website.)

Further on in the testimony, Clinton is questioned about Lewinsky's earlier affidavit that she had had no sexual relationship with the president. What definition could Lewinsky have used? Clinton points out that there is a common understanding of *sexual relationship* as implying intercourse:

> I believe at the time that she filled out this affidavit, if she believed that the definition of sexual relationship was two people having intercourse, then this is accurate. And I believe that is the definition that most ordinary Americans would give it.
> If you said Jane and Harry have a sexual relationship, and you're not talking about people being drawn into a lawsuit and being given definitions, and then a great effort to trick them in some way, but you are just talking about people in ordinary conversations, I'll bet the grand jurors, if they were talking about two people they know, and said they have a sexual relationship, they meant they were sleeping together; they meant they were having intercourse together.

From the point of view of Cognitive Semantics and a prototype-theoretical conception of semantic structure, the tension between the questions of the Grand Jury and Clinton's line of defence is perfectly interpretable. The Grand Jury takes a broad, perhaps even schematic view of the category, in the sense in which any type of sexual activity might be the basis for talking about a sexual relationship. Conversely, Clinton takes a restrictive view by focusing on intercourse as the prototype case of sexual activity, in the sense in which at least, though not exclusively, intercourse has to be present. Restricting the category to the prototype allows Clinton to specify intercourse as a necessary and sufficient condition for a sexual relationship. The view of the grand jurors, on the other hand, seems to encompass the full range of the prototype concept, including less prototypical forms of sexual activity as characteristic of a sexual relationship.

The semantic agility of president Clinton does not stop there. Elsewhere in the testimony, he exploits the spatial vagueness of the term *alone* (is he alone with Ms Lewinsky when they are the only people in the Oval Office but when there are other people present in the White House?), and there is also some discussion about the temporal range of the present continuous. (For an in-depth analysis of the Clinton testimony, see Morgan (2001). She makes clear that the semantic issues involved in the debate extend to definitions of speech acts such as *apology* and *lie*, and the legal definition of *perjury*.) The lesson to be learned from a theoretical point of view is clear, though: the semantic diversity of a prototype-theoretical concept is not just the basis for the communicative flexibility of lexical categories, but it may also lead to conflicts about the interpretation of words – about the *correct* interpretation of words, to be more precise. Communicatively speaking, semantic flexibility and diversity may not only help, they may also hinder, when they engender interpretative conflicts.

Such conflicts have only received a restricted amount of interest from Cognitive Linguistics. Karol Janicki in particular, in a number of publications (1987, 1999, 2003) has pointed out that the non-essentialist conception that is inherent in prototype theory (and a number of other semantic theories) provides an interesting framework for talking about linguistic misunderstanding and conflict. The recognition that language users may define words differently implies not just that there is no one correct definition, but also that conflicts may arise. Janicki, however, devotes surprisingly little attention to the way in which such conflicts may get resolved: are there any norms at all that come into play when interpretations clash? Janicki tends to blame essentialism as such (the belief that there is an essential reading to any term in the language) for the emergence of conflicts, but clearly, the Clinton case would not be solved if all parties concerned were simply to agree, in a non-essentialist metalinguistic stance, that *sexual relationship* may receive different interpretations: the question which interpretation to adhere to in the circumstances would still arise, and there would be no need for norms settling the issue. Referring to the debates that were held in the Polish parliament about the legal status of abortion, Janicki (2003) notes that both the pro-lifers and the pro-choicers take an essentialist stance: the former claim that legalizing abortion violates human rights, viz. the rights of unborn children, whereas the latter equally argue that legalizing abortion violates human rights, viz. the rights of women. Both try to make the notion of human rights more precise than it usually is – and, in Janicki's view, than it intrinsically and irremediably is. But if such a position implies that making a concept more precise is never possible nor perhaps even required, how could conflicts be settled at all? How would it be possible at all that every once in a while, people do agree on a more precise interpretation?

An approach that does address these issues (albeit a decidedly essentialist one) is the theory developed by the philosopher Hilary Putnam (1975, 1979, 1999), whose views on the "linguistic division of labor" constitute one of the theoretically most articulate (and certainly one of the best known) conceptions of the socially normative aspects of meaning. In this paper, a prototype-theoretical conception of meaning will be compared with Putnam's theory. The point of departure is Putnam's notion of "stereotype", which bears a superficial resemblance to the notion of "prototype". The argumentation proceeds in three steps. First, Putnam's approach is presented. Second, prototypicality and Putnamian stereotypicality are compared, the crucial point being that prototypicality is basically a psychological notion, whereas stereotypicality is a sociolinguistic notion. However, there are various reasons why this initial comparison, which seems to suggest a useful complementarity between the two approaches, is somewhat misleading and should be supplemented with a more thorough analysis. The third step, then, argues that Putnam's conception of a division of linguistic labor, however important it may be as an addition to the indifference of much prototype-theoretical work to the social aspects of meaning, itself needs to be refined. Next to the division of linguistic labor, other forces have to be identified as shaping the social dynamics of meaning – including conflicts of interest as represented by the Clinton example.

The gist of the present paper goes back to Geeraerts (1982, 1985: 160–165), where an initial attempt was made to compare stereotypicality and prototypicality, and more specifically to Geeraerts (1989: 163–173), where the necessity of an extended conception of the social dynamics of meaning, comprising the three types of social semantics that will be mentioned in paragraph 4, was first described.

2. Rigid designation, stereotypes, and the division of linguistic labor

Let us first present Putnam's conception of meaning as expounded in his highly influential paper "The meaning of meaning" (1975). Three concepts are crucial: the theory of rigid designation, the division of linguistic labor, and the notion of stereotype.

The core of Putnam's argumentation is an attack on the intensionalist view of meaning. According to Putnam, this view rests on two major tenets: first, the assumption that knowing the meaning of an expression is a particular psychological state, and second, the view that the intension (the meaning) of an expression determines its extension (its referent). He then goes on to show that both assumptions cannot be maintained at the same time, because there are situations in which two individuals are in the same psychological state, i.e. attach the same intension to an expression, but nevertheless refer to different extensions. A fictitious 'Twin Earth' serves to give an example of such a situation. Twin Earth resembles earth in all respects, except for the fact that what we call *water* is represented on Twin Earth by a liquid that has the same appearance and properties as earthly water, but that does not have the chemical composition H_2O. Rather, its chemical composition is very complex; it is symbolized by the formula *XYZ*. Putnam further argues as follows.

The expression *water* has a different extension on earth than on Twin Earth, because the set of molecules referred to by the formula *XYZ* is distinct from the set of molecules referred to by H_2O. Now, imagine that Twin Earth is visited by a human being A who is living around 1750, and who is therefore unaware of the fact that one molecule of (earthly) water consists of two molecules of hydrogen and one molecule of oxygen. In analogous circumstances, a native B of Twin Earth visits the earth. Because the only difference between the liquids referred to by *water* on both planets is not yet discovered, A and B have the same convictions and beliefs with regard to the liquids in question; they are in the same psychological state. Still, the extensions of *water* in English and Twin English differ: A refers to H_2O, and B to *XYZ*. In this way, Putnam exemplifies that the two crucial assumptions of intensionalism mentioned above need not always be true simultaneously.

Putnam then suggests that it is not the intension, but the internal essence of a category that determines the use of the expression referring to that category. If a human observer would be able to make out that *XYZ* isn't really H_2O, terminologies would have to change. Following Kripke (1972), Putnam defends the thesis that natural kind terms such as *water* are *rigid designators*; because they implicitly refer to one and the same, uniquely determined category with one and the same internal essence, they more or less function like proper names, which refer to one and the same individual, regardless of what is intensionally known about that individual. Natural kind terms refer to a class of entities that share a particular hidden structure (such as H_2O or *XYZ*).

However, not all members of a linguistic community are required to know the hidden structure of the extension of an expression of their language. A *division of linguistic labor* ensures that there are societal experts who know that water is H_2O, that there is a difference between pyrites and gold, what the specific differences between elms and beeches are, and so on. On the other hand, laymen attune their own linguistic usage to that of the expert scientists and technicians. The members of the non-specialized group are not required to have expert knowledge, but they are supposed to know the *stereotype* connected with a category if they are to be regarded as full-fledged members of the linguistic community. A stereotype is a socially determined minimum set of data with regard to the extension of a category. For the category *water* (H_2O), the stereotype includes the information that it refers to a natural kind that is a colorless, transparent, tasteless, thirst-quenching liquid that boils at 100° Celsius and that freezes when the temperature drops below 0° Celsius. For the natural kind *tiger (Felis tigris)*, the stereotype includes the information that it is a yellowish, black-striped, catlike, dangerous predatory animal.

The two crucial aspects of Putnam's views are also known under other names than the ones used in the previous lines. The rigid designation theory is know as *semantic externalism* (meanings are external, i.e. not in the head), and the division of linguistic labor is known as *semantic deference* (in order to decide on questions of meaning, we defer the question to experts).

3. Stereotypes and/or prototypes?

Given Putnam's theory as described in the previous paragraph, could it be linked in any relevant way to the prototypical rather than stereotypical conception of semantic structure that is customary in Cognitive Linguistics? The question arises naturally from the recognition that stereotypes bear a certain relationship to the prototypes (i.e. the core cases of a prototypically structured category) of Cognitive Linguistics. Stereotypes and prototypes alike involve semantic information that is salient within a category but that is not sufficient to adequately characterize the category as a whole. The stereotype of *water* contains the information that water is a transparent, tasteless, thirst-quenching liquid (and so on), but it is the scientific definition of water as H_2O that ultimately counts. Likewise, prototypes may cover the most central, dominant applications of a linguistic category, but they do not exhaust the full range of possibilities for using a category. Furthermore, it is easy to imagine that the actual characteristics that are mentioned as belonging to a stereotype would feature in the prototype of the categories in question. What, in fact, would be the prototype case of *water*? No doubt, a transparent, thirst-quenching liquid without taste, and so on.

Stereotypes, in other words, seem to find a natural place in a prototypically structured category: if the kind of conceptual information that constitutes the prototype is essentially the same as the information that goes into the stereotype, *stereotypes are prototypes seen from a social angle*. Prototypes are primarily psychological notions with an individual status. Stereotypes, on the other hand, are social entities; they indicate what the adult citizen is supposed to know about the referents of the categories he uses, given the principle of the division of linguistic labor. Stereotypes involve the social, prototypes the psychological organization of knowledge, but to the extent that they coincide, prototypes/stereotypes constitute a link between the psychological and the social organization of semantic knowledge. (Note, incidentally, that the social nature of Putnamian stereotypes as meant here does not imply that they equal what are commonly known as “social stereotypes”, i.e. a more or less prejudiced and rigidly applied conception of certain social groups and their members. The latter concept of “stereotype” derives from social psychology, the former from philosophical epistemology.)

More generally, an overall combination of the stereotypical and the prototypical approaches would seem to be possible if not just stereotypes, but cases of rigid designation as well could be incorporated into the prototypically structured network of semantic values. In fact, the scientific or the technical definition of a concept can be seen as one of the contextual variations incorporated into the prototypical cluster. Prototypically organized conceptual categories will have to provide room for particular, rigid nuances in any case: next to scientific or technical definitions of the concept, juridical interpretations of a category can be cited as an example of a more technical kind of specification that will have to be included in the prototypical cluster. The possibility of incorporating rigid nuances as contextually specific applications in a prototypically organized cluster of senses is also supported by the recognition that it is possible to enforce a rigid interpretation of almost any natural kind category by putting hedged questions such as: 'Is thing x *properly speaking* still a member of category *A*? ('Properly speaking, Twin Earth water isn't water at all', and so on.)

However, this combination of prototypicality and stereotypicality (a combination that basically takes the form of an incorporation of stereotypes and rigidly referring meanings into the prototypical model) is rather too facile. There is also a considerable difference between stereotypes and prototypes that needs to be spelled out and that will call for a more thorough analysis. Both aspects of Putnam's approach, in fact, contrast sharply with specific features of prototypicality as it is usually conceived of.

To begin with, the division of linguistic labor implies that linguistic communities are not homogeneous: by definition, semantic knowledge is unevenly distributed over the members of the speech community. Prototype-theoretical studies, on the other hand, generally tend to ignore the question whether and to what extent the prototype structure of the category is shared by all the speakers of the language. This is remarkable, because the prototypical model of category structure might be plausibly interpreted as involving social variation over individuals rather than just psychological variation over contexts of use. For instance, if a lexical category consists of a core reading A and peripheral senses A_1, A_2, and A_3, the subconcepts might be variously distributed over subgroups of the linguistic community. A natural assumption could be that at least the core reading A would be shared by all, and only the peripheral senses A_1, A_2, and A_3 would be distributed in different combinations over different individuals or groups. According to such a model, the central application of the prototypically structured concept, the prototype, implicitly receives a social function rather than a purely psychological one. The shared knowledge of the speakers of the language then consists of a common central reading plus rules of semantic extension that could lead to either A_1, A_2, or A_3. But whether a particular individual ever puts rule 1 into practice to derive A_1 from A (and further, whether he or she subsequently stores A_1 in his long-term semantic memory) would depend on the specific circumstances of the individual's linguistic history, i.e. on whether he or she ever experienced a context in which A_1 was relevant.

In most actual studies of prototypicality in linguistics, however, the social interpretation is largely ignored. (For an exception, see Geeraerts, Grondelaers and Bakema 1994.) Rather, prototypicality research more often than not assumes the homogeneity of the speech community – a somewhat naïve assumption, but one that has a considerable pedigree in theoretical linguistics. Putnam, incidentally, does allow for variation in stereotypicality, in the sense that there might be, in his terms, 'idiolectal' variation in the constitution of a stereotype. Some speakers, for instance, might regard the information that tigers have stripes as optional but regard the fact that they live in jungles as obligatory. This form of social variability involves stereotypicality but not the rigid designation part of the model.

If we accept, more realistically than most prototype-theoretical studies, that the type of semantic knowledge that linguists describe in prototype-theoretical models need not be uniformly distributed, what exactly are the mechanisms that determine its distribution? To what extent is there such a thing as semantic deference, i.e. a division of semantic labor that requires speakers to refer to experts for the definition of certain terms? And to what extent does the expert definition exhibit rigid designation? If we take a slightly broader view, we can now appreciate that the two pillars of Putnam's approach – rigid designation and the division of linguistic labor – are logically independent. We can define four configurations in which rigid designation and social deference of meaning are either absent or not. If + SEMANTIC EXTERNALISM, + SEMANTIC DEFERENCE characterizes the situation described by Putnam, the following configurations may be distinguished.

+ SEMANTIC EXTERNALISM, – SEMANTIC DEFERENCE
Imagine an egalitarian society in which all have the same degree of schooling and in which all attain the same level of proficiency in the sciences: the kind of community of uomini universali, in brief, that academics tend to dream of, a scientific and scholarly elite with no lesser beings around. In such a community, no division of semantic labor would be necessary, since all would be experts. At the same time, assuming that scientific discourse is indeed determined by an attempt to capture the hidden essence of natural kinds, rigid designation would play a role apart from a division of linguistic labor.

– SEMANTIC EXTERNALISM, + SEMANTIC DEFERENCE
Imagine a theocratic society in which a caste of priests guards the Holy Shrine together with the linguistic taboos. The tabooed items are known to the community at large, by reference to the linguistic practices maintained and propagated by the theocratic elite. But the taboo language

need not be fixed for eternity. Every once in a while, such as when a new invention appears, the question would arise whether the new thing falls under one of the existing taboo categories. The decision would not necessarily be one in which hidden essences of the kind meant by Putnam play a role, but it would be a decision taken by the societal "experts in taboo", the priests. The decision could even be made arbitrarily (arbitrary decisions being the purest signal of power), but the common people would accept and adopt the new practice in accordance with the division of linguistic labor. (Less exotic illustrations may be imagined, by the way. Suppose the speakers of French were to follow the linguistic decrees of the Académie Française unconditionally and systematically: this would illustrate linguistic deference, but the honourable members of the Académie would be experts and legislators of the language and its evolution only, not scientists applying principles of rigid designation.)

– SEMANTIC EXTERNALISM, – SEMANTIC DEFERENCE
Imagine a completely homogeneous language community, with ideal speakers-hearers who know their language perfectly – the well-known Chomskyan idealization, in short. If we accept that the categories of the language are used flexibly, in accordance with the mechanisms highlighted by prototype theory, then this would be a situation in which the absence of a division of linguistic labor (because all speakers participate equally in the language) combines with the absence of rigid designation (because scientific or technical readings do no specifically restrain the language). This, of course, is the situation tacitly assumed by prototype-theoretical analyses that assume linguistic homogeneity.

In addition to the argumentation that establishes the logical independence of rigid designation and the division of linguistic labor, there are a number of empirical observations that suggest that Putnam's conception of sociosemantics is too limited. There are three basic points, which may already be found in Ware's (1978) early reaction to Putnam's views.

First, to the extent that semantic deference plays a role at all, the relevant experts are not always scientists. Putnam's theory holds only for natural kind terms, but most of the words in the language do not involve natural kind terms. Still, they may be subject to semantic normativity effects.

> We will depend on certain linguists to distinguish cases and categories; some rhetoricians will be able to tell the difference between simile and metaphor or spondees and trochees; certain boat builders can tell the dif-

> ference between schooners and sloops; chefs or gourmets will distinguish daubes and stews for us; and probably some philosophers are the best we have for distinguishing reference and extension for us. There are people of various groups who serve as authoritative members of the society with respect to various words. Dictionaries often indicate the variety of authorities by noting whether a definition is one of architecture, archaeology, or whatever. (Ware 1978: 42)

Second, the extent to which speakers rely on the experts may differ according to the specific purposes and interests of the speakers.

> It is these other purposes and interests that will also lead a speakers' community to abandon some or all aspects of their dependence on authorities of any kind. A case in point is that of 'water', an example of a natural kind term used by Putnam. As I understand it, 'water' is scientifically defined as being chemically H_2O (or essentially similar), and anything which is H_2O (or essentially similar) is water no matter what state it is in. [...] On the other hand, when I ask for whiskey with ice, I am not asking for whiskey with water. In an ordinary sense of 'water' we make an exception in our dependence on a scientific distinction. (Ware 1978: 46)

The priority of rigid designation would imply that natural language would follow the developments and discoveries of science in a strict fashion, which is not true. In practice, the informational contents of natural language is not only determined by the state of affairs in the sciences, but also by the communicative and cognitive exigencies of the linguistic community in its own right. One of Putnam's own examples can be used as an illustration. Although science has discovered that *jade* refers to two kinds of materials, one with the hidden structure of being a silicate of calcium and magnesium, the other being a silicate of sodium and aluminium, ordinary usage continues to refer to both substances indiscriminately as *jade*. If the communicative purposes of the linguistic community can entail that not all scientifically discovered facts have to be included in the individual's cognitive system, they can also entail that everyday usage lumps together categories that should be distinguished from a purely scientific point of view. Kripke, the founding father of the theory of rigid designation, implicitly accepts the existence of two ways of speaking, a rigid one and a vague one, where he admits that it is possible to designate things in a non-rigid manner, 'speaking loosely' (1972: 332). Similar remarks concerning the relative autonomy of natural language vis-à-vis scientific essentialism (and conversely, concerning the observation that the division of linguistic labor may involve other experts than just scientists) may be found in Evans (1977) and Dupré (1981). Braisby, Franks and Hampton (1996) provide experimental evidence for the view that natural kind terms are often used in a non-essentialist way.

Third, as the Clinton example shows, conflicts may arise.

> If we are not definite about who our authorities are, there are likely to be uncertainties arising from conflicts of authorities [...] Such uncertainties can, of course, arise about fruits and vegetables, but they will also arise about atoms and quarks [...] Besides uncertainties of meaning arising from the conflicts of authorities, there will also be differences of meaning, since our authorities think different things about what kinds of things there are.
> (Ware 1978: 53–54)

The latter remark undermines one of the crucial aspects of rigid designation, viz. the idea that the world itself is the ultimate basis of categorization, at least to the extent that the existence of any particular natural kind is dictated by the world itself. Natural kinds are not arbitrary: they have an *objective* existence, and to the extent that scientific categorization tries to be objective, its categories are in principle fixed by the world itself. In ordinary language, this need not be the case with the same stringency, and the independence of natural language categorization vis-à-vis scientific categorization establishes as much. But could it be the case that the objective restriction does not even hold within science? At least some researchers suggest that the notion of a natural kind is less objective than Putnam implies. Douven and Van Brakel (1998) note that whether two things belong to the same natural kind in the Putnamian sense depends on whether they obey the same objective laws. These objective laws cannot just be the laws of physics: the laws that are relevant for the demarcation of a natural kind term like *multiple sclerosis* include the principles of the medical and biological sciences rather than just physics. But the limits of these sciences, and therefore the identification of the laws that belong to them, may be subject to discussion and social variation: what is considered medicine, for instance, is not simply and straightforwardly objectively given but may depend on social values. Hence, Douven and Van Brakel argue, the demarcation of natural kinds may be less determined by the real world and more by the perspective of the researchers than Putnam would be likely to suggest.

The argumentation developed by Douven and Van Brakel makes clear that even in the epistemological heart of Putnam's approach (as distinct from the sociosemantic elaboration of the theory that is the prime focus of the present article), rigidity and essentialism may not have as firm a position as Putnam implies. We may note, in addition, that Putnam's rejection of intensions is not inevitable either. Putnam formulates semantic externalism as a way of avoiding Twin Earth-like problems, i.e. situations in which speakers are in the same psychological state but still refer to different referents. But Putnam's argumentation can only be upheld if the psychological states in question consist of descriptive knowledge concerning the intended referents. If the relevant psychological states may include references to the social distribution of expertise, then it would seem that psychological states do indeed determine reference. My descriptive knowledge of elms may not be sufficient to distinguish them from other trees, but if it is part of my knowledge about elms that I may resort to botanists for a precise identification, then my personal concept of elms would at least in principle be sufficient to identify the reference of *elm*. If it is part of my concept of *elm* that an elm is the kind of tree that botanists would call *elm* (or, in still other words, that the kind of tree that I intend to refer to is the same kind of tree that specialists refer to with the same word), then my concept does indeed, although indirectly, uniquely determine reference (this point as well may be found in Ware 1978).

To summarize, we may formulate the following intermediate conclusions. First, prototype-theoretical research should abandon the naïve idea of a completely homogeneous linguistic community. The distribution of the different elements of a prototypically organized category over the members of a speech community is likely to be heterogeneous. This automatically implies that it will be necessary to investigate the mechanisms that ensure semantic coordination within a speech community and the forces that shape the distribution of the readings – to incorporate, in other words, sociosemantic mechanisms of the kind described by Putnam into the prototype-theoretical model of linguistic categories.

Second, however, rigid designation and the division of linguistic labor are mutually independent, which means that the specific proposal made by Putnam as the basis of a sociosemantic theory should not be accepted without further consideration. So, can we define a sociosemantic model that realistically extends Putnam's approach?

4. Authority, conflict and cooperation

A fundamental step in the development of an alternative sociosemantic model would be to link the central notion of prototypicality itself to some form of normativity. We know from what went before that the relationship between certain elements within a prototypically organized category may be subject to normative forces: a more loosely defined reading of a term may, in certain circumstances, be recognized as less normative than the more authoritative strict reading that is the scientist's or the technician's or another expert's; and in other circumstances, there may be Clintonian normative conflicts between a loose and a strict reading that even recourse to an expert would not easily settle. But is there any normativity to the very fact that different readings, more narrowly defined ones and more loosely defined ones, may be combined into a single lexical category? What is the sociosemantic motivation for having prototypically structured categories at all?

We started off, at the beginning of the previous paragraph, by thinking of prototypicality as a model for the psychological, cognitive organization of meaning, and of stereotypicality as a model for the social organization of meaning. Such a fairly straightforward complementarity of perspectives is not entirely adequate, however, among other things because the idealization behind the cognitive model (the idealization, that is, of a homogeneous language community) implies that prototypicality might also receive a sociosemantic reading. What would be the way of making that sociosemantic interpretation of prototypicality explicit?

The most articulate theory to date of the normativity of ordinary (rather than scientific or technical) concepts is Renate Bartsch's theory of linguistic norms (1987). Her starting-point is a communicative one: linguistic activity is geared towards communication, and the norms of language arise from the fact that communication requires some form of coordination. The efficient transfer of information requires rules and guidelines for speakers and hearers, and these rules are the norms that speakers and hearers abide with (at least to the extent that it is their purpose to achieve successful communication at all). Importantly, within the set of linguistic norms, a distinction has to be made between the highest norm of communication and lower norms. The "highest norm of communication" is defined as follows:

> All specific linguistic norms are justified relative to the highest norm of communication, which is: 'Express yourself in such a way that what you say is recognizable and interpretable by your partner in agreement with what you intend him to understand'. And, correspondingly, for the hearer it is: 'Interpret such that the interpretation will be in agreement with what the speaker intends'. (1987: 212)

The activities of a speaker expressing himself, and the receptive activities of the hearer interpreting the message are not arbitrary. In order to guarantee efficiency, expression and interpretation have to be constrained by a shared agreement about the communicative value of the linguistic means of expression. In order to comply with the highest norm of communication, the speaker will have to code the information he wishes to transmit in a format that he knows to be interpretable for the hearer. Conversely, the hearer will only be able to reconstruct the speaker's intentions adequately if he is familiar with the value that the speaker attaches to the means of expression that he employs. The specific agreements that exist concerning the communicative value of the linguistic means of expression are the "lower linguistic norms". Among other things, these involve the meanings that may be attached to individual words.

Crucially, Bartsch accepts the semantic flexibility of the language: lower linguistic norms may be breached when the highest norm of communication requires as much. How can new meanings arise at all? Any time a word is used with a new meaning, the given norms of the language are broken, or at least, the *lower* norms of the language are broken, but the highest norm may still be intact: using a word flexibly with a new nuance may be important precisely because of communicative exigencies. When speakers are expressing new attitudes, evaluations or points of view, when they develop new scientific insights or when they communicate new technical developments, in all of these circumstances the new context may not be easily communicated by remaining with the existing lower norms. When the lower norms of the language are too narrow, they may be creatively infringed by the speaker, and the hearer should be flexible enough to accept the violation. In specific contexts, then, the highest norm of communication may lead to breaking the lower level norms.

And the structural characteristics of linguistic categories reflect this situation. The semantic flexibility that is descriptively elaborated by prototype theory is interpreted by Bartsch as a necessary feature of the sociosemantic function of categories. Linguistic categories have to possess a potential of semantic flexibility and even vagueness, precisely because the highest norm of communication may require going beyond existing usage.

> The necessary tolerance in the application of semantic norms is the vehicle of semantic change. Semantic norms structurally carry the possibility of change with them. Because of this, we can adjust our language to change in our physical and social world. If vagueness and context-dependence of

> meaning were not part of the meanings of words, language would be a less efficient means of communication. (1987: 215)

So, if we accept the Bartschian model, the prototype-based semantic fabric of linguistic categories has a normative background: it derives from the hierarchy of communicative norms and the communicative necessity to contextually override the lower linguistic norms.

Could we now combine Bartsch's inspiring interpretation of prototypicality effects in normative terms with what we had already learned about sociosemantic norms? It appears that there are basically three types of sociosemantic relations: cooperation as described by Bartsch, compliance with authorities as described by Putnam, and conflict as described by the Clinton example:

– The *semantics of cooperation* generally underlies the unproblematic prototype-based expansion of meaning as described by Bartsch. Existing norms for linguistic behavior are stretched towards novel ways of using words, but the departure from the existing norms is socially acceptable because it conforms to the highest norm of communication.
– The *semantics of authority* comes into play when discussions and debated issues are settled by deference to recognized experts. Although these need not be scientific experts, as in Putnam's theory of the division of linguistic labor, the semantics of authority generally follows the model of semantic deference put forward by Putnam.
– The *semantics of conflict and competition* plays a role when semantic choices are implicitly questioned or explicitly debated. Such debates may be settled by invoking the semantics of authority, but they may also occur in the absence of a mutually accepted authority that could settle the discussion.

We may suggest, in other words, that the sociosemantic model described by Putnam in terms of stereotypes and the division of linguistic labor has to be expanded into a model incorporating cooperation and conflict next to deference to authority. The three fundamental sociosemantic forces are basic ones in sociological terms: they respectively involve collaboration, power, and competition. With considerable simplification and keeping in mind the metaphorical nature of the comparison, we could see a similarity with different basic types of social structure: a socialist, an authoritarian, and a capitalist organization of society.

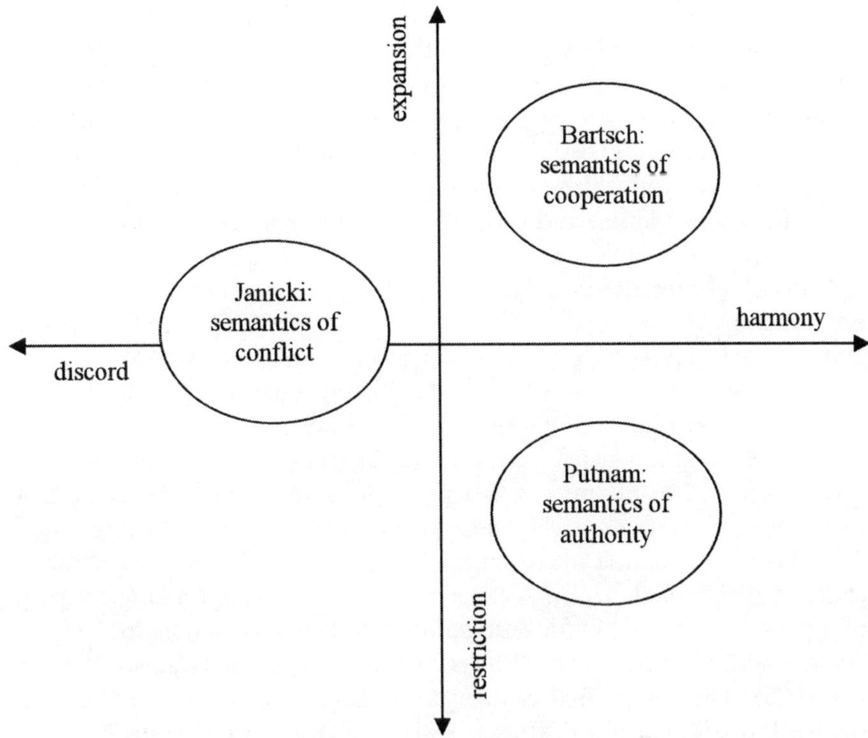

Figure 1. The relationship between the basic sociosemantic forces

Overall, the different sociosemantic forces push the evolution of a category in different directions. The semantics of cooperation generally leads to a prototype-based expansion of categories, to flexibility and vagueness, as described by Bartsch; it is the normative source for "speaking loosely". The semantics of authority works rather in the opposite direction, restricting meaning to expert definitions that are usually more narrowly circumscribed than ordinary usage; it is the normative source for precisification. The semantics of conflict would seem to occupy a middle ground in this respect, to the extent that discussions might involve both the claim to restrict the range of application of a category as the acceptability of extending it; again, this is illustrated by the Clinton case.

The different tendencies represented by the three sociosemantic forces lead to the summary representation in Figure 1, in which the three types of sociosemantic mechanisms are plotted against two underlying dimensions. One dimension distinguishes between harmony and discord: the semantics of conflict is situated at the discord end, while the semantics of cooperation and the semantics of authority are both situated at the harmony end; the absence of conflict may be due to obedient deference to authorities or to the cooperation between equals. The other dimension distinguishes semantic expansion, as the natural tendency resulting from the cooperative application of the highest norm of communication, from the semantic restriction and precisification that is usually involved in expert definitions.

The model presented here bears a considerable resemblance to the one proposed by Gärdenfors (1993, 1999), but was developed independently from it; see Geeraerts (1989). Gärdenfors combines two of the three forces brought together in Figure 1. He distinguishes between an "oligarchic" or "dictatorial" and a "democratic" power structure, the latter governing the common usage parts of the language. In contrast with the model sketched in Figure 1, Gärdenfors does not include a specific conflictual model, but conversely, he adds an important point that is absent from Figure 1, viz. the idea that the configuration of forces may take a contextually variable form. A language does not exhibit a single picture of interacting sociosemantic forces, but a language is "a conglomerate of several sublanguages, each with its own conditions of linguistic power" (1999: 28). This contextual element also occupies an important place in the work of Eikmeyer and Rieser (1981, 1983). Elaborating on Putnam's views, their formal semantic model includes an ordered set of contexts, connected by a relation "is more specialized than". Context changes are responsible for precisification, i.e. for making vague expressions more precise.

5. Sociosemantics and Cognitive Linguistics

Having derived an initial model of the social dynamics of meaning, we may now come back to our starting-point: Bill Clinton may be an implicit cognitive linguist, but how explicit is Cognitive Linguistics at large about the social dynamics of meaning? To put the matter in a wider perspective, how exactly does Cognitive Linguistics deal with the social aspects of language?

Language variation has been studied in Cognitive Linguistics (and adjacent approaches) primarily from three points of view: from a diachronic perspective, including grammaticalization research (see e.g. Heine 1991; Hopper and Traugott 1993; Geeraerts 1997; Bybee 2001), from a comparative and anthropological point of view (see e.g. Palmer 1996; Pederson 1998; Kövecses 2000; Levinson 2003), and from a developmental point of view (see Tomasello 2003). Language-internal variation and sociolinguistic diversity have been much less studied, but still, we may note a number of developments within Cognitive Linguistics that are likely to contribute to an increased interest in sociolinguistic research.

First, there is the interest in cultural models and the way in which they may compete within a community: see e.g. many of the papers collected in Dirven, Frank and Pütz (2003), and earlier work collected in Holland and Quinn (1987). In work such as Lakoff (1996), this approach takes on a critical aspect that brings it close to the tradition of ideological analysis known as Critical Discourse Analysis. More examples of this approach may be found in Dirven, Hawkins and Sandikcioglu (2001) and Dirven, Frank and Ilie (2001). Further, it has been pointed out (Berthele 2001; Geeraerts 2003) that such models may also characterize the beliefs that language users entertain regarding language and language varieties. In this way, Cognitive Linguistics may link up with existing sociolinguistic research about language attitudes.

Second, there is a growing tendency in the theoretical conception of language entertained by Cognitive Linguistics to stress the social nature of language. Researchers like Sinha (1999; Sinha and Jensen de López 2000), Zlatev (2003), and Harder (2003) emphasize that the experientialist nature of Cognitive Linguistics does not only refer to material factors (taking embodiment in a physical and physiological sense) but that the cultural environment and the socially interactive nature of language should be recognized as primary elements of a cognitive approach.

Within this sociolinguistically oriented type of Cognitive Linguistics, sociosemantic norms have hardly received any attention, with the exception of Janicki's work mentioned earlier. We may expect that the growing interest in socially oriented forms of Cognitive Linguistics will naturally raise the attention for the interplay between the semantics of conflict, the semantics of authority, and the semantics of cooperation, but at the same time, we have to recognize that a number of steps will have to be taken before the heightened interest may lead to a full-fledged research programme.

To begin with, the idealization of a completely homogeneous language community has to be given up, together with the tendency to think of conceptual knowledge only in referentially descriptive terms: our knowledge about any thing may include the knowledge that other people's knowledge about that thing is superior (or inferior, for that matter). The former point (the *heterogeneity of linguistic knowledge*) calls for an empirical investigation into the actual distribution of semantic and lexical knowledge. The latter point (the *reciprocity of meaning*) calls for an investigation into the forces that could change – through the resolution of conflicts, through compliance with authorities, through communicative cooperativeness – the existing distribution.

But while the schematic picture drawn in Figure 1 may have an immediate appeal for philosophers in search of fundamental principles, such empirical investigations require an adequate methodology, one that is able to go beyond anecdotal evidence and individual case studies, that is meticulous enough to capture the relevant factors, and that is broad enough to allow for generalizations – the type of quantitative empirical methodology, in other words, that is dominant in sociolinguistic research at large. However, quantitative empirical studies of variational phenomena are relatively scarce in Cognitive Linguistics. In the realm of lexicological investigations, the research tradition started in Geeraerts, Grondelaers and Bakema (1994) and continued in works such as Geeraerts, Grondelaers and Speelman (1999), Speelman, Grondelaers and Geeraerts (2003), integrates theoretical ideas from Cognitive Linguistics with a variational perspective and a corpus-based methodology. Further, a number of researchers have started to investigate social variation outside the lexical realm: see e.g. the work by Kristiansen on phonetic variation (2003), the studies carried out by Berthele (2004) on differences in syntactic construal between dialects, and work by Grondelaers (Grondelaers, Brysbaert, Speelman and Geeraerts 2002) on grammatical phenomena whose distribution is determined by a combination of internal (structural or semantic) and external (contextual or sociolinguistic) factors. All in all, however, these attempts to merge a sociolinguistic interest with an empirical methodology within the overall framework of Cognitive Linguistics are far from dominant.

In short, we have only started to scratch the surface of the social dynamics of meaning, but if we are to dig deeper, in the methodologically sound way that the topic requires, selecting or inventing the appropriate empirical instruments is the next priority to tackle.

References

Bartsch, Renate
1987 *Norms of Language. Theoretical and Practical Aspects.* London/New York: Longman.

Berthele, Raphael
2001 *A tool, a bond or a territory. Language ideologies in the US and in Switzerland.* LAUD Paper 533. Essen: Linguistic Agency of the University of Duisburg-Essen.
2004 The typology of motion and posture verbs: A variationist account. In: Bernd Kortmann (ed.), *Dialectology Meets Typology. Dialect Grammar from a Cross-linguistic Perspective*, 93–126. Berlin/New York: Mouton de Gruyter

Braisby, Nick, Bradley Franks and James Hampton
1996 Essentialism, word use, and concepts. *Cognition* 59: 247–274.

Bybee, Joan
2001 *Phonology and Language Use.* Cambridge: Cambridge University Press.

Dirven, René, Bruce Hawkins and Esra Sandikcioglu (eds.)
2001 *Language and Ideology. Volume I: Theoretical Cognitive Linguistic Approaches.* Amsterdam/Philadelphia: Benjamins.

Dirven, René, Roslyn Frank and Cornelia Ilie (eds.)
2001 *Language and Ideology. Volume II: Descriptive Cognitive Approaches.* Amsterdam/Philadelphia: Benjamins.

Dirven, René, Roslyn Frank and Martin Pütz (eds.)
2003 *Cognitive Models in Language and Thought. Ideology, Metaphors and Meanings.* Berlin/New York: Mouton de Gruyter.

Douven, Igor and Jaap Van Brakel
1998 Can the world help us in fixing the reference of natural kind terms? *Journal for General Philosophy of Science* 29: 59–70.

Dupré, John
1981 Natural kinds and biological taxa. *Philosophical Review* 90: 66–90.

Eikmeyer, Hans-Jürgen and Hannes Rieser
1981 Meanings, intensions, and stereotypes. A new approach to linguistic meaning. In: Hans-Jürgen Eikmeyer and Hannes Rieser (eds.), *Words, Worlds, and Contexts*, 133–150. Berlin: Walter de Gruyter.
1983 A formal theory of context dependance and context change. In: Theo Ballmer and Manfred Pinkal (eds.), *Approaching Vagueness*, 131–188. Amsterdam: North Holland Publishing Company.

Evans, Gareth
1977 The causal theory of names. In: Stephen P. Schwartz (ed.), *Naming, Necessity, and Natural Kinds*, 192–215. Ithaca: Cornell University Press.

Gärdenfors, Peter
1993 The emergence of meaning. *Linguistics and Philosophy* 16: 285–309.
1999 Some tenets of cognitive semantics. In: Jens Allwood and Peter Gärdenfors (eds.), *Cognitive Semantics. Meaning and Cognition*, 19–36. Amsterdam/Philadelphia: Benjamins.

Geeraerts, Dirk
1982 Prototypes en stereotypes. *Forum der Letteren* 23: 248–248.

1985 *Paradigm and Paradox. Explorations into a Paradigmatic Theory of Meaning and its Epistemological Background.* Leuven: Universitaire Pers.

1989 *Wat er in een Woord zit. Facetten van de Lexicale Semantiek.* Leuven: Peeters.

1997 *Diachronic Prototype Semantics. A Contribution to Historical Lexicology.* Oxford: Clarendon Press.

2003 Cultural models of linguistic standardization. In: René Dirven, Roslyn Frank and Martin Pütz (eds.), *Cognitive Models in Language and Thought. Ideology, Metaphors and Meanings*, 25–68. Berlin/New York: Mouton de Gruyter.

Geeraerts, Dirk, Stefan Grondelaers and Peter Bakema

1994 *The Structure of Lexical Variation. Meaning, Naming, and Context.* Berlin/New York: Mouton de Gruyter.

Geeraerts, Dirk, Stefan Grondelaers and Dirk Speelman

1999 *Convergentie en Divergentie in de Nederlandse Woordenschat. Een Onderzoek naar Kleding- en Voetbaltermen.* Amsterdam: Meertens-instituut.

Grondelaers, Stefan, Marc Brysbaert, Dirk Speelman and Dirk Geeraerts

2002 'Er' als accessibility marker: on- en offline evidentie voor een procedurele interpretatie van presentatieve zinnen. *Gramma/TTT* 9: 1–22.

Harder, Peter

2003 The status of linguistic facts. Rethinking the relation between cognition, social institution and utterance from a functional point of view. *Mind and Language* 18: 52–76.

Heine, Bernd

1991 *Grammaticalization: A Conceptual Framework.* Chicago: University of Chicago Press.

Holland, Dorothy and Naomi Quinn (eds.)

1987 *Cultural Models in Language and Thought.* Cambridge: Cambridge University Press.

Hopper, Paul J. and Elizabeth C. Traugott

1993 *Grammaticalization.* Cambridge: Cambridge University Press.

Janicki, Karol

1987 On understanding misunderstanding. Some further support for prototype linguistics. *Folia Linguistica* 21: 463–470.

1999 *Against Essentialism: Toward Language Awareness.* München: Lincom Europa.

2003 The ever-stifling essentialism: Language and conflict in Poland (1991–1993). In: Hubert Cuyckens, Thomas Berg, René Dirven and Klaus-Uwe Panther (eds.), *Motivation in Language*, 273–295. Amsterdam/Philadelphia: Benjamins.

Kövecses, Zoltan

2000 *Metaphor and Emotion: Language, Culture, and Body in Human Feeling.* Cambridge: Cambridge University Press.

Kristiansen, Gitte
2003 How to do things with allophones: linguistic stereotypes as cognitive reference points in social cognition. In: René Dirven, Roslyn Frank and Martin Pütz (eds.), *Cognitive Models in Language and Thought. Ideology, Metaphors and Meanings*, 69–120. Berlin/New York: Mouton de Gruyter.

Kripke, Saul
1972 Naming and necessity. In: Donald Davidson and Gilbert Harman (eds.), *Semantics of Natural Language*, 253–355. Dordrecht: Reidel.

Lakoff, George
1996 *Moral Politics. How Liberals and Conservatives Think*. Chicago: The University of Chicago Press.

Levinson, Stephen
2003 *Space in Language and Cognition*. Cambridge: Cambridge University Press.

Morgan, Pamela
2001 The semantics of impeachment: meaning and models in a political conflict. In: René Dirven, Roslyn Frank and Cornelia Ilie (eds.), *Language and ideology. Volume II: Descriptive cognitive approaches*, 77–105. Amsterdam/Philadelphia: Benjamins.

Palmer, Gary B.
1996 *Toward a Theory of Cultural Linguistics*. Austin: University of Texas Press.

Pederson, Eric
1998 Spatial language, reasoning, and variation across Tamil communities. In: Petr Zima and Vladimír Tax (eds.), *Language and Location in Space and Time*, 111–119. München: Lincom Europa.

Putnam, Hilary
1975 The meaning of meaning. In: Keith Gunderson (ed.), *Language, Mind and Knowledge*, 131–193. Minnesota: University of Minnesota Press.
1979 *Meaning and the Moral Sciences*. Boston, London/Henley: Routledge and Kegan Paul.
1999 Is semantics possible? In: Eric Margolis and Stephen Laurence (eds.), *Concepts. Core Readings*, 177–187. Cambridge, Mass.: The M.I.T. Press.

Sinha, Chris
1999 Situated selves. In: Joan Bliss, Roger Säljö and Paul Light (eds.), *Learning Sites: Social and Technological Resources for Learning*, 32–46. Oxford: Pergamon.

Sinha, Chris and Kristina Jensen de López
2000 Language, culture and the embodiment of spatial cognition. *Cognitive Linguistics* 11: 17–41.

Speelman, Dirk, Stefan Grondelaers and Dirk Geeraerts
2003 Profile-based linguistic uniformity as a generic method for comparing language varieties. *Computers and the Humanities* 37: 317–337.

Tomasello, Michael
2003 *Constructing a Language. A Usage-based Theory of Language Acquisition*. Harvard: Harvard University Press.

Ware, Robert
1978 The division of linguistic labor and speaker competence. *Philosophical Studies* 34: 37–61.

Zlatev, Jordan
2003 Beyond cognitive determination. Interactionism in the acquisition of spatial semantics. In: Jonathan Leather and Jet van Dam (eds.), *Ecology of Language Acquisition*, 83–107. Amsterdam: Kluwer Academic Publishers.

Style-shifting and shifting styles: A socio-cognitive approach to lectal variation

Gitte Kristiansen

LIBRARY, UNIVERSITY OF CHESTER

Abstract

Dialectology and diachronic phonology constitute areas which are generally understudied in Cognitive Linguistics. However, the mechanisms by means of which language users categorize speech and the ways in which knowledge about the social significance of speech variants is put to use are fields of study which merit attention within a framework which places an emphasis on meaning construction and perspectivization. This paper analyses lectal varieties (e. g. those categories we traditionally label as *dialects, accents, sociolects, registers, speech styles* etc.) from a CL perspective and examines the processes by means of which speakers shift towards codes or styles that are different from their own – or perhaps already form part of their habitual repertoire.

The paper first explains why prototype theory and the notion of "cognitive reference point" may contribute substantially to a deeper understanding of what an accent is. It is argued that clusters of perceptually salient (subphonemic or transphonemic) contrasts serve as ideal triggers of social meaning and that social and lectal categorizations constitute prototype categories which are systematically related within a wider frame by means of a metonymic link. LANGUAGE STANDS FOR SOCIAL IDENTITIES.

Then the paper goes on to examine the notion of "shifts", focusing less on receptive competence of speech styles, (i.e. Hearer's ability to locate Speaker on social or regional dimensions), and more on Speaker's possibilities of actively positioning him/herself. LANGUAGE IS A TOOL FOR EXPRESSING SOCIAL IDENTITIES.

Keywords: cognitive sociolinguistics, dialectology, lectal variation, cognitive reference point, subjectification, social deixis, diachronic prototype phonology.

1. Why do we need a CL theory of lectal variation?

We need to apply a Cognitive Linguistics framework to lectal variation for at least three reasons. First and foremost because CL is a usage-based model of linguistics. Second, because the study of structured variation at the level of lectal categories is highly relevant for other areas of research, including phonology, morphology, syntax and semantics. And third, because without such a theory, as linguists we would hardly be able to answer a number of pressing questions concerning the link between language and society. Let us proceed stepwise and briefly examine these three claims in turn.

1.1. Lectal variation and usage-based Cognitive Linguistics

One of the cornerstones of Cognitive Linguistics is its usage-based orientation. As Langacker (1999: 91) phrased it:

> In a usage-based model, substantial importance is given to the actual use of the linguistic system and a speaker's knowledge of this use; the grammar is held responsible for a speaker's knowledge of the full range of linguistic conventions, regardless of whether these conventions can be subsumed under more general statements. It is a non-reductive approach to linguistic structure that employs fully articulated schematic networks and emphasizes the importance of low-level schemas.

Also Taylor (2002: 27) emphasizes the relationship between a usage-based grammar and language acquisition:

> It is assumed that the input to language acquisition are encounters with actual linguistic expressions, fully specified in their phonological, semantic, and symbolic aspects. Knowledge of a language is based in knowledge of actual usage and of generalizations made over usage events. Language acquisition is therefore a bottom-up process, driven by linguistic experience.

But Cognitive Linguistics is also usage-based in a slightly different sense. It necessarily follows that the kind of language to be investigated within a CL framework is language as it is actually used by real speakers in real situations. As Geeraerts (2001: 53) explains, a truly usage-based model naturally entails an examination of the social variation we encounter in real speech:

> As has been explained many times, most forcefully by Ron Langacker, Cognitive Linguistics is a usage-based model: it takes actual language use as its starting-point, and investigates the cognitive reality behind those facts of use. But if the methodological movement of Cognitive Linguistics so to speak goes from *parole* to *langue*, it should be obvious that sociolinguistic variation in the broadest sense will have to be included in the investigation of actual use; it is impossible to take seriously the claim that Cognitive

Linguistics is a usage-based approach and at the same to neglect the social aspects of language use.

Needless to say, Cognitive Linguistics also endeavours to study actual language use *empirically*, and solid work is certainly being carried out in this respect. The kind of structured variation which shows up in written texts has successfully been analysed by means of large corpora (cf. Geeraerts, Grondelaers and Bakema 1994; Geeraerts, Grondelaers and Speelman 1999; Barlow and Kemmer 2000; Gries 2003; Stefanowitsch and Gries 2003). However, this enterprise remains programmatic in the case of spoken variation – to some extent due to the lack of spoken corpora which reflect not only phonological, but also phonetic transcriptions. Actual language use is a complex affair, involving both spoken and written production, but it is unfortunately only part of the variation in which linguists might take an interest which is detectable when our data are drawn from written texts exclusively. Much structured variation is masked by the use of a standard written variety, and if we reduce our study of a given language to the study of its standard variety as we observe it in the written form, we obtain no more than a partial picture.

In line with the claims that language acquisition is a bottom-up process and that CL and sociolinguistics, rather than being incompatible disciplines, complement and need each other, in this paper we shall direct our attention to the existence of low-level and high-level schemas between *parole* (language as individual performance) and *langue* (language as a collective system).

1.2. Lectal variation and implications for other areas of linguistic research

A lectal variety (i.e. any given speech style, including those categories traditionally labelled as standard varieties, regional dialects, sociolects, basilects, acrolects, registers and styles) is composed of a structured series of linguistic forms from a variety of levels of linguistic structure such as lexis, syntax, morphology or phonology. Whenever we use language, we necessarily draw upon such structured sets of paradigmatic variants. At this stage we need to distinguish between two different approaches to lectal variation:

1. Lectal varieties constitute formally distinct but conceptually analogous systems. Linguistic triggers (e.g. phonetic or lexical variants) from different varieties thus evoke the same conceptual targets. Allo-

phonic variants, for instance, are processed as phonemes which combine to form morphemes. Phonetic detail is discarded. Since this is the case, lectal varieties constitute interchangeable paradigms whose formal distinctiveness adds no meaning to the utterance or the speech situation in which they occur.

2. Lectal varieties form part of the same general system. Together they constitute a given language and interact in dynamic ways within it. The variants from different varieties largely evoke the same conceptual targets, but in addition they trigger a number of social schemata which on further consideration also turn out to be meaningful. Lectal variation thus overrides the linear constraints of language by adding meaningful aspects to a proposition or a speech situation, without the necessity of recurring to further syntagmatic components.

These two perspectives – or models – are not necessarily mutually exclusive. While Chomskyan linguistics opted for a homogeneous speech community, systematically eradicating social variation as if weed in an ornamental garden, Halliday (1978) solved "the problem" by dividing language into "language as system" (language as a system analysable in terms of levels of linguistic structure) and "language as institution" (language as constituted by independently formed varieties). According to Halliday, stylistic variation and registers belong to "language as system" and regional and social varieties (regiolects, sociolects, accents) to "language as institution". Such a division conveniently includes styles and registers within the study of language as system, but it excludes dialectal variation. Both models ultimately turn out to be reductionist, as neither focuses on language as it is globally and actually used in real situations by multilectal speakers.

In preparation for a more fundamental discussion, let us now briefly and schematically outline the consequences of applying each of the two models to the areas of phonology, morphology and semantics.

1.1.1. Lectal varieties and phonology

Consider the lexeme *butter*. (1) below represents the word-form, i.e. a string of written graphs, (2) the phonological transcription and (3)–(7) a variety of specific phonetic realizations:

(1) <butter>
(2) /'bʌtə/
(3) ['bʌtʰə]

(4) ['bʊt^{h}ə]
(5) ['bʌt^{s}ə]
(6) ['bʌdəɹ]
(7) ['bʌʔə]

The transcription in (2) stems from Daniel Jones' English Pronouncing Dictionary (1979, 14th ed.). Accordingly, it constitutes a phonemic slot-based representation ultimately modelled on a British prestige accent (RP[1]) which, as it attempts to convey commonalities at a fairly high level of granularity, fails to reveal more specific realizations. (3)–(7) correspond to the (proto)typical phonetic realizations of <butter> in a series of large-scale lectal categories. (3) reflects British RP, revealing the fact that non-prevocalic /r/ is unpronounced and intervocalic /t/ realized as a slightly aspirated [t^{h}] in this accent. (4) represents a typical northern English realization,[2] (5) Estuary English[3] with its highly aspirated intervocalic /t/, (6) General American with flapped intervocalic /t/ and non-prevocalic /r/, and (7) Cockney (and many southern English urban lects) with intervocalic /t/ realized as a glottal stop. Note that these phonetic realizations also constitute abstractions, in the sense that variation within such large-scale lectal categories[4] is left out of the picture, but they never-

1. It has been estimated (Trudgill 1979) that only around 3 per cent of the Bristish English population speak with an RP accent.
2. Cf. Kristiansen (2003) for more details about the northern-southern /ʌ/-/ʊ/ contrast – a linguistic expression of the north-south divide.
3. In very broad terms, Estuary English is a relatively fast-spreading middle-class accent which originated in the speech of the middle-class in the area known as the Thames Estuary. From the point of view of its formal characteristics, it emerged as an independent lectal category drawing upon resources from both RP and Cockney.
4. A realistic picture of actual usage would furthermore account for not only qualitative, but also quantitative variation. Within the same region, social groups differ in their linguistic production in ways that can be quantitatively measured. Cf. Petyt's (1977) study (in Hughes and Trudgill 1987: 7) on the relative elision of initial /h/ in the Bradford area of Yorkshire:

	% aitches dropped
Upper middle class	12
Lower middle class	28
Upper working class	67
Middle working class	89
Lower working class	93

theless reflect real usage in a far more accurate way than a phonological transcription.

Returning to our two models of the role of lectal variation within a language, we can observe that according to model 1, lectal variants are functionally and conceptually equivalent. As each social or regional realization becomes processed by language users as a given phoneme, phonetic detail is discarded. But say that speakers often concomitantly process realizations as those described in (3)–(7) as instantiations of RP, northern English, Estuary English, General American or Cockney, respectively. If, in other words, speakers possess **receptive competence** of lectal varieties (cf. Kristiansen *to appear* for an empirical study on lectal acquisition and lectal awareness), then model 2 is the one we must opt for. Receptive competence (the term is more suitable than "passive competence" as the ability to process data and correlate tokens with types is quite an active process – which does not imply that it should necessarily take place above the level of conscious awareness) involves the ability to on the one hand categorize speech as such and on the other hand relate lectal categories to social categories. In more precise terms, it involves the step from a linguistic trigger to a social schema, activating stored encyclopaedic knowledge in the broad sense, including ideological aspects and psychological attributes associated with the group in question. Model 2 is thus consistent with the view that social and regional phonetic variants adopt a dual functional role: on the one hand they realize a phoneme, but on the other hand they also lead us, through structured and systematic *linguistic* variation, to structured and systematic *social* variation. To the extent that cognitive phonology is really usage-based, regional and social variants must surely be considered as an integral part of phonemic categories (for implications for a prototype-theoretical conception of phonemic categories cf. Kristiansen 2006).

1.1.2. Lectal varieties and morphology

Now consider the following pairs of sentences[5]:

(8) It needs washing
(9) It needs washed

5. Examples drawn from Hughes and Trudgill (1987: 22)

(10) She gave it to him
(11) She gave it him

The examples in (8) and (10) correspond to Standard English as spoken in the south of England. However, (9) and (11) are not incorrect. Sentence (9) reflects the typical realization of the proposition conveyed in (8) in the speech of many[6] educated speakers from the north of England. (11) in turn is how many educated Scottish speakers convey the proposition reflected in (10). In formal writing, these constructions tend not to be used, but they are as part of the English language as those in use in Southern Standard British English.

When Grondelaers (2000) examined Dutch adjunct-initial presentatives as construed either with or without insertion of the particle *er* (English *there*), he also investigated whether *er*-insertion occurs in similar ways in Netherlandic Dutch and in Belgian Dutch. The effect of adjunct-type proved to be significantly stronger in the Netherlands than in Belgium. When Fanego (2004) investigated English sentential complements, she conducted a computer search of four matching corpora of written British and American English (LOB, BROWN, FLOB and FROWN). The fact that there is an interval of thirty years between the two first corpora and their updates allowed her to identify and document linguistic change in real time, distributed across two major regional varieties of English. The choice of to-infinitives and gerunds after certain verbs displayed significant regional differences. Grondelaers and Fanego thus both chose to incorporate regional variation within their studies as a natural variable which added further dimensions to the phenomena under scrutiny (and which naturally also called for an explanation). A usage-based grammar will not limit itself to an analysis carried out at the level of idealized speech communities, but rather take a most natural interest in fine-grained, language-internal variation.

6. To avoid an oversimplified picture, let us once again point to the fact that when alternative constructions exist, speakers of social and regional varieties often, but not always, as already noted in Labov's study on Martha's Vineyard, display quantitative variation. To the extent that speakers are aware of the social significance of the variants they use, they will be sensitive to contextual factors or not. In the latter case, each of a set of co-existing options will be in use to a certain degree.

1.1.3. Lectal varieties and lexical variation

In a paper on lectal variation and empirical data, Geeraerts (2005) argues in favour of incorporating lectal variation as an integral part of the usage-based approach, precisely because the social aspects of meaning constitute a specific form of meaning. A study of denotational meaning (i.e. cognitive, logical, referential or descriptive meaning), it is argued, does not always suffice for the description of the meaning of a lexical item:

(12) bicycle
(13) bike
(14) Mexican
(15) greaser

While (12) and (13) are denotationally synonymous, they differ in STYLISTIC meaning. (14) and (15), denotational synonyms as well, illustrate the EMOTIVE meaning of lexical items. The informative content of a lexical item is accordingly often composed of denotational meaning together with some kind of non-denotational meaning (e.g. emotive, stylistic or discursive). Dialectal variation is as much part of a language system perceived as a diasystem (a conglomerate of lects mastered to varying degrees by individual speakers) as stylistic variation – and the difference between a dialectal form and a standard form is as expressive as the difference between stylistic variants.

The same lexical item can furthermore have quite different meanings for different social groups. As in the case of the different varieties of English as a global language, when the members of different cultural groups make use of common core vocabulary items such as "family", "home" or "ancestor" (cf. Sharifian *this volume*), they often "mean" different things. The word-forms in question may be written in exactly the same way and even be pronounced in exactly the same way, but nevertheless denote different concepts. In other words, the Cultural Cognitive Models (Holland and Quinn 1987) associated with the same word-form can be fundamentally different. This adds further complexity to the picture. Variation in form reflects variation at the conceptual pole, but variation may occur at the conceptual pole and not necessarily at the same time at the pole of the linguistic trigger. Such differences are often analysed in terms of onomasiological and semasiological approaches, but the case in question is not a "simple" case of polysemy. It is a case of culturally distributed, conceptual variation masked by invariance in the formal, linguistic aspect.

In this section it has been argued that as much as we need a proper theory of lectal variation and lectal categorization, the fields of cognitive phonology, morphology and semantics would also benefit from taking social and regional variation more into account, especially to the extent that Cognitive Linguistics wishes to engage in a really serious manner in issues such as language variation and change.

1.3. Lectal variation and the language-society link

On many occasions scholars resort to philosophy for answers when the question of how language relates to culture is raised. Yet what we surely (also) need are explanations involving a more linguistically-oriented theoretical framework and a solid empirical basis.

Accents, for instance, are socially diagnostic, but in many disciplines, to some degree Sociolinguistics included, it has very simply been assumed that speech forms *can* trigger social meaning. Accordingly it is a fairly unproblematic issue. Other disciplines, in turn, have consistently denied that the lectal variety-society link should have any kind of bearing on the systematic configuration of linguistic codes. In the first case, there seems to be no real problem to solve. The link exists and it is obvious. In the second case, the link obviously does not exist. In neither case do we seem to have a topic. One of the purposes of this chapter is to show that, when viewed from a Cognitive Linguistics perspective, the link between lectal and social categories is a complex and intriguing affair. Its emphasis on conceptual structure and mechanisms provided, Cognitive Linguistics is furthermore a perspective on language which would want to provide convincing answers to the many questions which arise from statements such as the following:

> Just as **upper-class English evokes in many people's minds an image** of Hooray Henry's and Henriettas, chinless wonders, Land Rovers, green wellies and -in the case of the women- Jacqmar scarves and velvet headbands, so **Estuary English evokes a similarly stereotypical image** of shell suits, beer bellies, Ford Escorts, chunky gold chains, flats in Marbella (at least for those in the dodgy dealings end of the spectrum) and -again in the case of the women- white, high-heeled shoes preferably worn with no tights.
> (Coggle 1993: 73)

> Upper- and middle-class young people often feel that **a flavour of Estuary identifies them as being more ordinary and less privileged than they really are**. Women may feel that **a hint of Estuary helps them come over as tougher**

> **and more positive**, and so on. [...] The difficulty is in striking the right balance in order to achieve a positive image. There is a delicate path to tread between avoiding the **negative connotations of conservative RP** on the one hand and the totally but equally **negative connotations of broad Cockney** on the other. (Ibid.: 86–87)

The highlighted statements (my emphasis) present us with a whole series of assumptions regarding the link between speech and society, but the relationship as such is nowhere explained in a principled, technical way. The following questions naturally arise: what do we mean by *accents* and *linguistic stereotypes*, and what is the relationship between such notions? What do we mean by *social group*, *social identity* and *social stereotype*? How can accents "*evoke stereotyped images*"? By means of which mechanisms can an accent have *negative* (or *positive*) *connotations*? How exactly does a linguistic stereotype lead to a social stereotype?

From research on popular entertainment we receive similar signals as those found in Coggle's characterizations. The following quotation (Lippi-Green 1997: 85, my emphases) contains claims about the link between accents and stereotypes which likewise need to be brought under scrutiny:

> In animated film, even more so than is the case with live-action entertainment, **language is used as a quick way to build character and reaffirm stereotype**. [...] the hypothesis is a simple one: animated films entertain, but they are also **a way to teach children to associate specific characters and life styles with special social groups, by means of language variation**. [...] On the surface it is quite obvious that Disney films present children with **a range of social and linguistic stereotypes**, from *Lady and the Tramp*'s cheerful, musical Italian chefs to *Treasure of the lost Lamp*'s stingy, Scottish-accented McScrooge.

2. Lectal categorization

As we have already observed, little attention has so far been paid to lectal variation in Cognitive Linguistics. Let us assume, however, that our linguistic environment is as effectively organized into categories and stored as our natural environment. It is in this sense that we shall use the term *lectal categorization*. But let us begin the discussion by considering the notions "language" and "phoneme" in the first place.

2.1. Levels of abstraction: language and phonemes as superordinate categories

Whenever we speak a language, we inevitably speak a given variety of the language in question. *English*, like *fruit* or *furniture* can only be realized through a specific instantiation. Then, at successively more specific levels of abstraction, further specifications can be made by means of subsequent subcategorizations. Language – in the sense of *a* language, i.e. not the general human capacity, nor an assembly of constructions – constitutes a *superordinate* category and a *schematic* concept:

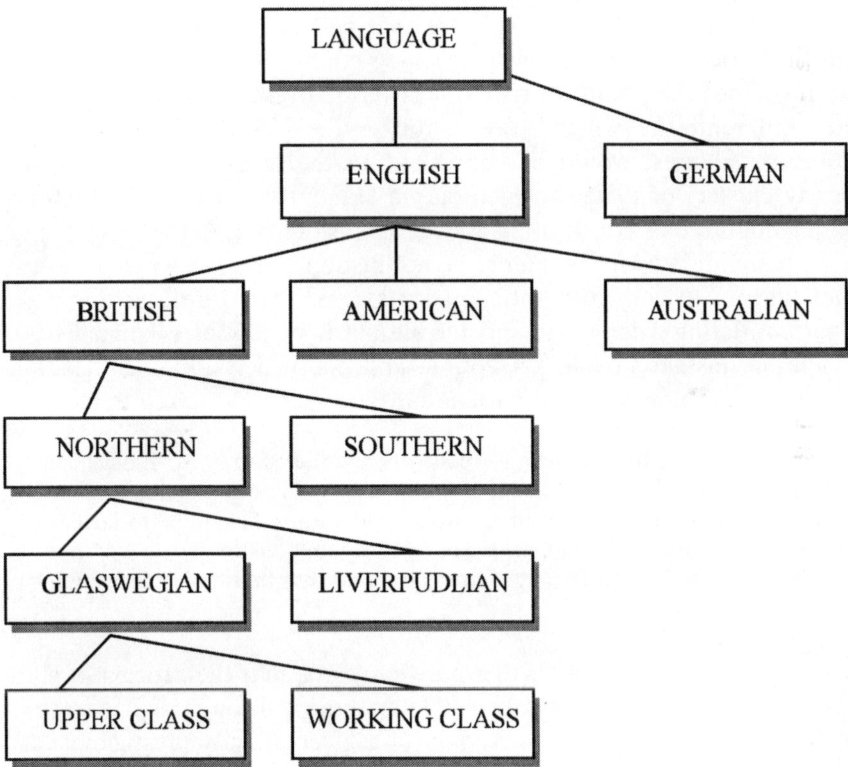

Figure 1. A taxonomy of lectal categories

The picture is highly schematic and thus fairly simplistic, as more – and increasingly more subtle – schema-instance relations could readily be added as we move further down the hierarchy. Yet, for the present purposes the illustration will have to do.

Let us note at this stage that defining and delimiting the concept of *a language* has not been an easy affair for a number of sociolinguists. More than one scholar eventually surrendered, drawing the conclusion that "there is no such thing." Hudson (1980: 30–37), for instance, observed that from the point of view of folk perception (i.e. from a non-expert perspective) it is common to distinguish between the concepts of *language* and *dialect*, but in reality, from the point of view of the linguist, such a distinction cannot be established. *Size*, for a start, or so at least Hudson (1980: 34–5) argues, is a relative variable; a language is supposedly "larger" than a dialect, but while the variety containing all the variants used in Great Britain would seem "big" in comparison with the Cockney variety or the standard variety, it would be "small" when compared to all the varieties used in English-speaking countries.

If on the other hand we apply the criterion of *prestige* we do not arrive at a differentiation which is satisfactory, either. The standard variety, the most prestigious, would be equivalent to the language, but there are many clusters of dialects which lack a standard variety and which are still recognized as constituting a language. Moreover, in the case of English, there are numerous standards, not just one, and these can obviously not be said to constitute different languages. Let us note at this point that conflating a language and the standard variety of a language is a common mistake in folk perception, and one which ultimately leads to the view that non-standard varieties are incorrect:

> Standard English, moreover, is frequently considered to be *the* English language, which inevitably leads to the view that other varieties of English are some kind of deviation from a norm, the deviation being due to laziness, ignorance or lack of intelligence. In this way millions of people who have English as their mother-tongue are persuaded that they "can't speak English". (Trudgill 1982: 19–29)

A diachronic analysis furthermore shows us that the process of standardization involves active, social intervention through the four steps defined by Haugen (1966): *selection* (of a given already prestigious variety), (formal) *codification*, *elaboration of functions* (rendering the variety omnifunctional in all the relevant domains of the society in question) and *acceptance* (on the part of the whole linguistic community, including those speakers who do not have immediate access to the variety in question).

In the third place, the obvious candidate for a more valid criterion would be *mutual intelligibility*. If two speakers of different varieties can understand each other, they speak the same language. Yet this is as relative a criterion as that of size. How intelligible does a variety have to be to be considered a dialect of a given language? Intelligibility is a gradable concept, involving *motivation* (the desire to understand or not), *familiarity* and the degree of *similarity* of a given variety with respect to one's own. The Scandinavian languages, for instance, are mutually intelligible, at least to a degree depending on the varieties chosen. Chinese, in contrast, consists of numerous dialects which fail to be mutually intelligible, and yet it still counts as a language. These arguments provided, Hudson concludes that there exist no formal or technical criteria which allow us to distinguish between the concepts of *language* and *dialect.* The concept "language X" accordingly "has no part to play in sociolinguistics – nor, for exactly the same reasons, can it have any place in linguistics" (p. 37). Not being able to use neither the item nor the concept "language X" in linguistics undoubtedly appears as too radical a position to adopt (and more so when Hudson himself in the rest of his book repeatedly refers to "language Y" or "language X"). *Language* is a conventional notion and a practical one, allowing us to distinguish between codes which are as different as those that we label "English" and "Chinese". Whether our linguistic analyses are to be carried out at such general levels of granularity is another question.

Trudgill (1982: 15) in turn proposes that it is not so much linguistic, but political and cultural factors which determine whether a variety should be categorized as part of this or that language. He applies the notions *heteronomous* and *autonomous* in order to describe the relative dependency of non-standard varieties on a given standard variety. The sum of an autonomous variety (i.e. the standardized one) and a series of heteronomous varietes (non-standard varieties dependent on the standard) together constitute a language. As Trudgill argues (pp. 15–16) the nonstandard dialects of Germany, Austria and German-speaking Switzerland are heteronomous with respect to standard German because speakers of these dialects look to German as their standard language; they read, write and listen to German in their everyday use of language. Speakers of dialects on the Dutch side of the border, in the same way, will read and write in Dutch, and standardizing changes in their dialects will take place in the direction of standard Dutch, not standard German.

Though it appears to be a plausible explanation, it is not without flaws: in great parts of the world there is no written standard variety which could take on the role of an autonomous variety. *A language* is perhaps best described as a superordinate category which cannot be defined on the basis of linguistic criteria only. The decision whether a variety "belongs" to language X or to language Y is often ultimately a political and a social question. The basic criteria, as it often happens in superordinate categorization, seem to be basically functional rather than formal.

[LANGUAGE] is thus schematic for its instances, and "speaking a language" invariably implies speaking a given variety of that language. However, there is still a widespread tendency to apply a model according to which the standard variety equals the language that it forms part of, and that model is not only at work in folk perception, but also in many branches of linguistics. The impression that we are working at the level of *langue* (see also endnote 1) when standard varieties form the basis of our analysis, but at the level of *parole* when the object of study is a nonstandard variety, is obviously misleading, if both of them are just that: varieties of the same language.

Not only languages, but also phonemes constitute superordinate categories. A phoneme such as /t/ can only be actualized through one of its phonetic variants, through instances of the more schematic unit (cf. Taylor 2002 ch. 8). Obviously, regional and social allophonic variation will in a most natural way form part of any descriptive analysis of a phonemic category. In cognitive phonology, phonetic variation has been analyzed in terms of the radial network model, according to which phoneme categories are perceived in terms of mental units of extensions of relatively similar variants (e.g. Nathan 1986, 1996; Dirven and Verspoor 2004). However, the variants of the same phoneme can be perceptually very distinct, and even though it is still possible on theoretical grounds to apply such a framework, it is hardly satisfactory to remain at a purely descriptive level. The motivation behind the presence of very dissimilar variants is an intriguing matter which definitely merits attention from the perspective of Sociolinguistics and Cognitive Linguists alike.

In this respect, I have argued (Kristiansen 2003, 2006) that speakers gradually acquire receptive (and to a minor extent also active) competence of a wide range of different speech styles. This knowledge, which is experientially grounded (see Kristiansen *to appear* for empirical evidence) goes hand in hand with the ability to relate speech styles to the corresponding social groups. Accents, in short, are socially diagnostic.

In line with some of the tenets of Social Identity Theory (Tajfel 1969, 1978, 1981) and Speech Accommodation Theory (Giles *et al.* 1987) we may readily assume that subphonemic prototypes (salient contrasts within a phonemic category) and transphonemic contrasts (variants used in lexical sets where others would be expected, e.g. [aɪ] for [eɪ]) constitute ideal triggers of social meaning, and that social groups this way achieve social distinctiveness through psycholinguistic distinctiveness. Accordingly, if allophonic variants, apart from realizing phonemes, also serve as clues to social categorization, then our analysis of phoneme categories (even phoneme inventories) will in a natural way involve a closer examination of "social variants" and the type of social meaning they evoke (cf. Kristiansen 2003, 2006, *to appear*).

2.2. Converging sociolinguistics and cognitive linguistics: Lectal varieties as prototype categories

If defining the notion *language* turns out to be a laborious affair, the very same problem arises in an intensified way when the object to become defined and delimited is that of *variety*. As Chambers and Trudgill (1998) once observed, varieties often form part of a *dialect continuum*. In such a chaining relationship, adjacent varieties are mutually intelligible, but as the chain grows, varieties chosen from each end of the chain no longer are. Examples of dialect continua in Europe include one stretching from Paris to southern Italy and one from Amsterdam to Vienna.

Furthermore, lectal varieties do not constitute discrete entities with well-defined characteristics. Isoglosses overlap and there are no strict boundaries between each category:

> If you travel from Norfolk into Suffolk, investigating conservative rural dialects as you go, you will find, at least at some points, that the linguistic characteristics of these dialects change gradually from place to place. There is no clear linguistic break between Norfolk and Suffolk dialects. It is not possible to state in linguistic terms where people stop speaking Norfolk dialect and start speaking Suffolk dialect. If we choose to place the dividing line between the two at the county boundary, then we are basing our decision on social (in this case local-government-political) rather than on linguistic facts. (Trudgill 1982: 14–15)

What is at work, in Cognitive Linguistics terminology, seem to be the principles of centrality gradience and membership gradience (Lakoff 1987, following Rosch). Lectal categories, in short, constitute prototype categories. If lectal varieties constitute prototype categories, some realizations will be more "typical" or "central" or "better examples" of a given variety than others. As Wells (1982: 301) once phrased it:

> Some people deny that RP exists. This seems to me like denying that the colour red exists. We may have difficulty in circumscribing it, in deciding whether particular shades verging on pink or orange counts as "red", "near-red", or "non-red"; the human race disagrees on what to call red, some preferring *rosso* or *krasnyj*, *pupa* or *ruĝa* rather than our red, but we all agree in identifying fresh blood as typically having this colour, and almost all have a name for it (Berlin & Kay 1969). Similarly we may hesitate about a particular person's speech which might or might not be "RP" or "Near-RP"; we may prefer to call it "BBC English", "southern British Standard", "General British", "a la-di-la accent" or even "Standard English", and define it more narrowly or more widely than I have done, but anyone who has grown up in England knows it when he hears a typical instance of it.

The knowledge which allows us to classify a stretch of speech as an instance of a given lectal variety is bound to be experientially grounded. Yet from the point of view of language acquisition, it seems to be a relatively late discovery. While 3 year olds already know how to speak and process their mother tongue, when it comes to lectal acquisition the leap from 6 to 8 and from 8 to 12 are quite significant (cf. Kristiansen *to appear*). However, at the age of 6 children already begin to convey – in ways that are statistically significant – that they know how certain other groups speak. At 8 the picture becomes not only wider but more accurate. Further, children now overtly imitate the speech styles of many other speech communities. In order to do so, they must have both receptive and active competence of a number of perceptually distinctive features – those which effectively set styles off as distinct speech categories.

Bell (1999: 525–526) addresses precisely this question in the following quotation:

> The notion of 'styling the other' presupposes that a variety has a distinguishable and rather stable core of linguistic features in order for it to be modelled at all. For me to be able to 'sound American' or 'sound RP' requires that there are some features (or cluster of features) of those varieties which are distinctive. The distinctive core consists of those features that set the variety off from the majority of other dialects.

Also in Speech Accommodation Theory (Giles *et al.* 1987), it has been acknowledged that speakers often realize that they are using a given style when they converge to or diverge from the style of the addressee. For this awareness to exist, "speakers must have beliefs or other cognitive structure, for example, various schemata, that indicate just how speech can be similar to or different from that of others" (ibid: 37).

Humans have receptive competence of lectal varieties, but the images formed are not necessarily accurate, at least from the perspective of experts such as linguists. It is in this sense that I use the term "linguistic stereotype"; an instance of folk perception with respect to the distinctive features of a speech variety. Linguistic stereotypes, rather than representing exaggerated and distorted images, constitute useful *cognitive reference point constructions* which allow us not only to categorize our linguistic environment but also to categorize and characterize our social environment. As I have previously argued (Kristiansen 2003), linguistic stereotypes metonymically evoke the social stereotypes associated with the group in question. Accents are thus not only regionally and socially diagnostic; they also serve to characterize speakers in very significant ways.

Let us for instance consider the ways in which Trudgill (1999: 52–66) classifies the modern non-standard varieties of British English. The classification is based on relative sharedness of a total of 7 differential features:

1. /ʊ/ realized as [ʌ] or [ʊ] in words such as <*butter, love, some, other, cup, up*>
2. non-prevocalic /r/ realized as [ɹ] or θ in words such as <*arm, car*>
3. <ng> realized as [ŋ] or [ŋg] in words such as <*singer, Birmingham*>
4. /u:/ realized as [u:] or [ju:] in words such as <*super, news, few, music, tune*>
5. <-i> realized as [ɪ] or [i:] in words such as <*coffee, city, seedy* y *money*>
6. Retention of the monophthong [e:] instead of the diphthong [eɪ] in words such as <*gate, face*>
7. Vocalization of "dark" [ɫ] in words such as <*hill, milk*>: [miʊɫk] – or [miʊk] as [ɫ] often drops; already "expressed" by [ʊ] it becomes a redundant element.

What allow us to differentiate the 16 modern dialects of England are combinations of these seven features, with the following versions (forming chaining relationships) of the same phrase as the result (see Table 1 on p. 62).

The fact that Trudgill based his distinction on precisely these features and at this level of abstraction indicates that what we are facing is a major first-scale division based on particularly salient features, subject to multiple successive subcategorizations. Each combination of distinctive features seems to constitute a model, or type. Not all speakers of, say the

Table 1. Pronunciation characteristics of the sixteen Modern Dialect regions of England: regional versions of the utterance Very few cars made it up the long hill (Trudgill 1999: 68)

Northeast:	Veree few cahs mehd it oop the long hill /veriː fjuː kaːz meːd ɪt ʊp ðə lɒŋ hɪl/
Central North:	Veri few cahs mehd it oop the long ill /verɪ fjuː kaːz meːd ɪt ʊp ðə lɒŋ ɪl/
Central Lancashire:	Veri few carrs mehd it oop the longg ill /verɪ fjuː kaːrz meː d ɪt ʊp ðə lɒŋ ɪl/
Humberside:	Veree few cahs mehd it oop the long ill /veriː fjuː kaːz meː d ɪt ʊp ðə lɒŋ ɪl/
Merseyside:	Veree few cahs mayd it oop the longg ill /veriː fjuː kaːz meɪd ɪt ʊp ðə lɒŋg ɪl/
Northwest Midlands:	Veri few cahs mayd it oop the longg ill /verɪ fjuː kaːz meɪd ɪt ʊp ðə lɒŋg ɪl/
West Midlands:	Veree few cahs mayd it oop the longg ill /veriː fjuː kaːz meɪd ɪt ʊp ðə lɒŋg ɪl/
Central Midlands:	Veri few cahs mayd it oop the long ill /verɪ fjuː kaːz meɪd ɪt ʊp ðə lɒŋ ɪl/
Northeast Midlands:	Veree few cahs mayd it oop the long ill /veriː fjuː kaːz meɪd ɪt ʊp ðə lɒŋ ɪl/
East Midlands:	Veree foo cahs mayd it oop the long ill /veriː fuː kaːz meɪd ɪt ʊp ðə lɒŋ ɪl/
Upper Southwest:	Veree few carrs mayd it up the long ill /veriː fjuː kaːrz meɪd ɪt ʌp ðə lɒŋ ɪl/
Central Southwest:	Veree few carrs mayd it up the long iooll /veriː fjuː kaːrz meɪd ɪt ʌp ðə lɒŋ ɪʊl/
Lower Southwest:	Veree few carrs mehd it up the long ill /veriː fjuː kaːrz meːd ɪt ʌp ðə lɒŋ ɪl/
South Midlands:	Veree foo cahs mayd it up the long iooll /veriː fuː kaːz meɪd ɪt ʌp ðə lɒŋ ɪʊl/
East Anglia:	Veree foo cahs mayd it up the long (h)ill /veriː fuː kaːz meɪd ɪt ʌp ðə lɒŋ (h)ɪl/
Home Counties:	Veree few cahs mayd it up the long iooll /veriː fjuː kaːz meɪd ɪt ʌp ðə lɒŋ ɪʊl/

East Midlands, drop their aitches and yods in words like <hill> and <few> and pronounce <up> with /ʊ/ instead of /ʌ/, but it would not be far-fetched to say that this is what prototypical East Midlands speech sounds like. If so, the central image of a variety seems to involve a complex cluster of acoustic-perceptual contrasts which is distinct with respect to the central images of neighbouring lectal categories, and effectively sets the accent off as different:

Table 2. Complex clusters of acoustic-perceptual contrasts in RP, Estuary English and Cockney. Data drawn from Altendorf (1999), Coggle (1993) and Wells (1994, 1997)

Perceptual contrast	RP	EE	Cockney
Th-fronting: [fɪŋk] for <think>	–	–	+
Realization of intervocalic /t/	t^h	t^s	ʔ
Glottalization of final /t/: [gæʔwɪk] for <Gatwick>	–/+	–/+	+
Vocalization of non-prevocalic [ɫ]: [miuk] for <milk>	–	+	+
h-elision: [ɑ:m] for <harm>	–	–	+
Diphthong change in /eɪ, aɪ, əʊ/ as in <face, price, goat>	/eɪ, aɪ, əʊ/	/ʌɪ, aɪ, ʌʊ~œʊ/	/aɪ, ɒɪ, ʌʊ/
Yod coalescence: [tʃu:n] for <tune>	–	+	–
Yod elision: [tu:n] for <tune>	–	–	+
Diphthongization of /i:, u:/: <sea, blue>	/i:u:/	/ɪi, ʊu/	/əɪ, əu:/
Realization of /aʊ/ as in <mouth>	/aʊ/	/œʊ/	/œ:/

Speakers of RP, Estuary English or Cockney may of course depart from such highly schematized and prototypical realizations[7], conform to them to various degrees or even place themselves in a fuzzy area between adjacent categories. What is important to understand is that the central image of each lectal and social categorization constitutes a cognitive reference point construction that guides both speaker and hearer, allowing them not only to locate each other regionally and socially, but also, as we shall see in section 5, position themselves in more active ways.

7. Lectal varieties are not homogeneous entities. The cluster of features listed in each case represents an abstraction which reflects the typical speech of a salient subcategory within the lectal category in question. Formal Cockney, for instance, lacks four of the traits of broad Cockney, the variants described in this table. In the case of RP, there are at least four distinguishable subvarieties (Wells 1982: 279):

> It is convenient to recognize first of all a central tendency which I shall call mainstream RP. We can define it negatively, by recognizing two other tendencies or types of RP, which are part of RP as a whole but distinct from mainstream RP. One is U-RP [...], the other adoptive RP. It is also convenient to recognize a rather vaguer entity, Near-RP, comprising accents which are not exactly RP though not very different from it.

3. The target: Social categories, social stereotypes and cultural models

Accents are socially diagnostic, but what is it that structured speech patterns call up in our minds? Let us assume that what in everyday terminology is referred to as *language*, *accent*, *dialect*, *style* and *social group* constitute concepts; categorizations and schemas on different levels of abstractions that relate to one another in the sense that they form part of a larger frame, or Cognitive Cultural Model. Not only speech styles, but also non-linguistic triggers of social meaning seem to form part of such frames: song, dance, property, social activities, dress and manners also "index" social group membership. Let us at this stage recall that Social Identity Theory (*cf.* Tajfel 1969, 1981) adopted a positive approach to social stereotypes, arguing that stereotyping constitutes an inevitable and natural (thus not necessarily negative) side-effect of the general process of categorization. Accordingly, when human beings categorize other humans into a series of social categories and subcategories, simplified images representing what such groups are like develop. These images are social stereotypes. Psychological attributes certainly form part of such frames; as shown in the study by Lambert *et al.* (1960)[8], speech patterns related with social categorizations characterize speakers as intelligent, friendly, assertive and of course also in much less positive terms.

Yet viewing social stereotypes as a natural categorization effect alone would undoubtedly assign too passive a role to such construals. As Rosch (1999: 72) has stated, "concepts and categories do not represent the world in the mind; they are a *participating part* of the mind-world whole of which the sense of mind (of having a mind that is seeing or thinking) is one pole, and the objects of mind (such as visible objects, sounds, thoughts, emotions, and so on) are the other pole." From the perspective of Sociolinguistics, a number of scholars have also called for approaches which assign a more active and dynamic role to linguistic variants and social concepts. Le Page (1980) argues that speech is not just a reflection of identity, but a *projection* of it. In the same line of thought, Eckert (2004) argues in favor of a dynamic conception of speech styles:

8. Lambert's matched-guise technique constituted an innovation with respect to the instrument of investigation, but following Allport (1954) it was still based on an arbitrary adjective list. Both Labov (1966) and Trudgill (1974) later on used the matched-guise technique and adopted more realistic value scales.

[...] the meaning of variation lies in its role in the construction of styles, and what I am proposing here is a study of the role of variation in stylistic practice. This involves not simply placing variables in styles, but in understanding this placement as an integral part of the construction of social meaning. This has several implications for our view of variation. First, variables do not come into a style with a specific, fixed meaning, but take on such meaning in the process of construction of the style. This leads to the second point, that style (like language) is not a *thing* but a *practice*. It is the activity in which people create social meaning, as style is the visible manifestation of social meaning. And inasmuch as social meaning is not static, neither are styles.

Eckert thus adopts a more radical approach to the style-social meaning relationship than what is reflected in what we might label as the data-gathering tenet of Sociolinguistics; style does not just *reflect* social meaning, but actively *construes* it.

Quite interestingly, Morgan (2001) relates speech styles directly to Cultural Cognitive Models:

The 'Just Plain Folks' CCM (see Morgan 1997a, 1997b), an enduringly important American CCM, appeared rhetorically less often in the impeachment process than did the 'High Oratory (Nineteenth Century)' (genre-based) CCM. For example, 'Just Plain Folks' appeared briefly when House Judiciary Chairman Hyde thanked the expert witnesses on the perjury issue:

(31) Even when you disagreed with us, which is most of the time, you helped us. You're here because you're darn good citizens and you want to contribute to this awful task we are grappling with, and you have made a great contribution. (*Impeachment* 1999: 66)

"Darn good" and "awful", as well as the 'dangling preposition' syntax of "grappling with" (proscribed in 'standard American English': 'Never end a sentence with a preposition', understood as including particles) mark this as very nearly a prototypical example of 'Just Plain Folks' language, linked here with the 'Good Citizen' CCM. ('Just Plain Folks' are traditionally and prototypically the best examples of 'Good Citizens', possessing as they do all the 'Traditional American Values', such as 'honesty', 'dependability', 'generosity', 'patriotism', 'lack of affectation', etc.)

That a speech style should develop in order to "express" a CCM and the ideology that nurtures it certainly makes sense; CCMs, as intangible as the concepts evoked by lexical items, can only be effectively instantiated by means of tangible triggers in e.g. the visual or auditory dimensions.

Speech as a trigger of social meaning furthermore seems to form part of a wider frame. To Wells (1982: 29) accents constitute an important part of social stereotypes; speech patterns forms part of a wider social frame, and we only realize how intimate the relationship between speech styles and social frames are when an instance runs counter to our expectations:

> [...] stereotypes are simplified and standardized conceptions of kinds of people, conceptions we share with other members of our community. Few people in Britain have ever met a genuine working cowboy: but we have our stereotyped view of what a cowboy is like. We know what he wears, the way he behaves, the kind of food he is likely to eat, and the way he talks. And if we come across someone dressed as a cowboy, hitching his horse to the wooden rail outside the saloon, then swaggering in and up to the bar to order a whisky in an U-RP accent [...] we should notice that something was wrong. Accents constitute an important part of many stereotypes. We use the indexical information we collect from listening to a person speak in order to slot him into an appropriate stereotype.

Yet stereotypes are not shared by all the members of a social group, at least to the same degree. As Lo (1999: 461) reminds us:

> Irvine (1987) notes that no social group [...] is internally linguistically homogeneous in practice. Silverstein (1997) has argued that membership in a speech community is itself gradient; while speakers who are members of the same speech community may share orientations towards norms and presuppositions, this sharedness itself varies by degree.

While such construals are spread within a social group, they are shared only to a degree; as Sharifian (2003) reports, the elements of cultural schemas are not shared by all members of a cultural network, but rather distributed across the minds. It is not by virtue of the knowledge of (or perhaps rather the belief in) only one schema that one becomes a member of a cultural group, as two people can share more elements from one cultural schema and less from another. It is the overall degree of how much a person draws on various cultural schemas that makes an individual more or less representative of a cultural group. Cultural schemas thus constitute an emergent property of cognition at the level of cultural group, rather than at the level of the individual. Schemas thrive within groups and the group emerges as such, shaped and brought into existence by relatively shared beliefs, values and norms. In similar ways, the group also determines and is determined by speech patterns such as "dialects", "accents" and "styles".

4. The semiotic link: From linguistic trigger to social target

4.1. The metonymic link

Viewing both lectal and social categorizations as prototype categories whose central images relate to each other furthermore provides us with a better understanding of the process by means of which an accent triggers a series of psychological attributes, associated with a social categorization (Lambert *et al.* 1960). Adopting a frame-oriented approach, we may say that a linguistic stereotype leads us efficiently, directly and rapidly to the corresponding social stereotype with all its value-laden components because a source-in-target PRODUCER-PRODUCT or CAUSE-EFFECT metonymic schema is at work: the speech pattern associated with a particular group leads hearer to the wider frame of the social group itself, to the social stereotype associated with it (psychological attributes included) and all the encyclopaedic knowledge hearer has about the group in question. Typical speech patterns apart, encyclopaedic knowledge is likely to involve social habits, ideological values, dance, song and physical appearance such as dress and other markers of group membership:

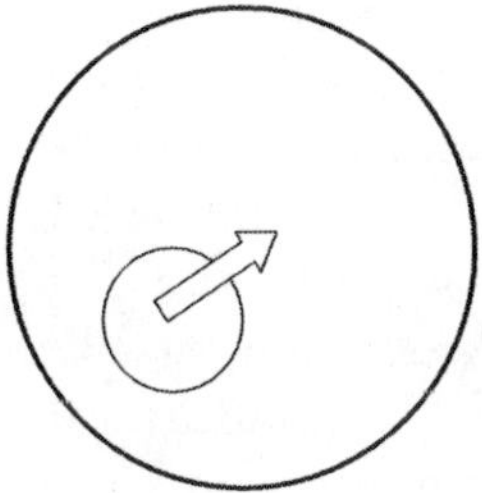

Figure 2. Metonymic source-in-target link between linguistic stereotypes and social groups

The claim that accents relate metonymically to their social target is justified by the domain-internal nature of the mapping. According to Ruiz de Mendoza Ibáñez and Pérez Hernández (2001: 323–327) metonymies are domain-internal mappings which can be subclassified into two main types: source-in-target metonymies (cases of domain expansion because part of a domain invokes the domain as such) and target-in-source metonymies (cases of domain reduction because a subdomain of a wider domain is highlighted). Accents form part of such a wider domain (or frame), as the use of a given accent leads Hearer to classify Speaker as belonging to or stemming from the social group which originated the accent in question. Accents are *diagnostic* because they are reliable, i.e. they are not easily changed, and *socially* diagnostic because the patterns acquired were effected by our social category membership in early childhood.

4.2. Receptive competence

Whether we have receptive competence of lectal schemata and the ability to relate them to the social groups that brought them about is not a trivial question. However, scholars in Cognitive Phonology have not yet reached consensus as to the existence of receptive competence. While Nathan (1996) seems disinclined to believe that phonetic detail is retained and put to constructive use, Taylor (2002: 483) is in favour of such an explanation:

> Storage of even minute phonetic detail is suggested by another consideration. Speakers of a language are remarkably good at detecting minor variations in accent, often as markers of regional provenance. This ability would be inexplicable if linguistic forms were associated only with schematic phonological representations, which abstract away from phonetic detail.

There is empirical evidence which validates the latter view: an empirical study on accent identification (Purnell, Idsardi and Baugh 1999) has shown that a two-syllable word ("hello") is enough for subjects to successfully establish the link between an accent and the social group to which the speaker belongs. This indicates that (a) hearers perceive very subtle differences in speech production, (b) store these in systematic ways as instances of a particular accent (lectal categorization), (c) have receptive competence of a range of different accents and (d) possess the ability to relate accents to specific social groups.

Returning to the models on lectal variation presented in section 1.2, let us observe that even if such implications are accepted, there are still two fundamentally different ways of viewing accents in terms of structured group-related variation:

- in consonance with model 1, even if we assume that we have receptive competence of lectal varieties, these do not originate as such for any particular purpose. We are able to distinguish those varieties that coincidentally happen to be perceptually salient and contrastive enough for us to do so.
- in consonance with model 2, lectal differentiation is in part caused by speakers' desire to express social meaning. In the case of accents, speakers achieve social distinctiveness through psycholinguistic distinctiveness. Varieties thus interact in dynamic ways.

Note that according to the first view, to push the argument even further, sound change could be considered as systematic, but socially unmotivated. The second view, on the contrary, holds that sound change is not only systematic, but often also socially motivated.

4.3. Meaningfulness at the level of speech sounds?

That elements below the level of the morpheme should be meaningful in at least some situations, to speaker, to hearer, or both, is a statement which is at variance with most current linguistic theories. And yet, if speech sounds *do* turn out to be meaningful on a variety of occasions, there should also be a way to reconcile actual language usage with the theoretical frameworks that we employ.

4.3.1. Functions of language and symbolic units

Langacker (1991: 105) posits three, and only three, broad facets of linguistic structure: semantic, phonological, and symbolic. Symbolic units are bipolar and consist of a semantic unit at one pole in symbolic association with a phonological unit at the other:

> Consider the morpheme *dog*. At the phonological pole, it is complex, being assembled out of the smaller phonological units [d], [ɔ] and [g]. We can represent this complex phonological unit as [[d]-[ɔ]-[g]], where hyphens between the components indicate that these smaller units combine "syntagmatically" to form the complex, higher-order phonological unit represented by the outermost set of square brackets. The semantic pole of *dog* is similarly complex, but for now I will simply abbreviate it as [DOG]. The morpheme as a whole, then, is a higher-order symbolic unit formed by putting [DOG] and [[d]-[ɔ]-[g]] in symbolic association, i.e. [[DOG]/[[d]-[ɔ]-[g]]]. Both poles are internally complex, but each has unit status and can be manipulated as a whole. Only at the level of the whole do they enter into a symbolic relationship (i.e. *dog* is not analyzable into smaller meaningful parts).

In structuralist, functionalist and cognitive phonology alike, there exists a clear dichotomy of meaning-making and meaning-building elements: meaning-construction begins at the level of morphology. The phoneme is perceived as the minimal successive distinctive unit in language – a builder of meaning at the morphemic level. The allophone is a mere phonemic slot-filler, never a meaning-making unit. Now, if allophonic variation is totally devoid of "meaning", then how can we explain that accents are socially diagnostic, that a two-syllable word is enough to evoke social meaning successfully? In other words, would there be a way of rendering the Cognitive Linguistics conception of meaning-construction described above compatible with the view that variation at the level of phonetics *can*, on many occasions, be socially meaning-making?

There certainly seems to be, if only one brings the claim that Cognitive Linguistics is also inherently *functionally oriented* into the perspective as well. Just think about how often we engage in conversations in which the primary goal can hardly be said to be the exchange of factual information. When we meet people for the first time, engage in the maintenance of social relationships or the negotiation of social roles and positions, the so-called ideational, message-bearing or referential function of language is secondary with respect to the so-called social, phatic or interpersonal function. Language is not just a tool for ideational communication. It is also an important vehicle for social communication. It enables us to identify and characterize unknown individuals, convey and preserve our own relative position on a given hierarchical scale and define ourselves as ingroup or outgroup members of relevant social categorizations.

These various functions of language have been described the following way:

Table 3. The functions of language as reported by Thrane (1980: 2)

Bühler	Lyons	Halliday	Jakobson	Popper
Ausdruck	Expressive	Interpersonal	Emotive	Expressive
–	Social	Interpersonal	Phatic	–
Appell	–	Interpersonal	Conative	Stimulative
Darstellung	Descriptive	Ideational	Referential	Descriptive
–	–	Textual	–	–
–	–	–	Metalingual	–
–	–	–	Poetic	–
–	–	–	–	Argumentative

As we have posited in this paper, lectal variation involves structured patterns of variants associated not only with the social groups that effected them, but also with the social stereotypes construed to portray them. And as argued in Kristiansen (2003), the whole cluster of salient contrasts that compose a lect can be metonymically evoked by the use of just one of its components.

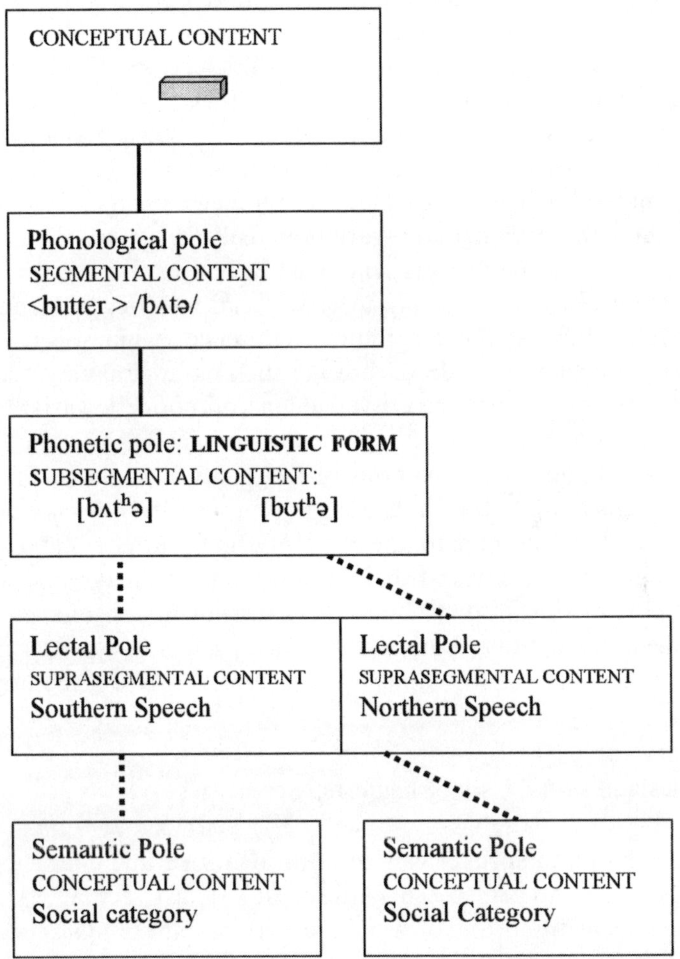

Figure 3. Meaning-construction through structured paradigmatic variation

Just in case it needs saying, let me hasten to draw attention to the following point: the claim that allophonic variation should be meaningful in general constitutes a gross misunderstanding of the phenomenon we are bringing under scrutiny. Most phonetic variants probably fulfill just one function: once processed and categorized as instantiations of a particular "phoneme" they serve as builders of meaning at the morphemic level of linguistic structure. But as the dotted lines indicate, they may also concomitantly relate metonymically to larger constructs such as the **lectal category** they form part of, and then in turn to the corresponding social categories. As we have argued, certain salient variants may become associated with a given social group and serve to effectively evoke in the mind of the hearer the group itself, its characteristics, ideological values and hierarchical position.

Needless to say, the symbolic relationship between phonological pole and semantic pole in most cases[9] remains unchanged. The same semantic content 'butter' will be evoked by the phonetic variants in [bʌtʰə] and [bʊtʰə]. And the paradigmatic variation realized by [bʌtʰə] and [bʊtʰə] does not evoke social concepts symbolically, but it still evokes concepts – to the extent that one is willing to view social meaning in terms of concepts. Metonymic reference is indirect reference – but still reference – and a very efficient one indeed; through such paradigmatic variation, the linear constraint of language is overridden and phonetic variants such as [ʌ] and [ʊ] adopt a dual functional role, complying at the same time with the ideational and social functions of language. It might be argued that what is at work are two different levels of granularity: socially indexical phonetic variants pertain to the level of lectal varieties (and hence to dialectology), phonetic variation in general to phonology – but that type of clear-cut division into structural levels is not in consonance with the basic tenets of Cognitive Linguistics, which prefers to consider meaningfulness in terms of constructions and assemblies across structural levels.

5. Styles and shifts: Uses of linguistic stereotypes

As we have seen, a speaker can be both identified and characterized on the basis of his or her speech pattern. In the last section we explored the mechanisms by means of which accents constitute markers of social meaning. Accents, dialects and social stereotypes, it was argued, are prototype categories which relate to one another within a wider frame. This wider frame comprises not only ideological components, but markers

9. Unless, of course, culture-specific conceptualisations are at work.

from a wide variety of dimensions, including speech, dress, dance, song and physical appearance. The "meaning" of social group membership may thus be invoked by means of either linguistic or non-linguistic triggers through what is ultimately a usage-based metonymic operation. Humans may efficiently not only categorize, but also identify and characterize a given speaker on the basis of his or her speech pattern.

Hearer's categorization and evaluation of Speaker, however, only make up the starting-point of the story, a picture which needs further elaboration. Let us observe, to begin with, that *awareness* and *attention* constitute important factors as regards the possibility of more active uses of speech patterns. It is a curious coincidence, moreover, that both William Labov and Ronald W. Langacker have built up a theoretical framework around these notions. While Langacker's insight concerns subjectification, scope, construal and perspective, Labov's model, often referred to as the "attention paid to speech" model, investigates how speech styles vary according to situation. Assuming that speakers adjust their speech to contextual factors whenever they are aware of these, attention can be viewed as a determining factor which links linguistic variants to social variables. Labov aimed at eliciting "real" unmonitored speech by drawing the speaker's attention away from situational factors.

A certain degree of awareness is certainly a prerequisite for active meaning construction, but (though it at first sight sounds ambiguous) this awareness need not be conscious. As Labov explained, the inhabitants of Martha's Vineyard who changed their pronunciation of certain diphthongs to make them distinct with respect to that of the visitors from the mainland were not aware of the fact that they were using linguistic variants loaded with social meaning (which is supposedly why their pronunciation did not vary according to situational factors). In the New York City study on certain variants of /r/, speakers did vary their choice of variants in different situations (i.e. they made contextual use of the two variants in question) because they were more aware of the social meaning attached to each variant. Bearing in mind that awareness is a gradable dimension, the following possibilities regarding receptive and active uses of patterns involved in speech categorization and speech perception can now tentatively be outlined:

a) Hearer locates Speaker socially and regionally on the basis of his/her speech pattern in a general way.
b) Hearer locates Speaker socially and regionally in more specific ways.
c) Hearer locates Speaker relative to him/herself.

d) Hearer changes his/her relative position with respect to Speaker.
e) Hearer changes his/her speech style towards an existing pattern.
f) Hearer develops a new style, exploiting existing speech patterns.

5.1. General lectal and social categorization of speaker

In the situation described in (a) and depicted in figure 4 below, Hearer makes use of his receptive competence of a wide range of different "speech styles" and his ability to relate that knowledge to a series of corresponding social categorizations:

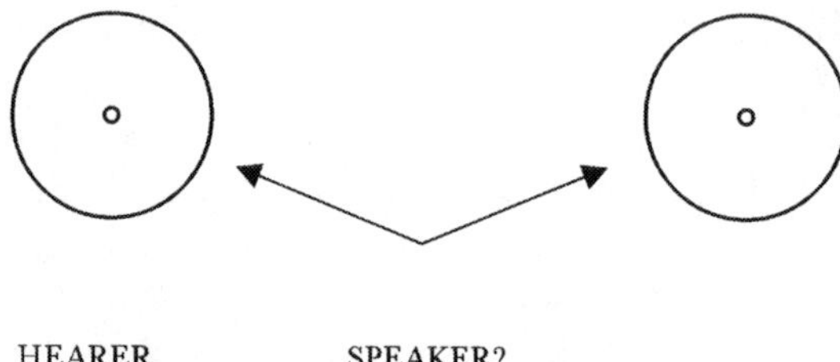

Figure 4. Hearer locates Speaker socially and regionally on the basis of his/her speech pattern in a general way

We assume that Hearer categorizes the speech pattern of Speaker and evokes an entrenched, metonymic schema concerning the speech style in question and the social categorization that effected it. The central images of both lectal and social categorizations operate as cognitive reference point-constructions. Such categories are presumably naturally organised around clusters of elements in the visual or auditory modalities which are distinctive enough to establish perceptual contrast with neighbouring categories. Lectal categorization thus seems to involve a conceptualizer who correlates a token (stretch of unidentified speech) with a number of idealized speech models (linguistic stereo*types*). The similarity may be relative, of course; two people who "speak with the same accent" obviously do not speak exactly the same way. Rather, their intonation patterns, phonetic realizations and phonemic slots are judged to be relatively similar when compared to an abstract model. When similar instantiations of speech are categorized as "sort of the same thing", minor differences become discarded as irrelevant, at least for the purposes of first-hand ad hoc categorization.

5.2. More precise lectal and social categorization

The situation described in (b), however, departs from that of a general process of categorization. Say that, once two Speakers have been categorized as speaking "sort of the same accent", we realize that one of them speaks an accent which is "purer" than the other one. Accents constitute, like many non-linguistic triggers of social meaning, gradable notions and a token of speech may lead us to a central or less central instantiations of the type, depending on how far or close to the reference point construction of the category the token is judged. Accents, for instance, can be "strong, (really) heavy, slight, weak, pure, broad, (really) thick, nearby" or "foreign." Even in the case of a foreign accent, the speaker's L1 is often recognizable:

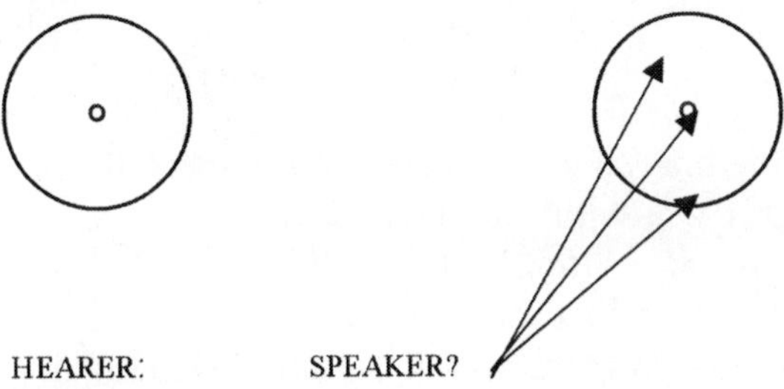

Figure 5. Hearer locates Speaker socially and regionally in more specific ways

In (b) then, Hearer identifies the relative position of Speaker with respect to a central image, the purest instantiation of an accent. As Rosch (1975: 545) once said "[...] the best examples of a category can serve as reference points in relation to which other category members are judged." In Langacker's (1993b) terms, the reference point – as the focus of the conceptualizer's attention – allows for further activation of instances within its dominion. This is probably what cognitive reference points are all about; as perceptually salient and maximally contrastive variants, they constitute natural landmarks that enable us to "navigate" in the cognitive sense from one domain to another or focus our attention on a subdomain.

5.3. Hearer locates Speaker relative to herself himself: Styles, shifts and subjectification

The situation in (c) is fundamentally different from the rest. For a start it involves a (more or less conscious) process of **self**-categorizing of

Hearer. Once both participants have been categorized on the part of at least one of the two conceptualizers, a relative positioning of Hearer with respect to Speaker which is absent in (a) and (b) now forms part of the speech event:

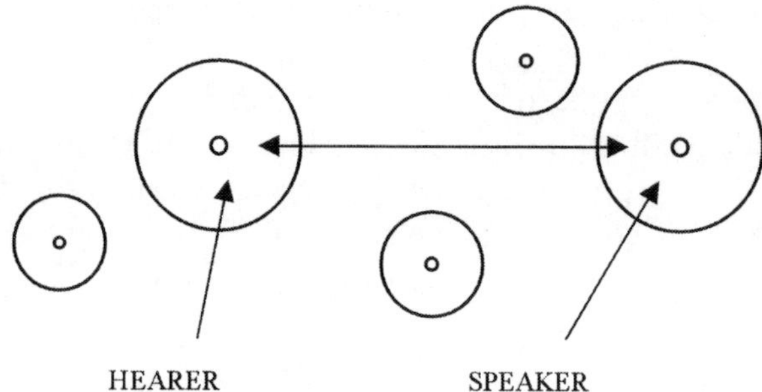

Figure 6. Hearer locates Speaker relative to him/herself

And if "something is somewhere with respect to another entity" – Speaker is at a Place with respect to Hearer – it is not far-fetched to speak of a *deictic* operation. When Fillmore (1982: 43) analysed the use of ostensive "this", as in *I just bought this* (a Locative Expression with an Identifying function), he applied Talmy's (1980) notions of *Figure*, *Place* and *Ground*:

> […] an expression by which a Figure is said to be at a Place identified with reference to a Ground. In the particular case of *deictic* Locating Expressions, the Ground is the Speaker's (or in some cases the Hearer's) body.

At first sight the situations described in (a) and (b) resemble a deictic operation, too. In these cases, however, it seems to be relative *perceptual similarity* – i.e. the relative degree of identity – between reference-point and an unidentified element that enables us to categorize a token as a type. In the case of a spatial deictic operation, the Figure is not *similar* to the Ground. Rather, we are able to locate or identify the Figure because of factors such as *relative distance, relative orientation,* or *active zones.* Furthermore, in deixis the Ground (i.e. an element known to the decoder of the message, a reference point construction) forms part of the immediate context, the speech situation itself. As Fillmore (1975: 38) explained, deictic aspects of language require *contextualization*:

> […] lexical items and grammatical forms which can be interpreted only when the sentences in which they occur are understood as being anchored

in some social context, that context defined in such a way as to identify the participants in the communication act, their location in space, and the time during which the communication act is performed.

In (a) and (b) Hearer does not make use of an immediate social context in order to identify Speaker socially. Rather, he applies his knowledge about the central images of lectal categories. The conceptualizer makes use of a much wider, stable and entrenched kind of "context" which is not dependent upon factors involved in the speech event as such. In (c), however, Speaker is located **relative to Hearer**, who thus no longer limits himself to categorizing Speaker lectally and socially. This, of course, is a multidimensional picture.

An enlightening framework within which this situation can be analysed has been provided by Langacker (1990, 1991b, 1993a; 1993b). "Context" is a complex notion, indeed, and in this respect Langacker's (1990: 9–11) distinction between *Ground* – "the speech event, its participant, and its immediate circumstances (such as the time and place of speaking)" and *Landmark* – "a salient entity other than the trajector" is useful in the sense that it provides us with more complex tools. For the sake of clarity and since Langacker's terminology differs with respect to that of Talmy and Fillmore, let us briefly schematize the correspondences:

Table 4. Correspondences between terms used to describe spatial relationships

Talmy/ Fillmore	Figure		Place	Ground	
Langacker	Trajector	Path		Landmark	Ground
	Localized entity	*Direction*	*Location of entity*	*Reference point*	*Situation, participants, conceptualizer*

Langacker's dynamic model brings in additional dimensions. In his analysis of the sentence "Mulroney was sitting across the table" (1993a: 54) he observes that the speaker (or conceptualizer) follows a path *subjectively*: "he traces along it mentally in order to specify the trajector's location with respect to some reference point (*R*). The Trajector (*Mulroney*), in other words, is located not only with respect to a known object, the Landmark (*table*) but also with respect to an element which forms part of the Ground: the conceptualizer himself. As Langacker (1993a: 52) explains, in the alternative construal "Mulroney was sitting across the table from me," the explicit mentioning of the conceptualizer has an objectifying impact: the scene is portrayed in rather neutral terms, as when one describes a photograph to someone else. In similar terms, we might say that Hearer conceptualizes Speaker in a rather subjective way in both (a) and (b). In (c), however, Speaker is more objectively construed. And crucially, as in the case of "someone sitting across the table", **two different reference point constructions** are clearly at work at the same time: the same contextually stable schemata that also operate in (a) and (b) to categorise Speaker lectally and socially and a contextual variable that forms part of the speech event, the Ground, itself: Speaker is perceived relative to the position of Hearer. It is this relative awareness of the fact that both Hearer and Speaker are onstage in the same speech event which gives rise to the situations in (d)–(f).

5.4. Hearer changes his/her relative position with respect to Speaker

If Hearer and Speaker both form part of the Ground, Hearer may now, in the terminology of Speech Accommodation Theory, henceforth SAT, (Giles *et al.* 1987), *converge towards*, *diverge from* or *maintain his position with respect to* Speaker's style (or his perception of Speaker's style):

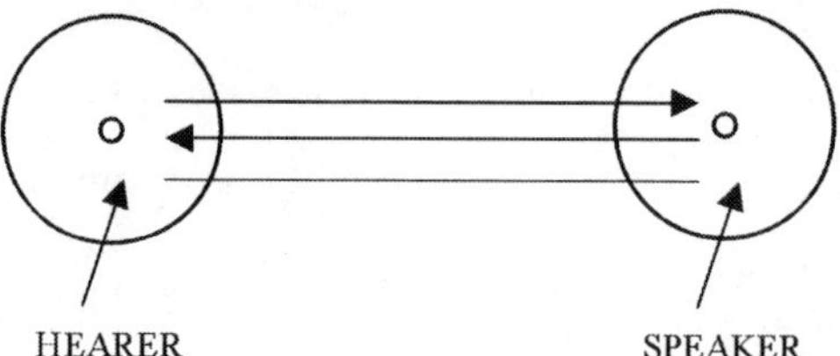

Figure 7. Hearer changes his/her code with respect to that of Speaker

The logic behind such moves seems to be that linguistic distance eventually equals social distance – after all like things are categorized together as basically the same thing. It is clear that the roles now become inverted; Hearer, either above or below the level of consciousness, exploits Speaker's own role as Hearer, his receptive competence and ability to locate people on a linguistic trigger-social target axis. In SAT, ***convergence*** is "a linguistic strategy by means of which individuals adapt to each other's speech by means of a wide range of linguistic features, including speech rates, pauses and utterance length, pronunciations and so on" (Giles *et al.* 1987: 14). Since convergence is to be expected in all positively oriented speech situations, ***maintenance***, i.e. absence of convergence, is in itself a negative sign. ***Divergence***, on the other hand, involves "the way in which speakers accentuate vocal differences between themselves and others" (*Ibid.*). Speech divergence is an intergroup process by means of which speakers achieve 'psycholinguistic distinctiveness'. Convergence can be mutual (A → ← B) and eventually produce similarity between styles, or less frequently lead to change in speech styles (A →B; A ← B). Convergence may also not be mutual (A → B). Both participants may maintain their respective speech styles (A – B). Divergence can be mutual (← A B →) or not (← A B) and a participant can engage in convergence and the other in divergence (← A ← B). It is important to realize that in SAT, when a speaker converges, diverges, or maintains his speech pattern, it is to be regarded as an *action*.

5.5. Hearer changes his/her speech style towards an existing stereotypical pattern

Hearer can also try to adopt the typical speech pattern of a group or individual which is different from that of both Hearer and Speaker:

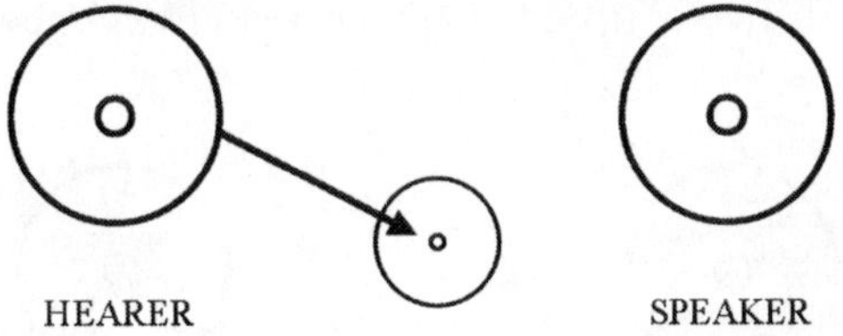

Figure 8. Hearer changes his/her speech style towards an existing pattern

Neither Bell's (1984; 1999) Audience Design model nor Wolfram and Schilling-Estes' (1998) Speaker Design model distinguish between codes and styles at all; we shift (style or code) when we take on certain roles and project social identities. These may be different from those of Speaker and Hearer (Bell's 'referee design'). The possibility of adopting the speech pattern of a non-present "participant" undoubtedly adds further dimensions to the picture drawn so far. For a start, as Hearer does not limit himself to an imitation of speech produced in the speech situation *in situ*, it strengthens the argument that humans possess receptive and active competence of speech styles which are stored in our long-term memory. We seem to be able to draw upon knowledge about relatively entrenched lectal schemata[10] and their relationship to social categories

10. By 'entrenched lectal schemata' I mean knowledge of speech styles which hearer builds up determined by his social and regional situatedness. Much

or social situations in order to bring about an effect on Hearer. Or even in order to count on emotive support in a given speech situation, as the presence of any third party which is important for us may be invoked effectively through an imitation of the speech pattern in question. Change towards a speech pattern which does not coincide with that of the interlocutor also involves cases of more persistent change towards the features and values of a community with which our Hearer/Speaker wishes to identify on a permanent basis (e.g. cases of regional or social mobility). When the features of a particular accent begin to spread throughout the social and regional dimensions of a country, it is because there are speakers who choose to adopt the features. The link between linguistic feature and social meaning is an obvious motivating factor and one which serves to throw doubt on the belief that sound change is systematic but socially unmotivated.

5.6. Hearer develops a new style, exploiting existing speech patterns

Entrenched, wide-scale socio-regional styles may also be exploited for other purposes; drawing upon available resources, new local identities may be set up:

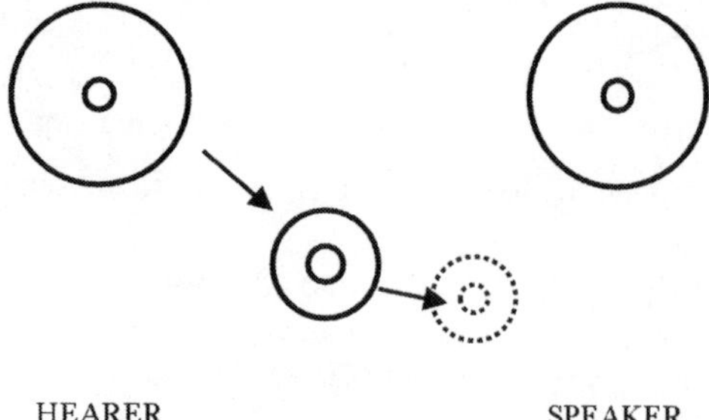

Figure 9. Hearer develops a new style, exploiting existing speech patterns

As Eckert (2004) reports, British English released final /t/ (i.e. a stop where the airstream is not only retained but afterwards released in a way which is audible to the hearer) and the psychological attributes associated

---

as in the case of social stereotypes, it is not a question of acquisition of ready-made packets of knowledge, but a situated and relational process involving real speakers, real situations, a real historical moment and an environment with a series of real social and physical resources. Lectal schemata, in other words, are experientially grounded.

with such a typical British feature has been put to various uses by American speakers:

> British speakers of English regularly release their /t/s, and Americans adopt this feature when imitating British English. The age-old stereotype of the British, and British English, as superior, intelligent and educated is no doubt at work here. A distinction made at the international level, then, seems to be providing American speakers with a resource for signaling superiority of a variety of sorts, but it seems to be primarily limited to intelligence, education, and articulateness.

The uses to which these meaningful correlations are put include the following (Eckert 2004):

(a) to convey the superiority and intellectuality of a group of high school girls:

> Mary Bucholtz (1996) has noted the use of this variable by a group of high school girls fashioning themselves as geeks. These girls saw themselves as intelligent – not as goody-goody good students, but as smarter than their teachers. Their use of /t/ release was a prominent resource in their development of a distinctive "intellectual" verbal style.

(b) to convey orthodox Jewishness and in part also masculinity:

> /t/ release is also often heard as Jewish, and particularly as Orthodox. Sarah Benor (2001) examined this variable in a study of kids in an Orthodox community and found that it indexed masculinity, inasmuch as masculinity is tied with Talmudic study. Further, she found that – among both boys and girls – those who had been to Yeshiva released /t/ more than those who had not.

(c) to convey gay identity:

> Comparing the language of a medical student, in the clinic with patients and at a barbecue with his friends, Podesva (2004) found a subtle pattern in the use of /t/ release. The medical student, Heath, adopts a highly competent and educated persona in the clinic, but a playful "bitchy diva" persona among his friends at the barbecue. As it turns out, he uses significantly more /t/ release in the clinic than at the barbecue, in keeping with the meaning of preciseness, intelligence and education that one would certainly want to evoke when functioning as a physician. At the barbecue, however, the bursts of the /t/ releases are rarer but significantly longer.

Entrenched styles and the entrenched social meanings which go with them may thus serve as the basis of new styles and relatively new meanings.

6. Conclusions

Once we realize that lectal and social categorizations are intimately related, we may begin to explore the possible functions and uses of speech styles. In this paper I have tried to reach a deeper understanding of the things that we do when we "style-shift". It is clear that linguistic competence, both active and receptive, is not just a question of access (to education, to literacy or to a better job), but also a subtle question of social categorization, social characterization and social positioning.

We might even wish to begin to consider the possibility of a diachronic prototype dialectology. At any given moment, a non-salient variety may gain prestige on any relevant dimension, and prestigious varieties may become increasingly non-central. In both cases, speakers who acknowledge the existence of entrenched relationships between linguistic and social schemata may engage in style-shifting or gradually adopt a number of the most prominent features. Social identities, in short, can be profiled because structured linguistic patterns relate in systematic ways to social meaning. Eventually, linguistic inventories may undergo changes, as well. Some features spread as the result of having gained prestige (or acquired other functional qualities), either on a global societal level or within the low-level strata of a community (cf. Labov 2001, 2007). Other features drop out of a language altogether, or become reduced to small speech communities. Such a perspective, which is not at odds with more structurally-oriented explanations such as chain-shifts and moves involving intra-systemic phonemic slots (cf. Labov 1994), constitutes a scenario within which the study of speech styles as socially motivated construals finds a most natural place.

Notes

1. To do full justice to Saussure, one must first read his *Cours de Linguistique Générale* in detail and understand his aims and achievements as an early 20th century linguist. Saussure *was* aware of the importance of cultural factors on language and of the role of language in constituting culture ([...] c' est dans une large mesure la langue que fait la nation. CLG: 40), but the discovery that a language can (far more easily) be systematically analysed when one operates at rather high levels of abstraction (*langue*) turned Saussure posthumously into the father of structuralism. As Saussure, in this paper we look into structured variation at the level of the group, but at intermediate levels with respect to Saussure's *langue* (a social construct, but one shared by *all* the members of a speech community) and *parole* (a purely individual and momentary manifestation; Il n'y a donc rien de collectif dans la parole; les manifesta-

tions sont individuelles et momentanées. CLG: 38) Regarding the relationship between oral and written language, Saussure (CLG: 45) wrote the following:

> Langue et écriture sont deux systèmes de signes distincts; l'unique raison d'être du second est de représenter le premier; l'objet linguistique n'est pas défini par la combinaison du mot écrit et du mot parlé; ce dernier constitue à lui seul cet objet. Mais le mot écrit se mêle si intimement au mot parlé dont il est l'image, qu'il finit par usurper le rôle principal; on en vient à donner autant et plus d'importance à la représentation du signe vocal qu'à ce signe lui-même. C'est comme si l'on croyait que, pour connaître quelqu'un, il vaut mieux regarder sa photographie que son visage.

2. Traditionally, dialectologists studied *regional* dialects. However, the discovery made by urban dialectology that language varies as much socially (i.e. within the same area) as regionally, led to a division into regional dialects and *social-class dialects.* Also the notion of regional dialect had to become restructured (Trudgill 1999) into *traditional dialects* (regional dialects or local dialects) and *mainstream dialects* (the standard variety and modern dialects), more influenced by social stratification. Traditional dialects present more differences amongst themselves and with respect to the standard variety of British English than mainstream dialects (cp. *she bain't a-comin, hoo inno comin* and *her idden comin* for the mainstream versions *she's not coming, she isn't coming* and *she ain't comin*). Traditional dialects are spoken in remote, rural areas, and are in the process of becoming extinct as the once self-contained agrarian communities have become more mobile and subject to urban, even "globalized" lifestyles. Compulsory education (from the last quarter of the 19th century in the case of Britain), the influence of mass media (last quarter of the 20th century onwards) also constitute converging factors. The result was a series of processes involving dialect levelling and dialect mixing. Consequently a new subcategory of similar dialects, labelled mainstream dialects, arose, which began to absorb the traditional dialects. Mainstream dialects include the standard variety and a wide range of *modern dialects.* These are spoken in non-rural areas and are more similar to one another and to the standard variety than traditional dialects. The standard variety, in spite of being the most prestigious in Britain and most of the English-speaking world is spoken by a rather small percentage (between 12 and 15 per cent) of the population as a "mother dialect."

References

Allport, Gordon W.
1954 *The Nature of Prejudice.* Cambridge, MA: Addison Wesley.

Altendorf, Ulrike
1999 Estuary English: Is English going Cockney? *Moderna Språk* XCIII: 1–11.

Barlow, Michael and Suzanne Kemmer (eds.)
2000 *Usage-based Models of Language*. Stanford, Cal.: CSLI Publications.

Bell, Allan
1984 Language style as audience design. *Language in Society* 13: 145–204.
1999 Styling the other to define the self: A study in New Zealand identity making. *Journal of Sociolinguistics* 3 (4): 523–541.

Chambers, Jack K. and Peter Trudgill
1998 *Dialectology*. Cambridge: Cambridge University Press.

Coggle, Paul
1993 *Do you Speak Estuary? The New Standard English. How to Spot it and Speak it*. London: Bloomsbury Publishing Ltd.

Dirven, René and Marjolijn H. Verspoor
2004 *Cognitive Explorations of Language and Linguistics*. Amsterdam/Philadelphia: Benjamins.

Eckert, Penelope
2004 The meaning of style. Online document: accessed November 11, 2007: http://www.stanford.edu/~eckert/PDF/salsa2003.pdf

Fanego, Teresa
2004 Is Cognitive Grammar a usage-based model? Towards a realistic account of English sentential complements. Miscelánea. A Journal of English and American Studies 29: 23–58.

Fillmore, Charles J.
1975 *Santa Cruz Lectures on Deixis 1971*. Bloomington, Indiana: Indiana University Linguistics Club.
1982 Towards a descriptive framework for spatial deixis. In: Robert Jarvella and Wolfgang Klein (eds.), *Speech, Place, & Action. Studies in Deixis and Related Topics*, 31–59. Chichester: John Wiley & Sons Ltd.

Geeraerts, Dirk
2001 On measuring lexical convergence. In: Augusto Soares da Silva (ed.), *Linguagem e Cognição*, 51–61. Braga: Associação Portuguesa de Linguística.
2005 Lectal variation and empirical data in Cognitive Linguistics. In: Francisco J. Ruiz de Mendoza Ibáñez and M. Sandra Peña Cervel (eds), *Cognitive Linguistics. Internal Dynamics and Interdisciplinary Interaction*, 163–190. Cognitive Linguistics Research 32. Berlin/New York: Mouton de Gruyter.

Geeraerts, Dirk, Stefan Grondelaers and Peter Bakema
1994 *The Structure of Lexical Variation: Meaning, Naming, and Context*. Berlin/New York: Mouton de Gruyter.

Geeraerts, Dirk, Stefan Grondelaers and Dirk Speelman
1999 *Convergentie en Divergentie in de Nederlandse Woordenschat. Een Onderzoek naar Kleding- en Voetbaltermen*. Amsterdam: Meertens Institut.

Giles, Howard, Anthony Mulac, James J. Bradac and Patricia Johnson
1987 Speech accommodation theory. The next decade and beyond. In: Margaret L. McLaughlin (ed.), *Communication Yearbook* 10: 13–48. Beverly Hills: Sage.

Gries, Stefan Th.
2003 *Multifactorial Analysis in Corpus Linguistics. A Study of Particle Placement*. London/New York: Continuum Press.

Grondelaers, Stefan
2000 *De distributie van niet-anaforisch er buiten de eerste zinplaats: Sociolexicologische, functionele en psycholinguïstische aspecten van er's status als presentatief signaal.* Unpublished PhD thesis, K.U. Leuven.

Halliday, Michael A. K.
1978 *Language as Social Semiotic*. London: Edward Arnold.

Haugen, Einer
1966 Dialect, language, nation. *American Anthropologist* 68: 922–935.

Holland, Dorothy and Naomi Quinn
1987 *Cultural Models in Language and Thought.* Cambridge: Cambridge University Press.

Hudson, Richard, A.
1980 *Sociolinguistics*. Cambridge: Cambridge University Press.

Hughes, Arthur and Peter Trudgill
1987 *English Accents and Dialects. An Introduction to Social and Regional Varieties of British English.* 2nd ed. London: Edward Arnold.

Jones, Daniel
1979 *English Pronouncing Dictionary.* 14th ed. London: J. M. Dent & Sons Ltd.

Kristiansen, Gitte
2003 How to do things with allophones: Linguistic stereotypes as cognitive reference points in social cognition. In: René Dirven, Martin Pütz and Roslyn M. Frank (eds.), *Cognitive Models in Language and Thought. Ideology, Metaphors, and Meanings*, 69–120. Cognitive Linguistics Research 24. Berlin/New York: Mouton de Gruyter.
2006 Towards a usage-based cognitive phonology. *International Journal of English Studies* 6 (2): 107–140.
2008 Idealized cultural models: The group as variable in the development of cognitive schemata. In: Roslyn M. Frank, René Dirven, Tom Ziemke and Enrique Bernárdez (eds.), *Body, Language, and Mind. Volume II: Sociocultural Situatedness*. Cognitive Linguistics Research. Berlin/New York: Mouton de Gruyter.
to appear Lectal varieties and child language acquisition. Paper derived from the theme session Cognitive Sociolinguistics: Language-internal variation, Cognition and Cognitive Representations, ICLC10, Krakow, July 2007.

Labov, William
1966 *The Social Stratification of English in New York City.* Washington, DC: Center for Applied Linguistics.
1994 *Principles of Linguistic change.* Vol I. Internal Factors. Oxford: Blackwell.
2001 *Principles of Linguistic change.* Vol II. Social Factors. Oxford: Blackwell.
2007 Transmission and diffusion. *Language* 83: 344–387.

Lakoff, George
1987 *Women, Fire, and Dangerous Things. What Categories Reveal about the Mind.* Chicago: The University of Chicago Press.

Lambert, Wallace E., Richard Hodgson, Robert C. Gardner and Samuel Fillenbaum
1960 Evaluational reactions to spoken languages. *Journal of Abnormal and Social Psychology* 60: 44–51.

Langacker, Ronald W.
1990 Subjectification. *Cognitive Linguistics* 1-1: 5–38.
1991 *Concept, Image, and Symbol. The Cognitive basis of Grammar.* Berlin/New York: Mouton de Gruyter.
1993a Deixis and subjectivity. In: S. K. Verma and S. Prakasam (eds.), *New Horizons in Functional Linguistics*, 43–58. Hyderabad: Booklinks Corporations.
1993b Reference-point constructions. *Cognitive Linguistics* 4 (1): 1–38.
1999 *Grammar and Conceptualization.* Berlin/New York: Mouton de Gruyter.

Le Page, Robert
1980 'Projection, focussing, diffusion' or, steps towards a sociolinguistic theory of language. *York Papers in Linguistics* 9: 9–31.

Lippi-Green, Rosina
1997 *English with an Accent. Language, Ideology, and Discrimination in the United States.* London: Routledge.

Lo, Adrienne
1999 Codeswitching, speech community membership, and the construction of ethnic identity. *Journal of Sociolinguistics* 3 (4): 461–479.

Morgan, Pamela
2001 The Semantics of Impeachment: Meanings and Models in a Political Conflict. In: René Dirven, Roslyn Frank and Cornelia Ilie (eds.), *Language and Ideology. Volume II: Descriptive Cognitive Approaches*, 77–106. Amsterdam/Philadelphia: Benjamins.

Nathan, Geoffrey S.
1986 Phonemes as mental categories. *Proceedings of the Berkeley Linguistic Society* 12: 212–223.
1996 Steps towards a cognitive phonology. In: Bernhard Hurch and Richard Rhodes (eds.), *Natural Phonology: The State of the Art*, 107–120. Berlin/New York: Mouton de Gruyter.

Petyt, Keith M.
1977 'Dialect'and 'accent' in the Industrial West Riding. Reading University. Unpublished Ph.D. thesis.
Purnell, Thomas, William J. Idsardi and John Baugh
1999 Perceptual and phonetic experiments on American English dialect identification. *Journal of Language and Social Psychology* 18: 10–30.
Ruiz de Mendoza Ibáñez, Francisco José and Lorena Pérez Hernández
2001 Metonymy and the grammar: motivation, constraints and interaction. *Language & Communication* 21: 321–357.
Rosch, Eleanor
1975 Cognitive Reference Points. *Cognitive Psychology* 7: 532–547.
1999 Reclaiming concepts. *Journal of Consciousness Studies* 6 (11): 61–77.
Saussure, Ferdinand de
1969 [1916] *Cours de Linguistique Générale*. 3rd ed. published by Charles Bally and Albert Sechehaye. Paris: Payot.
Searle, John, R.
1979 *Expression and Meaning: Studies in the Theory of Speech Acts*. Cambridge: Cambridge University Press.
Sharifian, Farzad
2003 On cultural conceptualisations. *Journal of Cognition and Culture* 3 (3): 187–206.
this vol. Cultural models of Home in Aboriginal children's English.
Stefanowitsch, Anatol and Stefan Th. Gries
2003 Collostructions: Investigating the interaction of words and constructions. *International Journal of Corpus Linguistics* 8: 209–244.
Tajfel, Henri
1969 Cognitive aspects of prejudice. *Journal of Social Issues* 25: 79–97.
1978 Social categorization, social identity and social comparison. In: Henri Tajfel (ed.), *Differentiation between Social Groups*, 61–76. London: Academic Press.
1981 *Human groups and social categories*. Cambridge: Cambridge University Press.
Talmy, Leonard
1980 *The Representation of Space by Language*. Manuscript. Cognitive Science Program. University of California at San Diego.
Taylor, John R.
2002 *Cognitive Grammar*. Oxford: Oxford University Press.
Thrane, Torben
1980 *Referential-Semantic Analysis. Aspects of a Theory of Linguistic Reference*. Cambridge: Cambridge University Press.
Trudgill, Peter
1974 The Social Differentiation of English in Norwich. Cambridge: Cambridge University Press.

1979 Standard and non-standard dialects of English in the United Kingdom: problems and policies. *International Journal of the Sociology of Language* 21: 9–24.
1982 *Sociolinguistics.* Cambridge: Cambridge University Press.
1999 *The Dialects of England*, 2nd ed. Oxford: Basil Blackwell. Original edition, Oxford: Basil Blackwell, 1990.

Wells, John C.
1982 *Accents of English.* Cambridge: Cambridge University Press.
1994 Transcribing Estuary English: a discussion document. *Speech, Hearing and Language: UCL Work in Progress* 8: 259–267.
1997 What is Estuary English? *English Teaching Professional* 3: 46–47.
1999 http://www.phon.ucl.ac.uk/home/estuary/home.htm (ed.) On-line documents on Estuary English. Accessed August 17, 2008.

Wolfram, Wolfram and Natalie Schilling-Estes
1998 *American English: Dialects and Variation.* Oxford: Blackwell.

Part two
Usage-based variation research

Methodological issues in corpus-based Cognitive Linguistics

Kris Heylen, José Tummers and Dirk Geeraerts

Abstract

A current trend in Cognitive Linguistics is the growing interest in empirical methods for linguistic analysis. Two groups of researchers, centred around Gries and Stefanowitsch (G&S[1]) and around Geeraerts, Speelman and Grondelaers (QLVL[2]), have relatively independently from each other tried to develop a methodology for empirical research in Cognitive Linguistics that is based on thorough quantitative analysis of corpus data. This article discusses a number of case studies into syntactic variation of both approaches. It points out some of the methodological differences between them and compares how they deal with the inherent challenges posed by the spontaneous usage represented in corpora: Both approaches use multivariate statistics to deal with the simultaneous effect of multiple factors, but G&S have additionally developed methods to study the interaction between lexical variability and syntactic variation. On the other hand, G&S take a strongly psycholinguistic perspective on syntactic variation that tends to disregard the offline nature and sociolinguistic heterogeneity of corpus data. These latter two properties are a central concern of QLVL.

Keywords: linguistic methodology, quantitative corpus analysis, variation studies.

1. Corpus-based Cognitive Linguistics

Recently, there has been an increased interest in methodological issues within the Cognitive Linguistics community[3]. More and more researchers

1. Stefan Gries is associate professor at the University of California, Santa Barbara: http://www.linguistics.ucsb.edu/faculty/stgries. Anatol Stefanowitsch is full professor at the University of Bremen (Germany): http://www-user.zfn.uni-bremen.de/~anatol/.
2. Research Unit *Quantitative Lexicology and Variational Linguistics* at the University of Leuven (Belgium): http://wwwling.arts.kuleuven.be/qlvl.
3. Illustrated by the *Empirical Methods in Cognitive Linguistics* workshop at Cornell University (NY, USA) in May 2003, by the theme session on the use

feel that traditional methods of linguistic enquiry, relying mainly on introspective analysis, are not sufficient for the study of cognitive grammar or conceptualization processes. Several alternatives to broaden the empirical basis of Cognitive Linguistics are currently being explored[4], but since Cognitive Linguistics is essentially a usage-based approach, corpora containing naturally occurring language use play a central role[5]. In an effort to investigate complex usage patterns with maximal objectivity, a number of studies have introduced sophisticated quantitative methods to analyse corpus data. These studies rely on explanatory notions adopted by the Cognitive Linguistics framework, but operationalize them in such a way that their relevance for a given linguistic phenomenon can be empirically validated in large corpora by means of advanced statistical techniques. Often, these statistical techniques have been developed in computational linguistics or the wider field of corpus linguistics but for purposes other than the explanation of the human cognitive language system. The merit of these studies then, lies mainly in the bringing together of a powerful theoretical framework (Cognitive Linguistics) with powerful empirical methods of analysis (quantitative corpus analysis).

The methodology of "cognitive linguistically inspired" quantitative corpus analysis has been developed relatively independently by two main groups of researchers: Gries, Stefanowitsch and colleagues (G&S) on the one hand and Geeraerts, Speelman, Grondelaers and colleagues (QLVL) on the other. Both approaches are very comparable, although there are some differences in the investigated phenomena, the explanatory perspec-

---

of corpora at ICLC 2003 in Logroño (Spain), by the CSDL 2004 conference theme *Experimental and Empirical Methods* at the University of Alberta (Canada), the upcoming theme session "Language System and Language Use: Corpus-Based Approaches" at ICLC 2005 in Seoul, or by the drawn-out discussion on empirical methods on the COGLING mailing list (started by Suzie Bartsch, July 4th 2004).

4. Interestingly, a similar discussion about methodological innovation is taking place in the Generative Grammar community exemplified by events like the workshop on *Quantitative Investigations in Theoretical Linguistics* (Osnabrück, Germany, October 2002) or the *Conference on Linguistic Evidence* (Tübingen, Germany, January 2004), and by publications like Schütze (1996), Cowart (1997), Sorace and Keller (2005) or Wasow (2002).
5. The Neural Theory of Language project developed by Feldman, Lakoff, Shastri and others (see http://www.icsi.berkeley.edu/NTL/) can also be seen as an evolution towards more empirical research methods, viz. neurolinguistic experiments.

tive and the precise statistical techniques. Nonetheless, these two approaches have the potential to converge into a single promising methodology for empirical usage-based research and, in the long run, a fully-fledged methodological framework for corpus-based Cognitive Linguistics. This paper tries to contribute to that evolution by discussing the methodological differences between both approaches and by exploring how they can complement each other. To allow a direct comparison, we look at a number of case studies that have occupied a central position within both approaches and that have applied the methodology to a similar type of linguistic phenomenon, viz. syntactic variation. As a benchmark, we use some of the inherent challenges that corpus data pose for a usage-based analysis and we compare how both approaches deal with these challenges. They include the multifactorial complexity of spontaneous usage, the offline nature of corpus data, and the cultural and situational diversity represented in most corpora.

The article is structured as follows. In section 2, we introduce a central case study of syntactic variation for each approach. Section 3 outlines some fundamental properties of corpus data viz. multifactorial complexity, offline nature and lectal diversity, and compares how each approach deals with these. Section 4 discusses how the differences in dealing with these properties are partly due to an underlying difference in perspective. Finally in section 5, we draw some conclusions about the merits of both approaches and about the challenges that still lie ahead.

Although we try to make an objective comparison of both approaches, it should be pointed out that the present authors are affiliated with the QLVL research group. Even though the authors do not discuss their own research directly, this affiliation will inevitably introduce a bias towards those issues that are felt to be important by the research group at large. However, the aim of the article is to contribute to the ongoing discussion about methodological innovation in Cognitive Linguistics. We believe that a confrontation between different methodological approaches is vital for such a discussion.

This paper is part of a set of articles exploring the methodology of usage-based linguistics. Geeraerts (2005) discusses from a theoretical and epistemological point of view why a usage-based linguistics has to combine empirical enquiry with a sociolinguistic perspective. Tummers, Heylen and Geeraerts (2005) present an overview of the methodological state of the art in usage-based linguistics, charting the different levels of empirical and quantitative-technical sophistication displayed by research conducted under the heading 'usage-based'. The present article zooms in on what could be called the methodologically most advanced quantitative case studies of syntactic variation and explores the issues that arise when actual methodological choices have to be made.

2. Corpus-based Cognitive Linguistics

Although G&S and QLVL have both focussed on combining quantitative corpus analysis with explanatory notions from Cognitive Linguistic, they have covered quite different areas of linguistic research. With their *collostructional analysis*, G&S have explored the lexical properties of constructions as defined in Construction Grammar (Stefanowitsch and Gries 2003, 2005; Gries and Stefanowitsch 2004a, 2004b) They have also done quantitative corpus analyses of *morphological variation* (Gries 2003b), *blending* (Gries 2004a, 2004b, 2004c) and *metaphorical mappings* (Stefanowitsch 2004, 2005). QLVL's main focus has been on research into *lexicological variation* (Geeraerts, Grondelaers and Bakema 1994) and *sociolexicology* (Geeraerts, Grondelaers and Speelman 1999) with extensions to *register profiling* (Grondelaers, Geeraerts, Speelman and Tummers 2001; Speelman, Grondelaers and Geeraerts 2003) and *morphological variation* (Tummers, Speelman and Geeraerts 2004). However, there is one area of linguistic research that has occupied an important position in both groups, viz. **syntactic variation**. Within the G&S group, there have been studies into several types of syntactic variation in English like *particle placement* (Gries 1999, 2001a, 2001c, 2002a, 2003a, 2003c), *dative shift* (Gries and Stefanowitsch 2004a; Gries 2007, Stefanowitsch and Gries 2005), *genitive alternation* (Gries 2002b; Stefanowitsch 2003) and *adjective order* (Wulff 2003). Within the QLVL group, there have been syntactic variation studies into *Dutch presentatives* (Grondelaers and Brysbaert 1996; Grondelaers 2000; Grondelaers, Speelman and Carbonez 2001; Grondelaers, Brysbaert, Speelman and Geeraerts 2001; Grondelaers, Speelman, Drieghe, Geeraerts and Brysbaert *submitted*), *the word order in Dutch verb clusters* (De Sutter, Speelman, Geeraerts and Grondelaers 2003) and *verb argument order in German* (Heylen and Speelman 2003).

In the remainder of the article we will concentrate on the studies within this shared field of interest because the comparison between the two approaches is most straightforward there. Nevertheless, in both approaches there are interactions between the syntactic variation research and the other strands of research so that the latter will still be alluded to occasionally. In what follows, we shortly present the two most elaborate case studies of syntactic variation within the respective approaches, viz. particle placement in English, as studied by Stefan Gries, and Dutch presentatives, as studied by Stefan Grondelaers[6].

2.1. Particle placement in English

Particle placement in English[7] is a type of word order variation that occurs with transitive phrasal verbs, i.e. composite transitive verbs that are made up of a verb and a verb particle. The verb particle can either precede the direct object (ex. 1) or follow it (ex. 2).

(1) *Fred picked up the book*
(2) *Fred picked the book up*

Previous studies have proposed a large amount of variables that might influence particle placement, including phonological, morphosyntactic, semantic and discourse-functional factors. As Gries (2003c: 12–43) points out, previous studies have not been able to give a clear picture of the exact effect of many variables, nor have they given an adequate explanation that integrates the different variables. This seems mainly due to methodological deficiencies. The majority of studies relies on notoriously unreliable introspective analyses of made-up sentences and intuitive acceptability judgements. Furthermore, most studies consider only one factor at a time, not doing justice to the variation's multifactorial complexity. Apart from formulating a cognitive-functional explanation of particle placement, Gries therefore aims "to establish new methods for analysing syntactic variation and show that many new insights can be gained by combining multifactorial statistical procedures and a cognitively oriented perspective" (Gries 2003c: 46).

For the cognitive-functional explanation of particle placement, Gries takes a psycholinguistic perspective, i.e. "the perspective of online speech production" (2003c: 7). He puts forward the *Processing Hypothesis* (Gries

6. Since Grondelaers is the main author of the research into Dutch presentatives, we will mainly refer to him in the discussion, but it should be noted that much of the research was done in close collaboration with Dirk Speelman. Most notably, Dirk Speelman is responsible for the statistical analyses.
7. A book-length treatment of Gries' research of particle placement is Gries 2003c. An overview article (19 pages) is provided by Gries 2002a.

2003c: 48–66) which states that the speaker will subconsciously choose the order of verb particle and direct object in a way that minimizes cognitive processing effort. Most variables from the literature are hypothesized to have in common that they influence processing cost and, via processing cost, particle placement. For most variables this means that the verb particle will precede the direct object when the direct object requires a lot of processing effort, whereas the verb particle will follow the direct object when the latter requires little processing effort[8]. For example, the direct object in ex. 2 above requires little processing effort because it is both short and concrete so that object-particle is the preferred order. In ex. 3 below on the other hand, the direct object is fairly long and abstract and thus fairly demanding in processing terms. Speakers will in this case probably use the particle-object order.

(3) *He thought up a new and complicated theory of syntactic change*

To test the Processing Hypothesis, Gries (2003c) performs a multifactorial corpus analysis. 403 instances of particle placement, i.e. clauses containing a transitive phrasal verb and a direct object (DO), are extracted from the British National Corpus. The instances are nearly equally distributed between written and spoken materials. Next, the instances are annotated for the response variable (order of the DO and verb particle) and for 21 explanatory variables. Most of the explanatory variables are taken from previous studies, but they are operationalized in such a way that every instance can be assigned one value per explanatory variable[9]. They include variables like *length of the DO*, *NP-type of the DO*, *complexity of the DO*, *concreteness of the DO's referent*, *idiomaticity of the verb*, *times of preceding mention of the DO's referent in discourse*,

8. In the penultimate chapter of his book on particle placement (2003c: 157–184), Gries reinterprets the Processing Hypothesis in terms of Interactive Activation Models. There, the notion of processing cost is replaced by activation: lower processing cost of the direct object leads to earlier and stronger activation and earlier production.
9. Operationalization of variables is a non-trivial task. Gries operationalizes some variables from the literature in more than one way, e.g. *length of the direct object* is both measured in words and syllables. Some variables, like *phonetic shape of the verb*, are not operationalized, because they cannot be measured reliably. Gries also refines operationalizations over time: e.g. the operationalization of *entrenchment* (1999) is replaced by a set of other variables like *animacy* and *concreteness of the DO's referent* (2003c).

times of subsequent mention of the DO's referent in discourse, and *Channel* (spoken vs. written). With the annotation completed, the separate effect of each variable on particle placement is statistically tested. The results are argued to be in line with the Processing Hypothesis: the morpho-syntactic variables (length, complexity), the semantic variables (idiomaticity, concreteness), discourse-functional variables pertaining to the preceding discourse (preceding mention) have a very significant effect, whereas discourse-functional variables pertaining to the following discourse (subsequent mention) have little effect. Particle placement appears also to be dependent on the channel difference spoken vs. written. Although it is very informative to know what the exact effect is of each separate variable, all of these variables influence particle placement simultaneously in actual language use. Therefore, Gries also investigates the combined effect of the variables. First, he analyses the strength of each variable relative to the other variables by pair-wise comparing variable values with conflicting word order preferences. The variable value that can 'impose' its word order preference most frequently can then be said to have the strongest relative effect on particle placement. Next, the combined effect of all explanatory variables is modelled with a multifactorial statistical technique called Linear Discriminant Analysis. The model assigns a weight to each variable which gives a measure of the contribution of that variable to the combined effect. The weights of the different variables are again argued to be in line with the Processing Hypothesis. The model also allows predicting particle placement for each instance. Prediction accuracy is then an indication how well the model accounts for the variation. A by all standards high, cross-validated prediction accuracy of 82,9% leads Gries to the conclusion that the Processing Hypothesis is indeed very well borne out by the empirical data and has to be accepted.

In later work and on a different data set (2443 instances culled from the *International Corpus of English – Great Britain*), Gries and Stefanowitsch (2004) have also studied the effect of lexical variability on particle placement with a statistical technique developed within their collostructional analysis framework. With a *distinctive collexeme analysis*, Gries and Stefanowitsch investigate for individual phrasal verbs whether one of the two word orders occurs significantly more frequently with that verb than on average. Verbs that are significantly linked to one order are called distinctive collexemes of that order. The distribution of distinctive verb collexemes over the word orders mirrors the effect of the variable *idiomaticity* studied in the multifactorial corpus analysis: idiomatic verbs are typical of the particle-DO order, whereas literal verbs are characteristic of the DO-particle order. On the same data set, Gries (2005, 2007) also studies the effect of syntactic priming and rhythmic alternation. Results from the priming study indicate that the use of a specific particle-DO order primes the use of that same order with subsequent transitive phrasal verbs. Results from the rhythmic alternation study suggest that particle placement is influenced by the preference for alternating stressed and unstressed syllables.

2.2. Dutch presentatives

Grondelaers (2000) investigates Dutch adjunct-initial presentatives. These can be construed either with or without the particle *er* in post-verbal position.

(4) *Op de hoek van de straat is* ***(er)*** *een winkel*
on the corner of the street is **(there)** a shop
"At the corner of the street, there is a shop"

Some previous studies regard *er* as just a dummy particle; others have suggested a number of variables that might influence *er*-insertion, including language-internal variables, like verb type and adjunct type, and language-external[10] variables, like stylistic or regional differences. Yet the overall picture remains vague, so that the Dutch standard reference grammar maintains that "no strict rules can be given" (ANS 1997: 473). Those previous studies also suffered from severe methodological drawbacks: some used unreliable grammaticality judgements and most studied only one variable in isolation.

To overcome these shortcomings, Grondelaers[11] (2000) carries out a multifactorial corpus analysis. 2748 instances of adjunct-initial presentatives are extracted from the ConDiv corpus of written Dutch. The observations are annotated for the language-internal variables *adjunct type* (locative vs. temporal) and *verbal specificity*[12], and for the language-ex-

---

10. Language-internal variables pertain to phonetic, morpho-syntactic, semantic or pragmatic properties. Language-external variables include socio-cultural, regional and situational differences.
11. An overview article in English is Grondelaers, Speelman and Geeraerts (2002).
12. Operationalized as the size of the class of possible subject referents for which the verb subcategorizes. The variable constrasts the Levin (1993) classes VERBS OF EXISTENCE and VERBS OF APPEARANCE, which typically co-occur with specific entities (e.g. sit co-occurs with 'person' and 'chair'), with the unspe-

ternal factors *region* (Netherlands vs. Belgium) and *register formality* (on the cline Internet Relay Chat, usenet, popular newspapers, quality newspapers). First, a statistical analysis for each variable separately shows that all variables have a significant effect on *er*-insertion. Next, the combined effect of the variables is analysed using a multifactorial statistical technique called Logistic Regression Modelling, which models the combined effect of the variables on the odds in favour of *er*-insertion. The model assigns to every variable an effect parameter that gives a measure of the strength of that variable's contribution to the combined effect and that can be interpreted as an odds ratio, i.e. the variable's influence on the odds in favour of *er*-insertion. The model also includes significant interactions between variables. The language-internal variables have the strongest effect, but the external variables also have significant effects. Interestingly, there is also an interaction between adjunct-type and region. This leads Grondelaers to investigate whether *er*-insertion happens the same way in The Netherlands and Belgium. Separate logistic regression models for the two national varieties show that the effect of adjunct-type is significantly stronger in Netherlandic Dutch than in Belgian Dutch. The logistic regression model also allows predicting *er*-insertion for each instance. Prediction accuracy can then be used as an indication how well the model accounts for the variation. An overall accuracy of 85.2% indicates a fairly good (statistical) explanation of the variation, but the separate models for the two national varieties indicate that the Netherlandic presentatives can be better modelled (89.5%) than the Belgian ones (85.1%). In an additional corpus study, Grondelaers then zooms in on Belgian presentatives with a locative initial adjunct and investigates whether *topicality of the adjunct* and *spatial specificity of the adjunct* can help to improve the statistical explanation of *er*-insertion in Belgian Dutch. A logistic regression model confirms that *verbal specificity* is still the strongest variable, but the two adjunct related variables have a significant effect too. In a later study (Grondelaers, Speelman and Geeraerts 2003), a regression analysis of 1048 adjunct initial presentatives from the Corpus of Spoken Dutch confirmed the general findings from the written data[13].

---

cific verb *zijn* "to be". There is also an intermediary class of verbs which impose minimal restrictions on the subject referent like "exist".

13. As a result of the predominance of formal standard language in the corpus, regional tendencies could not be replicated.

Grondelaers (2000) interprets the function of *er* in adjunct-initial presentatives in the light of Langacker's reference point theory. He hypothesizes that the results from the corpus analysis suggest that the presence of *er* reflects how well the initial adjunct and the verb serve as a reference point to situate the subject referent. With the insertion of *er*, the speaker signals that the hearer cannot situate the subject referent very well on the basis of the adjunct and the verb, thus preparing the hearer for a subject that will require quite a lot of processing. Because corpus data can only offer indirect evidence for processing differences, Grondelaers tests this hypothesis further with a number of psycholinguistic reading experiments that by and large confirm the relation between *adjunct topicality, adjunct specificity* and *verbal specificity* (as indicators of reference point potential) and processing cost (as measured by reaction times). A later study (Grondelaers, Brysbaert, Speelman and Geeraerts 2001) refines this cognitive-functional hypothesis by characterizing *er* as an accessibility marker in the sense of Ariel (1990). An additional set of psycholinguistic experiments confirms that the refinement of the initial hypothesis was justified.

2.3. Differences in approach

It is clear from the previous two sections that the two approaches to quantitative corpus analysis as applied to syntactic variation are very similar. Both annotate relevant observations for a number of explanatory variables and then statistically analyse the separate and the combined effect of those variables. Both use a multifactorial statistical model to quantify the contribution of each explanatory variable to the overall effect and to measure how well the variation can be explained given the selected variables. However, there are some differences between both approaches: Firstly, they investigate different types of explanatory variables. Gries focuses on language-internal variables and, in later work, on the effect of lexical variability on syntactic variation. He has only a secondary interest for one external variable, viz. the difference between spoken and written usage. Grondelaers examines language-internal variables too (though a smaller number than Gries), but the effect of external variables and their interaction with internal variables are also central points of interest. On the other hand, Grondelaers pays little attention to the effect of individual lexical items on syntactic variation. Secondly, there are some marked differences in interpretation of the results of the quantitative corpus analysis. Gries draws strong conclusions about underlying online processes on the basis of his corpus findings. Grondelaers on the other hand, sees his corpus results as first empirical facts that lead to a cognitive interpretation that has to be tested further with psycholinguistic experiments.

Given these differences in the choice of variables and interpretations, the question arises whether some of these choices and interpretations are more warranted than others. To answer that question, the next section will look at some basic properties of corpus data and at how they constrain the choice of variables and the possible interpretations.

3. Properties of corpus data

Corpus data has some inherent properties that any corpus analysis must take into account because they largely determine which conclusions can be supported by the data and which explanatory variables should be included in the analysis. Here are three of them:

1. **Complexity in spontaneous usage**: corpus data has the advantage that it allows to study language use as it occurs naturally in real life and it avoids the potential problems with elicited usage that can contain biases due to artificially controlled examples or unnatural experimental settings. Yet, unlike in controlled experimental settings, a researcher cannot select beforehand which explanatory variables he wants to study and which he wants to keep constant. All variables are at work simultaneously in spontaneous usage and thus also in corpus data.
2. **Offline usage**: corpora only contain the physical offline outcome (as sound waves or writing) of a production process[14] with many underlying online cognitive processes. Offline corpus data does not allow direct observation of these underlying online processes. They can only be studied indirectly.
3. **Socio-cultural diversity**: most corpora strive to contain a representative sample of usage from different communicative situations and from different portions of the native speaker population. This means that corpus data will display sociolectal, regiolectal and register vari-

14. This has to be nuanced for spoken corpora: if the original recordings are available or the corpus has been annotated with time-stamps or disfluencies, some information about online processes is more directly observable.

ation. A corpus analysis will have to take these language-external or "lectal" variables into account, even if only to factor them out from the language-internal analysis.

In the remainder of this section, we will discuss in more detail how Gries and Grondelaers deal with each of these properties and which methodological choices are better warranted given these properties.

3.1. Complexity in spontaneous usage

Corpora can be considered as the primary data type in linguistics because they contain language as it presents itself in real life. Corpora can be used to study naturally occurring, spontaneous language use, whereas with other data types, like psycholinguistic experiments or surveys, there is always a risk of introducing unwanted artefacts due to artificial experimental settings or biased survey questions. Moreover, for a usage-based approach to grammar, the spontaneous usage in corpora is also primary from a theoretical point of view because grammar is considered to emerge from usage. However, this big advantage of corpus data also gives rise to its biggest challenge: In spontaneous usage, language displays its full complexity. In the elicited usage of psycholinguistic experiments or surveys, the conditions of usage can be controlled: An analysis can focus on the effect of a limited set of explanatory variables while keeping other variables constant. In spontaneous usage, all possible variables exert their influence simultaneously and their effect is distributed over the data. This leads to high, multifactorial complexity. A corpus analysis (and any usage-based analysis for that matter) has to take this fundamental property of spontaneous language use into account by including multiple variables in the analysis of a linguistic phenomenon. Both Gries and Grondelaers take this challenge seriously by systematically investigating the effect of a number of explanatory variables on syntactic variation in corpus data.

Although taking into account multiple variables is a necessary precondition for a descriptively adequate account of a syntactic variation, it is not enough. The effect of different variables should not only be studied in isolation but also in combination. This is where the full potential of a quantitative corpus analysis becomes clear. Using multifactorial statistical techniques, both Gries and Grondelaers are able to examine the combined effect of explanatory variables on syntactic variation. Gries examines the relative strength of variables by pair-wise comparison. Both Gries and Grondelaers use a multifactorial model to assess how well the variation can be explained on the basis of the included variables and to quantify and compare the contribution of each variable. However, there are also some more specific methodological challenges posed by the simultaneous effect of multiple variables. These include the problem of spurious effects, the possibility of interactions and the problem of lexical variability. Gries and Grondelaers deal differently with these difficulties.

Spurious effects occur when an explanatory variable only has an effect because it is intercorrelated with another variable. For example, the animacy of the constituent's referent may seem to influence whether the constituent precedes or follows the verb in English clauses. Yet the effect of animacy may be solely due to the fact that subjects, which (nearly) always precede the verb, tend to be animate whereas objects, which (nearly) always follow the verb, tend to be inanimate. Animacy is then a spurious effect because it merely reflects the effect of grammatical function. Of course, this is a very obvious example, but spurious effects can be more subtle. Gries, for example, examines both the effect of concreteness and animacy of the DO's referent. Both variables considered separately have a very significant effect, but of course concreteness and animacy are highly intercorrelated because all animate referents are also concrete. It would be wrong to say that both variables have an effect, because they actually reflect the same effect. Often it is difficult to say which variable has the real and which one has the spurious effect. In this case, Gries's partial correlation analysis suggests that animacy stops having an effect when concreteness is partialled out, whereas the reverse is not true, so that concreteness could be said to be the real effect. The problem of spurious effects also plays a role when the combined effect of variables is examined in a multifactorial model. Variables that appear to have a significant effect when considered separately can turn out to be unimportant for the combined effect because they are correlated with one or more other variables. In that case, it is unnecessary and undesirable to include them in the model because they do not help to explain the variation. It is clear that spurious effects can only be identified and discarded when multiple variables are examined in combination. Gries and Grondelaers differ in the extent to which they systematically check for spurious variables. Out of 20 variables, Gries only explicitly checks intercorrelation for two pairs of variables: animacy and concreteness as mentioned above (2003c: 89), and noun type and determiner (Gries 2003c: 86–87)[15]. Animacy and de-

15. Prior to the actual statistical analysis of explanatory variables, Gries (2003c: 30) also checks the intercorrelation between *entrenchment*, an operationalization he used in previous research (Gries 1999), and its constituative subparts

terminer are found to have only a spurious effect and are therefore removed from the multifactorial model. Other spurious variables (e.g. *mention of the DO's referent in subsequent discourse*) are discarded from the model mainly "on theoretical grounds" (Gries 2003c: 113), i.e. because they cannot be subsumed under the proposed processing hypothesis. Statistically, these discarded variables also show a low contribution to the general effect, but so do other variables (e.g. *disfluency* or *definiteness*) that are nonetheless kept in the model because they do fit the proposed hypothesis. Gries does not test whether any of the discarded variables made a statistically significant contribution to the model or not (which is the standard way to decide whether a variable should be kept in the model). He only observes that the prediction accuracy of the model is not compromised by leaving these variables out and thus he concludes that they are dispensable. But again, so might other variables that are still in the model. From a statistical point of view, this is a somewhat unprincipled way of identifying the relevant variables for a multifactorial model and excluding the spurious ones[16]. Grondelaers does not explicitly check the intercorrelation between different variables either, but he does use a more principled method to discard unnecessary variables from the model. He uses a technique called stepwise selection that statistically checks for every variable whether it contributes significantly to the overall effect and if not, the variable is removed from the model.

Although Gries lacks a systematic way for dealing with intercorrelations between explanatory variables, he does use an interesting technique called Structural Equation Modelling (SEM) that has no counterpart in Grondelaers. SEM can help to find out how the intercorrelations between some of the variables are structured. For example, Gries's corpus

---

animacy, concreteness and nountype. This anlaysis exposes entrenchment as a spurious variable so that the subparts are used as separate variables in the further analysis.

16. Gries [personal communication] points out that the goal of a researcher is not necessarily to identify the smallest set of explanatory variables (by removing spurious variables from the multifactorial model), but can also be to determine whether the variables that do exhibit an effect can be subsumed under a proposed theoretical explanation. However, this theory-based selection does take away part of the function of corpus data as empirical touchstone for model building. Moreover, it is also statistically questionalable whether comparing the predictive power of two models, one with and one without an individual variable can be used to assess whether that variable contributes significantly to the model.

analysis has shown that morphosyntactic variables (*length of the DO, complexity of the DO*) are strongly correlated with particle placement whereas discourse-functional variables (*times of previous mention, distance to previous mention, cohesiveness to previous discourse*) are somewhat weaker correlated. Both types of explanatory variables are also intercorrelated. Given this constellation, three types of causal relations are possible (Gries 2003c: 146–152): (1) only morphosyntactic variables have a direct causal relation to particle placement, whereas the discourse functional variables are only spuriously correlated with the morphosyntactic variables; (2) the discourse-functional variables have a causal relation to the morphosyntactic variables (e.g. recent mention in discourse causes a referent to be coded by a short pronoun) and in their turn the morphosyntactic variables are a causally related to particle placement, resulting in an indirect causal relation between the discourse-functional variables and particle placement; (3) the discourse-functional variables have an indirect causal link to particle placement via the morphosyntactic variables like in 2, but additionally they also have a direct causal effect on particle placement[17]. Structural Equation Modelling can help to determine which of these three scenarios is most likely given the correlations observed in the data. In this case (Gries 2003c: 178–180), SEM supports scenario 3.

A second specific methodological problem is the possible **interaction** between explanatory variables. The effect of one explanatory variable might be conditioned by a second variable. In the case of *er* in Dutch presentatives, the effect of verbal specificity might be different depending on the type of adjunct with which the clause begins. If adjunct and verb help to increase the accessibility of the subject referent, it might well be that a locative adjunct does this well enough so that the specificity of the verb does not matter much, whereas a temporal adjunct is a worse accessibility enhancer so that the verb specificity plays a more important role in that context. The effect of the explanatory variable *verb specificity* would then be different for different values of the explanatory variable *adjunct type*. This kind of interaction is exactly what Grondelaers finds for Netherlandic Dutch. He can trace such interactions by testing whether they make a significant contribution to the multifactorial model. Gries compares the separate effect of internal variables in written vs.

17. The other logical possibilities in which the morphosyntactic variables have a causal effect on the discourse-functional variables, are excluded because such a relation would have to work backwards in time: current morphosyntactic realization of a referent cannot affect its previous mention in discourse.

spoken data to see whether there is an interaction. Yet he does not consider interactions between internal variables[18], nor does he analyse interactions in his multifactorial model. However, it is clear that all these types of interactions are important to understanding the exact nature of usage patterns.

A third complicating factor in spontaneous usage is the **lexical variability**. Alternating schematic constructions like the ones studied by Gries (ex. 5) and Grondelaers (ex. 6) are of course instantiated by specific lexemes in actual usage.

(5) *[VERB][PARTICLE][OBJ] vs. [VERB][OBL][PARTICLE]*
(6) *[ADJNCT][VERB][SUBJ] vs. [ADJNCT][VERB][er][SUBJ]*

Each schematic slot in the construction can be filled by a wide range of different lexemes and each specific lexeme may introduce a bias towards a specific syntactic variant, i.e. a bias that is not taken into account by the explanatory variables that capture more general properties[19]. A corpus analysis of syntactic variation will have to take this potential lexical bias into account. Although Grondelaers studies the effect of more general verb classes, he fails to consider the effect of individual lexical items. Gries and Stefanowitsch (2004) have come up with a method to do exactly that: Distinctive Collexeme Analysis was developed within their broader collostructions research framework and it tests for every lexeme occurring in a schematic slot whether it introduces a significant bias towards a syntactic variant. If so, that lexeme is called a distinctive collexeme of that particular variant. Of course, it may happen that each vari-

18. As dicussed above, Gries does make pair-wise comparisons of conflicting variable values. However, these comparisons assess which variables have the stronger effect but not whether the effect of one variable is reinforced or inhibited by another variable. Apart from Linear Discriminat Analysis, Gries also uses a Classification Tree for multifactorial modelling. Classification Trees have the property of automatically taking interactions into account. However, Gries does not use this information in the discussion of variable effects.
19. Since Clark's (1973) influential paper "The language-as-fixed-effect fallacy", statistical procedures in psycholinguistics take this possibility of lexical bias into account by performing separate analyses for the effect of conditions over lexical items (F_2), as well as over subjects (F_1). See Raaijmakers (1999) for a discussion and critique of this methodological solution to the problem of lexical bias.

ant's distinctive collexemes have some more general property in common, that can then be included as an explanatory variable in the multifactorial analysis. For particle placement, Gries and Stefanowitsch point out that the distinctive verb collexemes of the particle-object order tend to have an idiomatic meaning, whereas those of the object-particle order tend refer to literal actions. In other words, the distinctive collexemes reflect the explanatory variable *verb idiomaticity*. Distinctive Collexeme Analysis is a very promising technique not only because is solves a methodological problem, but also from a theoretical point of view: a usage-based grammar model assumes that syntactic constructions are entrenched schematizations of lexically instantiated usage-events. Specific syntactic constructions may therefore well be more strongly associated with specific lexemes.

3.2. Offline usage

Language use is determined by numerous and complex cognitive processes such as conceptualization, retrieval of constructions from long term memory, their integration in short term memory and the assignment of a phonetic representation. The resulting physical output of these processes can be directly observed in corpus data in the form of writing or sound waves, but the underlying cognitive processes cannot. Corpora contain offline usage and the underlying online processes can only be studied indirectly in corpus data. A corpus analysis can ascertain correlations between a number of offline observable linguistic variables. A researcher, especially a researcher in Cognitive Linguistics, may wish to interpret these correlations in terms of online cognitive processes, but corpus data alone cannot provide insight into the exact nature of the cognitive processes involved. For example, Grondelaers interprets the correlations between explanatory variables and *er*-insertion found as related to the accessibility and ease of online processing of the subject. But as he points out, it is impossible to get independent confirmation for this hypothesis in corpus data and therefore he turns to psycholinguistic experiments:

> In the remainder of this article we make use of experimental linguistic data instead of corpus data. This has to do with the fact that the comprehension processes put forward in the hypotheses cannot be measured offline: It is impossible to find an independent variable that allows to ascertain whether a hearer needs more time to process constituent y in context a than in context b. (Grondelaers, Brysbaert, Speelman and Geeraerts 2001: 10)

Gries on the other hand does use his corpus analysis to study the online processes involved in syntactic variation. Despite the offline nature of corpus data, he wants "to investigate particle placement from the perspective of online speech production" (2003c: 7). His aim is to find out what "lies behind the subconscious decisions of native speakers" (2003c: 44). Gries puts forward the Processing Hypothesis to explain the variation. It states that particle placement is determined by online processing cost and that the explanatory variables influence processing cost, hence their effect on particle placement. Gries quite adamantly argues that his corpus analysis provides strong support for this hypothesis. His line of reasoning is the following: First, he argues that most explanatory variables affect processing cost (premise 1). Next, he formulates the hypothesis that particle placement is determined by processing cost (premise 2). Given these two premises, he then predicts that there will be a correlation between the explanatory variables and particle placement in usage. Since these predictions are borne out by his corpus analysis, he concludes that the hypothesis is confirmed[20]. The problem is that this argumentation[21] starts from an uncertain premise: "The relation between the [explanatory] variables and the Processing Hypothesis has only been established on an argumentative basis" (Gries 2003c: 61), i.e. with little independent evidence that the explanatory variables have the relation to processing cost proposed in premise 1. Although many of the proposed relations are quite plausible and some get support from psycholinguistic research (e.g. *length of the DO*)[22], many variables might nonetheless have a different

20. This procedure whereby a researcher first makes predictions on the basis of some hypothesis and then tests them against data is called *a-priori hypothesis testing*. It provides much stronger proof for a hypothesis than *a-posteriori* interpretation of the data because the hypothesis cannot be bent to fit data.
21. Note also that this is an inductive type of reasoning whereby the general statement "particle placement is determined by processing cost" is induced from the regular co-occurrence of phenomena (variables influencing processing cost and variables correlating with particle placement). Unlike deduction, induction does not lead to logical necessity, but nonetheless induction is the implicit reasoning behind most scientific research.
22. Gries [personal communication] points out that the proposed relations between the explanatory variables and processing cost are well established in the literature. However, most of the references that Gries (2003c, Ch. 4) provides to back up these claims, do not base themselves on online data either. Most of them use offline data and then give processing cost as a possible explanation. Some that do use online data (e.g. McDonald et al. 1993) do not reach univocal conclusions.

or no relation to processing cost (e.g. *Concreteness of the DO's referent*). For some explanatory variables like *mention in subsequent discourse*, Gries himself (1999) first states that they have an effect on processing cost, but later (2003c) changes his mind basing himself again on offline corpus data[23]. Without certainty about premise 1, the whole argumentation that it must be online processing cost that explains particle placement becomes quite shaky. One could easily find another cognitive hypothesis to explain the correlations between the explantory variables and particle placement observed by Gries in his corpus data[24]. For example, one could argue that the correlations have their basis somewhere else in the cognitive system, e.g. in long term memory rather than in short term memory: for instance, the almost obligatory use of the object-particle order with pronominally realized direct objects might well be entrenched in long term memory, rather than being a consequence of the low online processing cost of pronouns in short term memory. Similar entrenchments in long term memory could exist for other variables.

Gries is aware of the problem that offline correlations observed in corpus data can be explained by multiple hypotheses, but he dismisses it nonetheless:

> The statistical techniques used so far make it difficult to choose among competing hypotheses that make identical claims as to the strength and direction of the relationship between the independent variables and particle placement. Yet, this valid objection is much less of a problem than it might look at first: it holds for nearly every analysis using inferential statistics. Whenever a researcher has some hypothesis (H_1), analyses some data using inferential statistics and obtains a result supporting his H_1, it is with hind-

23. This casts doubts on whether Gries' procedure can be really called a-priori hypothesis testing. He modifies his 1999 hypothesis on the basis of a corpus analysis and then uses the same data later on to test that modified hypothesis. Of course, the hypothesis is then no longer formulated without beforehand knowledge of the data.
24. Interestingly, Gries' own results also give an indication that online processing alone might not suffice to explain the relation between explanatory variables and particle placement. The prediction accuracy of the multifactorial model is much better for written than for spoken data. However, as Gries himself points out (Gries 2003c: 40) spoken language is much more subject to online processing constraints than written language. If the explanatory variables only have an influence via online processing cost, one would expect the model to be better at predicting spoken material than written material, rather than the other way around.

> sight, possible to argue that the researcher's H_1 is not the correct one, but some other H_1 that is equally compatible with the data. That is, if we take this to the extreme, it would not be possible to ever accept some H_1 as there are, at least theoretically, always competing alternative hypotheses that could be responsible for the outcome of the investigation and cannot be ruled out because they make fully identical predictions. Strictly speaking, one might even say that this dilemma is inbuilt in the paradigm of falsificatory testing: since we only attempt to falsify H_0, the logical counterpart of our own hypothesis, a result conforming to our hypothesis only rules out H_0 but does not pick out one among many particular alternative hypotheses making identical predictions. Nevertheless, it is common to accept one's own hypothesis if the corresponding null hypothesis is not supported significantly by the data, and in this study, I simply follow this generally accepted practice. (Gries 2003c: 124)

Gries argues that the possibility of explaining the correlations in corpus data with competing hypotheses does not pose a problem, because (1) competing hypotheses are always possible and (2) this is inherent to statistical testing procedures. Although true to a certain extent, both arguments miss the point. Let us first discuss argument (1), viz. that multiple hypotheses are always possible. In modern scientific methodology, it is indeed assumed that a hypothesis can never be definitively proven and that it can only "withstand falsification for the time being". A hypothesis is considered to be corroborated, when it is not proven wrong or *falsified* by the currently available data. But even when corroborated, a hypothesis remains provisional. Hence, there is indeed always some margin left for other hypotheses that can account for the same data. However, the relevant question is: how much margin is left? Obviously, the principled "provisionalness" of any hypothesis does not mean that all hypotheses that currently cannot be proven wrong are equally well corroborated. There are degrees of corroboration: the less margin there is left for alternative hypotheses, the more corroborated a hypothesis will be. Although a corpus analysis already restricts the possible cognitive hypotheses in the sense that every hypothesis will have to account for the correlations found in corpus data, it does not offer a high degree of corroboration for a specific cognitive hypothesis in terms of online processes because the margin for alternative cognitive hypotheses is quite "large". It would be a perversion of the falsification paradigm to pick out one hypothesis and simply acquiesce in the fact that the data can still accommodate a wide range of alternative cognitive hypotheses. Rather, the aim of research is to narrow down the range of alternative hypotheses by confronting them with data for which they make different predictions[25]. It is clear that offline corpus data is less suitable to do so for processing hypotheses.

Let us now turn to Gries's second argument, viz. that the possibility of competing hypotheses is inherent to statistical testing procedures. More specifically, Gries argues that competing hypotheses exist because only the null-hypothesis (H_0) is statistically tested, not the researcher's hypothesis (H_1). However, Gries confuses two distinct types of hypotheses here, viz. research hypotheses and statistical hypotheses. A research hypothesis gives a theoretical explanation for some phenomenon, just like the Processing Hypothesis does for particle placement. Statistical hypotheses on the other hand state an expected value for some observable variable, e.g. the average length of the direct object. The H_1 or alternative hypothesis in testing procedures is a statistical hypothesis, *not* a research hypothesis. Rather H_1 is a statistical hypothesis *derived* from the research hypothesis. In principle, it is possible to derive an infinite number of statistical hypotheses from one research hypothesis, which is the actual reason why a research hypothesis can never be definitely proven: a research hypothesis can never be exhaustively confirmed. Even if H_1 would be directly tested instead of H_0, this still would not make much of a difference because it will still be possible to formulate alternative research hypotheses that can account for the same data[26]. So Gries is right when he says

25. Gries [personal communication] rightfully points out that it is not the task of individual researchers to invest all possible alternative hypotheses. Rather, their task is to put forward one hypothesis and check whether it is supported by the data. Other researchers can then try to improve on that hypothesis by putting forward an alternative that is equally or better supported by the (existing or new) data. However, it might also be considered the task of the individual researcher to make sure that the type of data used is suited to support the kind of hypothesis proposed, all the more so in a discipline that is still in full methodological development. From a publication that has the explicit goal of setting new standards in methodological rigour, one might also expect a critical assessment of the epistemological possibilities of the datatype that is promoted.
26. Incidentally, it is possible although uncommon to test H_1 directly, if highly specific predictions can be derived from the research hypothesis, e.g. "the average length of the direct object in construction$_0$ is 2.34 words" or "the average length of the direct object is 6.21 times bigger in construction$_0$ than in construction$_1$". Usually such a specific H_1 is not available and there is only a more general prediction that a dependent variable value will not be the same for different levels of an explanatory variable. In this case, it is more practical to test the logical counterpart (H_0) that states the variable value will be the same for all levels of the explanatory variable.

that statistical testing "does not pick out one among many particular alternative [research] hypotheses making identical predictions", but this is not due[27] to testing H_0 instead of H_1.

With his corpus analysis, Gries has attained an unprecedented level of adequacy in the description of particle placement but he draws conclusions from his analysis that clearly go beyond what is warranted by corpus data alone. His Processing Hypothesis is a plausible cognitive interpretation of his corpus findings, but its claims about the online processing of particle placement await further confirmation by online psycholinguistic research.

Although offline corpus data is for the time being not very suitable to empirically test hypotheses about cognitive processes, this does not mean that investigating such hypotheses through corpus data is impossible in principle. Once we have gained a clear understanding of the processing properties of a linguistic variable from other empirical methods, that variable could be used as an explanatory variable to investigate processing effects in corpus data. However, a lot of work still has to be done before we have determined the psycholinguistic properties of the variables that linguists usually use in their studies. In recent work, Gries has contributed to this by studying the psycholinguistic properties of his measure of collostructional strength (Gries, Hampe and Schönefeld 2005, *in press*). He has also studied the comparability of corpus and psycholinguistic analysis of syntactic priming (Gries 2005, 2007).

3.3. Socio-cultural diversity

Especially relevant within the context of the current volume is the fact that most corpora aim to be representative for different socio-cultural contexts in which language is put to use. More specifically, these contexts can be distinguished from each other by factors like the region or social stratum that speakers originate from, or the communicative situation that they find themselves in (e.g. formal vs. informal or speaking vs.

---

27. Testing H_0 instead of H_1 may unnecessarily increase the uncertainty margin. Within the research community of experimental psychology, there is a lively discussion about the reliability of Null-Hypothesis Significance Testing (NHST) (for an overview of objections, see Loftus 1996). In fact, some researchers have even called for NHST to be banned from all journals published by the authorative *American Psychological Association* (Shrout 1997). Several alternatives to NHST have been proposed (see Denis 2003 for an overview).

writing). A well known reference corpus like the British National Corpus (BNC) describes its contents in the following way[28]:

> The Corpus is designed to represent as wide a range of modern British English as possible. The written part (90%) includes, for example, extracts from regional and national newspapers, specialist periodicals and journals for all ages and interests, academic books and popular fiction, published and unpublished letters and memoranda, school and university essays, among many other kinds of text. The spoken part (10%) includes a large amount of unscripted informal conversation, recordeded [sic] by volunteers selected from different age, region and social classes in a demographically balanced way, together with spoken language collected in all kinds of different contexts, ranging from formal business or government meetings to radio shows and phone-ins.

Corpora like the BNC try to reflect this – in a broad sense – cultural and situational diversity for good reasons. It is well known that language-external factors lead to actual differences in language use. They cause dialectal, regiolectal, sociolectal, idiolectal and register variation. In short, this kind of "lectal" diversity is also an inherent property of spontaneous usage and a corpus analysis will have to take it into account.

External factors are well known to have also an effect on syntactic variation. They are also a central concern for Grondelaers (2000) and he tries to incorporate them systematically into in his corpus analysis. Hence, he studies the external factors that are represented in the ConDiv corpus of written Dutch: regional variation (Belgium vs. the Netherlands) and register variation between informal vs. formal styles of writing[29]. Gries bases his corpus analysis on a random sample from the BNC, but he does not systematically investigate the different external factors that are represented in the BNC (see above). He picks out one external factor, viz. the difference between spoken and written channel of communication (which he calls REGISTER), but he is aware that external factors are very important for the understanding of syntactic variation:

> Additionally, we have, extending the work by Biber et al. (1999), also shown how REGISTER influences particle placement to such a degree that, I dare say, analyses of particle placement neglecting register influences can

28. From the "Introduction" on the BNC webpage: http://www.natcorp.ox.ac.uk/
29. A later study on spoken data (Grondelaers, Speelman and Geeraerts 2003) additionally investigated the external (sociological) factors *Birth Region* and *Education Level*, but these did not reach statistical significance.

> definitely not be descriptively adequate, if, by *descriptively adequate* it is meant that we really know 'what is going on' (Gries 2003c: 100)

External factors can have an effect on (syntactic) variation in three different ways. Firstly, they can influence variation indirectly because they are **correlated** with a number of language-internal explanatory variables. This is what Gries suggests for the spoken/written distinction (but see Stefanowitsch and Gries *this volume*):

> Of course, the question arises as to why the register has the influence it has – one would probably hesitate to assume that there is a direct causal relationship between REGISTER and particle placement. Apart from the characteristics of different registers, one can examine whether REGISTER is related to other variables that in turn causally influence particle placement. Upon doing that, we find that REGISTER correlates very significantly with Idiomacity (Somer's d = .309; $p < .001$), Complex (Somer's d = .144; p = .003) and LengthS (r_{pbis} = .237; t_{401} = 4.88; $p < .003$) … Since we have seen that exactly those variables are among the most influential ones determining particle placement, the correlation between REGISTER and particle placement comes as no surprise: it follows naturally from characteristics of oral and written discourse. (Gries 2003c: 100–101)

In this case, the effect of external factors is an interesting fact for the *description* of the use of syntactic variants, but it is not directly relevant for the *explanation* of the variation, because the external factors do not have a causal effect. They merely reflect the effect of language-internal variables. However, this is not the only way in which external factors can affect variation and the quite substantial lower prediction accuracy of Gries's multifactorial model for spoken compared to written observations suggests that channel may also influence particle placement more directly.

A second way in which external factors can have an effect is through **interaction** with internal variables. The effect of an internal explanatory variable might not be the same in all lectal varieties. For example, Grondelaers finds that the effect of adjunct type on *er*-insertion is not the same in Belgium and the Netherlands. Apparently locative adjuncts are a much stronger cue to omit *er* for Netherlandic speakers of Dutch than for Belgian speakers. A similar interaction between channel and the explanatory variables might be at play with particle placement in English. If particle placement is determined by processing cost, it might well be that explanatory variables adding to processing cost have less effect in written discourse because there the limitations of short term memory play less of a role than in spoken discourse. This is also suggested by a number of interactions between channel and explanatory variables that Gries (2003c) finds in his corpus data. In this case, external variables have a causal effect because they change the conditions that are relevant for the effect of internal variables. With the spoken/written distinction these changed conditions may pertain to the limitations of short-term memory, whereas with the regional difference, they may have to do with how the function of syntactic variants gets entrenched in different communities.

Thirdly, external factors may also have a direct **independent effect** on variation. Speakers of different varieties may alternate between variants for the same language-internal reasons, but speakers of one variety may simple use one variant more often than speakers of another variety. In that case, the effect of internal explanatory variables is the same in both varieties, and the effect of external variables is not simply due to correlations with internal variables. External variables can have this independent causal effect, because the use of syntactic variants might be entrenched differently in different lectal varieties. This seems to happen with *er*-insertion: Grondelaers shows an independent effect of register in both Belgian and Netherlandic Dutch. *Er* is used more in informal contexts and may partially be an informality-marker.

Grondelaers investigates the three types of external effects described above systematically in his multifactorial analysis. If an external variable only reflects the effect of internal variables through intercorrelation, that external variable will not be included in the multifactorial model by the stepwise selection procedure because it only has a spurious effect (cf. section 3.1). If an external variable interacts with an internal variable, this will show up as a significant interaction term in the model. Grondelaers further analyses interactions by testing separate models per variety and by checking statistically whether these models are significantly different. Finally, if an external variable has an independent effect, it will be taken up as a significant independent variable in the multifactorial model. Gries analyses the effect of the spoken/written distinction somewhat less systematically. He does check for interactions by comparing graphically the separate effect of each internal variable in spoken and written data, but he does not check whether the observed interactions are statistically significant. Although these graphical checks indicate prima facie that there are at least some interactions, he does not take up the spoken/written distinction in his multifactorial model either. In a footnote (Gries 2003c: 130, fn. 33) he does mention that he has tested separate multifactorial models for spoken and written data, but he then only states that the contributions of the internal variables to the model were roughly the same in both models, without statistically checking this.

Taking into account external factors is not only a methodological necessity to deal with the cultural diversity in corpus data, in Cognitive Linguistics it also makes sense from a theoretical point of view: In a usage-based grammar, constructions emerge from actual usage and become entrenched through frequency of use. If the usage is different in different lectal varieties, it is logical that constructions and their functions can be entrenched differently in different varieties. Since there are an enormous number of external factors, the question arises, which of those are really relevant for linguistic analysis, i.e. which external factors really define distinct varieties. In another strand of research, Geeraerts, Speelman and Grondelaers have developed techniques to measure the distance between varieties (Speelman, Grondelaers and Geeraerts 2003). Their approach is akin to that of Biber (1995), but unlike Biber, they try to filter out thematic bias.

4. Different perspectives

Gries (2003c) and Grondelaers (2000) take a quite different perspective on syntactic variation in their corpus studies. More specifically, they use quantitative corpus analysis to test hypotheses at different *explanatory levels*. With his corpus analysis, Gries tries to examine the online psycholinguistic processes that determine a speaker's subconscious choice of word order. Grondelaers uses his corpus analysis primarily to explore how linguistic variables are correlated in different parts of the speaker population and in different registers. Ultimately, he is also interested in how these linguistic variables affect online psycholinguistic processes, but to answer those questions, he uses another methodological paradigm, viz. psycholinguistic reading experiments. In short, Gries uses quantitative corpus analysis to investigate the speaker's choice of a specific syntactic variant at the *level of online cognitive processes*, whereas Grondelaers uses quantitative corpus analysis to uncover the linguistically relevant distributional properties of syntactic variants at *the level of offline data*.

The underlying difference in perspective explains many of the differences in implementation between Gries and Grondelaers we have described above. First of all, it explains why Gries and Grondelaers concentrate on different types of variables. Grondelaers attaches great importance to both external and internal variables, because they both have important effects on the distribution of syntactic variants. Gries on the other hand focuses on internal variables and has only a secondary interest for external variables because it is not straightforward within his psycholinguistic perspective how external variables can have a direct impact on online cognitive processes (cf. the quote in section 3.3). Indeed, if syntactic variation is only determined by processing cost and the limitations of short term memory, it is difficult to see how speakers could make their "subconscious choices" differently depending on the region or social stratum they originate from. After all, short term memory limitations are supposed to be the same for all native speakers.

Secondly, the difference in perspective also explains the different choice of statistical technique, both for analyzing the separate and the combined effect of explanatory variables. From Gries's perspective, the relevant question is how well an explanatory variable helps to determine a speaker's subconscious choice of word order. He is therefore interested in how an explanatory variable affects the *predictability* of word order in individual usage events of particle placement. Consequently, he quantifies the separate effect of nominal explanatory variables with the λ-measure, which measures increase in predictability given an explanatory variable. Grondelaers on the other hand is interested in how an explanatory variable affects the distribution of the syntactic variants. Hence, he quantifies the effect of nominal explanatory variables with an odds ratio, which measures how strongly the distribution of cases with and without *er* differs between two values of an explanatory variable. The difference between both measures becomes clear with explanatory variables that have a statistically significant effect, but that do not change the preferred variant. For example, a distribution of 70% word order A and 30% word order B with a topical referent versus a distribution of 54% word order A and 46% word order B with a non-topical referent results in a statistically very significant effect (given a large enough data sample). Yet, the λ-measure would quantify the effect as zero, because a speaker is predicted to use word order A with both topical and non-topical referents, since that is the dominant order in both cases[30]. An odds ratio on the other hand would indicate a quite strong effect (1.98), because the distribution of word orders is very different for topical and non-topical referents.

To examine the combined effect of variables, Gries first uses pair-wise comparison of variable values with conflicting word order preferences. Here again, the analysis is based on categorical decision making. First of

30. This is a real example from Peters' (1999) as discussed in Gries (2003c: 28). Gries follows the same reasoning presented here to dismiss the statistically significant effect of givenness found by Peters.

all, a variable is only relevant when it increases predictability as measured by the λ-measure, otherwise its values cannot have conflicting word order preferences that can be compared with other variable values. Again, despite its statistically significant effect, topicality as described above would not be included in this type of pair-wise analysis. Secondly, the measure derived from the pair-wise comparison is based on how often a variable value can impose its word order preference over the preference of another variable value *in categorical decisions*. From Gries's perspective of studying the subconscious decisions of speakers, this is highly relevant information, whereas from Grondelaers's point of view, this analysis only obfuscates the more subtle underlying distribution differences by imposing categoricity.

A similar difference in perspective exists between the multifactorial models that Gries and Grondelaers use. The Linear Discriminant Analysis, which Gries uses, is foremost a classification technique. The linear discriminant model tries to make a categorical decision between two variants based on a number of explanatory variables. The weights that are assigned to the explanatory variables in the model (based on underlying probabilities) quantify how well the variables help to make that categorical division. From Gries's perspective, this categorical decision making corresponds exactly to what a speaker has to do every time he uses a transitive phrasal verb. On the other hand, the Logistic Regression as used by Grondelaers models the odds of encountering a specific variant given a number of explanatory variables. In other words, the Logistic Regression models the combined effect of explanatory variables on the probability distribution of the two variants. The weights assigned to the variables can be interpreted as odds ratios and this distributional information of course fits Grondelaers's research interest very well. The clash between both perspectives and the resulting choice of statistical technique becomes especially clear when Gries explicitly dismisses Labov and Sankoff's variable rule model, which is a (simplified) version[31] of a Logistic Regression Model, exactly because it outputs distributional probabilities rather than categorical decisions:

31. The extended possibilities of Logistic Regression versus Variable Rules include the possibility to specify a probability cut-off value for categorical classification and to include interaction terms into the model. Compared to Linear Discriminant Analysis (LDS), Logistic Regression (LR) has the advantage that it puts less strict conditions on the data. Unlike LR, LDS requires a multivariate normal distribution of variable values, which is often not the case in linguistic data, as Gries (2003c: 115) also points out for his data.

> the present approach does not share some of the weaknesses of variable rules (cf. ... the introduction of a threshold level yielding categorical speaker decisions as output rather than probabilities)
>
> (Gries 2003c: 145–146)

Finally, it has to be noted that the divergence in perspectives between both approaches is also partly due to a difference in background. Gries (2003c: 157–184) shows a strong interest in processing theories, especially connectionist theories like Rumelhart and McClelland's Interactive Activation Models. This background partly explains why Gries focuses on the production and subconscious decision process that underlies each individual use of a transitive phrasal verb. Geeraerts, Speelman and Grondelaers on the other hand have done extensive research into prototypical lexical categories. They studied the distribution of conceptual features in lexical categories, first from a diachronic (Geeraerts 1997) and then from a synchronic perspective (Geeraerts, Grondelaers and Bakema 1994). In recent work they compared the feature distributions of lexical categories in different language varieties (Geeraerts, Grondelaers and Speelman 1999). Given this background, the interest in the distributional and populational properties of linguistic categories and constructions comes quite natural.

5. Conclusions

Unlike in other (cognitive) sciences, the systematic statistical analysis of empirical data is not yet very common in theoretical linguistics. In the previous sections we have discussed two approaches that are in the empirical vanguard of Cognitive Linguistics by their introduction of quantitative methods for analyzing what can be considered the primary data type in language research, viz. spontaneous usage collected in corpora. For a theoretical framework like Cognitive Linguistics that proposes a usage-based model of grammar, it is of course fundamental to systematically investigate actual usage and quantitative corpus analysis is an important methodology to do so. In this article, we have concentrated on one specific strand of research that these two quantitative approaches have in common, viz. syntactic variation. Both the Gries-Stefanowisch group and the Geeraerts-Speelman-Grondelaers group have also covered a range of other linguistic phenomena, but we nevertheless hope to have given an idea of the potential of quantitative corpus analysis for studying actual language use.

The comparison of Gries's work on particle placement in English and Grondelaers's work on Dutch presentatives has shown that there is a large degree of convergence between both approaches and that they complement each other fairly well. Yet, there are still some methodological issues that need further clarification and that are related to the three properties of corpus data discussed in section 3.

First of all, there are some aspects of the *multifactorial complexity in spontaneous usage* that are still in need of a more systematic analysis. We have seen that both approaches study the effect of multiple explanatory variables on the use of syntactic variants, but the internal relations between explanatory variables and how these relate to syntactic variation is not yet analysed systematically. Yet, this is important not only, as we have discussed above, to identify spurious effects and interactions, but also to investigate the precedence relationships between variables or to deal with so-called latent variables, i.e. explanatory variables, often called factors, that are themselves a function of multiple observable variables, e.g. referent topicality which is a function of distance to previous mention, frequency of previous mention and conceptual cohesiveness to previous discourse. Both Gries (2003c) and Grondelaers (2000) have made some attempts to take the correlation structure of multiple explanatory variables into account, using partial correlations, Structural Equation Modelling, Stepwise Selection and interaction terms. But this could be done more systematically using statistical techniques like Cochran-Mantel-Haenszel methods (Agresti 1996, Ch. 3), Log-linear Analysis (Agresti 1996, Ch. 6), Configural Frequency Analysis (Krauth 1993), Correspondence Analysis (Clausen 1998), Latent Class Analysis (Hagenaars and McCutcheon 2002), (Categorical) Principal Component Analysis (Jolliffe 2002), additional applications of Structural Equation Modelling (Loehlin 1998), etc. In short, there is still a large potential left for making use of advanced statistical methods to get a better grip on the complexity in language use.

Also the complexity introduced by lexical variability deserves further consideration. Gries and Stefanowitsch have already developed a number of techniques under the heading of collostructional analysis to identify lexemes that typically occur in constructions and constructional variants (Stefanowitsch and Gries 2003; Gries and Stefanowitsch 2004a). Currently they are extending this to the identification of typical pairs of lexemes (Gries and Stefanowitsch 2004b; Stefanowitsch and Gries 2005). Of course, these types of analysis are also highly relevant for syntactic variation. Furthermore, it would be interesting to have a principled way to know whether the set of individual collexemes can be generalized to (semantic) classes of lexemes, which would mean that a construction can be associated with a schematic semantic meaning. Gries and Stefanowitsch have previously tried to make these generalisations ad hoc but they (Gries and Stefanowitsch *in press*) are currently objectifying this process with the help of hierarchical clustering techniques. Yet another question is how strong a construction is lexically constrained, i.e. where it is situated on the continuum ranging from fully lexical words and idioms to highly schematic constructions. Geeraerts et al. try to quantify degree of lexicalisation by comparing the number of construction uses instantiated by significant and non-significant collexemes (Tummers, Speelman and Geeraerts 2004). The higher the percentage of uses instantiated by significant collexemes, the more lexically constrained the construction is. A high percentage of collexeme pairs would then indicate even stronger lexical constraints. Finally, we still need to find multifactorial methods to compare lexeme-specific effects with the effect of other explanatory variables that determine the use of constructions or syntactic variants.

Relating to the second property of corpus data that we discussed, viz. *offline usage*, there are still questions about which aspects of the language system can be fruitfully studied through corpus analysis. More generally, there is a need to integrate quantitative corpus analysis with other empirical methodologies into a coherent methodological framework for research into the cognitive aspects of language. Quantitative corpus analysis and psycholinguistic reaction time experiments complement each other fairly well: quantitative corpus analysis can (relatively easily) collect large amounts of data to study the effect of multiple variables simultaneously, but it can only measure offline effects. Reading time experiments measure the effects of online processes more directly, but they are too time-consuming to gather enough data to study the effect of a large number of variables. A division of labour could be to first identify relevant variables through quantitative corpus analysis and then investigate the online properties of variables in a more targeted way through psycholinguistic experiments. On the other hand, corpus analysis has the advantage that it relies on spontaneous, naturally occurring language use, whereas psycholinguistic experiments are often forced to use constructed examples. Validating experimental results against corpus data can be a way to avoid experimental artefacts. Grondelaers et al. (Grondelaers and Brysbaert 1996; Grondelaers 2000; Grondelaers, Brysbaert, Speelman and Geeraerts 2001) have tried from the beginning to integrate corpus-based and experimental findings, but also Gries et al. (Gries 2002b, 2005,

2007; Gries, Hampe and Schönefeld 2005, *in press*) have recently started to compare corpus-based with experimental methodologies.

Finally, the biggest challenge ahead is probably posed by the third property of corpus data discussed above, viz. the *socio-cultural diversity* in language use. In section 3.3, we discussed three general ways in which external variables can influence usage, yet there are many different types of external variables: regiolectal variation, sociolectal variation, register variation, stylistic variation, variation due to differences in communication channel, etc. Moreover, there are quite important qualitative differences between these types of external variables. For example, most or all speakers of a language have mastered different stylistic registers, but most speakers use only one regional variety. Also, the socially determined difference in register formality is quite different from the 'technical' distinctions between channels of communication (e.g. speaking vs. writing vs. internet relay chat).

It is still an open question how these different types of external variables should be integrated in the linguistic system as a whole. First of all, it is clear that qualitatively different external variables will influence usage and interact with internal variables in different ways. As we discussed earlier, it is hard to imagine how regional differences could interact with internal variables related to the limitations of short term memory, because these limitations are the same for all humans. Yet, differences in communication medium might very well change the impact of these limitations. On the other hand, communication medium probably does not alter the core semantics of a construction (cf. Stefanowitsch and Gries, this volume)[32], but regional differences might (Grondelaers 2000; Wulff, Gries and Stefanowitsch 2005). Methodologically speaking, this means that it can be appropriate to have different multifactorial models for the choice of syntactic variant depending on the regional variety; Register differences on the other hand might well be included in the model together with internal variables[33].

32. Grondelaers [personal communication] points out that the specific channel properties of internet relay chat (time pressure) can prevent optional *er* from being used and thus from exerting its usual communicative function (see Grondelaers 2000: 67).
33. Stefanowitsch and Gries (2005, *this volume*), Wulff, Gries and Stefanowitsch (2005) discuss how configural frequency analysis can be used to that end; Grondelaers (2000) Grondelaers Geeraerts and Speelman (2002) include register in the logistic regression model.

The qualitative properties of some external variables also blur the traditional distinction between internal and external variables made in the Variable Rule tradition (initiated by Labov 1969). For example, register formality is not simply a language-external factor that constrains the application of the linguistic system; rather it is internalized into the system so that formality is even explicitly expressed by certain constructions and lexemes (e.g. modal distancing or personal pronouns). The same is true for some other 'external' variables. Obviously, individual language users have (un)conscious cognitive models about the language variation found in the speaker population as a whole and these socio-cultural models can be tightly associated with the use of constructions or lexemes. With its interest in both the bodily and cultural experience that determines language use, and in both the cognitive and social functioning of language, Cognitive Linguistics is ideally suited to integrate internal and external variables into a coherent theoretical framework: the framework of Cognitive Sociolinguistics. Such a framework can provide crucial concepts to refine corpus-based methodologies and, conversely, hypotheses formulated within the framework can be tested and validated through quantitative corpus analysis.

References

Agresti, Alan
1996 *An Introduction to Categorical Data Analysis*. New York: Wiley.

ANS = Algemene Nederlandse Spraakkunst
1997 Walter Haeseryn, K. Romijn, G. Geerts, J. de Rooij and M.C. Van de Toorn (eds). Groningen/Deurne: Nijhoff, Plantyn.

Biber, Douglas
1995 *Dimensions of Register Variation*. Cambridge: Cambridge University Press.

Clark, Herbert H.
1973 The language-as-fixed-effect fallacy: A critique of language statistics in psychological research. *Journal of Verbal Learning and Verbal Behavior* 12: 335–359.

Clausen, Sten-Erik
1998 *Applied Correspondence Analysis: An Introduction*. Thousand Oaks (CA): Sage.

Cowart, Wayne
1997 *Experimental Syntax. Applying Objective Methods to Sentence Judgments*. London: Sage.

Denis, Daniel J.
2003 Alternatives to null hypothesis significance testing. *Theory and Science* 4 (1) (http://theoryandscience.icaap.org)
De Sutter, Gert, Dirk Speelman, Dirk Geeraerts and Stefan Grondelaers
2003 Woordvolgordevariatie in tweeledige werkwoordelijke eindgroepen. Naar een statistische evaluatie van zes factoren. In: Tom Koole, Jacomine Nortier and Bert Tahitu (eds.), *Artikelen van de Vierde Sociolinguistische Conferentie* 111–119. Delft: Eburon.
Geeraerts, Dirk
1997 *Diachronic Prototype Semantics. A Contribution to Historical Lexicology.* Oxford: Clarendon Press.
2005 Lectal variation and empirical data in cognitive linguistics. In: Francisco J. Ruiz de Mendoza Ibáñez and M. Sandra Peña Cervel (eds.), *Cognitive Linguistics: Internal dynamics and interdisciplinary interaction*, 163–190. Berlin/New York: Mouton de Gruyter.
Geeraerts, Dirk, Stefan Grondelaers and Peter Bakema
1994 *The Structure of Lexical Variation. Meaning, Naming, and Context.* Berlin: Mouton de Gruyter.
Geeraerts, Dirk, Stefan Grondelaers and Dirk Speelman
1999 *Convergentie en Divergentie in de Nederlandse Woordenschat. Een Onderzoek naar Kleding- en Voetbaltermen.* Amsterdam: Meertens Instituut.
Gries, Stefan Th.
1999 Particle movement: A cognitive and functional approach. *Cognitive Linguistics* 10 (2): 105–145.
2001a A multifactorial analysis of syntactic variation: Particle movement revisited. *Journal of Quantitative Linguistics* 8 (1): 33–50.
2001b A corpus-linguistic analysis of *-ic* and *-ical* adjectives. *ICAME Journal* 25: 65–108.
2001c Particle placement in English: A multifactorial investigation. In: Ruth M. Brend, Alan K. Melby and Arle R. Lommel (eds.), *LACUS Forum XXVII: Speaking and Comprehending*, 19–32. Fullerton (CA): LACUS.
2002a The influence of processing on grammatical variation: Particle placement in English. In: Nicole Dehé, Ray Jackendoff, Andrew McIntyre, and Silke Urban (eds.), *Verb-Particle Explorations*, 269–88. Berlin/New York: Mouton de Gruyter.
2002b Evidence in Linguistics: Three approaches to genitives in English. In: Ruth M. Brend, William J. Sullivan and Arle R. Lommel (eds.), *LACUS Forum XXVIII: What Constitutes Evidence in Linguistics?*, 17–31. Fullerton (CA): LACUS.
2003a Grammatical variation in English: A question of 'structure vs. function'? In: Günter Rohdenburg and Britta Mondorf (eds.), *Determinants of Grammatical Variation in English*, 155–173. Berlin/New York: Mouton de Gruyter.

2003b Testing the sub-test: A collocational-overlap analysis of English *-ic* and *-ical* adjectives. *International Journal of Corpus Linguistics* 8 (1): 31–61.

2003c *Multifactorial Analysis in Corpus Linguistics: A Study of Particle Placement*. London/New York: Continuum Press.

2003d Towards a corpus-based identification of prototypical instances of constructions. *Annual Review of Cognitive Linguistics* 1: 1–27.

2004a Shouldn't it be breakfunch? A quantitative analysis of the structure of blends. *Linguistics* 42 (3): 639–667.

2004b Isn't that fantabulous? How similarity motivates intentional morphological blends in English. In: Michel Achard and Suzanne Kemmer (eds.), *Language, Culture, and Mind*, 415–428. Stanford, CA: CSLI.

2004c Some characteristics of English morphological blends. In: Mary Andronis, Erin Debenport, Anne Pycha and Keiko Yoshimura (eds.), *Papers from the 38th Regional Meeting of the Chicago Linguistics Society: Vol. II. The Panels*, 201–216. Chicago, IL: Chicago Linguistics Society.

2005 Syntactic priming: A corpus-based approach. *Journal of Psycholinguistic Research* 34 (4): 365–399.

2007 New perspectives on old alternations. In: Jonathan E. Cihlar, Amy L. Franklin, David W. Kaiser and Irene Kimbara (eds.), *Papers from the 39th Regional Meeting of the Chicago Linguistics Society: Vol. II. The Panels*, 274–292. Chicago, IL: Chicago Linguistics Society.

Gries, Stefan Th., Beate Hampe and Doris Schönefeld

2005 Converging evidence: Bringing together experimental and corpus data on the association of verbs and constructions. *Cognitive Linguistics* 16 (4): 635–676.

in press Converging evidence II: More on the association of verbs and constructions. In: John Newman and Sally Rice (eds.), *Experimental and Empirical Methods in the Study of Conceptual Structure, Discourse, and Language*. Stanford, CA: CSLI.

Gries, Stefan Th. and Anatol Stefanowitsch

2004a Extending collostructional analysis: A corpus-based perspectives on 'alternations'. *International Journal of Corpus Linguistics* 9 (1): 97–129.

2004b Co-varying collexemes in the *into*-causative. In: Michel Achard and Suzanne Kemmer (eds.), *Language, Culture, and Mind*, 225–236. Stanford (CA): CSLI.

in press Cluster analysis and the identification of collexeme classes. In: John Newman and Sally Rice (eds.), *Experimental and Empirical Methods in the Study of Conceptual Structure, Discourse, and Language*. Stanford, CA: CSLI.

Grondelaers, Stefan
2000 De distributie van niet-anaforisch *er* buiten de eerste zinplaats : Sociolexicologische, functionele en psycholinguïstische aspecten van er's status als presentatief signaal. Unpublished Ph.D. thesis, K.U. Leuven.
Grondelaers, Stefan and Marc Brysbaert
1996 De distributie van het presentatieve *er* buiten de eerste zinsplaats. *Nederlandse Taalkunde* 1 (4): 280–305.
Grondelaers, Stefan, Dirk Speelman and An Carbonez
2001 Regionale Variatie in de postverbale distributie van persentatief *er*. *Neerlandistiek.nl* 1(4) (www.neerlandistiek.nl)
Grondelaers, Stefan, Dirk Speelman and Dirk Geeraerts
2002 Regressing on *er.* Statistical analysis of texts and language variation. In: Anne Morin and Pascal Sébillot (eds.), *6th International Conference on the Statistical Analysis of Textual Data*, 335–346. Rennes: Institut de Recherche en Informatique et en Automatique.
2003 De distributie van *er* in het gesproken Nederlands. Paper presented at the workshop *Spraakmakende Spraak (Corpus Gesproken Nederlands).* Nijmegen, May 2003.
Grondelaers, Stefan, Dirk Geeraerts, Dirk Speelman and José Tummers
2001 Lexical standardisation in internet conversations. Comparing Belgium and The Netherlands. In: Josep M. Fontana, Louise McNally, M. Teresa Turell and Enric Vallduví (eds.), *Proceedings of the First International Conference on Language Variation in Europe*, 90–100. Barcelona: Universitat Pompeu Fabra, Institut Universitari de Lingüística Aplicada, Unitat de Investigació de Variació Lingüística.
Grondelaers, Stefan, Marc Brysbaert, Dirk Speelman and Dirk Geeraerts
2001 *Er* als accessibility marker: on- en offline evidnetie voor een procedurele interpretatie van presentatieve zinnen. *Gramma/TTT* 9 (1): 1–22.
Grondelaers, Stefan, Dirk Speelman, Dennis Drieghe, Dirk Geeraerts and Marc Brysbaert
subm. The use of presentative *er* "there" as an accessibility marker: a processing approach to indefinite reference. *Discourse Processes.*
Hagenaars, Jacques A. and Allan L. McCutcheon
2002 *Applied Latent Class Analysis.* Cambridge: Cambridge University Press.
Heylen, Kris and Dirk Speelman
2003 A corpus-based analysis of word order variation: the order of verb arguments in the German middle field. In: Dawn Archer, Paul Rayson, Andrew Wilson and Tony McEnery (eds.), *Proceedings of the Corpus Linguistics 2003 conference*, 320–329. Lancaster: UCREL.
Jolliffe, Ian T.
2002 *Principal Component Analysis.* New York: Springer.

Krauth, Joachim
1993 *Einführung in die Konfigurationsfrequenzanalyse (KFA)*. Weinheim: Beltz, Psychologie-Verlags-Union.

Labov, William
1969 Contraction, deletion and inherent variability of the English copula. *Language* 45: 715–762.

Loehlin, John C.
1998 *Latent Variable Models: An Introduction to Factor, Path, and Structural Analysis*. Mahwah, NJ: Lawrence Erlbaum.

Loftus, Geoffrey R.
1996 Psychology will be a much better science when we change the way we analyze data. *Current Directions in Psychological Science* 5 (6): 161–171.

McDonald, Janet L., Kathryn Bock and Michael H. Kelly
1993 Word and world order: Semantic, phonological, and metrical determinants of serial position. *Cognition Psychology* 25: 188–230.

Peters, J.
1999 Discourse factors influencing the ordering of constituents in the verb particle construction. Unpublished MA thesis, University of Alberta.

Raaijmakers, Jeroen G. W.
1999 How to deal with "The Language-as-Fixed-Effect Fallacy": Common misconceptions and alternative solutions. *Journal of Memory and Language* 41: 416–426.

Schütze, Carson T.
1996 *The Empirical Base of Linguistics: Grammaticality Judgments and Linguistic Methodology*. Chicago: Chicago University Press.

Shrout, Patrick E.
1997 Should significance tests be banned? Introduction to a special section exploring the pros and cons. *Psychological Science* 8 (1): 1–2.

Sorace, Antonella and Frank Keller
2005 Gradience in linguistic data. *Lingua* 115 (1): 1497–1524

Speelman, Dirk, Stefan Grondelaers and Dirk Geeraerts
2003 Profile-based linguistic uniformity as a generic method for comparing language varieties. *Computer and the Humanities* 37: 317–337.

Stefanowitsch, Anatol
2003 Constructional semantics as a limit to grammatical alternation: The two genitives of English. In: Günter Rohdenburg and Britta Mohndorf (eds), *Determinants of Grammatical Variation in English*, 413–441. Berlin/New York: Mouton de Gruyter.
2004 HAPPINESS in English and German: A metaphorical-pattern analysis. In: Michel Achard and Suzanne Kemmer (eds.), *Language, Culture, and Mind*, 137–149. Stanford: CSLI.
2005 The function of metaphor: developing a corpus-based perspective. *International Journal of Corpus Linguistics* 10 (2): 161–198.

Stefanowitsch, Anatol and Stefan Th. Gries
2003 Collostructions: Investigating the interaction between words and constructions. *International Journal of Corpus Linguistics* 8 (2): 209–243.
2005 Covarying collexemes. *Corpus Linguistics and Linguistic Theory* 1 (1): 1–46.
this vol. Channel and constructional meaning: A collostructional case study.
Tummers, José, Dirk Speelman and Dirk Geeraerts
2004 Quantifying and evaluating semantic effects: The impact of lexical collocations on the inflectional variation of Dutch attributive adjectives. In: Gérald Purnelle, Cédrick Fairon and Anne Dister (eds.), *Le Poids des Mots. Actes des 7*[es] *Journées Internationales d'Analyse Statistique des Données Textuelles*, 1080–1089. Louvain-la-Neuve: Presses Universitaires de Louvain.
Tummers, José, Kris Heylen and Dirk Geeraerts
2005 Usage-based approaches in Cognitive Linguistics: A technical state of the art. *Corpus Linguistics and Linguistic Theory* 1 (2): 225–261.
Wasow, Thomas
2002 *Postverbal Behaviour.* Stanford, CA: CSLI.
Wulff, Stefanie
2003 A multifactorial corpus analysis of adjective order in English. *International Journal of Corpus Linguistics* 8 (2): 245–282.
Wulff, Stefanie, Stefan Th. Gries and Anatol Stefanowitsch
2005 Brutal Brits and argumentative Americans: What collostructional analysis can tell us about lectal variation. Paper presented at the International Cognitive Linguistics Conference 2005, Seoul, Korea.

Channel and constructional meaning: A collostructional case study

Anatol Stefanowitsch and Stefan Th. Gries

Abstract

Research on grammatical structure, including construction-based research, is sometimes criticized for not paying sufficient attention to variational dimensions such as register, channel, etc. Our recent research on constructions, which is based on a set of quantitative corpus methods that we refer to as *collostructional analysis*, is theoretically subject to such criticism, as we have investigated the meaning of a range of constructions without paying attention to these variables at all. In this paper, we address this potential criticism. Using recent methodological extensions of our method, we show how variables like channel can be included in collostructional analysis. On the basis of three case studies, we show that (i) constructions may display channel-specific associations to individual lexical items, (ii) constructions differ with respect to their channel sensitivity, and (iii) the meaning of a given construction does not vary across channels. We argue that the inclusion of channel-specific information is a necessary addition to the specification of a construction's properties even though it does not interact substantially with constructional semantics.

Keywords: collostructional analysis, configural frequency analysis, quantitative corpus linguistics, construction grammar, channel, spoken vs. written language.

1. Introduction

Researchers interested in language structure, especially syntacticians, are sometimes criticized by broadly usage-oriented linguists for failing to include in their analyses a range of usage-related aspects such as social meaning, interactional meaning, or – most importantly for the present paper – register (i.e. contextually induced variation) and channel (i.e. variation induced by the choice of spoken vs. written language) (see, for example, Tummers et al. 2006; Grondelaers this volume; Speelman this volume).

This criticism potentially also applies to a strand of research that we have developed in a series of recent publications (Stefanowitsch and Gries 2003, 2005; Gries and Stefanowitsch 2004a, 2004b, in press). In this work, we have outlined a usage-based procedure for investigating the semantics of constructions (in the Construction Grammar sense of the term, cf. Goldberg 1995: 4, cf. also Croft 2001: 18 ff.).

Construction grammar is a cover term for a group of more or less closely related linguistic theories most of which all share two assumptions: first, that grammatical structures are meaningful linguistic signs, and second, that these signs, referred to as *grammatical constructions*, are the basic units of grammar. Grammatical constructions can vary in complexity and schematicity, ranging over the following broad types (cf. the discussion in Croft 2001: 17 f.):

- *simple specific*, i.e. morphemes such as *give* or *-ing*;
- *simple schematic*, i.e. grammatical categories – for example, word classes (NOUN, VERB, etc.) or grammatical relations (SUBJECT, OBJECT, etc.);
- *complex specific*, i.e. multimorphemic words (like *caregiver* or *give up*) or fixed expressions (like *Don't give up the day job* or *He gives twice who gives quickly*);
- *complex schematic*, i.e. partially filled expressions (like SUBJECT be given to NP, as in *Billy is given to hasty decisions*) or fully abstract grammatical structures (like the ditransitive construction SUBJECT + VERB + OBJECT + OBJECT, as in *Billy gave Diane a diamond ring*).

Most of these theories take a broad approach to meaning, taking this notion to cover not just semantics proper (i.e. propositional semantics and frame semantics) but also 'contexts of use' (cf. Goldberg 1995: 229), which, presumably, include channel, register, etc. In any theory attributing meaning to grammatical structure, it is desirable to have empirical discovery procedures that allow the researcher to uncover this meaning.

Our procedure, which is based on a quantitative corpus-linguistic method referred to as *collostructional analysis*, essentially involves identifying the association strength between a given construction and the lexical items occurring in one (or more) particular slot(s) in that construction (i.e. the strength of the preference of lexical items to occur in particular constructional slots); the lexical items are then ranked according to their association strength and grouped into semantic classes (typically on the basis of common-sense criteria arrived at inductively, but cf. Gries and

Stefanowitsch in press for a more objective procedure based on hierarchical cluster analysis). These classes can then guide the researcher in uncovering the meaning or meanings of the construction in question as well as allowing statements about the relative importance or centrality of particular subsenses as compared to others.

On the basis of this method, we have (among other things) uncovered systematic and semantically highly coherent distributional differences between members of 'alternating' pairs of constructions in English such as active/passive (*Billy wrote this poem* vs. *This poem was written by Billy*), ditransitive/*to*-dative (*Billy sent Diane a poem* vs. *Billy sent a poem to Diane*), *s*-genitive/*of*-construction (*the poem's beauty* vs. *the beauty of the poem*), the *will*-future and the *going-to*-future (*Diane will marry Billy* vs. *Diane is going to marry Billy*), and the two verb-particle constructions (*Diane's father gave away the bride* vs. *Diane's father gave the bride away*).

Let us give a concrete example to illustrate this method and introduce some crucial terminology. Consider the alternation between the ditransitive and the *to*-dative. Many verbs in English can occur in both of these constructions (for example, *give*, *tell*, *bring*, *teach*, *send*, etc.), a fact which has led a number of researchers to claim that the two constructions are purely formal variants. However, the fact that a large number of verbs *can* occur in both constructions does not warrant the conclusion that all of these verbs actually *do* so randomly. Instead, some or all of these verbs may have significant preferences towards one of the two (we call words that have such a significant preference to one member of a given pair of constructions (*significant*) *distinctive collexemes* of that construction). Take the verb *give*, which is actually one of the most frequently found verbs in both constructions. More precisely, in the British Component of the *International Corpus of English* (ICE-GB), it occurs in the ditransitive 461 times and there are 574 occurrences of this construction with other verbs, and it occurs in the *to*-dative 146 times and there are 1,773 occurrences of this construction with other verbs. In order to test whether this distribution shows a significant association to one of the two constructions, these frequencies are entered into a two-by-two contingency table, which can then be submitted to a distributional statistic such as the chi-square test or the Fisher-Yates exact test (in our work, we use the latter, since, as its name suggests, it is an exact test, cf. Stefanowitsch and Gries 2003 and Gries and Stefanowitsch 2004 for details on the statistical test and extensive justification). Table 1 shows the relevant contingency table (for expository reasons, the table also shows the frequencies expected from chance alone in parentheses; these were, of course, derived by the

Table 1. The distribution of *give* in the ditransitive and the *to*-dative

	give	Other Verbs	Row Totals
Ditransitive	461 (213)	574 (822)	1,035
To-dative	146 (394)	1,773 (1,525)	1,919
COLUMN TOTALS	607	2,347	2,954

standard procedure of multiplying the marginal frequencies for each cell and dividing the results by the table total).

Submitting these frequencies to the Fisher-Yates exact test yields a p-value of 1.84E-120. This p-value shows that *give* is significantly associated with one of the two constructions; however, it does not in itself tell us with which of the two. In order to determine this, we need to compare the observed frequencies with the expected ones. This comparison shows that *give* occurs in the ditransitive more than twice as frequently as expected, but only occurs about two thirds as frequently as expected in the *to*-dative. Thus, *give* is significantly associated with – is a (*significant*) *distinctive collexeme* of – the ditransitive construction. Since the comparison is only between these two constructions, this automatically entails that *give* is repelled by the *to*-dative. One can now apply the same procedure to all verbs that occur at least once in each of the two constructions in the ICE-GB, and rank the results in descending order of the p-values.

Table 2 shows the significantly distinctive collexemes for each construction.

Table 2. Distinctive collexemes in the ditransitive and the *to*-dative

DITRANSITIVE		*To*-DATIVE	
COLLEXEME	p	COLLEXEME	p
give (461:146)	1.84E-120	*bring* (7:82)	1.47E-09
tell (128:2)	8.77E-58	*play* (1:37)	1.46E-06
show (49:15)	8.32E-12	*take* (12:63)	2.00E-04
offer (43:15)	9.95E-10	*pass* (2:29)	2.00E-04
cost (20:1)	9.71E-09	*make* (3:23)	6.80E-03
teach (15:1)	1.49E-06	*sell* (1:14)	1.39E-02
wish (9:1)	5.00E-04	*do* (10:40)	1.51E-02
ask (12:4)	1.30E-03	*supply* (1:12)	2.91E-02
promise (7:1)	3.60E-03		
deny (8:3)	1.22E-02		
award (7:3)	2.60E-02		

Clearly, the distinctive collexemes of both constructions encode the notion 'transfer' (either literally or metaphorically). However, the collexemes of the ditransitive all encode a relatively direct transfer of an object from an agent to a recipient in a face-to-face situation; in contrast, the collexemes of the *to*-dative encode a transfer of an object over some distance to some location (note that the verb *play*, whose presence in this list may seem puzzling at first, occurs in these constructions frequently in sports commentary (e.g. *Billy plays the ball to Diane*). This semantic contrast between the two sets of distinctive collexemes reflects a corresponding semantic contrast between the two constructions that has been posited by a number of authors (for example, Goldberg 1995).

In all our previous analyses, we have taken a relatively narrow approach to constructional meaning, restricting ourselves to semantics proper (in the sense defined above) and, occasionally, some general pragmatic aspects such as illocutionary force or discourse structure. We have almost completely ignored differences concerning channel or register. We assumed that these variables would not interact significantly with constructional semantics proper; however, we did note in passing that the specific verbs instantiating the semantic classes identified by our procedure were possibly influenced by asymmetries in the distribution of a given construction across channels (Gries and Stefanowitsch 2004: 128 f., cf. also Stefanowitsch and Gries 2003: 233 f.).

In this paper, we take initial steps toward a systematic inclusion of channel variation into collostructional analysis by extending the method of distinctive collexeme analyses first introduced in Gries and Stefanowitsch (2004a), specifically, the three-dimensional version introduced in Stefanowitsch and Gries (2005). We focus on three questions, namely (i) whether there are channel-specific associations between constructions and individual lexical items (i.e., whether there are verbs that are associated with a given construction in channel X, but not in channel Y), (ii) whether constructions differ with respect to such associations (i.e. whether some constructions display more cases of such channel-specific associations to individual lexical items), and (iii) whether these associations point to channel-specific differences in the meaning of constructions (i.e. whether the individual lexical items associated with a given construction in channel X form a different semantic class than those items associated with the same construction in channel Y). With these tests, we can determine whether constructional semantics is in fact sensitive to channel differences or not.

In order to investigate these questions, we need to operationalize the notion *channel* in a manner suitable to the requirements of collostructional analysis. Collostructional analysis in any of its manifestations requires an exhaustive and thus largely manual retrieval of the construction(s) in question, and thus large amounts of syntactically annotated corpus data are needed. Such data are hard to come by: one of the few corpora annotated in sufficient detail is the British component of the *International Corpus of English* (ICE-GB) already mentioned above, which is a mere one million words in size (cf. Greenbaum 1996 for detailed descriptions of this corpus). The files in the ICE-GB are classified according to a variety of dimensions that would allow us to categorize them into different sub-channels or even registers (or register-like entities) in various ways, but even a moderately sophisticated approach to this task would result in sub-corpora too small for quantitative analysis. Thus, we are forced to settle on a very general operationalization and simply draw the broadest distinction that the ICE-GB allows us to draw, that between spoken and written language. Note that this distinction will – to some extent – correlate with classes of registers that are more likely to be associated with one or the other of these channels, but this correlation will, of course, not be a perfect one.

2. Case studies

Aims and Methods. In order to investigate the potential influence of channel on constructional semantics, we chose three pairs of constructions from among those analyzed in our previous work that have been claimed to interact with channel or register: active vs. passive voice, the two verb-particle constructions, and two English future-tense constructions; since we have already investigated these constructions in earlier work, we will be in a position to compare the results of these case studies to the earlier analyses, where channel was not included.

With respect to passives there is by now general agreement that they are distributed asymmetrically across channel: while several early studies (Blankenship 1962; Poole and Field 1976) failed to find clear preferences of the passive for either spoken or written language, more recent work has consistently reported that passives are more frequent in writing (cf. Chafe 1982; Brown and Yule 1983; Biber et al. 1999: 938). In addition, Biber et al. (1999: 937) observe that in English "short dynamic *be*-passives are sharply differentiated by register, with conversation and academic prose at opposite poles"; specifically, they report that in conversation stative and dynamic passives are about equally frequent while in academic writing dynamic passives are seven times as frequent as stative ones.

With respect to the two verb-particle constructions, there is little previous work on their distribution across channel or register. In one recent corpus-based study, Gries (2003: 97) finds that the verb-particle construction in which the particle precedes the direct object (which we will refer to as the *particle-first variant* here) is significantly more frequent in writing while the construction in which the particle follows the direct object (which we will refer to as the (*object-first variant*), is significantly more frequent in speaking. However, Gries also argues that this correlation does not reflect a direct causal relation between channel and constructional choice, but that it is an epiphenomenon arising from the interaction of other factors.

Finally, with respect to the two future-tense constructions, there also appears to be general agreement that *will* and *going-to* are distributed asymmetrically across written and spoken channels, with the latter occurring more frequently in speech and speech-like texts (cf. e.g. Quirk et al. 1985, § 4.43, and Berglund 1997 for corpus-based verification). At the same time, most reference works agree that there is a semantic difference between the two constructions, with the *going-to* future expressing a greater degree of premeditation, certainty, and/or immediacy than *will* (e.g. Thompson and Martinet 1986: 185; Murphy 1986: 16). In addition, Quirk et al. (1985, § 4.43) claim that *going-to* is associated with more agentive events (cf. Gries and Stefanowitsch 2004: 113 ff. for corpus-based verification).

For each of the three constructions, we followed the procedure outlined in Stefanowitsch and Gries (2005) for three-dimensional collostructional analysis. This procedure is based on Configural Frequency Analysis (cf. von Eye 1990), in particular, the binomial version discussed in Krauth (1993, Sec. 1.10) (the binomial test is an exact test used to determine the probability to obtain x hits out of n trials when the probability of each hit is p). Our procedure involves constructing a three-dimensional frequency table for each potential collexeme along the dimensions COLLEXEME × CONSTRUCTION × CONTEXT. What precisely constitutes a CONTEXT variable depends on the research question. It may be an additional collexeme (as in covarying-collexeme analysis, cf. Stefanowitsch and Gries 2005), it may be regional dialect (as in Wulff, Gries, and Stefanowitsch 2007), or it may be any other variable that can be systematically assessed on the basis of corpus data.

For the present study, we chose the variables COLLEXEME (specified as lemma of the verb occurring in the finite verb slot of the construction vs.

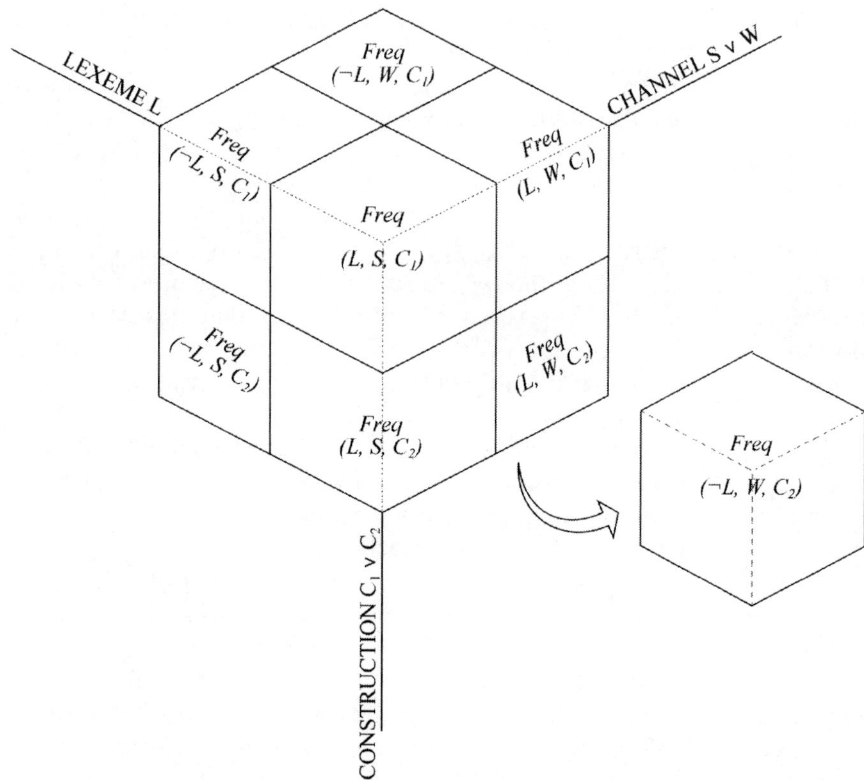

Figure 1. Three-dimensional distinctive collexeme analysis with the variables LEXEME × CONSTRUCTION × CHANNEL

all other verb lemmas), CONSTRUCTION, (specified, respectively, as Active vs. Passive, V-OBJ-Prt vs. V-Prt-OBJ, and *will*-future vs. *going-to*-future), and CHANNEL (specified as spoken vs. written language). This gives us the design COLLEXEME × CONSTRUCTION × CHANNEL. The three-dimensional frequency table that needs to be constructed for each verb in this design is represented schematically in Figure 1 (the extra cell shown at the bottom right of the table is the one opposite the top cell).

Once such tables are constructed for each verb lemma, a binomial test is performed for each cell (i.e., each combination of values of the three dimensions) to test whether its observed frequency deviates significantly from the expected one. The p-values resulting from these tests are taken to reflect the degree of association of the combination in question (cf. Stefanowitsch and Gries 2003, 2005, Gries and Stefanowitsch 2004a, b for extensive discussion and justification). For reasons that are partly mathematical and partly expository, these p-values are then transformed into their base ten logarithms and then the sign of the resulting value is set to plus for positive associations – i.e., for cases where the observed frequency is greater than expected –, and to minus for negative associations – i.e. for cases where the observed frequency is smaller than expected (these reasons cannot be discussed here; the mathematically-minded reader will find a discussion in Stefanowitsch and Gries 2005, and in Gries, Hampe, and Schönefeld 2005 n. 13).

The result of this procedure is a measure of association for each combination of values of the three dimensions. The final step of the analysis consists in choosing a relevant set of comparisons between these combinations and then drawing these comparisons by calculating the difference between the values corresponding to these combinations. In the present study, we focused on three comparisons, namely:

(1) CONSTRUCTION 1 VS. CONSTRUCTION 2 by CHANNEL: this will show us which verbs are distinctive for each of the two constructions in the spoken channel and which verbs are distinctive for each of the two constructions in the written channel – no direct comparison between the two channels takes place;
(2) SPOKEN CHANNEL VS. WRITTEN CHANNEL by CONSTRUCTION: this will show us which verbs are distinctive for each of the two channels in the first construction and which verbs are distinctive for each of the two channels in the second construction – no direct comparison between the two constructions takes place;
(3) CHANNEL S/W by CONSTRUCTION 1/2: this will show us which verbs display crossover effects, i.e. which verbs are associated with construction 1 in speaking but with construction 2 in writing or vice versa.

While the first two comparisons are meant to yield potential general differences between the behavior of the two constructions in the two channels, the third comparison is the one that most directly tests the hypothesis that the meaning of constructions may vary across channels.

Let us briefly illustrate our procedure by means of an example, namely the distribution of the verb *have* across the active and the passive construction and across the two channels. The three-dimensional table for this verb is shown in Table 3 (for details concerning extraction and lemmatization of the data see further below).

Table 3. Three-dimensional frequency table HAVE × CONSTRUCTION × CHANNEL

VERB	CONSTRUCTION	CHANNEL	Obs. frequency
have	active	spoken	2,642
have	active	written	1,291
have	passive	spoken	0
have	passive	written	1
other verbs	active	spoken	29,893
other verbs	active	written	19,335
other verbs	passive	spoken	4,886
other verbs	passive	written	7,046

As outlined above, we then computed for each of these configurations of VERB × CONSTRUCTION × CHANNEL (i) the expected frequency, and (ii) the probability to obtain the observed frequency by means of an exact one-tailed binomial test (whose p-value was then transformed into the base ten logarithms reflecting the strength and the direction of association). These interim results are shown in Table 4.

Table 4. Computing association strengths for HAVE × CONSTRUCTION × CHANNEL

Configuration	Observed frequency	Expected frequency	$p_{binomial}$	log_{10} $p_{bin.}$ with +/− for attraction/ repulsion
have active spoken	2,642	1,847	5.57E-70	69.25
have active written	1,291	1,365.8	2.03E-02	−1.69
have passive spoken	0	414.6	2.35E-181	−180.63
have passive written	1	306.6	1.06E-131	−130.97
other active spoken	29,893	28,714	7.67E-21	20.12
other active written	19,335	21,234.2	6.13E-58	−57.21
other passive spoken	4,886	6,445.4	9.09E-101	−100.04
other passive written	7,046	4,766.4	1.44E-227	226.84

From the upper half of Table 4, each of the configurations with *have* can now be evaluated in isolation. For example, the configuration [*have* active spoken] is significantly more frequent than expected on the basis of complete independence of the three variables while the configuration [*have* passive spoken] is significantly less frequent than expected. However, there is more this data can offer since one can now also perform the pairwise comparisons mentioned above. Thus, while the use of loglinear analysis and similar methods was ruled out given the many tables with extremely low observed frequencies, it is still possible to measure individual preferences by simply subtracting the logarithms of the p-values of the configurations to be compared.

For example, in the spoken channel, *have* is strongly preferred in the active (as indicated by the positive value of 69.25) and strongly dispreferred in the passive (as indicated by the negative value of −180.63) so that the difference of the two (69.25− (−180.63) = 249.88) reflects that, within this channel (the variable that is held constant in the subtraction) – *have* exhibits a strong preference of the active.

We can perform similar comparisons by simply choosing the appropriate values for subtraction accordingly. For example, while the above subtraction aimed at identifying the preference of *have* in speaking, it is equally possible to determine the preference of *have* in writing: we simply subtract the value −130.97 (which indicates a very strong avoidance of have in the passive in writing) from the value −1.69 (which indicates a slight avoidance of *have* in the active in writing), yielding the value 129.28, which indicates that, just as in speaking, *have* also exhibits a strong preference for the active in writing.

Before we discuss the results of these and additional comparisons in quite some detail, note that a highly positive value such as 128.93 for *have* in writing does not necessarily mean that *have* strongly prefers actives in writing and strongly disprefers passives in writing: as is obvious from the above values, *have* in writing is dispreferred in actives (cf. −1.69) *as well as* in passives (−130.97). The dispreference in passive constructions is simply much stronger than that in active constructions and thus outweighs the much weaker one for actives, yielding the strong overall preference of *have* for actives.

2.1. Active and passive voice

We first extracted all main verbs from the ICE-GB and generated separate lemmatized frequency lists for the spoken and written channels (lemmatization was done manually). We then repeated the process for all main verbs in the passive voice, based on the annotation provided in the ICE-GB. By subtracting the passive frequencies from the overall frequencies for each verb, we calculated the active frequencies (active voice is not explicitly coded in the ICE-GB's annotation). We then followed the general procedure outlined above. The resulting association measures served as a basis of two comparisons: (i) a separate comparison of the active and the passive construction for each of the two channels, and (ii) a separate comparison of the spoken and the written channel for each of the two constructions.

2.1.1. Results

The results of the first comparison are shown in Table 5, where the verbs are rank-ordered in each column (i.e., for each construction); in other words, when one compares active vs. passive in speaking, the verb *have* is the verb most strongly associated with active while *concern* is most strongly associated with passive etc.

Table 5. Comparison of active and passive by channel

SPOKEN		WRITTEN	
ACTIVE	PASSIVE	ACTIVE	PASSIVE
have (249.88)	*concern* (43.74)	*have* (129.28)	*base* (55.42)
think (240.41)	*base* (29.99)	*want* (22.85)	*think* (54.36)
get (182.67)	*involve* (29.77)	*thank* (13.46)	*use* (52.95)
say (128.44)	*bear* (21.98)	*hope* (11.9)	*do* (47.13)
do (120.23)	*use* (13.7)	*include* (11.57)	*associate* (24.44)
want (91.94)	*engage* (13.35)	*try* (11.53)	*make* (18.87)
know (71.73)	*publish* (11.83)	*wish* (11.11)	*publish* (17.45)
see (62.04)	*enclose* (10.6)	*mean* (10.74)	*entitle* (16.84)
like (43.59)	*marry* (10.1)	*enclose* (9.87)	*deposit* (15.52)
mean (42.31)	*associate* (9.7)	*ensure* (9.4)	*relate* (15.32)
try (36.32)	*damage* (9.34)	*see* (8.26)	*design* (14.85)
remember (20.24)	*confine* (9.3)	*get* (8.12)	*derive* (14.7)
read (14.21)	*design* (9.2)	*provide* (8.02)	*require* (13.81)
believe (12.71)	*aim* (9.13)	*like* (7.98)	*report* (12.3)
suppose (12.69)	*distribute* (8.66)	*know* (7.7)	*store* (12)
feel (11.63)	*compare* (8.41)	*contain* (7.02)	*confine* (11.98)
take (11.07)	*release* (8.14)	*help* (6.96)	*engage* (11.34)
hope (9.29)	*injure* (7.17)	*reach* (6.68)	*link* (10.83)
hear (8.19)	*build* (6.98)	*believe* (6.22)	*record* (10.46)
find (7.58)	*entitle* (6.96)	*increase* (4.98)	*concern* (10.45)

In Gries and Stefanowitsch (2004a: 108 ff.) we showed that the active construction prefers low-dynamicity verbs whose logical objects are not easily construable as patients (i.e. verbs encoding states like *want* or *know* or time-stable processes like *see* or *remember*) while the passive construction prefers high-dynamicity verbs whose patients will be in a salient and typically permanent end state as a result of the event (i.e. verbs encoding actions involving transfer of energy like *damage* or *melt*). The results in Table 5 essentially confirm these observations: the top twenty distinctive collexemes for the active construction consist mainly of stative (often mental) verbs, with only five exceptions in the spoken data (*say*, *do*, *try*, *read*, and *take*); the trend is less clear in the written data, where only half of the top twenty collexemes are stative while the other half are relatively dynamic (*thank*, *include*, *try*, *enclose*, *ensure*, *get*, *provide*, *help*, *reach*, *increase*). For the passive construction, the distinctive collexemes are almost exclusively dynamic in both the spoken and the written data (with the exception of *think* and possibly *relate* in the latter).

Crucially for our research questions, the two channels behave essentially identically with respect to the dynamicity contrast between active and passive, even though it seems slightly more pronounced in the spoken data. The two constructions do not differ greatly across channels with respect to specific associations to individual verbs either; there is a substantial overlap of verbs (active: *have*, *get*, *want*, *know*, *see*, *like*, *mean*, *try*, *believe*; passive: *base*, *use*, *engage*, *publish*, *associate*, *design*, *entitle*). Even the collexemes that do differ in their distribution across channels do not show any obvious channel specificity, but such differences would be more likely to emerge in the second comparison, to which we will turn presently. Before we do so, note that there are three apparent cases of crossover, i.e., of verbs that are associated with one construction in one channel and the other construction in the other: *think*, *do*, and *enclose*. However, as pointed out above, it is not strictly speaking possible to contrast an individual construction across the two channels on the basis of the data in Table 5. Instead, the identification of crossover effects has to be done separately on the basis of the original cell values (see further below). Briefly, the reason is that the values in Table 5 are based on channel-internal contrasts between the two constructions, and thus the fact that, for example, *think* is listed for *active-spoken* and *passive-written* does not mean that it is generally associated with these two combinations, but only that it is vastly more strongly associated with *active-spoken* than with *active-written* and vastly more strongly with *passive-written* than with *passive-spoken* (recall the discussion of *have* in writing above). A direct comparison of channels shows, however, that *think* is so frequent with *active-written* that all other combinations occur less frequently than expected with all other combinations.

The results of the second of the three possible comparisons introduced above are shown in Table 6, where the verbs are once again rank-ordered within columns so that, for example, when one looks only at the active verbs in order to compare spoken vs. written language, *think* is the verb most strongly associated with the spoken channel whereas *enclose* is most strongly associated with the written channel.

Table 6. Comparison of channels by active/passive

ACTIVE		PASSIVE	
SPOKEN	WRITTEN	SPOKEN	WRITTEN
think (280.16)	*enclose* (23.91)	*concern* (23.73)	*use* (54.91)
do (178.84)	*provide* (23.25)	*involve* (13.63)	*have* (49.65)
get (157.08)	*include* (21.29)	*do* (11.48)	*see* (32.93)
say (122.35)	*use* (15.66)	*bear* (7.35)	*base* (25.8)
have (70.95)	*thank* (13.34)	*marry* (7.31)	*associate* (20.67)
want (57.93)	*contain* (11.84)	*arrest* (4.61)	*know* (19.35)
know (44.69)	*display* (11.64)	*crossexamine* (4.49)	*get* (17.47)
like (27.99)	*increase* (10.79)	*cube* (4.49)	*make* (17.23)
mean (23.49)	*involve* (10.02)	*readmit* (4.49)	*require* (15.62)
see (20.85)	*produce* (9.76)	*put* (4.21)	*think* (14.62)
read (19.83)	*receive* (9.61)	*knock* (3.99)	*entitle* (13.97)
try (16.07)	*concern* (9.57)	*hear* (3.6)	*deposit* (12.65)
put (15.28)	*satisfy* (8.42)	*inspire* (3.23)	*provide* (11.94)
remember (9.49)	*wish* (8.09)	*found* (3.23)	*derive* (11.94)
suppose (9.04)	*reach* (8.02)	*addict* (3.16)	*report* (11.47)
measure (8.91)	*fold* (7.88)	*adduce* (3.16)	*want* (11.15)
hear (7.34)	*bear* (7.75)	*extrude* (3.16)	*describe* (10.82)
believe (5.74)	*influence* (7.67)	*win* (3.04)	*store* (10.79)
take (5.59)	*ensure* (7.57)	*damage* (3.04)	*channel* (10.45)
make (5.34)	*require* (7.54)	*dress* (2.88)	*replace* (10.03)

This comparison confirms our observations concerning dynamicity: again, the active construction is clearly associated with stative (low-dynamicity) verbs and the passive construction with dynamic verbs. However, in this direct comparison of each construction across channels, clear formality differences emerge in the case of the active construction. In the spoken channel, it tends to occur with short (mostly monosyllabic) verbs of Germanic origin, while in the written channel it tends to occur with polysyllabic verbs of Romance/Latinate origin. This is, of course, the kind of formality difference that we would expect to characterize these two channels in general, so it is, perhaps, not altogether surprising to see it emerge in an individual construction. However, this difference does *not* emerge in the case of the passive construction, which occurs with both formal and informal vocabulary to approximately the same degree in both channels. In this case, there does seem to be an interaction of an individual construction and channel: the passive construction itself seems to be associated with formal vocabulary to a higher degree than the active construction, and it retains this association even in the more informal registers likely to be found in spoken language.

Finally, let us return to the crossover effects mentioned above. These are properly identified by identifying verbs for which the following conditions hold: (i) in each channel, they are significantly attracted to one and only one of the constructions in question, and (ii) they are attracted to different constructions in the different channels. For the active/passive comparison, only two such verbs were identified: *find* and *work* are significantly attracted to the combinations spoken/active and written/passive (the opposite case did not occur at all). However, both verbs point to an interaction between lexical semantics and channel rather than differences in constructional semantics: a closer examination reveals that we are dealing with different senses of these words in the two channels. While *work* in the written/passive combination occurred mainly with the meaning 'use' (e.g. *work one's muscles, work the sails*), its main use in the spoken/active combination is the phrasal verb *to work out sth*. Similarly, while *find* in the written/passive combination occurred mainly with the meaning 'exist' (e.g. *The fibres of group B are found in the autonomic nervous system* [ICE-GB W2A-026]), its main meaning in the spoken/active combination is 'realize' (e.g. *I found that I was not behaving well* [ICE-GB S1A-072]).

2.1.2. Discussion

In sum, the results of channel-sensitive collostructional analysis are essentially identical to those yielded by a 'channel-ignorant' analysis as far as constructional meaning in the narrow sense is concerned: we found no interaction between channel and semantics proper at all. This suggests that, in this respect, the method is comparable to the narrower procedure used in our previous work. With respect to channel-specific vocabulary, however, we did find a general tendency of the active construction, but not of the passive, to occur with channel-specific vocabulary: the passive construction occurs relatively frequently with formal vocabulary in both channels. This result clearly could not have been arrived at by the narrower method used in our previous work.

2.2. Verb-particle constructions

We extracted all verb phrases containing a phrasal adverb (the ICE-GBs label for particles) and a direct object from the ICE-GB based on the annotation provided and manually annotated the results as cases of either the object-first or the particle-first variant. We then generated separate lemmatized frequency lists for each channel and each variant; as before, lemmatization was done manually. We then followed the procedure outlined above. Again, the resulting association measures served as a basis for (i) a separate comparison of the two verb-particle constructions for each channel, and (ii) a separate comparison of spoken and written language for each construction.

2.2.1. Results

The results of the first comparison are shown in Table 7 (rank-ordered within columns as above).

Table 7. Comparison of the two verb-particle constructions by channel

SPOKEN		WRITTEN	
V-PRT-OBJ	V-OBJ-PRT	V-PRT-OBJ	V-OBJ-PRT
carry out (8.94)	*get back* (5.61)	*carry out* (6.79)	*get out* (1.95)
find out (5.83)	*play back* (4.74)	*set up* (6.14)	*get in* (1.81)
point out (5.67)	*get out* (4.51)	*point out* (5.82)	*get back* (1.56)
give up (3.72)	*turn off* (4.09)	*find out* (5.77)	*cheer up* (1.54)
work out (3.25)	*ring up* (3.64)	*take on* (5.13)	*fold across* (1.54)
set up (3.1)	*take out* (3.2)	*take up* (4.23)	*lock in* (1.54)
set out (3.03)	*get on* (3.07)	*build up* (3.61)	*psyche up* (1.54)
take on (2.85)	*get together* (3.07)	*rule out* (3.19)	*shove back* (1.54)
bring out (2.83)	*put up* (2.68)	*wipe out* (2.88)	*slow down* (1.54)
build up (2.53)	*put in* (2.58)	*pull off* (2.61)	*put back* (1.51)
take up (2.19)	*follow up* (2.45)	*write off* (2.61)	*put out* (1.51)
bring about (2.06)	*take off* (2.43)	*bring in* (2.46)	*hold together* (1.31)
poke out (1.85)	*phone up* (2.36)	*hold up* (2.29)	*have back* (1.09)
cut down (1.66)	*play forward* (2.32)	*scrape down* (2.06)	*trace back* (1.09)
hold off (1.6)	*turn round* (2.32)	*put on* (2.04)	*send out* (1.05)
cut off (1.51)	*let down* (2.19)	*leave out* (2.01)	*send back* (1.02)
radiate away (1.48)	*write down* (2.06)	*make out* (2.01)	*bring back* (0.97)
strike out (1.48)	*chip forward* (1.94)	*fill in* (1.98)	*ask home* (0.91)
type in (1.48)	*get up* (1.94)	*give up* (1.84)	*attract back* (0.91)
make out (1.37)	*have off* (1.94)	*keep up* (1.84)	*bang in* (0.91)

In Gries and Stefanowitsch (2004a), we showed that the particle-first variant is mainly associated with idiomatic verb-particle combinations, while the object-first variant is mainly associated with spatial and/or resultative readings where the particle encodes a final location or state (cf. also Gries 2003: 87 f. on data from the BNC). As before, this result is confirmed by the data in Table 7, and the two channels behave identically with respect to this semantic difference. Again, there is also a substantial overlap of individual collexemes for the particle-first variant (nine of the top twenty collexemes are shared – *carry out*, *find out*, *point out*, *give up*, *set up*, *take on*, *build up*, *take up*, and *make out*); interestingly, however there is very little overlap for the object-first variant. There seem to be a few channel-specific lexical choices, but their number is far from overwhelming – *poke out*, *phone up*, *turn 'round* and *have off* have an informal flavor, while *rule out* or *write off* could perhaps be argued to be more formal; however, both the spoken and the written data contain a substantial number of informal verb-particle combinations, especially in the case of the object-first variant. The results of the second comparison are shown in Table 8.

Table 8. Comparison of channels by the two verb-particle constructions

V-PRT-OBJ		V-OBJ-PRT	
SPOKEN	WRITTEN	SPOKEN	WRITTEN
work out (2.61)	*set up* (3.81)	*put in* (3.77)	*carry out* (4.78)
bring out (1.79)	*keep up* (3.03)	*play back* (3.65)	*give up* (2.8)
hold off (1.64)	*hold up* (2.96)	*take out* (3.52)	*lay down* (1.88)
send out (1.57)	*pull off* (2.94)	*ring up* (3.35)	*cheer up* (1.69)
poke out (1.56)	*write off* (2.94)	*turn off* (3.02)	*fold across* (1.69)
give out (1.5)	*wipe out* (2.89)	*get back* (2.61)	*lock in* (1.69)
put in (1.32)	*carry out* (2.63)	*get on* (2.48)	*psyche up* (1.69)
set out (1.27)	*rule out* (2.36)	*get together* (2.48)	*shove back* (1.69)
radiate away (1.27)	*scrape down* (2.32)	*get out* (2.32)	*slow down* (1.69)
strike out (1.27)	*lay down* (2.31)	*phone up* (2.27)	*curl up* (1.52)
type in (1.27)	*hand out* (2.14)	*write down* (2.12)	*find out* (1.37)
miss out (1.23)	*follow up* (2.09)	*tidy up* (1.96)	*bring about* (1.27)
blow out (0.95)	*leave behind* (2.05)	*play forward* (1.91)	*bring back* (1.25)
feed in (0.95)	*leave out* (2.05)	*turn round* (1.91)	*keep up* (1.14)
lay aside (0.95)	*bring together* (1.94)	*put up* (1.77)	*call in* (1.03)
line up (0.95)	*carry on* (1.76)	*bring in* (1.7)	*call up* (1.01)
mix up (0.95)	*put up* (1.74)	*follow up* (1.69)	*ask home* (0.98)
pack away (0.95)	*put on* (1.73)	*make up* (1.65)	*attract back* (0.98)
pass over (0.95)	*build up* (1.67)	*take off* (1.62)	*bang in* (0.98)
pull in (0.95)	*build in* (1.67)	*chip forward* (1.61)	*bend back* (0.98)

These results confirm the impression that idiomaticity is a determining factor for the choice between the constructions in both channels. In fact, Gries (2003: 100f., 196) found that the effect of idiomaticity is slightly stronger in written language. These results also confirm the impression that channel does not strongly influence lexical choice in the verb-particle construction: there are no clear formality differences for either variant. There do seem to be some choices that are plausibly tied to situations that are more likely to be verbalized in one channel than the other (for example, *get together*, or *play back* and *play forward*, both of which occur exclusively in live football commentary in the ICE-GB); however, even these differences are not overwhelmingly obvious.

Finally, note that in the case of the verb-particle constructions, there was not a single crossover effect, i.e. there was not a single verb-particle combination that was significantly attracted only to object-first/spoken and particle-first/written (or vice versa).

2.2.2. *Discussion*

Two aspects of our results seem particularly noteworthy. First, that, again, neither of the two variants show evidence for channel-specific semantics, and that, in fact, there does not even seem to be a general tendency towards channel-specific vocabulary (instead, the vocabulary in both registers is relatively informal). Second, and more importantly for our present purposes, however, the two variants of the verb-particle construction nevertheless behave asymmetrically with respect to the variable *channel*: the particle-first variant is clearly less sensitive to channel influences than the object-first variant (as witnessed by the vastly higher lexical overlap for this variant). It seems to be the case that the strong association of the particle-first variant to idiomatic verb-particle combinations overrides channel influences in the same way as was the case for the strong association of the passive to formal verbs in the preceding section.

2.3. *Will*-future vs. *going-to*-future

We extracted from the ICE-GB all main verbs following the modal auxiliary *will* and all verbs following the string *going to* (either directly, or after some intermediate material). The latter were manually post-edited to remove false hits. We generated separate lemmatized frequency lists for each construction in each channel (as before, lemmatization was done manually). We then followed the procedure outlined above, with the same two comparisons as before.

2.3.1. *Results*

The results of the first comparison are shown in Table 9 (rank-ordered within columns).

Table 9. Comparison of the two future constructions by channel

SPOKEN		WRITTEN	
will	*going to*	*will*	*going to*
see (4.38)	*say* (16.06)	*be* (17.71)	*do* (4.76)
know (2.32)	*be* (14.7)	*give* (3.7)	*let* (1.38)
want (2.24)	*have* (9.33)	*find* (3.57)	*chubb lock* (1.27)
notice (1.86)	*do* (9.16)	*have* (3.41)	*conduct* (1.27)
read (1.55)	*go* (6.03)	*make* (2.95)	*extradite* (1.27)
find (1.42)	*happen* (5.99)	*consider* (2.83)	*spoil* (1.27)
speak (1.32)	*use* (4.87)	*increase* (2.76)	*go* (1.26)
agree (1.27)	*win* (4.22)	*receive* (2.64)	*say* (1.14)
explain (1.27)	*stay* (3.97)	*depend* (2.48)	*manage* (1.11)
recall (1.23)	*get* (3.71)	*send* (2.28)	*deliver* (1.1)
learn (1.23)	*buy* (3.41)	*add* (2.25)	*feed* (1.1)
lie (1.23)	*show* (3.39)	*include* (2.25)	*talk* (0.81)
teach (1.23)	*put* (2.94)	*write* (2.24)	*die* (0.73)
hear (1.15)	*increase* (2.79)	*become* (2.24)	*hit* (0.73)
ring (1.11)	*ask* (2.68)	*provide* (2.21)	*mention* (0.7)
take (1.11)	*suggest* (2.63)	*pay* (2.19)	*win* (0.61)
give (1.07)	*talk* (2.52)	*occur* (2.08)	*develop* (0.61)
work (1.07)	*pass* (2.24)	*reach* (1.97)	*move* (0.56)
mention (1.07)	*pay* (2.22)	*cause* (1.94)	*spend* (0.53)
answer (1.06)	*cause* (2)	*wait* (1.81)	*introduce* (0.48)

In Gries and Stefanowitsch (2004a), we were able to confirm earlier claims that the *going-to*-future has a much stronger preference for verbs encoding dynamic actions than the *will*-future. These results are further confirmed by the data in Table 9. Among the top twenty distinctive collexemes of the *going-to*-future there are only three low-dynamicity verbs in the spoken data (*be*, *have*, *stay*) and one in the written data (*die*); in contrast, among the top twenty distinctive collexemes of the *will*-future there are nine low-dynamicity verbs in the spoken data (*see*, *know*, *want*, *notice*, *find*, *agree*, *recall*, *learn*, and *hear*), and the same number in the written data (*be*, *find*, *have*, *consider*, *receive*, *depend*, *become*, *occur*, and *reach*). As before, then, we find the same semantic contrast in both channels. Also as before, we do not find strong channel influences on lexical choice; but recall that these are really only expected to emerge in the direct comparison of channels, to which we now turn. The results of the second comparison are shown in Table 10.

Table 10. Comparison of channels by the two future constructions

will		*going to*	
SPOKEN	WRITTEN	SPOKEN	WRITTEN
do (4.89)	*be* (12.57)	*be* (19.83)	*chubb lock* (1.21)
see (4.8)	*increase* (5.01)	*say* (16.22)	*conduct* (1.21)
go (4.51)	*pay* (3.5)	*have* (11.88)	*extradite* (1.21)
come (3.61)	*consider* (3.41)	*do* (9.29)	*spoil* (1.21)
want (2.39)	*receive* (3)	*go* (9.28)	*deliver* (0.98)
tell (2.15)	*add* (3)	*happen* (5.01)	*feed* (0.98)
know (2.07)	*cause* (2.95)	*use* (4.63)	*bear* (0.85)
talk (1.95)	*write* (2.84)	*get* (4.05)	*tour* (0.83)
notice (1.92)	*occur* (2.75)	*show* (3.96)	*serve* (0.81)
mention (1.87)	*depend* (2.66)	*talk* (3.66)	*close* (0.51)
hear (1.8)	*include* (2.64)	*win* (3.54)	*move* (0.51)
introduce (1.75)	*assist* (2.48)	*put* (3.41)	*provide* (0.47)
develop (1.65)	*base* (2.48)	*come* (3.26)	*depend* (0.42)
read (1.55)	*last* (2.48)	*stay* (3.19)	*let* (0.41)
speak (1.53)	*qualify* (2.48)	*ask* (3.15)	*receive* (0.39)
learn (1.53)	*understand* (2.48)	*make* (3.01)	*consider* (0.36)
lie (1.53)	*apply* (2.3)	*buy* (2.73)	*remain* (0.36)
teach (1.53)	*entitle* (2.3)	*tell* (2.21)	*finish* (0.33)
spend (1.42)	*reach* (2.26)	*suggest* (1.86)	*include* (0.3)
try (1.39)		*play* (1.71)	*hold* (0.3)

The dynamicity differences show up less clearly than before in this comparison, but instead, clear formality differences emerge between the channels for both constructions: the top collexemes in the spoken data consist mainly (though not exclusively) of short words of Germanic origin while in writing the collexemes tend to be longer Romance or Latinate words.

Finally, there was one case of crossover: the verb *be* is significantly associated with *going-to*/spoken and with *will*/written. Given the wide range of functions served by this verb, it is impossible to come up with an explanation for this without a more detailed investigation

2.3.2. Discussion

The results of this case study do not differ fundamentally from those of the previous two, and thus there is little to say about them beyond what was already said above. One noteworthy fact is that in this case both constructions showed a relatively high sensitivity to channel with respect to lexical choice in that their top collexemes in the written data were much more formal than those in the spoken data. Thus, none of the two constructions seems to have its own formality preferences (unlike in the previous two case studies).

3. General discussion

Despite possible overgeneralizations in the way in which 'channel' was operationalized in the present study, three important conclusions follow from the results presented above.

The first conclusion is that there is no evidence so far to suggest that constructional semantics in the narrow sense interacts with channel in such a way that there are differences in a construction's meaning across channels. The semantic characterizations of the constructions in question arrived at in earlier work were found to hold in both spoken and written language. This was shown in each case by the two major comparisons we drew (CONSTRUCTION 1 VS. CONSTRUCTION 2 by CHANNEL and SPOKEN CHANNEL VS. WRITTEN CHANNEL by CONSTRUCTION) as well as by our investigation of crossover effects. To be fair, two caveats are in order, one concerning the major comparisons, and one concerning the investigation of crossover effects. With respect to the comparisons, the method employed here (like corpus-based methods in general) is necessarily superficial in two important respects: first, it only captures those semantic differences that have consequences for lexical choice, and second, it ignores the polysemy of lexical items and constructions. More fine-grained annotation of large corpora may allow future research to overcome this problem, but for now, corpus linguists will have to live with it. With respect to the crossover effects, it has to be kept in mind that the criterion we apply here is extremely strict since we only accept cases where a word is significantly associated to a single construction in each channel. It is conceivable to take a less categorical approach and to accept cases whose association strengths exhibit crossover effects.

Even given these caveats, however, the results seem plausible and are perhaps not entirely unexpected. Linguistic signs may differ in their connotative meaning and thus have different likelihoods of occurrence in different channels. The (invariant) meaning of a given sign may certainly be exploited to yield different communicative effects in different contexts, and future construction-based research would certainly profit from taking this into account (cf. Stefanowitsch and Gries 2005 for a brief discussion of one such case). However, if meaning itself were to differ according to context, this would seriously threaten the integrity of the linguistic system and hence its usefulness for communication. This is true of lexical items, which are relatively accessible to conscious introspection and hence to meta-linguistic discourse; how much more true should we expect it to be of grammatical constructions, which are inaccessible to conscious introspection.

The second conclusion is that there can be channel-specific associations between constructions and individual lexical items. Again, this is perhaps not entirely surprising, since it is a well-known fact that channel may influence lexical selection (it is, in fact, reflected in most modern dictionaries by labels such as *formal*, *informal*, *colloquial*, etc.) Since spoken and written channels differ in vocabulary, they inevitably also differ in terms of specific collostructional relationships between words and constructions. Such specific collostructional relationships are doubtless of theoretical and of practical interest and thus could fruitfully be integrated into any collostructional analysis and into construction-based research in general.

The final, and perhaps most important conclusion from a construction-grammar viewpoint is that different constructions differ with respect to the degree to which they exhibit channel-specific collostructional relationships: while some constructions (the active construction, the particle-first variant of the verb-particle construction, and the two future-tense constructions) are relatively sensitive to the formality differences associated with spoken vs. written channels, other constructions are rather insensitive, and seem to have their own, construction-specific preferences which they retain regardless of the channel they are used in (the passive construction always has a relative preference for formal lexical items, the particle-first variant of the verb-particle construction always has a relative preference for informal, idiomatic lexical items. Such differences in the degree to which lexical choices within a given construction reflect either general properties of a particular channel or specific properties of the construction itself constitute an important fact about it that has to be recorded as part of the construction's specification if construction grammar takes serious its commitment to a broad understanding of meaning.

References

Berglund, Ylva
1997 Future in Present-day English: Corpus-based evidence on the rivalry of expressions. *ICAME Journal* 21: 7–19.

Biber, Douglas, Stig Johansson, Geoffrey Leech, Susan Conrad and Edward Finegan
1999 *Longman Grammar of Spoken and Written English.* London: Longman.

Blankenship, Jane
1962 A linguistic analysis of oral and written style. *Quarterly Journal of Speech* 48: 419–422.

Brown, Gillian and George Yule
1983 *Discourse Analysis.* Cambridge: Cambridge University Press.

Chafe, Wallace L.
1982 Integration and involvement in speaking, writing, and oral literature. In: Deborah Tannen (ed.), *Spoken and Written Language: Exploring Orality and Literacy,* 35–54. Norwood, NJ: Ablex.

Croft, William
2001 *Radical Construction Grammar. Syntactic Theory in Typological Perspective.* Oxford: Oxford University Press.

Eye, Alexander von
1990 *Introduction to Configural Frequency Analysis: The Search for Types and Antitypes in Cross-classifications.* Cambridge: Cambridge University Press.

Goldberg, Adele E.
1995 *Constructions. A Construction-Grammar Approach to Argument-Structure Constructions.* Chicago/London: The University of Chicago Press.

Greenbaum, Sidney (ed.)
1996 *Comparing English Worldwide: The International Corpus of English.* Oxford: Clarendon Press.

Gries, Stefan Th.
2003 *Multifactorial Analysis in Corpus Linguistics: A Study of Particle Placement.* London/New York: Continuum.

Gries, Stefan Th., Beate Hampe and Doris Schönefeld
2005 Converging evidence: Bringing together experimental and corpus data on the association between verbs and constructions. *Cognitive Linguistics,* 16.4: 635–676.

Gries, Stefan Th. and Anatol Stefanowitsch
2004a Extending collostructional analysis: A corpus-based perspectives on 'alternations'. *International Journal of Corpus Linguistics* 9.1: 97–129.
2004b Co-varying collexemes in the *into*-causative. In: Michel Achard and Suzanne Kemmer (eds.), *Language, Culture, and Mind,* 225–236. Stanford, CA: CSLI
in press Cluster analysis and the identification of collexeme classes. In: John Newman and Sally Rice (eds.), *Experimental and Empirical Methods in the Study of Conceptual Structure, Discourse, and Language.* Stanford, CA: CSLI Publications.

Grondelaers, Stefan
this volume National variation in the use of *er* "there". Regional and diachronic constraints on cognitive explanations Regional constraints on cognitive explanations.
Krauth, Joachim
1993 *Einführung in die Konfigurationsfrequenzanalyse (KFA)*. Weinheim: Beltz.
Murphy, Raymond
1986 *English Grammar in Use*. 4th rev. ed. Cambridge: Cambridge University Press.
Poole, Millicent E. and T.W. Field
1976 A comparison of oral and written code elaboration. *Language and Speech* 19: 305–311.
Quirk, Randolph, Sidney Greenbaum, Geoffrey Leech, and Jan Svartvik
1985 *A Comprehensive Grammar of the English Language*. London: Longman.
Siegel, Sidney.
1956 *Nonparametric Statistics for the Behavioral Sciences*. Tokyo: McGraw-Hill & Kogakusha Ltd.
Speelman, Dirk
this volume Variation in the choice of adjectives in the two main national varieties of Dutch.
Stefanowitsch, Anatol and Stefan Th. Gries
2003 Collostructions: Investigating the interaction between words and constructions. *International Journal of Corpus Linguistics* 8.2: 209–243.
2005 Co-varying collexemes. *Corpus Linguistics and Linguistic Theory* 1.1: 1–46.
Thompson, Audrey J. and Agnes V. Martinet
1986 *A Practical English Grammar*. 4th ed. Oxford: Oxford University Press.
Tummers, José, Kris Heylen, and Dirk Geeraerts
2006 Usage-based approaches in Cognitive Linguistics: A technical state of the art. *Corpus Linguistics and Linguistic Theory* 1.2: 225–261
Wulff, Stefanie, Anatol Stefanowitsch, and Stefan Th. Gries
2007 Brutal Brits and Persuasive Americans: Variety-specific Meaning Constructions in the into-causative. In: Radden, Günter, Klaus-Michael Köpcke, Thomas Berg, and Peter Siemund (eds). *Aspects of Meaning Construction in Lexicon and Grammar*, 265–81. Amsterdam, Philadelphia: Benjamins.

National variation in the use of *er* "there". Regional and diachronic constraints on cognitive explanations

Stefan Grondelaers, Dirk Speelman and Dirk Geeraerts

Abstract

Since cognitive linguists believe that "fundamental cognitive abilities and experientially derived cognitive models have direct and pervasive linguistic manifestations" (Langacker 1993: 1), the core business of Cognitive Linguistics is to investigate how cognitive structure determines the syntactic surface of natural language. This chapter focuses on the hazards associated with the one-on-one relation which is tacitly assumed in Cognitive Linguistics between underlying cognitive mechanisms and their linguistic manifestations. As a case study, we will investigate the notoriously complex distribution of *er* "there" in adjunct-initial sentences such as *In ons land is (er) nog altijd geen openbaar golfterrein* "In our country there still is no public golf course". Although this distribution is reputed to be sensitive to national variation, we will demonstrate that there are no underlying functional differences between *er*'s Belgian and Netherlandic distribution: the cognitive "motor" of both is the human reference point ability (Langacker 1993, Taylor 1996), and both are triggered by the same discursive and syntactic parameters of that ability. Since the different distribution of *er* in the national varieties of Dutch is not functionally motivated, we attribute divergent *er*-preferences in Netherlandic and Belgian Dutch to the *delayed linguistic standardization* of the latter, which was blocked in the 16th C as a result of political and social factors, resuming its course only in the 20th C. The key concept in the evolution from unsteady Belgian *er*-preferences to the more balanced Netherlandic distribution of *er*, will be argued to be *functional specialisation*, viz. the progression from *subjective evaluation* of the functional properties of a class of elements to speaker-and-hearer-shared *objective knowledge* about the functional properties of that class of elements.

Keywords: presentative sentences, reference point constructions, regional and register variation, linguistic standardization, multivariate corpus analysis.

1. Introduction

One of the basic tenets of Cognitive Linguistics is that "fundamental cognitive abilities and experientially derived cognitive models have direct and pervasive linguistic manifestations" (Langacker 1993: 1). A pivotal case in point is the human *reference point ability*, a phenomenon so ubiquitous in the perception of our surroundings that we are largely oblivious to it. Langacker (1991: 170, but see also Taylor 1996: 17–19) introduces the reference point phenomenon as follows:

> The world is conceived as being populated by countless objects of diverse character. The objects vary greatly in their salience to a given observer; like stars in the nighttime sky, some are immediately apparent to the viewer, whereas others become apparent only if special effort is devoted in seeking them out. Salient objects serve as reference points for this purpose: if the viewer knows that a non-salient object lies near a salient one, he can find it by directing his attention to the latter and searching in its vicinity.

This reference point ability has been found to be the cognitive motor of very diverse linguistic phenomena: building on the perceptual and conceptual aspects of the reference point Gestalt, cognitively oriented linguists have been able to account for the syntactic, semantic and pragmatic peculiarities of such diverse phenomena as possessive constructions (Langacker 1993; Taylor 1996), topic constructions (Langacker 1993), and, more recently, adjunct-initial presentative sentences (Grondelaers 2000; Grondelaers and Brysbaert 1996; Grondelaers, Brysbaert, Speelman and Geeraerts 2002).

Although this interest in cognitive structure has furnished researchers with a rewarding way into the processing machinery behind a great number of poorly understood constructions, some aspects of the relation between cognitive structure and its linguistic manifestation are as yet too shadowy to have absolute methodological confidence in the type of functional explanations propounded in mainstream cognitive work. This paper therefore focuses on some of the *constraints* which eclipse the causal link between cognitive phenomena and their linguistic surface realizations. Building on an extensive investigation into the distribution of presentative *er* "there" in Belgian and Netherlandic Dutch presentative sentences with a preposed adjunct (*In ons land is (er) nog altijd geen openbaar golfterrein* "In our country there still is no public golf course"), we will demonstrate that, despite its ubiquity and universality, the human reference point ability appears to generate perceptibly different presentative constructions in the national varieties of one small language, viz.

Dutch. While these functional differences may reflect alternate construal patterns (it is well-established that construal is culture-dependent, see especially Pederson et al. 1998), they may equally well indicate that the tacitly assumed one-on-one relation between underlying cognitive mechanisms and their linguistic manifestations is an oversimplification. In both cases, the researcher must be extremely cautious that his functional explanations do not overgeneralize: they may be *externally* constrained (to national, regional, or social *varieties* of a language instead of the whole language for which they are designed), or they may be *internally* constrained, and *not* offer direct access into underlying cognitive machinery because the processing motivation for a constructional pattern may have "fossilized" to some extent in, for instance, a process of linguistic standardization. In the case study reported here we will collect quantifiable offline data to reveal what sort of constraints – external or internal – lead to, or have led to, the different presentative mechanisms in Belgian and Netherlandic Dutch.

In doing so, we will also demonstrate that an eminently non-objectivist research topic such as cognitive motivation can be studied by means of an objectivist methodology, viz. a corpus-based regression analysis. To many cognitive linguists, such an approach will reek of exactly the objectivist attitude Cognitive Linguistics wanted to get rid off in the first place. This uneasiness, however, is based on a category mistake. It is not because the cognitive processes that we describe on the object level are non-objectivist that our description on the theoretical metalevel will necessarily be unable to achieve objectivity. And even if a non-objectivist methodology is residually unavoidable (see Geeraerts 1985 for the intricacies of the relationship between epistemological levels and metalevels), general principles of repeatability and comparability of results favor an empirical approach spiring towards maximal objectivity.

This does not mean, to be sure, that our corpus research will be independent of the hermeneutic, interpretative features that are typical of a non-objectivist methodology ("we have to understand what people mean when they mean, and such an understanding requires interpretation"). Our investigation neither denies nor ignores the necessity of interpretations, but it takes on a *helix-like* structure of a gradual refinement of interpretations through a repeated confrontation with empirical data. The latter, in a nutshell, is the track we have followed in our investigation of presentative constructions in Belgian Dutch (see Grondelaers 2000; Grondelaers and Brysbaert 1996; Grondelaers, Brysbaert, Speelman and Geeraerts 2002; Grondelaers, Speelman, Drieghe, Geeraerts and Brysbaert *submitted*). A first set of multivariate analyses of the factors which determine the syntax of presentative sentences revealed underlying cognitive motivations (see especially Grondelaers 2000) which were further tested and refined in psycho-experimental designs (see Grondelaers, Brysbaert, Speelman and Geeraerts 2002; Grondelaers, Speelman, Drieghe, Geeraerts and Brysbaert *submitted*) and new multivariate analyses (see Grondelaers and Speelman 2007). The time has come now to find out whether we can extend the analysis of presentative constructions which was hitherto restricted to Belgian Dutch to Netherlandic Dutch.

This is how we will proceed. In the next section we focus on some of the problems traditionally associated with the analysis of presentative sentences in Dutch, and in particular on the postverbal distribution of *er* in adjunct-initial presentative sentences. Whereas section 3 compactly summarizes the basic features of the first multivariate analysis (materials, methods, and initial results), section 4 reiterates how the regression findings lead to our hypothesis about the reference point function of adjunct-initial sentences and *er*'s *inaccessibility marking* role therein. In section 5, we propose quantifiable parameters of these functions which will subsequently be tested in separate regression analyses of *er*'s distribution in Belgian and Netherlandic Dutch. Section 6 analyses the consequences of our findings for this paper's main issue, viz. the exact nature of the cognitive motivation of linguistic structure. Without pre-empting the discussion, it will be shown that regional differences between Belgian and Netherlandic Dutch are *diachronically*, rather than *functionally* motivated.

2. Presentative sentences and presentative *er*

Few linguistic phenomena have given rise to such fiery theoretical controversy as presentative sentences and, in particular, presentative *er* "there" (cognitive approaches to *there* can be found a.o. in Lakoff 1987; Kirsner 1979 is an early example of a cognitive analysis of Dutch *er*). Examples (1)–(3) illustrate the standard type of presentative sentence in Dutch, which is to a high extent isomorphous with English *there*-sentences. The sentence-initial *er* in this construction type has been dubbed "plaatsonderwerp" (topical subject), "repletive *er*", "presentative *er*" (Haeseryn et al. 1997: 464, 467 ff.), and "existential *er*":

(1) Er bevonden zich geen paparazzi vlak voor, naast of achter de *wagen*.
"There were no paparazzi right in front of, next to, or behind the car."

(2) *Er* zijn *op dit moment* 11.500 invalide zelfstandigen.
There are at this moment 11.500 disabled small businessmen
"There are 11.500 disabled small businessmen at this moment."

Linguistic approaches to sentence-initial *er* have for the most part been dominated by two views. In the structuralist and generative tradition, *er* is regarded as a mechanically inserted, semantically empty dummy which occupies subject position when the actual, ontological subject follows the main verb (Bech 1952: 13 ff.; Paardekoper 1963: 34 ff.; Nieuwborg 1968: 285 and, more recently, Leys 1979: 244 and Swiggers and Van den Eynde 1985). Although early transformational descriptions (Kraak 1966[1]; Verkuyl e.a. 1974: De Haan 1974; De Haan, Koefoed and Des Tombe 1975; Pollmann 1975 and Van den Toorn 1976) also regard *er* as a placeholder for the real subject, they resort to *there*-insertion to account for the syntactic properties of presentative sentences: *there*-insertion moves non-generically interpreted indefinite subjects to a VP-governed NP, and inserts a "dummy subject" into the vacated subject position[2]. In the Government and Binding stage of generative syntax, *er*'s distribution continues to be governed by a mechanical insertion rule (Den Besten 1981, 1982, 1983; Reuland 1983; Hoekstra 1984).

Analysts in the functionalist tradition strongly reject the dummy subject view and attribute to *er* fairly equivalent propositional and discursive meanings. According to Kirsner (1979: 71), presentative *er* denotes "the spatio-temporal context or circumstances surrounding the event and its participants" (similar views can be found in Van Es and Van Caspel 1971; De Schutter 1974; Schermer-Vermeer 1986; Blom 1992). This unanimity extends to functionalist thinking on *er*'s discursive function: according to

1. Kraak (1966) makes no explicit mention of *er*-insertion, but his view of a purely mechanical operation triggered by the indefiniteness of the subject, is very much in the spirit of that transformation.
2. The popularity of the *there*-insertion transformation should not obscure the existence – since the beginning of the '70-ies – of alternative analyses in which *there* is a "base-generated postcopular subject" (see for instance Jenkins 1975) which need not be removed from the subject slot. Bennis (1986) is an influential generative alternative to *there*-insertion. According to Bennis (1986), Dutch word order basically instantiates a presupposition-focus structure, and *er* fills the presupposition when no other element is available to do so, in order to satisfy the "Empty Presupposition Principle", which stipulates that pragmatically well-formed sentences mandatorily contain an overt constituent which is presuppositional (1986: 225).

Geerts et al. (1984: 395) and Haeseryn et al. (1997: 467, 1273), *er*-clauses are used to introduce a subject which contains new, important information. De Schutter (1974: 349) suggests that the construction with *er* introduces and situates "an entity unknown in some respect (viz. nature, individuality, characteristics, and/or number" (for related opinions, cf. also Elffers 1977: 420 ff. and Schermer-Vermeer 1985: 80 and note 24).

This case study, however, predominantly concentrates on the distribution of *er* in the adjunct-initial presentative sentence type. When an adjunct is topicalized in Dutch presentatives, *er* emerges postverbally, if it emerges at all: it has often been observed that *er* can in certain cases be deleted in adjunct-initial presentative sentences (see Haeseryn et al. 1997 and De Rooij 1991 for Dutch, and Bolinger 1977 for English).

(3) In 1977 was *er* een fusie tussen Materne en Confilux.
In 1977 was *er* a merger between Materne and Confilux
"In 1977 there followed a merger between Materne and Confilux."

(4) Morgen volgt een extra ministerraad.
Tomorrow follows an additional cabinet meeting
"Tomorrow there is an additional cabinet meeting."

(5) In het redactielokaal staan enkele flessen wijn en wat borrelhapjes.
In the newsroom stand some bottles of wine and some appetizers
"In the newsroom there are some bottles of wine and some appetizers."

(6) In ons land is *er* nog altijd geen openbaar golfterrein.
In our country is *er* still no public golf course.
"In our country there still is no public golf course."

The restriction to adjunct sentences has the pivotal methodological advantage – first observed in Bolinger's groundbreaking study on the distribution of *there* in English adjunct-initial presentatives (1977: 93) – that any syntactic, semantic or functional difference between sentence variants with and without *er* can only be attributed to the presence or absence of *er*. We believe that by identifying such syntactic, semantic and functional differences between variants with and without *er*, we can "tease out" the true function sense of *er*.

Teasing out *er*'s true function from adjunct-initial "minimal pairs" has so far proved to be a frustrating enterprise; *er*'s postverbal distribution has given rise to a good deal of descriptive vagueness in the linguistic literature. According to the Algemene Nederlandse Spraakkunst (ANS) – the standard grammar of Dutch (see Haeseryn et al. 1997) – no strict rules can be given for the presence or absence of postverbal *er*: "it can be optional, there may be semantic or stylistic differences involved, and there is a lot of individual and sometimes also regional variation in its use" (1997: 473). Only a handful of factors have hitherto been identified (mostly on the basis of introspection). On p. 477, specifically in connection with the optionality of postverbal *er* in adjunct-initial sentences, the ANS states: "in the standard language, *er* is more easily deleted in sentences with a fronted locative than in other cases" (see also De Rooij 1991 and Van Es and Van Caspel 1971). All sources, however, hasten to add that this is no more than a tendency: our own corpus data (see especially Grondelaers, Speelman, and Geeraerts 1992) confirm that locative adjunct sentence retain *er* in more than 25% of all cases (cf. infra). Another observation (made a.o. in De Rooij 1991) which converges well with native speakers' intuitions is the idea that the preference for *er* correlates negatively with the taxonomical specificity of the main verb: the more specific the verb, the less *er* (this correlation, again, is no categorical constraint but a strong tendency). To complicate matters further, there are outspoken regional and stylistic tendencies in *er*'s postverbal distribution: Belgian Dutch is known to be much more tolerant towards *er* than Netherlandic Dutch (cf. De Rooij 1991; Haeseryn et al. 1997), and *er* is attested significantly more often in *informal* register (Haeseryn et al. 1997).

The observation that a substantial portion of locative adjunct sentences are attested *with er* in our corpus data, and the fact that *er*'s presence or absence will be shown to be highly predictable, constitutes the strongest evidence against structuralist and generative analyses which view *er* as no more than a dummy placeholder, but also against functionalist approaches which attribute some vague locative meaning to it. If *er* is no more than a "placeholder" for the genuine subject, why should it in some cases appear postverbally when another constituent, viz. an adjunct, holds the first place? And why should sentences with an initial locative benefit from the "zooming out" to the much more general situational reference coded by *er*? More particularly, if locative adjuncts are indeed a suitable "'handle' on an event which otherwise would be difficult to picture" (Kirsner 1979: 103–104), there is no reason why an even more suitable, but vaguer handle – presentative *er* – should be realized postverbally when an appropriate "grip" is already available. Kirsner seems to be aware of this shortcoming when he observes that "while it is also possible for such 'fronted locatives' to introduce 'expletive' *er*, sentences such as (6a) below – [*In de tuin blaft er een hond* "In the garden there barks a dog"] – are quite rare in discourse". This apologetic observation, however, is clearly wrong: our corpus data (Grondelaers, Speelman, and Geeraerts 2002) prove that Belgian and Netherlandic presentative sentences with a preposed locative adjunct contain *er* in respectively 19.1 and 33,3 % of all attestations. In what follows, we will moreover demonstrate that there are good reasons for *er* to emerge postverbally in some locative adjunct sentences.

Crucially, the function we will unveil for postverbal *er* in this paper can be shown to apply to preverbal, sentence-initial *er* as well. Although space limitations preclude a detailed analysis, we argue in section 7 that *er*-initial presentative sentences as a whole inherit their constructional meaning and function from postverbal *er*[3]. First, however, let us re-evaluate what is known about postverbal *er*'s distribution in a more reliable way.

3. Regressing on the known determinants of *er*'s postverbal distribution

Confronted with postverbal *er*'s distributional complexity and the scarce facts thus far available, how can we proceed to investigate *er*'s distribution in an empirically more responsible way? In the next section we will outline and operationalize a functional hypothesis which will subsequently be verified on the basis of an extensive corpus of written Dutch. Let us first, however, reconsider the four factors mentioned in the previous paragraph (ADJUNCT TYPE, VERBAL SPECIFICITY, REGION, and REGISTER) in a quantitatively more dependable way, in order to be able to feed them

3. It will be obvious by now that we concentrate on uncovering *er*'s *function* in this paper, rather than suggest a "lexical" or "referential" meaning for it. While the minimal pair-approach is eminently suited to expose *er*'s impact on other constituents of the adjunct-initial construction (which helps us to flesh out its function), we do not endorse Bolinger's (1977) claim that it offers direct access into *er*'s proper *denotatum*. Although we do not wish to exclude in advance that *er* has a proper meaning or referent apart from the function we attribute to it, the latter will be shown to rule out any proposal which has been made so far in the literature: it is highly unlikely that *er* should refer to the "spatio-temporal setting surrounding the event and its participants" – to name the most elaborate proposal (Kirsner 1979) – and at the same time play the extremely specific information processing role which all our online and offline data findings point to.

into the hypothesis. For now, it is essential that we find a reliable answer to the following questions. First, are the four factors really significant determinants of *er*'s distribution? All of them are compatible with speaker judgements, but none of them constitute clear-cut rules: example (6) is an obvious counterexample to the "rule" that locative adjunct sentences are preferably constructed without *er*. Second, what is their respective impact on *er*'s distribution? This question is especially relevant in this context, since the factors involved come in two types: whereas ADJUNCT TYPE and VERBAL SPECIFICITY are *language-structural factors* which – when succesfully identified and operationalized – help solve *er*'s distribution, REGION and REGISTER are *contextual factors*, which traditionally belong to the domain of sociolinguistics, and which constrain our explanations to one region or register. More specifically, when we find that ADJUNCT TYPE *does* have an impact, we are one step closer to our goal, viz. determining *er*'s distribution; if, by contrast, the statistical analysis reveals that, for instance, REGION has a significant influence on *er*, we know that our account is restricted to Belgian or Netherlandic Dutch, which greatly complicates matters. It is therefore pivotal that we learn which factors are significant, and which factors – language-structural or contextual – have the greatest impact. Third, how much variation can be explained and predicted on the basis of these four factors? Are they already sufficiently powerful predictors, or do we need additional features?

A reliable answer to these questions necessitates a sophisticated corpus design. In the absence of a fully stratified corpus of Dutch, we compiled the ConDiv-corpus, an extensive text-database tailored to the needs of various corpus-based sociolinguistic investigations (see Grondelaers, Deygers, Van Aken, Van Den Heede, and Speelman 2000 for design details). The ConDiv-corpus not only contains Netherlandic as well as Belgian Dutch texts, it is also structured along an important register dimension. The corpus basically consists of two types of attested language use. In the newspaper component a distinction is made between quality newspapers such as *De Standaard* and *NRC Handelsblad* and popular newspapers such as *De Telegraaf* and *Het Laatste Nieuws*. There are national popular papers – *Het Laatste Nieuws en De Telegraaf* –, but also regional popular papers such as *Het Belang van Limburg* or *De Gazet van Antwerpen*. The lowest position on the register scale is represented in this study by language data attested on UseNet, an Internet forum on which surfers debate in "newsgroups", by means of e-mail messages they add to an ongoing discussion. Since e-mail is offline – so that users can re-

read their contributions before adding them to a "thread" – and since academic Internet operators only tolerate (relatively) serious newsgroups on their net –, the UseNet register is not as informal as Internet Relay Chat, a module in which anonymous users debate online (a detailed motivation for the restriction to UseNet materials can be found in Grondelaers, Speelman, and Geeraerts 2002).

From this corpus, we extracted all presentative main sentences constructed either with a sentence-initial locative or a temporal adjunct. The distribution of the observations over the different sources in the corpus is given in Table 1:

Table 1. Distribution of observations over the sources in the corpus

	UseNet	Popular Newspapers		Quality Newspapers
N	n = 192	*Telegraaf* n = 227		*NRC* n = 263
B	n = 225	*Het Belang van Limburg* n = 397	*Het Laatste Nieuws* n = 198	*De Standaard* n = 403

The preference for *er* was subsequently quantified as the ratio between the absolute frequency of the adjunct-initial clauses attested with *er* in a source, and the total frequency of adjunct-initial clauses in that source. This calculation returns the maximal *er*-preference value for adjunct-initial clause types which always contain *er* and the minimal value for clauses which are never attested with *er*.

The implementation of the contextual independent variables is unproblematic in this analysis, for REGION – Belgian vs. Netherlandic Dutch – and REGISTER – UseNet vs. popular newspapers vs. quality papers – are reflected in the structure of the corpus. The extracted observations were then tagged for the language-structural variables ADJUNCT TYPE and VERBAL SPECIFICITY. ADJUNCT TYPE was operationalized straightforwardly by contrasting observations with a locative and a temporal adjunct. The VERBAL SPECIFICITY FACTOR, by contrast, does not translate easily into an operational parameter. Although adjunct-initial presentative sentences allow only a limited number of verbal classes, the specificity of those verbs may be determined by any of the three conceptual ingredients their semantics presuppose, viz. the subject, the setting coded by the adjunct, and the verbal relation between both. Because of the conceptual inseparability of a verbal process from its subject and its setting, we have operationalised the VERBAL SPECIFICITY-FACTOR on the basis of the size of the class of possible subjects the different verbs in adjunct-initial presentatives subcategorise. Building on this criterion, the lowest level of specificity is represented by the verb *to be*, which imposes no restrictions at all on process, setting and subject. In this respect it is hardly surprising that almost all the verbs we encounter in adjunct-initial presentative sentences are hyponyms of *to be*. The highest level of specificity, by contrast, is represented by verbs which are constructed with a limited set of subjects. These include Levin's (1993) VERBS OF ENTITY-SPECIFIC MODES OF BEING, (*vloeien* "flow", *branden* "burn"), VERBS OF MODES OF BEING INVOLVING MOTION (*wapperen* "flutter"), MEANDER VERBS (*meanderen* "meander"), VERBS OF SOUND EXISTENCE (*echoën* "echo"), VERBS OF GROUP EXISTENCE (*dansen* "dance" in reference to bees), VERBS OF SPATIAL CONFIGURATION (*sit*, *stand*, *lie*, and *hang*), and VERBS OF APPEARANCE, DISAPPEARANCE AND OCCURRENCE (*verschijnen* "appear", *perish* "vergaan", *plaatsvinden* "occur", *aan de gang zijn* "take place"). Contrary to Van Es and Van Caspel (1971), De Rooij (1991), and Grondelaers and Brysbaert (1996), we add an intermediate level represented by a small group of (frequently attested) verbs, which impose a minimal restriction on one of their conceptual ingredients (*bestaan* "exist" is slightly more specific than zijn "to be" because it situates its subject within the metaphysical boundaries of this world, *ontstaan* "to come into being" adds an inchoative aspect to zijn, *blijven* "remain" an imperfective aspect, *voorbij gaan* "to pass" and *eindigen* "to end" a perfective aspect).

Data were collected in order to answer three questions in connection with the distribution of postverbal *er*. First, is the impact of the individual variables on *er*'s distribution statistically significant? Second, which factor's impact is the most outspoken? Third, is the explanatory and predictive power of the model which contains these variables as poor as traditional analyses – notably Haeseryn et al. (1997) and De Rooij (1991) – would like us to believe? Table 2 contains the output of the logistic regression analysis to which we subjected our data in order to answer these questions (the technical details are not important here; see Rietveld and Van Hout 1993: 330 for an overview). The analysis returns *p-values* (in the second column) which reflect the statistical significance of each factor (a value below .05 indicates that the impact of a factor is significant), as well as *Odds Ratios* (in the third column) which reflect the relative importance of each factor's impact on the variation at issue. To give an example: if the analysis returns Odds Ratio "6" for an independent variable, the use of *er* vs. the non-use of *er* is predicted to increase 6 times as a result of the impact of that independent variable.

Table 2. P-values and Odds Ratios of the independent variables which explain *er*'s distribution in the global database

	p	Odds Ratio
adjunct type	0.0001	40.2
verbal specificity 1	0.0001	68.8
verbal specificity 2	0.0001	3.27
region	0.0001	3.36
register 1	0.0001	2.68
register 2	0.0051	1.55

Before we go into the data in table 2, it should be noticed that all factors are interpreted as nominal variables, a consequence of which is that our analysis returns two estimates for variables with three values (VERBAL SPECIFICITY and REGISTER): a first one for the impact on *er*'s distribution of the opposition between values "1" and "3" (in the case of, for instance, VERBAL SPECIFICITY, between the main verb *to be* and a main verb of the EXISTENCE & APPEARANCE-type), and a second for the impact on *er*'s distribution of the opposition between values "2" en "3" (the difference between intermediary verbs and EXISTENCE & APPEARANCE-verbs). Again, the technical details are of no great concern.

Much more important is the confirmation in table 2 that the impact of all factors is highly significant. For the language-structural variables ADJUNCT TYPE and VERBAL SPECIFICITY, whose impact on *er* can be intuitively verified, this outspoken statistical significance could be predicted. The high significance of REGISTER 1, REGISTER 2, and REGION from now on necessitates extreme caution when interpreting the global data.

Despite their outspoken significance, the respective impact of these variables on *er*'s distribution differs noticeably. Our statistical tool returns extremely high Odds Ratios for ADJUNCT TYPE and especially VERBAL SPECIFICITY 1, which suggests that the choice of verb and adjunct is decisive for *er*'s distribution. The impact of the contextual variables, by contrast, is much more limited.

The analysis also returns estimates of the global explanatory and predictive quality of our factors. A simple model which includes the four factors correctly predicts *er*'s distribution in no less then 84.4% of all cases, and this contrasts sharply with the "no strict rules" pessimism traditionally propounded in the linguistic literature (Haeseryn et al. 1977: 477). Though none of our factors constitutes a categorical constraint, their cumulative predictive efficiency can be translated into a simple algorithm, which correctly predicts *er*'s distribution in the overwhelming majority of adjunct-initial presentative sentences: in a temporal adjunct sentence with main verb *zijn* "to be", *er* is preferably inserted; in a locative adjunct sentence with a more specific verb, *er* need not be present (although, as we shall see, there are compelling reasons to insert it, even where it is not necessary for grammaticality).

There are, however, regional constraints on this predictive success (the statistical significance of REGION already was a provisional indication). A separate regression analysis of the Belgian and Netherlandic data indicates that *er*'s distribution is much more predictable in Netherlandic Dutch. In the latter, ADJUNCT TYPE and VERBAL SPECIFICITY are absolutely dominant: Netherlandic adjunct sentences can typically do without *er* when they have an initial locative adjunct, and the verbal factor blocks *er*-preferences in the rare cases where the locative adjunct has not already done so. In addition, there is no significant REGISTER-variation in the Netherlandic distribution of *er*. As a result, the predictive success rate of the Netherlandic model is as high as 89.5%. In the Belgian model, by contrast, the effect of ADJUNCT TYPE and VERBAL SPECIFICITY on *er*'s predictability is much less outspoken (locative adjunct sentences and adjunct sentences with specific main verbs are frequently attested with *er*), and the factors barely interact. In addition, REGISTER *does* play a role: the more informal the Belgian source, the more frequently adjunct sentences will contain *er*. The cumulative predictive success rate of the three variables in Belgian adjunct sentences is no more than 85.1%.

It is premature at this stage to draw far-reaching conclusions about differences in cognitive architecture between Belgian and Netherlandic presentative strategies. In order to eventually gain access into how Belgian and Netherlandic speakers of Dutch construe and structure the introduction of new information in discourse (for that is the major function of adjunct-initial presentative sentences), let us first outline an encompassing functional hypothesis about the discoursal role of presentative sentences and presentative *er* in Belgian Dutch, and test this hypothesis in a controlled experimental design. If we find independent evidence for the reference point function of adjunct-initial sentences, we can then go on to find quantifiable corpus parameters of this reference point function (*and er*'s inaccessibility marking function) which can subsequently be tested in a series of new regression analyses of *er*'s distribution in Belgian and Netherlandic Dutch.

4. Reference points and (in)accessibility markers

Recall that one of the basic axioms of Cognitive Linguistics is the non-autonomous character of linguistic structure, because "fundamental cognitive abilities and experientially derived cognitive models have direct and pervasive linguistic manifestations, and conversely, (...) language structure furnishes important clues concerning basic mental phenomena" (Langacker 1993: 1). In the final decades, cognitive linguists found evidence for a number of phenomena whose relevance is not restricted to language (like Talmy's *force dynamics* (1988) and Lakoff's *image schemas* (1987)). A recent discovery in this field was the "reference point scenario" (cf. supra), a ubiquitous cognitive phenomenon considered to be "the abstract basis" for semantically diverse prenominal possessives such as *the boy's watch, the girl's uncle, the dog's tail, the cat's fleas* or *Lincoln's assassination.* What all these constructions have in common is "that one entity (the one we call the *possessor*) is invoked as a reference point for purposes of establishing mental contact with another (the *possessed*)" (Langacker 1993: 8–9). Take the example *the girl's uncle*: "the very purpose of a kinship term is to situate people – socially and genealogically – with respect to a reference individual ("ego"). Only in relation to a particular ego does it make sense to call someone a *cousin*, an *uncle*, a *sister*, or a *stepson*; a person is not a *cousin* or a an *uncle* autonomously (...)." In the same way, it does only makes sense to refer to a part in the context of a whole "which functions as a natural reference point for its conception and characterization". The notion "possession" also is

> clearly asymmetrical and lends itself very naturally to reference-point function. We know and recognize people as individuals, but for the most part we do not have comparable individual familiarity with their possessions (except our own). Moreover, a given person has numerous possessions, each of which he uniquely controls (according to our idealized cognitive model), and for any general type of object (e.g. watches) there are many exemplars that we know nothing about except that each belongs to a particular individual. Hence a person is naturally invoked as a "mental address" providing access to the cluster of items he possesses.
>
> (Langacker 1993: 9)

The linguistic relevance of the reference point strategy is not restricted – according to Langacker (1993: 26 ff.) – to possessive constructions, because "certain presentational constructions that serve to introduce an element into the scene are reasonably attributed reference-point function" (ibid.). A case in point, Langacker continues, are the adjunct-initial clauses represented in (7)–(9):

(7) On the table sat a nervous calico cat.[4]
(8) Beside the pond stood an enormous marble sculpture.
(9) In her room were many exquisite paintings.

Since the prepositional constituent focuses the hearer's attention on a specific location, in which a new entity is subsequently introduced, it is attractive to regard the preposed adjuncts in these clauses as reference points for the conception of a subject entity which is new and hence non-salient. Notice that just as in possessive constructions, constituent ordering in adjunct-initial presentatives "iconically diagrams the mental route that the conceptualizer needs to follow in order to identify" the located element (Taylor 1996: 18): the fact that the adjunct is clause-initial symbolizes that the hearer is first invited to conceptualize the adjunct as a "mental adress" at which the new entity can then be found.

The reference point scenario not only has a *conceptual* dimension to it (as sketched in the previous paragraph), but also a *discoursal* dimension (elaborated for the most part in Taylor 1996: 193 ff.). On the discourse level, the facilitating impact of a reference point is the result of the referential restrictions the reference point imposes on the target entity: "an effective reference point is one which will limit the choice of possible targets" (Taylor 1996: 193). The difference in that light between target entities in possessive constructions and presentatives is reflected in the fact that possessees are typically marked definite whereas adjunct clause subjects are predominantly indefinite, which is the result of a difference in referential efficiency between the two types of reference points: "the possessor nominal (...) delimits the referential possibility of the possessee nominal – prototypically, down to a single, uniquely identifiable entity"

4. In the systemic-functionalist tradition (see Downing and Locke 2002), a distinction is made between *Circumstantial relational clauses* – basically the clause type in (7) –, which are fully reversible (*A nervous calico cat sat on the table*), and *Existential clauses* such as *There sat a nervous, calico cat on the table*, which need not always retain *there* when reversed, as is borne out by the grammaticality of (7), see in particular Bolinger (1977). We will come back to this distinction in section 7, where it will be shown that the present classification in Circumstantial relational clauses and Existential clauses has to be reconsidered, at least for Dutch.

(Taylor 1996: 207). "In the optimal case, there will only be one possible target; the reference point is such that there is a *unique relation* between it and the intended target" (o.c.: 193). In presentative sentences, by contrast, there rarely is a unique relation between reference point and target: "good" reference points narrow down the set of *nominal types* that can be coded by the subject NP head:

(10) a. In the refrigerator was a sausage
b. In the refrigerator was milk
c. ? In the refrigerator was bread
d. ?? In the refrigerator was a toothbrush

An adjunct such as "refrigerator" typically selects its subject from the relatively small class of "food stuffs limited in size which have to be refrigerated in order to remain fresh". Although this category contains more than one member (as shown by 10a. and b.), its mental activation prior to its actual realization greatly speeds up the processing of the compatible target entities in 10a. and b. (evidence to this effect will shortly be presented); incompatible target entities such as *bread* in 10c. (which needs not be refrigerated) and *a toothbrush* (no food), were shown to be processed significanty slower in the psycholinguistic literature. The psychological key concepts in this respect are *contextual constraint* – "the degree to which a sentence constrains the reader's expectations for possible completions" (Schwanenflugel 1986: 363) – and *predictive inferencing* (Altmann and Kamide 1999), the view that unfolding context functions as an incremental *filter* (updated on a constituent-by-constituent basis) which reduces the postverbal domain of reference on the basis of semantic and real-world knowledge emanating from the verb and initially realized arguments (in this case the adjunct).

Unfortunately, Langacker does not explicitly specify the relevant linguistic characteristics of "good" reference points, except that they have "a certain cognitive salience, either intrinsic or contextually determined" (1993: 6). And Taylor (1996: 210) does not go beyond suggesting that good reference points are highly accessible, i.e. topical. We will therefore have to operationalize the reference point phenomenon ourselves, and find quantifiable parameters of "good" reference points. Now, if good reference points enhance the processing of the subject entity by imposing restrictions on the referential potential of the subject nominal, then locative adjuncts will be better reference points than temporal adjuncts, because they situate their subjects in a spatial setting which generates more useful inferences about the upcoming subject (concerning its concreteness, size, etc.) than temporal settings, which do not constrain the entities they situate in any considerable way. Adjuncts such as *gisteren* "yesterday" or even the much more concrete *Vorige week dinsdag om tien over half negen* "last Tuesday at 8:40 AM" do not impose many restrictions on forthcoming subject entities, which can be abstract or concrete, of any conceivable nature or size:

(11) Vorige week dinsdag om tien over half negen was *er* een documentaire over Kenya op televisie.
"Last Tuesday at 8:40 AM there was a documentary on Kenya on"

(12) Vorige week dinsdag om tien over half negen was *er* plots een zwarte vrachtwagen.
"Last Tuesday at 8:40 AM there suddenly was a black lorry."

(13) Vorige week dinsdag om tien over half negen was *er* eindelijk rust.
"Last Tuesday at 8:40 AM there suddenly was peace."

It should be noticed at this point that the subject reduction realized in adjunct-initial clauses is not only effected by the reference point – viz. the adjunct – itself: referential restrictions on the subject also emanate from the verb. Recall in this respect that the factor VERBAL SPECIFICITY was implemented exactly in terms of the size of the class of potential subjects the different verbs subcategorize: the verb *zijn* "to be" does not constrain its subjects in any way, intermediary verbs impose only schematic restrictions, and EXISTENCE & APPEARANCE verbs are attested exclusively with a limited class of subjects. In the light of the "extended" reference point hypothesis outlined in this paragraph – reference point facilitation is the responsibility of the adjunct *and* the verb – we suggest that the more specific a verb, the more suitable as a reference point: EXISTENCE & APPEARANCE verbs constitute better reference points than intermediary verbs, which themselves are better reference points than any form of the verb *zijn*.

Let us now move on to a hypothesis about *er*'s function in adjunct-initial sentences, and recall that *er* is attested predominantly in the context of poor reference points, viz. temporal adjuncts, and unspecific main verbs. Clauses which feature a locative adjunct and a specific main verb, by contrast, can do very well without *er*. *Er*, in other words, appears to be a "diagnostic indicator" of poor reference point potential, of limited inferential access into the upcoming subject. We will therefore provisionally refer to it as an *inaccessibility marker* (notice that Bolinger 1977: 92 also mentions the absence of proper contextual anticipation of the subject as a *there*-triggering factor).

In (14)–(15) we propose working hypotheses on the function of adjunct-initial clauses, and the function of *er* in such clauses:

(14) Some adjunct sentences represent an important linguistic manifestation of our cognitive reference point potential, because they are semantically and syntactically structured to enhance inferential access into a subject entity which is new and therefore difficult to process.

(15) Adjunct sentences tend to contain *er* when one or more of their ingredients contributes insufficiently to enhancing the inferential accessibility of the subject entity. *Er* can therefore be considered as an "inaccessibility marker".

While (14)–(15) account for the language-structural factors ADJUNCT TYPE and VERBAL SPECIFICITY in an integrated way, the latter factors do not – according to the estimates about model quality which our statistical analysis returned – explain all the variation observed in our data: especially in Belgian Dutch, there remain substantial *er*-residues in clauses with a locative adjunct and a specific matrix verb, i.e. in contexts which are supposed to *block* the preference for *er* according to (15). Unless we are prepared to abandon the latter hypothesis, we have to look for additional observable parameters of *er*'s alleged function as an inaccessibility marker. Since the distribution of *er* in temporal adjunct clauses is more or less fully predictable, we will from now on concentrate our search for extra factors on locative adjunct sentences, in which *er*'s distribution is far less predictable.

First, however, we have to overcome one of corpus linguistics' major limitations, viz. the fact that it is impossible to find direct corpus evidence in support of hypotheses such as (14). Phenomena such as processing speed cannot reliably be measured offline: in a corpus design, there is no dependent variable which allows us to determine whether the hearer needs more time for the processing of constituent *y* in context *a* than in context *b*. And yet it is pivotal for two reasons that we should find independent evidence for (14). Purely theoretically, it is only after "we have gained a clear understanding of the processing properties of a linguistic variable from other empirical methods, that [that] variable could be used as an explanatory variable to investigate processing effects in corpus data" (Heylen, Tummers, and Geeraerts this volume: 18[5]). In the specific context of this argument, however, independent evidence for (14) is indispensable in order to avoid deductive circularity: given the proposed correlation between poor reference point potential and *er*, it is attractive to use the presence of *er* precisely as a dependent variable of insufficient potential on the part of the adjunct to enhance subject accessibility. Yet, *er*'s impact on subject processing in the context of poor reference points can only be studied after it has been independently established that some adjuncts and verbs facilitate the processing of the subject to a higher extent than others.

The self-paced reading (or subject-paced reading) technique we used in Grondelaers and Brysbaert (1996) and Grondelaers (2000: 197 ff.) offers dependable online indications of processing difficulty or speed. Self-paced reading is a test paradigm in which participants read a sentence or short text on a computer screen, while pressing the spacebar to control the presentation of the successive segments of the sentence or text. In all our designs, the experimental stimuli were presented as follows:

```
(16) -- --- ------- --- --- ------ -------. (sb)
     In het tuintje --- --- ------ -------. (sb)
     -- --- ------- was --- ------ -------. (sb)
     -- --- ------- --- een immense plataan. (sb)
```

The first screen contains a sequence of dots which correspond to the letters of the words of the test sentence. A spacebar hit produces the first segment, which disappears when the participant taps the spacebar to indicate that s/he has read it; simultaneously, the next segment appears on the screen, which disappears with the next spacebar tap and until the participant has read the whole sentence. The time interval between two spacebar taps (i.e. the time it takes the participant to read the segment) is registered in milliseconds and recorded in a database, the underlying assumption being "that this measure reflects the time taken to execute at least some of the major processes associated with analysing the material in the display" (Mitchell 1984: 70).

If (14) is correct, then we can expect that *een zoutvat* "a salt tub" will be read faster in (17) than in (18):

5. Heylen, Tummers, and Geeraerts (this volume) contains an indepth evaluation (in section 3.2.) of the value of offline evidence in support of online processing hypotheses.

(17) In de keukenkast was een zoutvat
"In the kitchen cupboard was a salt tub."

(18) In het toneelstuk was een zoutvat
"In the play was a salt tub."

In de keukenkast "in the kitchen cupboard" referentially restricts the subject to the set of material objects associated with the preparation of food which are small enough to fit in a kitchen cupboard; since this category is not very large, and salt tubs represent a prototypical member of it, the subject in (17) will be processed effortlessly. In (18), by contrast, the adjunct confines the subject referent to the class of "objects, persons, and phenomena associated with the theatre", a category which is so large and heterogeneous that marginal stage props such as a salt tub will in all likelihood confound the hearer. This confusion, we assume in (14), will surface in a relatively longer processing time.

Grondelaers and Brysbaert (1996) report a self-paced reading experiment which confirms this expectation. We compared subject reading times in 24 sentences, which divided in two sets on the basis of the variable "reference point potential of the adjunct": 12 sentences were constructed with a high-constraint adjunct such as *in het koffertje* "in the briefcase", which coded a three-dimensional, material container; 12 sentences were constructed with a low-constraint adjunct such as *in het toneelstuk* "in the play", which coded metaphorical inclusion in vague or abstract unbounded spaces. 54 undergraduate students from the Faculty of Arts of the University of Leuven – all native speakers with normal or corrected eyesight – participated voluntarily.

The statistical analysis of the reading data revealed a facilitating impact on subject processing of high constraint adjuncts (*high constraint* 778 ms. < *low constraint* 832 ms., p1 and p2 < 0.05). This effect – which was replicated in three other experiments – clearly demonstrates that the accessibility of indefinite subject NP's is variable but – crucially – manipulable. Even relatively minor manipulations within an adjunct NP lead to perceptible subject processing differences: high-constraint adjuncts restrict the referential potential of the subject which, as a result, is processed faster. Low-constraint adjuncts, which do not, inhibit subject processing[6].

6. All of the experiments mentioned in this paragraph also confirmed *er*'s facilating impact on subject processing in the context of low-constraint adjuncts (see Grondelaers, Brysbaert, Speelman and Geeraerts 2002: 15 and Grondelaers, Speelman, Drieghe, Brysbaert and Geeraerts *submitted*).

We can therefore proceed with the offline substantiation of *er*'s function as sketched in (15). Section 5.1. focuses on outlining and implementing two quantifiable parameters of the reference point potential of preposed adjuncts. In section 5.2. we present the corpus materials used in the new study, and the dataset extracted from them. Section 5.3 sketches two alternative models in anticipation of the regression findings, and then goes on to diagram *er*'s distribution as a function of the new adjunct parameters for a provisional evaluation of these models. Section 5.4. discusses the stepwise regression analysis carried out for a more dependable substantiation of the research questions. In section 6, we summarize the findings into a comprehensive diagram of *er*'s Belgian and Netherlandic distribution as a function of *all* the adjunct and verb distinctions introduced in this paper. We will then review the consequences of our data for the issues at hand in this paper, and propose separate processing models for *er*'s Belgian and Netherlandic distribution to account for the differences observed. First, however, let us concentrate on finding relevant and tangible adjunct distinctions which can be used to substantiate the reference point potential of adjunct-initial presentative sentences (and *er*'s inaccessibility marking function in these sentences) in a methodologically responsible way.

5. Inaccessibility marking in Belgian and Netherlandic Dutch

5.1. Two reference point parameters

In the previous paragraph we suggested that locative adjuncts are more efficient reference points than temporal adjuncts because they generate more useful predictive inferences about the forthcoming subject[7]. The

7. An alternative elaboration of Langacker's reference-point scenario can be found in Chen (2003), an extensive investigation into the syntactic, semantic, and pragmatic aspects of English "full verb inversion" constructions such as *On my left was Tom Lopez* (2003: 3). Although many of the conclusions of Chen's approach are confirmed by our own quantitative on- and offline data, we take issue with his specific brand of cognitive-linguistic analysis. Our main objection is Chen's commitment to a non-quantitative use of corpus data and, in the same vein, his total disregard of external variation in the language he investigates. Although Chen uses a corpus of 1132 examples, he does "not make statistical claims" (2003: 42), for it is his "belief that such corpus-based statistical claims will eventually suffer from the limitations of the representativeness of the corpus itself, regardless of how large it may be" (2003: 42–43). The latter is further justified by Chen's admission that his

experimental data cited just now, however, indicate that inference generation is restricted to locative adjuncts which denote concrete threedimensional locations such as *keukenkast* "kitchen cupboard" or *ijskast* "refrigerator", that is locatives which heavily constrain their subjects with respect to size and dimensionality. The majority of locatives, however, does not refer to such state-of-the-art reference points, and in the light of the hypothesis in (15), it would be instructive to discover whether ADJUNCT CONCRETENESS – a potential operational definition of Langacker's *intrinsic salience* – correlates negatively with a preference for *er*. In order to find out, all adjuncts in the dataset (to be discussed in 5.2.) were coded on the basis of the *concreteness taxonomy* developed in Grondelaers (2000: 176–177), an operational parameter which breaks up into five distinct values. The maximal value was assigned to adjuncts which refer to the physical aspects of the speech situation, by definition the most

---

data collection "has been a journey of surprise. Quite a few times, I discovered counter-examples to my thinking of a particular issue that had been formulated a few days earlier, one time even the night before" (2003: 279, footnote 23). Observe, first, that Chen's lack of faith in a statistical exploitation of his corpus does not absolve him from the epistemological requirement of *compiling* a representative one, at least if he wishes to take seriously his ambition to use his database as a means of validating his hypotheses ("as a place to look for counterexamples to my own arguments", 2003: 43). The haphazard collection of sources from which his examples derive will not only yield incidental counterexamples at best: in the absence of balanced and representative sampling, it is impossible to detect whether these counterexamples are representative of a specific variety or register of English, as a consequence of which it is difficult to advance one's insights by integrating the counterexamples at issue into a new hypothesis. In addition, Chen's rejection of statistical claims does not keep him from rejecting (2003: 15–25) the statistically supported "information packaging" account of inversion, as proposed in a.o. Birner (1996). According to Birner, inversion is predominantly used to "entrench" new information in ongoing discourse through the use of a preposed "hanger" entity which typically codes old information; inversion, in other words, is used "to allow the new element to be processed in terms of its relationship to the (preceding) evoked element" (Birner 1996: 90, quoted in Chen 2003: 21). Although Birner's corpus counts suggest that the postponed element in inverted sentences is ostensibly "newer" than the initial adjunct in no less than 80% of all cases, Chen rejects the information packaging account on the basis of the residual 20%. However, all the psycholinguistic evidence we collected in support of our own version of the reference-point hypothesis (cf. the references in footnote 6) clearly confirms the validity of the information packaging account.

salient and stable reference point available to the language user. Value 2 was assigned to bounded two- or threedimensional concrete entities, and value 3 to unbounded concrete entities spaces. Value 4 was reserved for locations which cannot be straightforwardly categorized as either concrete or abstract. In a sentence such as *Bij de BOB is er een gebrek aan personeel* "At the Belgian Criminal Investigation Bureau there is a staff shortage", *de BOB* "The Belgian Criminal Investigation Bureau" refers to a metaphorical location which can nevertheless be metonymically interpreted as referring to the "the building in which the BOB resides". Value 5, finally, was restricted to abstract locations which allow no spatial interpretation whatsoever.

In the same vein, it would be revealing to find out whether Langacker's "contextually determined salience" equates ADJUNCT TOPICALITY (as suggested, for instance, in Taylor 1996: 209). Do adjunct topicality and *er*-preference also correlate negatively? Notice that the latter is extremely plausible in our reference point account of adjunct sentences: a higly topical adjunct "entrenches" the adjunct sentence in the preceding context, as a result of which the subject constraining potential which emanates from the adjunct is extended to the preceding sentences, which considerably increases the subject reducing potential of the adjunct clause. Consider in this respect the following sentence:

(19) The visitors of the folk-museum feasted their eyes on the beautifully restored farmhouse; on the rough, oak-wood table stood a basket of fresh apples and *suspended from the roof-beam hung an enormous ham.*

Without the context, the constraining potential of the italicized adjunct clause is relatively restricted, since many things can be suspended from roof-beams. In the context of (19), however, *roof-beam* is metonymically inferred from *farmhouse* (and indirectly also from *folk-museum*), which dramatically reduces the class of roof-beam suspendable objects. The first clause focuses the hearer's attention on the type of historical farmhouses he knows from period movies or novels; *a basket of apples* in the next clause zooms in on, or strongly suggests that the narrative will continue with, the gastronomical aspects of former farming. The adjunct *from the roof-beam* directs the comprehender's attention to the category of "foodstuffs associated with former farming which are suspended from roof-beams", and this category virtually coincides with the nominal type "ham".

ADJUNCT TOPICALITY was operationalized on the basis of a newly developed given-new taxonomy with 10 values (space limitations preclude an in-depth description, but details can be found in Grondelaers 2000: 156). Due to the relatively small size of the dataset, this 10 value-taxonomy was later reduced to 5 for statistical convenience. On the basis of its syntactic structure, length, and the distance between referring expression and antecedent, adjuncts were attributed value 1 when immediately and automatically available because referring to the *ground*, value 2 when available in the *recent linguistic context* (referents of pronouns or definite NP's available in the same clause as their referring expression or in the previous clause), value 3 when *available in the remote linguistic context* (referents of definite NP's anticipating their referring expression between 2 and 20 clauses in discourse), value 4 when referring to *discourse-new* entities (referents of proper names or referents of definite NP's previously unavailable in the context), and value 5 when referring to *new* entities (non-generic indefinite NP's).

Before we move on to the materials used in the offline evaluation of the reference-point hypothesis and the role of *er*, we elaborate on two factor types which will not be included in the new analysis. Observe, first, that the remainder of this paper will focus exclusively on locative adjunct sentences. The original analysis revealed that there is almost no residual *er*-variation (including regional variation) in adjunct sentences with a preposed temporal constituent: all remaining *er*-variation was found in locative adjunct sentences (see Grondelaers, Speelman and Geeraerts 2002). Also, it is practically unfeasible to classify temporal adjuncts in terms of concreteness and topicality in a reliable way, as a result of which they are of little value for an analysis whose prime ambition is to access the cognitive machinery which motivates the semantics and syntax of presentative sentences (machinery of which ADJUNCT CONCRETENESS and ADJUNCT TOPICALITY are the alleged surface parameters).

In addition, and more importantly, we restrict the analysis to aspects of the *contextual accessibility* of the subject, and ignore for the time being the parameters of the subject's *intrinsic accessibility*. We will, in other words, not include any subject features in the forthcoming regression. At first sight, this decision appears to be theoretically unjustifiable. If "not every nominal is equally suited to serve as a reference point" (Taylor 1996: 205), it is logical to surmise that "not every nominal is in equal need of support by a reference point" (idem). More concretely, the need for reference-point support appears to correlate with a nominal's lack of inherent salience (or "automatic salience", cf. Deane 1992: 194–195).

Animate entities possess a higher degree of automatic salience than non-animate physical entities (Deane: idem, but cf. also Taylor 1996: 219–220), whereas the lowest degree of inherent salience is found in "abstract concepts, that is, concepts that are non-human, non-animate, non-concrete, non-manipulated, non-individuated" (Taylor 1996: 220). Given that the hypothesis in (15) – pertaining to the correlation between contextually inaccessible subjects and *er* – is correct, we may also expect a correlation between *inherently inaccessible* subjects and *er*. And if inherent inaccessibility equates non-salience, we may anticipate that abstract subjects will attract *er* to a higher degree than more salient entities. That is exactly what a corpus count in the Belgian Dutch sources reveals: there is a significant correlation (Spearman correlation coefficient = 0.1961) between SUBJECT CONCRETENESS (implemented as the distinction between "animate", "sharply bounded physical entities", "fuzzily bounded physical entities", and "abstract entities") and *er*-preference (Grondelaers 2000: 204 ff.). Since, however, SUBJECT CONCRETENESS correlates even more significantly with ADJUNCT CONCRETENESS, to the extent that physical adjuncts typically introduce physical subjects, whereas abstract adjuncts typically attract abstract subjects (Spearman correlation coefficient = 0,3614), it is impossible to determine on the basis of these data whether it is ADJUNCT or SUBJECT CONCRETENESS which engenders the high *er*-preferences. A restriction to attestations with concrete adjuncts – in which high *er*-frequencies cannot be attributed to adjunct quality – neither confirms the impact of SUBJECT CONCRETENESS on the frequency of *er* (Grondelaers 2000: 207). In order to solve this indeterminacy, we ran a replication of the psycholinguistic experiment outlined at the end of section 4 (cf. Grondelaers 2000: 208 ff.), in which we not only distinguished between concrete and non-concrete adjuncts, but also between concrete and non-concrete subjects; the statistical analysis of the reading data revealed no independent effect whatsoever of SUBJECT CONCRETENESS on *er*-preferences.

Crucially, what seems to be at issue here is not the "domain" (concrete or abstract, cf. Langacker 1990: 61 ff.) against which an entity is characterized, but whether or not it is "bounded" in that domain ("bounding" is used here in the technical sense of Langacker 1990: 63 ff.). Nouns like *circle* and *triangle* select bounded regions in two-dimensional space, whereas *sphere* and *cylinder* are comparable terms for three-dimensional space. The noun *January* delineates a well-delineated region in the domain of time, and nouns like *beep* and *flash* require a combination of domains for their characterization (resp. of time and pitch, and time, color space, and the visual field, cf. Langacker: idem). What all these nouns have in common, however, is that they profile bounded regions in these domains, and this "boundedness" appears to be among the crucial parameters of an entity's inherent or automatic accessibility. It certainly is a major parameter of an entity's inherent *visual* accessibility. Cognitive Psychology confirms the pervasiveness of the figure/ground gestalt in human perception, viz. the fact that some component of a heterogeneous visual field (the figure) automatically and distinctively stands out from the other parts (the ground) because of its higher visual accessibility. Among the properties Reinhart (1984) and Wallace (1982), both cited in Chen (2003: 46–47), list for prototypical figures, are "closure" and "continuation in shape": closed areas with continuous contours are much more likely to be selected as figures. Given that the centrality of the figure/ground gestalt is not restricted to vision, but extends to cognition – Cognitive Linguistics has repeatedly invoked the gestalt to account for linguistic structure (see Chen 2003: 44 for an overview) –, it is plausible to presume that bounded entities are intrinsically and conceptually more accessible than unbounded entities.

Whether less accessible unbounded entitities attract more *er* in adjunct-initial sentences (independent of the available adjunct triggers) can be easily tested, since "bounding" constitutes the semantic characterization of count nouns like *chair* or *explosion* vs. mass nouns such as *milk* or *peace* (Langacker 1990: 69–74). We classified the subjects of 1461 adjunct sentences from the Belgian Usenet logs, the regional popular newspaper *Het Belang van Limburg*, the national popular newspaper *Het Laatste Nieuws*, and the quality newspaper *De Standaard* into count vs. mass nouns (count nouns can be constructed without an indefinite determiner – although they allow indefinite determiners when qualified, cf. *Uit de grijze lucht valt een ijskoude regen* "out of the grey sky falls a chilling rain" – and they do not take a plural). Whereas, interestingly, about half (45,09 %) of the clauses with a count noun subject contains *er*, 67,66 % of clauses with a mass noun subject attract *er* (χ^2 = 34,44; 1 df; p < 0,001). This time higher *er*-proportions in the mass noun clauses cannot be attributed to adjunct factors: when we restrict the calculation to clauses with a locative adjunct and a main verb more specific than *zijn* "to be", *er* is still three times more frequent with mass than with count nouns (35 % vs. 13,2 %; χ^2 = 24,61; 1 df; p < 0,001).

These data therefore lend provisional credence to the hypothesis that some nominals are intrinsically less accessible, and need reference-point support or *er*-cueing to a higher extent than others. Before, however, we can enter features of the subject into a regression analysis of *er*'s distribution, we need independent, psycholinguistic evidence that mass nouns do indeed take longer to process than concrete nouns. The attested psycholinguistic correlation between an adjunct's poor reference point potential and *er* need not signify that *er* also directly facilitates inaccessible subjects. In order to avoid using *er* as a dependent variable of low intrinsic subject accessibility (recall the argument preceding (16)), we had better find out first whether mass nouns are indeed less accessible than count nouns. For the time being, we will therefore stick to adjunct factors, whose impact on subject processing has already been psycholinguistically established.

5.2. Materials

In order to test the impact of ADJUNCT CONCRETENESS and ADJUNCT TOPICALITY on *er*'s distribution, a portion of the original dataset included in the first regression was reanalyzed for those parameters. All in all, we reexamined 555 Belgian adjunct sentences from the Belgian UseNet logs (n = 147), the Belgian nation wide popular paper *Het Laatste Nieuws* (n = 115), and the Belgian nation wide quality paper *De Standaard* (n = 293). In addition, three matching Netherlandic sources were reconsidered, yielding 98 locative adjunct clauses from the Netherlandic UseNet logs, 100 from the nation wide popular paper *De Telegraaf*, and 99 from the nation wide quality paper *NRC Handelsblad*[8].

Target sentences were extracted by means of the browser *Abundantia Verborum*, developed by the second author (Speelman 1997; for more information about the browser, and how to obtain a free copy of it, please consult http://wwwling.arts.kuleuven.ac.be/qlvl/abundant). Observations like *Bij die ramp vielen 34 doden* "In this disaster 34 people were killed" demonstrate that the definition of what constitutes a locative adjunct is not unproblematic, because *bij die ramp* allows at the same time a locative (on the place of the disaster) and a temporal interpretation (at the time of the disaster). Because of its low frequency, observations with this intermediary adjunct type were excluded from the original as well as

8. In contrast to the first regression, we did not include materials from the regional popular newspaper *Het Belang van Limburg* in the new analysis. These materials were excluded in order to maintain a stylistically and regionally balanced corpus structure, with three stylistically different nation wide sources on the Belgian as well as on the Dutch side.

the present analysis. And for reasons which have become clear in section 4, we are primarily interested in constructions with one overt subject, as a result of which impersonal passives such as *Op het feest werd (er) gedanst* "there was dancing at the party" – which need not contain such a subject in Dutch – were barred.

5.3. Models and proportions

In section 5.4., we report on separate regression analyses of *er*'s distribution in the Belgian and the Netherlandic dataset, in order to find out to what extent these distributions overlap. Since we are especially interested at this stage in the respective impact on Belgian and Netherlandic *er*-preferences of the new adjunct factors, we will carry out a one-by-one comparison of these factors on the basis of the Belgian and Netherlandic *input* regression models (which feature *all* the factors fed into the analysis, not only those retained by the analysis as significant determinants of *er*'s distribution). For each factor, the regression returns significance estimates which can subsequently be used to assess whether there are proportional and/or structural differences between the Belgian and the Netherlandic *er*-model.

Let us, in anticipation of the actual regression data, outline a number of possible scenarios to account for *er*-distributional differences between Belgian and Netherlandic Dutch, based on whether or not the Belgian and Netherlandic *er*-models coincide. And let us, given the psycholinguistic evidence discussed in section 4, and in order to reduce the set of possible scenarios, anticipate that ADJUNCT CONCRETENESS and ADJUNCT TOPICALITY will be significant determinants of *er*'s distribution in Belgian Dutch. If this is indeed the case, and the regression *does* return proportionally or structurally different Belgian and Netherlandic *er*-models, we have reliable statistical evidence for *functionally motivated* differences between those varieties. The processing properties of ADJUNCT CONCRETENESS and ADJUNCT TOPICALITY in the context of reference point facilitation have been sufficiently confirmed (and replicated) in psycholinguistic analyses of Belgian Dutch, to guarantee that the offline manifestation of these factors reflects underlying reference point construal. In the same vein, failure to confirm these variables in Netherlandic Dutch strongly suggests that *er*'s distribution is *not* motivated by reference point construal in that variety.

If, conversely, the regression returns *overlapping er*-models for Belgian and Netherlandic Dutch (with significant adjunct factors in both models), we have no reason to suspect cognitively motivated differences between *er*'s distribution in those varieties. If that scenario applied, the inevitable conclusion would be that *not all* syntactic surface differences have a direct and pervasive cognitive motivation, as a consequence of which we would have to resort to another explanation for the distributional differences at issue in this paper.

Table 3. Netherlandic and Belgian *er*-proportions as a function of ADJUNCT CONCRETENESS

	N	B
two- or threedimensional concrete	9.84	9.68
unbounded concrete	7.02	18.81
vaguely spatial	27.03	34.67
abstract	36.67	47.54

Table 4. Netherlandic and Belgian *er*-proportions as a function of ADJUNCT TOPICALITY

	N	B
recent linguistic context	7.75	19.19
remote linguistic context	28.33	18.18
discourse-new	41.54	40.6
new	20.69	33.33

While these proportions seem to suggest that ADJUNCT CONCRETENESS and ADJUNCT TOPICALITY are determinants of *er*'s distribution in Belgian *as well as* in Netherlandic Dutch (because decrease in topicality and concreteness perceptibly leads to increase of *er*), there appears to be little uniformity between the distributions. One important observation leaps out though: in Netherlandic Dutch, factor values neatly split up between low and high *er*-proportions, reflecting clear, functional distinctions. In Netherlandic adjunct sentences, *er* appears to be triggered by abstract adjuncts rather than by concrete adjuncts (observe the low *er*-proportions for both types of concrete adjuncts and the much higher proportions for semi- and fully abstract adjuncts), and by adjunct referents which were activated prior to the current or previous clause. It is cognitively significant in the latter respect that the cut-off point between *er* and no *er* should coincide – as far as adjunct topicality is concerned – with the distinction between referents activated in the recent linguistic context, and *older* or *non*-activated referents: it has often been suggested (see for instance Ariel 1990: 12) that the (most) recent context coincides with the linguistic materials held in *short term memory*: "independent of other factors, the last clause processed grants the entities it mentions a privileged place in working memory. They are readily available to be referred to by nouns or pronouns" (Clark and Sengul 1979: 35). For all non-recent materials, which are unavailable in short term memory, it goes that they attract significantly more *er* in Netherlandic Dutch.

In the Belgian materials, by contrast, there is a much more continuous relationship between ADJUNCT CONCRETENESS and *er*-preference. And the split impact on *er*-preferences of entities available in the linguistic context (values 1 and 2) and (discourse)-new entities (values 3 and 4) is far less cognitively motivated than both Netherlandic adjunct**er*-correlations. If Short Term Memory can hold no more than the materials communicated in the previous sentence (cf. supra), then the Remote Linguistic Context and the Encyclopaedic Context are, at best, only quantitatively different. In order to operationalize the difference between both, we used the somewhat arbitrary criteria introduced by functional linguists such as Givon (1983) and Brown (1983). On the basis of extensive corpus data from different languages, Givon (1983: 36, note 2) concludes that "the average values for the most *dis*continuous definite-topic devices, i.e. those used to return a topic into the register after a relatively long gap of absence, is around 15–17 clauses". All referents activated more than 20 clauses prior to their referring expression are considered to be "maximally discontinuous" by Givon, and it is significant that no distinction is made in this respect between "indefinites introduced for the first time" and "definite topics returning into the register after a long gap of absence".

We will come back to this issue in section 6, but first we turn to the regression analyses, which yield more reliable indications of significance and impact.

5.4. Regression findings

These are the factors that were entered in the regression analyses of the distribution of postverbal *er* in locative adjunct sentences in Belgian and Netherlandic Dutch: ADJUNCT CONCRETENESS, ADJUNCT TOPICALITY, VERBAL SPECIFICITY, and REGISTER (since the latter two factors were identified as significant determinants of *er*'s distribution in earlier analyses, it goes without saying that they are also included in the present analysis). Table 5 contains Odds Ratios, p-values, and confidence intervals for these four factors:

Table 5. P-values, Odds Ratios and confidence intervals for 4 potential determinants of *er*'s distribution in Netherlandic (N) and Belgian (B) adjunct sentences.

	N				B			
	p	O.R.	C.I.		p	O.R.	C.I.	
register	0.323	0.81	0.53	1.24	0.000	0.68	0.57	0.81
adjunct topicality	0.013	1.28	1.05	1.56	0.001	1.37	1.19	1.57
adjunct concreteness	0.052	1.48	1	2.21	0.002	1.45	1.09	1.94
verbal specificity	0.000	0.17	0.1	0.3	0.003	0.23	0.16	0.32

Observe first that the significance of REGISTER in Belgian Dutch (p = .000), but not in Netherlandic Dutch (p = .323), confirms earlier evidence for national constraints on stylistic *er*-effects (Grondelaers 2000; Grondelaers, Geeraerts and Speelman 2002). Whereas *er*'s distribution is quite stable over registers in Netherlandic Dutch, it is heavily register-dependent in Belgian Dutch: the more informal a Belgian source, the more it will contain *er* (we will come back to this asymmetry below).

Much more crucial is the confirmation that ADJUNCT CONCRETENESS and ADJUNCT TOPICALITY are not only significant determinants of *er*'s distribution in Belgian Dutch (p = .002 and p = .001 respectively), but also in Netherlandic Dutch (p = .013 and p = .052): although locative adjunct sentences are but rarely attested with *er* in Netherlandic Dutch, it is typically abstract and discourse-new locations which trigger it. Moreover, in spite of the outspoken differences observed between the Belgian and Netherlandic distribution of *er* in the first regression, the Belgian and Netherlandic models of *er*'s distribution in locative adjunct sentences appear to be highly comparable as far as the relative *impact* of the different variables is concerned. A pre-statistical indication of this equivalence is the fact that the regression returns more or less equivalent Odds Ratios for the three language-structural factors in both models. A more reliable confirmation of model equivalence is obtained by comparing the *confidence intervals* of the Netherlandic and Belgian Odds Ratios for the language-structural variables, which delimit the interval in which the Odds Ratio finds itself, given the variance in the data and the significance level: if these intervals do not overlap, we have statistical evidence that there is at least a proportional difference between the models evaluated. When we compare the Netherlandic and Belgian confidence intervals per factor, however, it turns out that they *do* overlap, which indicates that there are no proportional differences between the Belgian and the Netherlandic models of *er*'s distribution. For additional corroboration, we carried out separate stepwise regressions of *er*-preferences in the Belgian and the Netherlandic database (ignoring REGISTER in both samples): the regression selected the same ingredients in both models, in exactly the same order.

No matter how comparable Belgian and Netherlandic *er*-preferences in locative adjunct sentences appear to be, the respective success rates of the national *er*- models reveal that predictive progress is *much more outspoken* in the Belgian one. The paucity of *er* in Netherlandic locative adjunct sentences makes for a high initial predictability of *er*'s distribution (the *naive* model without the factors we fed into it predicts *er*'s distribution is no less than 79.32 % of all cases), so that addition of the factors ADJUNCT CONCRETENESS, ADJUNCT TOPICALITY and VERBAL SPECIFICITY increases the model's predictive power by "only" 6.78 %. The Belgian model, by contrast, starts out at no more than 70.96 % of initial predictability (due to a much larger *er*-residue and register variation), but proceeds as much as 13.61 %, to end at a success rate comparable to that of the Netherlandic model, viz. 84.57 %.

6. Interpretation and discussion

Let us, before moving on to the general discussion, review all the findings:

- The regression data prove that distributional *er*-differences between Belgian and Netherlandic Dutch are *not* motivated by differences in underlying cognitive architecture: the significance in both varieties of the *er*-triggers ADJUNCT CONCRETENESS and ADJUNCT TOPICALITY clearly indicates that *er* functions as an inaccessibility marker in Netherlandic as well as in Belgian Dutch adjunct sentences, which, in both varieties, are pervasive linguistic manifestations of our reference point ability. The remainder of this paper will therefore be devoted to an alternative explanation of national constraints on *er*-preferences.
- This explanation will have to take into account outspoken *national differences* in the division of labour between low-level and high-level adjunct factors. Although *er*'s distribution is identically motivated in Belgian and Netherlandic Dutch, and although the same set of factors leads to high predictability of *er*-preferences in both varieties, the bulk of the variation is accounted for in Netherlandic Dutch by the opposi-

tion between locative and temporal adjuncts: temporal adjuncts typically trigger *er* in Netherlandic Dutch, whereas locative adjuncts typically don't, especially when they feature a more specific verb than *zijn* "to be" (any other verb than *to be* will dramatically reduce remaining inclinations towards using *er*). Hence, fine-grained semantic considerations – no matter how significant they turned out to be in the regression analysis – play but a relatively minor role in Netherlandic *er*-preferences, and it is revealing that these "high level" factors come in the shape of clear-cut, functionally motivated distinctions (without "grey" areas) between concrete and abstract adjuncts, and between extremely highly activated adjunct referents (kept in working memory) and all other adjuncts. Summarizing: *er*'s distribution is determined in Netherlandic Dutch by an algorithm of interacting, discontinuous factors which resolve practically all the variation to be accounted for. This explanatory and predictive rigidity should encourage the compilers of the *Algemene Nederlandse Spraakkunst (ANS)* (Haeseryn et al. 1997) to propose a transparent description/prescription of *er*'s distribution – at least in Netherlandic Dutch – for the benefit of second language learners to whom the variation at issue in this paper represents one of the major obstacles on their way to fluent Dutch.

– In Belgian Dutch, by contrast, the effect of ADJUNCT TYPE and VERBAL SPECIFICITY on *er*'s predictability is much less outspoken, because locative adjuncts and specific main verbs are frequently attested *with er*, and the factors barely interact. A consequence of this distributional uncertainty is a substantial residue of unexplained *er*-variation. In order to account for this remaining variation, we had to resort to semantic and pragmatic factors which do not break up into sharply delineated functional categories: ADJUNCT CONCRETENESS and ADJUNCT TOPICALITY are continuous parameters which do not allow us to determine clear cut-off points between *er* and its absence. To complicate matters even further, *er*'s distribution is not only internally, but also externally *unstable* in Belgian Dutch: on all levels of analysis, REGISTER-considerations play a significant role, because the more informal a Belgian source, the more frequently adjunct sentences will contain *er*. As a consequence, our model of *er*'s Belgian distribution is little more than a set of causally unrelated, individual "more or less" options, whose cumulative *er*-predictability is high, but does not translate easily into a serviceable and helpful grammar item.

How then can we account for the fact that *er*'s distribution in Belgian and Netherlandic Dutch appears to be near-identically motivated from a functional and cognitive point of view, but surfaces so differently in those varieties? In order to answer this question, let us first notice that the register differences which characterize *er*'s distribution in Belgian but not in Netherlandic Dutch converge well with similar findings from a series of sociolinguistic investigations into the linguistic history of Netherlandic and Belgian Dutch, which is known to be characterized by a *delayed standardization*. Whereas – in a nutshell – Netherlandic Dutch benefitted from a normal standardization which was finished at the beginning of the 20th C, the standardization of Belgian Dutch was blocked in the 16th C as a result of political and social factors, resuming its course only in the 20th C. In an extensive corpus-based investigation of lexical convergence and divergence processes in Belgian and Netherlandic Dutch (see especially Geeraerts, Grondelaers and Speelman 1999 for a detailed historical overview (in chapter 2) and the initial results of the investigation), we found that lexical choices in the domain of clothing and football terms were much more *stable across registers* in Netherlandic than in Belgian Dutch. This finding was later replicated (see Grondelaers, Van Aken, Speelman and Geeraerts 2002) with alternations in verb-preposition collocations such as *vragen naar/achter* "to ask for/(lit.) after": the systematic comparison of different registers by means of a newly developed uniformity measure revealed that prepositional choices in Netherlandic Dutch were virtually identical in highly informal chat data, moderately informal UseNet data, and formal newspaper materials; in Belgian Dutch, by contrast, prepositional choices revealed huge differences between these registers. Given that a larger lexical or grammatical distance between registers is thought to be characteristic of a delayed standardization (see Geeraerts, Grondelaers and Speelman 1999: 45–47), it is attractive to attribute the reported register effects on Belgian *er*-preferences to the greater inherent variability of lesser standardized varieties.

We will argue in the remainder of this paper that the much more predictable Netherlandic distribution of *er* – characterized by formal rather than by semantic distinctions and by sharp(er) cut-off points – *also* reflects the more advanced standardization of that variety. The evidence available at this point converges on the view that the effect of linguistic standardization on the correlation between reference point construal and *er*-preference amounts to *functional specialization.*

In order to substantiate that claim, we will try and translate all the available on- and offline data into processing models of *er*'s distribution

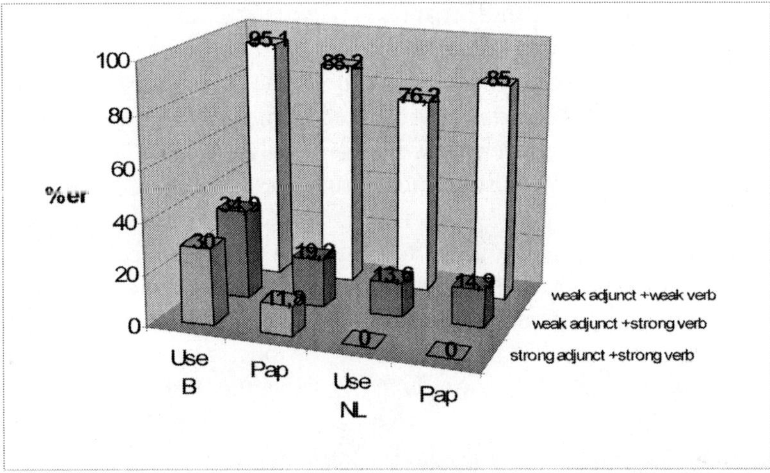

Figure 1. Er-preferences in the major functional categories of locative adjunct sentences.

in Belgian and Netherlandic Dutch. By way of leg up to these models, let us first focus on a more graphic representation of the exact differences between Belgian and Netherlandic *er*-use. Figure 1 diagrams *er*-preferences over the major functional categories of locative adjunct sentences, as outlined in this paper. It compares *er*-proportions over regions (Belgium and The Netherlands) and registers (newspaper materials and UseNet logs) in adjunct sentences with a "weak" adjunct (viz. a lowly activated, abstract locative) and a weak verb (viz. *zijn* "to be"), in adjunct sentences with a weak locative and with a strong verb (i.e. more specific than *zijn* "to be"), and in adjunct sentences with a strong locative (containing a highly activated, concrete adjunct referent) and a strong verb[9].

Two important caveats have to be mentioned in connection with figure 1. Since, for reasons of statistical convenience, the figure diagrams feature clusters rather than individual factors, the respective impact of

9. "Highly activated" is defined in this context as referring to the recent linguistic context; "concrete" adjuncts refer to two- or threedimensional containers. Observe that the fourth logical combination – of strong adjuncts and weak verbs – was omitted from figure 1 for frequency reasons (n = 6). The rare occurrence of this collocation constitutes extra evidence for the reference point hypothesis: a speaker who selects a strong adjunct in order to enhance subject accessibility, will almost certainly also select a strong verb for additional guidance.

ADJUNCT CONCRETENESS and ADJUNCT TOPICALITY, as attested in the regression analysis, is not directly visible. More importantly, the much larger impact of the adjunct factors on Belgian *er*-preferences which transpires from the regression data is obscured in figure 1 by our proportional representation of *er*-preferences (which conceals the fact that absolute *er*-frequencies in Netherlandic Dutch are much lower than in Belgian Dutch).

All other regression findings, however, are neatly reflected in the figure. Observe, to begin with, the sheer size of the individual, and especially the cumulative impact of strong adjuncts and strong verbs on *er*-preferences: selecting a specific main verb on top of a contextually available, concrete adjunct referent severely constrains the use of *er* in Belgian Dutch, and blocks it altogether in Netherlandic Dutch. Equally perceptible is the impact of REGISTER on Belgian, but not on Netherlandic *er*-preferences: in Belgian Dutch, there is a consistent negative correlation between *er*-use and formality over the different functional categories of adjunct sentences, which is totally absent in Netherlandic Dutch.

Most crucial in figure 1, however, is the observation that regional variation is unevenly distributed over the different adjunct sentence types. Recall from the final paragraph of section 5.1. that *er*-preferences in temporal adjunct sentences were not affected by regional variation. The same apparently goes for most locative sentence types: there is some evidence of regional bias in adjunct sentences with a weak adjunct and a strong verb, but *outspoken* regional differences are restricted to adjunct sentences which are strong in every respect. Whereas this sentence type is never attested with *er* in the Netherlandic data, there remain substantial *er*-residues in Belgian strong-strong adjunct sentences.

The distribution of regional variation as observed in figure 1 will be argued to be indicative of a major difference in the way Belgian and Netherlandic speakers and hearers cooperate in the processing of new information. Observe, first, that in Netherlandic "strong" adjunct sentences, *er*'s distribution is fully predictable on the basis of the adjunct and verb features hitherto identified. The Belgian data, by contrast, demonstrate than an intrinsically strong adjunct and an intrinsically strong verb do not always suffice to enhance subject accessibility in such a way that remedial cueing by *er* is unnecessary. The attestation of *er* in a context which should in fact *block* its presence converges well with psycholinguistic evidence (see especially Grondelaers, Brysbaert, Speelman, and Geeraerts 2002: 12 ff.; Grondelaers, Speelman, Drieghe, Geeraerts and Brysbaert *in press*) which shows that *er* is preferred in Belgian "strong adjunct-strong verb" sequences when inferential *mismatch* is imminent. This is the case in stimuli such as *Op de envelop zat een schildpad* "On the envelope was a tortoise", which represent the mismatched condition of *Op de envelop zat een postzegel* "On the envelope was a stamp". The mismatched condition characteristically leads to significantly higher subject reading times than the match condition, unless *er* is inserted to deactivate the garden path to the expected subject.

Moving on now from offline distributions to online processing, it will be obvious that deciding when to insert *er* is a much more complicated matter in Belgian than in Netherlandic Dutch. Let us assume, with Sperber and Wilson (1986) and Ariel (1990), that Belgian and Netherlandic speakers of Dutch are guided in their *er*-use by "Optimal Relevance", viz. the natural inclination "to opt for that choice which is least costly for the addressee" (Ariel 1990: 175). In order to attain Optimal Relevance, the Belgian speaker has to take into simultaneous consideration a great number of syntactic, semantic, and pragmatic adjunct, verb and subject features (which, as we know, rarely break up into well-delineated, functionally motivated values), *as well as* decide whether the predictive inferences projected by adjuncts and verbs are *compatible* with the upcoming materials to be realized. An inevitable consequence of such complex deliberations is a noticeable lack of inter-speaker consensus about what constitutes a good reference point, and when to cue with *er*. It is revealing in this respect that F1-significance – viz. significance over experimental subjects – was much more difficult to attain in the psycholinguistic experiments than F2-significance – significance over test stimuli[10]. So all in all, it is the Belgian speaker's subjective assessment of the quality of contextually available inferences, *not* the adjunct's compliance with a checklist of necessary-and-sufficient conditions, which determines whether or not the subject is deemed accessible enough to do without *er*-decontextualization.

What do the available data tell us about how speakers of Netherlandic Dutch organize and process the introduction of a new subject? Although the absence of experimental data partially precludes access into the processing facets which constitute the Belgian model in the previous paragraph, the meanwhile accummulated offline findings conjure up a provisional "model" which remains to be tested in subsequent psycholinguistic

10. This finding represents a rare counterexample to general psycholinguistic knowledge that inter-subject significance is the least "conservative" of both types of signifance.

investigations, but which accounts nicely for some of the findings hitherto unexplained.

Compared to the situation in Belgian Dutch, deciding whether or not to insert *er* appears to be a comparatively straightforward matter in Netherlandic Dutch. Since, to begin with, *er* is triggered only by adjunct and verb features, it does not appear to signal *inferential incompatibility* in Netherlandic Dutch. As a consequence, there is no need to access syntactic, semantic, pragmatic, and real world features of *all* the constituents to see whether they match sufficiently to render the subject accessible. So, Netherlandic speakers not only have noticeably *less* considerations to make; decision making itself[11] is also much easier because of the fact that the dominant consideration is a *syntactic* distinction (temporal adjuncts typically take *er*, whereas locative adjuncts rarely do) complemented with comfortably discontinuous high-level factors which, again, correlate more or less categorically with presence and absence of *er*, especially when in combination. If inaccessibility marking by means of *er* is "case-based" in Belgian Dutch, it appears to be "rule-based" in Netherlandic Dutch: a Netherlandic adjunct's compliance with a checklist of necessary-and-sufficient conditions *does* seem to determine whether or not it will be followed by *er*.

Now, if the amount of inter-speaker consensus about what consitutes a good reference point is determined by the number and the complexity of the features the speaker has to check, then we can assume that Dutch speakers and hearers have much more shared knowledge about the predictive success of their adjunct-initial constructions than Belgian speakers. That in itself explains why *er*-cueing in Netherlandic Dutch is less necessary and much more predictable. Yet, we wish to take the explanation one step further, and claim that reference potential is, as it were, "wired into" some Netherlandic instantiations of the adjunct-initial construction template (notably those with a strong adjunct or a strong verb, or – even more so – the combination of both): the activation of an adjunct-initial sentence with a strong adjunct and a strong verb simultaneously activates the expectation, on the part of the hearer, that the adjunct clause will *succesfully* guide him towards the intended subject.

The latter constitutes, we believe, the main difference between how Belgian and Netherlandic speakers of Dutch tackle the processing of new information: whereas in the former variety an adjunct-initial template

11. Please bear in mind that we continue to refer here to *subconscious* evaluations.

with an intrinsically strong adjunct and verb can still garden-path the hearer to the *wrong* entity (a situation which can be remedied in the light of Optimal Relevance by deactivation of the template's reference point load by means of *er*), in Netherlandic Dutch the adjunct-initial template is reserved – we believe – for the introduction of subjects which are *known beforehand* by the speaker to be compatible with the inferences he is about to project. Optimal Relevance is assured in Netherlandic Dutch by a *division of labour* between presentative strategies: whereas adjunct-initial templates are reserved for the introduction of materials which *can* be made accessible by means of predictive inferencing (viz. materials which are contextually inferable), the introduction of non-inferable materials is established by means of the *er*-initial template.

We will refer to this process as *functional specialization*, viz. the emergence of speaker-hearer shared knowledge about the function of a construction (or class of constructions) which leads to rationalization(s) in the linguistic system. It goes without saying that at this point, this account represents no more than a research hypothesis which has to be verified in an experimental design[12]. For now, we will have to content ourselves with provisional indications that the proposed development is not only plausible, but also explanatorily adequate, in that it offers an explanation for the observed register differences.

Observe, first, that although we have found no proof of comparable functional-pragmatic specialization phenomena in Netherlandic Dutch, there is evidence that the more advanced standardization of that variety has lead to other types of specialization leading to rationalizations in the linguistic system. In this light we refer to *onomasiological specialization*, viz. speaker-hearer consensus about a preferred name for a given concept, rather than a whole set of competing names. Building on a newly developed statistical measure of onomasiological homogeneity, Geeraerts, Grondelaers and Speelman (1999: 46) have demonstrated that internal onomasiological uniformity in the lexical fields of clothing and football is consistently higher in Netherlandic than in Belgian Dutch (1999: 75).

12. Contextual constraint and expectation are processing phenomena which cannot be tested offline, since there are no objective norms to decide whether, and to what extent, a subject is expected in a certain context. In the psycholinguistic designs cited in connection with the situation in Belgian Dutch (see Grondelaers, Brysbaert, Speelman and Geeraerts 2002; Grondelaers, Speelman, Drieghe, Geeraerts and Brysbaert *submitted*), the degree of "expectedness" of a subject was determined in a prior Cloze task.

The fact that linguistic standardization *does* correlate with reduction of internal variability increases the plausibility that speaker-hearer consensus about the functional charge of a constructional template will also lead to linguistic simplification.

The suggestion that speaker-hearer consensus about the inferential potential of an element or construction leads to various sorts of linguistic change, has been abundantly documented. Building on the emergence and codification of the conditional meaning of *as long as*, Traugott (1998) and Traugott and Dasher (2002) describe a recurrent three-stage process of grammaticalization in the framework of the *Invited Inferencing Theory of Semantic Change* (IITSC). The diachronic evolution of presentative constructions which is synchronically reflected in the difference between Belgian and Netherlandic *er*-preferences is highly reminiscent of this grammaticalization pattern. From the perspective of IITSC, the process could be summarized as follows: in the first stage of the development (which corresponds roughly to the situation in Belgian Dutch), the hearer is "invited" by the speaker to make use of subject-facilitating inferences generated by the adjunct-initial template; since the quality of these inferences is heavily context-dependent, they can be "cancelled" (1998: 95) by means of specific cues (in our case *er*). In the second stage (corresponding to the situation in Netherlandic Dutch), invited inferences become "generalized" as "preferred meanings, conventions of use" (1998: 95) which are no longer context-dependent: wired into an adjunct-initial template with a strong locative and a strong verb is the entailment that it will *always* afford access into an upcoming subject. Although Traugott (1998: 45) maintains that generalized inferences can still be cancelled, the need to do so decreases when the quality of a specific inference (succesful subject facilitation) is no longer context-dependent, but known in advance (because entailed by the template).

Crucially, if "successful subject facilitation" is a context-independent "preferred" meaning, wired into some instantiations of the Netherlandic Dutch adjunct-initial template, then that preferred meaning is "linguistically based" (Traugott 1998: 95) and invariant over register. This may well explain why *er*-preferences are register-independent in Netherlandic, but register-*dependent* in Belgian Dutch. If our hypothesis that the reference point potential of an adjunct-initial construction in the latter variety is evaluated "on the spot" by the speaker (and cancelled when there is a risk that ineffective inferencing will overburden the hearer's processing resources), then we can readily see why *er*-use correlates negatively with register in Belgian Dutch: whereas newspaper language can be carefully planned to *maximize* contextual access into new materials (so that remedial cueing by means of *er* can be reduced to a minimum), internet materials feature more informal, unedited language which does not offer much in the way of inferential access into upcoming materials. Besides, the highly fragmented context of the UseNet forum (which typically features e-mail contributions with abundant *quoting* from earlicr mcssages) does not lend itself to efficient contextual anticipation either.

7. Conclusion

In this paper, we have investigated the notoriously complex distribution of presentative *er* in Belgian and Netherlandic Dutch presentative adjunct sentences, focusing especially on the question whether or not the regional differences traditionally observed are cognitively motivated. By way of alternative to existing, largely unsuccesful approaches, we have tried to demonstrate that a corpus-based variationist approach can unveil the underlying cognitive motors of the investigated variation in the respective varieties. As a first step, we summarized earlier regression findings (reported for the most part in Grondelaers, Speelman and Geeraerts 2002), which confirmed that there are outspoken proportional and structural differences between the Belgian and Netherlandic distribution of *er*: the Netherlandic distribution is much more predictable, with more formal distinctions and clearer cut-off points. Next, we reviewed psycholinguistic evidence in support of the hypothesis that adjunct sentences represent a linguistic manifestation of the human reference point ability to gain access into non-salient entities (in this case a new subject referent), whereas *er* is a *meta-reference point*, signalling how (in)accessible the subject is on the basis of predictive inferences projected by the adjunct and the verb; a series of self-paced reading designs confirmed both hypotheses.

The core of this paper consisted of a series of new regression analyses in support of the hypothesis that ADJUNCT CONCRETENESS and ADJUNCT TOPICALITY are quantifiable parameters of the reference point function of presentative adjunct sentences and *er*'s inaccessibility marking function in these sentences. A first analysis confirmed that both parameters are significant factors which markedly improve *er*'s predictability in Belgian Dutch (which is hardly surprising considering the prior psycholinguistic evidence). Much more surprising is the fact that a second regression analysis demonstrates beyond any doubt that *er* is also an inaccessibility marker in Netherlandic Dutch, which suggests that the outspoken distributional differences between *er*-preferences in Belgian and Netherlandic Dutch are *not* functionally nor cognitively motivated: both instantiate the human reference point ability, albeit in a somewhat different way.

Given the nature of the distributional differences, and building on additional data from our sociolinguistic work (notably Geeraerts, Grondelaers and Speelman 1999), we hypothesized that divergent *er*-preferences in Belgian and Netherlandic Dutch reflect the different degree of linguistic standardization of these varieties. Whereas all the on- and off-line data suggest that *er*-preferences in Belgian Dutch are based on individual, case-based assessments of the reference point potential of every separate adjunct sentence, the more advanced linguistic standardization of Netherlandic Dutch shows up – we have argued – in shared knowledge about the reference point potential of classes of adjuncts, and hence in a reduction in the need for remedial cueing by means of *er*. More generally, we suggest that *functional specialization* – the emergence of knowledge shared between speaker and hearer about the functional load of a class of items – is a key concept in linguistic standardization.

On the methodological level, which is crucial in this paper, these findings have two important consequences. First and foremost, they substantiate the claim that even the most elusive aspects of linguistic structure which concern cognitive linguists are amenable to rigourous quantitative analysis on the basis of attested language data, provided that the processing properties of the factors included in the analysis are independently confirmed in prior experimental designs. We have shown that the underlying cognitive structures which motivate syntactic variation are accessible to statistical research methods, and that the data yielded by those techniques can be used to verify pretty sophisticated processing hypotheses. And if a hypothesis is not yet in the stage of direct verification – as in the case of our views on *functional specialization* as a mechanism which short-circuits the causal relation between cognitive motivation and syntactic symbolisation – the available quantitative data offer provisional cues about how hypotheses can be fleshed out and fine-tuned.

As a case in point of how an analysis of syntactic surface variation can access the functional core of a grammatical construction – the "nerve centre" which motivates the syntax and semantics of that construction – let us briefly focus on a word order variation pattern which has largely gone unnoticed in the description of Dutch[13]:

13. Our observations here will inevitably be sketchy and selective. A full account of this intricate issue can be found in Grondelaers and Speelman 2007).

(20) *Er* bevonden zich geen paparazzi vlak voor, naast of achter de wagen.
"There were no paparazzi right in front, next to, or behind the car."

(21) *Er* is in mijn leven iets belangrijks gebeurd.
There has in my life something important happened
"Something important has happened in my life."

In Dutch *er*-initial presentatives, locative adjuncts typically follow the subject, as in (20). The alternative ordering in (21), with the adjunct preceding the subject, represents the statistically marked option, and is moreover restricted to adjuncts denoting an abstract or unprecise concrete location. This need not surprise us: if we hypothesize that sentence-initial *er* is an inference deactivator (like its sentence-internal sibling), it makes sense that concrete locative adjuncts – a major source of inferential access into the subject (cf. the experiment at the end of section 4) – should be in a position where they have *no impact* on the processing of the subject. It would indeed be ambiguous to announce *decontextualisation* of the subject by means of *er*, and at the same time *recontextualize* the subject by means of a subject-preceding concrete locative. In the same vein, it is perfectly logical why abstract location-denoting adjuncts – which were found to generate few useful inferences with respect to the upcoming subject – *can* precede the subject without creating an ambiguous signal. Interestingly, a regression analysis confirms the significance and impact of ADJUNCT CONCRETENESS on word order in *er*-initial sentences (adjuncts referring to physical containers almost never precede the subject, cf. Grondelaers and Speelman 2007), but indicates at the same time that there is a more important reordering motivation. The main reason why constituents are sentence-final in *er*-initial sentences appears to be their INFORMATIONAL PROMINENCE: it is the more informative constituent (measured in terms of Givon's "persistence", cf. 1983: 14 ff.) which is awarded sentence-final position, whereas less informative constituents tend to be "demoted" to penultimate position. The Concreteness Constraint, the main parameter of the decontextualizing effected by the *er*-initial template, *conditions* the operation of the "downgrade unimportant materials" principle: uninformative constituents which are undeserving of sentence-final position can only precede the subject provided that they do not generate too many predictive inferences with respect to that subject. Yet, the constructional semantics of the *er*-initial template do more than curtail the template's focus-promoting function: in the inferential vacuum established in an *er*-initial sentence, nominal entities are decontextualized to the extent that they are "stripped off" of contextually accumulated features which are incompatible with focus-status (such as high accessibility through repeated mention, cf. Grondelaers and Speelman 2007: 182–185).

Given their common decontextualizing function, it would be attractive to lump *er*-initial clauses and adjunct-clauses with *er* in Dutch together in a category of *Existential Sentences* (as is done in the systemic-functionalist tradition, cf. Downing and Locke 2002), to be distinguished from adjunct-initial clauses without *er*, which are *Circumstantial Relational Clauses* in the same tradition. English and Dutch differ with respect to the subject-verb inversion which is typical of Dutch, but not of English adjunct-initial clauses: *On the table there sat *(there) a nervous, calico cat.* English, in other words, does not distinguish structurally between *there*-initial clauses and adjunct-initial clauses with *there*. In the absence of this structural isomorphy, the only reason to regard adjunct-initial clauses with *er* as Existential Clauses is the presence in these sentences of *er*. In view of its function as an inaccessibility marker, however, *er* should not be used as a constructional indicator, especially not in Belgian Dutch. In Netherlandic Dutch, the distribution of *er* was shown to evolve into a constructional choice between the *er*-initial sentence type (for inaccessible materials) and the adjunct-initial type (for accessible materials), and one could conjecture that Netherlandic Dutch is moving towards a binary system with existential clauses which always have a sentence-initial *er*, and adjunct clauses which never contain *er*. In present-day Belgian Dutch, on the other hand, the use of *er* does not amount to a syntactic or constructional choice: *er* is so entrenched as an inference-deactivator in adjunct-initial sentences, that a categorical constructional separation into *er*-initial sentences and *er*-less adjunct-initial sentences is totally unimaginable. Given these regional differences, we are confident that no linguist would ever endorse a nomenclature which can be applied to Netherlandic, but not to Belgian Dutch. If, therefore, one must abide by traditional clause type categorizations, we would (albeit reluctantly) suggest a distinction between *er*-initial Existential clauses and Circumstantial relational clauses with an optional *er*.

The latter brings us to the main point of the paper, the observation that cognitive and functional linguists should be extremely cautious about the scope of the cognitive explanations and generalizations they posit. We have found clear evidence that the same cognitive motivation need not lead to identical syntactic behaviour: the fact that Belgian and Dutch adjunct sentences represent a pervasive linguistic manifestation of our reference point ability which is in some cases switched off by *er*, need not imply or predict that the latter will be used identically in varieties whose diachronic status is so different as that of the national varieties of Dutch. In Netherlandic Dutch, increased speaker-hearer consensus about the reference-point load of "strong" instantiations of the adjunct-initial template has streamlined the processing of new information, and has lead to a rationalization in the linguistic system.

As a methodological consequence, identifying the underlying cognitive motor of a surface phenomenon – the core business of cognitive linguistics – is but one part of the linguistic characterization of that phenomenon, which should be complemented with an investigation into *all* phenomena which may obscure the one-one-one relation between cognitive processes and their linguistic expression. In this respect, it is not only necessary to focus on *functional specialization* and *entrenchment* processes (used here in the sense of Deane 1992 and Geeraerts, Grondelaers and Bakema 1994), which conventionalize or fossilize the relation between a function and its symbolization, for it is not only functional reduction which leads to different expression of identical cognitive content. Cognitive-linguistic attention is also due to types of variation traditionally associated with the field of sociolinguistics: it has become increasingly obvious, even within Cognitive Linguistics, that the linguistic expression of *any* concept or function is sensitive to *contextual* factors, pertaining to age, sex, regional, or professional factors, to name but a few (see Geeraerts, Grondelaers and Bakema 1994 for a cognitively oriented, corpus-based investigation of various contextual factors which affect lexical selection).

References

Altmann, Gerry T. M., and Yuki Kamide
1999 Incremental interpretation at verbs: restricting the domain of subsequent reference. *Cognition* 73: 247–264.

Ariel, Mira
1990 *Accessing Noun-phrase Antecedents.* London/New York: Routledge.

Barlow, Michael, and Suzanne Kemmer (eds.)
2000 *Usage-based Models of Language.* Stanford: CSLI.

Bech, Günnar
1952 Über das Niederländische Adverbialpronomen *er. Travaux du cercle linguistique de Copenhague* 8, 5–32. Kopenhagen/Amsterdam.

Bennis, Hans
1986 *Gaps and Dummies*. Dordrecht: ICG Printing.

Besten, Hans den
1981 Government, syntaktischen Struktur und Kasus. In: Manfred Kohrt and Jürgen Lenerz (eds.), *Sprache: Formen und Strukturen. Akten des 15. Linguistischen Kolloquiums*, 97–107. Tübingen: Niemeyer.
1982 Some remarks on the ergative hypothesis. *Groninger Arbeiten zur Germanistischen Linguistik* 21: 61–82.
1983 On the interaction of root transformations and lexical deletive rules. In: Werner Abraham (ed.), *On the Formal Syntax of the Westgermania. Papers from the 3rd Groningen Grammar Talks*, 47–131. Amsterdam/Philadelphia: Benjamins.

Birner, Betty
1996 *The Discourse Function of Inversion in English*. New York: Garland.

Blom, Alied
1992 Wat gebeurde er in Lobith? In: Everdina C. Schermer-Vermeer, Wim G. Klooster and Arjen F. Florijn (eds.), *De kunst van de grammatica, artikelen aangeboden aan Frida Balk-Smit Duyzentkunst*, 15–26. Amsterdam: Universiteit van Amsterdam, Vakgroep Nederlandse Taalkunde.

Bolinger, Dwight
1977 *Meaning and Form*. London: Longman.

Brown, Cheryl
1983 Topic continuity in written English narrative. In: Talmy Givon (ed.), *Topic Continuity in Discourse. A Quantitative Cross-language Study*, 313–337. Amsterdam/Philadelphia: Benjamins.

Bybee, Joan, and Paul Hopper (eds.)
2001a *Frequency and the Emergence of Linguistic Structure*. Amsterdam/Philadelphia: Benjamins.

Bybee, Joan, and Paul Hopper
2001b Introduction. In: Joan Bybee and Paul Hopper (eds.), *Frequency and the Emergence of Linguistic Structure*, 1–24. Amsterdam/Philadelphia: Benjamins.

Chen, Rong
2003 *English Inversion. A Ground-before-Figure Construction* (Cognitive Linguistics Research 25). Berlin/New York: Mouton de Gruyter

Clark, Herbert H., and C. J. Sengul
1979 In search of referents for nouns and pronouns. *Memory and Cognition* 7: 35–41.

Croft, William, and D. Allan Cruse
2004 *Cognitive Linguistics*. Cambridge: Cambridge University Press.

Deane, Paul D.
1992 *Grammar in Mind and Brain. Explorations in Cognitive Syntax*. Berlin/New York: Mouton de Gruyter.

Dirven, René, and John Taylor
1988 The conceptualisation of vertical space in English: the case of *tall.* In: Brygida Rudzka-Ostyn (ed.), *Topics in Cognitive Linguistics,* 379–402. Amsterdam/Philadelphia: Benjamins.
Downing, Angela, and Philip Locke
2002 *A University Grammar of English.* Oxford: Routledge
Elffers, Els
1977 *Er*-verkenningen. *Spektator* 6: 417–422.
Es, Gustaaf A. van, and Paulus P. J. van Caspel
1971 "De patronen van de zinspotente groepen; grondtype A en zijn varianten II". *Publicaties van het archief voor de Nederlandse syntaxis.* Groningen: Rijksuniversiteit.
Geeraerts, Dirk
1985 *Paradigm and Paradox. Explorations into a Paradigmatic Theory of Meaning and its Epistemological Background.* Leuven: Universitaire Pers.
1999 Noch standaard, noch dialect. 'Tussentaal' in Vlaanderen en Nederland. *Onze Taal* 68: 232–235.
Geeraerts, Dirk, Stefan Grondelaers, and Peter Bakema
1994 *The Structure of Lexical Variation. Meaning, Naming, and Context.* Berlin/New York: Mouton de Gruyter.
Geeraerts, Dirk, Stefan Grondelaers, and Dirk Speelman
1999 *Convergentie en Divergentie in de Nederlandse Woordenschat. Een Onderzoek naar Kleding- en Voetbalnamen.* Amsterdam: Meertensinstituut.
Geerts, Guido, Walter Haeseryn, Jaap de Rooij, and Maarten C. van den Toorn
1984 *Algemene Nederlandse Spraakkunst.* Groningen/Leuven: Wolters-Noordhoff.
Givon, Talmy
1983 Topic continuity in discourse. An introduction. In: Talmy Givon (ed.), *Topic Continuity in Discourse. A Quantitative Cross-language Study,* 1–43. Amsterdam/Philadelphia: Benjamins.
Goossens, Louis
1990 Metaphtonymy: The interaction of metaphor and metonymy in expressions for linguistic actions. *Cognitive Linguistics* 1: 323–340.
Gries, Stefan Th.
2003 *Multifactorial Analysis in Corpus Linguistics: A Study of Particle Placement.* London: Continuum Press.
Grondelaers, Stefan
2000 De distributie van niet-anaforisch *er* buiten de eerste zinsplaats. Sociolectische, functionele en psycholinguistische aspecten van *er*'s status als presentatief signaal. Ph.D. diss., Department of Linguistics, University of Leuven.
Grondelaers, Stefan, and Marc Brysbaert
1996 De distributie van het presentatieve *er* buiten de eerste zinsplaats. *Nederlandse Taalkunde* 1: 280–305.

Grondelaers, Stefan, Marc Brysbaert, Dirk Speelman, and Dirk Geeraerts
2002 *Er* als accessibility marker: on- en offline evidentie voor een procedurele interpretatie van presentatieve zinnen. *Gramma/TTT* 9: 1–22.
Grondelaers, Stefan, Katrien Deygers, Hilde Van Aken, Vicky Van den Heede, and Dirk Speelman
2000 Het CONDIV-corpus geschreven Nederlands. *Nederlandse Taalkunde* 5: 356–363.
Grondelaers, Stefan, Dirk Speelman, Denis Drieghe, Dirk Geeraerts, and Marc Brysbaert
submitted Modelling indefinite reference processing: Converging evidence for predictive inferencing and remedial cueing. To appear in *Acta Psychologica.*
Grondelaers, Stefan and Dirk Speelman
2007 A variationist account of constituent ordering in presentative sentences in Belgian Dutch. *Corpus Linguistics and Linguistic Theory* 3: 161–193.
Grondelaers, Stefan, Dirk Speelman, and Dirk Geeraerts
2002 Regressing on *er.* Statistical analysis of texts and language variation." In: Annie Morin, and Pascale Sébillot (eds.), *6th International Conference on the Statistical Analysis of Textual Data,* 335–346. Rennes: Institut National de Recherche en Informatique et en Automatique.
Grondelaers, Stefan, Hilde Van Aken, Dirk Speelman, and Dirk Geeraerts
2001 "Inhoudswoorden en preposities als standaardiserings-indicatoren. De diachrone en synchrone status van het Belgische Nederlands. *Nederlandse Taalkunde* 6: 179–202.
Haeseryn, Walter, Kirsten Romijn, Guido Geerts, Jaap de Rooij, and Maarten C. van den Toorn
1997 *Algemene Nederlandse Spraakkunst.* Groningen and Deurne: Martinus Nijhoff–Wolters Plantyn.
Haan, Germen J. de
1974 "On extraposition". *Spektator* 4: 161–183.
Haan, Germen J. de, Gerard A. T. Koefoed, and Louis Des Tombe
1975 *Basiskursus Algemene Taalwetenschap.* Assen: Van Gorcum.
Heylen, Kris, José Tummers, and Dirk Geeraerts
this volume Methodological issues in corpus-based Cognitive Linguistics.
Hoekstra, Teun
1984 *Transitivity. Grammatical Relations in Government-Binding Theory.* Dordrecht: Foris.
Hüllen, Werner, and Rainer Schulze (eds.)
1988 *Understanding the Lexicon: Meaning, Sense and World Knowledge in Lexical Semantics.* Tübingen: Max Niemeyer Verlag.
Istendael, Geert Van
1993 *Het Belgisch Labyrinth. Wakker Worden in een ander Land.* Amsterdam: De Arbeiderspers.

Jenkins, Lyle
1975 *The English Existential.* Tübingen: Niemeyer.
Kemmer, Suzanne, and Michael Barlow
2000 Introduction. In: Michael Barlow, and Suzanne Kemmer (eds.), *Usage-based Models of Language*, vii–xxviii. Stanford: CSLI.
Kirsner, Robert S.
1979 *The Problem of Presentative Sentences in Modern Dutch.* Amsterdam: North Holland.
Kraak, Albert
1966 *Negatieve Zinnen; een Methodologische en Grammaticale Analyse.* Hilversum: W. de Haan.
Lakoff, George
1987 *Women, Fire, and Dangerous Things: What Categories Reveal about the Mind.* Chicago: University of Chicago Press.
Langacker, Ronald W.
1990 *Concept, Image, and Symbol. The Cognitive Basis of Grammar* (Cognitive Linguistics Research 1). Berlin: Mouton de Gruyter.
1991 *Foundations of Cognitive Grammar. Volume 2: Descriptive application.* Stanford: Stanford University Press.
1993 Reference point constructions. *Cognitive Linguistics* 4: 1–38.
Levin, Beth
1993 *English Verb Classes and Alternations. A Preliminary Investigation.* Chicago and London: The Chicago University Press.
Leys, Odo
1979 De bepaling van het voornaamwoordelijk bijwoord en de systematisering van het Nederlands *er. De Nieuwe Taalgids* 72: 240–246.
Milroy, Lesley, and Matthew Gordon
2003 *Sociolinguistics. Method and Interpretation.* Oxford: Blackwell.
Mitchell, Don
1984 An evaluation of subject-paced reading tasks and other methods for investigating immediate processes in reading. In: David E. Kieras and Marcel A. Just (eds.), *New methods in reading comprehension research*, 69–89. Hillsdale: Erlbaum.
Nieuwborg, Eli
1968 *De Distributie van het Onderwerp en het Lijdend Voorwerp in het Huidige Geschreven Nederlands in zijn A.B.-vorm.* Antwerpen: Plantijn.
Paardekoper, Piet
1963 *Beknopte ABN-syntaksis.* Den Bosch: Malmberg
Pederson, Eric, Eve Danziger, David Wilkins, Stephen Levinson, Sotaro Kita, and Gunter Senft
1998 Semantic typology and spatial conceptualization. *Language* 74: 557–589.
Pollmann, Thijs
1975 Oorzaak en handelende persoon: de beschrijving van passieve zinnen in de Nederlandse Grammatica. Ph.D. diss., Department of Linguistics, University of Nijmegen.

Reinhart, Tanya
1984 Principles of gestalt perception in the temporal organization of narrative text. *Linguistics* 22: 779–809.
Reuland, Erik
1983 Movement vs. merger: relations between inflection and verb. *Proceedings N.E.L.S.* XIII.
Rietveld, Toni, and Roeland Van Hout
1993 *Statistical Techniques for the Study of Language and Language Behaviour.* Berlin: de Gruyter.
Rohdenburg, Günter, and Britta Mondorf (eds.)
2003 *Determinants of Grammatical Variation.* Berlin/New York: Mouton de Gruyter.
Rooij, Jaap De
1991 Regionale variatie in het gebruik van *er* III. *Taal en Tongval* 43: 113–136.
Schermer-Vermeer, Everdina C.
1985 De onthullende status van *er* in de generatieve grammatica. *Spektator* 15: 65–84.
Schulze, Rainer
1988 A short story of *down.* In: Werner Hülllen and Rainer Schulze (eds.), *Understanding the Lexicon: Meaning, Sense and World Knowledge in Lexical Semantics*, 394–410. Tübingen:Max Niemeyer Verlag. 394–410.
Schutter, Georges de
1974 *De Nederlandse Zin. Poging tot Beschrijving van zijn Struktuur.* Brugge: De Tempel.
Schwanenflugel, Paula J.
1986 Completion norms for final words of sentences using a multiple production measure. *Behavior Research Methods, Instruments, & Computers* 18: 363–371.
Swiggers, Piet, and Karel Van den Eynde
1985 Distributie- en combinatiemogelijkheden van Nederlands *er*: een studie in syntactische classificatie. *Linguistics in Belgium* 7: 67–86.
Speelman, Dirk
1997 Abundantia Verborum. A computer tool for carrying out corpus-based linguistic case studies. Ph.D. diss., Department of Linguistics, University of Leuven.
Speelman, Dirk, Stefan Grondelaers, and Dirk Geeraerts
2003 Profile-based linguistic uniformity as a generic method for comparing language varieties. *Computers and the Humanities* 37: 317–337.
Sperber, Dan, and Deirdre Wilson
1986 *Relevance: Communication and Cognition.* Cambridge: Harvard University Press.
Stefanowitsch, Anatol
2003 Constructional semantics as a limit to grammatical alternation: The two genitives of English. In: Günter Rohdenburg, and Britta

Mondorf (eds.), *Determinants of Grammatical Variation*, 413–444. Berlin/New York: Mouton de Gruyter.

Stefanowitsch, Anatol, and Stefan Th. Gries
2003 Collostructions: Investigating the interaction between words and constructions. *International Journal of Corpus Linguistics* 8: 209–243.

Taeldeman, Johan
1992 Welk Nederlands voor de Vlamingen? *Nederlands van Nu* 40: 33–52.

Talmy, Leonard
1988 Force dynamics in language and cognition. *Cognitive Science* 12: 49–100.

Tomasello, Michael
2000 First steps toward a usage-based theory of language acquisition. *Cognitive Linguistics* 11: 61–82.

Taylor, John
1996 *Possessives in English. An Exploration in Cognitive Grammar*. Oxford: Clarendon.

Toorn, Maarten C. van den
1976 *Nederlandse Grammatica*. Groningen: Tjeenk Willink.

Traugott, Elisabeth C.
1998 The role of pragmatics in semantic change. In: Jef Verschuren (ed.), *Pragmatics in Semantic Change*, 93–102. Antwerp: International Pragmatics Association.

Traugott, Elisabeth C., and Richard B. Dasher
2002 *Regularity in Semantic Change*. Cambridge: Cambridge University Press.

Verhagen, Arie, and Jeroen van de Weijer (eds.)
2003 *Usage-Based Approaches to Dutch*. Utrecht: LOT.

Verkuyl, Henk J.
1998 O corpora, O mores. *Nederlandse Taalkunde* 3: 60–63.

Verkuyl, Henk J., Geert E. Booij, Els H. C. Elffers-Van Ketel, Wim G. Klooster, Johannes H. J. Luif, and Everdina C. Schermer-Vermeer
1974 *Transformationele Taalkunde*. Utrecht: Het Spectrum.

Wallace, Stephen
1982 Figure and ground: the interrelationships of linguistic categories. In: Paul Hopper (ed.), *Tense-Aspect: Between Semantics and Pragmatics*, 201–223. Amsterdam/Philadelphia: Benjamins.

Variation in the choice of adjectives in the two main national varieties of Dutch

Dirk Speelman, Stefan Grondelaers and Dirk Geeraerts

Abstract

In this paper we investigate, and defend, the "pattern revealing" potential of *stable lexical marker analysis*, a (word frequency list based) method for comparing corpora. We use the method to compare the choice of adjectives in Netherlandic Dutch and Belgian Dutch in the Spoken Dutch Corpus (CGN). A global comparison of both varieties shows three stable sources of lexical differences: *formal variation*, *topic variation* and *subjective vs. objective perspective*. Additional comparisons for specific registers reveal that these globally identified sources are mostly stable across registers[1]. A final series of analyses, in which nation internal differences between registers are investigated, show a striking resemblance between the observed differences across both nations. In short, taken together, the analyses in this paper reveal robust national differences across registers, as well as robust register differences across nations. With respect to the method of stable lexical markers, the case studies in the paper confirm that the method indeed is a useful exploratory technique for detecting patterns of variation and for identifying different sources of variation.

Keywords: keyword, key keyword, stable lexical marker, quantitative corpus linguistics, register analysis, regional variation

1. Introduction

The comparison of word frequency lists derived from different corpora can reveal several types of differences between these corpora. A broad

1. In this text we use 'register' as a broad cover term that covers various sorts of distinctions. Following Biber (1988, 1989), we use the term 'register' to refer to 'a particular situational and/or contextual setting', which is defined in terms of 'external' criteria such as e.g. spoken versus written, dialogue versus monologue, etc. The 'internal' linguistic characteristics of different texts that belong to one and the same specific register can vary significantly between texts.

range of different sources of variation may lead to lexical variation. To name just a few such sources: stylistic considerations and adaptation to genre-rules on the part of the language user may have a substantial influence on lexical choices; topic variability in the corpora may also play an important role; regional differences in the language varieties that are used, as well as social differences among the language users (sex, age, education ...), may also lead to different word choices, and in these different choices differences in conceptualisation may or may not be involved; etc.[2] This broad coverage of phenomena is at the same time the strength and the weakness of word frequency list based comparisons. The strength lies in the fact that, in principle, a wide range of types of variation can, to some extent, be studied with one and the same straightforward instrument[3]. The weakness lies in the fact that the instrument provides no obvious way to disentangle the different sources of variation.

In this paper we want to investigate, and defend, the "pattern revealing" potential of one specific word frequency list based method for comparing corpora. Our claim will be that, in spite of the aforementioned difficulties to disentangle different sources of variation, a carefully designed application of word frequency list comparison can be an effective exploratory tool. The method we will use is called 'stable lexical marker analysis' (Speelman et al. 2006). This method, which elaborates on the concepts 'keywords' and 'key keywords' (Scott 1997), is designed to compare two sets of subcorpora and to identify the most consistent lexical differences between those two sets. In Speelman et al. (2006) the method was used to compare a set of Dutch *computer mediated communication* subcorpora to a set of Dutch *newspaper* subcorpora. In this paper we will use the same method to compare two sets of subcorpora that contain Dutch spoken language data from The Netherlands and from Belgium respectively. Unlike Speelman et al. (2006), where the complete lexicon is taken into consideration, this paper zooms in on a specific word class: adjectives.

2. For an elaborate classification of the different types of lexical variation we refer to Geeraerts et al. (1994).
3. An interesting illustration of the range of types of variation that can be studied on the basis of frequency lists alone, can be found in Xiao and McEnery (2005). The authors illustrate that many of the findings of a multi-dimensional analysis of register – a method introduced by Biber (1988) and further elaborated in later work, e.g. Biber (1995) – can be approximated by means of a keyword and key keyword analysis.

We chose to compare the use of adjectives in the two national varieties because adjectives, more than other word classes, make explicit how we qualify things, which perspective on things we choose, and sometimes also which attitude towards things we have. The concrete questions we will try to answer in the study in this paper are the following:

- From a global perspective, summarising over specific registers, how many systematic differences are there in the use of adjectives in both national varieties, and what are the sources of these differences?
- Zooming in on more specific registers, do the same globally detected systematic differences show up again and again, or is it rather the case that different registers are characterised by different differences between the nations?
- Do the nation-internal differences between registers differ in the two nations?

The more general background for these concrete questions is the search for differences between both varieties in the use of, the distances between, and perhaps even the attitude[4] towards specific registers. From a methodological point of view, this paper addresses the 'pattern revealing' potential of stable lexical marker analysis, one possible exploratory tool in search for such differences.

The structure of this paper is as follows. In section 2 we descibe the method and materials that are used in the case study. In section 3 we report on the case study. In section 4 we summarize the methodological issues that were raised in the paper, by summing up the strengths and weaknesses of the 'stable lexical marker analyses'. Section 5 finally contains the overall conclusions of the paper.

2. Methods and materials

In this section we will first introduce the method of 'stable lexical markers' and the rationale behind it. Next we will describe the structure of the Spoken Dutch Corpus (*CGN – Corpus Gesproken Nederlands*), which is the corpus we used in the case study. In this context we will also introduce a notation for easy reference to specific parts of the Spoken

4. An example would be differences with respect to implicit conventions for what is appropriate in a specific register.

Dutch Corpus and to a specific stable lexical marker analysis of these parts. We will also give some details about the procedure we followed to derive frequency lists from the corpus.

2.1. Keywords and key keywords

2.1.1. Keywords

As was already mentioned, the method of 'stable lexical markers' elaborates on the concepts 'keywords' and 'key keywords'. Mike Scott (1997) proposes the use of categorical data analysis, more precisely of *chi squared* analysis, to automatically generate the list of *keywords* of a particular text. By keywords he means the words that are either surprisingly frequent or surprisingly infrequent in that text. In order to establish what is 'surprising', a large and balanced reference corpus is used – for instance, a typical reference corpus for contemporary British English would be the complete British National Corpus. More concretely, the word frequency list of the text under scrutiny is compared to the word frequency list of the reference corpus. For each word *W* that appears in at least one of the two frequency lists, a contingency table similar to Table 1 is created.

Table 1. The frequencies that determine the keyness of word W for text T

	text *T*	reference corpus *R*
word *W*	*a* (frequency of *W* in *T*)	*b* (frequency of *W* in *R*)
other words	*c* (size of *T* minus *a*)	*d* (size of *R* minus *b*)

The 'keyness' of word *W* for text *T*, which is a measure for the extent to which its frequency is surprising, is then calculated on the basis of the cell frequencies *a*, *b*, *c* and *d* in Table 1. Informally speaking, one could state that the keyness measure expresses how much evidence we have that the observed popularity $a / (a + c)$ of *W* in *T* differs from its observed reference popularity $b / (b + d)$ in a way that cannot be attributed to chance alone. Formally speaking, Scott uses the *chi squared* test statistic (derived from a chi squared analysis of the two-by-two table) as measure for the keyness of the word. Having established the keyness of all words, the list of words which occur in *T* and *R* can be ordered by the keyness of the words. In addition, a cut off point in this list can be identified that marks the borderline between significant and non-significant deviations from the reference corpus, given some significance level[5]. The words with a significant deviation are the 'keywords' of the text.

The keyness measure itself does not distinguish between the two possible directions of the deviation: surprisingly high frequency in text *T* versus surprisingly low frequency in text *T*. However, the 'direction' of the keyness of a word *W* in a text *T* can easily be established by comparing the popularity $a / (a + c)$ of *W* in *T* to its reference popularity $b / (b + d)$. If the former is higher than the latter, the keyness is said to be positive. If the latter is higher than the former, the keyness is said to be negative. In a similar vein, we speak of the positive keywords of text *T* (words attracted by *T*) and the negative keywords of *T* (words repelled by *T*).

Since their introduction, keyword lists have been used by many researchers[6]. Apart from the most obvious application, which is topic analysis of texts, they have been used for many different purposes, including genre analysis (e.g. Xiao and McEnery 2005).

2.1.2. *Key keywords*

The purpose for which keywords are introduced in Scott (1997) is not so much the study of the (lexical) characteristics of particular texts, but rather the study of co-occurrence patterns between keywords across many texts. He starts from a design in which for many texts (hundreds or thousands), that collectively cover a wide range of topics, the keywords are identified, each time using the same reference corpus. Then, having obtained a separate keywords list for each text, he subsequently investigates which keywords often co-occur in the same keywords list. Of course, a keyword can only play an important role in such co-occurrence patterns if it is a keyword in many texts. Therefore Scott (1997) proposes

5. By significance level we mean the 'calculated risk' we accept for making alpha-type errors in the chi squared analysis, i.e. the risk for rejecting the null hypothesis of 'no difference' whereas in fact there is no difference. Typical values for the significance level in a chi squared analysis are 0.05 or 0.01, although in the specific context of keyword analyses sometimes more restrictive significance levels (e.g. 0.001, 0.0001, 0.00001) are used, which leads to a smaller number of keywords.
6. One factor that undoubtedly contributed a lot to the popularity of the keywords method is the fact that the method is supported by the popular and user friendly software package WordSmith Tools (Scott, 1999).

to base the analysis of these co-occurrence patterns on those keywords that occur in many keywords lists (in other words, that are keywords in many texts). He calls these keywords the 'key keywords' for a collection of texts.

Given a particular key keyword, Scott first identifies all words that co-occur with that key keyword in at least one keywords list (meaning that the word and the key keyword both are a keyword for the same text), and calls these words the associates of the key keyword. Next he clusters these associates into smaller groups, which he calls 'clumps', the members of which co-occur with each other and with the key keyword in many keywords lists. His claim then is that these 'clumps' reveal stereotypical associations between words, i.e. socially determined networks of links between words.

Scott compares the analysis of co-occurrences of keywords with a key keyword in a keywords list to the (more traditional) analysis of co-occurrences of collocates with a node in a word span[7]. He claims that the former type of co-occurrence analysis can reveal semantic associations between words that have proved to be very difficult to trace in the latter type of co-occurrence analysis.

2.2. Stable lexical markers

The use of 'stable lexical markers' in this paper is technically related to the key keywords concept, but the purpose of the method is different. We start from a set A of subcorpora A_1, A_2, ..., A_n and a set B of subcorpora B_1, B_2, ..., B_m. All subcorpora in set A share some external feature or feature set F_A, and all subcorpora in set B share some external feature or feature set F_B. Examples of external features are contextual, situational, sociolinguistic or regional specifications. In the case study in section 3 of this paper the external features will be "Belgian Dutch" and "Netherlandic Dutch", "spontaneous private dialogue", "public dialogue" and "prepared public monologue". Apart from the shared feature(s), the subcorpora in a set may be, and preferably are, very different.

7. In this traditional approach a target word (the node) is investigated by considering all occurrences of this word in a corpus and by examining, in each of these occurrences, which words (the collocates) occur in the vicinity of the target word. The 'vicinity' (the span) that is investigated is typically specified as a word range [n,m], which means 'the range that spans from n words to the left of the target word up to m words to the right of the target word'.

Given these two sets A and B, the next step is that for each couple (A_i, B_j), with A_i an element of A and B_j an element of B, the set of positive keywords of A_i is calculated, using B_j as a reference corpus. Note that in this design the meaning of the term 'reference' is restricted to the technical meaning of 'reference point'; in contrast to the methods in 2.1, the language use in the reference corpus B_j typically does not represent 'some general standard', but instead it typically is just as specialised as the language use in A_i; also in contrast to the methods in 2.1, there is not a single corpus that is used as reference corpus for all keyword lists, but instead different keyword lists are based on different reference corpora. The comparison of all these couples (A_i, B_j) renders *n* x *m* positive keyword lists. Stable lexical markers of set A, when compared to set B, are words that occur in many of these positive keyword lists.

2.3. The corpus

The subcorpora we use in the case study are drawn from the Spoken Dutch Corpus (*CGN – Corpus Gesproken Nederlands*)[8]. The Spoken Dutch Corpus, compiled between 1998 and 2003, contains about 9 million tokens of contemporary spoken standard Dutch. It contains 14 different registers[9], called the 'components' of the corpus, labelled A through N. They are listed in Table 2.

The first column in Table 2 contains the label of the component. The second contains a short description. The other columns indicate which components contain dialogues of multilogues (DIA/MUL) and which contain monologues (MONO), which are spoken in a private context (PRIV) and which are spoken in a public context (PUB), and, finally, which contain spontaneous speech (SPON) and which contain more or less prepared speech (PREP).

In order to be able to construct subcorpora of the Spoken Dutch Corpus, we split up the corpus data on the basis of the components and the national varieties. Table 3 shows the number of tokens in each cell that we obtain on the basis of this operation.

8. See, for instance, Oostdijk (2002) and Schuurman et al. (2003).
9. Actually there is a 15th component, component O, but this contains written language read aloud, and so is useless in the present study. Since this 15th component contains a bit more than 900000 words, the part of the CGN that we do use in this paper, contains a bit more that 8 million words.

Table 2. The components of the Spoken Dutch Corpus

<table>
<tr><td>A</td><td>Spontaneous conversations ('face-to-face')</td><td rowspan="8">DIA/ MUL</td><td rowspan="5">PRIV</td><td rowspan="5">SPONT</td></tr>
<tr><td>B</td><td>Interviews with teachers of Dutch</td></tr>
<tr><td>C</td><td>Spontaneous telephone dialogues (recorded via a switchboard)</td></tr>
<tr><td>D</td><td>Spontaneous telephone dialogues (recorded on MD with local interface)</td></tr>
<tr><td>E</td><td>Simulated business negotations</td></tr>
<tr><td>F</td><td>Interviews/ discussions/debates (broadcast)</td><td rowspan="9">PUB</td><td>PREP</td></tr>
<tr><td>G</td><td>(political) Discussions/debates/ meetings (non-broadcast)</td><td rowspan="3">SPONT</td></tr>
<tr><td>H</td><td>Lessons recorded in the classroom</td></tr>
<tr><td>I</td><td>Live (e.g. sports) commentaries (broadcast)</td><td rowspan="6">MONO</td></tr>
<tr><td>J</td><td>Newsreports/reportages (broadcast)</td><td rowspan="5">PREP</td></tr>
<tr><td>K</td><td>News (broadcast)</td></tr>
<tr><td>L</td><td>Commentaries/columns/reviews (broadcast)</td></tr>
<tr><td>M</td><td>Ceremonious speeches/sermons</td></tr>
<tr><td>N</td><td>Lectures/seminars</td></tr>
</table>

2.4. Some notation

For ease of reference, we introduce a simple notation for referring to parts of the Spoken Dutch Corpus (CGN), and for identifying a specific stable lexical marker analysis. First, we introduce names for individual subcorpora of the Spoken Dutch Corpus (CGN):

- CGN-N_A, CGN-N_B, CGN-N_C, …, CGN-N_N: the Netherlandic components A to N
- CGN-B_A, CGN-B_B, CGN-B_C, …, CGN-B_N: the Belgian components A to N

Next, we introduce names for sets of subcorpora:

Table 3. Size (nr of tokens) of the Spoken Dutch Corpus data, by component and national variety

	The Netherlands	Belgium	*total*
A	1,752,614	882,696	2,635,310
B	250,232	316,524	566,756
C	745,396	467,850	1,213,246
D	511,676	345,177	856,853
E	136,679	0	136,679
F	540,036	251,066	791,102
G	221,583	138,891	360,474
H	300,483	105,605	406,088
I	130,428	78,164	208,592
J	90,926	95,252	186,178
K	285,316	82,875	368,191
L	80,198	65,400	145,598
M	5,571	12,512	18,083
N	61,865	79,131	140,996
total	5,113,003	2,921,143	8,034,146

- CGN-N ≡ {CGN-N_A, CGN-N_B, …, CGN-N_N}
- CGN-B ≡ {CGN-B_A, CGN-B_B, …, CGN-B_N}

More specific sets will be specified with multiple subscripts, e.g.

- CGN-$N_{A,C,D}$ ≡ {CGN-N_A, CGN-N_C, CGN-N_D}

Finally, a stable lexical marker analysis of the sets A and B will be notated as SLM(A, B), e.g.

- SLM(CGN-B, CGN-N): the stable lexical marker analysis of the A-set CGN-B and the B-set CGN-N.

2.5. Generation of the frequency lists

In this last subsection of the “Methods and materials” section we briefly sketch the process of the generation of the adjective keywords lists in the case study. The following are the steps in this process[10]:

10. The whole process was automated by means of a series of scripts written in the open source programming language Python [http://www.python.org]. For the numerical and statistical aspects of the algorithm the Python libraries

- The CGN is an annotated corpus: each token in the CGN is annotated with lemma-information and part-of-speech-information. On the basis of this annotation we have converted each token in the corpus to a string of the form "lemma/word-class-code", for instance "goed/ADJ" (good/ADJ), "hebben/WW" (have/V) or "de/LID" (the/DET).
- Next we have generated separate frequency lists of these "lemma/word-class-code" strings (all of them, not just the adjectives) for all relevant parts of the CGN.
- The stable lexical marker analysis was then conducted on the complete frequency lists (not just the adjectives). Instead of chi squared, the log likelihood ratio statistic (see Dunning 1993) was used to establish the keyness of a word. In all analyses a significance level of 0.05 was used to identify the keywords. And, as stated before, only positive keywords are used in stable lexical marker analysis, so the negative keywords were disregarded.
- In the last step the keywords lists of the stable lexical marker analysis were filtered, and only the keywords that are adjectives (according to the CGN annotation) were retained (i.e. the keywords that end with "/ADJ").

3. Case study: comparison of the national varieties

3.1. Global comparison of both national varieties

In the global comparison **SLM(CGN-N, CGN-B)** there are *14* × *14*, i.e. 196, different couples (A_i, B_j). By consequence, the highest possible 'stability' is 196. It turns out that the highest observed stability for adjectives is 165, and that there are 45 adjectival markers with a stability of 80 or higher[11]. They are listed in Table 4, ordered by their stability. For each

---

Numerical Python [http://numeric.scipy.org] and SciPy [http://www.scipy.org] were used.

11. The number 80 is an arbitrary number. In the present and subsequent analyses we each time choose an arbitrary cut off point to see just enough of the top layer of the stable markers. But it should be mentioned that we have conducted several tests with slightly or (if possible) even significantly lower cut off points (accepting more markers) to verify that the patterns reported on in the paper do not stand or fall with the arbitrary choice of a particular cut off point.

Table 4. Markers of SLM(CGN-N, CGN-B) with stability ≥ 80

verder (161) 'further'[12]	*gelijk* (115) 'equal'	*goed* (89) 'good' ***[S]***
later (155) 'later'	*jammer* (105) 'regrettable' ***[S]***	*druk* (89) 'busy'
aardig (141) 'nice' ***[S]***	*mooi* (104) 'beautiful' ***[S]***	*tegenwoordig* (87) 'present'
leuk (139) 'cool, amusing, funny, pleasant' ***[S]***	*anders* (100) 'different'	*handig* (86) 'handy'
gewoon (137) 'usual, common'	*vreselijk* (97) 'terrible' ***[S]***	*keurig* (86) 'nice, exquisite' ***[S]***
erg (136) 'bad' ***[S]***	*kwijt* (97) 'missing, lost'	*gauw* (85) 'quick'
lekker (131) 'nice, delicious' ***[S]***	*gek* (96) 'crazy, silly, odd' ***[S]***	*langzaam* (84) 'slow'
eerder (130) 'previous, sooner'	*echt* (96) 'real'	*Nederlands* (84) 'from The Netherlands'
heel (128) 'entire, whole'	*heerlijk* (96) 'lovely' ***[S]***	*extra* (83) 'extra'
makkelijk (128) 'easy'	*vervelend* (95) 'annoying' ***[S]***	*prachtig* (82) 'wonderful' ***[S]***
prima (120) 'excellent, first-rate' ***[S]***	*Voldoende* (95) 'sufficient'	*flink* (82) 'good, considerable, fine' ***[S]***
geweldig (118) 'enormous, great' ***[S]***	*behoorlijk* (94) 'decent, proper, fitting'	*vaak* (82) 'frequent(ly)'[13]
ontzettend (117) 'tremendous, awesome' ***[S]***	*allerlei* (94) 'various'	*net* (82) 'clean, neat'
laatst (116) 'last'	*natuurlijk* (90) 'natural'	*hard* (81) 'hard'
precies (115) 'precise(ly)'	*prettig* (90) 'pleasant' ***[S]***	*gezellig* (81) 'cosy, pleasant' ***[S]***

marker the lemma is shown (without the "/ADJ"), followed by its stability, followed by a translation. In the opposite comparison

12. We chose to show the lists exactly as they were generated by the automated procedure, without postprocessing. It should be noted, though, that in the interpretation of the patterns in the lists we disregard a few words in the lists, since their presence is an artefact of subtle features of the CGN lemmatisation procedure. In Table 4 and Table 5 these words are *voldoende* 'sufficient' (N) and *voldoend* 'sufficient' (B), *later* 'later' (N), *laatst* 'latest' (N) and *laat* 'late' (B), and *verder* 'further' (N).
13. The CGN part of speech annotation also assigns the word class 'adjective' to adverbially used adjectives (in most cases, Dutch has no formal indication of adverbial use, such as -ly in English). By consequence, these cases of adverbial use are included in our counts. In this text, we will add "(ly)" to examples that are predominanty used adverbially.

Table 5. Markers of SLM(CGN-B, CGN-N) with stability ≥ 80.

gans (154) 'whole, all'	*bepaald* (105) 'definite'	*voorbij* (90) 'previous'
Vlaams (150) 'Flemish'	*eigenlijk* (105) 'actual' ***[O]***	*cultureel* (89) 'cultural'
plots (145) 'sudden'	*spijtig* (105) 'regrettable'	*vroeger* (89) 'earlier'
blijkbaar (136) 'apparent, evident' ***[O]***	*tamelijk* (104) 'fair, passable'	*eventueel* (87) 'possible, potential' ***[O]***
Belgisch (131) 'Belgian'	*volledig* (100) 'complete' ***[O]***	*belangrijk* (86) 'important' ***[O]***
gemakkelijk (125) 'easy'	*federaal* (100) 'federal'	*uiteindelijk* (86) 'eventual'
zeker (123) 'certain, sure' ***[O]***	*jong* (100) 'young'	*Franstalig* (86) 'French-speaking'
onmiddellijk (122) 'immediate'	*perfect* (99) 'perfect' ***[O]***	*overdreven* (84) 'exagerated' ***[O]***
vlug (122) 'quick'	*ongetwijfeld* (98) 'doubtless' ***[O]***	*concreet* (83) 'concrete'
waarschijnlijk (116) 'probable' ***[O]***	*Europees* (96) 'European'	*gewoonlijk* (83) 'usual' ***[O]***
zodanig (114) 'such'	*evident* (96) 'evident' ***[O]***	*plezant* (83) 'pleasant, funny'
verschillend (114) 'different'	*sociaal* (96) 'social'	*zwaar* (82) 'heavy'
Antwerps (112) 'from Antwerp'	*laat* (95) 'late'	*politiek* (81) 'political'
voldoend (109) 'sufficient'	*rap* (95) 'quick'	*zogezegd* (81) 'so-called, would be' ***[O]***
vorig (109) 'previous'	*juist* (91) 'right, correct' ***[O]***	*sterk* (80) 'strong'

SLM(CGN-B, CGN-N), which also has a maximum stability of 196, the highest observed stability for adjectives is 154, and here too there happen to be 45 adjectival markers with a stability of 80 or higher. These markers are shown in Table 5. For now, please ignore the symbols ***[S]*** and ***[O]*** in tables 4 and 5. They will be explained later on when we propose a classification of the markers.

Looking into these two lists, we identified three recurrent sources/ types of variation:

- formal variation
- topic variation
- objective versus subjective perspective

By *formal variation* we mean cases where the same concept or property can be lexicalised in different ways, without there being a clear difference in conceptualisation. Examples in the above lists are:

- *makkelijk* (N) versus *gemakkelijk* (B) 'easy'
- *jammer* (N) versus *spijtig* (B) 'regrettable'
- *gauw* (N) versus *rap* and *vlug* (B) 'quick'
- *leuk* (N) versus *plezant* (B) 'pleasant'
- *gans* (N) versus *heel* (B) 'whole'

In each of these examples, both/all variants are known and used in both nations, but the difference in preference for different variants in the two national varieties is so outspoken that in both lists the preferred variants show up as stable lexical markers. Of course, in general, formal variation need not be so outspoken and symmetric that it shows up in both lists, and indeed the lists in Table 4 and Table 5 contain words that can be seen as cases of asymmetric formal variation. However, at this point we only discuss the symmetric cases, because we want to restrict ourselves to patterns that can be detected in the lists themselves.

By *topic variation* we mean words that refer to topics that are of greater national concern in one of the two nations. Examples are:

- *Nederlands* 'from the Netherlands' (N)
- *Vlaams* 'Flemish', *Belgisch* 'Belgian', *federaal* 'federal', *Franstalig* 'French-speaking', *Europees* 'European', *Antwerps* 'from Antwerp' (B)

These examples either refer to local places or to a specific local political or institutional situation. Examples of the latter are *federaal* 'federal' (Belgium has a federal government) and probably also *Europees* 'European' (which we assume is in the list because Brussels happens to be in Belgium).

In contrast to the previous two items, the third item, *objective versus subjective perspective*, is not something that we had expected to show up as a source/type of variation before we generated the lists. But when looking at the lists, we noticed that in the Netherlandic list there are quite a few words that express a *subjective appreciation*, often in a way that merely expresses the resulting *emotion* and does not allude to any reason, argument or motif for the subjective appreciation. In the Belgian list, on the other hand, quite a few words convey a qualification that expresses *a particular type of relationship to the truth or the objective facts* (e.g.

certainty, probability), and if the qualification does express an evaluation, then this is often done by referring to *some accepted norm or convention or some (rational) argument* (e.g. correctness, importance, necessity).

In the Netherlandic list in Table 4 approximately[14] one third of all markers express a subjective perspective whereas hardly any items express an objective perspective (we identify three):

- subjective perspective: the items with ***[S]*** in Table 4
- objective perspective: *gewoon* 'usual, common', *behoorlijk* 'decent, proper, fitting', *echt* 'real'.

In the Belgian list in Table 5 about one third of all markers express an objective perspective, and we identify only two items that express a subjective perspective. Moreover, the latter two are both examples of formal varation, so in fact there is not a single 'pure' example of a subjective perspective:

- objective perspective: the items with ***[O]*** in Table 5
- subjective perspective: *spijtig* 'regrettable', *plezant* 'pleasant'

Although, as we stated before, the item *objective versus subjective perspective* was not anticipated beforehand, it is, in retrospect, compatible with existing stereotypes about (spoken) language use in both nations. It is a cliché that, in line with social behaviour in general, language use in The Netherlands typically is more extrovert and 'self-confident' than in Belgium. This difference, still according to the stereotype, is assumed to be most outspoken in spoken language. One could argue that a less 'self-confident' attitude is more likely to go together with the 'safer' objective perspective and that a more 'self-confident' attitude is more likely to go together with a 'less timid' or even 'more assertive' subjective perspective. However, a thorough attempt to explain the exact nature of the phenomenon would be far beyond the scope of this paper. In this text, we restrict ourselves to establishing and exploring the pattern.

---

14. We write 'approximately' because the classification is inexact, since (a) it relies on the subjective judgement of the researcher, (b) our categories *objective perspective* and *subjective perspective* have fuzzy boundaries, and (c) the judgements are made on the basis of words in isolation, instead of on the basis of words in context. But even if the numbers are inexact, we still would claim that the overall pattern is clear enough to be considered a 'tangible' pattern.

To sum up this subsection: among the stable markers obtained from the global comparisons of the 'spoken register' of Netherlandic Dutch and Belgian Dutch, three recurrent sources/types of variation were identified: formal variation, topic variation and objective versus subjective perspective. Because more than one type is involved, and because none of the types approximate the maximum possible stability, it certainly is worthwhile to make additional comparisons that are restricted to specific subsets of the CGN. This may show whether some of the identified types of variation are more typical of specific registers than others. In addition, it may also point to additional types of variation that did not show up in the general comparisons, because they are register specific, and hence less 'stable' in the global comparison.

3.2. Comparisons of both national varieties for specific registers

First, we zoom in on the spontaneous private dialogue part in the CGN. By dialogue we henceforth mean anything that is not a monologue, so the multilogues are included in our category "dialogue". More in particular, we now look at the components **A**, **C** and **D**. We do not include component **B**, because teachers of Dutch constitute a category of expert language users. Neither do we include component **E**, which is small and lacks Belgian data. The markers we obtain on the basis of **SLM(CGN-**$\mathbf{N_{A,C,D}}$**, CGN-**$\mathbf{B_{A,C,D}}$**)** and **SLM(CGN-**$\mathbf{B_{A,C,D}}$**, CGN-**$\mathbf{N_{A,C,D}}$**)** reveal that 59 Belgian markers and 61 Netherlandic markers have the maximum possible stability of 9. So there are some clear differences between the sets CGN-$N_{A,C,D}$ and CGN-$B_{A,C,D}$. In the following description, we look at these 59 plus 61 markers with maximum stability.

Formal variation appears to be a bit more important and outspoken here than in the general comparisons of 3.1. The following are the symmetric examples (note that all examples from 3.1 show up again):

- *net* (N) versus *proper* (B) 'neat, tidy, clean'
- *klaar* (N) versus *gereed* (B) 'ready'
- *dadelijk* (N) versus *direct* (B) 'immediate(ly)'[15]
- *makkelijk* (N) versus *gemakkelijk* (B) 'easy'
- *jammer* and *sneu* (N) versus *spijtig* (B) 'regrettable'
- *gauw* and *snel* (N) versus *rap* and *vlug* (B) 'quick'

15. See note 12.

- *leuk* (N) versus *plezant* and *tof* (B) 'pleasant'
- *gans* (N) versus *heel* (B) 'whole'
- *heerlijk* (N) versus *zalig* (B) 'lovely'

An extra dimension that shows up at the level of spontaneous private dialogue is that of the *French origin of words*. We treat this dimension at this point in the text, because it is mostly a matter of formal variation, although in most cases it does not show up symmetrically in the lists. Several Belgian markers are of French origin[16], with only two counterexamples in the Netherlandic list.

- (B) *serieus* 'serious', *proper* 'clean', *akkoord* 'in agreement', *ferm* 'sound, firm', *ambetant* 'annoying', *evident* 'evident', *direct* 'immediate', *plastieken*[17] 'plastic', *plezant* 'pleasant', *content* 'satisfied, pleased', *eventueel* 'possible'
- (N) *mobiel* 'mobile', *precies* 'exact(ly), precise(ly)'

This dimension certainly was not clear in the general analyses in section 3.1. Looking back at these lists now, however, we do see some modest traces of it: *eventeel* 'possible', *evident* 'evident' and *plezant* 'pleasant' are also in Table 5, and so is *concreet* 'concrete', which is also of French origin; there is one counterexample in Table 4: *net* 'clean', also of French origin.

A look at the contexts of the counterexamples in the present analyses reveals that neither of them is in fact a true counterexample. The word *mobiel* turns out to be used exclusively in the context of mobile phones, so, although the word iself is of French origin, the specific usage of the word is probably borrowed from English. In the Netherlandic material, the word *precies* turns out to be used predominantly in particular adverbial uses, in contexts where *precisely* can easily be used in English, and where *précisément* cannot be used in French (see note 12).

16. Many of the words listed here exist in English too, in some form or another, but in the context of Dutch, they all clearly are borrowed from, and are still associated with, French.
17. Because it is perhaps less obvious for this example than for the others, we point out that here there is indeed variation in the naming of PLASTIC in Dutch: the alternative to the Dutch *plastieken*, with French origin and French-like pronunciation, is the Dutch *plastic*, with English-like pronunciation. The latter variant is preferred in The Netherlands.

The presence of words of French origin in the Belgian list is not surprising. In the past, French has been the language of prestige in Flanders for a long time, and the influence of French on Dutch in Flanders is still very strongly entrenched in the lexicon of Flemish dialects. So it should not come as a surprise that this history is also visible at the level of (colloquial) standard Dutch.

Another phenomenon that could have been expected is a stronger preference for English words in The Netherlands. It is a common belief that The Netherlands have a stronger orientation towards English-speaking countries than Belgium has. However, no pattern shows up in the lists. In the Belgian list no English words were found, and in the Netherlandic list only one English word was found: *relaxed.* Even if *mobiel* 'mobile' and *precies* 'exact(ly), precise(ly)' are interpreted as additional evidence (cf. supra), the evidence is still too anecdotic to call it a pattern.

The second source of variation identified in 3.1, *topic variation,* is missing in the spontaneous, private dialogue part in the CGN. The only remaining 'trace' is *Belgisch* 'Belgian' in the Belgian list.

The third source of variation identified in 3.1, on the other hand, *subjective versus objective perspective*, does seem to be relevant in the spontaneous, private dialogue part of the CGN, even if the situation is not identical to that found in 3.1. Compared to 3.1, the positions of the two national varieties both seem to have shifted a bit towards the subjective pole, but there still is a clear difference between the two. The Belgian list seems to be almost "in balance" with a comparable number of subjective and objective qualifications:

- subjective: *zalig* 'lovely, heavenly', *tof* 'amusing, funny, pleasant', *ambetant* 'annoying', *triestig* 'sad', *wreed* 'cruel', *onnozel* 'silly', *plezant* 'pleasant', *zot* 'stupid', *content* 'satisfied, pleased'
- objective: *zogezegd* 'so-called', *eventueel* 'possible', *juist* 'correct, right', *eigenlijk* 'actual', *evident* 'evident', *waarschijnlijk* 'probable', *gewoonlijk* 'usual', *totaal* 'total', *volledig* 'complete', *blijkbaar* 'apparent, evident', *waar* 'true'

In the Netherlandic list the subjective qualifications are clearly in the majority:

- subjective: *zielig* 'sad, pathetic', *vreselijk* 'terrible', *gek* 'crazy', *mooi* 'beautiful', *lullig* 'lousy', *geweldig* 'great', *waardeloos* 'worthless', *kut* 'lousy', *ontzettend* 'terrible', *aardig* 'nice', *gaaf* 'cool', *erg* 'bad', *grap-*

pig 'funny', *geinig* 'funny', *onwijs* 'stupid', *sneu* 'regrettable', *chagrijnig* 'unsatisfied', *lekker* 'nice, delicious', *irritant* 'irritating', *heerlijk* 'lovely', *gezellig* 'cosy', *heftig* 'heavy', *prima* 'first-rate', *vrolijk* 'cheerful', *leuk* 'pleasant', *suf* 'stupid', *vervelend* 'boring, annoying', *prettig* 'pleasant', *naar* 'unpleasant'
- objective: *precies* 'precise', *heus* 'true, real', *gewoon* 'normal', *behoorlijk* 'decent', *kennelijk* 'obvious'

We now move to the public dialogue part of the CGN (spontaneous as well as prepared), with the analyses **SLM(CGN-N$_{F,G,H}$, CGN-B$_{F,G,H}$)** and **SLM(CGN-B$_{F,G,H}$, CGN-N$_{F,G,H}$)**. The following patterns show up. In the Netherlandic list there are 7 words with the maximum possible stability of 9, and 48 words with a stability of 6 or higher. In the Belgian list there are 10 words with the maximum possible stability of 9, and 60 words with a stability of 6 or more. So in all, these comparisons reveal weaker differences than the comparisons of spontaneous, private dialogue part. In our search for patterns, we will take into account all words with a stability of 6 or higher.

Formal *variation* is less outspoken than in the spontaneous private dialogues. The list of symmetric cases is a bit smaller than that in the general analysis in 3.1. The following is the list, together with the stability of the words:

- *makkelijk* (7 in N) versus *gemakkelijk* (9 in B) 'easy'
- *jammer* (7 in N) versus *spijtig* (6 in B) 'regrettable'
- *gauw* (6 in N) versus *vlug* (9 in B) 'quick'
- *gans* (9 in N) versus *heel* (7 in B) 'whole'

Apart from that, there also are some asymmetric 'traces' of examples we saw in a symmetric form in other analyses: *net* 'clean' (6 in N), *leuk* 'pleasant' (7 in N).

The dimension *French origin of words,* on the other hand, is relatively strong in this register. There are no words of French origin in the Netherlandic list. The following are the words of French origin in the Belgian list, with their stability:

- (B) *akkoord* (9) 'in agreement', *momenteel* (7) 'momentary', *quasi* (6) 'seeming', *eventueel* (6) 'possible', *fier* (6) 'proud', *abnormaal* (6) 'abnormal', *efficiënt* (6) 'efficient', *effectief* (6) 'effective', *totaal* (6) 'complete', *fameus* (6) 'famous, enormous, splendid'

There are no words of English origin in either one of the lists. The next source of variation identified in 3.1, *topic variation*, is visible in the public dialogues. The following are the topic variation markers.

- (B) *Antwerps* (9) 'from Antwerp', *Vlaams* (9) 'Flemish', *Belgisch* (9) 'Belgian', *federaal* (6) 'federal', *Gents* (6) 'from Ghent', *Waals* (6) 'Walloon', *socialistisch* (6) 'socialist', *Brussels* (6) 'from Brussels', *Franstalig* (6) 'French-speaking', *interparlementair* (6) 'inter-parliamentary', *Nederlandstalig* (6) 'Dutch-speaking'
- (N) *Nederlands* (6) 'Netherlands', *katholiek* (6) 'catholic'

For most words in the list the reason for their presence is straightforward. Only for *socialistisch* 'socialist' (B) and *katholiek* 'catholic' (N) the situation is not so clear. For *socialistisch* 'socialist' (B) we see no convincing reason why it would be that much more important in Belgian political discussions than in Netherlandic political discussions. So this may be an idiosyncratic pattern. Futher analysis on the basis of additional corpora would be needed to bring clarity. For *katholiek* 'catholic' (N) we assume the word is in the list because it has a higher discriminative importance in The Netherlands (which has an important protestant community as well as an important catholic community), not because it has a higher absolute importance (in Belgium the catholic community is by far the most important religious community).

The last source of variation identified in 3.1, *objective versus subjective perspective*, is visible in the public dialogues, but once again the two national varieties both seem to have shifted a bit, this time towards the objective pole. The Netherlandic situation seems to be almost in balance between subjective and objective markers. The Belgian situation is objective only (with the exception of *spijtig* 'regrettable' (B), which as was said before, is also, and foremost, a case of formal variation). These are the words in the Netherlandic list:

- subjective perspective: *lastig* (9) 'annoying', *geweldig* (8) 'great', *erg* (8) 'bad', *vervelend* (8) 'annoying', *vreselijk* (7) 'terrible', *ontzettend* (7) 'dreadful', *aardig* (7) 'nice', *leuk* (7) 'pleasant', *jammer* (7) 'regrettable', *bang* (6) 'afraid', *lekker* (6) 'nice, delicious', *prima* (6) 'first-rate'
- objective perspective: *precies* (9) 'precise', *gewoon* (7) 'normal', *kennelijk* (7) 'obvious', *feitelijk* (7) 'actual', *daadwerkelijk* (6) 'real', *behoorlijk* (6) 'proper', *zakelijk* (6) 'essential, real, objective', *formeel* (6) 'formal', *echt* (6) 'real', *extreem* (6) 'extreme'

These are the words in the Belgian list:

- subjective perspective: *spijtig* (6) 'regrettable'
- objective perspective: *perfect* (9) 'perfect', *blijkbaar* (9) 'apparent', *volledig* (8) 'complete', *juist* (7) 'right', *overdreven* (7) 'exagerated', *zeker* (7) 'certain', *eigenaardig* (7) 'strange, odd', *waarschijnlijk* (7) 'probable', *belangrijk* (6) 'important', *duidelijk* (6) 'clear', *zogezegd* (6) 'so-called', *quasi* (6) 'seeming', *eventueel* (6) 'possible', *eigenlijk* (6) 'actual', *abnormaal* (6) 'abnormal', *efficiënt* (6) 'efficient', *effectief* (6) 'effective', *totaal* (6) 'complete', *ongetwijfeld* (6) 'certain'

Finally we zoom in on the prepared public monologue part of the CGN, with the analyses **SLM(CGN-N$_{J,K,L}$, CGN-B$_{J,K,L}$)** and **SLM-(CGN-B$_{J,K,L}$, CGN-N$_{J,K,L}$)**. We did not include the components **M** and **N**, which contain a lot of material from very specialised, and marked registers. Here the differences are even weaker than in the previous comparison: 1 Netherlandic marker and 3 Belgian markers have the maximum possible stability of 9; 24 Netherlandic markers and 42 Belgian markers have a stability of 6 or higher. In our presentation of the patterns, we will take into account all words with a stability of 6 or higher.

Formal variation is almost completely lacking. The only symmetric example is *gans* (6 in N) versus *heel* (6 in B) 'whole'. The only asymmetric example is *leuk* (6 in N) 'pleasant'. Neither can a clear dimension *French origin of words* be distinguished, although there still are three Belgian markers of French origin (*ultiem* (6) 'ultimate', *concreet* (6) 'concrete', *perfect* (6) 'perfect'), versus none in the Netherlandic list.

Topic variation on the other hand is more clearly present:

- (N) *Nederlands* (7) 'Netherlandic', *Nijmeegs* (6) 'from Nijmegen', *Fries* (6) 'Frisian', *Rotterdams* (6) 'from Rotterdam'
- (B) *federaal* (9) 'federal', *Antwerps* (9) 'from Antwerp', *Vlaams* (9) 'Flemish', *Belgisch* (8) 'Belgian', *Brussels* (8) 'from Brussels', *Franstalig* (8) 'French-speaking', *Europees* (7) 'European', *Gents* (6) 'from Ghent', *Waals* (6) 'Walloon', *Congolees* (6) 'Congolese', *communautair* (6) 'community-related', *paars-groen* (6) 'purple-green'

The last item in the Belgian list refers to a coalition of political parties. New in this analysis, when compared to the previous ones, is the presence of additional topic variation that is harder to interpret, and that probably is due to more temporary and coincidental differences in (especially) news coverage in both nations that happen to be captured in the CGN. The following are some words that we would put in this category. The word *geel* 'yellow' refers to the yellow shirt of the leader in the sports event Tour de France:

- (N) *geel* (8) 'yellow'
- (B) *Brits* (6) 'Britisch', *archeologisch* (6) 'archeological', *christen-democratisch* (6) 'christian democratic', *militair* (6) 'military'

The source *subjective versus objective perspective*, finally, still stands, but is a bit slimmer than in the other analyses. The Netherlandic words are:

- subjective perspective: *flink* (7) 'good, considerable, fine', *lekker* (7) 'nice, delicious', *mooi* (6) 'beautiful', *aardig* (6) 'nice', *leuk* (6) 'pleasant', *erg* (6) 'bad', *prachtig* (6) 'wonderful', *naar* (6) 'unpleasant'
- objective perspective: *gewoon* (6) 'normal'

The Belgian list contains no *subjective perspective* words. The *objective perspective* words are:

- objective perspective: *blijkbaar* (8) 'apparent, evident', *bevoegd* (6) 'competent, qualified', *duidelijk* (6) 'clear', *beperkt* (6) 'limited', *ultiem* (6) 'ultimate', *gans* (6) 'complete', *concreet* (6) 'concrete', *ongetwijfeld* (6) 'certain', *perfect* (6) 'perfect'

To sum up this subsection: the same sources of variation that were observed in the global 'spoken register' (formal variation, topic variation and subjective versus objective perspective), show up again and again in the more specific comparisons of 'spontaneous private dialogue', 'public dialogue' and 'prepared public monologue', even if not all sources are equally strong in all registers (in two registers one source is even missing: topic variation in 'spontaneous private dialogue', and formal variation in 'prepared public monologue'). Apart from the observation that in dialogue, especially in spontaneous private dialogue, several Belgian markers are *words of French origin*, no additional patterns/sources of variation were detected at the level of the more specific registers.

3.3. Comparison of the internal relation between registers within both national varieties

Up to this point we have been making direct comparisons of Belgian and Netherlandic material. An alternative, more indirect perspective is to compare registers within one nation and to repeat this exercise for the other nation. In this section we will examine the nation-internal differences between CGN-$N_{A,C,D}$, CGN-$N_{F,G,H}$ and CGN-$N_{J,K,L}$, both in Belgium and in The Netherlands. We could have chosen to make all possible pairwise comparisons of the three sets, but instead we will choose the slightly broader approach of comparing each set to the union of the other two sets. First we zoom in on the spontaneous private dialogues, and see how they stand out from the other registers. The relevant comparisons are **SLM(CGN-$B_{A,C,D}$, CGN-$B_{F,G,H,J,K,L}$)** for Belgium and **SLM(CGN-$N_{A,C,D}$, CGN-$N_{F,G,H,J,K,L}$)** for The Netherlands.

In the Netherlandic list 7 words have the maximum possible stability of 18 and 38 words have a stability of 14 or higher. In the Belgian list 7 words have the maximum possible stability of 18, and 25 words have a stability of 14 or higher. We will look at all markers with a stability of 14 or higher.

The most striking observation is the large overlap of the Belgian list and the Netherlandic list. No fewer than 11 words occur in both lists:

– *echt* (18 in N; 18 in B) 'real', *tof* (14 in N; 18 in B) 'pleasant', *gewoon* (18 in N; 18 in B) 'normal', *waar* (16 in N; 18 in B) 'true', *stom* (18 in N; 17 in B) 'stupid', *moe* (15 in N; 16 in B) 'tired', *raar* (15 in N; 16 in B) 'strange, odd', *leuk* (18 in N; 16 in B) 'pleasant', *grappig* (18 in N; 14 in B) 'funny', *goed* (17 in N; 14 in B) 'good', *lekker* (18 in N; 14 in B) 'nice, delicious'

The lexical specificity of the register 'spontaneous private dialogue' seems to be very similar in both nations. It is worthwhile to note that some nation-specific markers that we encountered in sections 3.1 and 3.2 now show up in the lists of both nations. The examples are *echt* (N-marker in 3.1 and 3.2) 'real', *gewoon* (N-marker in 3.1 and 3.2) 'normal' and *lekker* (N-marker in 3.1 and 3.2) 'nice, delicious', and even the formal variants *tof* (B-marker in 3.2) 'pleasant' and *leuk* (N-marker in 3.1 and 3.2) 'pleasant'. In other words, some concepts, such as PLEASANT, are so typical of the spontaneous private dialogue register that not only the more preferred formal variant for referring to the concept, but also the less preferred formal variant shows up as a marker of the register.

On the other hand, other national markers that we know from 3.1 and 3.2 remain specific for one nation in the present lists. The examples are:

- (B) *plezant* (18) 'pleasant', *rap* (18) 'quick', *ambetant* (17) 'annoying', *content* (17) 'satisfied', *direct* (18) 'direct'
- (N) *jammer* (14) 'regrettable'

Apart from *rap* 'quick', all examples in the above Belgian list are words of French origin.

Next, we explore what sets apart the public dialogue register. The relevant comparisons are **SLM(CGN-B$_{F,G,H}$, CGN-B$_{A,C,D,J,K,L}$)** for Belgium and **SLM(CGN-N$_{F,G,H}$, CGN-N$_{A,C,D,J,K,L}$)** for The Netherlands. In the Netherlandic list no words have the maximum possible stability of 18 and 51 words have a stability of 12 or higher. In the Belgian list no words have the maximum possible stability of 18, and only 15 words have a stability of 12 or higher. We will look at all markers with a stability of 12 or higher.

Again, the most striking observation is the overlap of the lists. The following words are markers in both lists:

- *duidelijk* (17 in N; 15 in B) 'clear', *bepaald* (16 in N; 15 in B) 'definite', *belangrijk* (13 in N; 15 in B) 'important', *ander* (14 in N; 13 in B) 'other, different', *specifiek* (15 in N; 12 in B) 'specific', *fundamenteel* (14 in N; 12 in B) 'fundamental', *cultureel* (15 in N; 12 in B) 'cultural', *financieel* (12 in N; 12 in B) 'financial'

Even if the rather modest stability of the markers indicates that the lexical specificity of the public dialogue register could have been more pronounced, the amount of overlap between the Belgian list and the Netherlandic list indicates that this lexical specificity does seem to be stable across both nations. Apart from *cultureel* 'cultural' and *financieel* 'financial', which refer to typical topics of debates or discussions, all words in the above lists refer to concepts that are important for any argument in any debate or discussion, and in this way are typical of the public dialogue register as such (which, at least in the Spoken Dutch Corpus, more often than not has the form of a debate or discussion).

Finally we look at the prepared public monologue register. The relevant comparisons are **SLM(CGN-B$_{J,K,L}$, CGN-B$_{A,C,D,F,G,H}$)** for Belgium and **SLM(CGN-N$_{J,K,L}$, CGN-N$_{A,C,D,F,G,H}$)** for The Netherlands. In the Netherlandic list 3 words have the maximum possible stability of 18 and 25 words have a stability of 14 or higher. In the Belgian list 4 words have the maximum possible stability of 18, and 26 words have a stability of 14 or higher. We will look at all markers with a stability of 14 or higher.

Again, there is a clear overlap of the lists of both nations, even if it may be slightly more modest than in the previous analyses. The following words are markers in both lists:

- *Amerikaans* (17 in N; 18 in B) 'American', *groot* (17 in N; 16 in B) 'big, great', *gewond* (17 in N; 18 in B) 'wounded', *dood* (16 in N; 18 in B) 'dead', *hoog* (14 in N; 14 in B) 'high', *medisch* (14 in N; 15 in B) 'medical', *jong* (14 in N; 16 in B) 'young'

Apart from *Amerikaans* 'American', which refers to a frequent news topic, the other words refer to features that are shared by many new items (and which unfortunately typically are related to negative things such as casualties). The non-overlapping parts of the lists also mostly refer either to frequent news topics or to characteristics shared by many news topics. One concrete example is the appearance, in the non-overlapping parts of the lists as well as in the overlapping parts, of several names that refer to countries or other places:

- (N) *Amsterdams* (18) 'from Amsterdam', *Amerikaans* (17) 'American', *Duits* (15) 'German', *Nederlands* (14) 'from The Netherlands'
- (B) *Amerikaans* (18) 'American', *Brits* (18) 'British', *Belgisch* (16) 'Belgian', *Brussels* (16) 'from Brussels', *Spaans* (15) 'Spanish', *Europees* (15) 'European', *Oostenrijks* (15) 'Austrian', *Frans* (15) 'French'

Surprisingly there is hardly any overlap in the lists (only *Amerikaans* 'American' appears in both lists), but that is in part due to the arbitrary stability threshold of 14. If we relaxed that threshold criterion, the overlap would increase.

To sum up this subsection, the nation-internal differences that were detected between the specific registers 'spontaneous private dialogue', 'public dialogue' and 'prepared public monologue', were found to be not nation-specific at all. In both nations very similar, and often even identical markers set these specific registers apart from each other.

4. Strengths and weaknesses

We believe that the case study in section 3 has illustrated that stable lexical markers represent a useful technique which enables the exploration of large amounts of data and the extraction from these data, by means of straightforward and time efficient[18] computations, of those phenomena that from the perspective of stability are most noteworthy. The selection procedure, which is fair but strict, results in lists that are convenient and tractable for thorough manual analysis, which is an obvious practical advantage. At the same time, the lists turn out to be sufficiently substantial for successfully bringing to light various dimensions of variation, and illustrating how these sources of variation interact in the registers under scrutiny.

It should be noticed that *additional automation could take the technique a few steps further* than what was done in the present study. A first example pertains to the automated selection of analyses. In this paper the sets A and B in an analysis of type SLM(A, B) were always chosen manually on the basis of external criteria, inspired by prior expectations about which comparisons make most sense from a linguistic point of view. However, an alternative, or complementary approach would be to automatically iterate over many possible sets A and B, and have the algorithm identify those couples (A, B) that stand out on the basis of a more internal, data-driven criterion, such as, for example, 'number of stable lexical markers which exceed a given threshold level of stability'[19]. As a second example, the automatic generation of graphical reprentations could also be helpful in further unveiling certain hitherto implicit features of the observed phenomena. For instance, Venn-diagrams with links between specific set members could be useful for highlighting which couples of subcorpora contribute to the stability of a particular stable lexical marker, thus visualising the spread of the keyword status (or keyness) of this marker. As a third example, certain comparisons that turned out to be relevant in the manual analyses in section 3 in this paper, can easily be automated. For instance, the intersection of two lists of stable lexical markers – a concept that was crucial in section 3.3 – can easily be calculated automatically. This would not only be a useful addition to a manual analysis, but it could also be incorporated in a broader type of advanced automation that is very similar to our first example, *viz.* the automatic selection of couples of analyses SLM(A_1,B_1) and SLM(A_2,B_2), on the basis of some data-driven criterion such as 'the relative (or abso-

18. The initial compilation of the database of all keyword lists took several hours, but this has to be done only once. From that point onwards the generation of specific lists of stable lexical markers is (almost) instantaneous.
19. This approach has already been explored to some extent in Speelman et al. (2006).

lute) size of the intersection of the two lists of stable lexical markers (above some given stability threshold)'.

In spite of these positive results and suggestions for further extensions, it is nevertheless crucial to bear in mind the intrinsic limitations of the technique. First, it has become clear – at many points in section 3 – that the last step in the process, the *interpretation of the lists* of stable lexical markers, requires significant 'manual' contribution by the researcher, both at the level of digging into the corpus (and looking at the contexts in which a particular marker occurs), and at the level of the classification of the markers. At the level of the individual markers, there is a danger of jumping to conclusions too soon. Each and every marker raises the difficult question of why it shows up in the list, and the answer to such a question requires individual, careful investigation. This continues to be true when one no longer relies on individual markers, but on patterns of co-occurring markers, which is the approach adopted in this paper. Moreover, the classification of (co-occurring) markers raises another pivotal question: which level of consistency of classification can be obtained across analyses and across researchers? Clearly, there is a big need for cross-validation at this level.

Second, one should bear in mind that the method is based on a radical selection of phenomena. From the perspective of stability, the 'layer of variation' that is operationally selected by the method could indeed be considered as the 'top layer', on which the major dimensions of variation obtain. However, variation which is more sensitive to all sorts of interactions (and which, as a consequence, is less stable), may be called less systematic, but it is nonetheless very real. In other words, the selection procedure which is at the heart of our technique, is not equally sensitive to all types of variation, as a consequence of which only the 'strongest' types are detected. The way to compensate for this is by complementing global analyses such as the one in 3.1 with several 'local' analyses such as the ones in 3.2 and 3.3 and by comparing the analyses.

Third, the method is course-grained by design, because it *starts out with units which are often ambiguous.* Strings of the form "lemma/word-class-code" do not distinguish between the different meanings or syntactic functions a word may have, and neither do they take into account any other aspect of the context of a word that may be important to distinguish between different uses of the word. Inevitable as it is in a corpus which is not enriched with independently accessible semantic information this ambiguity may well lead to important markers not being detected, and sometimes also to the generation of spurious markers. By its very own nature, the method therefore is incapable of attaining the level of detail and sophistication of techniques which incorporate a more carefully designed data retrieval step. A well-known example of such a method is the multidimensional analysis by Biber (e.g. 1988, 1995), which implies the construction of a specialised tagger for the accurate identification of a wide range of phenomena in the corpora. It should be noted though that Biber mostly focusses on other phenomena than those in the lexicon: the majority of the phenomena analysed by Biber are not lexical as such. A more lexically oriented example is *profile-based analysis* (Speelman et al. 2003, Speelman et al. 2006), which builds on a careful classification of 'words (or other phenomena) in context' into onomasiological profiles as the first step of the analysis. Compared to these more sophisticated, but also much more time-consuming and laborious methods, stable lexical marker analysis should be regarded as a powerful exploratory tool. Depending on the context and the needs, this exploratory tool can either be sufficient in its own right, or it can serve as a first step to explore not only whether, but also where exactly, a more thorough analysis with more elaborate methods is in order[20].

5. Conclusions

This paper has empirical as well as methodological conclusions. As far as the case study is concerned, we can state, with some amount of confidence, that spoken Dutch – as represented by the Spoken Dutch Corpus – is characterised by several stable patterns of variation in the choice of adjectives. A global comparison of Netherlandic and Belgian spoken Dutch manifests three sources of lexical differences: *formal variation*, *topic variation* and *subjective versus objective perspective*. Additional analyses that compare Netherlandic and Belgian Dutch in three more specific registers (spontaneous private dialogue, public dialogue and prepared public monologue) demonstrate that the cited sources of variation recur in each of these registers, albeit that their individual strength may vary across the registers (and that in two cases one of the three sources

20. A comparable position, mutatis mutandis, is defended more elaborately by Xiao and McEnery (2005) in their comparison of the virtues of the (easily used and yet powerful) keyword method and the (more comprehensive but more demanding) multidimensionsal analysis for register studies. See also note 2.

is even absent). Moreover, no noteworthy additional sources of variation show up in these more specific registers, with the exception of the factor *French origin of words* which characterises several Belgian markers of *(formal) variation* in the dialogues. A final series of analyses, in which nation-internal differences between registers were investigated, show strikingly similar patterns in both nations. In other words, although in each register the lexicon in Belgium and The Netherlands is consistently different, the way registers differ *within* each country is consistently identical across both countries: to a large extent, exactly the same words show up as markers of specific registers in both countries. In short, we found robust nation differences across registers, as well as robust register differences across nations.

With respect to the methodology of stable lexical markers, it has been shown that the method has a high 'pattern-revealing' potential. It has proved itself to be an excellent exploratory tool, which, depending on the context and the needs, may either be sufficient in its own right, or may serve as a first step to explore whether, or where exactly, a more thorough analysis with more elaborate methods, such as multidimensional analysis or profile-based analysis, is in place.

References

Biber, Douglas
1988 *Variation across Speech and Writing*. Cambridge: Cambridge University Press.

Biber, Douglas
1989 A typology of English texts. *Linguistics* 27: 3–43.

Biber, Douglas
1995 *Dimensions in Register Variation*. Cambridge: Cambridge University Press.

Dunning, Ted
1993 Accurate methods for the statistics of surprise and coincidence. *Computational Linguistics* 19 (1): 61–74.

Geeraerts, Dirk, Stefan Grondelaers and Peter Bakema
1994 *The Structure of Lexical Variation. Meaning, Naming and Context*. Berlin: Mouton de Gruyter.

Oostdijk, Nelleke
2002 The design of the Spoken Dutch Corpus. In: Pam Peters, Peter Collins and Adam Smith (eds.), *New Frontiers of Corpus Research*, 105–112. Amsterdam: Rodopi.

Scott, Mike
1997 Pc analysis of key words – and key key words. *System* 25: 233–245.

Scott, Mike
1999 *WordSmith Tools*. Oxford: Oxford University Press.

Schuurman, Ineke, Machteld Schouppe, Heleen Hoekstra and Ton Van der Wouden
2003 CGN, an annotated corpus of spoken Dutch. In: Anne Abeillé, Silvia Hansen-Schirra and Hans Uszkoreit (eds.), *Proceedings of the 4th International Workshop on Linguistically Interpreted Corpora,* 101–108. Budapest, Hungary.

Speelman, Dirk, Stefan Grondelaers and Dirk Geeraerts
2003 Profile-based linguistic uniformity as a generic method for comparing language varieties. *Computers and the Humanities* 37: 317–337.

Speelman, Dirk, Stefan Grondelaers and Dirk Geeraerts
2006 A profile-based calculation of region and register variation: the synchronic and diachronic status of the two main national varieties of Dutch. In: Andrew Wilson, Paul Rayson and Dawn Archer (eds.), *Corpus Linguistics Around the World,* 195–202. Amsterdam: Rodopi.

Xiao, Zhonghua and Anthony McEnery
2005 Two approaches to genre analysis: Three genres in modern American English. *Journal of English Linguistics* 33: 62–82.

Part three

Cultural models of language and language policy

Rationalist or romantic model in globalisation?

Frank Polzenhagen and René Dirven

Abstract

There is a heated and ongoing debate – both among linguists and non-linguists – on the effects current processes of globalisation have on language(s) and linguistic situations world-wide and on the role played by language(s) in these processes. Various and often conflicting positions have been taken towards these issues and a whole set of arguments has been put forward in order to back the different positions. In our paper, we review key arguments made in this debate. We are, however, less concerned with the question of whether or not or in which specific contexts they may be valid. Rather, we primarily take a discourse-analytic and metatheoretical perspective and discuss these arguments against the background of the conceptions of language they reflect and the politico-philosophical traditions they are rooted in. Our focus is on views of global languages, notably English. In line with and leaning on Geeraerts' (2003) parallel cognitive-linguistic analysis of views of standard languages, we regard the underlying politico-philosophical positions and conceptions of language as pertaining to two central competing cognitive cultural models in Western thinking, namely the rationalist model and the romantic model. Hence, in our discussion, we relate the key arguments made in the current debate on global languages to conceptualisations that are characteristic of these two models, in particular to specific metaphoric and metonymic conceptualisations of language (e.g. LANGUAGE AS A TOOL in the rationalist and LANGUAGE AS AN IDENTITY MARKER in the romantic model). Along with the cognitive-linguistic analysis of these conceptualisations we provide a critical discussion of the ideologies inherent in the two models and in their corresponding views of globalisation.

Keywords: Metaphor/metonymy in science; cultural models of globalisation; romantic model; rationalist model; conceptualisations of language; biological model of language; Neo-Whorfianism; global English.

1. Rationalist and romantic models in evolution

Language policies in most countries of the world have traditionally been guided by the ideas of monolingualism and social homogeneity. It is becoming increasingly evident that these tenets fail to respond adequately to the multilingual and multicultural realities in most regions of the world. The rapid social changes in the present world, especially modern forms of globalisation[1] and, closely connected to it, large-scale migrations, induce even more linguistic and cultural diversification at all levels of society. Given this factual situation, language policies that aim at upholding these monolingual ideas and tenets have increasingly detrimental and oppressive effects. For decades, such ideals have been vehemently criticised by linguists of various persuasions and proposals have been made to develop multilingual language policies that may cope with the present challenges. Although these proposals break with established tenets in a number of crucial respects, they are often still embedded in a long tradition of dominant competing models or ideologies in linguistics and the social sciences in general. With Geeraerts (2003), two models may be identified in which these trends are, globally, situated. On the one hand, there is the rationalist model, which has its roots in Enlightenment thinking. On the other hand, there is the romantic model, which derives its basic assumptions from the 18th and 19th century romantic tradition. Both models underwent significant changes over the last centuries, which are carefully outlined in Geeraerts (2003). For our present concern, these historical transformations are not of immediate interest (see, however, below). Rather, we focus on the views advocated by contemporary proponents of these models, which attempt to account for the multilingual and multicultural realities against the background of the romantic and rationalist models.

It may be in order to recall, first of all, the basic assumptions of the two models in their present pronunciation, as identified by Geeraerts (2003: 40). Table 1 below presents Geeraerts' systematisation, in a slightly adapted form.

It needs to be stressed that these models are meant to characterise certain positions rather than to label individual authors. As cultural cognitive models,[2] they are entrenched idealised systems of thought with a particular perspective on the phenomenon they conceptualise. And as cultural models, they truly emerge only in discourse, rather than necessarily and fully pertaining to individuals. In fact, few scholars, if any, would exclusively subscribe to either perspective. And evidently, the academic

1. Globalisation as such is, of course, not a new phenomenon. See, e.g., Mufwene (2002) on earlier forms of globalisation.
2. For a review of the notion of "cultural model" see Dirven, Wolf and Polzenhagen (2007).

Table 1. Rationalist versus romantic model: The multilingual stage

	The rationalist model	The romantic model
linguistic-philosophical basis	language as a medium of communication	language as a medium of expression
conception of standardisation and globalisation	a democratic ideal: standard / global language as a neutral medium of social participation and emancipation	anti-ideological criticism: standard / global language as a medium of social exclusion and a threat to local identities
conception of language variation	language variation / multilingualism as functional specialisation	language variation / multilingualism as expressing different and layered identities

debate has produced a more differentiated picture than the postulation of these models may suggest. The authors we discuss in this paper, for instance, represent, to varying degrees, mid-positions between the two models. In the actual academic discourse, the models are thus poles on a continuum. Still, they capture the two dominant vantage points in the present debate and they may signal in which direction any single author tends to look and to think. However, they are drawn upon by the individual scholars according to the specific needs and purpose of their argument.[3] Here, it is important to notice that a critical assessment of a certain position is readily pronounced in the logic of the opposed model. This observation also holds true for the present paper. We take this to be an independent justification for actually postulating the two global models as idealised entrenched systems of thought, i.e. as cultural cognitive models. Further justification for positing the two models comes from the fact that the differentiated ideas of academic discourse are more often than not absent in actual language policies. Language policies, evidently, involve decision-makers without any linguistic background, who seek,

3. Two papers that are cited in our further discussion, House (2001) and Phillipson (2001), provide a clear illustration of this point. Published in *The Guardian*, the two articles are contributions to the public debate on language policy and global languages rather than to the more narrowly linguistic discourse. They are explicitly meant to present the two conflicting positions in a fairly straightforward pro-and-contra way. The individual statements they contain should not be taken as the basis of attaching labels like "rationalist" or "romanticist" to their authors, labels to which they would often and rightly object.

first of all, linguistic support for their particular political strategies. What comes to the fore here is that the two models correspond to more general, competing ideologies. And consequently, a strong orientation to either of them is dominant in actual language policies.

What is intriguing about the two models is that their advantages and disadvantages, respectively, are almost complementary. The rationalist model's emphasis on the promotion of national standard languages and on global communication fosters and ensures, at least ideally, democratisation, emancipation and broad access to social participation at the national level and beyond. However, it does so to the possible detriment of local and minority languages, and in some negligence of the cultural dimension of language. The promotion of one or a few languages entails the danger of what has been termed, in biological metaphors, "language attrition" and "language death" among the non-promoted ones. In actual language policies, this neglect in linguistic matters is more often than not part of a general disregard of local and "non-mainstream" cultures. In turn, the romantic model's emphasis on the local and on the cultural dimension of language allows for, again ideally at least, the preservation and expression of one's own identity and the recognition of others' identities. However, it faces the inherent danger of fostering isolation from the nation and from global communication, and, furthermore, the threat of nationalistic excesses. It needs to be stressed that the above pitfalls are, with both models, often unintended. Rather, they constitute instances of what Geeraerts (2003: 34f., 49), leaning on Horkheimer and Adorno, calls "negative dialectics" of the two models, i.e. the paradox that the models tend to become subverted and to contradict at least some of their own original starting points.

In our paper, we focus on the discussion of conceptualisations underlying the linguistic bases of the two models, as reflected in their metalanguage, on their views of global languages,[4] on ideological implications, and on possible points of contact between the two approaches.

Geeraerts (2003) rightly identifies the underlying linguistic assumptions of the rationalist and romantic models by the opposition between the views of language as a medium of communication and as a medium of expressing identity, respectively (cf. Table 1). These foci are characteristic of the two models over the centuries.[5] The primary perspective of

4. Also see Wolf (*this volume*) for a related analysis.
5. The two perspectives are, of course, older than the models.

the romantic model, for instance, is equally expressed in the following quote from Herder, the model's historical key figure:

> Der schönste Versuch über die Geschichte und mannigfaltige Charakteristik des menschlichen Verstandes und Herzens wäre also eine philosophische Vergleichung der Sprachen; denn in jede derselben ist der Verstand eines Volkes und sein Charakter eingeprägt. [The most superb approach to the history and the manifold characteristics of the human mind and heart would thus be the philosophical comparison of the languages, for in each of them is inscribed a people's mind and character].
>
> (Herder 1991 [1784–1791]: 185; our translation)

and the following parallel statement by Pattanayak (2003a), a contemporary proponent of romantic positions:

> The mother tongue is the expression of one's own identity as well as of one's primary group identity. Knowledge and experience are shared among the primary group members through language. (Pattanayak 2003a: 25)

Likewise, the view of language as, primarily, a medium of communication is as fundamental to early proponents of the rationalist model, e.g. Grégoire (see Geeraerts 2003 for discussion), as it is to contemporary rationalist approaches, as evidenced by numerous quotations throughout our paper.

From the cognitive-linguistic perspective we take in our subsequent discussion, the models' different foci may be captured by two conceptual metaphors: LANGUAGE AS A TOOL on the one hand, and LANGUAGE AS IDENTITY MARKER, on the other hand.[6] It has been noted elsewhere (see e.g. Dirven, Polzenhagen and Wolf 2007) that scientific theories may generally be characterised by specific underlying conceptual metaphors. These metaphors convey and express the particular perspectives these theories take on their subject matter. In Dirven, Polzenhagen and Wolf (2007), we distinguish between the heuristic function of such metaphors, with a limited scope, and the paradigmatic status, where a particular set of metaphors plays a truly constitutive role in a theory.[7]

---

6. For the case of English, further specific metaphors that guided the view of this language over the centuries are outlined by various authors, e.g. Eggington (1997), Romaine (1997), Yajun (2002), and Berthele (*this volume*).
7. Furthermore, scientific theories frequently seek their source domains in other sciences. Consider the case of the highly frequent language metaphors in modern biology, as discussed in Dirven, Polzenhagen and Wolf (2007). *Inter alia*, strong analogies between living beings and the Saussurian model of

One may argue that the two above metaphors are too vague to adequately capture the linguistic bases of the models. In particular, the tool metaphor may well be seen as guiding a specific pronunciation of the romantic conception, too. Language would then be metaphorised, against a functionalist background, as a TOOL FOR EXPRESSING IDENTITY.[8] We accept this possible criticism to a large extent and make it the input for some considerations on the issue of the language-identity link.

The tool metaphor in the strict rationalist sense implies that the relation between language and identity is, in principle, arbitrary. As we will see, all the rationalist core views of global languages are derived from this premise. From the perspective of the romantic model, however, the identity-language link would rather be assumed to be indexical, i.e. that particular linguistic features are used as markers that signal group membership in social (re)cognition. Labov (1972), in his seminal studies on vowel peculiarities in Martha's Vineyard and on the distribution of the r-sounds in New York department stores, was the first to give a systematic account of linguistic features along these lines. And Kristiansen (*this volume* and 2003) provides a fully-fledged cognitive-linguistic framework for the analysis of the role and status of such markers in social cognition and categorisation. It is important to notice that the emphasis on the identity-marking function of language is, in this respect, in line with the folk perception of language: For the individual speaker or a given group the language-identity link is "psychologically real" and certainly bound to specific markers. We take it to be a particular strength of the romantic approach that it strives to capture and valorise this folk perception of the language-identity relationship and to give it a scientific treatment.

---

language have been suggested. Here, mappings are proposed, amongst other things, from *langue* to *genotype*, *parole* to *phenotype*, *new words* to *new mutations*, *linguistic communication* to *genetic communication, signifiant* to *DNA triplets*, *morpheme* to *gene*. Note the advantages and limits of these mappings. If, for instance, the gene is seen in analogy to a morpheme as the smallest meaning-bearing unit, this fails to account for the substantial and not abstract nature of a gene and misses the fact that a gene is only truly meaningful through and in the process of its biochemical interpretation. Without the appropriate interpretation device, it is no more than a DNA sequence. The language metaphors in biology have a counterpart in linguistics, namely the biological model of language to be discussed later in our paper.

8. We are indebted to Gitte Kristiansen for drawing our attention to this crucial point in a personal comment.

Seeing the link between identity and linguistic markers as indexical, however, implies contiguity of the two, and precisely not arbitrariness.[9] Language, then, is not just a mere tool. Here, the romantic conception differs decisively from the rationalist premise. Contiguity, however, is a broad notion, covering several types of relation and various degrees of closeness. In a strong interpretation of contiguity, the expression of identity would not be regarded as a *function* but rather as a *property* of language. Then, the underlying conceptualisation of the relation between language and identity is that of an interchangeable metonymy: LANGUAGE FOR IDENTITY and IDENTITY FOR LANGUAGE, respectively. As we shall see later, this "property" view frequently results in an undue leap from the functions of language to language itself, conflating language, language use and language user.[10] With respect to the immediate concern of our paper, this perspective may lead proponents of the romantic model to the interpretation of language shift as a *per se* threat to and loss of one's identity.

In fact, however, also from a romantic point of view, identity markers may be perceived as "largely arbitrary" when a diachronic and dynamic perspective is taken. Diachronically speaking, such markers will always come up and change, and from the global perspective of a social group there is virtually no threat of losing or running short of them. Most importantly, there is thus no intrinsic link to a specific form with which identity is marked linguistically. Against the background of such a dynamic functional view, one may hence speak of the TOOL metaphor (expressing identity) also within the LANGUAGE AS IDENTITY MARKER paradigm. Kristiansen (2003) is representative of this approach.

In sum, there are good reasons for maintaining the tool metaphor in order to capture the conflicting views. The dividing line, however, is not just between the two models, but rather inside the romantic one, too. The former yields the distinction between the dominant conception of language as a TOOL FOR COMMUNICATION on the rationalist side and as

9. For Cognitive Linguistics, contiguity, be it causal, spatial or else, is the common denominator of all phenomena that fall within the range of the indexical principle, including metonymy in its various forms. The indexical principle is distinguished from the iconic principle, where the form-meaning relation is motivated, roughly speaking, by analogy or similarity, and the symbolic principle with an arbitrary meaning-form relation (cf. Dirven and Verspoor 2004).
10. It needs to be stressed that authors like Labov and Kristiansen are completely alien to such a conflation.

a TOOL FOR EXPESSING IDENTITY in the dynamic romantic model. Both perspectives take a functional approach to language. The latter dividing line distinguishes, within the romantic model, the static property view, on the one hand, and the dynamic functional TOOL interpretation on the other hand. This distinction may be captured in the following table:

Table 2. The romantic model: Conceptions of language

	The romantic model
general focus	expression of identity
function view	focus on identity/expressive function language as a tool for expressing identity
property view	language for identity identity for language

Generally speaking, it is difficult to perceive how these two perspectives – the dynamic functional view and the static property view – are compatible against a romantic background. In actual language policy, they may lead to virtually opposite paths: The static property interpretation yields a strict preservationist approach, whereas the dynamic interpretation would not subscribe to this imperative.

Earlier in this section, we noted that scientific theories may generally be characterised by the conceptual metaphors they draw upon, as these metaphors convey and express the specific perspectives these theories take on their subject matter. We argue for the heuristic function and value of conceptual metaphors in science and, at the same time, strive to draw attention to their limits. Most importantly, conceptual metaphors are well known to display particular highlighting-and-hiding effects, i.e. they emphasise certain aspects of their target domain and, in turn, bar other perspectives on the target. Thus the exclusive recourse to a certain set of metaphors faces the inherent danger of yielding a one-sided perspective on the target domain. Our subsequent discussion needs to be read against this background. Both metaphors, the rationalist LANGUAGE AS A TOOL FOR COMMUNICATION and the romantic LANGUAGE AS IDENTITY MARKER, represent fully legitimate, fruitful and, from a heuristic point of view, equally valuable perspectives on the target language and it is not our endeavour to man the barricade on either side. We do, however, strictly argue against the static property interpretation outlined above.

The above considerations suggest that the two models are mutually exclusive and that there is no meeting place between them. Historically, however, there was a remarkable convergence in the issues of nation building and of national languages during the 19th century (cf. Geeraerts 2003 from a linguistic vantage point; and Koenig 1999 from the perspective of a political and social analyst), and this convergence is still observable in present language policies. The notion of nationalism as such (i.e., generally speaking, the ideology that a state should be nation; Gccraerts 2003: 45) was agreeable to both models, though from different perspectives. In the logic of the rationalist model, as Koenig (1999: I.2) rightly observes, the modern nation state promised to replace bonds of particularistic solidarity by formal citizenship founded on presupposed universalistic norms, especially individual rights. The ideal was hence a civic model of a nation state, with a de-ethnicised public space in which social integration may be achieved and in which social conflicts may be resolved democratically. This civic nation state thus derives its legitimacy through a system of political representation and through active participation by the citizens (Geeraerts 2003: 45). From the perspective of the romantic model, the notion of a nation state was agreeable, as it promised the articulation of the shared cultural identity of a people, the "Volksgeist", characterised by common historical origin and destiny, shared culture, mentality and customs and, not least, a common language (Koenig 1999: I.2). This "identity nationalism", as Geeraerts (2003: 45 f.) calls it, thus envisaged an ethnic nation state, which derives its legitimacy from a people's cultural identity.

It is important to notice that both models of nationalism and nation building, the civic and the ethnic, have supposed a strong degree of cohesion on the societal level (Koenig 1999: I.2). With respect to language policy, this is manifest in their strict upholding of the ideal of monolingualism. In their assumption of homogeneity, both models contain an inherent oppressive element in their attitude towards social and linguistic groups that do not conform to the presupposed cohesion of society. Koenig (1999: II.2) distinguishes between two variants of this oppressive element: the assimilationist approach, which seeks to integrate and absorb "deviant" social and linguistic groups that threaten social cohesion into the politically dominant "mainstream", and the differentialist, i.e. exclusionist, approach, which strives at defending the pre-defined social mainstream by systematically excluding "deviant" groups. Assimilationist and exclusionist approaches pertain to both the rationalist and the romantic model in their nationalist pronunciation.

The nationalist stages of the two models may thus be summarised in the following table based on Geeraerts (2003: 40, 55):

Table 3. Rationalist versus romantic model: The nationalist stage

	The rationalist model	The romantic model
conception of the nation	the nation as the basis of a liberal democracy	the nation as the focus of cultural identity
conception of national language	national language as a neutral medium of social participation and emancipation	national language as the medium of expressing a common "Volksgeist"
conception of language variation	language variation / multilingualism as an impediment to emancipation	language variation / multilingualism as an impediment to common identity

The supposition of cohesion and homogeneity certainly was no more than a comfortable illusion even in the 19th century, and it proves to be the more untenable faced with the post-modern experience of diversity and diversification. Still, both nationalist models continue to guide contemporary language policies in a considerable number of countries. A discussion of two case studies is given in Dirven and Polzenhagen (2004): the official-English policy in the U.S. vis-à-vis immigrant groups, which would count, in Koenig's (1999) terms, as an assimilationist approach against the background of the civic model (also see Berthele *this volume*), and the Kyrgyz language policy in the early 1990s, which illustrates an exclusionist approach based on the ethnic model. These two case studies also illustrate two of the present multilingual challenges: a multilingual situation in a traditionally multi-ethnic region and, respectively, a multilingual situation arising from large-scale migration. A third, and closely related challenge is globalisation, which is the specific focus of our present paper.

2. Rationalist and romantic views of global languages

Geeraerts (2003: 52) cautiously expresses the view that multiculturalism and multilingualism may become a second possible meeting place between the two models. Ideally, this would lead to the mutual reinforcement of efforts in favour of a global pluralist approach. However, in the present state of the discussions, the two transformed versions of the models are only about to be developed. Consequently, the debate is often characterised by programmatic statements which tend to stress diverging points rather than seek common ground with the adversary approach. In our discussion, we focus on two issues which we perceive to erect frontiers between the two competing models. They are closely related and, to a significant degree, legacies of earlier stages of the models. Firstly, we observe, among proponents of the two approaches, the withdrawal to narrow understandings of the linguistic-philosophical basis of the respective model. Secondly, and this will be discussed more specifically in section 4, we notice the tendency to measure languages along some ideologically motivated value matrix. We argue that these two issues need to be critically reconsidered in the further development of the two models. It needs to be stressed that we are not concerned with approaches that still uphold the monolingual principle; rather, we focus on approaches that have incorporated a positive understanding of multilingualism and multiculturalism. In the following, we provide a discussion of rationalist and romantic views of global languages, against the background of the underlying LANGUAGE AS A TOOL and LANGUAGE AS IDENTITY MARKER conceptions, respectively.

In line with the strong commitment to the functionalist tradition, the views held by the rationalist model focus on the role of language as an instrument for wider communication crystallised in the key metaphor of LANGUAGE AS A TOOL (cf. section 1). Historically, this rationalist view got its first political realisation in the French Revolution with its programme of taking the Enlightenment ideals of liberty of the citizen and his thoughts, of bourgeois equality, and of national and international brotherhood to the whole country and even to the whole world. We find clear echoes of these ideals in the American discourse on spreading the benefits of present-day democratisation, e.g. to Asia and Africa. In both instances, this expansion has led to rationalist policies aiming at monolingualism and overall homogeneity. Still, this monolingualist interpretation of the rationalist model is rather the conservative one. A more progressive interpretation of the rationalist model takes into account the exigencies of language needs both in the primary and secondary domains of life, which can be served by different varieties of one and the same language or by different languages. Here we can and must also distinguish between the international and the national levels.

With respect to the international level, global languages such as English are seen as neutral means of world-wide communication, most prominently by authors like Kachru (e.g. 1986) and Crystal (1997).[11] In con-

11. Note that the identity function of language is fully recognised in Crystal (1997), too. In his more recent publications, the language-as-identity perspective is even more prominent, and the author also adopts some of the biological metaphors.

trast to romantic positions discussed below, the rationalist model does not see any intrinsic correlation nor causal link between the use of a particular 'bridge' language and extra-linguistic factors such as power or socio-cultural identity. Language is regarded, in principle, as dissociated and detachable from these symbolic factors, i.e. merely functioning as a TOOL OF WIDER COMMUNICATION. With respect to global English, this *lingua franca* function is expressed in the following statements by House (2001):

> True, there may still be attempts by "inner circle" English native speakers to perpetuate old dichotomies of "us and them", of one-way translation avenues, of controlling access to professional organisations and publications. *But this has nothing to do with the English language itself, which is neutral.* Such imbalance simply reflects unequal power resulting from differences in social, economic, political, or scientific conditions.
> (House 2001: n.p.; our emphasis)

According to House, English already serves this *lingua franca* role, for instance, in Europe:

> English as a lingua franca is nothing more than a *useful tool*: it is a "language for communication", a medium that is given substance with the different national, regional, local and individual cultural identities its speakers bring to it. *English itself does not carry such identities, it is not a "language for identification".* (House 2001: n.p.; our emphasis)[12]

Seen in this perspective, the tool metaphor does not deny issues of power relations and identity. At the national level, national or native languages can still be seen and are seen as truly embedded in the respective socio-cultural and political settings and the analysis of these settings is, of course, an integral part of the rationalist-functionalist approach.

From the rationalist perspective, the adoption of a language of wider communication for higher domains of life is first of all induced by the speakers' spontaneous, albeit often unconscious, cost-benefit considerations which must balance communicative, socio-economic and cultural

---

12. On the notions "language for identification" and "language for communication" see House (2003).

needs.[13] The emphasis is thus on the speakers' priorities and potential gains rather than on their potential losses, which are often estimated incorrectly in romantic approaches, as we shall see later. This more general difference in focus is vividly emphasised in the following statements by Mufwene (2002),[14] who is speaking on the basis of his African experience:

> Linguists have typically bemoaned loss of linguistic, especially typological, diversity. Rarely have they focussed on speakers themselves in terms of motivation and costs and benefits to them in giving up their languages. Seldom have they addressed the question of whether the survival of a language would entail more adequate adaptations of its speakers to the changing socio-economic ecologies. They have decried the loss of ancestral cultures as if cultures were static systems and the emergence of new ones in response to changing ecologies was necessarily maladaptive.
> (Mufwene 2002: 21–22)

> To suggest that native speakers will maintain or preserve their culture if they continue speaking their language is to ignore the fact that in the first place they would not stop speaking it if they valued its association with their ancestral culture over their necessary adaptation to the current world order – a simple matter of prioritising things in their struggle for survival.
> (Mufwene 2002: 23)

Here, the cultural dimension of language is seen to be but one of several factors that need to be considered, and not necessarily the central one. Furthermore, and crucially, proponents of the rationalist model hold that cultural identity is not *per se* linked to a particular language, which means that one can change one's language, but keep one's cultural identity. Historical examples include the Irish, the Scots, and, to a lesser degree, the Welsh in the British Isles. On a wider plane, English has become the carrier of many cultures, religions, value systems, and of different,

---

13. Cases where a speech community gives up its language completely, in favour of another one, rather than shifting to bilingualism, would then also be seen as the result of a cost-benefit balancing. Mufwene (2002: 26), for instance, gives the following assessment of such cases: "Not everyone has a vested interest in speaking more than one language."
14. Mufwene (2002) represents a mid-position between the two models, in that he adopts much of the ecology-of-language view and, to a significant degree, the biological metaphors of language, but incorporates many of the rationalist arguments.

even antagonistic, political systems. As House (2001: n.p.) puts it, "The point is that we can no longer say that English is one monolithic, 'hegemonic' voice, it is a diversity of different voices." Mufwene (2002), in the same vein, criticises the romantic model's counter-position:

> The position in the average literature is also tantamount to assuming that language and culture go hand in hand, that only one language can best mirror or convey a particular culture, and that another language cannot be adapted to convey it. (Mufwene 2002: 23)

He cites the examples of African English and African French as illustrations of languages' cultural contextualisation. In some respect, this may be less felicitous, since one can hardly say that anywhere in Africa either English or French have completely taken over. They are still almost exclusively second-language varieties. And although spoken, with various degrees of proficiency, by up to 20 or 30 per cent of the indigenous population, they clearly are the languages of the elites, and serve, first of all, the higher domains in life.[15] Note, though, that these varieties show distinct marks of culture-specific conceptualisations (cf., e.g., Wolf 2001; Wolf and Polzenhagen 2007; Polzenhagen and Wolf 2007 for the case of African English). And cultural contextualisation does not necessarily imply the achievement of mother-tongue status, i.e. replacement of other languages. However the present and future role of the former colonial languages is to be assessed, from the perspective of the rationalist model, even the shift towards another language is not *per se* equated with the loss of the speakers' cultural identity, as attested most prominently by the Irish or the Scottish cultures.

It needs to be stressed that the objective of the progressive rationalist model is not to induce such shifts towards the dominant and socio-economically advantageous language. In contrast to earlier stages of the model, the LANGUAGE AS A TOOL metaphor is now employed for a positive perception of multilingualism, in terms of functional specialisation. In the context of English as a global language, this is illustrated by the following statement by House (2001):

---

15. It is a typical African phenomenon that 80 to 90 per cent of the population thus remain systematically excluded from participation in the power and knowledge structures of the nation, because these are accessible only in the former colonial languages. This is an absolute flouting of the rationalist commitment to broad social participation. See Dirven and Pütz (2007) for discussion.

> There is no need to set up an old-fashioned dichotomy between local languages and English as the "hegemonic aggressor": there is a place for both, because they fulfil different functions. To deny this is to uphold outdated concepts of monolingual societies and individuals. (House 2001: n.p.)

The identity function of language is then primarily ascribed to the national or local native languages. And, as House (2001) argues, the presence of a global language may even strengthen this identificational dimension:

> Paradox as this may seem, the very spread of English can motivate speakers of other languages to insist on their own local language for identification, for binding them emotionally to their own cultural and historical tradition. (House 2001: n.p.)

More precisely, the identity function resides in speech forms that mark group membership, and this even applies to social and regional varieties of the same language. While there is no denying the fact that local varieties of English, for instance, adopt features from the globally present external norms (AmE and BrE), there is a parallel development towards divergence and towards local distinctiveness.[16]

Against this background, the rationalist model's view of English as a global language is, though not uncritical, largely positive. Also, English and other international languages are not regarded as a *per se* lethal threat to local languages in the post-colonial world, as often assumed in the romantic model. Generally, this threat is seen to be less significant by proponents of the rational model.[17] Mufwene (2002), for instance, ob-

16. Meyerhoff and Niedzielski (2003) provide a critical discussion of the view of Global English as a "category killer" and its impact on variationist sociolinguistics. Specifically they make note the eagerness to attribute, against the background of this view, the emergence of certain features in local varieties of English to the pressure of the dominant external varieties AmE and BrE. They suggest that linguistic variables hitherto analysed as being the consequence of globalisation might partly be better thought of as reflecting a broadening of the vernacular base, i.e. as local processes. Their examples are recent developments in New Zealand English.
17. The same applies to the threat ascribed to standard languages with respect to non-standard varieties. Mufwene (2002), for instance, notes that the presence of an American English standard language does not seriously affect the "vitality", to apply a biological metaphor, of varieties like Appalachian English or African American Vernacular English (AAVE).

serves that the threat-scenario only applies to settings where English is spoken as a vernacular, i.e. in what he calls former "settlement colonies". In former "exploitation colonies", however, where the use of English had been restricted to a small set of domains and a relatively small number of speakers, the situation appears to be markedly different:

> Anyone who claims that the spread of English around the world endangers indigenous languages should explain how this is possible in countries where [as already hinted at before] it is only a lingua franca of an elite minority but is barely spoken by the vast majority, or a large proportion, of the population. (Mufwene 2002: 8; our addition)

In such settings, the shift to dominant prestigious local languages as national languages rather than a shift to English or French constitutes a potential threat to small indigenous languages. Examples of such dominant local languages include Wolof in Senegal / Gambia and Swahili in East Africa (see Mufwene 2002: 16; on Wolofisation see Peter and Wolf 2003). Thus, the decrease of linguistic diversity should not *per se* and not only be attributed to the impact of English and other international languages but equally well, and perhaps primarily, to the dominance of certain indigenous national language(s). Furthermore, proponents of the rationalist model point to the fact that globalisation has inspired and continues to inspire a specific new diversity, i.e. the diversification of the former colonial languages in indigenised, regional varieties of English, French, Portuguese, etc. As House (2001) observes:

> English is no longer "owned" by its native speakers because acculturation and nativisation processes have produced a remarkable diversification of the English language into many non-native varieties. (House 2001: n.p.)

A major objection against global English made by proponents of the romantic model is the claim that global languages, parallel to standard languages, are means of social exclusion and division (cf. Table 1). Advocates of the rationalist model do acknowledge this threat for third-world countries, where the socio-economic split may partially coincide with a language split. But in Europe and most parts of Asia, they argue, English may also have a unifying role, as expressed in the following statement by House (2001) with respect to English in Europe:

> Using English as a lingua franca in Europe does not inhibit linguistic diversity, and it unites more than it divides, simply because it may be "owned"

> by all Europeans – not as a cultural symbol, but a means of enabling understanding. (House 2001: n.p.)

The potential unifying function of English is, however, also observed in particular post-colonial contexts. It is, for instance, well-known that English functioned as the language of several liberation movements world-wide (see Brutt Griffler 2002 for discussion). A clear illustration is provided by the South African example, where English became the language of the anti-Apartheid movement, especially stimulated by the ANC (African National Congress), precisely because it allowed to bridge ethnic boundaries and counter the tribalisation policy under the Apartheid regime.[18] Here, after the 1976 Soweto revolt, whereby black pupils refused to be taught in Afrikaans as the medium of instruction, English became a symbolic counterweight against the oppressor language Afrikaans and even functioned, to a significant degree, as a symbol of group identity beyond ethnicity. Likewise, in the post-colonial context, numerous L2 English-speaking communities without a common mother tongue have emerged. Here, being anglophone may constitute a strong sense of group identity, as Wolf (2001) shows for the case of Cameroon, a country with a clear anglophone-francophone division.

In spite of its possible merits, from a critical perspective, some reservations need to be made with respect to the LANGUAGE AS A TOOL OF WIDER COMMUNICATION metaphor. When it is employed unduly, we observe two major possible shortcomings. The first, and most evident pitfall is that of functional reductionism, where the exclusive emphasis on the mere

18. South Africa is far from being the only example where English functioned as the language of a liberation movement. The underlying argument that English is, at least to a large degree, ethnically unmarked is generally made by proponents of the rationalist view in order to justify the special status and the promotion of English in post-colonial countries, as a common *lingua franca*, and also as a language of the public sphere. This argument is evidently weakened by the fact that English is not distributed evenly among the numerous ethnic groups. Closely related, the relative unmarkedness of English in ethnic terms sharply contrasts with the language's strong social markedness in these settings. From the perspective of the rationalist model, however, social markedness is certainly perceived to be the less problematic case, given, too, that this model's endeavours are directed precisely to the reduction of unequal access to social participation via the promotion of standardised languages of the public sphere. Ideally, social markedness would gradually diminish then, whereas attempts to reduce ethnic markedness and the related resentments appear to be a lost cause.

tool character of language may lead to a neglect of other dimensions of language, in particular its identity function. As the above discussion has shown, this is, however, less present in the progressive version of the rationalist model. The tool metaphor is, however, taken to its extreme by advocates of a "culturally neutral" or even a culture-free international English. This is an altogether dubious concept. If the notion of intercultural communication is supposed to be meaningful, it is precisely the understanding of one's and others' culture that is at stake. Furthermore, from a cognitive-linguistic perspective, the very notion of a "culturally neutral" language is an oddity. A speaker's underlying cultural models and cultural conceptualisations will always find expression in his or her specific language use. Linguistic material is never void of conceptual contents. The universality of certain conceptualisations notwithstanding, there is no set of "neutral" cognitive models among or in between those entrenched in the various cultures. And even if the same linguistic expressions are used, they may convey largely different conceptualisations embedded in the respective background culture.[19]

Secondly, certain well-known deterministic assumptions may be derived from the tool metaphor. Such claims maintain that particular languages are, due to their specific linguistic properties, more suitable tools of communication than others, either generally in all domains or, minimally, in specific domains. Pennycook (1998: Ch. 5) provides a critical review of such arguments made by certain advocates of English as a world language. Assumptions of this kind echo the well-known colonial discourse on the supremacy of the English language. These arguments include the alleged simplicity of English grammar and morphology, the size of its vocabulary, etc. Language-intrinsic arguments of this kind need to be seen as a distortion of the rationalist model, as they leave its functionalist basis. In many respects, this parallels the distortion we observe in the romantic model due to the adoption of what was termed the "property" view above (cf. Table 2). But it is certainly not justified to extend this reproach to proponents of the progressive stage of the rationalist model. Pennycook (1998: 134), for example, suggests remnants of the supremacy argument in the work of prominent authors like Crystal, who certainly represents many of the progressive rationalist positions. Here, Pennycook's reproach is difficult to comprehend, in the light of numerous

19. For cognitive-linguistic case studies on conceptual differences, similarities and universals across languages and cultures see, e.g., Alverson (1994), Yu (1998) and Kövecses (2002).

statements by Crystal, as the following most recent one, which is very explicit on this point:

> It is often suggested, for example, that there must be something inherently beautiful or logical about the structure of English, in order to explain why it is now so widely used. [...] Such arguments are misconceived. [...] A language does not become a global language because of its intrinsic structural properties, or because of the size of its vocabulary, or because it has been a vehicle of a great literature in the past, or because it was once associated with a great culture or religion. (Crystal 2003: 7, 9)

The supremacy argument, however, is certainly not absent in the public discourse. Here, its persistence and continuity in all its various forms that Pennycook (1998) sees and describes from the colonial to the present time, may indeed be observed. This may also extend to institutions, as targeted in the critical discussions by authors like Phillipson (1992) and Pennycook (1998).

As a general problem, the rationalist approach is often in conflict with the folk perception of language. Seeing global English as a "neutral" medium of communication, for instance, may certainly be justified from a linguistic point of view, given that in a *lingua franca* the communicative function is evidently foregrounded. However, the neutrality assumption is clearly at odds with the fact that in the perception of people all over the world the English language *is* charged with a whole range of associations and stereotypes. As Edwards (2004: 1, citing William Mackey) puts it: "A language is neutral only before God and the linguist." This points to yet another crucial dimension: One needs to distinguish between the public "folk" conception, the view held by institutions and the linguist's "expert" model of language and language policy. Each of these dimensions has its own matrix, driving forces and impact.

After having discussed key positions of the rationalist approach, we now turn to views held against the background of the romantic model. As Geeraerts (2003: 52) rightly observes, the overcoming of the nationalist thrust within this model and thus the shift to a positive understanding of multilingualism and multiculturalism is closely related to the postmodernist notion of "fragmented identity". The essence of this notion may be captured as follows, in terms of Social Identity Theory (e.g. Tajfel 1978): It is not a question of having *one* identity; rather we have *multiple* social identities (with respect to gender, regional origin, social background, etc.). A particular social identity may be salient at a given time and in a given context, and others may be backgrounded. Seen from the perspective of the LANGUAGE AS IDENTITY MARKER paradigm, a speaker can enact these identities through language, emphasising the particular "layers" of those multiple identities at his/her convenience, through the linguistic means available. This applies both at the monolingual level and at the multilingual level. In each language community there is ample inner sociolinguistic variation. Such dialectal or sociolectal variation may be an important instrument, as Kristiansen (2003) has shown, for social and regional identification. Dialects and sociolects in so-called monolingual countries thus serve in face-to-face interaction as answers to such questions as "Who is this speaker? Where is s/he from? How do I have to speak to him/her?". In strong contrast to most studies on stereotypes carried out so far, Kristiansen (2003) thus sees dialectal and sociolectal variation and the allophones marking a particular stereotype as cognitive reference points in social cognition. In this way phonetic variants form part of larger cognitive structures, which in turn relate to social categorisations and self-categorisation. Seen from a listener-oriented perspective, the cognitive need for social categorisation effects a need for dialectal and sociolectal variants, which cluster in a set of salient and uniquely identifying variants and are signifiers of social meaning. This positive view also holds for the stereotypes associated with wide-spread regional and social accents and the covert ideology encapsulated in them. A progressive version like e.g. Kristiansen's acknowledges the functional role and functional necessity of non-standard varieties and the standard variety alike.[20] By way of analogy, national languages and varieties also fulfil certain roles and needs that are not incompatible with the functional role of a super-national variety.

This insight can be applied to multilingual situations with more strongly differing languages or language forms as expressing the various layers of identification of an individual and a group, in line with the postmodernist notion of "fragmented identities". It is important to notice that these identities are not necessarily in conflict with each other. Such an interpretation comes close to views held, for instance, by Pattanayak (2003b):

20. An early statistical proof of multifunctionality is Labov's (1966) analysis of AAVE and Standard American English (AmE). AAVE was found to cover three of five speech styles (intimate, casual, informal) and AmE two styles (formal style, reading style).

> A monolingual identity stretches from an idiolect to a language.[21] A multilingual identity extends from the language of intimacy through the language of proximity to languages of regional, national and international identification. [...] In this scenario, each language can be seen as the medium of more than one culture, as each culture can find expression through more than one language. (Pattanayak 2003b: 33)

The identification function of language thus works at many levels, more precisely through different languages as much as through different group lects of one language.

This gives room for a more positive evaluation of globally spreading languages against the background of the romantic model. For instance, distinct L2 varieties of English that have developed or are about to develop in countries belonging to what Kachru (e.g. 1986) termed the "outer circle" would then be seen, parallel to dialectal and sociolectal variation in the English-speaking "inner circle" countries and to the core native varieties, as marking specific regional and cultural identities and as arising from the cognitive need of social categorisation. So far, however, this approach is only beginning to be explored in the field of the New Englishes. A beginning is also made in the exploration of how specific cultural conceptualisations are linguistically manifest in the second-language varieties.[22]

Generally, research on the New Englishes and on indigenisation processes, i.e. what Pennycook (2003a, 2003b) refers to as the "heterogeny" paradigm, is regarded with much reservation by proponents of the romantic approach. It is rather associated with the rationalist framework. Given the romantic model's emphasis on and commitment to linguistic diversity, it is altogether surprising that this dimension of diversity is widely ignored. Some exceptions need to be made here, in particular the ecolinguistic approach represented by Mühlhäusler, and the "worldliness" approach represented by Pennycook (e.g. 1994, 2003a, 2003b). Mühlhäusler (e.g. 1996a) adheres to a dynamic view of language, indebted to Humboldt,[23] and to a strongly functional view, indebted to

21. One may argue that one should rather stay at the level of group languages, which would not include "idiolect". Furthermore, idiolect is a primarily stylistic notion.
22. See Wolf and Polzenhagen (2007) and Polzenhagen and Wolf (2007) for some case studies on African English, and Sharifian (*this volume*, 2003) on Australian Aboriginal English.
23. On the ecolinguistic reading of Humboldt, see, however, Mühlhäusler (2000).

Einar Haugen and the tradition of functional sociolinguistics.[24] Both these perspectives are explicit in Mühlhäusler's central concern "how languages adapt to changing environmental conditions" (2001: 137). Postcolonial English and its nativisation processes are one of his major objects of study. For the settings he investigates, his assessment, however, is largely negative and he argues that the spread of Global English has further slowed down the adaptation process of the local forms of English. With respect to English in Pitcairn, for instance, Mühlhäusler (2003) states:

> The naturalization and adaptation of English, its adaptation to its new environment in the shape of the Pitkern language [the local English-related creole] was slowed down, suppressed and nearly eradicated as a consequence of the constant dominance of metropolitan language models.
> (Mühlhäusler 2003: 78)[25]

His conclusion is explicitly made in opposition to the rationalist key perception:

> The view that language is a neutral medium of intercommunication is a problematic one. English is not a language that can cope equally well with all situations – as an additional language English has clear limitations, as a replacement language it brings with it many dangers.
> (Mühlhäusler 2003: 78)

A more positive stance is taken by Pennycook (2003a, 2003b), against the background of the postmodernist notion of "worldliness". "Worldly English", for Pennycook (2003a: 15), is the English adopted, adapted, transformed, reinvented and rearticulated by the local people to their advantage (cf. also Blommaert 2003: 609–610). It is part of the process in which, to use the postmodernist diction, the global is enacted locally. This view rejects the simplistic homogeny paradigm[26] in that it recognises

24. It needs to be stressed that we fully share the commitment to a dynamic and functional view of language.
25. This addresses the controversial issue of standards. Here, an endonormative approach, which acknowledges, accounts for, and supports the nativisation process, is required rather than the upholding of exonormative standards.
26. Here, Pennycook argues against the tendency, in the romantic model, to see the global spread of languages like English from the "homogeny" position, i.e. the view that it is leading to the homogenising of world culture (see, e.g., most prominently Phillipson 1992).

the diversity of the effects of globalisation, including diversification of English. It goes beyond the heterogeny paradigm in that it sees worldly English explicitly as a resistance and counter-movement to globalisation and as part of the de-colonising process (see Brutt-Griffler 2002: 73, 144 f. for discussion):

> On the one hand, then, we have a way of focusing on the process of globalization that does not merely reduce it to homogenization. This is a far more complex version of the spread of English, its institutionalization, and its role relative to other languages, than some versions of globalization would suggest. But it is also a version that allows for a critique of this process: It does highlight the politics, the inequalities, the cultural effects of English. (Pennycook 2003a: 15)

Seeing the New Englishes positively as a response to the challenges of globalisation, is also the position expressed in the following statement by Romaine (1997):

> Because national identity is not a permanent or static possession, it has to be continually reinvented. World Englishes will continue to evolve to meet the challenge. (Romaine 1997: xv)

Our discussion so far reflects both the traditional focus of the romantic model, i.e. the language-identity link, and the strong commitment to anti-ideological criticism in the model's contemporary pronunciation (cf. Table 1). The latter focus is programmatically expressed in the following statement by Romaine (1997), with respect to the issue of standard languages:

> "contingencies of language, rhetoric, ideology and power need to be openly and honestly confronted." We must be fully conscious of how language standards and standard English especially have developed against particular ideological assumptions rather than take them as neutral, objective and universally valid.
> (Romaine 1997: xi, quoting Dissanayake in the same volume)

and this critical approach is extended to the issue of global languages. It has inspired a rich sociolinguistically oriented literature dealing critically with views of language and language policy on the various dimensions. To name only a few examples: Views held by national and international institutions and programmes are critically examined e.g. in Pennycook (1994) and Calvet (1998), including a historical perspective. Both authors also provide a criticism of "expert" models advocated by professional linguists over the centuries. Phillipson (1992) looks, more narrowly, at the ELT profession. Language legislation and its ideological implications are the scope of Skutnabb-Kangas (e.g. 2000). The latter also pays much attention to the folk perception of language and language policy. Many controversial aspects notwithstanding, this literature has produced valuable insights into the ideologies underlying language policies.

What marks these approaches as representative of the romantic paradigm is not only their critical concern with imperialist tendencies in Global English but mainly their metonymic substitution of LANGUAGE for IDENTITY. Further parallel conceptualisations include LANGUAGE FOR POWER, LANGUAGE FOR IDEOLOGY, LANGUAGE FOR WORLD-VIEW, etc. Global English then stands, e.g., for Western world-view, for Western (neo)imperialism, for globalisation, or historically, for Western colonialism. These metonymic associations constitute the decisive difference from the rationalist approach, where such relations, as we have seen, are regarded as, in principle, neutral and arbitrary.

It is extremely important to be aware of the limits and dangers of this dimension of the romantic approach, and of metonymic models in general. In metonymy, as in metaphor, we are dealing with imposed and conceived connections and correspondences between the source and the target. Metonymy, as metaphor, restricts the view of the phenomena involved to a particular perspective. It is, in fact, not just a stand-for relationship. Rather, its essence is that the source serves to sum up the whole of the target (Dirven 2004: 13). As we shall see in section 3, this leads some key proponents of the model to a reductionist view of the English language and its spread and to attacking the language in place of the targeted ideologies.

This interpretation is, however, not a necessary corollary of the LANGUAGE AS IDENTITY MARKER view. Kristiansen's approach to language variation outlined above, for instance, seeing linguistic features as being indicative, i.e. as markers of socio-cultural identity and analysing their role in social cognition, definitely rejects any such implications. Likewise, it is well-known that certain linguistic features may indicate particular ideologies, world-view and power relations (see Dirven, Polzenhagen and Wolf 2007 for an overview of critical cognitive-linguistic work done in this field).

3. Distortions of the romantic model: Neo-Whorfianism and the biological metaphor[27]

We need to stress that our following, highly critical account of certain positions held against the background of the romantic model is not directed against the LANGUAGE AS IDENTITY MARKER view *per se*. Rather, we object to two highly controversial linguistic concepts that have infiltrated the romantic model's linguistic basis, and which, we argue, are a serious distortion of the model's original values. Firstly, there is a certain neo-Whorfian line of argument, as an ingredient of what was called "property" view in section 1, and secondly, there is an almost complete re-adoption of a fully-fledged biological model of language. Both positions are highly intertwined. It must be stated that this mixing of the romantic model with the biological metaphor and determinism is by no means a necessary evolution. There are proponents of the LANGUAGE AS IDENTITY MARKER view, and implicitly, of the romantic model who are totally alien to the biological view of language and to determinism.

The biological metaphor of language has a long and well-known tradition in romantic thought (for its role in 19th century linguistics see, e.g., Kucharczik 1998).[28] In its modern form, it is most prominently associated with Einar Haugen and the ecology-of-language view he proposed as an alternative to the models based on the LANGUAGE AS STRUCTURE metaphor and the LANGUAGE AS A TOOL metaphor, respectively (Haugen 1972: 326). These two models became dominant in the second and third quarters of 20th century linguistics, with the rise and spread of structuralism and functionalism, respectively. It is important to notice that Haugen (1972) argues for the biological metaphors in their heuristic function. To put it in cognitive-linguistic terms: They may capture, i.e. "highlight", important aspects of language, which are in turn "hidden" by the models based on LANGUAGE AS STRUCTURE and LANGUAGE AS A TOOL.

Haugen's ecology-of-language view, coupled with a specific application of the LANGUAGE AS ORGANISM metaphor, is constitutive in the recent and meanwhile established ecolinguistic literature. And, inspired by ecol-

27. Whereas the discussion of negative distortions of the romantic model by some of its proponents is foregrounded in the present paper, Dirven and Pütz (2007) goes into the many conflict situations that have arisen as the outcome of the rationalist model.
28. See Dirven, Polzenhagen and Wolf (2007) for a brief discussion of biological metaphors in linguistics.

inguistics, the "Linguistic Human Rights" movement, too, is increasingly characterised by a massive adoption of the ORGANISM metaphor in its various pronunciations.[29] Here, we notice a decisive shift away from the view of biological metaphors as heuristic tools and thus away from the view originally advocated by Haugen (1972). In some dominant strands within the more recent ecolinguistically oriented literature the ecological metaphors are now taken, to a significant degree, literally. Maffi (1998, 2001b), for instance, in her survey of the movement's development, suggests that the relationship between language and ecology is a factual and, explicitly, not a metaphorical one:

> However, in these initial pronouncements, no significant attempt was made to go beyond such parallels and ask whether *there might be more than a metaphorical relationship* between these phenomena. It is only recently that this question has been explicitly asked and the idea proposed that, along with cultural diversity, linguistic diversity should also be seen as inextricably linked to biodiversity.
>
> (Maffi 1998: 12–13, cf. also Maffi 2001b: 7–8; our emphasis)

This view is echoed by organisations like Terralingua and the International Society of Ethnobiology (ISE). In the preamble to the Code of Ethics of the latter, we find the following statement, resonating Maffi (1998):[30]

> The ISE recognises that culture and language are intrinsically connected to land and territory, and cultural and linguistic diversity are inextricably linked to biological diversity. Therefore, the right of Indigenous Peoples to the preservation and continued development of their cultures and languages and to the control of their lands, territories and traditional resources are key to the perpetuation of all forms of diversity on Earth.
>
> (ISE 1998)

Proponents of this view base their argument on the observation that there are "remarkable overlaps between the areas of greatest biological and greatest linguistic and/or cultural diversity around the world" (Nettle

29. The strong recourse to the biological model is most noticeably reflected by the cover illustrations of recent publications by these authors, which use visual versions of the ORGANISM metaphor, e.g. Skutnabb-Kangas' (2000) book on "linguistic genocide", whose cover graphically contrasts prospering and decaying plants. This, however, also applies to Crystal (2000), who uses a visual representation of the "language death" metaphor.
30. Maffi is the president of Terralingua.

and Romaine 2000: 27, also see Harmon[31] 1996, 2001). Studies that follow this approach thus typically present tables that correlate the number of biological species and the number of languages and cultures in some region (for a review, see, e.g., Skutnabb-Kangas 2000: Ch. 2). The argument goes that language, culture and the biological world coevolve as parts of a common overarching ecology. Following the logics of the biological evolution model, they are seen as interrelated, as interdependent and even as determining each other. Skutnabb-Kangas (2000: 91 ff.), for instance, takes observations about a correspondence between the diversity of languages, cultures and biological species in some areas as her starting point to reason about a possible "causal" relationship between language and biological environment (for a discussion, see Lucko 2003).[32] Against the background of the biological model, languages are seen as SPECIES, as AGENTS in an overall ecological system (see below for discussion).

The biological model of language has strong affinities to neo-Whorfian positions. In this paper, we do not wish to add to the list of theoretical considerations on Whorfian and neo-Whorfian positions, – although a clear distinction between these two is in order – nor on the issue of relativity in general.[33] Rather, we focus on some distinguishable relativist and deterministic – also here a clear distinction is needed – strands in the recent literature on post-colonial English. We sketch some basic assumptions of these positions in a rather straightforward way, certainly at the risk of oversimplifying. Such positions are traceable in the ecolinguistic criticism of post-colonial English (e.g. Mühlhäusler 1996a, 1996b,

31. Harmon is the secretary of Terralingua.
32. Some correspondence between these levels of diversity is not surprising (see, e.g., Harmon 1996 and Smith 2001: 105 f. on factors that contribute to this correlation). However, even some ecolinguists caution to assume a too direct relationship. Smith (2001), for instance, who presents data on the correlation between biodiversity and linguistic/cultural diversity in the Native North American Culture area, concludes that "the findings do not seem to support the idea that biodiversity is robustly correlated with either cultural or linguistic diversity" (Smith 2001: 104).
33. For a detailed discussion of Whorf's views, see Lee (1996, 1998). Our own position on the issue of linguistic relativity is close to the one held by Bickel (2000). Recent considerations on the issue of relativity and determinism from a cognitive linguistics perspective are collected in the twin volumes by Pütz and Verspoor (2000) and Niemeier and Dirven (2000). Also see the articles in Gumperz and Levinson (1996).

2001). Again, the "Linguistic Human Rights" movement (e.g. Skutnabb-Kangas and Phillipson 1994; Skutnabb-Kangas 2000; Maffi 2001) and the criticism of so-called "linguistic imperialism" (Phillipson 1992) make use of related arguments. Inherent in these approaches is a highly critical, and often negative, view of the socio-cultural role and function of the English language in the postcolonial context. Basically, English is taken to be isomorphic with Western culture, in line with the logic of what was called "property view" in section 1. These approaches may be termed, with Schmied (1991: 104), "alienationist". Alienationist in two respects: They regard English as "alien" to the respective settings[34] and English is claimed to "alienate" people in the post-colonial world from their own socio-cultural background.

The first claim that is guided by this conception may be termed "habitus" argument, a view which we find expressed in Phillipson (1992: 166). It follows the romantic view of standard and global languages as means of exclusion and domination (cf. Table 1) and makes reference to Bourdieu's (1982) well-known notions of "habitus" and "linguistic market". In Bourdieu's terms, language cannot be detached from the socio-political system that allows for its existence and thus cannot be discussed without considering the impact of power structures and the respective institutions like school, bureaucracy, etc. The socio-political dimension is taken to be linguistically crucial. According to Bourdieu, its norms are internalised ("embodied") and constitute a system of dispositions that are reproduced by the speaker in any of his/her linguistic acts – the "linguistic habitus."[35] Transferring Bourdieu's (1982) criticism of the historical French policy of standard language to the global spread of English, Phillipson (1992: 166) states that "what is at stake when English spreads is not merely the substitution or displacement of one language by another but the imposition of new 'mental structures' through English" (Phillipson 1992: 166). Generally, Phillipson (1992) sees English as inseparable

34. When coupled with the biological model of language, this view regards English just like in evolutionary biology alien species are seen as "invading species".

35. We wish to stress that our objections are not directed against Bourdieu. Note that Bourdieu is explicitly aiming at a non-deterministic view of culture (Bourdieu 1990: 55). Note, too, that, according to Bourdieu, the *habitus* is developed against and thus tied to a specific socio-cultural background. Evidently, the background of socialisation in post-colonial countries cannot be equated with the Western one, and, correspondingly, yields another specific *habitus*. Also, overt ideologies cannot be equated with *habitus*.

from what he calls Western "linguistic imperialism" and arrives at an almost exclusive interpretation of English in the post-colonial context in terms of power, control, and the reproduction of dispositions he identifies as imperialist and linguicist.[36] With regard to local power structures, English is regarded as a major medium of ensuring the hegemony of the elites. With respect to global power structures, English is seen, so to speak, as the Trojan horse of the West.[37] Phillipson's above statement, however, appears to go beyond this sociolinguistic interpretation. Speaking of the "imposition of new mental structures through English" suggests that he sees the English language as the *conceptual* Trojan horse of the West, too. Note that this is, in its essence, a strong deterministic position. The language English is regarded as having internalised, "embodied" (in the sense of Bourdieu), the Western value system, and the spread of the language is seen as the transfer of English thought processes. In the same vein, in the section outlining the aims of his book he states that it "looks specifically at the ideology transmitted *with*, *in*, and *through* the English language" (Phillipson 1992: 1, our emphasis). One may object that there are only a few passages in Phillipson (1992) which explicitly show his deterministic commitment. It would thus be unfair to build an argument on statements which are not altogether representative.[38] Note, however, that such positions are not singular. An even harsher version of this view is, for instance, expressed in Wollock's (2001) ecolinguistic criticism of "modern imperialism":

> A uniform language is imposed and, like everything else in the new system, becomes a global commodity, which immediately puts those who do not

36. Linguicism is defined as "ideologies, structures and practices which are used to legitimate, effectuate and reproduce an unequal division of power and (both material and non-material) resources between groups which are defined on the basis of language" (Phillipson 1992: 47). Linguicism and linguistic imperialism, besides being most valid theoretical sociolinguistic concepts, are unequivocal facts, both in history and in the present, and we do not imply any denial of their sad and devastating impact and consequences.
37. For a criticism of the conspiracy assumption underlying Phillipson's notion of "linguistic imperialism" see, however, Alatis and Straehle (1997).
38. Furthermore, Phillipson (1992) makes no explicit mention of the school of thought associated with linguistic relativism and determinism. Neither Whorf nor Sapir, for instance, are among his references. Rather, throughout his book, he is generally critical of what he calls "language-intrinsic" arguments, especially those that praise English as a "supreme language". Note, too, that Phillipson (1992) does not base his arguments on the biological model to be discussed below.

> speak it, or who speak it badly, at a grave disadvantage.[39] The new language embodies a system of values that conceives of land and nature as arbitrary signs, objects of domination and profit, a discourse in which maintenance of biodiversity (which it equates with foregoing monetary profit) is equated with 'waste' [...] As this language extends itself through compulsory education and mass media, both linguistic diversity and biodiversity decrease [...]. (Wollock 2001: 252)

The argument goes that languages like English,[40] as the bearer of a Western world-view and isomorphic with it, are therefore inadequate, alien and detrimental to the countries and regions in question.[41]

The second and, as the above quote from Wollock (2001) illustrates, closely related strand may be called the "mismatch" argument. The rationale behind it is that languages are "an integral part of a larger ecosystem" (Mühlhäusler 2001: 133; leaning on Haugen 1972). It regards languages as rooted in and adapted to a particular environment. Here, deterministic assumptions meet with the biological model of language advocated by these authors. In the colonial and postcolonial contexts, such arguments are employed against English in three major ways, depending on the respective interpretation of the notion of environment as "natural", "linguistic" and "cultural".

Firstly then, the English language is regarded, just like some invasive organic species, as not adapted and thus unfitted and detrimental to particular "natural" environments (for a discussion of the invasion rhetoric in evolutionary biology and of its underlying view of the interaction between species as competition, see Larson 2008 fc.). This metaphorical version of the 'mismatch' argument is prominently held by Mühlhäusler (e.g. 1996a, 2003) in his ecolinguistic account of English colonial settlements in the Pacific (for a critical discussion, see Lucko 2003). It needs to be stressed that Mühlhäusler's criticism is not exclusively directed against English and other European colonial languages, though these languages figure as prominent examples of the 'mismatch' hypothesis. Furthermore,

39. Here, the part "puts those who do not speak it, or who speak it badly, at a grave disadvantage" is, of course, most certainly true.
40. Wollock (2001) does not address specifically English, but generally speaks of languages of modern imperialism.
41. On a trivial cultural level, such authors speak of the "McDonaldisation" of the world, *inter alia* through, i.e. *by virtue of* English. The threat they see is that of homogenisation. See Pennycook (2003a, 2003b) for a critical discussion from within the movement itself.

it needs to be stressed that languages are not considered *per se* as incapable of adapting to a new setting, rather it is claimed that some languages did not undergo this process of adaptation. In the specific case of English (here in the Pacific region) the argument thus goes that, having failed to develop the linguistic resources appropriate to the specific environments, English failed and fails to provide suitable representations thereof and had and has largely detrimental effects on the ecological balance in the regions:

> The fact that an increasing number of well-adapted small local languages are being replaced by English is in all likelihood one of the reasons for global environmental deterioration. (Mühlhäusler 2003: 78)

Mühlhäusler (1996b: 105 f.) finds it plausible to attribute ecological disasters caused by the "outsiders", at least to a significant degree, to some 'mismatch' between their language and the new and unfamiliar environment they entered. Here the logical inferences drawn from metaphorical reasoning are no longer justified. Ecological disasters can be caused, if at all, only by organic species, not by artefacts such as languages. Specifically, Mühlhäusler assumes a direct causal link between what he calls "metaphorical naming" of particular local species and their extinction by colonial settlers:

> A particularly clear example of the consequences of such metaphorical naming is that of the numerous small marsupials which once inhabited the Australian Continent in prolific numbers. Most of them ended up being called bush rat or native rat and having got that name were regarded very much like a rat in Britain: at best useless, at worst dangerous pests that needed to be eradicated. (Mühlhäusler 1996b: 107)

Although it is basically true that once some species has been categorised as an animal with certain, for instance, negative, associations, it risks being treated accordingly, this is not necessarily so. Specifically, it is not a matter of the linguistic label given to a phenomenon.[42] Intended

42. In fact, instances of "metaphorical naming" (e.g. *sea-horse*) provide particularly clear examples that it is not a *per se* characteristic of metaphorical processes that entire patterns of human interaction with the source are transferred to the target. Here, the conceptual mapping is restricted to a few elements, usually to aspects like Gestalt or other particularly salient properties. The analogy cannot possibly be taken further.

or not, Mühlhäusler's statement contains a serious overrating of the role of language, in that it fails to make the necessary distinction between the knowledge a speaker or speech community has of a certain phenomenon, the way this phenomenon was initially conceptualised, and, finally, how it is expressed linguistically.[43] Lucko (2003) provides an illuminating discussion of a parallel example here:

> Analysing European languages that way would lead to the conclusion that their speakers adhere to, and are confined within, a Ptolemaic world view as virtually all of them use expressions corresponding to the English *The sun is rising*. These expressions – though not in keeping with our Copernican world view – have been retained because they are much more convenient than saying *Due to the rotation of the earth, the part of the earth's surface I'm on is moving into the light emitted by the sun*. (Let's hope there will never be a drive for "astronomically correct" language).
>
> (Lucko 2003: 156)

Thus, one should beware of deriving strong assumptions about world views and behaviour from linguistic data alone. What the rising-sun example may tell us about "world view", substantiated by numerous parallel expressions, is the well-known omnipresent anthropocentric way of perceiving and conceiving phenomena of the world, and correspondingly, the anthropocentric basis of numerous metaphoric expressions. Likewise, what the rat example may tell us is the salience of an entity's gestalt features in processes of analogy. Whether any other features of the source get transferred in the process of naming, however, remains to be seen. Therefore, any conclusions that go beyond this superficial level of "world view" require more than linguistic data alone. In its essence, Mühlhäusler's position again seems to be a strongly deterministic one. The assumption goes that language determines thought and that language imposes severe if not inescapable constraints on one's entire thinking and even behaviour. Compare also the following statement by Wollock (2001), echoing Mühlhäusler, in which a fully-fledged causal chain from language to human behaviour and its consequences is constructed: "language plays a key role in 'misreading the environment'. An inappropriate linguistic construct of nature will lead to inappropriate actions, like deforestation" (Wollock 2001: 255). These are classic neo-Whorfian stances, as most bluntly expressed in Weisgerber's well-known bon-mot "ob in einem Land Unkraut wächst, hängt von der Sprache seiner Bewohner

43. This distinction is of course precisely what is challenged by such approaches.

ab" (whether there is weed in a given country, depends on the language of its inhabitants).

In the second and closely related version of the mismatch argument, the English language is perceived as a threat not only to the natural environment but also to the "linguistic ecosystem" in the respective regions. In the tradition of the ORGANISM metaphor, languages are seen as SPECIES in an ecological system and, more specifically, as AGENTS in this ecosystem. Global languages as English are metaphorised as ALIEN SPECIES that invade[44] and, framed in the same militarist imagery, destroy native linguistic ecosystems,[45] as reflected in terms like *habitat destruction* (Mühlhäusler 1996a: 19), or, more drastically, *killer language*, *language murder* (Skutnabb-Kangas 2000, Mühlhäusler 1996a), *language war* and *linguistic cannibalism* (Calvet 1998), and *linguistic genocide* (e.g. Skutnabb-Kangas 2000). Here is a representative statement illustrating this metaphorical reasoning:

> While new trees can be planted and habitats restored, it is much more difficult to restore languages once they have been murdered. Languages are today disappearing at a faster pace than ever before in human history. What happens is linguistic genocide on a massive scale, with formal educa-

---

44. In biology, the invading-species metaphor is widely used. We cannot emphasise strongly enough that it results from the dubious, at best one-sided conception of biological systems, common among biologists, as being IN COMPETITION. The background metaphor, as Larson (2008 fc.) points out, is that of WARFARE. So when languages are metaphorised as alien invading species, there is an initial erroneous step of accepting awkward metaphors of biology as valid, which invalidates all further steps.
45. There is, of course, a high degree of arbitrariness in the characterisation of a language as *alien* (exoglottic) or *indigenous* (endoglottic) to a specific region. Clear-cut criteria are missing. Consider, for instance, that the colonial languages have been present in the respective contexts for hundreds of years now. The same arbitrariness is observable in the application of the term "colonisation". As Mufwene (2002: 26 f.) rightly remarks, it is, for instance, highly uncommon to refer to the dispersion of the Bantu population and languages from today's Nigeria and Cameroon to Central and Southern Africa as colonisation, although this dispersion had dramatic effects on the populations and languages in these regions. The same applies to the spread of the Indoeuropean languages and peoples to Europe. (Needless to say that our statement does not imply any attempt at justifying or playing down the atrocities of European colonialism.) The distinction between alien and indigenous is, however, highly appropriate with respect to the issue of standards (endonormative and exonormative, respectively).

> tion and media as the main concrete culprits but with the world's political, economic and military structures as the more basic causal factors. Big languages turn into killer languages, monsters that gobble up others, when they are learnt *at the cost* of the small ones.
>
> (Skutnabb-Kangas 2003: 33; emphasis in the original)

There is, of course, nothing wrong with metaphorically calling each language a species. Many linguists have done and do so. What is crucial, however, is that one does not transfer the inferences associated with real species to the domain of languages. Consider the following statement by Whorf (1956), in which the biological metaphor of "linguistic species" is employed in a fairly neutral manner: "The relatively few languages of the cultures which have attained to modern civilization promise to overspread the globe and cause the extinction of the hundreds of diverse exotic language species" (Whorf 1956: 84). What Whorf says is true: The spread of some few big languages for global communication will lead to the end of many smaller languages for local communication, but the big languages are not killers, murderers, etc. Whorf does not say less nor more than Jean Aitchison, who cannot be suspected of deterministic thinking nor adherence to the logic of the LANGUAGE AS ORGANISM view:

> Yet there is one extra worry to add in language loss. Ninety per cent of the world's languages may be in danger. Around 6,000 languages are currently spoken in the world. Of these, half are moribund in that they are no longer learned by the new generation of speakers. A further 2,500 are in a danger zone, in that they have fewer than a hundred thousand speakers. This leaves around 600, a mere ten per cent of the current total, as likely survivors a century from now. Of course, languages inevitably split, just as Latin eventually split into the various Romance languages. So some new languages may emerge. But the diversity will be much reduced. The splendiferous bouquet of current languages will be withered down to a small posy with only a few different flowers. (Aitchinson 1997: 95)

The logical error made in the specific rhetoric of killer language is that inferences drawn from the metaphorical system are taken literally. Hence, they are false, because the metaphors themselves must be taken as what they are, i.e. as images for diversity but not as literal ontological statements. This is crypto-Whorfianism like most, though not all, neo-Whorfianism is. Here are some of the numerous aspects where the analogy between language and species or language and living beings is wildly broken and hence the inferences drawn are wrong.

Where the LANGUAGE AS SPECIES metaphor goes fundamentally wrong is in the assumption that the various languages in the world are diverse species just like those in the fauna and flora. In fact, the familiar studies on the correlation of linguistic and biological diversity rest on this assumption. And the killer-victim classification of languages follows the same logic, metaphorising some languages as "predators" and some as "prey". But actually, speaking in metaphorical terms, language could at best be thought of as one species (language in general) with many subspecies (individual languages). And this metaphor, too, has its heuristic limits. A species in the biological world disappears when all its subspecies do. For a speech community, however, the loss of its language always means the shift to another one, except for the extreme case of real genocide. To repeat: There is nothing substantially wrong in metaphorically calling each language a species as long as one does not unduly transfer the inferences associated with real species to the domain of languages. Languages cannot and do not kill and certainly not cause a *linguistic genocide*, whatever that metaphor could mean.[46]

Metaphors like *killer language*, *language murder*, *linguistic cannibalism* and *linguistic genocide*, that are derived from the biological model, ascribe certain properties to their target domain LANGUAGE which languages do precisely not have. Authors proclaiming these terms are aware of this, as the following quote from Skutnabb-Kangas (2000: xxxi–xxxiii) shows:[47]

> A third argument against using 'language murder' is that it makes language a living organism with a life of its own. This can block our understanding of what happens/is done to languages because we may stretch the metaphor too far. Languages, after all, are not independent entities with their own lives, much as some linguists might like this to be the case. They are completely dependent on users. I accept this argument to a large extent.
> (Skutnabb-Kangas 2000: xxxiii)

Though accepting the counter-argument "to a large extent", she objects, in defence of the killer/murder metaphor, that conventional terms like *language death* have the same basis. Here, undue inferencing is made from the biological model. Be it a providential metaphor or not, the term *language death* differs from the killer/murder metaphor in one crucial

46. I have changed my opinion on the use of the genocide metaphor by analysing the metaphoric inferences. So I now take distance from my earlier opinion in Dirven and Pütz (2004: 10) [R.D.].
47. This quotation echoes Haugen's (1972) statements on the heuristic function of metaphor and his considerations on the LANGUAGE AS AN ORGANISM metaphor.

respect: As Skutnabb-Kangas (2000: xxxii) notes herself, it does not involve the notion of agency. Beside the evident fact that languages are not LIVING BEINGS (cf. Lucko 2003), that they are not a fleshy part of the world and cannot exist in themselves without human beings of flesh and blood, they are, more specifically, not AGENTS. They are thus not capable of a willful action like killing, as the murder metaphor suggests. This crucial point is also made by Mufwene (2002), who states that "languages have no lives that are independent of their speakers. Therefore, languages do not kill languages; their own speakers do, in giving them up"[48] (Mufwene 2002: 20).

Thus, from a heuristic point of view, the killer metaphor and its variants are hardly felicitous. They highlight an aspect which the target domain does not have. They unduly attach the notion of agency to language, and in doing so they conflate language and language user. From this perspective, the question is not whether the killer metaphor is too strong or 'stretched too far'. It is plainly inappropriate. Contrary to Skutnabb-Kangas' (2000: xxxii) declared intention it conceals rather than enlightens sociolinguistic realities and the real social agents and it is certainly at odds with her objective to "name realities".[49] This is highly detrimental to a critical approach, which should be determined to a clear allocation of causalities and responsibilities. In other word, just like in biology a false understanding of biological systems is introduced by awkward starter metaphors (see Larson 2008fc.), in this strand of critical linguistics, scientists arrive at and propagate wrong views of language because of their basic misunderstanding of metaphorical thought.

By some authors in the movement, the killer metaphor is even taken one step further. Mühlhäusler, for instance, elaborating on Phillipson (1992), goes that far as to provide a "list" of killer languages, cf.

> The definition [of linguistic imperialism] needs to be widened to include imperial languages other than English, in particular, 'killer languages' [...] such as Mandarin, Spanish, French and Indonesian.
>
> (Mühlhäusler 1996a: 20)

Such statements suggest that something inherent in a particular language makes it a "killer" or a "victim". There are good reasons for

48. Note that in the logic of the biological metaphor "giving them up" here would not be "killing them", but "letting them die". Compare Crystal (2000: 86), who speaks of "language suicide".
49. One may quarrel with the LANGUAGE AS A TOOL metaphor in many respects, but here it is the appropriate one.

criticising unsound language policies and (neo)-imperialist methods. However, such ideologies are not properties of a particular language and should not be attributed to it, neither factually nor metonymically.[50] Again, the killer metaphor conceals rather than enlightens socio-linguistic realities. If one strives to uncover causalities, one should address the right addressee. This should be the primary and vital interest of a critical approach to language.

The killer metaphor is taken to the extreme in Skutnabb-Kangas' (2000) specific notion of "linguistic genocide". Here, against the background of the language-as-expression view (see Table 1), culture, language, language use, and language user are almost fully conflated. Language is viewed as a PART OF A PERSON on a par with physical body parts, and the (forced) loss of their language is equated with the PHYSICAL DEATH OF THE SPEECH COMMUNITY (see Skutnabb-Kangas 2000: xxxii–xxxiii for her own view).

Thirdly, and again closely related, the 'mismatch' argument is applied to the cultural dimension. Languages are said not only to reflect culture, but also to harbour specific knowledge of a place, of respective modes of human interaction with it and of cultural practices. Going beyond this classic and undeniably true romantic view, this knowledge is, however, sometimes seen as essentially language-dependent and sometimes as more or less rigidly fixed in linguistic structures, which is again a crypto-neo-Whorfian position. On the basis of the "knowledge-in-language" argument, the wisdom assumed to be harboured in the indigenous languages is then regarded as ultimately lost with their disappearance:

> Each language encapsulates the world-view of its speakers – how they think, what they value, what they believe in, how they classify the world around them, how they order their lives. *Once a language dies, a part of human culture is lost – forever.* (Dixon 1997: 144; our emphasis)

The first part of this statement is, of course, fully agreeable. The second part, however, suggest the static view of human culture as an entity with parts that can get lost. Such a view tends to equate change with loss

50. The role of English in Africa clearly illustrates that such attribution is simply counterfactual. English was well the language of colonial power, but it was, for instance, also the language of liberation movements as the ANC during Apartheid. English had a unifying function in the latter case, allowing for a liberation movement across ethnic and linguistic boundaries. Such facts are rarely recognised by critics of "linguistic imperialism".

and is at odds with the dynamic nature of human culture(s) and of language. It would be much more appropriate to say that one particular manifestation of the human cultural potential is lost. Furthermore, it suggests that the expression of a specific culture or knowledge is bound to one particular language. This view is echoed, for instance, in the following statement by Maffi (2001b):

> local knowledge does not "translate" easily into the majority languages to which minority language speakers shift. Generally the replacing language does not represent an equivalent vehicle for linguistic expression and cultural maintenance. (Maffi 2001b: 6)

and in Nettle and Romaine's (2000: 50, 69) headlines 'lost words, lost worlds' and 'lost languages, lost knowledge'. Such statements need to be read with much caution. After all, local knowledge, for instance environmental, medical, and cultural knowledge, resides in the respective community. Certainly, this knowledge is by and large reflected in and indicated by a whole range of linguistic means. What can be deduced from labels for species, for instance, are aspects of gestalt or some other salient properties (see Nettle and Romaine 2000: 75 ff. for numerous examples). Further aspects that are encoded, to varying degrees of transparency, in the various linguistic means include culture-specific categorisation systems and specific modes of interaction with the respective environment. Yet the amount of information that is indeed formally and overtly encoded in these linguistic means alone is scarce. It needs primarily and indispensably extra-linguistic sources to interpret such linguistic data and to reveal the rich local background knowledge. Most importantly, without drawing on extra-linguistic evidence, the interpretation process may easily yield undue conclusions, as the above rising-sun example illustrates, i.e. the overtly available information may equally be misleading. Seen in this light, the "lost-words lost-worlds" argument turns out to be rather weak. It would be more appropriate to take the inverse stance and say that words get lost when worlds get lost, primarily in the sense that the cognitive content of linguistic units is affected when the material, cultural or mental worlds they are anchored in change. The deeper cause of lost local knowledge are socio-cultural shifts in a community, be they accompanied by language shift or not. Language shift may be a part of the problem, but it is not its root. Note, too, that when speakers shift towards another language, they do not simultaneously give up their culture-specific conceptual system. Rather, large segments or elements of their "cultural conceptualisations", as Sharifian (2003) calls it, then may find expression in the speakers' specific use of the language they shift to, albeit often in a formally different encoding, given the particular make-up of the languages involved. This has been shown, for instance, in recent cognitive-linguistic studies on second-language varieties, for Australian Aboriginal English by Sharifian (*this volume*, 2003) and for West African English by Wolf (2001) and Polzenhagen (2007). Importantly, this is a classic romantic stance, too, as expressed in Humboldt's statement that "jede Sprache besitzt die Geschmeidigkeit, alles in sich aufzunehmen und allem wieder Ausdruck aus sich verleihen zu können" [Every language has the adroitness to incorporate everything and to bear expression to everything] (Humboldt 1992 [1830–1835]: 206; our translation). This dimension receives no or little attention by proponents of the knowledge-in-language argument. Occasionally, it is recognised, as in the following passage from Nettle and Romaine's (2000: 69) discussion of the case of the Dyirbal people:

> One can also argue that some aspects of Aboriginal identity live on in the local and highly distinctive (though stigmatized) variety of English spoken among young people now. The version of the dominant language acquired in such cases of language shift is usually different from that used by the mainstream population in that it preserves traces of influence from the dying language. (Nettle and Romaine 2000: 69)

Yet, when the authors continue "that it is a different kind of identity than the one associated with the traditional Dyirbal", it is rather made part of the general loss-scenario and against a reference background to which the realities do no more correspond.

There is certainly no denying the fact that in language shift numerous genuine means of expression may get lost. Among them are means as diverse as lexical items, morphologically encoded classifier systems, culturally entrenched discourse patterns, specific phatic systems (e.g. respect and address systems) and poetic aspects of language. Means of expressing socio-cultural identity included. It is a clear merit of the romantically oriented literature that these potential losses and how they are perceived by the individual speakers are given full attention. It needs to be stressed, however, that these potential losses may also launch very creative linguistic and sociolinguistic processes in the adopted language. In other words: The argument should not stop with making an inventory of lost linguistic means but needs to proceed to a positive account of how the underlying concepts are expressed in the second or the replacement language. Again, change should not be equated with loss.

It is immediately apparent that in the romantic approach multilingualism and multiculturalism are highly valued. This positive perception is most noticeably expressed in the title of Haugen's well-known book *The Blessings of Babel.* In turn, however, in much of the recent literature, lack or loss of linguistic diversity are presented as a sign and threat of degeneration. This view is often based on an evolutionist argument:[51]

> When the field of diversity shrinks, the potential for distilling sameness from difference is impoverished commensurably. If, at some point, the impoverishment becomes acute enough, then, as I interpret it, our species will have passed a threshold. We will have become something other than human. By this view, diversity ought to be preserved because it provides the grounds for the continuance of *Homo sapiens.* (Harmon 2001: 64–65)

This inference from the biological metaphor is blatantly wrong when applied to language. In biology, the great diversity of subspecies within a given main species is a necessary precaution and self-protective evolutionary device. If, say, contagious insects infect one subspecies and the disease spreads, this may kill that whole subspecies, but not the various other subspecies of the main species. This danger does not exist for languages, hence the inference is wrong.[52]

The evolutionist argument is sometimes made in communion with the above knowledge-in-language view, as in:

> In the language of ecology, the strongest ecosystems are those that are the most diverse. That is, diversity is directly related to stability; variety is important for long-term survival. Our success on this planet has been due to an ability to adapt to different kinds of environment over thousands of years [...] Such ability is born out of diversity. Thus language and cultural diversity maximizes chances of human success and adaptability.
> (Baker 2001, cit. in Skutnabb-Kangas 2003: 39)

and in the following statement, which draws on the gene-pool metaphor of languages and knowledge:

---

51. See Skutnabb-Kangas (2003: 37 ff.) on the underlying notion of evolution.
52. Furthermore, the sustainability of an ecological system does not depend on the number of species in the first place but on the functioning of the relations between its elements. Thus, it is not just a matter of quantity. This is also accounted for in the ecolinguistic movement itself. Authors like Mühlhäusler, for instance, rather put their emphasis on the relational and functional aspect of linguistic "ecosystems".

> At the same time, when we consider the interrelationships between linguistic, cultural, and biological diversity, we may also begin to ask these questions as questions about the future, about the continued viability of humans on earth: "any reduction of language diversity diminishes the adaptational strength of our species because it lowers the pool of knowledge from which we can draw." (Maffi 2001b: 38; quoting Bernard 1992)

Such statements rest on the assumption that linguistic diversity is a necessary prerequisite for a diversity of knowledge systems and cultural plurality, and they hold that these dimensions of diversity all follow the pattern assumed for biological diversity. This generalisation is expressed in Pattanayak's often quoted statement that the "variety of forms is a prerequisite for biological survival. Monocultures are vulnerable and easily destroyed" and his resulting claim that "plurality in human ecology ***functions in the same way***" (cit., e.g., in Maffi 2001b: 39 and Mühlhäusler 1996a: 1; our emphasis added).[53] It is an undue generalisation when extended to language. As we have argued, the relationship between the biological world, language, and culture is non-analogous in many crucial respects.

4. The ideologies underlying the rationalist and romantic models

It is important to notice that both models have, in principle, strong egalitarian foundations and intentions, though their understanding of 'equality' differs significantly. In the case of the rationalist model, it is derived, as noted above, from a universalist, Enlightenment basis, and rests on the notion of equal social participation of all citizens.[54] The romantic

53. Against this background, linguistic diversity and multilingualism are seen as a value *per se*. This view is also expressed, though more cautiously, in Crystal's (2000) statement that "diversity, as we have seen, is a human evolutionary strength, and should be safeguarded as an end in itself" (Crystal 2000: 53). Here the metaphor of STRENGTH could again be seen as doubtful, though no inferences become clear in this utterance. If there had been "richness" instead of "strength", we would be in the vicinity of Aitchison's "bouquet" metaphor. What is generally dubious about the "diversity is good" and "diversity makes us human" claim (e.g. Harmon 2001: 64) is the explicit or implicit underlying value matrix. There is but a little step, then, to claim that, in turn, a monolingual individual and a largely monolingual society should be regarded as "less human". Furthermore, such statements generally ignore internal language variation, i.e. dialects, sociolects and other group languages, as a dimension of diversity.

model, by contrast, starts from the premise that all cultures are unique and equally valuable, and derives its egalitarian stance from this basis. Moreover, the romantic model saw the culture of a people embodied in the whole community, in the folk spirit ("Volksgeist"), the folk customs and folk 'lore'. From the discussion of the linguistic-philosophical bases of the two models, however, it should have become apparent that the egalitarian stance is seriously eclipsed and undermined by the one-sided focusing of the two models on either language functions, or on linguistic and cultural identity, respectively. Despite, and sometimes in disregard of, their egalitarian commitment, both models, in practice, have the inherent tendency to measure languages and language forms along some ideologically motivated value matrix. Even the transformed stages of the models are highly prone to such ideological biases.

We follow Geeraerts' (2003: 27) observation that cultural models (CMs) in the social sphere, including science, "may be ideologies in two different respects: either when their idealized character is forgotten (when the difference between the abstract model and the actual circumstances is neglected), or when they are used in a prescriptive and normative rather than a descriptive way." The first point Geeraerts makes may be put differently in the light of the above analysis: Scientific models are prone to shortcomings resulting from the ever-luring tendency to take the model for the realities it is supposed to capture, i.e. for the sake of maintaining the model, some parts of "reality" are obviously ignored or dubiously interpreted. And the second point Geeraerts makes may be restated as follows: A model is necessarily an idealisation. Problems arise when it is taken too literally as the basis of decision-making. One-sided interpretations of the model then yield one-sided policies. Here, power relations come heavily into play. This point leads us to a discussion of underlying, more global ideologies, in which the two models are embedded.

As for the rationalist model, the motivation behind explicit or implicit value judgements on languages is aptly described by Williams (1992):

> when the concept of social change as involving progress is invoked we have the [...] tendency to create dichotomies which involve norm/deviance within the context of social evolution. Invariably the norm involves the powerful element and the deviant involves the adversary which is placed in time

---

54. The historical French notion of "bourgeois 'citizen'", however, did not include all the people, but mainly the middle class bourgeoisie, not the lower classes, who only began to gain political weight long after the industrial revolution, say from the mid 19th century onwards.

> through dichotomies such as modern/traditional which derive from typological constructions which are assumed to reflect new and old forms, despite the fact that they both sit together at the same moment in time. Language is superimposed upon this vision of society by relating different language forms, whether they be languages or varieties, to the dichotomous relations of society. (Williams 1992: 233, cit. in Ouane 2003: 45)

In the logic of this model, progress and modernisation are highly valued and a language which is associated with these processes is ultimately rated above those that are not. This is reinforced by the model's almost exclusive focus on what has been termed "secondary or higher domains", i.e. domains that belong to the public sphere. The motivation of this emphasis is twofold: These are the domains where progress and modernisation are perceived to be located and these are the domains where the ideal of social participation in the economic and in the public sector is to be accomplished. And, intervention in the "primary domains", i.e. those pertaining to the private sphere (the home, hearth and heart areas), is, of course, only to some degree compatible with the model's commitment to individual rights. The focus on the secondary domains seems to get sociolinguistic justification by the fact that the impact of official language policy on the "primary domains" (e.g. on language use in the home, network of friends, club, church, etc.) is almost negligible. This resistance of the primary domains is, of course, also noticed by proponents of the romantic model (see, e.g., Romaine 2002: 3).

The rationalist model's focus on languages of ideological liberation and modernisation and on the secondary domains has well-known ideological implications. The promotion of these languages is, inevitably, at the same time a marginalisation of other languages, which are denied the same public space (cf. Romaine 2002: 6), for instance, in public education and public administration. And, evidently, this promotion is an enhancement of languages of power (cf. Bourdieu's 1982 seminal criticism). Modern advocates of rationalist positions are, however, fully aware of these problems and implications, cf., e.g., the following critical statement by House (2001) on the situation in the European Union: "Also, the supposed linguistic equality in the EU is a relative one: some languages are more clearly more equal than others, and minority languages inside the member states do not count at all" (House 2001: n.p.). Furthermore, and closely related, the model's commitment to the ideal of equal social participation is seriously undermined by the fact that the access to the languages of power is not equal. The model's pronounced democratic stance, moreover, is easily interpretable as a *per se* guarantee of majority rights: They are implicit, taken-for-granted, and minority rights are seen as special and in need of justification (Romaine 2002: 7). Pattanayak (2003a), responding to the rationalist key tenet of social participation from the perspective of the romantic model, thus concludes that it may rather be achieved through the emphasis on mother tongues:

> The mother tongue is the majority language of the community. And it is therefore the best defence of democracy. By providing greater participation for a greater number of people in the political process, by freeing communication from the grip of the few, by giving people a chance to participate in national reconstruction, mother tongues should count among the best resources of a country. It is most unfortunate that in our multi-layered social system the place of the colonial languages is considered high, but the place of the mother tongue low. (Pattanayak 2003a: 26–27)

More ideological implications may be and have been added in critical discussions of the rationalist model.

As exemplified in earlier sections, the romantic model, too, has become imbued with ideological biases, in particular with a pronounced anti-globalisation and anti-Western commitment (cf. Hutton 2001: 289–291). Some current strands even advocate an explicit taking-side approach (e.g. Mühlhäusler 1996a: 20 f.).[55] This comes to the fore in the alienationist criticism of the role of global languages like English, as discussed above. Here, languages are judged as sound or unsound, as adapted or alien, as "victims" or "killers". Further ethic and moral categories may be freely added to the list.[56] The argument goes, implicitly or sometimes explicitly,

55. Ironically, one of the movement's main tenets was precisely to reveal ideological underpinnings of the 'traditional' linguistics paradigm. Calvet (1998), for instance, traces the ideology of a dominant language and the neglect and even debasement of language variation in linguistic theory. Phillipson's notion of linguicism has a related objective, and much of Skutnabb-Kangas' (e.g. 2000) work is directed toward the uncovering of the impact of linguicist positions on language legislation. It is thus surprising that key notions of the movement's proponents are strongly founded on ideologically motivated assumptions. Essentially, such authors often replace the "myths" about language they identify in traditional linguistics by the respective opposites, i.e. they replace one ideology by another.
56. This tendency is a well-known legacy of the relativist heritage, which always had a strong idealising inclination. Recall Humboldt's notion of an ideal "Ursprache". Also note that his enthusiastic preference for inflection languages, for instance, was aesthetically motivated, cp. expressions like "der edlere Sprachbau" (Humboldt 1992: 198). Also note his considerations on

that some languages are more appropriate, some systems of knowledge (folk wisdom) more worthy than others, and that some cultures (the indigenous ones) are somehow superior (for a discussion, see Edwards 2002). As Mufwene (2002) rightly observes:

> We can perhaps argue that a language mirrors a culture because it is itself part of a culture. Changes affecting it reflect changes in a particular culture. Arguing for its maintenance when the population of its speakers behaves differently reflects a value judgement on the part of the linguist, who rates the ancestral culture more highly than the one that is being fashioned by the speaker's behaviour. (Mufwene 2002: 24)

The implications of Mufwene's position are, however, far-reaching. What he says boils down to leaving it up to any linguistic community to decide for themselves whether they want to give up their minority language for another language of wider or even national communication, or whether they want to fight and bring financial sacrifices for the survival of their own language. This means, in other words, can we leave it up to the linguistic communities themselves to decide on maintaining their language or not? The romantic model says "no", the rationalist model would tend to say "yes". But that is a merely speculative question. The real question is: Would the romantic model go so far as to say that faltering linguistic communities would have to be persuaded, if not obliged, to keep up their minority languages?

In the general antithesis between languages of wider, even global communication and the hundreds, if not thousands of threatened minority languages there is, in the conservative romantic view, a clear role pattern distribution: the stereotypical antagonistic roles of the cruel villain and the innocent princess. The parts are clearly allocated: English on the one hand, as the "villain", the language of colonialism, imperialism, globalisation, rationalism, and the "small" minority languages on the other hand, as the idyllic princess, living in harmony with nature, full of precious knowledge and sensitivity. Again, whereas such stereotypes, like all stereotypes, may appear exaggerated and offer too simplistic a picture, they contain a core of truth. The romantic views are multifaceted and heterogeneous, and the various authors do not necessarily subscribe to all of these positions. However, the ideological background is shared, to varying degrees, by many of them. And, despite assurances of the con-

---

the "character of languages", with attributes like "energisch", "träge", "vollkommen", "sinnlich", "intellektuell".

trary (e.g. Smith 2001: 105), these positions often have a distinct romanticist flavour.[57] As Edwards (2002: 8) rightly remarks, a "dislike of this world is usually the background, in fact, for arguments on behalf of 'indigenous' cultures" and "West-bashing", as Edwards calls it, is a major objective and ingredient of these approaches. The numerous pejorative statements on indigenous languages such authors rightly and vividly oppose are countered with equally derogative statements on languages like English, as manifest in the label *killer language* ("monsters that gobble up others", Skutnabb-Kangas 2003: 33) or in Wollock's (2001: 252) harsh attack on "imperialist languages" as embodying "a system of values that conceives of land and nature as arbitrary signs, objects of domination and profit". Here Whorf, in one of his more deterministic passages, may be seen as a distant prophet of romantic praise heaping on indigenous languages, in his case on the Hopi language: "Hopi can have verbs without subjects, and this gives to that language power as a logical system for understanding certain aspects of the cosmos. Scientific language, being founded on Western Indo-European and not on Hopi, does as we do, sees sometimes actions and forces where there may be only states" (Whorf 1956: 263).[58] And, parallel to Whorf's linguistically unjustified

57. That some romanticism comes in is certainly not an unfair reproach. Note, for instance, that the dedication line in Maffi (2001) reads "To the world's indigenous and traditional peoples, who hold the key to the inextricable link between language, knowledge, and the environment." On the dangers of romanticism, also see Mühlhäusler (2000: 97). Note, too, that romanticism is regarded, also from a post-modernist perspective, as a pitfall. Irrespective of the somewhat odd question of whether or not some presupposed idyllic state of harmony had ever existed, no culture is left unmarked by history. A nostalgia for lost origins may thus be highly detrimental to the critical exploration of present social realities.
58. This Whorf quotation is a rather strong version of the linguistic relativity theory and contains some over-generalisations. It is made the input for the following critical comment and assignments in Dirven and Verspoor (2004: 146–147):

    (a) Can you think of European languages that just like Hopi have verbs without subjects?
    (b) For English *It flashed* or *A light flashed*, Hopi just says *rehpi* 'flashes' or 'flashed'. Do you agree with Whorf that the English conceptualization includes a force, starting from the subject? (Have a look at Chapter 4.2.2. on the "happening" schema).
    (c) From a cognitive point of view there are no 'empty' words in the language. That is, *It* in *It flashed* does have a meaning. What could this meaning possibly be?

analysis of Hopi and English, the case for the indigenous languages is made as an explicit case against English. The enterprise of West-bashing is taken to the linguistic front as English-bashing. There are good reasons to be opposed to many aspects of Western value systems and policies and to criticise the often devastating impact they had and have at a global level. And, evidently, scientific work will always have ideological implications. But this is another issue; the crucial question is, whether "the good cause" justifies the means (cf. Lucko 2003).

The tendency to rate languages and language forms along some value matrix is in fact one of the most severe dangers within both models. If the positive understanding of multilingualism and multiculturalism is taken seriously, both models need to critically examine such positions.

5. Consequences

The previous sections focussed on points of divergence between the two models. The obvious and fundamental differences between the two approaches notwithstanding, there is, however, much factual and potential common ground between them, an area of exploration far beyond the mere programmatic commitment to multilingualism and multiculturalism. This observation is in line with the call, in the recent literature, for a "third way" (e.g. Pennycook 2003b; House 2003). We note several points of contact: Firstly, proponents of both models agree that a multilingual solution is heavily constrained by practical needs. Language policies that ignore practical constraints and issues of workability are evidently inappropriate. In highly multilingual settings, some, and often far-reaching, compromise is inevitable, and, here, the idealistic commitment to a fully egalitarian multilingual solution may turn out to be a counterproductive impediment. This is true for the national level as well as for the supranational one. Compromise solutions often appear to be agreeable to both models. Secondly, and this will be discussed in more detail below, we observe that the key concepts in a positive understanding of multilingualism, i.e. functional specialisation in the rationalist model and expression of multiple identities in the romantic model, are not incompatible. A third point shall be added to the debate: Within both models,

---

(d) For English scientific terms such as electricity, Hopi uses a verb, not a noun. This would support Whorf's opinion that English sees a state where there may only be a force. Do you agree with this analysis?

there is often an almost exclusive focus on languages rather than on their speakers. A shift towards a more speaker-centred approach may, on the one hand, produce more comprehensive accounts of socio-cultural and socio-political realities, and, on the other hand, it may yield further common ground between the two models.

As noted several times already, the rationalist model's response to multilingualism revolves around the notion of functional specialisation, i.e. that a given language or a given variety or speech form does not necessarily cover all domains of life, but may be restricted to only some of them. It needs to be stressed that, in contrast to the earlier view which saw multilingualism as an impediment to social participation, this multiple-functional view is an essentially positive understanding of diversity. The basic spirit of this approach is expressed in Mufwene's (2002) statement that "languages or dialects that have separate communicative or social functions can coexist quite happily" (Mufwene 2002: 39).[59]

Against the background of the rationalist model, the notion of functional specialisation presupposes an instrumental type of function, i.e. the view of language as a neutral instrument of communication as unequivocally stressed in the statement by House (2001), already quoted before, that "English as a lingua franca is nothing more than a *useful tool* [...] it is *not a 'language for identification'*" (House 2001, n.p.; our emphasis). In the same vein, Crystal (2003) states that

> factors, which include the recognition of global interdependence, the desire to have a voice in world affairs, and the value of multilingualism in attracting trade markets, all support the adoption of a functionalist account of English, where the *language is seen as a valuable instrument enabling people to achieve particular goals*. Local languages continue to perform an important set of functions (chiefly, the expression of local identity) and English is seen as the primary means of achieving a global presence.
> (Crystal 2003: 24; our emphasis)

This dissociation of language from certain functions, in particular the identity-symbolising function, is seen with reservation by some proponents of the romantic model. In the conservative camp, there used to be a tendency to regard functional specialisation in a negative way, as a sign of and a step towards impairment. With reference to the European

59. Skutnabb-Kangas (2000: 312), however, rightly notes that "unsupported coexistence mostly [...] leads to minority languages dying."

context,[60] Phillipson (2001), for instance, speaks of "domain losses" to global English as a threat to the "vitality" of other languages:[61]

> The market forces that are propelling English forward impact on the vitality and viability of other languages. English is capturing some of their territory, despite EU treaties and summit meetings proclaiming a commitment to diversity. (Phillipson 2001, n.p.)

He cites the Nordic countries as examples and states that work is now under way to ensure that Swedish, for instance, "remains a 'complete' language" (Phillipson 2001: n.p.), thus metaphorising the take-over by English in specific domains in the shape of the COMPLETENESS metaphor. The metaphor implies that language is an entity with parts and that some parts can be missing so that the entity is no longer complete. But in actual fact Phillipson does not refer to the language itself, but to the functions of language, and suggests inferences at the level of the ontological nature of language. The misleading step in the COMPLETENESS metaphor is again the leap from the functions of language to language itself. In the same context, Phillipson refers to the decline of German as a once dominant language of science, as documented by Ammon (1998, 2001). In German as a scientific language the COMPLETENESS metaphor makes way for the DECAY metaphor, probably the logical end of incompleteness.[62]

This, however, is a conservative interpretation of the romantic model. In spite of the different perspectives of the two models, the notion of functional specialisation may also be interpreted, to a significant degree, in terms of the language-as-identity view. As we have seen in section 2, this positive understanding of functional specialisation rests on the no-

60. For some more recent contributions to the debate on English in Europe, see the publications by the Language Policy Division of the Council of Europe (COE n.d.), e.g. Seidlhofer (2003), from the perspective of the rationalist model, and Skutnabb-Kangas (2002), from that of the perspective of the romantic model. Also see House (2003).
61. Phillipson's reservation also results from his view that language and power structures cannot or should not be dissociated.
62. Closely related is the common conceptualisation that the state of its language is indicative of and analogous to the state of a nation/society (cf. Romaine 1997). In the logic of the organism metaphor, a language's FAILING HEALTH mirrors the FAILING HEALTH of the body society. This conceptualisation also guides purist approaches to language and, in the specific context of Global English, conservative advocates of native exo-normative standards.

tion of "multiple identities" marked by and expressed through the various speech forms available. Such a progressive version acknowledges the functional role and functional necessity of non-standard speech forms, standard varieties and even supra-national languages alike. This is expressed in the following statement by Pattanayak (2003b):

> Each language is heteroglossic in the sense that it has complex stratification into genres, registers, styles, sociolects, dialects and mutual interaction between these categories. In a multilingual situation, not only are different languages used in defined domains, but selected variations of each language may be used for specific purposes. (Pattanayak 2003b: 31)

That functional specialisation and the language-as-identity view are not incompatible, is also reflected in actual language policies. Again, the South African example provides a good illustration of this point. Post-Apartheid language policy is, on the one hand, clearly guided by the emphasis on identity, as expressed in the key notion of the "Rainbow Nation".[63] This zeal is, of course, most readily reflected by the legal recognition of the country's eleven major languages as official languages, in the 1993 Interim Constitution and the 1996 Constitution. On the other hand, considerations in terms of functional specialisation play a significant role in the proposals that are developed in order to implement a plurilingualist policy. De Kadt (1997: 156 ff.) provides an exemplary discussion of the documents issued by the Language Plan Task Group (Langtag) established in 1995 and by other administrative bodies. The overall approach is that of an additive functional multilingualism, i.e. a policy of multilingualism which "does not imply that all languages have to be used for all functions, but rather that different languages may be appropriate for different functions" (Langtag 1996, cit. in de Kadt 1997: 165). Admittedly, as Neville Alexander points out in his contribution to the 2004 LAUD Symposium, the process of implementation is slow, due to many factors (also see de Kadt 1997 and Alexander 2003, for earlier discussions of this topic). *De facto*, it is English which has gained significantly in all domains, rather than the African languages, and at the expense of Afrikaans. However, as de Kadt (1997: 160 f.) cautiously argues, this may be seen as a short or medium term effect. If a revalorisation of African languages may indeed be achieved on all levels of society, the integration of these languages may be accomplished in the long

63. See Botha (2001) for an analysis of the language of modern South African political leaders.

run.[64] Alexander (2003: 17) reports some recent encouraging developments from the Western Cape Province, where an implementation plan for the introduction of seven years of mother-tongue based education and the acquisition of a third language is being drafted. Alexander calls this move "no less than revolutionary" in Sub-Saharan Africa, given, too, and most importantly, that the plan is accompanied by the required budget provision.[65]

Further common ground between the two models may be gained in a shift towards a more speaker-centred approach. As reflected in our discussion, there is, in the debate, an exaggerated emphasis on languages rather than on the speakers of these languages. This emphasis is manifest, first of all, in the legislative frameworks. The EU charter, for instance, does not grant rights to speakers or linguistic minority groups but, explicitly, to languages (cf. Romaine 2002: 9). Constitutions determine national and official languages. Education schemes decide on languages as subject or medium of instruction. And the endeavours of the Linguistic Human Rights movement were directed, in the last decades, primarily at the formal encoding of mother-tongue rights at the international and national levels. The more recent literature, from both models, rightly calls for a shift in focus. The formal recognition of linguistic rights, important as it is, does not guarantee a language's transmission to new generations.[66] Ultimately, this transmission depends on the speakers and their use of a language in the primary domains. And as Romaine (2002: 3), for instance, notes, the impact of official language policy on home use is almost negligible. Declaring a language official and giving it a place in the administrative and educational system is far easier to establish "than to get families to speak a threatened language to their children" (Ro-

64. Revalorisation is of course linked to sustaining the socio-economic status of the speech communities.
65. There is, of course, no lack of lip-service commitment to multilingual education throughout Africa. Even where permissive legal regulations exist, their implementation, however, is generally poorly financed.
66. This statement does not question at all the need of the legal recognition of linguistic rights. This objective is far from being reached, even in "established" Western democracies. Consider, as an example, the case of the U.S. and the ongoing English-Only debate in this country (see Dirven and Polzenhagen 2004 for discussion). Here, most tellingly, the turning down of an English-Only amendment in Arizona was achieved only after a ten-year legal combat and, significantly, under the First Amendment, given the absence of an explicit linguistic-rights legislation.

maine 2002: 3). Thus, what needs to be sustained is the social basis of the linguistic groups: "Conferring status on the language of a group relatively lacking in power doesn't necessarily ensure the reproduction of a language [...] conferring power on the people would be much more likely to do the trick" (Nettle and Romaine 2000: 39–40; cf. Romaine 2002: 2). And, closely related to socio-cultural issues, the focus in language policies needs to shift to economic factors. As Crystal (2003: 25) states: "Solutions are more likely to come from the domain of economic policy, not language policy." Romaine (2002), quoting Ó Riagáin, makes a similar point:

> the power of state language policies to produce intended outcomes is severely constrained by a variety of social, political and economic structures which sociolinguists have typically not addressed, even though their consequences are profound and of far more importance than language policies themselves. (Ó Riagáin 1997: 170–171; cit. in Romaine 2002: 19)

We argue that the role of language is often overestimated and the dominant emphasis on languages rather than on their speakers appears to be rooted in shortcomings in the philosophical-linguistic basis of the present models. Among proponents of the romantic model, we noted the strong tendency to view languages as agents with a life of their own, and to conflate language, language use, and language user. Furthermore, the strong equation of identity and culture with language suggests that the promotion of a language is the primary effort to be taken in the sustaining of a socio-cultural group. This has evidently led to some neglect of the factor speaker, a point strongly criticised by Mufwene (2002): "Because languages do not have independent lives from their speakers, it is bizarre that the hosts, whose socio-economic behaviours affect them, have been ignored" (Mufwene 2002: 22). Mufwene rightly notes that "even from an environmentalist perspective, in which all members of an econiche matter, speakers are far more important to our planet than their languages, which are being lost through their own communicative practices" (Mufwene 2002: 25). From the ecology-of-language perspective, too, the focus on language alone is altogether surprising, because any ecological system is not static, but dynamic in nature, and open to change:

> Linguists are thus different from environmentalists, who have realised that the survival of a particular species depends largely on restoring the ecology in which it thrives. Curiously, linguists' proposal for rescuing endangered languages (as articulated in, for example, Crystal 2000; Nettle and Ro-

> maine 2000) suggests that speakers must continue their traditional communicative behaviours regardless of changing socio-economic ecologies.
> (Mufwene 2002: 24)

Mufwene concludes that "solutions that focus on the victims rather than on the causes of their plights are just as bad as environmental solutions that would focus on affected species rather than on the ecologies that affect the species" (Mufwene 2002: 20).

A parallel overestimation of the language factor may be observed in the rationalist model. The LANGUAGE AS TOOL metaphor suggests that access to social participation may be ensured by providing the TOOL language for this. Providing the tool is certainly a prerequisite, but a group's social participation is ultimately, as its identity, dependent on a complex set of factors such as its historical experiences, its socio-economic status and its self-awareness.

Of the factors, it is probably the need to sustain the socio-economic basis of a speech community that should constitute the primary common ground between the models. From a theoretical perspective, we argue that the impact of socio-economic factors needs to find more consideration in the further development of the two models. From a practical perspective, socio-economic measures need to play a key role in actual language maintenance programmes and in actual language policies.

6. Conclusions

In our discussion, we reviewed and contrasted some of the dominant linguistic and sociolinguistic arguments made in the debate on global languages, and their underlying ideologies. We were not concerned with a fully-fledged analysis of the validity of these arguments. Rather, we intended to show that these views and ideologies are embedded in and derive from two competing general cultural models, the rationalist one and the romantic one, with their specific underlying metaphors and metonymies. While both models have their merits, they also and necessarily restrict, as any cultural model, our perspective on the phenomena and processes they conceptualise. Here, our specific emphasis was on the role of metaphorical reasoning in scientific thinking. Our critical account notwithstanding, this does not mean that science can proceed without metaphor. In this respect, we cannot agree with Fishman (2002) either, when he concludes his objections against certain biological and other metaphors in the following way:

> To some extent, our tendency to mystify and metaphorise our endeavours derives from our embarrassment that "language" is not yet a fully understood variable, not even in the so-called "Language sciences". [...] It is doubly difficult to precisely investigate and conceptualise the relationship between language and culture, for example when both variables are substantially metaphorised and thereby simplified, if not even more basically misunderstood. (Fishman 2002: 5)

This attitude of distrust of metaphor is out of touch with a general recognition that science is impossible without metaphor. Metaphor is used in all instances of scientific theory-building and subsequent experimental explorations test the implications of the metaphorical model. The problem is, as we hope to have shown, that one must be able to distinguish between the heuristic function of metaphors and the non-metaphorical inferences that can be drawn from them. In scientific-metaphorical reasoning, metaphors may abound at the descriptive level, but the inferences drawn from this reasoning ought to be non-metaphorical and related to scientifically controlled phenomena.

The two models will continue to develop and a critical assessment of their underlying conceptualisations may contribute to their further refinement. The metatheoretical criticism of such models is among the wide range of contributions and possible applications of Cognitive Linguistics, as put forward and illustrated in the present volume, to the field of sociolinguistics.

Note

This paper is a revised version of Dirven and Polzenhagen (2004) and Polzenhagen (2007: Ch. 4). While our present focus is on a critical discussion of a number of romantically oriented positions and on possible positive aspects of the contemporary rationalist approach, the complementary perspective is taken in Dirven and Pütz (2007), who review, in an exemplary way, the many conflict situations that have arisen from the application of the rationalist model and who emphasise the merits of the romantic approach.

References

Aitchinson, Jean
1997 *Language Change: Progress or Decay?* Cambridge: Cambridge University Press.

Alatis, James and Carolyn Straehle
1997 The universe of English: Imperialism, chauvinism, and paranoia. In: Larry E. Smith and Michael L. Forman (eds.), *World Englishes 2000*, 1–20. Honolulu: University of Hawaii and East-West Center.

Alexander, Neville
2003 Language education policy, national and sub-national identities in South Africa. Strasbourg: Council of Europe. [www.coe.int/T/E/Cultural_Co-operation/education/Languages/Language_Policy/Policy_development_activities/Studies/AlexanderEN.pdf access 10/02/04].
2004 Socio-political factors in the evolution of language policy in post-apartheid South Africa. Essen: LAUD, Paper N° 619.

Alverson, Hoyt
1994 *Semantics and Experience. Universal Metaphors of Time in English, Mandarin, Hindi and Sesotho*. Baltimore/London: Johns Hopkins University Press.

Ammon, Ulrich
1998 *Ist Deutsch noch Internationale Wissenschaftssprache?: Englisch auch für die Lehre an den Deutschsprachigen Hochschulen*. Berlin/New York: Mouton de Gruyter.
2001 English as a future language of teaching at German universities? A question of difficult consequences, posed by the decline of German as a language of science. In: Ulrich Ammon (ed.), *The Dominance of English as a Language of Science. Effects on Other Languages and Language Communities*, 343–362. Berlin/New York: Mouton de Gruyter.

Berthele, Raphael
this vol. A nation is a territory with one culture and one language: The role of metaphorical folk models in language policy debates.

Bickel, Balthasar
2000 Grammar and social practice: On the role of 'culture' in linguistic relativity. In: Susanne Niemeier and René Dirven (eds.), *Evidence for Linguistic Relativity*, 161–191. (Current Issues in Linguistic Theory 198). Amsterdam/Philadelphia: John Benjamins.

Blommaert, Jan
2003 Commentary: A sociolinguistics of globalisation. *Journal of Sociolinguistics* 7 (4): 607–623.

Botha, Willem
2001 The deictic foundation of ideology with reference to African Renaissance. In: René Dirven, Roslyn Frank and Cornelia Ilie (eds.), *Language and Ideology. Volume II: Descriptive Cognitive Approaches*, 51–76. (Current Issues in Linguistic Theory 205). Amsterdam/Philadelphia: John Benjamins.

Bourdieu, Pierre
1982 *Ce que parler veut dire. L'économie des échanges linguistiques*. Paris: Fayard.
1990 *The Logic of Practice*. Oxford: Polity Press.

Brutt-Griffler, Janina
2002 *World English: A Study of Its Development*. (Bilingual Education and Bilingualism 34). Clevedon: Multilingual Matters.

Calvet, Louis-Jean
1998 *Language Wars and Linguistic Politics*. Oxford: Oxford University Press.

COE (Council of Europe. Language Policy Division)
n.d. Studies on language policy. [www.coe.int/T/E/Cultural_Co-operation/education/Languages/Language_ Policy/Policy_development_activities/Studies/]

Crystal, David
1997 *English as a Global Language*. Cambridge: Cambridge University Press.
2000 *Language Death*. Cambridge: Cambridge University Press.
2003 *English as a Global Language*. 2nd ed. Cambridge: Cambridge University Press.

de Kadt, Elizabeth
1997 McWorld versus local cultures: English in South Africa at the turn of the millennium. In: Larry E. Smith and Michael L. Forman (eds.), *Word Englishes 2000*, 146–168. Honolulu: University of Hawaii and East-West Center.

Dirven, René
2004 Major strands in cognitive linguistics. Essen: LAUD, Paper N° 634.

Dirven, René and Frank Polzenhagen
2004 Rationalist or romantic model in language policy and globalisation. Essen: LAUD, Paper N° 622.

Dirven, René and Martin Pütz
2004 Der übergeordnete ideologische Rahmen der Sprachkonflikte weltweit. In: Katrin Bromber and Birgit Smieja (eds.), *Globalisation and African Languages: Risks and Benefits*, 9–30. New York: Mouton de Gruyter.
2007 Language conflict seen from the perspective of the rationalist and romantic models: New developments. *Southern African Linguistics and Applied Language Studies* 25 (3): 303–317. [Ed. by C. Jac Conradie (guest ed.)].

Dirven, René and Marjolijn Verspoor (eds.)
2004 *Cognitive Exploration of Language and Linguistics*. Second revised edition. (Cognitive Linguistics in Practice 1). Amsterdam/Philadelphia: John Benjamins.

Dirven, René, Roslyn Frank and Martin Pütz (eds.)
2003 *Cognitive Models in Language and Thought. Ideology, Metaphors and Meanings*. (Cognitive Linguistic Research 24). Berlin/New York: Mouton de Gruyter.

Dirven, René, Frank Polzenhagen and Hans-Georg Wolf
2007 Cognitive Linguistics, ideology, and Critical Discourse Analysis. In: Dirk Geeraerts and Hubert Cuyckens (eds.), *Handbook of Cognitive Linguistics*, 1222–1240. New York: Oxford University Press.

Dirven, René, Hans-Georg Wolf and Frank Polzenhagen
2007 Cognitive Linguistics and cultural studies. In: Dirk Geeraerts and Hubert Cuyckens (eds.), *Handbook of Cognitive Linguistics*, 1203–1221. New York: Oxford University Press.

Dixon, Robert
1997 *The Rise and Fall of Languages*. Cambridge: Cambridge University Press.

Edwards, John
2002 Ecolinguistic ideologies: A critical perspective. Essen: LAUD, Paper N° 531.
2004 The power of language, the language of power. Essen: LAUD, Paper N° 588.

Eggington, William
1997 The English language metaphors we plan by. In: William Eggington and Helen Wren (eds.), *Language Policy: Dominant English, Pluralistic Challenges*, 29–46. Amsterdam/Philadelphia: John Benjamins, Canberra: Language Australia.

Fill, Alwin
1993 *Ökolinguistik: Eine Einführung*. Tübingen: Gunter Narr.

Fill, Alwin (ed.)
1996 *Sprachökologie und Ökolinguistik*. Tübingen: Stauffenburg.

Fishman, Joshua
2002 Endangered minority languages: Prospects for sociolinguistic research. *International Journal on Multicultural Societies* 4 (2). Protecting Endangered Minority Languages: Sociolinguistic Perspectives. Ed. by Matthias Koenig. UNESCO. [www.unesco.org/most/vl4n2 f.ishman.pdf access 10/02/04].

Geeraerts, Dirk
2003 Cultural models of linguistic standardization. In: René Dirven, Roslyn Frank and Martin Pütz (eds.), *Cognitive Models in Language and Thought. Ideology, Metaphors and Meanings*, 25–68. (Cognitive Linguistic Research 24). Berlin/New York: Mouton de Gruyter.

Gumperz, John J. and Stephen C. Levinson (eds.)
1996 *Rethinking Linguistic Relativity*. Cambridge: Cambridge University Press.

Harmon, David
1996 Losing species, losing languages: Connections between biological and linguistic diversity. *Southwest Journal of Linguistics* 15: 89–108.
2001 On the meaning and moral imperative of diversity. In: Luisa Maffi (ed.), *On Biocultural Diversity. Linking Language, Knowledge, and the Environment*, 53–70. Washington/London: Smithsonian Institution Press.

Haugen, Einar
1972 The ecology of language. In: Anwar S. Oil (ed.), *The Ecology of Language. Essays by Einar Haugen*, 215–236. Stanford: Stanford University Press.

Herder, Johann Gottfried
1991 Extracts from *Ideen zur Philosophie der Geschichte der Menschheit.* In: Willi Oelmüller, Ruth Dölle-Oelmüller and Volker Steenblock (eds.), *Diskurs: Sprache.* (Philosophische Arbeitsbücher 8). UTB 1615. Paderborn: Ferdinand Schöningh. (Original publication: 1784–1791).

House, Juliane
2001 A stateless language that Europe must embrace. *The Guardian* online. 19th April, 2001. [www.guardian.co.uk/GWeekly/Story/0,3939,475288,00.html access 10/02/04]
2003 English as a lingua franca: A threat to multilingualism? *Journal of Sociolinguistics* 7 (4): 556–578.

Humboldt, Wilhelm von
1992 Extracts from *Über die Kawi-Sprache auf der Insel Java.* In: Wilhelm von Humboldt, *Schriften zur Sprache.* Edited by Michael Böhler. Stuttgart: Reclam. (Original publication: 1830–1835).

Hutton, Christopher
2001 Cultural and conceptual relativism, universalism and the politics of linguistics: Dilemmas of a would-be progressive linguistics. In: René Dirven, Bruce Hawkins and Esra Sandikcioglu (eds.), *Language and Ideology. Volume I: Theoretical Cognitive Approaches*, 277–296. (Current Issues in Linguistic Theory 204). Amsterdam/ Philadelphia: John Benjamins.

International Society of Ethnobiology (ISE)
1998 Code of Ethics. Preamble. [guallart.anthro.uga.edu/ISE/soceth.html access 10/01/05].

Kachru, Braj B.
1986 *The Alchemy of English: The Spread, Functions and Models of Non-native Englishes.* Oxford: Pergamon.

Koenig, Matthias
1999 Democratic governance in multicultural societies: Social conditions for the implementation of international human rights through multicultural policies. MOST Discussion Papers No. 30. [www.unesco.org/most/ln2pol2.htm access 10/02/04].

Kövecses, Zoltán
2002 *Metaphor. A Practical Introduction.* Oxford: Oxford University Press.

Kristiansen, Gitte
2003 How to do things with allophones: Linguistic stereotypes as cognitive reference points in social cognition. In: René Dirven, Roslyn Frank and Martin Pütz (eds.), *Cognitive Models in Language and*

Thought. Ideology, Metaphors and Meanings, 69–120. (Cognitive Linguistic Research 24). Berlin/New York: Mouton de Gruyter.

this vol. Style-shifting and shifting styles: A socio-cognitive approach to lectal variation.

Kucharczik, Kerstin

1998 'Organisch' – Um den beliebten aber vieldeutigen Ausdruck zu gebrauchen. Zur Organismusmetaphorik in der Sprachwissenschaft des 19. Jahrhunderts. *Sprachwissenschaft* 23 (1): 85–111.

Labov, William

1966 *The Social Stratification of English in New York City.* Washington, D.C.: Center for Applied Linguistics.

1972 *Sociolinguistic Patterns.* Philadelphia: University of Pennsylvania Press.

Larson, Brendon

2008 fc. Entangled biological, linguistic and cultural origins of the war on invasive species. In: Roslyn Frank, René Dirven, Tom Ziemke and Enrique Bernárdez (eds.), *Body, Language, Mind. Vol. II: Sociocultural Situatedness.* (Cognitive Linguistics Research 35.2). Berlin/New York: Mouton de Gruyter.

Lee, Penny

1996 *The Whorf Theory Complex: A Critical Reconstruction.* (Amsterdam Studies in Theory and History of Linguistic Science 81). Amsterdam/Philadelphia: John Benjamins.

1998 The operation of linguistic relativity in the cognitive domain. Essen: LAUD 1998. Paper N° 433.

Lucko, Peter

2003 Is English a killer language? In: Peter Lucko, Lothar Peter and Hans-Georg Wolf (eds.), *Studies in African Varieties of English*, 151–165. Berlin/Frankfurt (Main): Peter Lang.

Maffi, Luisa

1998 Language: A resource for nature. *Nature & Resources* 34 (4). [www.terralingua.org/DiscPapers/languagenature.pdf access 10/01/05].

2001b Introduction: On the interdependence of biological and cultural diversity. In: Luisa Maffi (ed.), *On Biocultural Diversity. Linking Language, Knowledge, and the Environment*, 1–50. Washington/London: Smithsonian Institution Press.

Maffi, Luisa (ed.)

2001a *On Biocultural Diversity. Linking Language, Knowledge, and the Environment.* Washington/London: Smithsonian Institution Press.

Mair, Christian (ed.)

2003 *The Politics of English as a World Language. New Horizons in Postcolonial Cultural Studies.* Amsterdam/New York: Rodopi.

Meyerhoff, Miriam and Nancy Niedzielski

2003 The globalisation of vernacular variation. *Journal of Sociolinguistics* 7 (4): 534–555.

Mufwene, Salikoko
2002 Colonisation, globalisation, and the future of languages in the twenty-first century. *International Journal on Multicultural Societies* 4(2). Protecting Endangered Minority Languages: Sociolinguistic Perspectives. Ed. by Matthias Koenig. UNESCO. [www.unesco.org/most/vl4n2mufwene.pdf access 10/02/04].

Mühlhäusler, Peter
1996a *Linguistic Ecology. Language Change and Linguistic Imperialism in the Pacific Region.* London: Routledge.
1996b Linguistic adaptation to changed environmental conditions: Some lessons from the past. In: Alwin Fill (ed.): *Sprachökologie und Ökolinguistik*, 105–130. Tübingen: Stauffenburg.
2000 Humboldt, Whorf and the roots of ecolinguistics. In: Martin Pütz and Marjolijn H. Verspoor (eds.), *Explorations in Linguistic Relativity*, 89–99. (Current Issues in Linguistic Theory 199). Amsterdam/Philadelphia: John Benjamins. (Prepubl. as LAUD Paper N° 442. Essen: LAUD, 1998).
2001 Ecolinguistics, linguistic diversity, ecological diversity. In: Luisa Maffi (ed.), *On Biocultural Diversity. Linking Language, Knowledge, and the Environment*, 133–144. Washington/London: Smithsonian Institution Press.
2003 English as an exotic language. In: Christian Mair (ed.), *The Politics of English as a World Language. New Horizons in Postcolonial Cultural Studies*, 67–86. Amsterdam/New York: Rodopi.

Nettle, Daniel
1999 *Linguistic Diversity.* Oxford: Oxford University Press.

Nettle, Daniel and Suzanne Romaine
2000 *Vanishing Voices: The Extinction of the World's Languages.* Oxford: Oxford University Press.

Niemeier, Susanne and René Dirven (eds.)
2000 *Evidence for Linguistic Relativity.* (Current Issues in Linguistic Theory 198). Amsterdam/Philadelphia: John Benjamins.

Ouane, Adama
2003 The discourse on mother tongues and national languages. In: Adama Ouane (ed.), *Towards a Multilingual Culture of Education*, 35–49. Hamburg: UNESCO Institute of Education.

Pattanayak, Debi Prasanna
2003a Mother tongues: The problem of definition and the educational challenge. In: Adama Ouane (ed.), *Towards a Multilingual Culture of Education*, 23–28. Hamburg: UNESCO Institute of Education.
2003b Multicultural contexts and their ethos. In: Adama Ouane (ed.), *Towards a Multilingual Culture of Education*, 29–34. Hamburg: UNESCO Institute of Education.

Pennycook, Alastair
1994 *The Cultural Politics of English as an International Language.* London: Longman.

1998 *English and the Discourse of Colonialism*. London: Routledge.
2003a Beyond homogeny and heterogeny: English as a global and worldly language. In: Christian Mair (ed.), *The Politics of English as a World Language. New Horizons in Postcolonial Cultural Studies*, 3–18. Amsterdam/New York: Rodopi.
2003b Global English, Rip Slyme, and performativity. *Journal of Sociolinguistics* 7 (4): 513–533.

Peter, Lothar and Hans-Georg Wolf
2003 Aku in The Gambia: Terminological problems, functional distribution and popular attitude. In: Peter Lucko, Lothar Peter and Hans-Georg Wolf (eds.), *Studies in African Varieties of English*, 119–127. Berlin/Frankfurt (Main): Peter Lang.

Phillipson, Robert
1992 *Linguistic Imperialism*. Oxford: Oxford University Press.
2001 English yes, but equal language rights first. *The Guardian* online. 19th April, 2001. [www.guardian.co.uk/GWeekly/Story/0,3939,475284,00.html access 10/02/04]
2003 English for the globe, or only for globe-trotters? In: Christian Mair (ed.), *The Politics of English as a World Language. New Horizons in Postcolonial Cultural Studies*, 19–30. Amsterdam/New York: Radopi.

Polzenhagen, Frank
2007 *Cultural Conceptualisations in West African English: A Cognitive-Linguistic Approach*. (Duisburger Arbeiten zur Sprach- und Kulturwissenschaft / Duisburg Papers on Research in Language and Culture). Berlin/Frankfurt (Main): Peter Lang.

Polzenhagen, Frank and Hans-Georg Wolf
2007 Culture-specific conceptualisations of corruption in African English: Linguistic analyses and pragmatic applications. In: Farzad Sharifian and Gary Palmer (eds.), *Applied Cultural Linguistics: Intercultural Communication and Second Language Learning and Teaching*, 125–168. (Converging Evidence in Communication and Language Research 7). Amsterdam/Philadelphia: John Benjamins.

Pütz, Martin and Marjolijn H. Verspoor (eds.)
2000 *Explorations in Linguistic Relativity*. (Current Issues in Linguistic Theory 199). Amsterdam/Philadelphia: John Benjamins.

Pütz, Martin, Susanne Niemeier and René Dirven (eds.)
2001 *Applied Cognitive Linguistics II: Language Pedagogy*. (Cognitive Linguistic Research 19.2). Berlin/New York: Mouton de Gruyter.

Romaine, Suzanne
1997 World Englishes: Standards and the new world order. In: Larry E. Smith and Michael L. Forman (eds.), *World Englishes 2000*, ix–xvi. Honolulu: University of Hawaii and East-West Center.
2002 The impact of language policy on endangered languages. *International Journal on Multicultural Societies* 4 (2). Protecting Endan-

gered Minority Languages: Sociolinguistic Perspectives. Ed. by Matthias Koenig. UNESCO.
[www.unesco.org/most/vl4n2romaine.pdf access 10/02/04].

Schmied, Josef
1991 *English in Africa: An Introduction*. Burnt Mill: Longman.

Seidlhofer, Barbara
2003 A concept of international English and related issues: From 'Real English' to 'Realistic English'. Strasbourg: Council of Europe. [www.coe.int/T/E/Cultural_Co-operation/education/Languages/Language_Policy/Policy_development_activities/Studies/SeidlhoferEn.pdf access 10/02/04].

Sharifian, Farzad
2003 On cultural conceptualisations. *Journal of Cognition and Culture* 3 (3): 187–207.
this vol. Cultural models of Home in Aboriginal children's English.

Skutnabb-Kangas, Tove
2000 *Linguistic Genocide in Education: Or the Worldwide Diversity and Human Rights?* Mahwah, N. J. – London: Erlbaum.
2002 Why should linguistic diversity be maintained and supported in Europe? Some arguments. Strasbourg: Council of Europe. [www.coe.int/T/E/Cultural_Co-operation/education/Languages/Language_Policy/Policy_development_activities/Studies/Skutnabb-KangasEN.pdf access 10/02/04].
2003 Linguistic diversity and biodiversity: The threat from killer languages. In: Christian Mair (ed.), *The Politics of English as a World Language. New Horizons in Postcolonial Cultural Studies*, 31–52. Amsterdam/New York: Rodopi.

Skutnabb-Kangas, Tove and Robert Phillipson (eds.)
1994 *Linguistic Human Rights. Overcoming Linguistic Discrimination.* (Contributions to the Sociology of Language 67). Berlin/New York: Mouton de Gruyter.

Smith, Eric A.
2001 On the coevolution of cultural, linguistic, and biological diversity. In: Luisa Maffi (ed.), *On Biocultural Diversity. Linking Language, Knowledge, and the Environment*, 95–117. Washington/London: Smithsonian Institution Press.

Tajfel, Henri
1978 Social categorization, social identity and social comparison. In: Henri Tajfel (ed.), *Differentiation between Social Groups*, 61–76. London: Academic Press.

Whorf, Benjamin L.
1956 *Language, Thought, and Reality*. Ed. by John Carrol. Cambridge, Mass.: MIT Press.

Wolf, Hans Georg
2001 *English in Cameroon*. (Contributions to the Sociology of Language 85). Berlin/New York: Mouton de Gruyter.

this vol. A cognitive linguistic approach to the cultures of World Englishes: The emergence of a new model.

Wolf, Hans Georg and Frank Polzenhagen
2007 Fixed expressions as manifestations of cultural conceptualizations: Examples from African varieties of English. In: Paul Skandera (ed.), *Phraseology and Culture in English*, 399–435. (Topics in English Linguistics 54). Berlin/New York: Mouton de Gruyter.

Wollock, Jeffrey
2001 Linguistic diversity and biodiversity: Some implications for the language sciences. In: Luisa Maffi (ed.), *On Biocultural Diversity. Linking Language, Knowledge, and the Environment*, 248–262. Washington/London: Smithsonian Institution Press.

Yajun, Jiang
2002 Metaphors the English language lives by. *English Today* 18 (3): 55–64.

Yu, Ning
1998 *The Contemporary Theory of Metaphor: A Perspective from Chinese*. Amsterdam/Philadelphia: John Benjamins.

A nation is a territory with one culture and one language: The role of metaphorical folk models in language policy debates*

Raphael Berthele

Abstract

This contribution is an updated and expanded attempt to come to terms with two examples of national language ideologies in the western world: The debates around the use and instruction of foreign language(s) in the US and in Switzerland (cf. Berthele 2001a). These debates pertain both to the essential political question of which languages "deserve" official status and/or are to be taught in public schools in a particular political entity. Whereas in the US the contentious issue is whether there is space for more than one official language (namely English), the currently most controversial issue in Switzerland is the space public schooling has to attribute to "non-native" languages, such as English, as opposed to the four national languages.

The main goals of this attempt is to make a substantial step towards a better understanding of the folk cultural models underlying attitudes towards particular languages or language-related issues. I use the term *folk models* by no means in a derogatory way. On the contrary, it mirrors the growing interest in pre-theoretic thinking about language, multilingualism and linguistic variation as a necessary prerequisite for understanding sociolinguistic processes in general. Along the same lines as Niedzielski and Preston (1999), I will argue that there is a set of particular tacit assumptions about the relationship of languages and socio-political entities, all of which have entailments for the ideological stances (i.e. the partisan points of view) taken in political debates involving language(s).

Starting from this genuinely anthropological and sociolinguistic interest in spontaneous theorizing about language and linguistic issues, elements from cognitive semantics will be shown to be useful in order to analyze metalinguistic discourse in the realm of language policy. A major point of the contribution will be that there are a number of recurrent *conceptual mappings* which allow construing the target domain of language. However,

* Acknowledgment: Many thanks to René Dirven and Gitte Kristiansen for their many helpful and well meaning comments on an earlier version of this chapter.

the differences in language policy issues cannot simply be boiled down to two or more different choices in metaphors for language. Rather, it is the precise way in which the metaphors are being used which displays and contributes to the opposing ideologies.

Keywords: conceptual metaphor, cognitive models, language policy, language ideology, multilingualism.

1. Introduction

Analogy as a central means of human theorizing and thinking has been acknowledged at least since Socrates' *Poetics*. In recent times, one particular framework from CL, the conceptual metaphor theory (Lakoff and Johnson 1980; Lakoff 1987; Lakoff and Johnson 1999) has had enormous success in the field. It is safe to assume that this framework does not need an in-depth introduction in the present volume. The following points have to be sufficient in order to justify why this framework is compatible with the general interest in folk theorizing and cultural models: metaphorical language is seen as not merely a matter of ornamental style. On the contrary, many domains of human culture are essentially metaphorical (Lakoff and Johnson 1980: 40) and we have probably no other way of thinking and speaking about them than by using metaphors. The analysis of the metaphors in a given discourse therefore should help to reveal the underlying, mostly unconscious conceptual processes.

The target domain LANGUAGE is difficult to conceptualize, and it is well known that even linguists do not agree on its nature – the different accounts range from an encapsulated modular competence in frameworks such as Generative Grammar to an epiphenomenon of social practice (e.g. the phenomenon of the third kind in Keller 1994). It is thus not far-fetched to expect a political discourse around language policy issues to be highly dependent on cognitive operations that link the complex and in some sense rather abstract domain (LANGUAGE) to more immediate domains. As I have shown elsewhere (Berthele 2002), there are a number of possible source domains for the conceptualization of language: Language can be understood in the terms of a BUILDING, of a TOOL, of a TERRITORY or simply of HOME, etc. Most of the mappings presented in the present paper are grounded in the pragmatic function of language (e.g. LANGUAGE IS A KEY). This has to do with the nature of the particular issues at stake: language policy addresses fundamental questions concerning official communication in a given political entity, questions of foreign language instruction in public schools, etc. (cf. Widmer et al. 2004). Whereas it is quite abstract and not very intuitive to think of LANGUAGE in terms of a SOCIAL PRACTICE (as sociolinguists generally do), it is much more common to focus on potential outcomes of the linguistic practice, e.g. its power to create communities (LANGUAGE IS A BOND) or to open up new OPPORTUNITIES (LANGUAGE IS A TOOL/KEY).

Metaphors and metonymies, together with image schemata and propositional structures (e.g. frames) form so-called Idealized Cognitive Models (ICMs, Lakoff 1987: 68 ff.). ICMs, in Lakoff's framework, are the major way in which our knowledge is organized. They organize the 'noisy' socio-physical world around us, serve as normative backgrounds, shape our expectations, and in some cases they determine to which differentiations we pay attention or not. ICMs are tied to lexical items (Lakoff 1987: 289) and form "the background against which the word is defined". In a famous example, Lakoff (1987: 74 ff.) spells out how the ICM of MOTHER is made out of a number of sub-parts, e.g. the birth model, the genetic model, the nurturance model, etc. Lakoff calls this type of complex model a CLUSTER MODEL:

> There need be no necessary and sufficient conditions for motherhood shared by normal biological mothers, donor mothers (who donate an egg), surrogate mothers (who bear the child, but may not have donated the egg), adoptive mothers, unwed mothers who give their children up for adoption, and stepmothers. They are all mothers by virtue of their relation to the ideal case, where the models converge. That ideal case is one of the many kinds of cases that give rise to prototype effects. (Lakoff 1987: 76)

Idealization is an extremely basic cognitive process, and there are arguments for its being an innate faculty of the human brain (Maratsos 2000: 751). In this paper, I will argue that Western language ideologies can be better understood if we consider them against a background of such idealizations, more precisely against an ICM of the nation-state. There is almost nothing new about this following model, if it weren't for the claim that we are dealing with an ICM of the type of Lakoff's cluster models. All other claims are well-known from the historical literature on European nation-building in the 19th century (cf. also Geeraerts 2003: 48). The ICM of the nation-state includes the following partial models:

- a nation is formed by people of one culture
- and one language,
- living in a contiguous, politically independent territory,
- looking back at their particular (heroic) history

The more of these partial models apply to a given case, the closer the case comes to the ideal case of the nation-state. In a related way, Kristiansen (2003: 106) points out that language is a crucial participant within the frame of social categorization.

There is probably not a single nation which perfectly matches all of these characteristics. Thus, the non-matching aspects of national reality or history tend to be erased (e.g. minority cultures and languages, not so heroic parts of the history, etc.). This cluster model is in some ways similar to Rubba's (1996: 241) ICM of territoriality, but in addition to the latter it explicitly applies to politically defined entities.

Geeraerts (2003) proposes two cultural models of linguistic standardization, the *RATIONALIST* and the *ROMANTIC* model. There are important connections and relationships between his very basic models and the more specific mental models discussed in the present text. To anticipate a way of bringing the two approaches together, standardization can be seen as an entailment of the ICM of the nation-state: Since a given nation-state is imagined as culturally homogenous, there is one common standard language which allows communication within the nation, and which opens up opportunities for all members of the nation. However, there are also possible ties to Geeraerts' other model, the Romantic Model, which puts particular emphasis on the expressive and identity-related function of language (Geeraerts 2003: 37): Since the ICM of the nation-state also includes the idea of a common cultural identity, it embraces also the romantic ideal of the national language expressing and encoding national/cultural identity. On the other hand, the Romantic Model is at first sight incompatible with the ICM with regards to the problem of linguistic variation and diversity. The positive attitude towards linguistic diversity within the Romantic Model opposes the homogenizing ICM of the nation-state. I will argue in section 5 that this incompatibility can be eliminated or at least reduced if we make finer-grained distinctions with respect to the level of abstraction our models apply to.

As has been argued above, it lies in the nature of idealized and idealizing models that they mask certain parts of the social, political and historical reality and tend to emphasize and generalize others. Language is only one part of this ICM, but as we will see, in political discourse it can play a crucial role in representing metonymically the whole model. It is only with respect to this model that most of the metaphorical and metonymical mappings discussed below make sense.

A last theoretical framework to be introduced here is the semiotic analysis of linguistic ideologies proposed by Gal and Irvine (1995) and

Irvine and Gal (2000). One of the central claims within this framework is that, in the ideological meta-linguistic discourse, selected features of the linguistic repertoire are seen as representing the 'essence' or 'inherent nature' of the social group. The ideological representation thus is a sign and takes part in a number of characteristic semiotic processes. There are three main processes: iconization, recursiveness, and erasure. Iconization and erasure are particularly interesting for our present purpose. Iconicity refers to a principled relation of "representation" or "depiction" between traits attributed to a particular social or ethnic group and evaluative judgments about this group's language (Irvine and Gal 2000: 37). Linguistic features are thus perceived as being a surface expression of essential properties of a social group. However, this form of iconicity seems to be rather a metaphorically construed relation between ethnic traits and linguistic features, since there is no immediate resemblance between sounds and cultural or ethnic properties. In the following, I prefer thus, following Kristiansen's (2003) frame-oriented approach, to assume that iconicity as introduced by Irvine and Gal should be understood as metonymic links between ethnic/social stereotypes and salient features of the corresponding lectal varieties: The linguistic feature stands metonymically for stereotypes which are tied to social and ethnic categories.

Erasure, following Irvine and Gal (2000), is the process according to which ideology simplifies the profiled representations. If, in a particular ideological context, the focus lies on a particular social category, there is a general tendency to homogenize the features attributed to the members of this category – and simultaneously increase the difference between members and non-members. Indeed, if metalinguistic and social categorizations work the same way as natural categorization does, then erasure is simply a consequence of the "process of accentuation of intragroup similarities" (Kristiansen 2003: 89). However, this last principle of erasure is closely related to the ICM of the nation-state which has just been introduced above: E.g., if membership in the national category is emphasized, the powerful majority language and culture tends to be represented as a homogeneous set of features and items, whereas minority languages and cultures tend to be "forgotten", i.e. erased.

2. Case study I: English-only

The first case to be examined here is the English-Only debate in the USA. The term *ENGLISH-ONLY* generally covers political actions both on the level of federal state as well as on the national level. The movement emerged in the aftermath of the new waves of immigration that began rolling in from about 1960 on. The declared goal of the English-Only proponents is to establish English as the only official language in the US. This means that all communication with official agencies, courts, administrations on the federal and on the state level be in English. Instruction in public schools should be exclusively in English and bilingual education must be abolished. Before this, there were, at least for five decades, virtually no language and immigration policy issues discussed in the US (Schmid 2001: 67). Historically, there have been variable degrees of official multilingualism in the US, e.g. many official documents were printed in German early in the republic, and many public school systems, from Ohio to Texas, offered German medium instruction. The most coercive suppression of non-English languages undoubtedly occurred for Native Americans, through boarding schools where other languages were not allowed. The enabling act of Congress that gave New Mexico and Arizona statehood in 1910 specified that the schools must be conducted in English. In 1906, Congress specified that aliens could not be naturalized without passing a test of oral English.

In the sixties, the interest in civil rights and pluralism reversed the trend of anti-foreignism in the twenties, and created Bilingual Education (e.g. in the Bilingual Education Act in 1968). The rather positive assessment of multilingualism in this latter act has been sharply corrected in the 2002 English Language Acquisition Act, as well as many other English-Only legislations, since the 1970s, in now more than half the U.S. states (cf. Crawford 2001 and Schmid 2001 for details). Although there are always exceptions to the rule, it is safe to attribute the English-Only efforts to a conservative political agenda and the defense or promotion of bi- and multilingualism to liberals (cf. the fight of the ACLU, the American Civil Liberties Union, against English-Only legislation; Rourke 2004: 109 ff.). Quite ironically, at a time when English rapidly increased its dominance on the international level, more and more people in the US started to fear immigrant and native languages. This is even more surprising if one considers that the rate of Anglicization of immigrants in the US increased during the last few decades (Veltman 1983, 1988).

2.1. English in danger: the English-Only proponents' point of view

In the texts, ads and banners provided by one of the major English-only organizations, US-English (cf. www.us-english.org), there are two main conceptualizations of language: LANGUAGE IS A BOND and LANGUAGE IS A

KEY/TOOL. Let us first turn to the latter, which is systematically used by the US-English Chairman Mauro E. Mujica:

> As an immigrant myself, I know that English is the key to opportunity in this country. (Mujica in a news release on Jan. 15, 2001)

> English is the key to opportunity in this country, and the first step on the road to success begins in the classroom. (http://www.us-english.org)

> English is the key to opportunity in this country. It empowers immigrants and makes us truly united as a people. (Mujica 2004: 108)

Here, the English language is the KEY to success, a TOOL that allows accessing the economic resources in the country. Understanding LANGUAGE AS A TOOL is one of the most traditional western cultural models, it goes back at least to Plato's Kratylos (cf. the notion of ORGANON). It is a *cultural* model since other cultures outside the Western world do not seem to put a similar emphasis on the usefulness of language (Haviland 1979: 209).

The related LANGUAGE IS A KEY metaphor suggests that a person needs the right key in order to open a particular lock, i.e. to achieve a goal, a variant of the PURPOSES ARE DESTINATIONS metaphor (Lakoff & Johnson 1999: 52). And this right key in the US is not Mandarin or Spanish or any other language than English. The LANGUAGE IS A TOOL metaphor has a similar entailment in the target domain: in order to achieve the intended goal one has to have adequate tools, and the only adequate tool in order to live the American Dream is the English language.

The second mapping found in the quote above implies that language is also what makes the people living in the US united, i.e. the LANGUAGE IS A BOND metaphor. A quote which is often used by US-English proponents is one by Alexis de Tocqueville (from the first volume of his "De la démocratie en Amérique"):

> The tie of language is perhaps the strongest and the most durable that can unite mankind.[1] (de Tocqueville 1835: 28)

The overtly presented argument is that, given the very different ethnic backgrounds of the members of the American society, there is a constant

1. "Le lien du langage est peut-être le plus fort et le plus durable qui puisse unir les hommes"

danger of lack of unity within the nation. The common language is what holds it all together. The LANGUAGE IS A BOND metaphor has been frequently used by S. I. Hayakawa, a linguist, former senator and chairman of the English-Only organization US-English:

> English, our common language, binds our diverse people.
> http://www.us-english.org/inc/official/quotes/quotes4.asp

> What is it that has made a society out of the hodge-podge of nationalities, races and colors represented in the immigrant hordes that people our nation? It is language, of course, that has made communication among all these elements possible. It is with a common language that we have dissolved distrust and fear. It is with language that we have drawn up the understandings and agreements and social contracts that make a society possible. (Hayakawa 1994: 15)

Alternatively, the common language is seen as the GLUE of an otherwise threatened nation:

> With all the divisive forces tearing at our country, we need language to help hold us together. (Bob Dole in 1995; cf. Crawford 2001: 35)

> America is not a nation of separation. All our citizens are Americans. The common denominator is our language. Our language is English. The glue that binds generation after generation is both our Constitution and our English language. Rep. James Traficant
> (cf. http://www.us-english.org/inc/official/quotes/quotes4.asp)

The mapping from the source domain BOND (or TIE or GLUE) onto the target domain LANGUAGE is not simply a mapping from a concrete source domain onto a more abstract target domain. The concept of a BOND, TIE or GLUE for the society involves another presupposed metaphorical mapping. The abstract construct SOCIETY is construed as a collection of elements which needs something that holds it all together. The primary metaphor which furnishes the experiential ground for this reasoning is RELATIONSHIPS ARE ENCLOSURES (Lakoff and Johnson 1999: 53). The abstract RELATIONSHIP between the members of a society is understood as having some common physical locus. If the society lacks this physical restraint, it is falling apart and it stops being a 'real' society. The argument which uses the LANGUAGE IS A BOND metaphor in the English-Only debate thus firstly builds on the metaphorical plausibility of RELATIONSHIPS ARE ENCLOSURES; it assumes that a society can only be a society if there is something which holds it together. Secondly, the LANGUAGE IS A BOND metaphor maps the entity which holds the society together onto language; this is why we could also call it the LANGUAGE IS PHYSICAL ENCLOSURE. Since there is no immediately perceivable physical enclosure which holds the society together, language is argued to be the key bond within any given society. It would be wrong to maintain that the English-Only proponents exclude any other concept as potential GLUE within the American society, but due to what is at stake in the particular debate, i.e. the question of which and how many languages merit official status in the US, the bond of LANGUAGE is profiled.

Obviously, if there is a factual lack of proficiency in English in certain immigrant communities, this is also a sign of ethnic and economic segregation. What the LANGUAGE IS A BOND metaphor probably means is that it is necessary to be potentially able to communicate with every other member of our nation, even if in reality we only interact with an infinitely small and sociologically restricted part of it. It is about an imagined community, not about a real community (Anderson 1983: 15).

The LANGUAGE IS A BOND metaphor is an important part of the ICM of the nation-state discussed above (section 1). According to this ICM, Language is one of the central cultural aspects shared within a nation-state, thus a prototypical nation-state has got its own exclusive official language. It is important to note that this is a prescriptive and ideological claim, since there are probably no examples of a nation which is entirely monolingual. Despite the discrepancy between actual reality and the ICM, Language can thus metonymically represent the nation-state as a whole, and the absence of a common language, seen from the collective point of view, is seen as putting the national cohesion into danger. From the point of view of the individual, the insistence on using languages other than English represents the construction of dangerous impediments which makes development, cultural and economic success impossible. In the US, there is an old tradition of this line of thinking, as the following quote from Indian Commissioner J. D. C. Atkins explains (the languages he is referring to the Native American languages):

> These languages [...] are a means of keeping them in their savage condition by perpetuating the traditions of carnage and superstition.
>
> (US Indian Office 1888: 15)

Thus, while the "good" official language is a necessary BOND that guarantees the unity of the nation, there is a flip side of the BOND-metaphor which entails that "bad" unofficial languages are PHYSICAL ENCLOSURES which prevent their speakers from being prosperous and civilized. This is the LANGUAGE IS A BARRIER metaphor.

> Official English benefits every resident of this wonderful melting pot called America. The melting pot works – because we have a common language.
> http://www.us-english.org/inc/

In the passage above it is very daring to use the LANGUAGE IS A BOND metaphor together with the notorious melting pot metaphor, since the latter suggests a mixing of cultures, ethnic groups, *and* languages, rather than adopting the idiom of the most successful one of the European colonizers. And a mixed language is definitely not what the authors are dreaming of, as the following ad used by the US-English organization shows clearly:

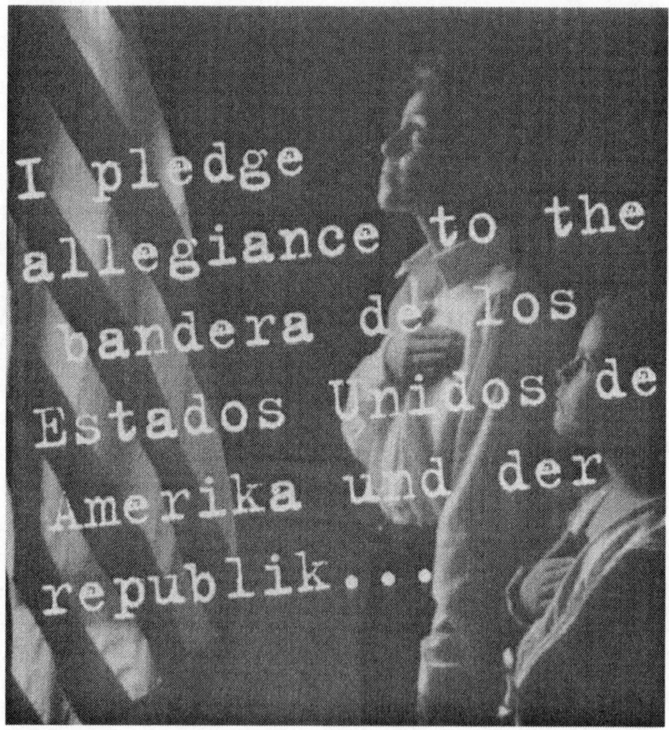

Figure 1. Anti-mixing ad used by the US-English organization (http://www.us-english.org/) The text below the picture continues: "Will it come to this? – We hope not".

This ad clearly alludes to linguistic purism. Purism is a quite natural entailment not necessarily of metaphorical mappings, but rather of prototype categories: a good language is a language which has typical features which allow a rapid and clear identification. Thus, languages which are perceived as mixed, impure etc. are bad languages. This is the cognitive basis for linguistic purism that advocates not only "pure English", but also "pure dialect" (cf. Haas 1992). According to the purist ideology, language is in constant decay due to mixing, careless use, and other "external" influences. Language used to be "pure" and "good" in earlier times and maybe still is pure (in the case of dialects) in remote, isolated communities (cf. Berthele 2001c), a folk belief which plays an important role in the romantic mystification of primitive cultures. The intended effect of the advertisement depicted in Figure 1 is to capitalize on the naturalness (from the point of view of categorization) of the purist argument; and its successful perlocution consists in creating a negative attitude towards multilingualism.[2]

To sum up, the mental model of language which operates for English-only proponents can be analyzed as being based firstly on general principles of natural categorization and secondly on metaphorical mappings from concrete source domains onto the abstract target domain LANGUAGE. The most important entailments are that one common language needs to function as a crucial bond in society, that it is easy to learn a language in an immersion setting, and that a language has to be pure, perfect, and perfectly mastered by its speakers. These cognitive patterns and mappings all fit in well with the ICM of the nation-state. Their relation to the Romantic and the Rationalist Model (Geeraerts 2003) will be discussed in the concluding section.

The US-English proponents do by no means assert that there is only one culture in the US. The cultural differences of the different immigrants and natives are acknowledged and in the same time erased by the evocation of "the American Dream of economic and social advancement" (English Language in Public Schools 1998) or the notion of the famous "melting pot". Thus, for the campaign in favor of Official English, the ICM postulates one nation, admittedly multicultural, but bound together by common values such as the American dream, probably certain basic political beliefs, one religion, and one language.

2. The bias against mixed languages should not be taken as a universal folk belief. As Rampton (1995: 57) shows, there are contexts in which mixed languages are positively evaluated as the "future language".

2.2. Multiculturalism in danger: the English-Only opponents' point of view

If we look at texts produced by the opponents of English-Only measures (e.g. as in the 150-page collection by Gallegos 1994), the first observation is that metaphors are much less likely to be used. As in the following example, the multilingualists' strive is rather one to prove that their opponents' metaphors are misleading:

> The common bond that unites Americans of all backgrounds, origins, and languages is our shared belief and commitment to freedom, democracy and liberty. That bond runs deeper than the English language.
> (Chen 2004: 119)

Multilingualists thus believe that multicultural America is not united by a common language, but by common ethical values:

> America is great not because we speak one language or the other, but because we are united by the fundamental principles than [sic] bind our people together: freedom, justice, equal opportunity for all, fairness, democracy. (Corrada 1992: 121)

The most frequent metaphor used in the pro-bilingualism writings is again LANGUAGE IS A TOOL. This metaphor is related to the usage-oriented claim within the Rationalist Model (Geeraerts 2003: 28 ff.), although it is obviously not used at all as an argument in favor of national monolingualism. Quite to the contrary, an entailment of this metaphor for a part of the bilingualism advocates is that a country with many languages is a country with more opportunities, a richer country:

> Rather than eliminate the second language of our immigrants, we need to help them learn English and maintain that valuable resource they already have, the use of a second language, and we need to teach our native English speakers a second language. (Stalker 1994: 50 f.)

Particularly when indigenous tongues are part of the argument, proponents of multilingualism argue that the English-Only policy is threatening a national 'treasure':

> But preventing the extinction of indigenous tongues must be understood as preserving cultural treasures that belong, in a sense, to all Americans – a public responsibility. (Crawford 1992: 260)

Sometimes a more modern variant of the TREASURE-mapping can be found, as in the following example from an article by Joseph Klein in the New Yorker:

> Do you realize that there are two hundred languages spoken in the Chicago school system? That's an asset, not a liability. (Klein 1997: 27)

Not all of the opponents of the English-Only movement are against English as the "unofficial" official language in the US. In some cases, bilingual education is advocated as a means of transition towards English, and thus bilingualism is not a goal but a necessary stage in the process of acculturation (Imhoff and Bikales 1994: 75).

Although I did not find any passage with the LANGUAGE IS A BOND metaphor, its use is not incompatible with the bilingualists' position. On the contrary, there is a parallel metonymy which is often evoked – the metonymy LANGUAGE STANDS FOR CULTURE/RACE:

> Opponents saw the imposition of official English as the potential destruction of their race and culture. (Gallegos 1994: 63)

The juxtaposition of language and culture is in fact ubiquitous in the multiculturalists' texts on bi- and multicultural education. Sometimes language is even seen as the most important locus of the ethnic culture:

> [T]he terms ["indigenous languages" and "heritage languages"] are used interchangeably in this document to refer to languages that originated in the particular region in which they are used (indigenous) and are the embodiment of the cultural heritage of that region.
> (Guidelines for the Strengthening Indigenous Languages 2001: 3)

Language is part of the frame of ethnicity, and the loss of language is equated with the loss of the native culture. In some cases, an extreme form of Whorfianism serves as an argument for denouncing forced English instruction as a form of mental mutilation:

> "Language," said the Spanish writer Miguel Unamuno, "is the blood of the spirit." He was right. We cannot do without our own tongue without brutally mutilating our individual consciousness, without being left without blood. (Montaner 1992: 164)

Thus, language is metonymically seen as being part of the individual and the collective identity. The novel metaphor LANGUAGE IS THE BLOOD

OF THE SPIRIT is an instance of an *xyz-metaphor* (Turner 1991: 198): Language is to the spirit as blood is to the whole organism. It entails that language is the essential 'organ' or bodily fluid which provides the basis for the functioning (the metabolism) of the spirit. Language – again – is the essential bond within immigrant or Native American communities, and the preservation of the native language within the community is seen as an important part of the preservation of the community's cultural heritage.

3. Two positions, one set of metaphors

As the analysis above shows, the mental models of language on both political sides turn out to be quite similar. The proponents of multilingualism use the ASSET, KEY or TOOL metaphor in order to express their belief that a society that has many different tools is not only a more colorful, but eventually also a more efficient society. The cost of bi- or multilingual institutions is the price the community has to pay for a sustained availability of those resources. The English-Only proponents use the TOOL metaphor in order to support only one but – in their view – the most powerful tool, the English language. Language, at the same time, is also the necessary BOND which holds the nation together. The monolingualists thus believe that common values have to be formulated in one common language.

In both views, language holds together a unit of politico-social organization. The main difference between the two discourses examined above is a different level of *granularity*: The English-Only proponents take a US-national vantage, treat the federal union as their ground and apply the mappings onto the whole population. One nation, one system of values, one language, very much like the Rationalist Model of the times of the French revolution (Geeraerts 2003: 30). This means that cultural differences and different ethnic traditions, be they native or immigrant, are erased in favor of a postulated uniting common culture, which is based on the common language. Thus, House Speaker Newt Gingrich, just before the House declared English the official language of the US government in August 1996, locates the common English language at the HEART of the American civilization:

> It is vital historically to assert and establish that English is the common language at the heart of our civilization.
> (cf. http://www.us-english.org/inc/official/quotes/quotes4.asp)

The multilingualists, on the other hand, argue on a higher level of granularity and take the ethnically defined community as their ground. It is important to note that, on the level of the ethnolinguistically defined community, the proponents of bilingualism apply some sort of a modified version of the ICM of the nation-state, stating that one ethnicity – internally – has one language. I will call this variant, which does not apply to a political nation, but to lower-level social communities, the *ICM OF TERRITORIALITY* (cf. Rubba 1996). In many ways, this stance is not so different from the English-Only arguments on the national level. The ICM of territoriality has also the capability to erase cultural differentiations within the ethnic category, and no fundamentally different view of ethnolinguistic identity, such as creolization, mixing of culture and language is proposed. It is very likely that both, the ICM of the nation-state as well as the ICM of territoriality are entailments of natural categorization (cf. section 1), or, in metaphorical terms, of a primary metaphor proposed by Grady (1997): since CATEGORIES ARE BOUNDED SPATIAL REGIONS, there have to be clear-cut distinctions between socio-ethnic categories. Due to their national point of view, English-Only advocates see double linguistic category-membership as an anomaly, whereas their opponents view bilingualism as a means to maintain ethnic plurality.

4. Case study II: Foreign language instruction in Switzerland

The second case to be analyzed here is debate about foreign language instruction in Switzerland. Since Switzerland is an officially quadrilingual country, there are two different types of foreign languages which do not benefit from equal privileges in public use and instruction: Firstly, the four national languages French, Italian, Romansh and German, and secondly, the "real" foreign languages such as English. There are several reasons why it is interesting and relevant to juxtapose the Swiss case and the English-Only debate. Both debates pertain to the ideologically explosive issue of language use and instruction and national coherence. Moreover, Switzerland served as an important argument for the proponents of a multilingual but unified America (e.g. Leibowicz 1992: 103; Chen 2003: 118). Correspondingly, Switzerland often figures as a counter-example to the "classical" one-nation-one-language ideology as stated in the ICM of the nation-state.

The particular political issue focused on in the following analysis is an intended change in foreign language instruction in some regions. Here, I am not going to give a comprehensive account of the Swiss language situation, as it has been described repeatedly and extensively elsewhere (e.g. Schläpfer and Bickel 2000; Rash 1998; Haas 1988, 2000; Berthele 2001b). There are four national languages, German, French, Italian and Romansh, the first three have the status of official languages, the fourth and smallest language, Romansh, has a so-called "semi-official" status (i.e. its usage is restricted to the communication between Romansh-speaking citizens and the federal administration). Romansh is clearly endangered, above all by a massive immigration of Swiss Germans into its territory. The speakers of Romansh are thus all bilingual with Romansh and Swiss German. With the exception of the more complicated case of Romansh, every language is seen as belonging to a particular territory, and the so-called 'principle of territoriality' (Fleiner 1991) states that within this territory the dominant language is to be used in schooling and for all official purposes. This principle is arguably some sort of a legal materialization of the ICM of territoriality introduced in section 1 above. The question of what defines the ethnolinguistic attribution of a territory is an intrinsically ideological issue that oscillates somewhere between (arbitrarily set) historical landmarks and demographic realities. The application of this principle of territoriality in Switzerland makes it appropriate to characterize the country as a federation of genuinely monolingual territories. Only in the Romansh-speaking areas and at the borders between the historical ethnolinguistic territories do we find aspects of bilingual practice in schools and administrations, but even there (as in the case of Fribourg, cf. Brohy 1992) the long tradition of bilingual practice does not necessarily mean that there is a coherent *official* policy of bilingualism.

Even though the Swiss are proud of their multilingual heritage, this does not mean that multilingualism per se is seen as a positive value: it depends on the languages involved. Immigrant languages and international languages such as English do not benefit from the same positive evaluation of multilingualism. It is thus not surprising to find the LANGUAGE IS A KEY metaphor also in debates on immigration (the following examples stem from newspaper articles on immigration and from a mission statement of one of the major political parties):

> As it were, language is the key for a successful participation in the life in the new home.[3] (Neue Zürcher Zeitung, 10. 06. 1997: 14)

---

3. "Die Sprache ist sozusagen der Schlüssel für eine erfolgreiche Teilnahme am Leben in der neuen Heimat."

The skillful mastery of the German language is the key to integration.[4]
(Neue Zürcher Zeitung, 23. 01. 2001: 69)

We expect from all foreigners more efforts in language acquisition: Language is the key to integration. A local national language must thus be learned in due time.[5]
(http://www.cvp.ch/deutsch/pdf/Gemeinschaft-Schweiz.pdf)

For our present context, the most important official symptom of the nation's multilingual identity was the rule that all schoolchildren had to learn one of the non-local national languages as their first L2 in school (the L2 instruction starts, depending on the canton, between the 3rd and the 5th year of elementary school). For the vast majority of German-speaking children, this means that they learned French, while French-speaking children learned German. Romansh- and Italian-speaking children often learn German *and* French. Other foreign languages were of course part of the curriculum, but their instruction started at the earliest two years later.

In 1997, the head of the education department in the canton of Zürich decided to launch a school reform project (called Schulprojekt 21). This project was conceived as a test for a small number of school classes. Among other things, it introduced early partial immersion in English from the beginning of the elementary school on. Thus, English would be learned before French or any other L2 is taught. The reaction across the country showed clearly that a national taboo had been broken. In the meantime, other cantons have followed this example and there are clear signs that by 2006/2007, major parts of German-speaking Switzerland will have switched to English as the first L2, whereas French or Italian will be taught somewhat later, e.g. from the 5th year on.[6]

The following sections are an attempt to render the most important arguments from both sides, with the corresponding conceptualizations of LANGUAGE.

---

4. "Der gekonnte Umgang mit der deutschen Sprache ist der Schlüssel zur Integration."
5. "Wir fordern von allen in der Schweiz Niedergelassenen mehr Anstrengungen beim Spracherwerb: Die Sprache ist der Schlüssel zur Integration. Wir erwarten, dass innert nützlicher Frist eine ortsübliche Landessprache erlernt wird."
6. cf. the press releases at the common homepage of the canton's educational ministries, http://www.edk.ch

4.1. The Early English proponents

The KEY/TOOL metaphor is the only really important metaphor underlying the texts by proponents of the early English instruction. Starting from the school's constitutionally anchored mission of teaching the essential abilities and knowledge for a successful career, the Zurich project aimed to emphasize autonomous learning, computer knowledge and English language skills. These three aspects of the new school profile are seen as important RESOURCES, TOOLS or KEYS to success in professional life:

> The mastery of computers and of the English language as well as the ability to be learning throughout the whole life are the indispensable key skills of tomorrow's society.
>
> (http://www.schulprojekt21.ch/projekt/summary.html)[7]

> English as key to the wide world.[8]
>
> (Neue Zürcher Zeitung, 20. 01. 2000: 45)

In the articles and letters by proponents of Early English instruction, the main issue is the unisonous evocation of globalized competition and the necessity to be proficient in English, the language of international economic, diplomatic and scientific exchange. If the other national languages are mentioned at all, then it is only to assure that their instruction remains unaltered or that the early teaching of English can help the subsequent acquisition of other languages.

The rationale behind this point of view, with its little emphasis on national language policy issues, can be seen as a direct consequence of the monolingual principle of territoriality: since, within the German-speaking territory, German is the official language of schools and local administrations, the choice of the first foreign language has to be a relevant one:

> The students should learn the language which serves them best in their youth. This is part of federalism.
>
> (Buschor in Weltwoche Nr. 38/00, 21. 9. 2000)[9]

---

7. "Die Beherrschung von Computer und Englisch sowie die Fähigkeit zum lebenslangen Lernen gehören zu den unabdingbaren Schlüsselqualifikationen der Gesellschaft von morgen"
8. "Englisch als Schlüssel zur weiten Welt / Zweisprachige Sekundarschule und Maturität am Freien Gymnasium."
9. "Sie [die SchülerInnen] sollen die Sprache lernen, die ihrer Jugend am meisten nützt. Das gehört zum Föderalismus."

Ernst Buschor is the former head of the education department of the canton of Zürich. Zürich, the by far economically most productive area of the country, generates at least half of its revenues in exchange with foreign countries – and English thus is perceived[10] as more useful than French.

4.2. The Early English opponents

Since the proponents of English as the first L2 intended to break a traditional rule regarding the sequence of foreign language instruction, the opponents immediately diagnosed an act of treason against national principles. For many journalists, historians, teachers and others, not only the knowledge of national partner languages is at stake, but the whole national coherence all of a sudden is endangered.

The opponents of the early English instruction do not question the Swiss tradition of territoriality, i.e. the primacy of the local language over all other languages, be they national or not. When they question the lack of priority attributed to a second national language, they are invoking the BRIDGE- and BOND-metaphors:

> Switzerland: land of official quadrilingualism and of cultural bridging[11]
> (Neue Zürcher Zeitung, 22. December 1998)

The solid knowledge of at least one additional national language is what allows building bridges across the monolingual territories within the nation. The headline of one of the major Francophone newspapers, when commenting on the issue of introducing English as the first L2 in Zürich, ran "La Suisse se meurt – Switzerland is born." (Le Matin, 11. 7. 2004). The mastery of at least one national language other than one's native tongue is construed as a THREAD or HAIRLINE that ties together the different parts of the country:

> [T]his invisible thread that links the people together.[12]
> (Le Matin, 11. 7. 2004).

10. It is important here to emphasize the *perceived* importance of languages. The actual functional value of English in Switzerland tends to be overestimated, as all studies on language usage in the national economy show very clearly.
11. "Land der offiziellen Viersprachigkeit und der kulturellen Brückenschläge"
12. "ce fil invisible qui relie les gens entre eux"

The wording is slightly different, but the conceptual mapping is identical to the LANGUAGE IS A BOND metaphor encountered in the first case study (section 2.1).

Of course, from an external, unhistorical point of view, there is no reason why English could not take over this bridging or linking function. The fear of English replacing the national languages in exolingual communication seems to be grounded in the commitment to tradition as well as to some sort of folk-Whorfianism, nicely expressed in the following quote:

> English is not part of the Swiss identity. [...] Would we still know why we are living together, if we spoke English with each other? Where is the respect for the linguistic minorities and the cultural differences? Language is the Soul of a people. (Ribeaud 1998: 56)[13]

This quote offers several metaphorical mappings and metonymies. The xyz-Metaphor (cf. section 2.2; Turner 1991) LANGUAGE IS THE SOUL OF A PEOPLE is actually a conflation of two mappings. LANGUAGE is to a politico-ethnic entity (a PEOPLE) what the SOUL is to the BODY. Thus, this mapping does not offer a more concrete source domain for the target domain LANGUAGE. On the contrary, the SOUL is a highly abstract entity whose very existence basically depends on philosophical and religious premises. The SOUL-LANGUAGE mapping is rather based on the ICM of territoriality (see above) and makes use of the fact that the borders of ethnic cultures often fall together with linguistic borders, and then it entails that a common native language is the *essential* part of the ethnic community. Another crucial entailment of this mapping is the claim that if we want to understand a particular ethnicity, we have to speak its language. This, ultimately, guarantees national coherence.

The last mapping to be discussed here is again a familiar one, LANGUAGE IS A TREASURE:

> But we are responsible that everybody, after leaving obligatory schooling, can communicate in one of the national languages, not because of nostalgic

13. "Englisch gehört nicht zur schweizerischen Identität. [...] Würden wir noch wissen, warum wir überhaupt zusammenleben, wenn wir miteinander englisch reden? Wo bleibt da der Respekt vor den sprachlichen Minderheiten und der kulturellen Eigenart? Die Sprache ist die Seele eines Volkes."

patriotism, but because we are convinced that quadrilingualism is part of the most precious treasures of our country.[14]

(Der FDP-Pressedienst Nr 44 – 02. 11. 2000)

To sum up, in these passages we discover a mental model very much related to the ICM of the nation-state described in section 1. This ICM is almost identical to the latter, only that there are several languages attributed to the nation in question. Thus, for a traditionally multilingual political entity like Switzerland, there are internal and external languages, and English is an external language which is not part of the cultural heritage. If it gains too much importance within the quadrilingual nation, the national coherence is in danger.

4.3. Diglossia and Early English instruction

In order to understand the energetic reaction particularly from the Francophone Swiss to the early English instruction, we have to take into consideration the diglossic nature of the German-speaking part of the country (cf. Ferguson 1959). The obligatory use of Standard German is restricted to particular domains: writing and more or less official situations. In most of everyday life, a Swiss German uses one of the various dialects, and many people claim that the dialect is even taking over some domains which were traditionally 'Standard language domains' (cf. Haas 2000: 81 ff.).[15] The Swiss German dialects are of course genetically related to the German standard language, but the distance is big enough to make smooth communication between inexperienced Germans and dialect-speaking Swiss impossible. Since the Francophone and other minority children in Switzerland are learning Standard German as an L2 in school, the fruit of their laborious studies has only limited communicative value in German-speaking Switzerland. In practice, therefore, there is a clear tendency towards the usage of French in exchanges across the linguistic

---

14. "Aber wir tragen die Verantwortung, dass sich alle nach der obligatorischen Schulzeit in einer Landessprache verständigen können, – und dies beileibe nicht aus nostalgischem Patriotismus, sondern aus der Überzeugung, dass die Vielsprachigkeit zu den kostbaren Schätzen unserer Schweiz gehört."
15. We lack empirical evidence for such claims. My guess is that, due to the considerable proportion of foreigners in the Swiss German part, the use of Standard German, in contexts formerly associated with the use of the dialects, increases as well. What we observe is thus an increasing overlap of dialect and standard language usage contexts (cf. Berthele 2004).

border: Because Swiss Germans often do not like speaking the standard variety and Francophones do not understand Swiss German, French seems to be the most natural choice. Now, if Swiss Germans all of a sudden stop learning (and liking) French, this choice becomes less natural and thus less likely, which is the main motive for the uproar in the Francophone territories against Early English.

From the point of view of metalinguistic ideologies and attitudes, the Francophones and the Swiss-German community could not be more opposed. In the French-speaking territories, starting in the 18th century, the Parisian norm of the French standard language has completely replaced the local (mostly Franco-provençal) dialects, and only relatively minor variation distinguishes the Swiss variant of the French language from the standard. But not only has the Parisian language been taken over, but also the rationalist view of linguistic variation and multilingualism described in Geeraerts (2003). Thus, a dialect is an improper language, and dialects have no grammar, are incorrect, rough and inelegant:

> The Swiss German's inferiority complex is amplified if he hears the precise and elegant German on German and Austrian television. [...] For most of the Swiss Germans it seems that the learning of correct German has no priority. (Ribeaud 1998: 48 f.)[16]

The author of this quote, José Ribeaud, is one of the best-known journalists in the Francophone part of Switzerland. He is not only a former main news anchor on Francophone public TV, but also a former editor-in-chief of the Francophone daily newspaper *la Liberté* (Fribourg). He has worked in the German-speaking areas, still lives partly near Zürich and – after his retirement – continues writing articles and books on domestic and other policy issues.

This example stands for a more widespread belief according to which non-standard languages have 'no grammar' or 'no rules', and therefore are a less valuable resource than the standard languages (Niedzielski and Preston 1999: 22 and 233). Therefore, there is an important incompatibility of linguistic values between dialect-speaking Swiss Germans and the standard-oriented Francophones. For the latter, the Swiss German dia-

16. "Sein [des Deutschschweizers] Minderwertigkeitskomplex wird noch verstärkt, wenn er auf deutschen und österreichischen Fernsehkanälen ein präzises und elegantes Deutsch hört. [...] Für sie wie für die meisten Schweizer deutscher Sprache scheint das Erlernen eines korrekten Deutsch keine Priorität zu geniessen."

lects are a bunch of coarse, primitive means of communication of an isolated, uncultivated group of speakers. The 'guttural' sounds of the language[17] are metonymically perceived as belonging to the general roughness of the people. And, if Swiss Germans use the standard language, they do it in a barbarian way:

> Across a barbaric pronunciation they are expressing deliberately the antipathy they resent towards their neighbors to north of the Rhine.
> (Ribeaud 1998: 49)[18]

From an outside perspective, one might suppose such statements to be ironic. However, the quoted passage is not ironic but serious, and it aptly reflects the stereotype shared by a large majority of the country's Francophone population. We have seen above that Ribeaud makes use of the LANGUAGE IS THE SOUL OF A PEOPLE metaphor in order to claim that mutual linguistic competence strengthens the bond among the Swiss. Since the Swiss Germans consider their native dialects their first language – a fact that Ribeaud knows very well – the soul of the German-speaking community (and as a consequence of the majority of the Swiss) is SWISS GERMAN. But the last quote makes it clear that Ribeaud does not advocate at all the teaching of Swiss German in the other parts of the country, which could also be an entailment from his LANGUAGE-SOUL-argument. We have to conclude that this is one of the examples where the folk theory lacks coherence. If we keep in mind the actual target of Ribeaud's article, it becomes clear that the point he makes is that the Swiss German majority should learn French as a first foreign language. The LANGUAGE IS THE SOUL OF A PEOPLE metaphor serves as an important argument, but only as long as it does not entail that Francophones have to learn Swiss German.

Ribeaud's text is particularly rich in metaphors for language in general and for Swiss German in particular. One of them, again preferentially applied to the Swiss German dialects, is the LANGUAGE IS A BARRIER metaphor (cf. section 2.1). Because the German-speaking majority insists on

---

17. Indeed, most Swiss German dialects have only has the velar [x] allophone where Standard German has positional alternatives [x] or [ç], and it has an additional [kx] allophone not present at all in Standard German.
18. "Sie drücken absichtlich durch eine barbarische Aussprache – oder können sie es nicht besser? – die Antipathie aus, die sie gegenüber ihren Nachbarn nördlich des Rheins empfinden."

the use of the dialects in all unmarked contexts, this language becomes a barrier both within the country as well as in the international context:

> Thus, the persistent use of Swiss German is one of the main reasons for the international isolation of our country, and it is a dangerous weapon in the battle against joining the European Union. (Ribeaud 1998: 63)[19]

Again, Ribeaud's text echoes a widely shared view in the Francophone parts of the country:

> Retreated in their dialect as in a fortress, the Swiss Germans are going to practice the mixed language that one still dares to call English.
> (Le Matin, 11. 7. 2004)[20]

The view of the dialects as physical enclosures and their isolating potential is also present in the self-criticizing texts of those Swiss German authors who advocate a more intensive use and cultivation of the German standard language:

> If the small nation of Switzerland wants to be integrated better into the circle of European nations [...], the Swiss Germans have to liberate themselves from the unilateral linguistic encapsulation.[21] (Gut 1990: 39)

It is in this very same strive for the cultivation of the standard language that we also find the LANGUAGE IS A KEY metaphor:

> It was the concern of another [participant in a discussion], that Standard High German needs to be maintained as a key to the culture of the whole German language world.[22] (Neue Zürcher Zeitung, 11. 11. 1993: 25)

The Swiss German dialects are associated with the rejection of institutional international integration of the country. From the French-speaking

19. "So bildet der ständige Gebrauch des Schweizerdeutschen einen der wichtigsten Gründe für die internationale Isolierung des Landes und eine gefährliche Waffe gegen den Beitritt zur Europäischen Union."
20. "Repliés dans leur dialecte comme dans une citadelle, les Alémaniques pratiqueront ce sabir international qu'on ose encore appeler l'anglais."
21. Denn wenn der Kleinstaat Schweiz sich stärker in den Kreis der europäischen Staaten einfügen will [...], so muss sich auch der Deutschschweizer aus der einseitigen sprachlichen Einkapselung befreien [...].
22. "Das Anliegen eines andern war es, dass Hochdeutsch besonders auch als Schluessel zur Kultur des ganzen deutschen Sprachraumes hochgehalten werden muss."

community's perspective, the way Swiss Germans speak is seen as standing in a metonymic relation to a salient stereotype they have towards Swiss Germans. The 'isolationist' attitude is less salient in the French-speaking parts of the country, a fact that has created a political divide along the linguistic boundaries. Francophone liberals feel particularly marginalized by a German-speaking majority that insists in a stubborn and anachronistic way on the special status of the Swiss confederation ('Sonderfall Schweiz').

4.4. Comparison of the two positions

Even within quadrilingual Switzerland, the ICM of the nation-state applies, with the important modification of attributing the monocultural and monolingual spaces not to the nation as a whole but to the four linguistically distinguished territories. The proponents of early English instruction focus on international competition and early acquisition of economically valuable skills. The LANGUAGE IS A TOOL metaphor is the surface symptom of this. The fact that the Early-English proponents only attribute second priority to the other national languages can be seen as an entailment of the principle of territoriality which dominated the Swiss language policy for the whole 150 years of the existence of the modern nation. The opponents, on the other hand, speak out against this economy-oriented point of view by invoking the national linguistic heritage. The "shared" languages, in this discourse, form the BOND which holds together the multicultural nation. The modified ICM of the nation-state also influences the Early-English opponent's discourse, in that Switzerland as a whole is construed as a territory with four native languages, where there is no prominent place for any other non-native language. It is a minimal degree of competence in at least one other national language that holds the country together.

5. Conclusions

The aim of this paper was to investigate the conceptualizations of the abstract entity LANGUAGE across opposing positions in national language policy debates. In the analysis of the two cases I tried to isolate the major conceptual structures which constitute the folk theory of language, at least as far as the choice of official languages is concerned. Since the focus of this study lies on the role the folk theories play in *language policy*, many other aspects of the folk theory of language had to be disregarded.

The metaphors used in the debates are surprisingly similar. Their usage of virtually each of them can be related to quite different ideological stances. The LANGUAGE IS A TOOL/KEY metaphor can be used in a restrictive way – in order to argue against bilingual education in the US – or on the contrary in an argument in favor of the instruction of an additional non-national language in Switzerland. The LANGUAGE IS A BOND/GLUE/TIE Metaphor, in the US, can be used as an argument against or in favor of bilingualism, depending on if it is applied to the nation as a whole or to ethnic minorities and their respective languages. In the Swiss debate, the BOND metaphor is mainly used by those who wish to strengthen the instruction and usage of the national languages. In both debates, the LANGUAGE IS A BARRIER metaphor is used as an argument against the use of unloved varieties/languages, be they foreign or domestic.

Table 1. "Restrictive" and "liberal" use of the main metaphors

	restrictive	*liberal*
BOND, GLUE, TIE	L is the indispensable national bond	L is an ethnic bond
TOOL, KEY	the official L is the crucial key to success	Ls are keys to intercultural understanding and success, the more you have, the better
BARRIER	foreign Ls/native dialects are segregating barriers	– [the barrier is NOT to speak other Ls than the dominating L]
SOUL	L is the soul of the nation	L is the soul and carrier of the ethnic culture

It would be wrong to emphasize conceptual similarities across the different positions without mentioning the differences in higher-level models of language, cultural and linguistic standardization, and society: English-Only proponents undoubtedly subscribe not only to a restrictive model closely related to Geeraerts' Rationalist Model (cf. Table 1), but also to clearly conservative, right-wing policies overall. The Swiss case displays less clear-cut political affiliations of the different positions, since the strong positions against English as the first foreign language (and against variation and non-standard languages, cf. section 4.3) do not entail a specific political color. However, the strong bias against both dialectal variation and English as expressed in statements from the (mainly Francophone) Early English foes can undoubtedly be assimilated to the Rationalist Model: The universal means of communication within the quadrilingual nation are the *standard* languages, they are seen as neutral and general in the sense of Geeraerts' (2003) Rationalist Model. At the same time, opponents of Early English use metaphors such as LANGUAGE IS THE SOUL OF A PEOPLE, which has a romantic flavor and may well be related to the Romantic Model. But, as the analysis in Section 4.2 has shown, this mapping is not used in a consistent way, but only in order to reaffirm the necessity to block the "invasion" of the English language, since it has got nothing to do with the "Swiss soul(s)". The full-blown romantic stance, which would value highly the emotional and authentic qualities of the dialects, is overtly rejected by the Francophone foes of Early English. Thus, they inherently advocate a Rationalist Model with some partial romantic disguise.

There is no direct path that leads from the metaphors and/or ICMs to the language policy stances expressed in the texts analyzed. The metaphors do not directly represent competing political models the way Lakoff (2002) claims for his STRICT FATHER VS. NURTURING PARENTS models. Quite the contrary, it turns out that there are a handful of recurrent mappings which are shared by all sides of the political struggles and multilaterally used. The difference between the partisan positions reside in (apparently) trivial details such as the choice of plural or singular (LANGUAGES ARE TOOLS or LANGUAGE IS A TOOL), in differences regarding what has been called the level of granularity of the socio-territorial entity to which the mappings are applied. There is a tendency following which the Rationalist Model leads to mappings and models aiming at the national level, whereas the Romantic Model focuses onto smaller units of ethnically defined communities. Within the entities in the scope of the mappings, the cognitive mechanisms such as prototype categorization, erasure, homogenization, iconization and indexicality are nevertheless similar.

ICMs, metaphors and metonymies play an important role in ideological discourse and they are worth studying for those who wish to uncover covert assumptions. However, language attitudes and other aspects of "sociolinguistic cognition" can only be fully understood if we manage to capture the role the metaphoric and other mappings play, together with low-level phenomena such as perception and categorization, in the construction of complex cultural models.

References

Anderson, Benedict R. O'Gorman
1983 *Imagined Communities: Reflections on the Origin and Spread of Nationalism*. London/New York: Verso.

Assembly of Alaska Native Educators
2001 *Guidelines for the Strengthening Indigenous Languages*. Anchorage: Alaska Native Knowledge Network.

Berthele, Raphael
2001a *A Tool, a Bond, or a Territory: Language Ideologies in the US and in Switzerland*. Essen: LAUD A 533.
2001b Die viersprachige Schweiz: Vorbild oder schlechtes Beispiel? In: Cees Debot, Sjaak Kroon, Peter H. Nelde and Hans van de Velde (eds.), *Institutional Status and Use of National Languages in Europe*, 109–130. Sankt Augustin: Asgard.
2001c On the history of sociolinguistic concepts: A continual search for mechanical solidarity. In: Josep Fontana, Louise McNally, M. Teresa Turell and Enric Vallduví (eds.), *Proceedings of the First International Conference on Language Variation in Europe. Barcelona (Spain), June 29–30/July 1, 2000*, 25–33. Barcelona: IULA/UPF.
2002 Attitudes and mental models of language: On the cognitive foundation of sociolinguistic practice. In: Gunnstein Akselberg (ed.), *Målbryting. Skrifter frå prosjektet Talemålsendring i Norge, Språkleg identitet og haldning*,6, 25–66. Bergen: Nordisk institutt, Universitetet i Bergen.
2004 Vor lauter Linguisten die Sprache nicht mehr sehen – Diglossie und Ideologie in der deutschsprachigen Schweiz. In: Helen Christen (ed.), *Dialekt, Regiolekt und Standardsprache im sozialen und zeitlichen Raum*, 111–136. Wien: Edition Praesens.

Brohy, Claudine
1992 *Das Sprachverhalten zweisprachiger Paare und Familien in Freiburg/Fribourg (Schweiz)*. Freiburg: Universitätsverlag.

Corrada, Baltasar
1992 Viva la Roja, Blanca y Azul. In: James Crawford (ed.), *Language Loyalties. A Source Book on the Official English Controversy*, 118–121. Chicago/London: University of Chicago Press.

Crawford, James
1992 *Hold Your Tongue. Bilingualism and the Politics of "English Only"*. Reading, Mass.: Addison-Wesley Publishing Company.
2001 *At War with Diversity. US Language Policy in an Age of Anxiety*. Clevedon, Buffalo, Toronto, Sidney: Multilingual Matters.

de Tocqueville, Alexis
1835 [1992] *De la démocratie en Amérique I + II*. Paris: Gallimard.

English Language in Public Schools
1998 *Initiative statute (Proposition 227)*. Available: http://Primary98.ss.ca.gov/VoterGuide/Propositions/227.htm

Ferguson, Charles A.
1959 Diglossia. *Word* 15: 325–340.
Fillmore, Charles J.
1971 Frame semantics. In: Linguistic Society of Korea (ed.), *Linguistics in the Morning Calm,* 111–138. Seoul: Hanshin.
Fleiner, Thomas
1991 Das sprachliche Territorialitätsprinzip in gemischtsprachigen Gebieten. *Gesetzgebung heute*, 93–107.
Gal, Susan and Judith T. Irvine
1995 The boundaries of languages and disciplines: How ideologies construct difference. *Social Research Social Research* 62 (4): 966–1001.
Geeraerts
2003 Cultural models of linguistic standardization. In: René Dirven, Roslyn Frank and Martin Pütz (eds.), *Cognitive Models in Language and Thougt. Ideology, Metaphors, and Meanings*, 25–68. Berlin/New York: Mouton de Gruyter.
Grady, Joseph E.
1997 *Foundations of Meaning: Primary Metaphors and Primary Scenes.* Ph.D. Dissertation, University of California, Berkeley.
Gut, Walter
1990 Über das gegenwärtige Ungleichgewicht zwischen Mundart und Hochdeutsch. In: Jean-Pierre Vouga (ed.), *La Suisse face à ses langues,* 34–39. Aarau, Frankfurt a. M., Salzburg: Sauerländer.
Haas, Walter
1988 Schweiz. – In: Ulrich Ammon, Norbert Dittmar and Klaus J. Mattheier (eds), *Soziolinguistik. Ein internationales Handbuch*, 1365–1383. Vol 2. Berlin/New York: Mouton de Gruyter.
1992 Reiner Dialekt. In: Harald Burger (ed.), *Verborum amor. Studien zur Geschichte und Kunst der deutschen Sprache*, 578–610. Berlin/New York: Mouton de Gruyter.
2000 Die deutschsprachige Schweiz. In: Robert Schläpfer and Hans Bickel (eds.), *Die viersprachige Schweiz*, 57–138. Aarau, Frankfurt am Main, Salzburg: Sauerländer.
Haviland, John
1979 How to talk to your brother-in-law in Guugu Yimidhirr. In: Timothy Shopen (ed.), *Languages and Their Speakers*, 161–240. Cambridge, Massachusetts: Winthrop Publishers.
Hayakawa, S. I.
1994 One nation ... indivisible? In: Bee Gallegos (ed.), *English – Our Official Language?*, 15–21. New York: Wilson.
Imhoff, Gary; Gerda Bikales
1994 The battle over preserving the English language. In: Bee Gallegos (ed.), *English – Our Official Language?*, 72–77. New York: Wilson.
Irvine, Judith and Susan Gal
2000 Language ideology and linguistic differentiation. In: Paul Kroskrity (ed.), *Regimes of language : ideologies, polities, and identities,* 35–83. Santa Fe, N.M.: School of American Research Press.

Keller, Rudi
1994 *On language change: The Invisible Hand in Language.* London and New York: Routledge

Klein, Joe
1997 Broken contract: Why Newt's followers no longer see him as the leader of the revolution. *New Yorker* 73 (4 August): 26–28.

Kristiansen, Gitte
2003 How to do things with allophones: Linguistic stereotypes as cognitive reference points in social cognition. In: René Dirven, Roslyn Frank and Martin Pütz (eds.), *Cognitive Models in Language and Thought. Ideology, Metaphors, and Meanings*, 69–122. Berlin/New York: de Gruyter.

Lakoff, George
1987 *Women, Fire, and Dangerous Things: What Categories Reveal about the Mind.* Chicago, London: University of Chicago Press.
2002 *Moral Politics. How Liberals and Conservatives Think.* Chicago: University of Chicago Press.

Lakoff, George and Mark Johnson
1980 *Metaphors we Live by.* Chicago, London: University of Chicago Press.
1999 *Philosophy in the Flesh.* New York: Basic Books.

Leibowicz, Joseph
1992 Official English: Another Americanization campaign? In: James Crawford (ed.), *Language Loyalties. A Source Book on the Official English Controversy*, 101–111. Chicago: University of Chicago Press.

Maratsos, Michael
2000 Disorderly nature. *Journal of Child Language* 27: 750–752.

Montaner, Carlos Alberto
1992 "Talk English – You are in the United States". In: James Crawford (ed.), *Language Loyalties. A Source Book on the Official English Controversy*, 163–165. Chicago: University of Chicago Press.

Mujica, Mauro E.
2004 Statement from the chairman of U.S. English. In: John T. Rourke (ed.), *You Decide! Current Debates in American Politics*, 105–108. New York: Longman

Niedzielski, Nancy and Dennis R. Preston
1999 *Folk linguistics.* Berlin/New York: Mouton de Gruyter.

Pedretti, Bruno
2000 *Die Beziehungen zwischen den schweizerischen Sprachregionen.* In: Robert Schläpfer and Hans Bickel (eds.), *Die Viersprachige Schweiz*, 269–308. Frankfurt a. M./Salzburg: Sauerländer.

Rampton, Ben
1995 *Crossing: Language and ethnicity among adolescents.* London: Longman.

Rash, Felicity
1998 *The German Language in Switzerland: Multilingualism, Diglossia and Variation*. Bern: Peter Lang.

Ribeaud, José
1998 Das schlechte Beispiel von Zürich: Die Schweiz ein Opfer des amerikanischen Sprachen-Imperialismus? In: Max Mittler (ed.), *Wieviel Englisch braucht die Schweiz? Unsere Schulen und die Not der Landessprachen*, 41–67. Frauenfeld: Huber.

Rubba, Jo
1996 Alternate grounds in the interpretation of deictic expressions. In: Gilles Fauconnier and Eve Sweeteser, *Spaces, Worlds, and Grammar,* 227–261. Chicago: University of Chicago Press.

Schmid, Carol
2001 *The Politics of Language: Conflict, Identity, and Cultural Pluralism in Comparative Perspective*. Oxford: Oxford University Press.

Stalker, James C.
1994 Official English or English only. In: Bee Gallegos (ed.), *English – Our Official Language?*, 44–52. New York: Wilson.

Turner, Mark
1991 *Reading Minds: The Study of English in the Age of Cognitive Science*. Princeton, N.J.: Princeton University Press.

US Indian Office
1888 *Correspondence on the Subject of Teaching the Vernacular in Indian Schools*. Washington, DC: Government Printing Office.

Veltman, Calvin
1983 *Language Shift in the United States*. Berlin/New York: Mouton de Gruyter.
1988 *The Future of the Spanish Language in the United States*. Washington, DC: Hispanic Policy Development Project.

Widmer, Jean, Renata Coray, Dunya Acklin Muji and Eric Godel
2004 *Die Schweizer Sprachenvielfalt im Öffentlichen Diskurs – La Diversité des Langues en Suisse dans le Débat Public*. Bern: Lang.

Cultural models of Home in Aboriginal children's English

Farzad Sharifian

Abstract

It is well known that students who speak 'non-standard' dialects are disempowered in education systems which recognise only the standard variety. In Australia this affects the majority of Aboriginal students, for whom Aboriginal English is the home language. The problem is, however, more subtle than simply one of linguistic interference, since many Aboriginal students, especially in metropolitan contexts, adopt the phonological and grammatical features of Australian English to express their Aboriginal cultural conceptualisations. In such cases, the Australian English speaking educators operate on the assumption that such students do not speak anything other than Australian English. This chapter provides a partial account of a study that addressed the validity of such claims by exploring conceptualisations that two groups of Aboriginal and Anglo-Australian students would associate with a number of English words such as *home*. The results provided evidence for the operation of two distinct, but overlapping, conceptual systems among the two cultural groups studied. The differences between the associative responses from the two groups largely reflected cultural models that usually characterise the two cultural groups, that is, Aboriginal and Anglo Australian. For example, many responses from the Aboriginal children to "home" referred to the members of their extended family and some responses referred to family obligations, whereas those from the Anglo-Australian children mainly referred to parts of the building where they resided and commodities such as TV. The similarities in the overall responses across the two groups appeared to arise from several phenomena such as experience in similar physical environments and access to 'modern' life style.

Keywords: Aboriginal English, cultural models, cultural cognition, cultural conceptualisation, non-standard dialects.

1. Introduction: Varieties of English

Like any other language, English is subject to variation depending on who speaks it, in what context, and for what purpose. Notions of prestige, esteem, social power, etc, also have a bearing on linguistic variation in English in the sense that they are the basic determiners of what gets constituted as the "standard" variety. The following section elaborates on this notion in the context of its educational implications, in particular with reference to Aboriginal English.

1.1. Standard vs. 'non-standard' varieties: Underlying cultural models

In many parts of the globe students who speak 'non-standard' varieties are disadvantaged as a result of the way they speak. Most educational systems idealise 'standard' varieties and promote them as part of a package for a better life. These standard varieties are usually put forward as a replacement for, and not a complement to, the 'non-standard' varieties that students bring to school.

The above position is in fact a realisation of a much wider cultural model that is referred to as "the rationalist cultural model" of language (Geeraerts 2003; Polzenhagen and Dirven this volume). This model views languages as a medium of "participation" and "emancipation", and also views 'standard' dialects as playing a key role in providing access to the world of learning and higher culture. Geeraerts contrasts this model of standardisation with the romantic model, which considers 'standard' varieties to constitute instruments of oppression and exclusion.

In Australia, educational systems largely subscribe to the rationalist model and promote the learning of Standard Australian English as the key to 'participation and success in wider society' among Aboriginal students. This is however mostly done with the implied ideology that the 'home' dialect that many Aboriginal students speak, that is Aboriginal English, is a deficient variety, which according to the rationalist model needs to be eradicated.

Thus far, the argument is classic and clear. There are however contexts in contemporary Australia in which some Aboriginal children appear to have largely adopted the phonological and grammatical features of Australian English to express their Aboriginal cultural conceptualisations. This is however not so transparent to some non-Aboriginal educators due to the fact that surface linguistic features are usually taken as the sole indicator of what language variety one speaks. This often leads non-Aboriginal teachers in the contexts described above to place the same expectations on these students as are placed on those who speak Australian English as their first dialect.

The above observation acted as an incentive for the author to move beyond the levels of phonology and grammar to explore conceptualisations that a number of English words would evoke in two groups of Aboriginal and Anglo-Australian students. This chapter provides a partial account of the study and briefly explores the educational implications of the findings.

The chapter begins by presenting a brief description of Aboriginal English, followed by a background section on the notions of *cultural cognition* and *cultural conceptualisations*. This is then followed by an account of research on Aboriginal cultural conceptualisations. The later sections of the chapter present details about the methodology that was employed in this study, along with the analysis of associative responses to the stimulus word *home*. The chapter concludes with a discussion of the educational implications of the findings.

1.2. Aboriginal English

Aboriginal English refers collectively to indigenised varieties of English spoken by Aboriginal Australians. For many speakers of Aboriginal English, this dialect is a successor of Aboriginal languages that are largely extinct now (Malcolm 2001). As Eades (1991: 57) observes, "Aboriginal English is a distinctive dialect of English which reflects, maintains and continually creates Aboriginal culture and identity". Aboriginal English includes features from Aboriginal languages. However, it should not be simply regarded as a simple mixture of the English and Aboriginal systems, but rather as a dynamic complex system with emergent features that belong neither to the former nor to the latter.

Aboriginal English is different from Australian English both at the surface levels of sound and syntax and also the deeper level of semantic content (e.g., Arthur 1996; Eades 1988, 1991, 1995; Harkins 1994, 2000; Malcolm 1994; Malcolm et al. 1999). Malcolm (2001) observes that Aboriginal English is mostly noted for its distinctive phonology by observers. Harkins (2000) notes that Aboriginal English is characterised by a high degree of variation in terms of its sound system. She observes that there is a continuum of accents in Aboriginal English, with a 'heavy' accent at one extreme and a 'light' accent at the other. The 'heavy' accent, appears to be close to the sound system of traditional Aboriginal languages and the 'light' accent is close to the sound system of Australian English (Harkins 2000; Malcolm 2001). Recent research has shown that various features of Aboriginal English largely instantiate conceptualisations that embody Aboriginal cultural experiences (Malcolm and Rochecouste 2000; Malcolm and Sharifian 2002; Sharifian 2001, 2002a,

2002b; Sharifian, Rochecouste and Malcolm 2004). As a preamble to the discussion of Aboriginal cultural conceptualisations the following section provides a brief background on the notion of 'cultural cognition', and more particularly, of 'cultural conceptualisations'.

2. Emergent cultural cognition

I have used the term *emergent cultural cognition* to refer to complex cognitive systems that are a property of cultural groups rather than individuals (Sharifian 2008). Cultural cognition is an *emergent* system (e.g. Johnson 2001) in that it results from the interactions between the members of a cultural group across time and space. In terms of its representation, cultural cognition is *heterogeneously represented* across the minds in a cultural group, rather than being repository of fixed representations that are equally imprinted in the minds of all the members. Figure 1 depicts this view of cultural cognition.

In this figure, the top, oval section represents the *emergent* level of cultural cognition. Cognition that emerges from the interactions between the members of a cultural group is often a complex system that may not be reducible to what is stored in the mind of each individual in a cultural group. The lower section of the figure, however, is meant to reflect the way in which cultural cognition is heterogeneously distributed across the minds in a cultural group. The figure highlights the fact that people in a cultural group may share some, but not all, elements of their cultural cognition, and what is shared between two members may not exactly be shared by others in the group. It is to be noted that in viewing cultural cognition as a heterogeneously distributed, emergent system I intend to a) present a view of cognition that goes beyond the level of the individual mind, and b) challenge the essentialist, deterministic views of culture while proposing a more dynamic and fluid view. Cultural cognition, as I view it, is constantly negotiated and renegotiated by the members of a cultural group and is distributed in people across time and space. This position is in consonance with some other recent trends which have called for an expanded view of cognition (e.g. Hutchins 1994). Hutchins (e.g. 1994), mainly emphasises the distribution of *cognitive processes* and includes the material environmental within the domain of cognitive processing. I emphasise the emergent nature of cultural cognition, which is primarily cultural knowledge, and I use the term "distributed" in conjunction with the term "heterogeneous" to highlight the view that cultural

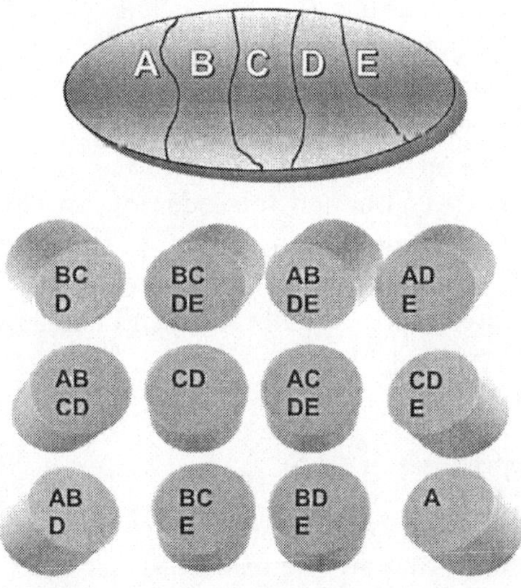

Figure 1. A model of distributed, emergent cultural cognition (Source: Sharifian 2008).

cognition is not equally imprinted in the minds of the people in a cultural group. Despite these differences in the focus of research, the two strands should be viewed as complimentary, particularly given the fact that Hutchins acknowledges that cognition is a cultural process. Kronenfeld (2002) also uses the notion of 'distributedness' in giving an account of culture. He observes that "culture has no existence outside of our individual representations of it, and since these representations are variable, there exists no single place where the whole of any culture is stored or represented. Thus, culture is necessarily and intrinsically a distributed system" (Kronenfeld 2002: 430).

The model of cultural cognition discussed here seems also to move in the direction of an ideational account of culture that Keesing (1987: 371) had in mind when he said, "An ideational theory of culture can look at cultural knowledge as distributed within a social system, can take into account the variation between individuals' knowledge of and vantage points on the cultural heritage of their people." It is this variation between individuals' knowledge of cultural conceptualisations that my use of the term 'heterogeneously distributed cultural cognition' is intended to highlight. It should be emphasised again that I do not view the ultimate level of cultural cognition in terms of fixed representations inside the mind of individuals but as emergent properties of the interactions between the members of a cultural group.

Two integral aspects of cultural cognition are conceptualisation and language. I maintain that although the locus of conceptualisation and language is the individual mind, their ultimate level of emergence is at the group level, be it a cultural group or a speech community. In what follows, I will elaborate on conceptualisation and language in relation to cultural cognition.

2.1. Cultural conceptualisations

The term *conceptualisations* captures various sub-configurations of human cognitive repertoire that are the result of basic perceptual and conceptual processes. *Image schemas, categories, schemas, metaphors,* and *models* are commonly discussed conceptualisations that have found their ways into several disciplines such as cognitive psychology, artificial intelligence, cognitive anthropology, cognitive linguistics, and cultural linguistics. The basis for human conceptualisation is multi-dimensional in the sense that our conceptual faculties, which might be largely universal and innate, derive from various sources of our experience including bodily, environmental, as well as cultural, to make sense of and organise new experience.

Cultural experience, including systems of belief that are usually termed 'worldview', largely provides a framework for human conceptualisation and may even underlie the way we conceptualise our body and our environment (Dirven, Frank and Putz 2003; Sharifian 2003). These conceptualisations act as the foundation for our emergent behaviour in our daily encounters.

A wealth of studies have shown how even very basic human actions, thoughts, and emotions may be construed through conceptualisations that appear to transcend individual cognition, but are socially or culturally constructed (e.g. D'Andrade 1995; Palmer 1996; Strauss and Quinn 1997). These conceptualisations, that I refer to as *cultural conceptualisations* (Sharifian 2003), are aspects of cultural cognition and as such are both 'emergent' and 'heterogeneously distributed'.

It may be useful at this point to make a distinction between three forms of cultural conceptualisations that will be relevant to the study presented in this chapter, that is *cultural categories, schemas and models.* Categories include *x is a kind of y* knowledge whereas schemas include conceptual knowledge that is based on other kinds of relationships, such as temporal, spatial, thematic, functional, etc. etc. (see further in Sharifian 2008). Schemas of a relatively higher degree of complexity are called *cultural models* (e.g. D'Andrade 1995). Cultural models may encompass a network of schemas, categories, and metaphors. An example of such models would be the cultural model of American Marriage (Quinn 1987). This cultural model includes conceptualisations such as GIVING AWAY schema, WEDDING GIFT category, and MARRIAGE AS JOURNEY metaphor.

2.2. Cultural conceptualisations and language

Cultural conceptualisations do not end in the cognitive domain and may be instantiated through various cultural artefacts, such as paintings, dance, ritual, etc. They may also be reflected in various features of human languages. Lexical items across different languages are largely associated with conceptualisations that embody cultural norms, knowledge, and experiences of the people who have spoken them throughout the history of these languages. Many morpho-syntactic features of human languages also appear to have been motivated by cultural conceptualisations (Enfield 2001; Palmer 1996). In the area of pragmatics, cultural conceptualisations largely provide for inferences that people make from the use of pragmatic devices of different kinds (Sharifian 2004).

As mentioned earlier, many features of Aboriginal English instantiate Aboriginal cultural conceptualisations. Malcolm and his colleagues (Malcolm and Rochecouste 2000; Malcolm and Sharifian 2002) explored cultural discourse schemas in more than 200 naturalistic oral narratives produced by Aboriginal children from Yamatji and Nyungar cultural subgroups living in urban and non-urban areas in Western Australia. The narratives revealed a number of culture-specific schemas and also a number of schemas that were reflective of contact experience. The culture-specific schemas were mainly associated with Aboriginal spiritual experience as well as cultural practices such as hunting and travelling. Sharifian (2001, 2002a) employed the notion of 'schema' in exploring various aspects of discourse structure in Aboriginal English, including the ordering of the events. The analysis revealed certain distinctive features among which was a non-reliance on chronological temporal schemas in determining the structure of discourse.

3. Empirical investigation of Aboriginal cultural models

In general, empirical investigations of Aboriginal cultural models embodied in Aboriginal English can contribute to our understanding of the relationship between language and cultural conceptualisation of experience and can also provide insights that would reduce the potential for miscommunication between Aboriginal and non-Aboriginal speakers in various settings from the court to the classroom. The study reported in the following section was a step in this direction.

3.1. Aims

As mentioned earlier, the present study was motivated by the observation that many non-Aboriginal educators in Perth dismissed the view that Aboriginal children attending metropolitan schools spoke an Indigenised variety of English. Since this position was based on similarities between the surface features of the speech of Aboriginal and Anglo-Australian students, the study targeted to explore the conceptual basis that the surface features would provide an index to. In particular, the study aimed at highlighting group-level conceptualisations that would emerge from the patterns of response by two groups of Aboriginal and Anglo-Australian students to a set of English words. The following section elaborates on the methodology that was employed to carry out the study.

3.2. Methodology

The study employed an ethnographic approach to the analysis of word associations. Word-association has so far been mainly used in quantitative studies of cognitive structures of various kinds. In this study the procedure was partly modified to suit the qualitative analysis targeted to explore cultural conceptualisations. The investigation was composed of two phases: the 'association' phase, in which a number of English words were used as prompts to evoke conceptualisations in participants, and the 'interpretation' phase, in which the associative responses given by the participants were analysed for the cultural conceptualisations that appeared to instantiate. The methodology may therefore be labelled *Association-Interpretation.*

The rationale for the recruitment of this method was that in a word-association task, the stimulus words appear to be able to elicit responses that largely reflect associative links in human conceptual system. These associative links are usually formed as a result of cognitive processes such as schematisation and categorisation. Thus, associative responses to a stimulus word should largely reflect elements and aspects of conceptualisations in an individual's conceptual system. When the task is administered to cultural groups, similarities and clusterings in associative responses are very likely to reflect *cultural* conceptualisations. Identification of cultural conceptualisations in associative responses would naturally need to be informed by *emic* (i.e., so-called insider's view) sources. The following sections elaborate on how such a methodology was employed in this study.

3.3. Participants

A group of 28 Nyungar, 1 Yamatji, and 1 Yamatji/Nyungar Aboriginal students from three metropolitan primary schools in Western Australia participated in this study. The students were from various grades, ranging from Grade 1 to Grade 7. The majority of Nyungars and Yamatjis speak English as their first language. A group of 30 non-Aboriginal Anglo Australian students also participated in this study as a reference group.

3.4. Instrument

A list of 32 words was prepared to be administered as part of the Association-Interpretation technique (see Appendix for the word lists). The words were chosen with help of an Aboriginal and an Anglo-Australian research assistant from everyday words of English that would be familiar to students across the two groups. The first two words were used as warm-up trials to establish a response mode in the participants and also to make sure that the participants understood the task.

3.5. Procedure

The investigator collected data from the participants on the school grounds and in the presence of an Aboriginal Islander Education Officer (AIEO), who helped with the administration of the task. The participants were briefed by the AIEO, who also assured them that the test was a group test and not a measure of individual performance.

The stimuli were presented orally and the responses were also required to be oral. The participants signalled the end of each response set, through utterances such as 'that's it'. Previous studies of word association mostly confined the size of responses to single words and this could in fact mask significant information regarding conceptual structures reflected in larger units of languages. In this study, there was no limit imposed on the size of the responses given by the participants. Previous studies of word associations mostly revealed a tendency for reducing to numbers the responses elicited and this does not appear to be maximally beneficial in terms of examining conceptualisations that underlie the use of language.

The responses given by the respondents were recorded using a cassette note-taker. The stimulus words were presented in a different random order for each participant. The task was made more interactive by either the investigator or the AIEO occasionally asking the participants to elaborate on their responses, at the end of a trial. The data collected were transcribed by the investigator and then subjected to the interpretive analysis.

3.6. The analysis of data

The study employed an ethnographic approach to the analysis of the responses given by the participants. The analysis viewed the responses in the context of conceptualisations that they appeared to instantiate. These conceptualisations were identified through what might be described as 'triangulated interpretation', which draws on a synthesis of several sources of information, such as the intuition of the participants and/or other members of the cultural group, a survey of the relevant published literature, and the expertise/intuition that the researcher has gained as a result of fieldwork and research. These sources of knowledge were employed in identifying conceptualisations that were reflected in the associative responses given to the stimuli.

4. Findings of the empirical investigation

Overall, the responses from the participants did not reflect conceptualisations that would be equally and totally shared by the members of each cultural group. This observation provides support for the view that cultural conceptualisations are represented in a 'heterogeneously distributed fashion' across a cultural group (Sharifian 2003). However, viewed at the emergent level of 'cultural cognition', the data suggested the operation of two distinct, but overlapping conceptual systems among the two cultural groups participating in this study. The two systems are integrally related to the dialects spoken by Aboriginal and Anglo-Australians, that is, Aboriginal English and Australian English. The discrepancies between the two systems largely appear to be rooted in the cultural systems that underlie many features of these dialects while the overlap between the two conceptual systems appears to arise from several phenomena, to be discussed later in this discussion.

For the sake of brevity, the following section only presents the analysis of the associative responses to the stimulus word *home*, in the light of the cultural conceptualisations that characterise the two cultural groups represented in this study. The analysis of the responses to the words *shame* and *family* is presented in Sharifian (2005) and a complete report of the study is presented in Sharifian (2002b).

4.1. Cultural conceptualisations of Home

A large number of responses from the participants in the two groups revealed conceptual discrepancies that appeared to arise from associating different cultural conceptualisations with the same English word-form. For example, many responses from the Aboriginal children to the word *home* referred to the members of their extended family and some responses referred to family obligations, whereas the Anglo-Australian children mainly referred to parts of the building where they resided and commodities such as TV. The patterns of response from the two groups are in consonance with cultural models of Home in the two cultures.

The Aboriginal cultural conceptualisations of Home are different from the Anglo-Australian conceptualisations of Home in several respects. The category of "home" for Aboriginal people is of much broader scope in the sense that *home* conjures up all the places where one usually stays, such as the houses in which members of one's extended family live. Thus, the houses that 'belong' to one's auntie or uncle may be considered as one's "home". Where Aboriginal people live next to each other, the concept of "home", therefore, may comprise part of a suburb.

For many Aboriginal people, the word *home* is associated with conceptualisations that profile the company of the extended family rather than a building and its contents. These conceptualisations are reflected in following responses from three Aboriginal participants to the word *home*.

(1) Stimulus: Home
Response:
– mum and dad, sisters an aunnies, an' uncles an' aunnies, and cousin, an' brothers.
– Families.
– I play playstation, I play nintendo, I play 64, wrestling,
F: (the researcher): you do wrestling at home?
P: (the participant): Yeah
F: With whom?
P: my brothers and my cousins and tonight tonight umm if you ask me the question about who's sleeping over, ask me that, say it.
F: Who's sleeping over?
P: My cousins, Stacy[1] and Broklin, she's Aboriginal, you know Beki?, you know Robbie?
F: They're coming over?
P: Yeah, and Kyle, they are my cousins.

For many Aboriginal people, the concept of 'home' may not be bounded by space and time. That is, the whole space in the house may often be shared by people who 'stay', in the Aboriginal sense, in the house and every person may not be given a dedicated room. Aboriginal children may stay up late playing with their cousins and sisters and brothers. There may not be a set time for various events happening in the house such as dinner, TV, bed, etc. This in fact appears to be associated with the cultural life style and norms, in the context of which it is not at all a deficiency. Aboriginal people often view putting children into their rooms at a set time and for a set period of time in darkness a "cruel" act, when they are asked to do so with their children (Glenys Collard, personal communication).

Several associative responses, such as the following, from the Aboriginal participants referred to 'keeping the house clean':

(2) Stimulus: Home
Response:
– Do dishes, cleaning up, be kind at home, sweeping, cleaning the table, cleaning the lounge room, cleaning your room, cleaning the laundry an the bathroom.
– Cleaning up at home.
– Keep your house clean, healthy.
– You look after it.

Several Aboriginal people suggested that the above responses might reflect reminders to Aboriginal children by their family members that

1. The names used in the data are pseudonyms.

they need to keep the house clean and tidy otherwise "they" [government authorities] would come and take them. This in fact is associated with conceptualisations of "stolen generation", which captures the sad events of taking Aboriginal children away by government authorities from their parents and putting them into white institutions. A common practice was simply to remove the child forcibly, often in the absence of the parent but sometimes even by taking the child from the mother's arms. Aboriginal people tell heart-rending stories about such events, such as the following:

> Our life pattern was created by the government policies and are forever with me, as though an invisible anchor around my neck. The moments that should be shared and rejoiced by a family unit, for [my brother] and mum and I are forever lost. The stolen years that are worth more than any treasure are irrecoverable.
>
> (A confidential submission to *Bringing Them Home*, 1997)

The Aboriginal cultural model of Home also embodies schemas that are associated with norms regarding responsibilities assumed by each member of the family within the context of 'home'. Overall, there is an emphasis in Aboriginal cultures on imparting a sense of self-reliance to children as soon as possible. Assistance, if needed, may be sought from older brothers and sisters, rather than from adults (Dunn 2001; Malin 1997). This is to give older children a chance to experience a sense of responsibility. Of course "self-reliance" as favoured by Aboriginal families is embedded with 'group-orientedness'. In other words, a person is encouraged to be self-sufficient but at the same time to attend to the needs of other members of the 'mob' and share willingly. This norm of conduct may be captured in a proposition schema which may be partly explicated as follows:

> It's good to be self-reliant but also help others, especially younger members of the family, if they need it.

Malin describes this schema as follows:

> Parents would allow their children both time and space to tackle new tasks and situations cautiously so to avoid making mistakes, and they would expect them to be both emotionally and physically resilient. To balance this independence, the parents encouraged their children to be affiliative –

> that is, to be affectionate and nurturant with those younger than themselves, to maintain an awareness of the whereabouts of everyone, to help those needing it and to trust that their peers will be similarly dependable.
> (Malin, 1997: 143)

The following responses from a six-year-old Aboriginal child instantiate the above-mentioned schema. In particular they suggest that Aboriginal children may assume the role of a carer for younger children from a very early age:

Stimulus: Home
Response:
– help them put their clothes on and their shoes
F: help who?
AIEO: What people do you help put on their shoes?
P: Katy (sister's name) and my cousin.

The associative responses from the Anglo-Australian participants largely instantiate the Anglo-Australian cultural model of Home, where everyone is allocated a separate bedroom and children spend a lot of time in their bedroom and play games. Unlike a good number of responses from Aboriginal children that refer to the members of the extended family, the responses from the Anglo-Australian students referred to different parts of their place of residence, activities carried out in the house, commodities such as TV, and to a much less degree to the members of the nuclear family. Consider the following responses from several Anglo-Australian participants:

Stimulus: Home
Response:
– Home you can sleep in, you can you can put your stuff in your house, you can have a dinner in your house, lunch, play sony, have fun.
– Bedroom, bed, backyard, shed, driveway, ceiling, garden.
– My nice bed, that's nice and soft and I like going to sleep, because I just like going to sleep, and I think about my family at home, an my cat [F: who's your family? I: my mum, my dad and my sister].
– My bedroom, kitchen, and the dining room
– Dog, person, a bed.
– Is where I go every time I finish school, where I can sit down relaxed lay on my bed, and do whatever I want, whenever I want, I don't have to live up to the standard or anything at home like at school, so I can basically relax.
– Has a roof, doors, carpet, trees at the back, tiles, and carpet, the kitchen, the rooms, beds, lights, clocks.

- It's a good place, play different games, TV, hobbies.
- It's like Nintendo, mainly my mum and dad big hug and kisses
- Place where I live, place where I go to have food an drink

It can be seen that a good number of responses refer to different parts and sections of the houses, specifically bedroom. It can also be seen that in terms of the activities carried out in the house, the responses mainly refer to 'eating', 'sleeping', and 'playing games'. People, if ever mentioned, are those of the nuclear family such as 'mum' and 'dad'. Apart from these differences, there are some elements common to the Aboriginal and the Anglo models of Home, which are reflected in various responses. The home model of many people from other countries may not include 'backyard', 'front-yard', 'shed', 'lounge', and 'laundry'

5. Overlapping cultural conceptualisations

As mentioned earlier, a number of responses across the two groups of participants suggested an overlap in the conceptualisations that were instantiated through the associative responses. The overlapping conceptualisations may be attributed in various degrees to several sources including the following:

- Experience in similar physical environments (i.e., school, park, etc)
- Membership of the same age group level
- Access to 'modern' life style
- Access to school materials
- Contact resulting in conceptual seepage.

It was observed in the analysis section that some responses from the two groups similarly referred to various aspects of school, shops, parks, etc. It is not surprising to observe such similarities in the responses given the fact that the two groups of participants have had access to these places. In fact, whoever lives in Perth and experiences going to parks, shopping centres, etc. will in time form similar conceptualisations of these places. However, subtle differences were observed between the two groups with respect to conceptualisations associated with school, park, and shops. The responses from the Aboriginal participants, for example, have revealed that physical environments mainly act as a base for profiling the cultural model of Family. It seems that it is the company of the extended family that gives significance to an event, not the place of the event or even the event itself. Aboriginal people often refer to localities and suburbs in terms of which family and 'mob' resides in them rather than where they are located in relation to the river, the city centre, or other suburbs.

Another set of responses that appeared to be similar across the two groups reflected cultural conceptualisations characterised by interests and practices of young age groups. It was observed that playing certain games and watching certain TV programs were considered by the participants across the two groups to be 'fun'. Members of other age groups may not necessarily find such games and programs to be entertaining. This means that two different age groups, even from the same culture, may have different conceptualisations of 'fun'. In other words, conceptual overlapping may derive from sharing various sub-cultures, such as the culture of age rather than anything else. It was again observed that there might be certain differences in the default elements of the conceptualisations that each group operate on. For Aboriginal children, for instance, it appears that the company of 'siblings' and 'cousins' in having fun experience is a default element and this does not appear to be so much so for Anglo Australians. Note that the words 'siblings' and 'cousins' in the Aboriginal sense may even refer to second cousins and more 'distant' relatives.

Some of the responses from the two groups were associated with cultural conceptualisations that reflect aspects of 'modern' life style, such as 'having fast food' and 'playing computer games'. A number of responses from both groups – more from Anglo-Australian participants – reflect conceptualisations that appear to have been derived from school materials or from the media. In other words, these conceptualisations appear to be school-based or TV-based and often relate to mediated rather than first-hand experience. For instance, mentioning the names of animals that are extinct, in response to the stimulus word *animal*, can be attributed to seeing their names and pictures in the books or their animations on movies.

6. Educational implications

There are significant implications arising from the way Aboriginal students conceptualise experience that can affect their school performance. For example, the way Aboriginal students conceptualise 'home' may have serious ramifications for school. There is anecdotal evidence showing that

Aboriginal students may refer to their aunts' and uncles' houses as 'home', and this has sometimes been misjudged as 'lying' by school staff.

It is also common among teachers to design classroom activities around students' home experience. In doing so, teachers may consider, as a starting point, their own cultural conceptualisations and form certain presuppositions about students' experience. A teacher reported, for instance, an incident where she asked an Aboriginal student to describe his bed, to which the child replied "I don't have a bed Miss, I sleep on the couch". Cases like this are clear evidence to potential miscommunication that can occur between Aboriginal children and their non-Aboriginal educators, due to their differences in conceptualisation of experience.

7. Acknowledgements

I wish to thank the Aboriginal and Anglo-Australian students who patiently participated in this study. Special thanks are also due to Nyungar Aboriginal educators, Colleen Sherratt, Denis Smith-Ali, and Michelle Ingram for their help with data collection and also for providing me with insights about Aboriginal cultural conceptualisations. Rene Dirven, Gitte Kristiansen, and Ian Malcolm also deserve special thanks for their helpful suggestions and comments on the earlier draft of this chapter. This chapter was written while the author was under the financial support from the Australian Research Council.

Appendix: The word list

1- Learn, 2- Tree, 3- Aboriginal, 4- Home, 5- Food, 6- People, 7- Fight, 8- Family, 9-Country, 10- Fun, 11- Australia, 12- Camping, 13- Story, 14- Birds, 15- Animal, 16- Mum, 17- Dream, 18- Watching, 19- Take-away, 20- Walk, 21- Deadly, 22- park, 23- White, 24- Shame, 25- Life, 26- Lovely, 27- Important, 28- kangaroo, 29- smash, 30- speaking, 31- hunting, 32- going out

References

Arthur, Jay
1996 *Aboriginal English: A Cultural Study*. Melbourne: Oxford University Press.

Bringing them Home
1997 Report of the national inquiry into the separation of Aboriginal and Torres Strait Islander children from their families. http://www.austlii.edu.au/au/special/rsjproject/rsjlibrary/hreoc/stolen/

D'Andrade Roy G.
1995 *The Development of Cognitive Anthropology*. Cambridge: Cambridge University Press.

Dirven, René, Roslyn M. Frank and Martin Pütz (eds.)
2003 *Cognitive Models in Language and Thought: Ideology, Metaphors and Meaning*. Berlin/New York: Mouton de Gruyter.

Dunn, Myra
2001 Aboriginal literacy: Reading the tracks. *The Reading Teacher* 54 (7): 678–687.

Eades, Diana
1988 They don't speak an Aboriginal language, or do they? In: Ian Keen (ed.), *Being Black: Aboriginal Cultures in 'Settled' Australia*, 97–115. Canberra: Aboriginal Studies Press.
1991 Aboriginal English: An introduction. *Vox* 5: 55–61.
1995 Cross-examination of Aboriginal children: The Pinkenba case. *Aboriginal Law Bulletin* 3 (75): 10–11.

Enfield, Nick
2001 *Ethnosyntax: Explorations in Grammar and Culture*. Oxford: Oxford University Press.

Geeraerts, Dirk
2003 Cultural models of linguistic standardization. In: René Dirven, Roslyn M. Frank and Martin Pütz (eds.), *Cognitive Models in Language and Thought: Ideology, Metaphors and Meaning*, 25–68. Berlin/New York: Mouton de Gruyter.

Harkins, Jean
1994 *Bridging Two Worlds: Aboriginal English and Cross-cultural Understanding*. St Lucia, Qld: University of Queensland Press.
2000 Structure and meaning in Australian Aboriginal English. *Asian Englishes* 3 (2): 60–81.

Hutchins, Edwin
1994 *Cognition in the Wild*. Cambridge, MA: The MIT Press.

Johnson, Stephen
2001 *Emergence: The Connected Lives of Ants, Brains, Cities, and Software*. New York: Scribner.

Keesing, Roger M.
1987 Models, "folk" and "cultural": Paradigms regained. In: Dorothy Holland and Naomi Quinn (eds.), *Cultural Models in Language and Thought*, 369–393. Cambridge: Cambridge University Press.

Kronenfeld, David
2002 Culture and society: The role of distributed cognition. In: Robert Trappl (ed.), *Cybernetics and Systems, Vol. 1.*, 430–431. Vienna: Austrian Society for Cybernetic Studies.

Malcolm, Ian G.
1994 Aboriginal English inside and outside the classroom. *Australian Review of Applied Linguistics* 17 (2): 147–180.
2001 Aboriginal English: Adopted code of a surviving culture. In: David Blair and Peter Collins (eds.), *English in Australia,* 201–222. Amsterdam: Benjamins.
Malcolm, Ian G., et al
1999 *Two-way English: Towards More User-friendly Education for Speakers of Aboriginal English.* Perth, WA: Education Department of Western Australia and Edith Cowan University.
Malcolm, Ian G. and Judith Rochecouste
2000 Event and story schemas in Australian Aboriginal English. *English World-Wide* 21 (2): 261–289.
Malcolm, Ian G. and Farzad Sharifian
2002 Aspects of Aboriginal English oral discourse: An application of cultural schema theory. *Discourse Studies* 4 (2): 169–181.
Malin, Merridy.
1997 Mrs. Eyers is no ogre: A micro-study in the exercise of power. In: Gillian Cowlishaw and Barry Morris (eds.), *Race Matters: Indigenous Australians and 'Our' Society*, 139–158. Canberra: Aboriginal Studies Press.
Palmer, Gary B.
1996 *Toward a Theory of Cultural Linguistics.* Austin: Universityof Texas Press.
Quinn, Naomi
1987 Convergent evidence for a cultural model of American marriage. In Dorothy Holland and Naomi Quinn (eds.), *Cultural Models in Language and Thought,* 173–192. Cambridge: Cambridge University Press.
Sharifian, Farzad
2001 Schema-based processing in Australian speakers of Aboriginal English. *Language and Intercultural Communication* 1 (2): 120–134.
2002a Chaos in Aboriginal English discourse. In: Andy Kirkpatrick (ed.), *Englishes in Asia: Communication, Identity, Power and Education*, 135–141. Melbourne: Language Australia.
2002b Conceptual-associative system in Aboriginal English. Unpublished Dissertation. Perth, Western Australia: Edith Cowan University.
2003 On cultural conceptualisations. *Journal of Cognition and Culture* 3 (3): 187–207.
2004 Cultural schemas and intercultural communication: A study of Persian. In: James Leigh and Eric Loo (eds.), *Outer Lim-its: A Reader in Communication and Behavior across Cul-tures*. Melbourne: Language Australia.
2008 Distributed, emergent cognition, conceptualisation, and language. In: Roslyn M. Frank, Enrique Bernárdez, René Dirven and Tom

Ziemke (eds.), *Body, Language, and Mind. Vol. 2: Sociocultural* Situatedness, 241–268. Berlin/New York: Mouton de Gruyter.

2005 Cultural conceptualisations in English words: A study of Aboriginal children in Perth. *Language and Education* 19 (1): 74–88.

Sharifian, Farzad, Judith Rochecouste and Ian G. Malcolm

2004 "It was all a bit confusing ...": Comprehending Aboriginal English texts. *Language, Culture, and Curriculum* 17 (3): 203–228

Strauss, Claudia and Naomi Quinn

1997 *A Cognitive Theory of Cultural Meaning*. New York: Cambridge University Press.

A Cognitive Linguistic approach to the cultures of World Englishes: The emergence of a new model[1]

Hans-Georg Wolf

Abstract

The "usage-based commitment" of Cognitive Linguistics leads by definition to a Cognitive Sociolinguistics emphasizing language variation (Geeraerts 2003). Therefore, Cognitive Linguistics has as one of its assignments the empirical study of World Englishes. Various pre-cognitive approaches to the study of World Englishes can be identified so far (see Bolton 2003), including (i) the British descriptive-historical and dialectological approaches, (ii) approaches highly critical of the role of English in the world, (iii) the "hybridizationist" approach, which highlights and promotes the pluricentricity of English and bilingual creativity in second language contexts (Kachru 1983, 1994). A typical contribution that a Cognitive Sociolinguistics can make to the field of World Englishes is in a crucial area, namely the study of culture expressed in the different varieties of English. One major assumption of Cognitive Linguistics is that the conceptualizations underlying language are systematic both in their universal and culture-specific dimensions. Although the common core of English grammar and lexis is used all over the world in the various World Englishes, the symbolizations these systems express may strongly reflect the variety-related conceptualizations of the speakers; essential components of the conceptualizations formerly expressed in the indigenous languages are now becoming associated with the symbolizations available in the structure of World Englishes. I will examine the studies done so far in this respect (e.g. by Hui 2004., Malcolm and Rochecouste 2000, Sharifian 2003, Wolf 2001) and point out the differences and commonalities with the other approaches to World Englishes.

Keywords: Cognitive Sociolinguistics, World Englishes paradigm, Cultural Linguistics, cultural schema, cultural model, conceptual metaphor, Australian Aboriginal English, African English, Chinese English.

1. I thank René Dirven and Frank Polzenhagen for their valuable comments on an earlier draft that found their way into this article.

1. Introduction

Since the 1980s, two major new paradigms have been put on the linguistic agenda world-wide. One is an evolution in the line of the globalization dynamism in the world. Linguistically, this movement has led to an ever-increasing interest in and the rise of a very large number of descriptive studies on the global varieties of English or *World Englishes* (cf. Bolton 2003: 2). Concurrently, the field of theoretical linguistics has witnessed the rise of the new paradigm of Cognitive Linguistics (CL), a similarly productive and wide-reaching research program, which has developed and brought forth a large number of revolutionary insights in the relation between language, cognition and culture, situated by and large at the antipode of the theoretical assumptions underlying most descriptive work in research on World Englishes (henceforth WE). In this research, the cultural component of WE is at best seen as optional in addition to formal descriptions, but it certainly has no legitimacy by itself. Such autonomous views of language go back to a strict Saussurean divide of language and cultural cognition. 'Langue' is defined as a system of forms and meanings "où tout se tient"[2], which has severed language from the conceptual world of its speakers and the culture that offers them the models and frames to live, think and act in. From a cognitive viewpoint this cultural-cognitive dimension is not just something that can be optionally included in or excluded from linguistic description, but it is the very existential ground, and often the motivation and the explanation for the narrowly defined descriptive facts. Since CL is not just another purely theoretical framework for the study of language, but defines itself as a usage-based theory, it is not surprising that it has developed a number of cognition-based insights and descriptive tools to deal with both the formal and cultural-cognitive dimensions of language. Some of the most relevant ones for a conceptual-constructional sociolinguistics are the following notions: 'prototype' (Rosch 1973, 1999), 'profile and base' and 'entrenchment' (Langacker 2002), 'conceptual metaphor' (Lakoff and Johnson 2003 [1980]), 'conceptual blends' (Fauconnier and Turner 1998), 'cultural model' (Holland and Quinn 1987). Moreover, in recent years one could witness various developments in CL towards a Cognitive Sociolinguistics (especially Geeraerts 2003; Kristiansen 2003; Kemmer and Barlow 2000; Achard and Kemmer 2004; Dirven, Frank and Pütz 2003).

2. On the origin of the phrase, see, e.g., LINGUIST *List* 14.1954. For a characterization of Saussure's divide, see Dirven, Wolf, and Polzenhagen (2007).

All this holds the challenge to bring research in WE and CL more closely together.

Thus, the aim of my paper is to explore how these two broad fields of linguistic inquiry can be fruitfully combined, and how Cognitive Sociolinguistics,[3] as a branch of CL, has the potential to become a new model within the wider context of WE, especially with respect to the higher-order research targets of cultural identity and cultural variation. In other words, the focus in the present paper will be specifically on these targets, i.e., studies with a cultural orientation. Consequently, my exploration will not include the notion of 'identity' as such (see Kristiansen 2003; this volume). Methods of CL have been applied to other kinds of investigations of varieties of English (e.g., Kristiansen 2003), yet a discussion of the general applicability of CL to the study of varieties of English would be beyond the scope of this paper.

Terminologically, the label 'World Englishes' mostly refers to the institutionalized second language varieties of English spoken around the world (and corresponds to the near-synonymous term 'New Englishes') or what Kachru (1985) has called the "outer circle" of English, like Indian English or Nigerian English. Given the global spread of English, the term WE may also be claimed to include the varieties of English emerging in the "expanding circle" as, for example, Japanese English (cf. Stanlaw 2004), as well as the "inner circle" varieties, like, most prominently, British or American English. WE studies – as opposed to those of a "World English," which is usually understood as some idealized norm of a uniform international and internationally intelligible English, "increasingly associated with the American print and electronic media" (Bolton 2003: 4; also see Johnson 1990) – concentrate on the differences between and the local identities of the various regional/national varieties. Thus, WE studies meet the assumption of sociolinguistics as the "linguistics of particularity" (Figueroa 1994: 5).

I will proceed as follows: First, I will characterize the theoretical approaches and positions within the field of WE thus far and will discuss their authors' perspective on culture and how they might agree or disagree with a cognitive sociolinguistic approach to WE. Then I will sketch the recent developments in CL which pave the way for a partial theoretical merger of the two linguistic enterprises CL and WE, before I proceed to analyze studies in which methods of Cultural Linguistics have already been applied to the investigation of WE.

3. The term Cognitive Sociolinguistics includes Cultural Linguistics here, see below.

2. Major approaches and positions within the study of World Englishes

In his book on Chinese Englishes, Bolton (2003: 7–36) has grouped the research on WE into some 10 categories and sub-categories (which I have slightly rearranged):

1. "The English studies approach," which has originated from English philology, the study of the history of English, and phonetics, and is exemplified by the work of British born linguists such as Robert Burchfield, David Crystal, Sidney Greenbaum, Tom McArthur, Randolph Quirk, and John Wells;
2. "English corpus linguistics," with the International Corpus of English (ICE) project (see Greenbaum 1996) being the most important compilation for the study of WE in its comparative outlook;
3. "The sociolinguistic approach," which Bolton further classifies into
   a. "the linguistic features approach," with a micro-sociolinguistic focus on linguistic variation in and among the different varieties of English, as found in the works of Trudgill and Hannah and Cheshire;
   b. "pidgins and creole studies," i.e., a languages in contact approach, whose objects of study are arguably structurally and sociolinguistically highly interwoven with some WE, such as Nigerian English and Cameroon English;
   c. "the socially realistic study of WE" by B. Kachru, which takes a macro-sociolinguistic perspective on the implications of the spread of English in culturally diverse settings and issues of linguistic creativity;
   d. "the sociology of language" approach, for which, most of all, Joshua Fishman stands;
4. "the lexicographical approach," which focuses on the compilation of variety-specific dictionaries and glossaries;
5. "applied linguistic approaches," which are mainly concerned with problems of bilingualism and interference in the teaching of English in second language contexts and the models of teaching; and, finally,
6. "popularizers, critical linguists, and futurologists," for Bolton a miscellaneous category of writers.

From a cognitive point of view and for present purposes, the various approaches outlined by Bolton can be usefully ordered into three prototype categories with partially overlapping clusters at their boundaries:

First, a purely *descriptive* approach to WE, which focuses on linguistic variation *per se* and descriptions of the linguistic situation in English-speaking countries (includes 1, 2, 3a, 3b, 4, possibly 5); second, a *critical* approach (includes 3d, 6, possibly 5), i.e., critical discussions of the role of English in the world subscribing to the view that the use of English alienates the second language speakers from the cultures of their mother tongues; and third, the *hybridizationist* approach (3c, possibly 5), i.e., the view of WE as culturally hybrid products of bilingual and bicultural speakers. Admittedly, the generalization that comes with these broad categories may not do justice to individual authors who may find themselves in an in-between position, yet individual instances do not impinge upon the heuristic value of my classification.

2.1. The descriptivist approach to World Englishes

Brown's (2001) survey of papers presented at past WE conferences and consultation of experts has shown that descriptive studies of WE dominate or are favored in the field. Indeed, numerous descriptivist works have been published which attest to the broad range of varieties of English and which have given shape to the paradigm itself.[4]

The descriptivist approach undoubtedly has the great merit of bringing to light and legitimizing the numerous varieties of English that exist, yet seems to be largely unaffected by the "cultural turn" in linguistics (see Auer 2000), and by Brown's (2001: 377) placing empirical studies on the culture of WE high on the research agenda of WE. In one of the latest resource book on World Englishes for students (Jenkins 2003), the word "culture" and its derivations do not appear in the index at all. The same holds true for the index to volumes 1–20 (1980–99) of *English World-Wide: A Journal of Varieties of English*, without any doubt one of the main journals in the field and the leading outlet of descriptivist studies on the varieties of English. The "aim and scope" of the journal is also mute on culture; articles are called for that "have a strong empirical and descriptive background" – referring, to be sure, only to "the forms and functions of varieties of English around the world." In the issues from 2000, 21(1) to 2004, 25(1), "cultural" appears only twice in the title of a

4. Recent ones include papers in Allerton, Skandera, and Tschichold (2002), and Lucko, Peter, and Wolf (2003), to name just a couple of collective volumes; some "classics" in the field are Bailey and Görlach (1982), Cheshire (1991), Hansen, Lucko, and Carls (1996), Pride (1982), Trudgill and Hannah (1986).

paper ("The use of vague language in intercultural conversations in Hong Kong," by Cheng and Warren, 2001; and "Tall poppies and egalitarianism in Australian discourse: From key words to cultural value," by Peeters 2004), though, to be fair, one article is published which has a cultural linguistic background ("Event and story schemas in Australian Aboriginal English discourse," by Malcolm and Rochecouste 2000, see below).

Interestingly enough, the scope of the journal seems to have become more restricted with the change in editorship. While Görlach, the first and former main editor, would include "topics from anthropological linguistics, ... the ethnography of speaking and the social psychology of language" (and makes note of "culture-bound specimens" and "different cultures" (Görlach 1980: 3–5), Schneider, the main editor of the journal from 1997 on, refers to it as being a "predominantly descriptively orientated journal" (Schneider 1998: 3) and makes no mention of culture or of the broad range of approaches highlighted by Görlach. I wish to state, though, that I highly respect Edgar Schneider and his work, and that my comments should not be taken as a personal critique but rather as a statement of a factual situation. A view expressed by Huber, author of a book on Ghanaian Pidgin English (Huber 1999) and former editorial assistant to *English World-Wide*, epitomizes the descriptivist stance: In his review of Wolf (2001), he does not agree with Wolf that a cognitive linguistic approach to WE is viable. He forms his opinion on the basis of the near absence of "linguistic peculiarities," i.e., formal differences, in the description of the worldview of Cameroonians expressed in their variety of English (Huber 2004: 209–210). This criticism highlights the fact that variation is narrowly understood, in the descriptivist view, with respect to linguistic form alone and that the cultural-cognitive dimension of variation is ignored or deliberately excluded.

Summarizingly, three shortcomings of descriptivism in WE become apparent:

1. As indicated, descriptivism has a narrow – from a CL perspective too narrow – understanding of "form" and of what counts as "linguistic peculiarities." This narrowness excludes, *inter alia*, "linguistic peculiarities" like cultural keywords, differences in prototypicality and entrenchment, and differences in frequency, traceable e.g., in corpus analyses. The methods developed in CL allow for a systematic investigation of these phenomena (see below).
2. The overemphasis of the description of linguistic "forms" leads to a neglect of the conceptual content these morpho-lexical and grammati-

cal forms express. It is a central tenet of CL that linguistic forms are never conceptually empty, and the conceptual content an item has for a particular socio-cultural group cannot be kept outside the scope of a comparative sociolinguistic account.

3. Extra-linguistic (e.g. socio-cognitive) data receives no attention in linguistic studies along the lines of the descriptive paradigm. Descriptivists provide at best a "thin" description of linguistic items in their embeddedness in a socio-cultural context. In this, as indicated above, they are heir to a Saussurian exclusive model of language in which only the "langue" as a self-contained system is of scientific interest (see Dirven, Wolf, and Polzenhagen 2007).

Given these limitations, it does not come as a surprise that such kind of descriptivism in the field of WE has not made much theoretical progress with respect to the description and understanding of culture in the last twenty-something years. A quote by Quirk (1981: 152), who, referring to Indian English, pointed out that "the natural processes of language-culture interaction have produced a large number of phonological, grammatical, lexical and stylistic features," attests to this narrow scope of linguistic interest in varieties of forms only. His claim is certainly true, but as I will show in section 3.2, there is a substantial amount more to language-culture interaction in varieties of English than the production of novel linguistic features and variety-specific lexicons (also see Wolf 2001: 2, 2004: 135).[5]

With the advancement of corpus linguistics and the compilation of variety-specific computer corpora, especially the ones compiled as part of the International Corpus of English (ICE) project (see, e.g., Nelson 2004), the comparative description of different cultures in WE can be conducted on a systematic and solid empirical basis. However, to the best

5. On a different level, the same narrow emphasis on "form" can be witnessed in discussions of "international English" and of the "intelligibility" of L2-speakers of English. The focus here is on syntactic divergence and phonological differences (see, e.g. Seidlhofer 2003; Atechi 2004). Culture is hardly ever assigned a prominent place in these discussions, or, worse, Western-based concepts are held to be a conceptually neutral base for an international English (see Johnson 1990). The discussion of an international English overlaps with studies of English as lingua franca interactions (see House 2003), and CL can make a valuable contribution to a meaning-oriented approach to intercultural communication as well (see Polzenhagen and Wolf 2007; Wolf and Polzenhagen 2006).

of my knowledge, only Leech and Fallon (1992), Wolf (2003), and Schmied (2004) have taken such an approach.[6] – The full potential of corpus linguistics in the descriptivist paradigms of both CL and WE is yet to be explored, but CL is well under way now not only to exploit the usage-based potential of large corpora but also to redefine itself, as the contribution by Stefanowitsch and Gries (this volume) documents. In corpus linguistics, understood not as a linguistic discipline in itself but rather as a method (see Rissanen 2004: 58), the interests of the descriptive sociolinguist and the cognitive linguist can be brought together (cf. below; Dirven 2004: 20–21; Rissanen 2004: 59). This, however, presupposes that the restricted understanding of "form" is abandoned.

2.2. The critical view

Studies that take a critical stance on the global role of English are the second category that can be identified. With respect to culture, authors in this camp are exponents of what Dirven and Polzenhagen (2004), leaning on Geeraerts (2003), have termed the romantic model.[7] Only the indigenous languages, i.e., the mother tongues of the second language speakers of English, are regarded as authentic bearers of autochthonous culture and as the medium to express cultural identity. The same romantic perspective, however, is not taken with respect to the second language varieties of English, in that the culture-specific patterns expressed in them are not fully recognized. A case in point is Mühlhäusler (1996b). According to his "mismatch hypothesis," which, from an ecological perspective refers to the supposed mismatch between a given natural environment and languages caused by outsiders, it takes about 300 years for a language to develop the necessary lexical resources to deal adequately with the environment (Mühlhäusler 1996b: 128; also see Polzenhagen and Dirven, this volume). Most, if not all, WE L2 standard varieties would thus

---

6. There is, however, a paper by Haase (2004) who uses, *inter alia*, the East African component of the ICE to investigate the lexical-semantic content of verbal constructions in different varieties from a cognitive perspective. Also, Skandera (2003) has used an expanded version of the ICE East Africa to look into the cultural dimension of idioms in East African English. A corpus approach to the study of metaphor, though not of varieties of English, is taken by Charteris-Black (2004).
7. For fuller summaries and a critique of the critical perspective beyond the aspect of culture, see, e.g., Mair 2002; Lucko 2003; Wolf and Igboanusi 2006; Polzenhagen and Dirven, this volume.

be excluded from being considered "ecologically adapted," so to say, if one concedes that the use of English on a broader scale by the indigenous population and the concurrent development of distinct varieties does not date back more than 40 to 50 years or so.[8]

"English" seems to be treated as a monolithic entity, whose linguistic structure embodies a Western worldview and whose adoption would lead to alienation from the culture embodied by the mother tongue. Alienationists thus pass over the findings of those descriptivists who have worked out the innumerable novel linguistic features of the second language varieties of English, which to a considerable extent go back to the cultural background of the speakers (albeit this background is not sufficiently accounted for in the work of the descriptivists). In so far as alienationists do not acknowledge linguistic variation in the varieties of English as a sign of their acculturation, they are fully at odds with hybridizationists, whose very research program is based on processes of sociocultural fusion in English, as will be discussed below. However, both groups converge in their "liberationist commitment."[9]

Alienationism cannot, in principle, agree with cognitive sociolinguistic studies of WE either, since the latter reveal the persistence of culture-specific conceptualizations in second language varieties of English (see below). Adherents of the critical view include, besides Mühlhäusler (1996a/b), for example Pennycook (1994, 2001); Phillipson (1992); Holborow (1999); Skutnabb-Kangas (2000), and Nettle and Romaine (2000), though I acknowledge that their positions differ in some major theoretical respects as well as ideological orientation. In fact, Pennycook's (2001: ch. 3) critique of the spread of English appears to be more differentiated than that of the other authors cited. He challenges the "determinism of some critical approaches" (Pennycook 2001: 71), yet cautions against

8. One could argue that distinct and recognizable national varieties fully emerged only with the end of colonialism, in that English was now institutionalized by the indigenous rulers (and not by the colonial ones anymore), alongside its increasing use in the "new" media like radio, television as well as in newspapers and literature.
9. The liberationist commitment could be defined as "forms of linguistic beliefs and practices … [being] rooted in contexts of social injustice … [seeking] to transform these contexts radically in the interest of the speakers of the 'other tongue'" (Bhatt 2001: 528). In that respect, the alienationsts concentrate on the endangered minority languages as "other tongues" – vis-à-vis English, while the hybridizationists focus on the liberation of the speakers of the non-standard forms of English.

what he finds an apolitical relativism of the WE linguistic hybridity advocates, in that they ignore "the broader political context of the spread of English" (Pennycook 2003: 516). Nevertheless, though he demands a "critical understanding of globalization" (Pennycook 2003: 518), to my mind, he never specifies what this critical understanding should look like in a wider political context.[10] What most alienationists fail to realize, though Pennycook may be an exception, is that the speakers of WE varieties do reflect and express essential aspects of their culture and thought through the medium of English.

2.3. Hybridizationism

The third paradigm within WE is "hybridizationism"; its key figure and founding father is B. Kachru (see, e.g., 1983, 1985, 1986, 1994). Arguably, it is the one that is theoretically, though not methodologically, closest to a cognitive sociolinguistic approach to WE. Culture is of central concern in this paradigm in that the structural and socio-cultural transformations English has undergone in the diverse colonial and post-colonial contexts are stressed, a concern which is reflected in terms like *nativization*, *Africanization*, *indigenization*, and *acculturation* used in reference to the processes shaping the varieties of English. Some even go as far as to speak of diverse "English *languages* [which] represent diverse linguistic, cultural and ideological voices" (Bhatt 2001: 527, italics mine). The emphasis on the structural changes induced by the diverse socio-cultural backgrounds also aligns this paradigm to some extent with the purely descriptive approach characterized above. A central theoretical construct in hybrid-oriented thought and research is the notion of the 'creative bilingual speaker," who "created new, cultural-sensitive and socially appropriate meanings ... by altering and manipulating the structure and functions of English in its new ecology" (Bhatt 2001: 534).

Literary creativity by post-colonial writers writing in English is taken as a foremost example for the acculturation of English (see, e.g., Lim 2002, Bhatt 2001: 537–538), and the hybridizationist enterprise is closely intertwined with the study of post-colonial literature. This subject has emerged as a new branch of literary studies (see, e.g., Ashcroft et. al 1989, 1995), which in turn brings hybridizationism close to cultural studies (see Dissanayake 2000). Hybridizationists discuss the work by post-colonial

10. See Holborow (1999: 80–86) for a longer critique of Pennycook; also see Wolf and Igboanusi (2006).

literary theorists (see, e.g., Y. Kachru and Nelson 2006), while B. Kachru is cited by post-colonial literary theorists (e.g., by Ashcroft 2001: 56).[11]

From a linguistic point of view, the problem for hybridizationists (and for post-colonial literary theorists, for that matter) is that "methodologies that are sensitive to multilingual and multicultural realities" (Bhatt 2001: 528) have been lacking within their own paradigm. Their approach has been referred to as "anecdotal" (Pennycook 2003: 518, citing Das Gupta 1993) or as a kind of "narrative linguistics" (Görlach 1999: 18). B. Kachru has rightly stated that second language varieties of English are "used in entirely different semiotic and cultural systems" (Kachru 1983: 9; also see Malcolm and Rochecouste 2000: 261–262). This means, on the one hand, that the traditional sociolinguistic variation approach is not sufficient to adequately capture this cultural dimension. Kachru (1986: 160) is fully aware that this cultural dimension has to be sought out at the cognitive level, when he speaks of "the underlying thought-patterns of bilinguals" being responsible for nativization. Yet while the cultural/cognitive linguistic perspective is already implied in Kachru's thought, any systematic empirical studies of the cultures of Englishes have not been set up by him. The main reasons, one can suppose, is that

11. The discussion of post-colonial literary theory in relation to WE would warrant a paper or book of its own and cannot be pursued further here. A good starting point would be Ashcroft (2001), whose notion of "transformation" establishes a link between linguistic form and literary function. Drawing from Ashcroft, Griffiths and Tiffen (1989), he writes: "The strategies by which a colonial language is transformed are extremely varied. Apart from direct glossing in the text, either by explanation or parenthetic insertions, such devices include syntactic fusion, in which the English prose is structured according to the syntactic principles of a first language; neologisms, new lexical forms in English which are informed by the semantic and morphological exigencies of a mother tongue; the direct inclusion of untranslated lexical items in the text; ethnorhythmic prose which constructs an English discourse according to the rhythm and texture of a first language; and the transcription of dialect and language variants of many different kinds, whether they come from diglossic, polydialectical or monolingual speaking communities" Ashcroft (2001: 78). This seems to reflect an understanding of linguistic variation similar to that of the descriptivists. Though for Ashcroft (2001: 78), these forms are cultural reproductions by a process of "metaphorical embodiment," and he considers such uses of language as "metonymic" in that these culture-specific forms stand for the culture they serve to represent, 'metaphor' and 'metonymy' refer only to (symbolic) literary functions but not to some conceptual structure of the second language speakers.

the descriptive tools of variationist sociolinguistics were not quite suited for that type of research, and that his original background as a literary scholar may have kept him from embracing the more technical methodology of CL.[12]

3. Cognitive Sociolinguistic and World Englishes

3.1. Theoretical background

The impotence of hybridizationism to produce methodologically rigorous and systematic studies of cultural conceptualizations developed through and expressed in varieties of English is the point where recent developments in CL come into play. In a programmatic paper presented at the *8th International Cognitive Linguistics Conference*, Geeraerts (2003) has argued that taking what might be called the "usage-based commitment" of CL seriously inevitably leads to a Cognitive Sociolinguistics with an emphasis on the study of language variation. Furthermore, he stressed the fact that CL has to study the role people's conceptualizations play in the constitution of social reality and, as an important methodological condition, he explicitly professed the necessary use of computer corpora in the cognitive study of variation.

The study of culture has always been part of the CL enterprise, but has been made programmatic in "Cultural Linguistics," as Palmer understands it, a socio-cultural approach within CL that is closely related to cognitive anthropology and its notion of cultural models, and rests on the assumption that culture-based conceptualizations underlying language or language varieties are systematic and can be studied by means of the methods developed in CL (see Palmer 1996, 2005; Dirven, Wolf, and Polzenhagen 2007; Wolf and Polzenhagen 2008fc.).

Both approaches are part of a Cognitive Sociolinguistics, as Dirven (2004) has described it. He argues that language variation should be at the heart of the research agenda of CL (Dirven 2004: 21). On the one

12. Yet another approach to WE needs to be mentioned, one that is close to the hybridizationist one, however difficult to access it is in terms of publications. Skybina (2004) has adopted a comparative-historical methodology to varieties of English and argues, based on the close scrutiny of historical texts, for a modification of English into the different national varieties, due to the exigencies of the new physical surroundings. In a way, this could be interpreted as a Marxist-influenced take on the shaping of English.

hand, WE is the ideal testing ground for the programmatic extension of CL, because variation can be studied among different varieties of one language, which still share a common core.[13] This eliminates problems of translatability and comparability which occur when variation across different languages is discussed. On the other hand, CL can contribute to a better understanding of cultural variation expressed in these varieties (cf. Dirven 2005: 272).

In the following, I will highlight and summarize some studies of varieties of English with a special focus on cultural variation which have been produced in the CL/Cultural Linguistics paradigm.

3.2. A review of some culture-orientated cognitive sociolinguistic studies of varieties of English

Apart from Grundy and Jiang's (2001) analysis of the link between grammatical constructions and an underlying ideological model in Hong Kong English,[14] and studies on cultural models in American English (Kövecses 1995, 2003; Csábi 2001), two research clusters stand out where cognitive sociolinguistic methods have been successfully applied to get a deeper understanding of the cultures underlying different varieties of English: Work on Aboriginal Australian English and Chinese Australian English, on the one hand, and on African English, on the other.[15] Though research was conceived independently of each other, both approaches share the same principles and the same outlook on WE.[16]

The article by Malcolm and Rochecouste (2000) on "event and story schemas in Australian Aboriginal English discourse" picks up on the no-

13. Thus, I would not go as far as to say that "Englishes" implies that the different varieties of English constitute different languages. For obvious reasons, the notion of a common lexical core of English is important for the comparative investigation of variety-specific corpora of English (see below).
14. See Dirven, Polzenhagen, and Wolf (2007) for a synopsis and further explanation of the ideological model in question.
15. I am aware of a cognitive linguistic research project at the English Department of the University Bayreuth, which aims to investigate the conceptual structure – specifically with respect to prototypes – of African languages and varieties, one of which is Nigerian English. However, other than a paper presented at the *8th International Cognitive Linguistics Conference* (see Schmied and Kopatsch 2003), I could not find any further material produced by this group on African English.
16. Note that Dirven (1994) applied the same principle and similar methods to his study of Afrikaans as a variety of Dutch.

tion of 'schema' as "a mental representation of regularity of our experiences," as being part of the "conceptual system that emerges from everyday experience," and as organizing perceptions and providing "bases for interpreting discourse" (Malcolm and Rochecouste 2000: 265, citing from Bregman 1990, Sweetser 1990, and Strauss 1992). To avoid terminological confusion, it is at place to point out that schema understood as "cultural schema" corresponds closely to the notion of "cultural model," which is more commonly used in CL. Strauss and Quinn (1997: 139–140, also see 49), for example, define "cultural models as complex cultural schemas."[17]

The significance of a cognitive approach to variation in WE becomes evident in the following quote:

> Recent research ... has shown how, even where Aboriginal English seems to employ the same vocabulary as Australian English, it is informed by a semantics deeply rooted in Aboriginal culture. The meanings of such everyday terms as *family, camp, dinner, granny* and *solid* are associated with different prototypes; there are contrasting schemas which lead to differing interpretations and uses of such terms as *long* (which can incorporate the vertical), *half* (which is simply less than the whole) and expressions such as *he's got plenty of money* (which refers not to possessions and assets, but simply to cash on the person). (Malcolm and Rochecouste 2000: 264)

From a corpus of forty oral narratives of 5- to 13-year-old speakers of Australian Aboriginal English recorded on cassette tape, Malcolm and Rochecouste by means of discourse analysis extracted four culture-specific 'schemas,' as they call it: 'travel,' 'hunting,' 'observing,' and 'encountering the unknown.' The following slightly modified excerpt is taken from Malcolm and Rochecouste (2000: 278–279). Passages in bold are instantiations of the hunting, respectively the traveling schema, italics indicate the discourse markers associated with the schema. The text in square brackets identifies the relevant schema or the discourse marker.

> 1. My name is Dean Samuel. 2. And ... *couple o months back...* [Time orientation] 3. Um ... *me an' my dad ... my brother ... and my uncle ...*

17. Malcolm and Rochecouste also refer to the work by Palmer (1996), Schank and Abelson (1977) and Wierzbicka (1992) and relate 'schema' to such concepts like 'scenarios,' 'scripts,' and 'cultural scripts.' For a further clarification of the terms 'cultural model' and 'schema,' see Polzenhagen and Wolf 2007).

> *Normie* ... [Participant. orientation] 4. ***we went up to dis creek***... (slight interruption) 5. ***went up to de creek*** [Travel] .[Moving segment marker "went up" Profiling marker "dis/de"] ... 6. and we was **lookin for** some bimba ... [Hunting] 7. but we **never found** any ... 8. so **we went an looks for** some kangaroos ... [Hunting] 9. and ... ***went up*** the creek [Travel] [Moving segment marker] 10. and we **saw**... a goanna ... and we **shot** it ... 11. **And it tried to go** 12. an it **ran** ... 13. **an it tried to go** in the 'ole ... 14. but my brother **grabbed** it ... 15. and ... then ... he **'old** it there ... 16. he moved some rocks away from the 'ole ... 17. and **pulled** it out of the 'ole. 18. An' when they chucked i' out 19. they **'it** it in the 'ead with the rock ... 20. an it **died** ... 21. an we ... and we **took** it ... [Hunting] 22. an put it in the car 23. and we ***went up*** the road ... 24. we ***was gonna*** go the other way ... 25. one way ... 26. but ... we ***turned around*** ...27. an went ***back down*** dis road ...28. and when ***we went to go through*** de creek ...[Travel] [Moving segment marker] 29. we ***pulled up*** ... [Stopping] [Stopping segment marker].

Though both the traveling schema and the hunting schema are involved, the hunting schema is in the foreground. The hunting episode is divided into three parts: "observing for prey" (6–8), "the chase" (10–18), and "the kill" (19–20) (Malcolm and Rochecouste 2000: 280–281). According to these researchers, "the chase" is the longest part, because in it the persistence of the hunter is shown.

They perceive these schemas to be reflections of ancestral survival strategies of a hunting-gathering people, "such as observation, orientation to time and space, avoidance of isolation from the group, persistence in hunting down game and caution with respect to the unknown" (Malcolm and Rochecouste 2000: 285). The authors rightly point to the educational value of their findings, as a bidialectal education (which is pursued by the State Education Department in Western Australia) that focuses only on lexical and syntactic variation would be too narrow in its scope to capture the full range of language-related cultural factors that impede Australian Aboriginal students' performance (Malcolm and Rochecouste 2000: 284–285).

The study by Malcolm and Rochecouste laid the ground for further work by Sharifian and also Hui. Sharifian broadened the cognitive linguistic investigation of Aboriginal Australian English, both in terms of the theoretical apparatus[18] and the conceptualizations underlying this variety. He speaks of a general "Aboriginal conceptual system" which "strongly revolves around cultural conceptualizations of Family," un-

18. See Sharifian (2003) on the problem of the distribution of cultural schemas in a given society.

derpinning "Aboriginal behaviours, thinking, and speaking" (Sharifian 2004: 14; also see this volume). "Family," in Aboriginal thought, is a wide network of relations, which goes far beyond the Western nuclear family, and is related to concomitant notions such as "home."

The Family schema is also at the center of Hui's work (2003, 2004) on differences between speakers of Chinese Australian English and, what she calls, "Anglo Australian English." She discovered that the evocation of this schema, which differs in both groups, can lead to misunderstandings in or even breakdown of interactions between speakers of these two varieties (also see below).

Concurrent with the studies of Australian varieties of English, cognitive linguistic investigations of African varieties of English were begun by Wolf and later joined by Polzenhagen. Unlike the Australian-based researchers just mentioned, whose method primarily comprises various types of interview techniques, Wolf and Polzenhagen get their data from an eclectic array of mostly written material, an important part of which is computer corpora. Their work has concentrated on a vast network of conceptualizations pertaining to the African cultural model of community (see, e.g., Wolf 1999, 2001; Wolf and Simo Bobda 2001; Wolf and Polzenhagen 2007; Polzenhagen and Wolf 2007). This cultural model involves a cosmology and relates to such notions as the continuation of the community, the members of the community, witchcraft, the acquisition of wealth, and corruption, which find expression in African English. Wolf and Polzenhagen's approach combines corpus linguistic methods and those developed in conceptual metaphor theory and blending theory; methodologically, they are thus at the heart of a Cognitive Sociolinguistics as envisaged by Geeraerts. From computer corpora,[19] they elicited cultural keywords which correspond to, or rather, are surface forms of culture-specific conceptualizations in varieties of African English. For example, the English form "family" is merely used to replace an indigenous word with highly culture-specific meaning and that meaning complex is now the symbolic value of the form "family" – the same holds true for "family" in Australian Aboriginal English (see above). The cultural significance of keywords has been forcefully argued for by Wierzbicka, who sees keywords "as focal points around which entire cultural domains

19. Wolf and Polzenhagen mostly used the Corpus of English in Cameroon and the East African English Corpus, compiled as part of the International Corpus of English (ICE) Project, but also smaller corpora, like Corpus Nigeria and Corpus Ghana, compiled at Humboldt-University, Berlin (for more information, see, e.g., Wolf and Polzenhagen 2007).

Table 1. Keywords in Cameroon English pertaining to the domain of kinship/community

word	CEC	FLOBFROWN	keyness	P-value
community	413	599	49.9	0.000000
communal	35	27	18.1	0.000021
marriage	189	281	20.7	0.000005
family	545	1,010	16.0	0.000063
relatives	44	43	15.5	0.000083
kin	35	11	40.9	0.000000
kinsman	9	3	10.2	0.001443
kinship	19	18	7.1	0.007773
lineage	18	16	7.5	0.006160
procreation	11	7	7.3	0.007078
birth	100	131	17.3	0.000033
child	1,057	1,480	146.0	0.000000
neonate	10	3	12.0	0.000535
newborn	9	5	6.8	0.008901
filial	9	2	12.5	0.000408
offspring	38	24	32.4	0.000000
childless	12	7	8.7	0.003202
elder	59	68	22.5	0.000002
ancestral	58	10	88.9	0.000000
ancestor	65	28	61.6	0.000000
ghost	60	64	17.7	0.000026
spirit	395	175	366.2	0.000000

are organized" (Wierzbicka 1997: 16–17). Thus, linking the study of keywords to the underlying conceptualizations derived by means of cognitive metaphor/blending theory greatly enhances the explanatory range of both corpus and cognitive linguistic approaches.

The table (1), adapted from Wolf (2006), and Wolf and Polzenhagen (2007) may serve as an illustration. It lists keywords pertaining to the domain of kinship/community, elicited from the Corpus of English in Cameroon (CEC), which was compiled as part of the International Corpus of English Project. The reference corpus was a combination of the FLOB corpus, based on British English, and the FROWN corpus, based on American English, together representing the two major "Western" varieties of English.[20] The columns of the table show the frequency of occurrence of lexical item in the two corpora, the "keyness," i.e., the statistical

20. For a detailed description of the methodology and corpus design, see Wolf (2003, 2006).

computation of the degree to which a word is a keyword, and the probability value of claiming a wrong relationship.[21]

These words, all of which belong to the common core of English, were found to be significantly more frequent in Cameroon English than in British English and American English.[22] The fact that they are 'key' highlights the prominent role of the kinship and community – which, in the African context, are not neatly distinguished – in Cameroonian society, and the importance that is placed on the continuation of the community. A close analysis of the texts the corpus consists of and of other sources shows that these words also appear as clusters/collocations. In terms of conceptual metaphor theory, the texts reveal, *inter alia*, an interchangeable set of metonymies, i.e., KINSHIP IS COMMUNITY and COMMUNITY IS KINSHIP in Cameroon English, evident in the following examples (taken from Wolf 2001: 280)[23]:

(1) I greet my fathers;

(2) my brothers and country people;

(3) to kill our own brothers and sisters, the suffering people;

(4) the family head of the Bakweri community;

(5) the health development of brothers and sisters in Cameroon;

(6) children are introduced to adult kin as 'other' fathers and mothers and to their children as brothers and sisters;

(7) the Santa CPDM [the branch of a political party] is planning a mass decamping because none of their sons was appointed in to [sic] the new government;

(8) Santa people whose son was a prime minister;

(9) three policemen molesting their grandson;

(10) all brothers and sisters are extending their warm greetings;

(11) they took bribes from their less fortunate brothers.

---

21. 0.05 is a 5% chance of error, usually deemed acceptable in the social sciences (see Scott & Oxford University Press).

22. One needs to bear in mind that WordSmith, the program used for the computations, factors in the size of the corpora – FLOBFROWN is more than twice that of the CEC. Therefore, looking at the items in this table in terms of absolute frequency would be misleading.

23. On the problem of "metonymy or metaphor" in WE, see Polzenhagen and Wolf (2007).

Judging from the work by Alo (1989) and Medubi (2003), one can find the same conceptualizations of kinship and community in Nigerian English, and evidence suggests that these conceptualizations are shared across "non-white" African varieties of English (see Wolf and Polzenhagen 2007).

Furthermore, ancestors, which are conceptualized as spirits or ghosts, are understood as members of the community who still exert a considerable influence on the (physiologically) living. *Ancestral spirit(s)* is a fixed expression in African English (see Wolf and Polzenhagen 2007), and the conceptualizations ANCESTORS ARE SPIRITS/GHOSTS and SPIRITS/GHOSTS ARE PART OF PRESENT REALITY are also expressed in the following examples (taken from Wolf 2001: 283–285):

(12) The frequent appearance of Mola's ghost affected the daily lives of the whole village community. The men had to accompany their wives to the farm. It had been rumoured that he had developed certain vices since his death. That he had become a sex maniac. He had molested his wife on many occasions. The villagers had to retire early to the safety of their homes as the ghost normally started its prowls at nine o'clock.

(13) I saw his ghost walking along the road.

(14) It is the duty and the right of every ancestor to torment or punish the living.

(15) Ancestors and gods keep a watchful eye on the living.

(16) I wish that everyone return home safely with our ancestors guiding you on the way.

(17) Cruelty to children is ... punishable by ancestral spirits.

(18) Spirits ... are also very sensitive to any acts of disrespect.

(19) The capriciousness of spirits.

(20) Ancestors intercede on behalf of their living kin.

(21) Nocturnal spirits are believed to use marketplaces as habitats.

These keywords and conceptualizations, as well as numerous other interrelated ones, which involve the domains of political leadership, witchcraft, health and illness, food, and money, occur in various varieties of African English, and are described in greater detail in Polzenhagen and Wolf (2007), and Wolf and Polzenhagen (2007). Wolf and Polzenhagen, and also Medubi (2003) demonstrate that these "peculiarities," to use the term again, are not something exotic or pertain only to traditional village life, but are pervasive and used to make sense of "modern" spheres like politics (also see Schatzberg 1986, 2001); after all, in Africa, English is primarily used in public and hence "modern" spheres.

Some initial findings on Hong Kong English – on the basis of some data I have collected from various sources (websites, films, newspaper, printed speeches) – seem to confirm the applicability of the cognitive sociolinguistic methods used in the study of African English to other WE as well. The most noticeable difference to Western varieties of English involve, again, the family domain. The importance of the family in Chinese culture is a well-known fact. Of the five important relations in Confucian thought (father and son, brothers and sisters, husband and wife, master and servant, friend and friend, see *World Religions* n.d.), three pertain to the family. As Hui (2004) has argued, "Chinese people foreground families in conceptualisations or knowledge configurations to the extent that Chinese families serve as an analogy for wider human relationships in the culture." Relevant metaphors in the Chinese language have been investigated in-depth by Liu (2002: ch. 6), who stresses the centrality of the family domain in Chinese conceptualizations pertaining to nation and society. The following examples from Hong Kong English confirm the point made by Hui and Liu. The first two express the conceptualization THE NATION IS A FAMILY:

(22) ... Cannot be tolerated by the sons and daughters of the Chinese nation (Chinese official on Taiwanese demonstrations for the right to hold a referendum. Radio and Television Hong Kong, Oct. 27, 2003, 8:00 news).

(23) We receiving gifts from our poor cousins [in Mainland China]. (Lee, Martin C.M. 2003: 12, "What can I do for Hong Kong?" Distinguished Alumni Lectures. The University of Hong Kong).

The following examples are instantiations of SOCIAL UNITS ARE FAMILIES:

(24) Hong Kong is our home, and we're proud of it. That's why we're committed to making direct contributions to the community in so

many ways .... What unites us is a shared vision to be the most admired airline in the world as well as a strong sense of belonging to our "family". (Homepage of Cathay Pacific Airways)

(25) The legendary Jockey Club 'Team Spirit' makes our group of employees more like a family than a workforce. But we're no ordinary family. (Homepage of the Hong Kong Jockey Club)

(26) To build a family of students, staff, parents, alumni, members of the Court, Council and HKU Foundation, benefactors and friends of the University, by facilitating interaction, dialogue, trust and cooperation among all members of the family.
(Homepage of The University of Hong Kong)

(27) Most corporations adopted a parental approach, a father-child arrangement. That means the boss would take good care of their employees and did not want them to speak up.
(*South China Morning Post*, Oct. 2003: 8)

(28) We are a family.
(A worker to a co-worker, *Troublesome Night 3*, Meih Ah Laser Disc Co. Ltd. 1998)

(29) Big brother
(the term for a recruiter or protector in a Chinese secret society, see Bolton 2002: 46, citing from *Grolier International Dictionary*).

Admittedly, it is not clear to what extent these conceptualizations are metaphoric. Informants did not agree whether family and, say, a company's work force one belongs to are clearly distinguishable domains; the size of the company may play a role, too. Either way, the salience of these expressions, and the fact that social units apparently are more readily conceptualized or metaphorized as a family in Hong Kong or, for that matter, Chinese culture, than in Western culture, are evidence of a cultural difference. Another, and perhaps more striking cultural difference to Western belief, is the metonymy ANCESTORS ARE SPIRITS, found in the following examples.

(30) Sister Ling says that with people, especially the younger generations, turning away from Chinese customs, she must burn extra incense and other offerings to the neglected spirits of ancestors whose own relatives no longer bother.
(*South China Morning Post*: Aug. 18, 2003: 2).

(31) Your mom's spirit is over there. It means she doesn't feel well. She comes back.
(*Troublesome Night 3*, Meih Ah Laser Disc Co. Ltd. 1998)

All ancestors are conceptualized as spirits or, more negatively (when spirits of unrelated deceased are referred to), as ghosts.[24] In fact, the Chinese beliefs relating to ancestors and spirits are very similar to the ones in African culture. The spirits continue to have human-like qualities and needs. Both in African and Chinese culture, for example, spirits are believed to be hungry and demanding food, which is offered by the living to appease them; in Hong Kong, the Yu Lan Festival (festival of the hungry ghosts) is celebrated. In this city, oranges and other fruits are presented in small shrines one can see in stores, on the streets, or at the entrance of apartments, and families prepare chicken for the ancestors (which, pragmatically, is then eaten by the families themselves). Furthermore, the spirits can interfere, positively or negatively, in the lives of the living. SPIRITS ARE HUMANS has generated the following passages:

(32) The older ghosts may enjoy watching Chinese opera, but times have changed and the younger generation of 'ghosts' like watching this type of performance.
(*South China Morning Post*: Aug. 28, 2003: 13)

(33) We are good friends, bless us to make a fortune. To bring so much sacrifices to worship you each month, it costs much.
(*Troublesome Night 3*, Meih Ah Laser Disc Co. Ltd. 1998)

(34) Old women burn candles, paper money and other gifts to appease the lonely spirits. (*South China Morning Post*: Aug. 18, 2003: 2)

The gifts for the spirits, more often than not, are paper models that represent a real object or person in the spirit world, and it is a pervasive custom to burn such paper models or paper money for the deceased.[25] Thus, A PAPER MODEL IS A REAL OBJECT OR PERSON IN THE SPIRIT WORLD, a conceptualization realized in the following expressions:

24. On beliefs in ghosts in Hong Kong, see Evans (1997).
25. When I first came to Hong Kong and saw paper models of airplanes, yachts, CD-players, electric fans, etc. being sold in various stores, I was wondering what the function of these objects was, as they did not look exactly like toys. As I found out, they are, in fact, bought and burned for use by the ancestors. See Scott (1997, 2007) on details of the paper model industry.

(35) We want to burn a paper woman to Ken [a 22 year old male, who had died], let's go.
(*Troublesome Night 3*, Meih Ah Laser Disc Co. Ltd. 1998)

(36) Mr. Wong is so rich, he won't live a [sic.] small house after his death. So we must burn him a big villa … I worry that he would feel lonely. So I will burn him two concubines.
(*Troublesome Night 3*, Meih Ah Laser Disc Co. Ltd. 1998)

With the release of the Hong Kong English sub-corpus of the International Corpus of English Project, more studies on cultural realizations in Hong Kong English along the line of Cognitive Sociolinguistics can be pursued. Briefly sketched, the situation in (36) can be characterized in terms of construction grammar as follows: the ditransitive or double-object construction (*offer somebody something*) is here lexically realized by the culturally determined expressions *burn somebody (a paper replica of) a villa*, which is one of the mourning rituals for the spirits of the deceased. Further investigations could show if words relating to the domains mentioned here will also appear as keywords.

As these examples from different varieties of English illustrate, there is a vast potential for cognitive sociolinguistic studies in WE. Not only do cognitive sociolinguistic studies of WE broaden the understanding of the linguistic varieties and the cultures associated with them, but also build a bridge to Applied Cognitive Linguistics, a similarly productive new branch of CL, since, as already hinted at, the findings introduced here are of immediate relevance to education and intercultural communication (see Pütz, Niemeier and Dirven 2001a/b, and also Wolf and Simo Bobda 2001).

4. Conclusion

This article argued for Cognitive Sociolinguistics as a new model within the field of World Englishes, with a special focus on the cultural dimension. With the programmatic tenet of CL, i.e., its insistence on the interrelation of language, thought, and culture, coupled with the variationist commitment of Cognitive Sociolinguistics, it is compelling to apply the principles and methods of CL, or, specifically, Cognitive Sociolinguistics, to the study of the varieties of English. The dominant orientations within WE studies so far were identified, namely formal descriptivism, a critical or alienationist view of English, and hybridizationism, and their basic theoretical assumptions, their mutual compatibility and their compatibility with Cognitive Sociolinguistics, were brought to light. More specifically, the following points have been revealed. First, Cognitive Sociolinguistics can explain culture-specific patterns like keywords, differences in prototypicality, and conceptualizations realized in these varieties, which descriptivists disregard due to their theoretical outlook or are incapable of explaining because they lack the appropriate methodology. Second, Cognitive Sociolinguistics does not share many points of contact with the proponents of the critical or alienationist view of English because of their denial of the pervasive influence of the indigenous cultures on the second language varieties of English. Third, Cognitive Sociolinguistics gets its findings by means of systematic and rigorous methods and on the basis of a broad database (such as computer corpora), which cannot be said of Kachru's hybridizationist approach to the cultures of WE.

To demonstrate the viability of this emerging model, different studies which apply the principles of Cognitive Sociolinguistics and which provide substantial novel insights into the cultures of WE were surveyed. These studies prove that Cognitive Sociolinguistics has a vitalizing effect on the WE paradigm and the potential to become the standard model for investigations of culture within it.

References

Achard, Michel and Suzanne Kemmer (eds.)
2004 *Language, Culture, and Mind.* Stanford: CSLI Publications.

Alatis, James E. (ed.)
1994 *Educational Linguistics, Crosscultural Communication, and Global Interdependence.* Georgetown: Georgetown University Press.

Allerton, D. J., Paul Skandera, and Cornelia Tschichold (eds.)
2002 *Perspectives on English as a World Language.* Basel: Schwabe & Co.

Alo, Moses
1989 A prototype approach to the analysis of meanings of kinship terms in non-native English. *Language Sciences* 11 (2): 159–176.

Ashcroft, Bill
2001 *Post-Colonial Transformation* [electronic resource]. London: Routledge.

Ashcroft, Bill, Gareth Griffiths, and Helen Tiffin (eds.)
1989 *The Empire Writes Back: Theory and Practice in Post-Colonial Literature.* London: Routledge.
1995 *The Post-Colonial Studies Reader.* London: Routledge.

Atechi, Samuel Ngwa
2004 The intelligibility of native and non-native English speech: A comparative analysis of Cameroon English and American and British English. PhD-thesis, Technical University Chemnitz. Available at http://archiv.tu-chemnitz.de/pub/2004/0088/data/ atechi_intelligibility.pdf

Auer, Peter
2000 Die Linguistik auf dem Weg zur Kulturwissenschaft? *Freiburger Universitätsblätter* 147: 55–68.

Bailey, Richard, and Manfred Görlach (eds.)
1982 *English as a World Language*. Ann Arbor: University of Michigan Press.

Bhatt, Rakesh M.
2001 World Englishes. *Annual Review of Anthropology* 30: 527–570.

Bolton, Kingsley
2002 The sociolinguistics of Hong Kong. In: Kingsley Bolton (ed.), *Hong Kong English: Autonomy and Creativity*, 29–55. Hong Kong: Hong Kong University Press.
2003 *Chinese Englishes: A Sociolinguistic History*. Cambridge: Cambridge University Press.

Bolton, Kingsley (ed.)
2003 *Hong Kong English: Autonomy and Creativity*. Hong Kong: Hong Kong University Press.

Brown, Kimberley
2001 World Englishes and the classroom: Research and practice agendas for the year 2000. In: Edwin Thumboo (ed.), *The Three Circles of English*, 371–382. Singapore: UniPress.

Charteris-Black, Jonathan
2004 *Corpus Approaches to Critical Metaphor Analysis*. Houndmills: Palgrave Macmillan.

Cheng, Winnie and Martin Warren
2001 The use of vague language in intercultural conversations in Hong Kong. *English World-Wide* 22 (1): 81–104.

Cheshire, Jenny (ed.)
1991 *English Around the World: Sociolinguistic Perspectives*. Cambridge: Cambridge University Press.

Csábi, Szilvia
2001 The concept of America in the Puritan mind. *Language and Literature* 10 (3): 195–209.

Dirven, René
1994 *Metaphor and Nation. Metaphors Afrikaners Live By*. (Duisburg Papers on Research in Language and Culture 22). Frankfurt: Peter Lang.
2004 Major strands in Cognitive Linguistics. *Linguistic Agency LAUD*. Series A: General & Theoretical Papers, No. 634.

2005 Review of Peter Trudgill. 2002. *Sociolinguistic Variation and Change*. Washington D.C.: Georgetown University Press. *Studies in Language* 29 (1): 269–273.

Dirven, René, Roslyn Frank, and Martin Pütz (eds.)
2003 *Cognitive Models in Language and Thought: Ideology, Metaphors and Meanings*. (Cognitive Linguistic Research 24). Berlin/New York: Mouton de Gruyter.

Dirven, René, Frank Polzenhagen, and Hans-Georg Wolf
2007 Cognitive Linguistics, Ideology, and Critical Discourse Analysis. In: Dirk Geeraerts and Hubert Cuyckens (eds.), *Handbook of Cognitive Linguistics*, 1222–1240. New York: Oxford University Press.

Dirven, René, Hans-Georg Wolf, and Frank Polzenhagen
2007 Cognitive Linguistics and cultural studies. In: Dirk Geeraerts and Hubert Cuyckens (eds), *Handbook of Cognitive Linguistics*, 1203–1221. New York: Oxford University Press.

Dissanayake, Wimal
1997 Cultural studies and World Englishes: Some topics for further exploration. In: Larry E. Smith and Michael L. Forman (eds.), *World Englishes 2000*, 126–145. Honolulu: University of Hawai'i Press.

English World-Wide: A Journal of Varieties of English.
2000 *Index to Volumes 1–20. 1980–1999.*
2000–2004 Volumes 21 (1)–25 (1).

Evans, Grant
1997 Ghosts and the new governor: The anthropology of a Hong Kong rumour. In: Grant Evans and Maria Tam (eds.), *Hong Kong: The Anthropology of a Chinese Metropolis*, 266–296. Richmond, England: Curzon Press.

Fauconnier, Gilles and Mark Turner
1998 Conceptual integration networks. *Cognitive Science* 22 (2): 133–187.

Figueroa, Esther
1994 *Sociolinguistic Metatheory*. New York: Elsevier.

Fill, Alwin (ed.)
1996 *Sprachökologie und Ökolinguistik*: *Referate des Symposions Sprachökologie und Ökolinguistik an der Universität Klagenfurt 27–28. Oktober 1995.* Tübingen: Stauffenburg Verlag.

Geeraerts, Dirk
2003 'Usage-based' implies 'variational': On the inevitability of cognitive sociolinguistics. Plenary lecture presented at the *8th International Cognitive Linguistics Conference: Cognitive Linguistics, Functionalism, Discourse Studies: Common Ground and New Directions*. Logroño, July 20–25, 2003.

Gnutzmann, Claus (ed.)
1999 *Teaching and Learning English as a Global Language: Native and Non-Native Perspectives.* Tübingen: Stauffenburg.

Görlach, Manfred
1980 Editorial. *English World-Wide: A Journal of Varieties of English* 1 (1): 3–7.
1999 Varieties of English and language teaching. In: Claus Gnutzmann (ed.), *Teaching and Learning English as a Global Language: Native and Non-Native Perspectives*, 3–21.Tübingen: Stauffenburg.

Greenbaum, Sidney (ed.)
1996 *Comparing English Worldwide: The International Corpus of English*. Oxford: Clarendon Press.

Grundy, Peter and Yan Jiang
2001 The bare past as an ideological construction in Hong Kong discourse. In: René Dirven, Roslyn Frank, and Cornillie Ilie (eds.), *Language and Ideology*. Volume II: Descriptive Cognitive Approaches, 117–134. (Current Issues in Linguistic Theory 205). Amsterdam/Philadelphia: Benjamins.

Haase, Christoph
2004 Conceptualization specifics in East African English: Quantitative arguments from the ICE-East Africa corpus. *World Englishes* 23 (2): 261–268.

Hansen, Klaus, Uwe Carls and Peter Lucko
1996 *Die Differenzierung des Englischen in Nationale Varianten: Eine Einführung*. Berlin: Erich Schmidt.

Holland, Dorothy and Naomi Quinn (eds.)
1987 *Cultural Models in Language and Thought*. Cambridge: Cambridge University Press.

Holborow, Marnie
1999 *The Politics of English: A Marxist View of Language*. London: Sage.

House, Juliane
2003 English as a lingua franca: A threat to multilingualism? *Journal of Sociolinguistics* 7 (4): 556–678.

Huber, Magnus
1999 *Ghanaian Pidgin English in its West African Context: A Sociohistorical and Structural Analysis*. (Varieties of English Around the World 24). Amsterdam/Philadelphia: Benjamins.
2004 Review of *English in Cameroon* (Contributions to the Sociology of Language 85), by Hans-Georg Wolf. *Journal of Pidgin and Creole Languages* 19 (1): 207–210.

Hui, Leng
2003 The influences of cultural schemas on intercultural communication between Chinese speakers of English and Anglo-Australians. *TESOL Links* 53: 6–11.
2004 Cultural knowledge and foreign language teaching and learning: A study of Chinese Family schemas in language, culture and intercultural communication. *Hong Kong Journal of Applied Linguistics* 9 (2): 17–37.

Jenkins, Jennifer
2003 *World Englishes: A Resource Book for Students*. London/New York: Routledge.
Johnson, Robert K.
1990 International English: Towards an acceptable, teachable target variety. *World Englishes* 9 (3): 301–315.
Kachru, Braj B.
1983 Introduction: The other side of English. In: Braj B. Kachru (ed.), *The Other Tongue: English Across Cultures*, 1–12. Oxford: Pergamon.
1985 Standards, codification and sociolinguistic realism: The English language in the outer circle. In: Randolph Quirk and H. G. Widdowson (eds.), *English in the World: Teaching and Learning the Languages and Literatures*, 11–30. Cambridge: University Press/The British Council.
1986 *The Alchemy of English: The Spread, Functions and Models of Non-Native Englishes*. Oxford: Pergamon Press.
1994 The speaking tree: a medium of plural canons. In: James E. Alatis (ed.), *Educational Linguistics, Crosscultural Communication, and Global Interdependence*, 6–22. Georgetown: Georgetown University Press.
Kachru, Braj B. (ed.)
1982 *The Other Tongue: English Across Cultures*. Oxford: Pergamon.
Kachru, Yamuna and Cecil L. Nelson
2006 *World Englishes in Asian Contexts: A Resource Book*. Hong Kong: Hong Kong University Press.
Kemmer, Suzanne and Michael Barlow
2000 Introduction: A usage-based conception of language. In: Michael Barlow and Suzanne Kemmer (eds.), *Usage-Based Models of Language*. Stanford, CA., CSLI Publications.
Kövecses, Zoltán
1995 American friendship and the scope of metaphor. *Cognitive Linguistics* 6 (4): 315–346.
2003 Language, figurative thought, and cross-cultural comparison. *Metaphor and Symbol* 18 (4): 311–320.
Kristiansen, Gitte
2003 How to do things with allophones: Linguistic stereotypes as cognitive reference points in social cognition. In: René Dirven, Roslyn Frank, and Martin Pütz (eds.), *Cognitive Models in Language and Thought: Ideology, Metaphors and Meanings*, 69–120. (Cognitive Linguistic Research 24). Berlin/New York: Mouton de Gruyter.
Lakoff, George and Mark Johnson
2003 [1980] *Metaphors We Live By*, 2nd ed. Chicago: Chicago University Press.
Langacker, Ronald W.
2002 *Concept, Image, and Symbol: The Cognitive Basis of Grammar*. Berlin/New York: Mouton de Gruyter.

Leech, Geoffrey and Roger Fallon
1992 Computer corpora – what do they tell us about culture? *ICAME Journal (Computers in English Linguistics)* 16: 29–50.

Lim, Shirley Geok-lin
2002 Cultural imagination and English in Hong Kong. In: Kingsley Bolton (ed.), *Hong Kong English: Autonomy and creativity*, 265–280. Hong Kong: Hong Kong University Press.

Linguist List
2003 Origin of 'un système où tout se tient.' 14. 1954. http://linguistlist.org/issues/14/14-1954.html. Accessed November 24. 11. 2004.

Liu, Dilin
2002 *Metaphor, Culture, and Worldview: The Case of American English and the Chinese Language*. Lanham/New York/Oxford: University Press of America.

Lucko, Peter
2003 Is English a "killer language"?' In: Peter Lucko, Lothar Peter, and Hans-Georg Wolf (eds.), *Studies in African Varieties of English*, 151–165. Frankfurt am Main: Peter Lang.

Lucko, Peter, Lothar Peter and Hans-Georg Wolf (eds.)
2003 *Studies in African Varieties of English*. Frankfurt/M.: Peter Lang.

Mair, Christian
2002 The continuing spread of English: Anglo-American conspiracy or global grassroots movement? In: D. J. Allerton, Paul Skandera, and Cornelia Tschichold (eds.), *Perspectives on English as a World Language*, 159–169. Basel: Schwabe & Co.

Malcolm, Ian and Judith Rochecouste
2000 Event and story schemas in Australian Aboriginal English discourse. *English World-Wide*, 21 (2): 261–289.

Medubi, Oyinkan
2003 Language and ideology in Nigerian cartoons. In: René Dirven, Roslyn Frank, and Martin Pütz (eds.), *Cognitive Models in Language and Thought: Ideology, Metaphors and Meanings*, 159–197. (Cognitive Linguistic Research 24). Berlin/New York: Mouton de Gruyter.

Mühlhäusler, Peter
1996a *Linguistic Ecology: Language Change and Linguistic Imperialism in the Pacific Region*. London: Routledge.
1996b Linguistic adaptation to changed environmental conditions: Some lessons from the past. In: Alwin Fill (ed.), *Sprachökologie und Ökolinguistik: Referate des Symposions Sprachökologie und Ökolinguistik an der Universität Klagenfurt 27.–28. Oktober 1995*. Tübingen: Stauffenburg Verlag.

Nelson, Gary
2004 Introduction. *World Englishes*, 23 (2): 256–226.

Nettle, Daniel and Suzanne Romaine
2000 *Vanishing Voices: The Extinction of the World's Languages*. Oxford: University Press.

Palmer, Gary B.
1996 *Toward a Theory of Cultural Linguistics*. Austin: University of Texas Press.
2007 Cognitive Linguistics and Anthropolical Linguistics. In: Dirk Geeraerts and Hubert Cuyckens (eds), *Handbook of Cognitive Linguistics*, 1045–1073. New York: Oxford University Press.

Peeters, Bert
2004 Tall poppies and egalitarianism in Australian discourse: From key word to cultural value. *English World-Wide* 25 (1): 1–25.

Pennycook, Alastair
1994 *The Cultural Politics of English as an International Language*. London: Longman.
2001 *Critical Applied Linguistics: A Critical Introduction*. Mahwah, NJ: Lawrence Erlbaum Associates.
2003 Global English, Rip Slyme, and performativity. *Journal of Sociolinguistics* 7 (4): 513–533.

Phillipson, Robert
1992 *Linguistic Imperialism*. Oxford: Oxford University Press.

Polzenhagen, Frank and Hans-Georg Wolf
2007 A case study on culture-specific conceptualisations: Linguistic expressions of corruption in African English. In: Gary Palmer and Farzad Sharifian (eds.), *Applied Cultural Linguistics*, 125–168. (Converging Evidence in Communication and Language Research 7). Amsterdam/Philadelphia: Benjamins.

Pride, John B. (ed.)
1982 *New Englishes*. Rowley, MA: Newbury House.

Pütz, Martin, Susanne Niemeier, and René Dirven
2001a *Applied Cognitive Linguistics I: Theory and Language Acquisition*. (Cognitive Linguistics Research 19.1.) Berlin/New York: Mouton de Gruyter.
2001b *Applied Cognitive Linguistics II: Language Pedagogy*. (Cognitive Linguistics Research 19.2). Berlin/New York: Mouton de Gruyter.

Quirk, Randolph
1981 International communication and the concept of nuclear English. In: Larry E. Smith (ed.), *English for Cross-Cultural Communication*, 151–165. London: Macmillan.

Quirk Randolph and H. G. Widdowson (eds.)
1985 *English in the World: Teaching and Learning the Languages and Literatures*, 11–30. Cambridge: University Press/The British Council.

Rissanen, Matti
2004 Computerized corpora and the study of the history of English. *Proceedings. 2004 International Conference in Commemoration of the 50th Anniversary. English Studies in an Era of Globalization*. June

15–18, 2004. The Academy of Korean Studies. The English Language and Literature Association of Korea.

Rosch, Eleanor
1973 Natural categories. *Cognitive Psychology*, 4: 328–350.
1999 Reclaiming concepts. *Journal of Consciousness Studies* 6 (11–12): 61–77.

Schatzberg, Michael G.
1986 The metaphors of father and family. In: Michael G. Schatzberg and I. William Zartman (eds.), *The Political Economy of Cameroon*, 1–19. New York: Praeger.
2001 *Political Legitimacy in Middle Africa: Father, Family, Food.* Bloomington: Indiana University Press.

Schmied, Hans-Joerg and Karina Kopatsch
2003 Conceptual structure of concrete nouns in Nigerian English. Paper presented at the *8th International Cognitive Linguistics Conference: Cognitive Linguistics, Functionalism, Discourse Studies: Common Ground and New Directions*. Logroño, July 20–25, 2003.

Schmied, Josef
2004 Cultural discourse in the Corpus of East African English and beyond: Possibilities and problems of lexical and collocational research in a one million-word corpus. *World Englishes*, 23 (2): 251–260.

Schneider, Edgar W.
1998 Editorial. *English World-Wide: A Journal of Varieties of English*, 19 (1): 1–5.

Scott, Janet Lee
1997 Traditional values and modern meanings in the paper offering industry of Hong Kong. In: Grant Evans and Maria Tam (eds.), *Hong Kong: The Anthropology of a Chinese Metropolis*, 223–242. Richmond, England: Curzon Press.
2007 For Gods, Ghosts and Ancestors: The Chinese Tradition of Paper Offerings. Hong Kong: Hong Kong University Press.

Scott, Mike and Oxford University Press.
1998 *WordSmith*. CD-ROM. Oxford: Oxford University Press.

Seidlhofer, Barbara
2003 A concept of international English and related issues: From 'real English' to 'realistic English.' Language Policy Division. DG IV – Directorate of School, Out-of-School and Higher Education. Strasbourg: Council of Europe. Available at: http://www.coe.int /T/E/ Cultural_Co-operation/education/Languages/Language_Policy/ Policy_development_activities/Studies/SeidlhoferEN.pdf?L=E

Sharifian, Farzad
2001 Schema-based processing in Australian speakers of Aboriginal English. *Language and Intercultural Communication* 1 (2): 120–134.
2003 On cultural conceptualisations. *Journal of Cognition and Culture* 3 (3): 187–206.

2004 Cultural conceptualizations in Aboriginal English: Empowering Aboriginal children in the classroom. *LAUD Linguistic Agency*, Series A: General & Theoretical Papers, No. 621.

Skandera, Paul
2003 *Drawing a Map of Africa: Idiom in Kenyan English.* (Language in Performance 26). Tübingen: Gunter Narr.

Skutnabb-Kangas, Tove
2000 *Linguistic Genocide in Education or Worldwide Diversity and Human Rights?* Mahwah, NJ: Lawrence Erlbaum Associates.

Skybina, Valentina
2004 Global language: What does it amount to? Paper presented at the *International Conference in Commemoration of the 50th Anniversary. English Studies in an Era of Globalization.* June 15–18, 2004. The Academy of Korean Studies. The English Language and Literature Association of Korea.

Smith, Larry E. (ed.)
1981 *English for Cross-Cultural Communication.* London: Macmillan.

Smith, Larry E. and Michael L. Forman (eds.)
1997 *World Englishes 2000.* Honolulu: University of Hawai'i Press.

Stanlaw, James
2004 *Japanese English: Language and Culture Contact.* Hong Kong: University Press.

Strauss, Claudia and Naomi Quinn
1997 *A Cognitive Theory of Cultural Meaning.* Cambridge: Cambridge University Press.

Thumboo, Edwin (ed.)
2002 *The Three Circles of English.* Singapore: UniPress.

Trudgill, Peter and Jean Hannah
1986 *International English. A Guide to Varieties of Standard English.* London: Edward Arnold.

Wierzbicka, Anna
1997 *Understanding Cultures Through their Key Words: English, Russian, Polish, German, and Japanese.* New York: Oxford University Press.

Wolf, Hans-Georg
1999 From mother tongue to second language: The cultural model of 'community' in African English. *La Langue Maternelle. Cahiers Charles V* 27: 75–91.
2001 *English in Cameroon.* (Contributions to the Sociology of Language 85). Berlin/New York: Mouton de Gruyter.
2003 The contextualization of common core terms in West African English: Evidence from computer corpora. In: Peter Lucko, Lothar Peter, and Hans-Georg Wolf (eds.), *Studies in African Varieties of English*, 3–20. Frankfurt/M.: P. Lang.
2004 Cultural approaches to second language varieties of English: A call for new methodologies and a review of some findings on (West) African English. In: Anne Schröder (ed.), *Crossing Borders: Inter-*

disciplinary Approaches to Africa (Afrikanische Studien 23), 133–149. Münster: LIT Verlag.

2006 Religion and traditional belief in West African English: A linguistic analysis. In Tope Omoniyi and Joshua Fishman (eds.), *Readings in the Sociology of Language and Religion*, 42–59. (Discourse Approaches to Politics, Society and Culture 20). Amsterdam/Philadelphia: Benjamins.

Wolf, Hans-Georg and Herbert Igboanusi

2006 Empowerment through English – a realistic view of the educational promotion of English in postcolonial contexts: The case of Nigeria. In: Martin Pütz, Joshua Fishman, and JoAnne Neff van Aertselaer (eds.). *Along the Routes to Power: Explorations of the Empowerment through Language*, 333–356. (Contributions to the Sociology of Language 92). Berlin/New York: Mouton de Gruyter.

Wolf, Hans-Georg and Frank Polzenhagen

2006 Intercultural communication in English: Arguments for a cognitive approach to intercultural pragmatics. *Intercultural Pragmatics* 3 (3): 285–321.

2007 Fixed expressions as manifestations of cultural conceptualizations: Examples from African varieties of English. In: Paul Skandera (ed.), *Phraseology and Culture in English,* 399–435. (Topics in English Linguistics 54) Berlin/New York: Mouton de Gruyter.

2008fc *Cognitive Linguistic Approaches to World Englishes: An Analysis of the Community Model in African English* (Applications of Cognitive Linguistics). Berlin/New York: Mouton de Gruyter.

Wolf, Hans-Georg and Augustin Simo Bobda

2001 The African cultural model of community in English language instruction in Cameroon: The need for more systematicity. In: Martin Pütz, Susanne Niemeier, and René Dirven (eds.), *Applied Cognitive Linguistics: Theory, Acquisition and Language Pedagogy*, 225–259. (Cognitive Linguistic Research 19.2.). Berlin/New York: Mouton de Gruyter.

World Religions

n.d. Confucian thought. http://wrc.lingnet.org/confuc.htm, accessed Nov. 24, 2004.

Part four

Socio-political systems

Corporate brands as socio-cognitive representations*

Veronika Koller

Abstract

This paper looks at the socio-cognitive representations that constitute corporate brands and at how these are instantiated in corporate discourse.

To this end, the study draws on earlier work on the cognitive construction of corporate identities in business media discourse (Koller 2004), comparing it to a corpus of mission statements as instances of companies' communicated identities, i.e. corporate brands. The methods employed in tracing these cognitive models include computer-assisted quantitative analysis as well as systemic-functional analysis of a sample text.

While the secondary discourse of the business media constructs companies in essentially metaphoric ways, notably as living organisms involved in evolutionary struggle, corporate discourse as instantiated in mission statements relies mostly on literalised concepts of partnership and emotion to convey the company's ideal self. This shift from other to self representation thus entails a move from competitive to cooperative models of business. In the social system constituted by companies and their stakeholders, as well as the relations between them, the former further endow themselves with additional meaning to reinforce their power vis-à-vis the latter.

Keywords: corporate brands, critical discourse analysis, mission statements, social cognition.

1. Introduction

This paper concentrates on social cognition and the way large corporations try to establish their identity in the minds of stakeholders such as employees, investors or customers. As such it reveals an essential layer in cognitive sociolinguistics, in that it appeals to the underlying cognitive patterns exploited by decision-makers in the corporate world.

---

* An earlier version of this paper was presented at the Discourse, Ideology and Ethics in Specialized Communication conference at the University of Milan, 11–13 November 2004. I am grateful to the editors for their helpful comments.

Corporations are paradoxical creatures: On the one hand, they are increasingly forcing their way into the private sphere of consumers and employees alike, as evidenced by aggressive direct marketing aimed at so-called target groups[1] and demands for complete commitment and identification on part of the workforce (Gee, Hull and Lankshear 1996: 31). On the other hand, corporations are highly introspective and concerned about their identity. Such soul-searching has given rise to a number of writings on Corporate Identity (CI). However, the majority of these either narrow down CI to its visual component (Dowdy 2003) or do not venture beyond case studies for the busy executive, selling CI as a new management tool (for a notable exception, see Berggold 2000). Although the two trajectories of corporate reach seem to point in different directions, they do meet in the notion of the corporate brand. Defined as the "outward oriented (i.e., projected) organizational identity" (Kapferer 2002: 185), a corporate brand is the image a company wishes to convey to it stakeholders. As such, it has to be distinguished from product brands: Although some corporations project both (e.g. Apple as corporate brand and iPod as one of its product brands), companies can communicate only corporate or only product brands as well. Examples are McDonald's as a corporate brand without particular product brands and, reversely, Ariel as one of the many product brands marketed by Procter & Gamble, which is not itself a corporate brand. Projecting both seems to be the exception rather than the rule, as such a duplication of images could ask too much of the cognitive capabilities of a consumer who is already faced with innumerable brands.

The present paper sets out to look at corporate brands in terms of their socio-cognitive structure. Social cognition, which first developed as a branch of social psychology in the early 1970s, represents the application of central concepts from cognitive psychology to the question of how individuals make sense of themselves and others. As such, it covers issues like categorization, attribution, self-schemata, scripts, memory as well as the relationship between cognition and affect, to name only the most central ones. Social cognition interprets social behaviour as functionally related to cognitive perception (Fiske and Taylor 1991: 9–10; see

1. Direct marketing comprises both telemarketing in the form of phone calls and customised email offers as well as personal selling. An extreme form of the latter is viral marketing, where private individuals are commissioned by companies to spread word-of-mouth messages about, and give out samples of, products in their respective peer groups (Grauel 2004).

also Kristiansen, this volume). An important strand in social cognition is represented by the theory of social representations (Moscovici 2000). In contrast to schemas, social representations, i.e. the cognitive structures jointly held by members of a particular group, are theorised to be the subject of "continual renegotiation [...] during the course of social interaction and communication" (Augoustinos and Walker 1995: 178). From a cognitive, discourse analytical viewpoint, such renegotiation is effected through intertextual chains, in which the respective representations are recontextualised and possibly enforced in discourse. Further, such socio-cognitive representations are said to provide a shared frame of reference so that communication can take place at all, i.e. make available the assumed shared background knowledge that tends to become naturalised as "common sense" in hegemonic discourses. In this context, Rothbart and Taylor's (1992) observation that social categories tend to be viewed in an essentialist fashion as homogeneous and unalterable is vital and will be taken up again later. Finally, socio-cognitive representations can be seen as establishing social identies and relationships by being communicated (Augoustinos and Walker 1995: 178, 180). In short, they fulfill both an ideational and an interpersonal metafunction in the Hallidayan sense and thus lend themselves very well to incorporation into cognitive sociolinguistics (see Method section).

In socio-cognitive terms then, a corporate brand constitutes the ideal self a company wishes to communicate to others. Ultimately, this ideal self is meant to converge with the "epistemic social schema" (Kristiansen 2008), i.e. the beliefs a social group, in the present case, stakeholders, has about the nature of another social group or entity, here, the company. The analysis carried out in this study will show how corporate brands are further constructed by drawing on an ought self (Kunda 1999: 472) or "deontic social schema" (Kristiansen 2008), i.e., the perceived view of stakeholders about what the company should be like. Moreover, CI constitutes a form of collective identity in that employees may construct their social self as "derive[d] from [their] membership in larger, more impersonal collectives" (Brewer and Gardner 1996: 83) such as the company they work for. Corporate brands, however, are better dealt with as a form of individual identity. Brands as intangible entities represent the cognitive-affective concepts stakeholders maintain about a particular product, service or, in the case of corporate brands, company. To make these abstract concepts graspable, companies seek to endow their brands with quasi-human "personality" (Christensen and Askegaard 2001: para.

27; Wee 2004), up to the point where brands become metaphorical persons interacting with stakeholders.[2]

Given the growing importance of brands in late capitalist consumer culture,[3] it has become a central task of corporate communication to "establish a strong and stable set of associations in the minds and memories of consumers" (Moore 2003: 335), i.e. to communicate and reinforce particular concepts through various texts. One site at which such impression management can be witnessed is the corporate mission statement. As the one genre in corporate discourse that acts most as "[carrier] of ideologies and institutional cultures" (Swales and Rogers 1995: 225), mission statements have the dual purpose of communicating executives' version of CI to employees, thus achieving identification and internal cohesion, and of persuading a multitude of external stakeholders of the inherent value of the company in question. As part of a wider discourse, the individual texts that fall within the boundaries of the mission statement genre draw on specific models to communicate a particular impression of a company into the social system that is business. As any social system, business, too, is constituted by agents,[4] their actions and the relations between them.[5] In that agents engage in a particular behaviour, including discursive behaviour, they re-enact and reproduce both their identities and their relations to other agents in the system. Actions that draw on particular socio-cognitive representations selectively in order to sustain or subvert power relations shall, for present purposes, be regarded as ideological. Investigating mission statements from a cognitive and discursive perspective, then, centres on the following questions: What socio-cognitive representations constitute corporate brands, and how does corporate discourse draw on those representations to communicate brands?

2. For an explanation in terms of metonymy, see Davidse (2002: 154).
3. The importance of brands is reflected in the fact that even in 2000, already more than 60 per cent of the value of fast-moving consumer goods (such as cosmetics or soft drinks) was accounted for by their brand value (Grauel 2000: 18).
4. Throughout this paper, "agent" will be used to denote a party to a social system, while "actor" will refer to a grammatically represented social actor (van Leeuwen 1996). The meaning of the two terms should therefore not be confused with that of participants in ergative and transitive clauses, respectively (Halliday and Matthiessen 2004: 289).
5. Although the definition of social sytems used in this study focuses on interaction within such a system, it tacitly follows Luhmann's notion of social systems as being constituted by their environment (1984: 242–243).

To answer these questions, I will first define and link the three key notions of cognition, ideology and discourse and outline how they impact on the understanding of corporate brands as socio-cognitive representations. Next, I will briefly introduce the corpus I worked with and the methods I used in its analysis. The next part will be dedicated to presenting both the quantitative results from analysing the corpus as a whole as well as the qualitative findings from the analysis of a selected sample text. Finally, I will round off the paper by discussing the role ideology and cognition play in the construction and communication of corporate brands in corporate discourse.

2. Theoretical considerations

Social systems can be understood as constituted by agents relating to each other under particular salient conditions and to specific ends. By engaging in relational behaviour, agents (re-)produce "a set of intercategory relationships, a set of [...] conditions [...] that are perceived to affect people because of their shared or different social category memberships" (Abrams 1999: 198). Moreover, by doing so, they also engender their identities as participants on that set. Vice versa, these identities also motivate relational behaviour. Applying these basic notions to business as a social system, we find "corporations" – the metonymic shorthand for the identities of, and relations between, executives as decision-makers and other employees implementing these decisions – engaging in relational behaviour with "stakeholders", an umbrella term for investors, clients, competitors, government agencies, NGOs and other groups and individuals. The salient conditions at work are the economic system of late capitalism in which the ultimate aim for corporations is to increase profits and thus shareholder value by promoting consumption of their goods and services, widening their market share at the expense of competitors and keeping costs, including labour costs, low. By pursuing this aim, corporations both actualise and constitute their sense of a self that is "potentially multi-leveled and multi-faceted, but [will] at any particular moment, [be] a specific product of a context-dependent comparison" (Abrams 1999: 206). As far as the same comparisons are drawn routinely, the corporate self, while still dynamic in principle, stabilises into a highly accessible socio-cognitive representation that will be used in future comparisons. Management literature refers to this corporate self as the Corporate Identity or CI. Most theorists in the field see CI as a form of strategic impression management in marketing communication, a tool that is based on a defined ideal image (Birkigt and Stadler 1985: 21). By contrast, this study regards CI as a collective representation that ideally originates from and transcends the notions executives and employees share about the company they are part of. As such, this study looks at the agents in the social system that is business.

2.1. Cognition and discourse

Corporate behaviour is manifold, ranging from obvious acts of buying and selling to lobbying in the political sphere and, increasingly, as the welfare state is being dismantled, philanthropy. For present purposes, the focus is on corporations' discursive behaviour, i.e., their textually mediated relational actions. Corporate texts are diverse, comprising both written and spoken ones, and are produced by various authors ranging from senior executives and PR managers to copywriters. They are distributed through various channels to, and interpreted by, different categories of stakeholders. Seen in its entirety, this highly complex process of text production, distribution and interpretation constitutes corporate discourse as a social practice (Fairclough 1995: 135). Discourse is linked to cognition in that mental models underlie both meaning-making processes and behaviour. These models include notions of the self, while behaviour obviously includes discursive behaviour. Linking these theoretical considerations back to the case at hand, CI models are posited as a basis for corporate communication.

It has been stated in the introduction that CI represents a form of collective identity that is metaphorically presented as an individual identity when projected as the corporate brand. Importantly, the brand "personality" is an instance of a "possible self" (Markus and Nurius 1986), more specifically, the ideal self the corporation wishes to become and convey. Possible selves have been defined as "specific representations of the self in future states [that] can serve important links to the articulation and realization of personal goals" (Fiske and Taylor 1991: 189). The text analysis will look at how these ideal future selves are presented as converging with actual, present selves and in how far perceived external expectations (the "ought self" or deontic schemata) have been incorporated into them.

In the highly complex formation that is corporate discourse, mission statements stand out as the genre that is perhaps most endowed with traces of the ideal corporate self, or corporate brand. According to

Balmer (2001: para. 122), a corporate brand as the communicated CI calls for "a clearly defined branding proposition [that] underpins organisational efforts to communicate, differentiate, and enhance the brand vis-à-vis key stakeholder groups". Given the variety of audiences, this proposition has to reconcile the needs and views of different target groups with the necessity to communicate a positive and credible company image (Gurau and McLaren 2003). Mission statements are ideally suited to act as such a branding proposition to various audiences as they are located at the interface between CI and corporate brand, actual and ideal self, internal and external corporate discourse. Indeed, internal and external audiences overlap to a considerable degree (Christensen and Askegaard 2001: para. 20). As a consequence, "much market-related communication [...] can be characterized as auto-communication, that is, communication through which the organization confirms and reinforces [...] its own culture" (Christensen and Askegaard 2001: para. 21). In that sense, mission statements are among the vehicles by which autopoietic systems (Luhmann 1984: 59–63) refer to and reproduce themselves. Consequently, the corporations that issue them become social systems within the larger social system of business that acts as its environment. The subsequent analysis will show in how far this self-referential nature of mission statements squares – or fails to square – with its purpose of persuading stakeholders of the company's inherent value.

2.2. Cognition and ideology

As mission statements originate within the social system they help to reproduce, they selectively draw on particular socio-cognitive representations that seem best suited to sustain or enhance that system and the identities and power relations within it. The selective instantiation of these representations imbues mission statements with ideology, here defined as a particular construction of reality which is encoded in textual representations.[6] As a selective actualisation of socio-cognitive representations in discourse, ideology can be seen as the interface between discourse and cognition. According to van Dijk (2003), it is particular models only that will be distributed in discourse, and they are disseminated

6. The self representations this paper addresses need to be distinguished from other representations (Morgan 1997). In the case of corporations, the other representations would e.g. be the coverage of companies in the business media (see section 3).

at the expense of other models which are equally cognitively available but less socially motivated. As such, cognitive models are not merely "an idealized set of cognitive objects, but a range of socially situated discursive practices" (Augoustinos and Walker 1995: 306). However, I do not see socio-cognitive representations as embedded in discourse in their entirety; rather, discourse instantiates aspects of underlying models strategically. According to the ideology prevailing in the broader socio-cultural formation that a given discourse is embedded in, such aspects of particular socio-cognitive representations may rise to prominence in that discourse. In a cyclical process, these prominent representations again inform discourse participants' cognition. The ultimate purpose for this selective drawing on socio-cognitive representations lies in sustaining or subverting power relations in the discourse community. Linking this to mission statements, it has been noted that "identities and images [...] are volatile social constructions that [...] base their existence and significance largely on the interpretive capabilities and preferences of their audiences" (Christensen and Askegaard 2001: para. 6), i.e. they partly thrive on representations already set up.

With regard to the study at hand, these considerations give rise to the following research questions: Aspects of what socio-cognitive representations are disseminated in business discourse to construct corporate brands, and how is this construction achieved at the textual level? Regarding discourses and their cognitive underpinnings as situated in, and constitutive of, social systems, this paper intends to support recent endeavours that employ cognitive linguistic theory to unravel ideological implications (Dirven, Frank and Pütz 2003; Dirven, Hawkins and Sandikcioglu 2001; Dirven, Polzenhagen and Wolf 2007). In doing so, it takes a post-modern perspective on CI and corporate brands and "seeks to disclose power relationships regarding business identity" (Balmer 2001: para. 29). The following section will outline the methods that were employed to that end.

3. Corpus and methods

3.1. The mission statements corpus

This study is based on a corpus of corporate mission statements. These were chosen as representing a company's ideal self and thus supplementing another staple of corporate websites representing the corporate self, namely the company history. The mission statements in question were taken from the websites of the 2003 Fortune Global 500, a list of the largest companies worldwide that is ascribed great importance by the business community. In particular, the texts comprise the top 50 and the bottom 50 companies, thus building a corpus of 29,925 words. Interestingly, the upper tier (i.e., numbers 1–50 of the Fortune list) shows a shorter average text length (286 words) than the lower tier (i.e., numbers 451–500), the texts in which are thus, at 401 words on average, more verbose. However, upper-tier companies are more likely to have self-presentation texts on their websites in the first place than are their counterparts from the lower tier. Thus, 86 per cent of all upper-tier companies feature a history section on their website and as many as 88 per cent have included a section on their mission, values or vision. By contrast, only 70 per cent of lower-tier companies provide information about their history, with the figure for mission and values being only slightly higher (78 per cent). Quite predictably, the lower tier also shows more broken links (hyperlinks that fail to direct the viewer to another page) and fewer English translations.[7]

However, mission/vision/values may score higher because they encompass a greater variety of texts, being generically heterogeneous in several regards. As for format, they range from simple no-frills text documents to audio files and sophisticated video presentations. Verbal texts in particular show considerable variation in length, ranging from 28 to 1,358 words across the corpus. Multimodal texts are predominantly used for meta-texts on CI, such as energy provider Total's "identity portal" (Total n.d.). In terms of text type, mission statements come under the headings of "Our Vision", "Message from the CEO" (a feature that is particularly popular with Japanese companies), "The essence of our company", "Strategy" or, indeed, "Our Mission" (see Swales and Rogers 1995: 226).[8] By using these headings interchangeably, companies corroborate Collins and Porras's observation of mission and vision statements as "a muddled stew of values, goals, purposes, philosophies, beliefs, aspirations, norms, strategies, practices, and descriptions" (1996: 77, quoted in Czerniawska 1997: 185) and also blur the boundaries between present mission and future vision.

---

7. Lack of English translations is not necessarily a sign of lower quality: After all, why should, for instance, a Dutch gas provider (Gasunie, ranking 491 in the list) provide a foreign-language version of its website?
8. Sections on Corporate Social Responsibility, which are usually clearly demarcated, were not considered.

3.2. Quantitative methods

The methods used to investigate this corpus are twofold, combining computer-assisted quantitative analysis of the whole corpus with functional qualitative analysis of selected sample texts. At this point, it should be noted that this paper developed out of previous work on business magazine articles dealing with mergers and acquisitions (M&A) (Koller 2004: 114–171). Following up on that work on other representations (Morgan 1997), the present study is intended to investigate in how far these converge with, or differ from, corporate self representation. Research on M&A discourse was chosen as a starting point since corporate restructuring directly affects a company's identity and almost always leads to a subsequent change in the corporate brand (referred to as "brand migration"), be it on part of the company acquired (as in the wake of the takeover of Mannesmann by mobile telecommunications company Vodafone) or of two merged companies (as in the creation of the DaimlerChrysler brand). Consequently, the findings for mission statements will be compared to those for the M&A texts. (For the respective corpus data, see Koller 2004: 45.) Given the origins of the present study, it seems reasonable to briefly outline the methodology employed in the earlier research.

Previous knowledge of, and familiarity with, business media discourse on M&A led to the hypothesis that texts on the topic would be dominated by other representations centering on a metaphor of EVOLUTIONARY STRUGGLE, which could be sub-divided into FIGHTING (expressed as, for instance, *hostile takeover*), MATING (e.g. *corporate marriage*) and FEEDING (e.g. *gobble up a company*). To avoid circularity of argument, the collection of magazine articles was checked for alternative metaphors as well. These were again suggested by anecdotal evidence and comprised DANCING (as in "the Asian automotive world's latest mating dance") and EMPIRE BUILDING (e.g. "part of the GM empire is Subaru"; both Thornton 2000). However, in terms of frequency, these turned out to be practically inexistent, recording less than three per cent of metaphoric tokens. In addition, the few instances there were tended to be co-opted into the dominant paradigm, as suggested by the above realisation of the DANCING metaphor combining dancing and mating, or by instantiations combining empire building and war (e.g. "she's […] killing fiefdoms", On top 2000: 56). The metaphor of EVOLUTIONARY STRUGGLE, posited as central to M&A discourse, is a culture-specific model inherent in capitalist societies: Interestingly, Urban (this volume) shows that Darwin originally relied on Adam Smith's economic writings for conceptualising the theory of natural selection. However, "the analogy is almost always made in the reverse direction", i.e. "motivated by the primacy of the natural in our Western dichotomy", the economic is redefined as following the alleged laws of nature. As such, EVOLUTIONARY STRUGGLE has become part of the COMPETITION model of business (Morgan, this volume).

This hypothesis of the central nature of the EVOLUTIONARY STRUGGLE metaphor in many areas of late capitalist society, but especially in the social (sub-)system that is business, called for an investigation into whether it is also used by companies projecting their ideal selves into the public sphere. Answering this question involved defining a field of 35 lexical items for each of the three sub-metaphors, relying on thesauri and glossaries in doing so. The lexical fields are reproduced in the appendix. Cognitively speaking, "overarching concepts [...] define [...] a lexical field" (Taylor 2002: 130), with the hypothesis here stating that these concepts would be used as source domains in the corpus. The ensuing 105 lemmas[9] were then run through the concordancing program of Word Smith Tools 3.0 to ascertain how many of them were actually realised as metaphoric expressions in the corpus, i.e. how many metaphoric types it featured. As the program only searches for a particular string of letters but cannot distinguish between literal and metaphoric usage of that string, the resulting concordance lines obviously required quite extensive manual reworking.[10] In a second step, the corpus was scrutinised for the relative frequency of metaphoric expressions (tokens) of FIGHTING, MATING and FEEDING metaphors. Finally, the present study also utilises another program from the WordSmith Tools suite to identify the respective key words in the two corpora. To that end, the program will generate frequency lists of words in the two corpora and cross-tabulate these against each other, thus arriving at the relatively frequent and hence central words and, by extension, concepts in the text collection.[11]

9. Contrary to Crystal's use of the term *lemma* (2003: 263), the term is here employed to mean a headword (for example *prey*) which can be split up into several lexemes, including phrasal ones (for example *prey*, *to prey [up]on*). These lexemes in turn comprise various word forms (for example *preying*, *preys*, *preyed*). Further, while a cognitive grammar approach would, in bottom-up fashion, start with the word forms (Taylor 2002: 172), the quantitative analysis in the original study was lemma-driven.
10. Another promising method to further prove the validity of the claims made in this study is the use of a semantic tagger to identify key domains of meaning, as those may function as the source domains of central metaphors (see Hardie et al. 2007).
11. For the statistical definition of keyness, see Scott (2001).

3.3. Qualitative methods

The qualitative analysis started out by identifying a sample text from the corpus that showed a high frequency of relevant metaphoric types and looked at it with regard to the role metaphoric and other models play in structuring it at the macro-level. Starting from the notion that metaphoric expressions come to structure text in the form of clusters and chains (Koller 2003), one can observe interrelations between the different instances as these can elaborate, extend or exemplify each other. On the other hand, they can call each other into question or, additionally, even negate each other (Kyratzis 1997). Apart from that, especially very frequent expressions, such as *target* or *hostile*, can simply echo each other by recurring throughout a text.

Supplementary qualitative analysis concerned social actors and process types in an attempt to shed further light on how corporations present their behaviour as agents in a social system. This part of the analysis is based on systemic-functional grammar and its key notion of "text [...] as actualized meaning potential" (Halliday 1978: 109), a coice which, in a volume on cognitive sociolinguistics, may require further explanation. In practical terms, functional grammar was chosen because it allows for concrete text parsing, which seems necessary when analysing a specific sample text. Generally speaking, it should be noted that this approach is indeed compatible with cognitive grammar as developed by Langacker (1987/1991) and Croft (1991). Functional grammar posits that language as a system incorporates three metafunctions: the textual (building cohesive discourse sequences), the interpersonal (enacting social roles and relationships) and the ideational (construing and categorising inner and outer experience) (Halliday and Matthiessen 2004: 29–30). Focusing on the latter two, the interpersonal covers the system of mood (Subjects and Finites) whereas the ideational is concerned with process types and agency. The ideational therefore spells out the cognitive aspects of the language system while the interpersonal addresses its social facets, with agency as a possible interface between the two.

Given the parallels between functional grammar – in particuar its ideational aspects – and cognitive grammar, it comes as no surprise that some authors have indeed combined the two approaches. Nuyts (2004: 135) points out that the "functional dimension refers to [...] what language as a behavioural system does for a human being [while the] cognitive dimension refers to what kind of system language is, in terms of the human 'biological' setup". Regarding the two as structurally related, he advances that a full account of language needs to integrate both dimensions, as shown in his work on epistemic modality (2001). Other studies start out from the ideational metafunction. Heyvaert (2001), for instance, discusses nominalisation, a phenomenon that has been referred to as an "ideational metaphor" rewording processes as entities (Halliday and Matthiessen 2004: 656). She points out how nominals with *-er* suffixes (*reader, grater*) in particular can both realise a number of ideational relations but also mirror the interpersonal link between Subject and Finite, thus combining cognitive with social aspects. Similarly, Davidse (2002) investigates the instantiating and grounding functions of the Subject and Finite (as well as their impact on the Complement) in transitive and ergative reflexive clauses, thus once more combining the ideational with the interpersonal, the cognitive with the social. On theoretical grounds then, it is the added benefit of the interpersonal in relation to the ideational that makes functional grammar appear as a suitable approach to investigating the socio-cognitive representations concrete texts draw upon.

Taken together, the quantitative analysis of the mission statements corpus and the qualitative investigation of the sample text are intended to infer the socio-cognitive representations prevailing in corporate discourse, in particular the way companies instantiate these to project their identities, i.e., communicate corporate brands.

4. Findings

4.1. Quantitative analysis

As described in the Method section, this first part of the empirical section comprises quantitative insights into the corpus of corporate mission statements, comparing these to business media texts on M&A.

Running the lemmas from the three lexical fields of fighting, mating and feeding through the concordancer, we can observe a clear dominance of mating: In terms of types, the field shows the highest number of items to be realised metaphorically, namely seven out of 35, or 20 per cent. It is followed by fighting (8.57 per cent) and feeding, which shows but one lemma in metaphoric use. By contrast, business media discourse on M&A is very much characterised by a predominant FIGHTING metaphor: From the pre-defined lexical field, a stunning 34 lemmas (97.14 per cent) were realised, to be followed by mating (28 out of 35, or 80 per cent) and feeding (16 types or 45.71 per cent). (Note that the highest percentage here is much higher than the one for the mission statement corpus.) As for tokens, it is again MATING which records the highest percentage in the mission statements: Of the combined 90 metaphoric expressions of evolutionary struggle in the mission statements compilation, MATING scores highest, accounting for 87.78 per cent. Again, expressions of mating are followed by fighting (ten tokens or 11.11 per cent) and feeding, which shows a single token. Comparing these findings with their counterpart from magazine articles shows that not only does the sub-field of fighting show the highest number of metaphoric types there, it also records most tokens: Of the combined 725 metaphoric expressions of fighting, mating and feeding in the magazine corpus, the first accounts for two thirds or 484 tokens (a figure that is much lower than the almost 90 per cent recorded for the MATING metaphor in the mission statement corpus). Again, the FIGHTING metaphor is, in business magazine articles, followed by MATING (173 tokens or 23.86 per cent), with FEEDING ranking third (68 tokens or 9.38 per cent).

Combining types and tokens yields the type-token ratio (TTR), a statistical measurement indicating lexical variety of a given text or concept: The higher the TTR, the more lexical variety do we find. In the mission statement corpus, TTRs record mating (.09) before fighting (.3) and feeding (1). On the whole, metaphoric expressions of mating are markedly over-represented in the corpus: Although the size of the collection of mission statements is only 18.19 per cent that of the magazine corpus, lemmas like *relationship* (110 per cent compared to the magazine corpus), *desire* (220 per cent) or *family* (250 per cent) feature in the corpus with disproportionately high frequencies. Other lemmas, such as *passion*, feature only in the mission statements. In the magazine articles, it is again FIGHTING which shows the lowest TTR (.07) and is thus least varied lexically. (MATING and FEEDING show TTRs of .16 and .24, respectively.)

A look at the collocations surrounding the MATING metaphor that is so prominent in the mission statements corpus shows it to be at least partly literalised: It is questionable whether the "passion for excellence" (Schering-Plough) or the "desire to be a leader" (Credit Suisse) are still metaphoric concepts. The qualitative analysis will take this point up again. The corpus of M&A articles shows a slightly different pattern: The TTR indicates variety in the way the FIGHTING metaphor is realised, yet the most frequent expressions it takes (*target*, *hostility* and *battle*, which account for over 40 per cent of all metaphoric expressions of fighting) are again rather conventional ones. On the other hand, journalists also come up with quite a few novel expressions, such as "he pulled the trigger on a merger" (Grant 1997: 86). It is those less entrenched metaphoric expressions which convey the underlying metaphor's productivity (Clausner and Croft 1997).

Briefly contrasting the two tiers in the mission statements corpus, i.e., the top 50 companies of the Fortune list with the bottom 50, it becomes clear that the former use even fewer FIGHTING tokens in their mission statements, while at the same time focusing on the non-romantic aspects of the MATING metaphor. Thus, rather than using expressions such as *passion* and *desire*, mentioned above, companies from the upper tier speak rather less eagerly about the "long term relationships with our customers" (Deutsche Bank) and their "family of brands" (Ford). Whatever its specific instantiations, however, it is the MATING metaphor which is central in the corpus as a whole. In that it is at least partly literalised, it may give way to a non-metaphoric representation of partnership and emotion, a point that will be addressed in the qualitative analysis (section 4.2). Another issue to be tackled there will be possible other traces – apart from a literalised concept of mating – that the EVOLUTIONARY STRUGGLE metaphor so central in business magazine articles on M&A may have left in mission statements. Could it be, for instance, that the metaphor is reflected in an attenuated form as LIVING ORGANISM? Checking the corpora for occurrences of *root**, *cultivat** and *grow** shows that these lemmas are indeed over-represented in the mission statements by up to 400 per cent. Again, the qualitative analysis will throw further light on this issue.

In quantitative terms then, it is the MATING metaphor that is most entrenched in the mission statement corpus, while media discourse on M&A shows the FIGHTING metaphor as a central feature. In either case, inferences can be drawn about writers' conceptualisations of corporations and their identities. Relating this to the communicative ends of the mission statements, the shift in metaphors between the two corpora suggests a reconceptualisation for purposes of impression management.

Finally, it can be seen that key words for mission statements are markedly different from those in business magazine articles on M&A: The former features the items *our*, *we*, *customers*, *products*, *global*, which signal a clear shift from the third person prominent in the latter (key words being *could, Internet*, *it*, *stock*, *he*, *would*, *his, it*, *I*). This finding is not overly surprising given the fact that mission statements were chosen precisely because they reflect a company's sense of self. However, this focus on the self is below shown to be at odds with the communicative purpose of the mission statement as a promotional genre.

4.2. Qualitative analysis

The second part of this paper's empirical section deals with a sample mission statement to see how the respective corporate brand is constructed by the company promoting its ideal self. Again, mission statements stand in contrast to magazine articles. In order to be able to draw comparisons, I will begin by summarising the way metaphor is used to structure a sample magazine article (Chen 2000; for a detailed analysis see Koller 2004: 130–160).

The text from *Fortune* magazine features all three metaphors in question: FIGHTING, MATING and FEEDING. Although it does not show any persistent use of one metaphor, we still find local metaphor chains, some of which fall into the questioning category by featuring different conceptualisations of a particular company. While the author of the article uses the FIGHTING metaphor as an unproblematic representation, alternative conceptualisations along the lines of the MATING metaphor are brought in by quoted corporate representatives. These representatives have to take the interests of various stakeholders into account, including the acquiree's, and are therefore much more reluctant to openly embrace an aggressive scenario, preferring to replace obliteration by incorporation. Here, corporate representatives use the media as a mouthpiece, seeking to attenuate any aggressiveness involved in the acquisition. In their case study of the media coverage of takeovers, Herrera and White (2000) notice that the WAR metaphor was at some point abandoned in favour of the MARRIAGE metaphor, as the latter was perceived as less face-threatening. In the words of the authors, "it downplays the loser dimension" (2000: 238). Mere questioning becomes downright negating when corporate representatives and journalists struggle over metaphoric meaning ("Should investors fear indigestion? 'We don't digest them, we integrate them'"). Metaphoric expressions thus prove to foster a conflict between primary corporate and secondary media discourse.

Quotes from corporate representatives make up about a fifth of the article. Apart from reconceptualising the prominent representations of companies in business magazines, they serve the additional function of redirecting the focus to the corporate *we*. While the article as a whole shows the third person orientation reflected in the keywords, the voices from primary corporate discourse bring in first person plural as an actor ("We had always thought", "We always take regulatory reviews seriously", "We don't digest them, we integrate them"). This shift is consistent with the key words for the mission statement corpus, which were dominated by first person plural pronouns. Further, the above examples show that these first person plural actors tend to feature in mental and affective processes.

By intertextually integrating, and thus recontextualising, corporate voices, the magazine article reflects typical features of mission statements. These are directly accessible by looking at a sample text from the corpus, the mission statement of upper-tier company IBM.

Text B1 (IBM n.d. Reprint courtesy of International Business Machines Corporation. Copyright 2004 © International Business Machines Corporation).

bold type: FIGHTING metaphor
bold italics: partnership and emotion
bold underlined: FEEDING metaphor
BOLD SMALL CAPS: **LIVING ORGANISM** metaphor (no word field)
An asterisk * indicates a relevant (metaphoric) expression that was not included in the word fields.

At IBM, we strive to lead in the invention, development and manufacture of the industry's most advanced information technologies, including computer systems, software, storage systems and microelectronics.We translate these advanced technologies into value for our customers through our professional solutions, services and consulting businesses worldwide.

Business value, and a company's values

We've been spending a great deal of time thinking, debating and determining the fundamentals of this company. It has been important to do so. When IBMers have been crystal clear and united about our strategies and purpose, it's amazing what we've been able to **CREATE** and accomplish. When we've been *___uncertain, conflicted or hesitant___, we've squandered opportunities and even made blunders that would have sunk smaller companies.

It may not surprise you, then, that last year we examined IBM's core values for the first time since the company's founding. In this time of great change, we needed to affirm IBM's reason for being, what sets the company apart and what should drive our actions as individual IB Mers. Importantly, we needed to find a way to *___engage___ everyone in the company and get them to speak up on these important issues. Given the realities of a smart, global, independent-minded, 21st-century workforce like ours, I don't believe something as vital and personal as values could be dictated from the top.

So, for 72 hours last summer, we invited all 319,000 IBMers around the world to * ***engage*** in an open "values jam" on our global intranet. IBMers by the tens of thousands weighed in. They were * ***thoughtful*** and ***passionate*** about the company they want to be a part of. They were also **brutally** honest. Some of what they wrote was * ***painful*** to read, because they pointed out all the bureaucratic and dysfunctional things that get in the way of serving clients, working as a team or implementing new ideas.

But we were resolute in keeping the dialog free-flowing and candid. And I don't think what resulted – broad, * ***enthusiastic***, GRASS-ROOTS consensus – could have been obtained in any other way.

In the end, IBMers determined that our actions will be driven by these values: * ***Dedication*** to every client's success

Innovation that matters, for our company and for the world

* ***Trust and personal responsibility*** in all ***relationships***

I must tell you, this process has been very meaningful to me. We are getting back in touch with what IBM has always been about – and always will be about – in a very concrete way. And I feel that I've been handed something every CEO * ***craves***: a mandate, for exactly the right kinds of transformation, from an entire workforce.

Where will this lead? It is a work in progress, and many of the implications remain to be discovered. What I can tell you is that we are rolling up our sleeves to BRING IBM's values TO LIFE in our policies, procedures and daily operations.

I've already touched on a number of things relating to clients and innovation, but our values of * ***trust and personal responsibility*** are being managed just as seriously – from changes in how we measure and reward performance, to how we equip and support IBMers' community volunteerism.

Our values underpin our ***relationships*** with investors as well. In late February, the board of directors approved sweeping changes in executive compensation. They include innovative programs that ensure investors first receive meaningful returns – a 10 percent increase in the stock price – before IBM's top 300 executives can realize a penny of profit from their stock option grants. Putting that into perspective, IBM's market value would have to increase by $17 billion before executives saw any benefit from this year's option awards. In addition, these executives will be able to acquire market-priced stock options only if they first invest their own money in IBM stock. We believe these programs are unprecedented, certainly in our industry and perhaps in business.

Clearly, leading by values is very different from some kinds of leadership demonstrated in the past by business. It is empowering, and I think that's much **HEALTHIER**. Rather than burden our people with excessive controls, we are ****trusting*** them to make decisions and to act based on values – values they themselves shaped.

To me, it's also just common sense. In today's world, where everyone is so interconnected and interdependent, it is simply essential that we work for each other's success. If we're going to solve the biggest, thorniest and most widespread problems in business and society, we have to innovate in ways that truly matter. And we have to do all this by taking personal ****responsibility*** for all of our ***relationships*** – with clients, colleagues, partners, investors and the public at large. This is IBM's mission as an enterprise, and a goal toward which we hope to work with many others, in our industry and beyond.

Samuel J. Palmisano

Chairman, President and Chief Executive Officer

The text includes a realisation the conventional COMPANIES ARE SHIPS metaphor ("blunders that would have sunk smaller companies", lines 13–14) as well as a few instantiations of the LIVING ORGANISM metaphor ("create" "bring to life" or "healthier" in lines 11, 46 and 66, respectively).[12] However, the sample is clearly dominated by lexis actualising the concepts of partnership and emotion. (Metaphoric expressions of fighting and feeding are virtually non-existent.) Importantly, the instances of partnership and emotion no longer express the MATING metaphor; in fact, they are not even linked to the metaphoric conceptualisation of the company as LIVING

12. The page on the IBM website where the text can be found features the picture of a helix in the corporate colour of "Big Blue", suggesting that values are the DNA of the organism that is the company.

ORGANISM. On the contrary, all instances of mating lexis in the magazine article briefly described above are clearly metaphoric (e.g., "SDL was the beautiful prom queen standing on the dance floor without a partner"). How do the literalised expressions of emotion and partnership combine to structure the IBM text then?

While relevant expressions occur throughout the text, they tend to cluster in its middle part, especially lines 24–53, forming two sets of interrelated chains (lines 12–28 and 33–74). Looking at those chains, we can see that the first chain begins in line 12 ("uncertain, conflicted or hesitant"), with the negatively evaluated emotional state being extended to "painful to read" in line 28. All other instances refer to positively connoted emotional states and processes, the first of which ("we needed to find a way to engage everyone" in line 19) being elaborated by "we invited all 319,000 IBMers [...] to engage" in lines 24–25. Even the "brutally honest" of line 28 is not entirely negative, since it functions as an elaboration of "thoughtful and passionate" in lines 26–27 and further describes an attitude that is helpful in achieving IBM's goals. The next set of chains starts in line 33, with "enthusiastic consensus" being extended to "dedication to every client's success" and "something every CEO craves" in lines 36 and 42, respectively. All three instances are linked by their intensive trajectory (Beaugrande 1997: 72). The widest-spanning chain starts with the sub-heading in line 38 ("trust and personal responsibility in all relationships"). Its three element all trigger chains across the remainder of the text: They are each echoed in lines 49 ("our values of trust and personal responsibility") and 53 ("our relationships with investors"), respectively. From there, the three concepts, while retaining their sequence, are spread still further apart, with "trust" being exemplified as "we are trusting [our people]" (line 67) and "responsibility" and "relationships" being echoed in line 74. As these three are the only items to be repeated in a three-link chain, they can be identified as the central concepts reflected in the text.

Notably absent are questioning or negating chains, as they would contravene the persuasive purpose of the text. Similar certainty is conveyed by the pronounced use of deontic modality (including "we needed to affirm" in line 17, "I must tell you", line 39, and "we have to innovate" in lines 72–73).

The above examples show one particularity of the IBM text, namely its use of direct address and first person singular (e.g. "I must tell you, this process has been very meaningful to me", line 39). As the linguistic equivalent of significant eye contact, these phrases are intented to engage the reader and lend further credibility to the text. (The latter function is also met by the narratives in lines 24–34 and 53–63 as well as by the inclusion of some negative evaluation such as "we've squandered opportunities" in line 13 or "all the bureaucratic and dysfunctional things" in line 29.) However, the most frequent personal actor is *we/our*, which occurs 38 times (as contrasted with 12 times for *they/them/their* and 9 times for *I/me*) and thus reflects its dominant status as key word in the corpus. Further, the first person plural actor is always found as acting, while second and third person also feature as affected entities.

Actor roles are ambiguous in that the predominant *we* refers to the categorised actor "IBMers" (lines 10–14) but is backgrounded everywhere else. Strikingly, IBMers are later allocated third-person status (lines 26–29), leaving the reader to infer that *we* refers to another categorised actor or, in cognitive grammar terms, relational noun (Taylor 2002: 209), namely the "board" or "executives". Still, these are referred to as *they* in lines 53–62 and set apart from "investors". It seems that the principal of the text, i.e. senior management, avoids fully identifying with either employees or executives, making *we* a paradoxical actor that is simultaneously inclusive and exclusive because backgrounded (Dieltjen and Heynderickx 2001).

Detached it may be, but the *we* still addresses the two most important audiences, namely employees and investors. In the first case, the top-down communication is potentially at odds with the intention to make employees identify with the corporate brand, a tension that is eased by positive politeness strategies such as compliments ("smart [...] independent-minded workforce", lines 21–22), showing interest ("we needed to [...] engage everyone", line 19), claiming common ground ("grass-roots consensus", lines 33–34) and claiming reciprocity ("keeping the dialog free-flowing", line 32). Investor communication in the latter half of the text is equally characterised by positive politeness, notably claims to reciprocity ("we work for each other's success", lines 70–71) and self-deprecation ("investors first receive meaningful returns [...] before [...] executives can realize a penny of profit", lines 55–57). Again, the lack of negative politeness ties in with the overall direct and unhedged nature of the text.

As for process types, the text echoes the quotes from corporate representatives in the magazine article in that the focus is on mental and affective processes ("I feel that I've been handed", lines 41–42; "I think that's much healthier", lines 65–66). Importantly, the tense used is the present, making the ideal self converge with the actual self.[13] The second narrative (lines

13. Mission statements of lower-tier companies feature markedly more tentative and volitional processes, such as "we intend to develop" or "[the company] aims for", thus replicating the findings of Mautner (2000).

53–63) also reflects perceived expectations of investors after the early 2000s flurry of corporate scandals, and thus incorporates the company's ought self.

To sum up, the text is, at its macro-level, structured by exemplifying, echoing, extending and elaborating chains formed by the central expressions of emotion and partnership. In line with the communicative purpose of the genre it represents, it further employs a number of persuasive devices, notably direct address, positive politeness and deontic modality. Most importantly, the corporate brand is presented as a reliable, fair and responsible partner (traits) who shows an engaging and trusting behaviour while putting themselves last (attitudes). Nevertheless, these persuasive devices clash with a narcissistic focus on the corporate self and a detached managerial class unwilling to identify themselves. The final section will discuss what this clash means for the corporate brand as socio-cognitive representation.

5. Discussion

The central concept to emerge in business magazines is clearly the FIGHTING metaphor, which is most frequent and most entrenched. As a masculinised scenario it is poised to reproduce business as a male-defined social area and practice. On top of that, we find the overarching EVOLUTIONARY STRUGGLE metaphor to naturalise this ideological agenda by veiling human agency: Corporate restructuring is no longer a socio-economic practice but a field where the laws of nature play out. While Luhmann (1984: 288) may perceive the metaphor that maps organisms onto social systems to have been a hackneyed concept for more than a century, it is certainly still very much used in contemporary business media discourse. In this context, Rothbart and Taylor's (1992) observation that social categories tend to be viewed in an essentialist fashion as homogeneous and unalterable natural kinds is crucial.[14] Interestingly, corporate voices integrated into media texts attenuate this central concept, thus using the media as a mouthpiece for stakeholder communication.

Direct stakeholder communication in the form of mission statements reflects the ideal corporate self, showing partnership and emotion as central

14. In this context, it is noteworthy that the term "evolutionary struggle" is itself an interpretation of evolutionary processes. Another view sees evolution not as brutal selection but as a principle for optimizing complex systems (Fischer and Lotter 2001: 81). See also Morgan (this volume).

concepts. These concepts make for an interdiscursive link between corporate and popular psychology discourse as well as between the genres of mission statements on the one hand and self-help guides on the other. The concepts are moreover literalised, perhaps in an attempt at sounding more serious and objective. Just like the FIGHTING metaphor, however, the emotion/partnership concept is highly gendered: In that the latter is feminised, it is set against the FIGHTING metaphor so prominent in media discourse, the two thus forming a virtual gender dichotomy. Although the mission statements also feature scenarios such as flow and open space (expressed by "transparency", "candid", "crystal clear") and forward movement (as in "goal"), partnership and emotion dominate, thus helping to manage the companies' impression on stakeholders by avoiding the FIGHTING metaphor and persuade the target audience of the companies' inherent value. To that end, the additional LIVING ORGANISM metaphor featured in the mission statements relates more to the aspect of caring and creation than struggle for survival.

The shift from business magazines to mission statements entails a shift from other to self representation, with the latter drawing on deontic schemata in constructing the company's ideal self. The ultimate aim in doing so is to anchor this ideal self as the epistemic schema of the company in the minds of its stakeholders. Although the schemata's instantiations in the mission statements corpus are partly literalised, other and self representations are both based on an underlying metaphor family of BUSINESS IS COMPETITION VS BUSINESS IS COOPERATION (Morgan, this volume). As Morgan points out, business as a social practice is neither; rather, it is discourse participants' assumptions that make business a competitive endeavour when viewed as other, or a cooperative effort when seen from inside. In this sense, even the FIGHTING metaphor could convey cooperation in striving to attain a shared goal. Expressions in the mission statements such as *brutally honest* bear witness to this fact.

In that their persuasive purpose clashes with their self-centred nature, mission statements, being more company than audience-oriented (Gurau and McLaren 2003), face an inherent communication problem and bring about a conceptual clash between primary and secondary business discourse. Notably, the readership for both business magazines and mission statements is likely to overlap to a large extent, in that the employees and investors addressed by the latter are the corporate representatives addressed (and quoted) by the former. As a result, readers are exposed to conflicting messages. (For the subsequent failure of value statements to generate employee identification, see Murphy and Davey 2002.) The question remains whether these conceptual clashes signal ideological change on a larger scale or merely outward attenuation of still persistent aggressive concepts.

It has been noted that "the relationship facet is particularly important for [...] corporate brands", with "the intimacy [being] based on shared values and visions, common commitments" (Kapferer 2002: 178, 179). (Similar notions can be found in popular management handbooks such as Davies 2002, Gobe 2001, Roberts 2004.) One relevant social change fuelling the focus on partnership and emotion in mission statements is the blending of the public and the private sphere. The invasion of the public by the private can be witnessed in the conversationalisation of public discourse, e.g. in the form of human-interest talk shows and other instances of "the routinised simulation of conversational spontaneity" (Chouliaraki and Fairclough 1999: 5). The reverse phenomenon, marketisation of private discourses and relationships, shows in, for instance, family counselling guidelines which rely on management discourse to rephrase parent-child dynamics (Pearce 2004). In the context of this paper, the construction of business relationships as private emotional relationships signals a further blurring of these boundaries: By drawing on private relationships to conceptualise business relations, the latter are relocated to a pseudo-private sphere. As a consequence, corporations endow themselves with meaning beyond mere profit generation. Indeed, they have recast themselves as brands supplying not only goods and services, but emotional support, bonding and community. By virtue of this added value, corporate representatives further reinforce the power of corporations as social systems within the larger interconnected social system that is late capitalism.

Appendix

Word fields

FIGHTING: armour/arms/army/to arm, (to) assault, (to) attack, to backfire, (to) battle/battlefield/battleground/embattled, to beleaguer, blood/bleed/bloody, bomb(shell)/to bomb(ard), (to) bruise, brutal(ity), casualty, (to) combat/combative, conqueror/conquest/to conquer, (to defeat), defence/to defend/defensive, enemy/inimical, fierce, (to)fight/fighter, front, hostility/hostile, killer/killing/to kill, (to) manoeuvre, (to)raid/raider, shootout/shot(gun)/to shoot, soldier(ly), (to) surrender, survival/survivor/to survive, (to) target, troops, veteran, victim, victory/victorious, vulnerability/vulnerable, war(fare)/warrior/warlike/warring, weapon(ry)

MATING: affair, affection(ate), altar, arms [body part], bed(fellow), bride-(groom)/bridal, consummation/consummate, court(ship)/to court/courtly, dalliance/to dally, (to) desire/desirable, divorce, (to) embrace, faith(ful), family, (to) flirt/flirtation/flirtatious/flirty, friend(ship)/friendly, heart, honeymoon, husband, infatuation/infatuated, (to) kiss, (to) love/lover/lovable, (to) lust/lustful, marriage/to marry, (to) mate, nuptials/nuptial, passion-(ate), relationship, romance/romantic, sex/sexy/sexual, spouse, suitor, wedding/to wed, wife, wooer/to woo

FEEDING: appetite/appetizer, (to) bite, to chew, course, delicious, to devour, (to) diet/dietary, (in)digestion/to digest/digestible, dinner/to dine, dish, eat/(un)eatable, (in)edible, (to) feast, food/feeder/to feed, glutton(y)/gluttonous, to gobble, to gorge, greed(y), (to) gulp, helping, (to) hunger/hungry, juicy, meal, morsel, (to) nibble, nourishment/to nourish, palatable, predator(y), (to) prey (on), ravenous, (in)satiable, to spit out, starvation/to starve, to swallow, (to) taste/tasting/tasty

References

Abrams, Dominic
1999 Social identity, social cognition, and the self: the flexibility and stability of self-categorization. In: Dominic Abrams and Michael A. Hogg (eds.), *Social Identity and Social Cognition*, 197–229. Oxford: Blackwell.

Augoustinos, Martha and Iain Walker
1995 *Social Cognition: an Integrated Introduction*. London: Sage.

Balmer, John M. T.
2001 Corporate identity, corporate branding and corporate marketing: seeing through the fog. *European Journal of Marketing* 35(3–4): 248–291. Available from http://proquest.umi.com/pqdweb?index=0&did=000000115925027&SrchMode=1&sid=1&Fmt=3&VInst=PROD&VType=PQD&RQT=309&VName=PQD&TS=1102435927&clientId=14829. Accessed 7 December 2004.

Beaugrande, Robert de
1997 *New Foundations for a Science of Text and Discourse: Cognition, Communication, and the Freedom of Access to Knowledge and Society* (Advances in Discourse Processes 61). Norwood, NJ: Ablex.

Berggold, Christian
2000 *Unternehmensidentität: Emergenz, Beobachtung und Identitätspolitik*. Berlin: Verlag für Wissenschaft und Forschung.

Birgikt, Klaus and Marinus M. Stadler
1985 Corporate Identity als unternehmerische Aufgabe. In: Klaus Birgikt and Marinus M. Stadler (eds.), *Corporate Identity: Grundlagen, Funktionen, Fallbeispiele*. 2nd edition. Landsberg am Lech: Verlag Moderne Industrie.

Brewer, Marilynn B. and Wendi Gardner
1996 Who is this "we"? Levels of collective identity and self representations. *Journal of Personality and Social Psychology* 71 (7): 83–93.

Chen, Christine Y.
2000 Gorilla in the midst. *Fortune*, 14 August. Available from http://www.fortune.com/fortune/investing/articles/0,15114,373533,0.html. Accessed 29 October 2004.

Chouliaraki, Lilie and Norman Fairclough
1999 *Discourse in Late Modernity*. Edinburgh: Edinburgh University Press.

Christensen, Lars Thoger and Soren Askegaard
2001 Corporate identity and corporate image revisited: a semiotic perspective. *European Journal of Marketing* 35 (3–4): 292–315. Available from
http://proquest.umi.com/pqdweb?RQT=309&VInst=PROD&VName=PQD&VType=PQD&sid=1&index=0&SrchMode=1&Fmt=3&did=000000115925016&clientId=14829. Accessed 8 December 2004.

Clausner, Timothy C. and William Croft
1997 Productivity and schematicity in metaphors. *Cognitive Science* 21 (3): 247–282.

Collins, James C. and Jerry I. Porras
1996 Building your company's vision. *Harvard Business Review* 74: 65–77.

Croft, William
1991 *Syntactic Categories and Grammatical Relations*. Chicago: University of Chicago Press.

Crystal, David
2003 *A Dictionary of Linguistics and Phonetics*. 5th edition. Oxford: Blackwell

Czerniawska, Fiona
1997 *Corporate Speak: the Use of Language in Business*. Basingstoke: Macmillan.

Davidse, Kristin
2002 Nominative and oblique in English: reflexive clauses as a test case for dictinct Agent-Patient models. In: Kristin Davidse and Béatrice Lamiroy (eds.), *The Nominative and Accusative and Their Counterpart* (Case and Grammatical Relations Across Languages 4). Amsterdam: Benjamins.

Davies, Melinda
2002 *The New Culture of Desire: 5 Radical New Strategies That Will Change Your Business and Your Life*. New York: The Free Press.

Dieltjen, Sylvain and Priscilla Heynderickx
2001 Evasive actions in top-down communication: strategies for avoiding direct sender and receiver references. *Document Design* 2 (2): 210–219.

Dirven, René, Roslyn Frank and Martin Pütz (eds.)
2003 *Cognitive Models in Language and Thought: Ideology, Metaphors and Meanings*. Berlin/New York: Mouton de Gruyter.

Dirven, René, Bruce Hawkins and Esra Sandikcioglu (eds.)
2001 *Language and Ideology: Theoretical Cognitive Approaches*. Amsterdam: Benjamins.

Dirven, René, Frank Polzenhagen and Hans-Georg Wolf
2007 Cognitive Linguistics, Ideology, and Critical Discourse Analysis. In: Dirk Geeraerts and Hubert Cuyckens (eds.), *Handbook of Cognitive Linguistics*, 1222–1240. New York: Oxford University Press.

Dowdy, Clare
2003 *Beyond Logos: New Definitions of Corporate Identity*. Mies: RotoVision.

Fairclough, Norman
1995 *Critical Discourse Analysis: the Critical Study of Language*. London: Longman.

Fischer, Gabriele and Wolf Lotter
2001 Von Zellen und Menschen (interview with Boris Steipe). *Brand eins*, February: 80–85.

Fiske, Susan T. and Shelley E. Taylor
1991 *Social Cognition*. 2nd edition. New York: McGraw-Hill.

Gee, James P., Glynda Hull and Colin Lankshear
1996 *The New Work Order: Behind the Language of New Capitalism*. St. Leonards, NSW: Allen & Unwin.

Gobe, Marc
2001 *Emotional Branding: the New Paradigm of Connecting Brands to People*. New York: Allworth Press.

Grant, Linda
1997 Why FedEx is flying high. *Fortune*, 10 November: 86–89.

Grauel, Ralf
2000 Die Macht der Marke. *Brand eins*, March: 16–24.
2004 Mitarbeiter des Monats: der Kunde. *Brand eins*, November: 18–20.

Gurau, Calin and Yvonne McLaren
2003 Corporate reputations in UK biotechnology: an analysis of on-line "company profile" texts. *Journal of Marketing Communication* 9 (4): 241–256.

Halliday, Michael A. K.
1978 *Language as Social Semiotic: the Social Interpretation of Language and Meaning*. London: Edward Arnold.

Halliday, Michael A. K. and Christian M. I. M. Matthiesen
2004 *An Introduction to Functional Grammar.* 3rd edition. London: Arnold.

Hardie, Andrew, Veronika Koller, Paul Rayson and Elena Semino
2007 Exploiting a semantic annotation tool for metaphor analysis. Proceedings of the Corpus Linguistics 2007 Conference. Birmingham, July 2007.

Herrera, Honesto and Michael White
2000 Business is war or the language of takeovers. In: Mercedes Fornés Guardia, Juan Manuel Molina Valero and Lorena Pérez Hernández (eds.), *Pragmática y Análisis del Discurso*, 231–239. Rioja: Universidad de la Rioja.

Heyvaert, Liesbet
2001 Nominalization as an "interpersonally driven" system. *Functions of Language* 8 (2): 283–324.

IBM
n.d. Our values at work. Available from http://www.ibm.com/ibm/values/us. Acessed 4 November 2004.

Kapferer, Jean-Noël
2002 Corporate brand and organizational identity. In: Bertrand Moingeon and Guillaume Soenen (eds.), *Corporate and Organizational Identities: Integrating Strategy, Marketing, Communication and Organisational Perspectives*, 175–193. London: Routledge.

Koller, Veronika
2003 Metaphor clusters, metaphor chains: analyzing the multifunctionality of metaphor in text. *metaphorik.de* 05: 115–134. Available at http://metaphorik.de/05/koller.pdf.
2004 *Metaphor and Gender in Business Media Discourse: a Critical Cognitive Study.* Basingstoke: Palgrave Macmillan.

Kristiansen, Gitte
2008 Idealized cultural models: The group as a variable in the development of cognitive schemata. In: Roslyn M. Frank, René Dirven, Tom Ziemke and Enrique Bernárdez (eds.), *Body, Language and Mind*, 409–432. Vol. II: Social Situatedness. Berlin/New York: Mouton de Gruyter.

Kunda, Ziva
1999 *Social Cognition: Making Sense of People.* Cambridge, MA: MIT Press.

Kyratzis, Sakis
1997 Metaphorically speaking: sex, politics and the Greeks. Ph.D. thesis, Lancaster University.

Langacker, Ronald W.
1987/1991 *Foundations of Cognitive Grammar.* 2 vols. Stanford: Stanford University Press.

Luhmann, Niklas
1984 *Soziale Systeme: Grundriß einer allgemeinen Theorie.* Frankfurt a. M.: Suhrkamp.

Markus, Hazel R. and Paula S. Nurius
1986 Possible selves. *American Psychologist* 41: 954–969.
Mautner, Gerlinde
2000 Market-driven education: the discourse of mission statements and Deans' messages on Business Schools' Internet web pages. Paper presented at the Annual Meeting of the British Association for Applied Linguistics, Cambridge, 7–9 September.
Moore, Robert E.
2003 From genericide to viral marketing: on "brand". *Language and Communication* 23 (3–4): 331–357.
Morgan, Pamela
1997 Self-presentation in a speech of Newt Gingrich. *Pragmatics* 7 (3): 275–308.
Moscovici, Serge
2000 *Social Representations: Explorations in Social Psychology.* Cambridge: Polity Press.
Murphy, Michael G. and Kate M. Davey
2002 Ambiguity, ambivalence and indifference in organisational values. *Human Resource Management Journal* 12 (1): 17–32.
Nuyts, Jan
2001 *Epistemic Modality, Language and Conceptualization: A Cognitive Pragmatic Perspective* (Human Cognitive Processing 5). Amsterdam: Benjamins.
2004 The cognitive-pragmatic approach. *Intercultural Pragmatics* 1 (1): 135–149.
On top of the world
2000 *Fortune,* 16 October: 38–59.
Pearce, Michael
2004 The marketization of discourse about education in UK general election manifestos. *Text* 24 (2): 245–265.
Roberts, Kevin
2004 *Lovemarks: the Future Beyond Brands.* New York: Powerhouse Cultural Entertainment Books.
Rothbart, Myron and Marjorie Taylor
1992 Category labels and social reality: Do we view social categories as natural kinds? In: Gün R. Semin and Klaus Fiedler (eds.), *Language, Interaction and Social Cognition*, 11–36. London: Sage.
Scott, Mike
2001 Comparing corpora and identifying key words, collocations, and frequency distributions through the WordSmith Tools suite of computer programs. In: Mohsen Ghadessy, Alex Henry and Robert Roseberry (eds.), *Small Corpus Studies and ELT: Theory and Practice*, 47–67. Amsterdam: Benjamins.
Swales, John and Priscilla S. Rogers
1995 Discourse and the projection of corporate culture: the Mission Statement. *Discourse & Society* 6 (2): 223–242.

Taylor, John R.
2002 *Cognitive Grammar*. Oxford: Oxford University Press.
Thornton, Emily
2000 Auto alliances in Japan: foreign buyers beware. *Business Week*, 27 March. Available from http://www.businessweek.com/@@AqsDnIcQ5rBxkwcA/2000/00_13/b3674233.htm. Accessed 12 December 2004.
Total
n.d. The Group's new visual identity. Available at http://www.total.com/identite/portail/en/index.htm. Acessed 15 July 2008.
van Dijk, Teun A.
2003 The discourse-knowledge interface. In: Gilbert Weiss and Ruth Wodak (eds.), *Critical Discourse Analysis: Theory and Interdisciplinarity*, 85–109. Basingstoke: Palgrave Macmillan.
van Leeuwen, Theo
1996 The representation of social actors. In: Carmen Caldas-Coulthard and R. Malcolm Coulthard (eds.), *Texts and Practices: Readings in Critical Discourse Analysis*, 32–71. London: Routledge.
Wee, Thomas Tan Tsu
2004 Extending human personality to brands: the stability factor. *Journal of Brand Management* 11 (4): 317–331.

Metaphorically speaking: Gender and classroom discourse[1]

Susan Fiksdal

Abstract

In order to study the ways in which metaphors are used in naturally occurring conversation, I analyzed the discourse of students commenting on their own videotaped seminar discussions. The participants were US undergraduate college students who participated in open-ended interviews while observing the videotapes. I test Reddy's (1979) formulation of the conduit metaphor, and show the way these speakers extended that framework by describing the shape of the discussion metaphorically. I found 7 metaphor clusters that indicate a distinct cultural schema or model—collaborative classroom discourse. When the metaphors were categorized by the speakers' gender, I found variation: the metaphorical expressions used by male students are grounded in the conceptual metaphor SEMINAR IS A GAME, whereas those used by female students are grounded in the conceptual metaphor SEMINAR IS A COMMUNITY. I suggest that the same goal of collaboration is present in the students' metaphors, regardless of gender, but gender differences in the formulations of metaphors highlight different alignments towards the discussion.

Keywords: cognitive sociolinguistics, discourse analysis, classroom discourse, conversation, gender, metalanguage, metaphor, communities of practice, alignment, cultural schema

1. Introduction

Within cognitive linguistics, the study of how metaphors are used has a well developed literature. The analysis is primarily based on introspection, linguistic resources within a given language (e.g. Lakoff and John-

1. This is a major revision of Fiksdal (1999) and is reprinted with kind permission of the editor of *Language Sciences*.

son 1980; Lakoff 1987; Johnson 1987; Dirven and Pörings 2003), or written texts (e.g. Boers 1999; Crisp 2002; Zinken 2003). Recently, researchers have begun to examine variation in the use of metaphor in naturally occurring conversation. In a study examining interviews with medical patients, Gülich (2003) found that patients used metaphors that were quite different from those used by medical practitioners to describe their condition, and that patients' metaphors yielded useful insights into their subjective experiences of illness. Cameron and Deignan (2003) compare speakers in two corpora and examine their use of hedges or "tuning devices" modifying their metaphors. They found variation according to the speakers' perceived expertise of the hearer.

In studies by ethnographers examining the ways in which cultural models frame experience, Quinn (1997: 137–144) classified the metaphors 11 couples used in extensive interviews describing their marriages into 8 broad categories. Balaban (1999) examined knowledge metaphors used by pilgrims at a Marian apparition site and found that pilgrims used more non-visual than visual metaphors, possibly to reduce their own agency and attribute divine authority to their experiences. Bialostok (2002) noted recurring metaphors used by parents regarding the literacy of their children. He focused on the conceptual metaphor LITERACY HAS MORAL WORTH and discovered little variation among the speakers in their use of this metaphor.

In this chapter I contribute to the research analyzing metaphor variation in naturally occurring conversation. I present a categorization of metaphor clusters as in previous studies, and I extend that analysis by examining the variation within each cluster based on gender. This analysis reveals a cultural schema or model of collaborative classroom discourse that is distinct from traditional classroom discourse, and it adds a new dimension of sociolinguistic variation to the notion of cultural schemas or models.

This research agenda evolved from questions I had about seminar discussions, a form of classroom discourse. In previous research I found students often leave a seminar discussion with varied perspectives on its success (Fiksdal 1993); therefore, I was interested in examining the discourse in these discussions from the students' point of view. In order to understand the meanings they were constructing through their talk, I categorized the metaphors they used to describe their seminar discussions. I expected to find variation based on their experience (measured by time spent in seminar discussions); instead, I found different alignments[2] to the talk based on gender.

1.1. Cultural schema of classroom discourse

Students clearly come into seminar discussions with a cultural schema or model of classroom discussion in the United States and Britain. Cultural schemas are highly flexible as Quinn (1997: 139) suggests: there are different degrees of sharedness in students' reasoning about the discussion. This particular schema can be described briefly by its structure and function. The general goal, or function, is teacher-centered learning. The communicative structure has been described as teacher initiation, student response and teacher follow-up (Sinclair and Coulthard 1975) and initiation, response and evaluation (Mehan 1979). This structure relies on a physical arrangement of students' seats facing towards the standing instructor. The teacher is the authority and is ratified as such through the interaction and seating arrangement. In addition, there are other characteristics having to do with the construction of identity through talk such as expectations of a particular display of knowledge. These elements can be found in classroom discourse from kindergarten through college. Students and professors alike also draw differentially on other cultural schemas such as in-depth informal conversations and debates.

At the college where I conducted the present study, professors actively work to facilitate a particular form of classroom discussion called the seminar, which is considered a forum for collaborative learning. It differs from the traditional cultural schema of classroom discourse in one major way: the goal is student-centered learning. The communicative structure relies on student-initiated comments similar to informal conversations. Students sit in a circle so that they can see each other (and respond to each other) and their professor, also part of the circle, is a facilitator or sometimes a mere observer if students are facilitating. Students are encouraged to talk to each other rather than to the professor, and to

2. I use the term *alignment* following Goffman (1981: 128) to signal a change in frames or stance towards the discourse. As Goffman points out, in the course of a conversation, speakers and hearers may change their alignments (or footings) often. However in the interviews under investigation here, each speaker is ratified to speak for the length of the interview and individually, they do not appear to change their alignment during that time, at least regarding the metaphors they use to describe the seminar discourse.

learn from each other. Because the structure is similar to conversation, the floor is ratified by the group rather than the instructor.

In my analysis of the metaphors students used to describe their seminars, I found evidence of a cultural schema for collaborative classroom discourse that is shared in some respects, but differentiated in others based on gender. This evidence is based on 7 metaphor clusters that are prominent in the discourse in terms of number, and in terms of variation in use by men and women. These clusters are IDEAS AS VALUABLE OBJECTS, IDEAS ARE MALLEABLE OBJECTS, IDEAS ARE THROWABLE OBJECTS, SEMINAR IS A JOURNEY, SEMINAR IS A BUILDING, SEMINAR IS A MACHINE, and SEMINAR IS WAR.

1.2. Gender differences

The literature on conversation and gender has demonstrated that gender differences exist in the ways men and women draw on linguistic resources. These differences can be lexical, phonological, syntactic, or specific discourse strategies such as turn allocation. For example, Tannen (1993) demonstrates that men and women use different conversational styles based on the function of their talk with women building networks and relationships and men concerned with establishing status and hierarchy. Research examining gender in conversation in recent years continues to focus on the social construction of gender through talk (e.g. Hall and Bucholtz 1995; Johnson and Meinhof 1997; Eckert and McConnell-Ginet 2003).

Turning to studies examining gender differences in classroom discourse, it is possible to trace gender differences in talk among students from kindergarten to the university. Children are clearly socialized by practices in the classroom. For example, researchers examining talk in elementary classrooms have found that boys have more turns at talk and talk more than girls (e.g. Sadker and Sadker 1994: 42–76). Swann (1988) found that although there have been many studies indicating the dominance of boys in turn allocations in the classroom, a careful examination of nonverbal interaction in a class of 11 and 12 year olds indicates that teachers may direct their attention (through gaze) to boys thus encouraging their more active participation in discussions in terms of turn allocation.

In work examining collaborative work among 14 year olds in a classroom, Davies (2003) found that girls demonstrated and solidified their social loyalties through the work while remaining on task; boys, on the other hand, challenged the work process with their demonstrations of social loyalties. Similarly, in a secondary school setting Baxter (2002) found that girls conformed more to rules of collaboration than boys; in addition, boys did not support girls' ideas but actively sought to undermine them.

At the college level, a study of engineering students (Bergvall, 1996) found that both men and women collaborated on group projects and both groups used assertive strategies usually found in research on men's speech such as interrupting and maintaining the floor. Women also facilitated the conversation more and made self effacing remarks. Bergvall attributes these behaviors to the need these women have to interact in a heavily male dominated field. In a study echoing the findings of task divergence and task continuance in classroom discussions, Bergvall and Remlinger (1996) found that men use more task-divergent behaviors such as humorous asides to resist both men and women who are on task. In a study of a post-graduate seminar, Kramarae and Treichler (1990) found that women were more interested in supporting their friends and in collaborative discussion while men were interested in individual expertise and presentation. The findings of Kramarae and Treichler are closest to the findings of the present study. However, collaboration is a major goal of the seminar discussions at the college where I gathered the data unlike most traditional classrooms.

1.3. Metalanguage

The analysis I present is drawn from metalanguage, or talk which refers to the conversation itself. The research in this area indicates that metalanguage functions in context with other strategies in conversation. Gumperz (1976) shows that metalanguage acts as a contextualization cue, signaling a frame for different moments in the discourse. For example *as I was saying*, is a signal the speaker is moving back in time to an earlier thought; or, *what I'm trying to figure out*, is a prelude for talk to come. Another perspective on metalanguage comes from Fiksdal (1990: 107–110), who shows that speakers use metastatements, as well as other cues, as a rapport-maintaining strategy in the face work between speakers. For example, the metastatement, *what I was trying to say*, functions to bring both speakers to agreement about the topic of the conversation. In a broader context, Reddy uses this notion of metalanguage as a beginning point in his argument about the Language as Conduit metaphor drawing on Weinrieich's observation, "Language is its own metalanguage (1979: 286)."

Because some of the students' comments about their own seminar discussions seemed to fit the conduit metaphor, after identifying metaphor clusters, I tested Reddy's (1979) framework for the conduit metaphor in my analysis. In his ground-breaking study Reddy examines the ways in which English speakers communicate about language, and identifies the conduit metaphor as central. In fact, he argues, using the conduit metaphor actually influences our thinking about communication. We can hardly avoid using these metaphors in talking about our communication with others; for example, *I think I'm getting your point. I can't grasp what you're saying.* Our metaphors indicate that we reify ideas, and that these ideas move between people, sometimes getting twisted out of recognition, or taken out of context.[3]

Reddy proposes major and minor frameworks of metaphor clusters for the conduit metaphor. The major framework describes ideas as residing in human heads or in words. It has four parts: 1) Language functions like a conduit, transferring thoughts from one person to another: *Give me your best idea.* 2) We insert our thoughts or feelings in the words we use – they are conveyers. One problem, then, is the insertion process: *I can't always put my ideas into words.* 3) Words accomplish the transfer by containing the thoughts and conveying them to others: *This idea shows up again and again.* 4) In listening or reading people extract the thoughts and feelings from the words (or fail to): *I got a lot out of that book.*

Reddy's minor framework for the container metaphor demonstrates that ideas flow out into an idea space: 1) A speaker or text puts thoughts and feelings into an idea space: *Put those ideas down on paper before you lose them.* 2) Thoughts and feelings are reified so they can exist independently of the speaker or text: *That idea has been floating around for a long time.* 3) Reified thoughts may or may not find their way into the heads of other people: *You have to absorb those ideas slowly.*

Two features of the data I analyzed call into question this categorization proposed for metalanguage. First, students drew on most metaphor clusters Reddy identified, but in particular ways. These are illustrated in the metaphor clusters IDEAS ARE VALUABLE OBJECTS, IDEAS ARE MALLEABLE OBJECTS, IDEAS ARE THROWABLE OBJECTS. Ideas in motion are important

3. Researchers have suggested some critiques of Reddy's formulation of the conduit metaphor. (See, for example, Taylor 1987; Goossens 1994; Gozzi 1998; Eubanks 2001.)

for these speakers and this is not indicated in Reddy's description. In addition, most of their metaphors do not fit in the major framework; instead, they fit the minor framework or describe the idea space. These findings indicate that labeling metaphor clusters as major and minor may need to be revisited. Second, because they are discussing talk in a particular context, it is not surprising that the students move beyond Reddy's conception to discuss what Lakoff (1993) terms the Event Structure in which the target domain is events (the seminar) and the source domain is space. Lakoff identifies long-term, purposeful activities as journeys. Students draw on SEMINAR IS A JOURNEY, but their metaphors also reveal other structures for the space: SEMINAR IS A BUILDING, SEMINAR IS A MACHINE, and SEMINAR IS WAR.

2. Methodology

The metaphors under investigation in this study come from 36 undergraduate college students (both traditional age and older) – 20 women and 16 men – whose comments were recorded as they watched edited versions of their own seminars (N = 10).

2.1. Seminar discussions

The seminar discussions took place at a small liberal arts institution, The Evergreen State College in the USA. Seminars at this college are an innovative and central feature of its curriculum emphasizing collaborative learning. Students typically engage in discussions on a text in the same group four hours each week, and are held responsible for the quality of the discussion. The faculty member acts as a facilitator only. For this reason students are usually concerned with the content of their comments in seminars, and the process of the seminar itself and they regularly discuss the seminar process in and outside of class. Clearly, then, the metalanguage I examine here is a well developed form of discourse for them.

These seminars are part of larger learning communities (of 2–3 seminar groups) and typically involve around twenty students and one professor. The seminars videotaped as part of a project (not reported on here) were part of the students' normal schedule and were not experimentally controlled except for the presence of a video camera and cameraperson. I edited the two-hour seminar discussions to thirty minutes, and students were invited to individually view the edited videotape and discuss the communication with me or my research assistant. We invited their comments and asked open-ended questions such as What were you thinking at this point? or Here you leaned back, what was going through your mind? And we always asked: What was your goal for the seminar? Was this a successful seminar? The individual sessions were audiotaped and transcribed and it is the conversation of the students in these individual sessions which provide the metaphors under investigation in this chapter.

2.2. Categorization of metaphor clusters

My analysis of metaphors evolved as I examined the transcripts. My research focus is the microanalysis of conversations, and I had hoped to find clues in these transcripts that would clarify the talk in the seminars themselves. However, what caught my attention were the rich metaphors students used to describe the talk in the seminars – the metalanguage. I looked for patterns in the metaphors, classified them into metaphor clusters, and then tested Reddy's framework with my results.

The total count of metaphors in my data is 371: 197 produced by men and 174 by women. In the analysis that follows in Section 3, I cite metaphors that are clearly illustrative and those highlighting the speaker's alignment. Unless I found at least 5 metaphors in a metaphor cluster I identified, I do not include that metaphor cluster in my analysis. The number of metaphors has to do with the topics of each open-ended interview and their length. I had several issues to resolve while counting and categorizing.

In categorizing these metaphors, I found a number of constraints. First, the naming of categories may influence that categorization. I used the traditional form introduced by Lakoff and Johnson (1980) of Abstract Noun is Concrete Noun; for example, SEMINARS ARE JOURNEYS. However, it would be more accurate, I believe, when referring to the idea space to use the term coined by faculty and students, *seminaring*. Using parallel structure, SEMINARING IS TRAVELING, would emphasize the process students are describing rather than the resulting structure. It would also capture more metaphors in the cluster with greater transparency. The notion of process that is introduced in these conceptual metaphors seems to better capture the notion of learning in a social context. And, it fits better with the notion of cultural schemas. As D'Andrade (1992) points out, schemas are processes not events. Because I do not have the space to discuss this point about labeling clusters in depth, I will not pursue this discussion further.

In counting metaphors I was faced with a number of decisions. For example, I found that many speakers repeat their metaphors. I decided to include these repeated metaphors in the overall count. In the context of the discourse, this repetition may serve to emphasize the importance of the metaphor to the speaker at that moment.[4] Restatements seem to serve the same function.[5] By merely listing the metaphors in a particular metaphor cluster as I do in the next section, their importance to a particular speaker is not clear nor is the possible repetition across speakers noted. Finally, in each student's discourse, there are varying topics that influence their use of metaphors. For example, there were 3 students who spoke rather elaborately about group dynamics, while 2 others confined their comments primarily to the content of the talk so these latter students produced only 1–2 metalinguistic metaphors. Two seminars did not go well according to the students who appeared for the interviews. These contextual factors may be important in considering the speakers' choice of metaphors, although that contextual aspect is not the focus of the present chapter.

It is important to note that extracting metaphors from naturally occurring discourse for the purpose of categorization is not a straightforward process. For example, one does not generally find well formed sentences in the transcripts. Instead there are chunks of grammatical speech, chunks of understandable ungrammatical speech, false starts, hedges, ellipses, word choices that do not seem appropriate, repetitions, paraphrases, self-interruptions, exterior interruptions (e.g. phone calls), etc. I used as examples only those metaphors that appeared in an understandable phrase in my corpus. Finally, in considering which examples to include as illustrative, I omitted those that did not seem typical.[6]

---

4. To illustrate repetition, one man uses the metaphor *tie in* as a way of connecting reified ideas: *at least they come in and tie some of it in ... Or someone says something that's kind of related but not really without some way to tie it in. I don't know that's frustrating for me ... It seems like when I try to tie it in ...*
5. Other speakers may restate rather than repeat. For example, a woman says, *I guess that's my big question all the time. Did anybody get that? Does anybody you know connect with what I was saying?*
6. I do not include a series of metaphors from one speaker as he is the only informant who uses them in this particular way. After viewing a few minutes of the seminar discussion, a man says: ... *we have a sense of how many beats you have before you can jump in and if you notice the – I don't think I've ever felt stomped on and um (that) was left hanging and ah somebody just came*

3. Speaker's alignment to the discourse

I identified ten underlying conceptual metaphors (Lakoff and Johnson 1980: 4) that the speakers used to describe the communication of the seminar: LANGUAGE IS A CONDUIT, IDEAS ARE THROWABLE OBJECTS, IDEAS ARE MALLEABLE OBJECTS, IDEAS ARE VALUABLE OBJECTS, SEMINAR IS A JOURNEY, SEMINAR IS A BULDING, SEMINAR IS A MACHINE, SEMINAR IS WAR, SEMINAR IS A CONTAINER, and SEMINAR IS A FLOW.

This finding of several underlying conceptual metaphors is not surprising given the extensive, introspective work on the conduit metaphor by Reddy (1979) and Lakoff and Johnson (1980: 10–13). What is interesting about these conceptual metaphors is that IDEAS ARE OBJECTS has entailments based on individual actions; and SEMINAR IS A JOURNEY, A BUILDING, A MACHINE, OR WAR has entailments based on group actions. Thus, an emphasis on the individual as agent and the collective as agent are both possible given the human experiential and cultural use of objects, journeys, buildings, machines and war. Flows and containers on the other hand do not need human agency or interaction, at least in these data. It appears that reified ideas can be put into them or taken out in particular ways, however.

Both men and women see the seminar group working together and moving toward a common goal; however, the metaphorical expressions they use construct a relationship between the self and other that is different in intriguing ways. The metaphorical expressions men use are grounded in the conceptual metaphor SEMINAR IS A GAME. A game entails having a clearly defined goal, collaboration, competition, rules, winning

---

over and you know filled the space. In this chunk of talk, the metaphors are *beats you have, jump in, felt stomped on, that was left hanging, and filled the space.* I will address two of the many questions that arise in interpreting this chunk of discourse. First, when he mentions beats, is he referring to the tempo of talk so that the thing he imagines jumping into is a flow or steam of talk? This rhythmic aspect is a possible interpretation because he speaks of a space, as in a musical score, and earlier (not cited here), he uses the term orchestrating in describing the professor's facilitation. Also, in my own work, I have found tempo to be a fundamental organizing factor in turn-taking (Fiksdal 1990: 71–93) and the student could have been aware of my work. The second question it raises regards the phrase *jumping in.* I categorized this metaphor when it was used by other speakers as an aspect of a container rather than a flow, but in this context, a flow seems to be more appropriate.

and losing. Speakers have some control over the game and therefore men's metaphors reveal an actor moving, carrying, manipulating ideas. The actor, the I, then, is salient.

In contrast, the metaphors women use do not fit as easily into the game metaphor; instead, their metaphors fit the conceptual metaphor SEMINAR IS A COMMUNITY. This metaphor entails sharing, valuing, and helping other seminar members. The goal is collaboration – it is not an end point as in a game. The *we* and collective *you* are more salient in this metaphor: individual actors are important only if they are helping in some way. It is the group or collective that is salient. Both of these conceptual metaphors entail cooperative action and communication although other entailments are quite different. To explore this finding, we will examine each of the ten identified conceptual metaphors and the specific metaphorical expressions men and women use.

3.1. Language is a conduit

As mentioned above, I found few examples of Reddy's major framework in my data, possibly because students are talking about talk rather than about writing. When language functions as a conduit it transfers thoughts and ideas from one person to another. I find this metaphor cluster exploited primarily by women (N = 6; 5 by women, 1 from a man):

(1) Most people got to get their points across.

(2) Everybody put in input that carried through.

(3) It's difficult to completely convey my ideas because sometimes they have many sides.

(4) It's easy to get my viewpoint across.

(5) I guess that's my big question all the time, Did anybody get that?

These metaphors refer to the successful or unsuccessful transfer of ideas. The concern women reveal with getting ideas across to others fits the conceptual metaphor SEMINAR IS A COMMUNITY: it highlights one's relationship to others. The only metaphor from a man which addressed this transfer of thoughts from one speaker to another indicates the responsibility of the agent as well:

(6) I cannot get my ideas across the way I wanted.

The adverbial phrase *the way I wanted* indicates the grounding for his use of the conceptual metaphor SEMINAR IS A GAME. In a game, each player has responsibilities to the team and actions have consequences for the goals of the game. The adverbial phrase of manner fits well with the game metaphor as each individual's play is as important as the team's as a whole.

3.1.1. Minor framework of language is a conduit

This next section examines the first aspect of Reddy's minor framework: speakers eject thoughts or ideas into an idea space. Most of the metaphors students used fall into this minor framework, raising the question of what is major and what is minor in conduit metaphor categorizations. For these students, a major concern appears to be getting ideas out. For example,

(7) I have urges to blurt something out but I usually restrain that and try to refine it. (man)

(8) I have something I really want to bring up. (man)

In these examples, the men see themselves as the principle guide to their ideas while the women seem to consider the context of others in their metaphors:

(9) I usually can come up with something that others can relate to. (woman)

(10) Usually if I do have a point I'm concerned about, it gets discussed so I don't have to bring it up. (woman)

Both men and women have trouble with their ideas coming out clearly:

(11) When I say something, the idea that I have in my head before I start talking never quite gets out in my words. (woman)

(12) Usually what I express in seminar comes out unclear. (man)

3.2. Ideas are valuable objects

Detailing further the metaphors in the first aspect of Reddy's minor framework, both men and women make extensive use of the metaphor

IDEAS ARE VALUABLE OBJECTS (N = 17; 9 from women, 8 from men). However, in these data primarily women use the verb *share*. Consider these examples:

(13) I am eager to share my ideas.

(14) I share my ideas and listen and learn from others.

(15) I like sharing ideas and learning alternative ways to look at something.

(16) I use seminars to share my ideas with others.

One man used the verb *share*, not as an opportunity, but as a personal challenge:

(17) That's a requirement of me being in seminar is that I have to share something.

In other metaphors indicating IDEAS ARE VALUABLE OBJECTS, the men seem to be focused on their own contributions or the value of others':

(18) I can often contribute significantly.

(19) I feel that I am an important primary contributor to the seminar, ego notwithstanding.

(20) I want there to be some substance to his words rather than, you know, just the power or the might of them.

There can be a sense of reciprocity when mentioning IDEAS AS VALUABLE OBJECTS:

(21) My goals were to put into it, contribute, expect the same of everybody else. (woman)

(22) I try to make an effort in seminar to help other people by giving my metaphors when I can and with that they would do the same thing and help me – show me your metaphor and I'll show you mine. (man)

At first glance, these latter two seem to be similar statements, but in his restatement the man (example 22) actually places himself in the position of waiting to get someone else's metaphor or idea before he gives his: *show me your metaphor and I'll show you mine.* His reformulation makes the reciprocity clear: it must be evenly distributed by individuals. By using the (understood) you and I, he also particularizes the reciprocity, as one might expect in a game. The woman, on the other hand, (example 21) speaks of others as a generalized whole (*everybody else*), reflecting the understanding of an existing community.

Metaphors regarding participation from everyone, which is required in a game, come mostly from men:

(23) You would need participation from everyone present.

(24) The more views you get the more information you have the more ideas you have to think about.

(25) I think I've actually learned more because I'm able to put my two cents in.

Women appear to focus on the community in the room. In both examples that follow, there is a valuing of contributions of others, an important aspect of community:

(26) I talk a lot because I am eager to share my ideas. I also listen to others. I feel that their insight is valuable to me so I may expand my own processes of understanding.

(27) If we're trying to conceptualize the world in new ways and not put the blinders on, [as] we were talking about there, we need to look at- value each person's input and so often what I see happening and what I feel seminar is about here is trying to take them off.

3.3. Ideas are malleable objects

Although Reddy does not mention it, I find that reified ideas can expand, become broader. Both men and women use metaphors indicating IDEAS ARE MALLEABLE OBJECTS ($N = 7$, 3 from women, 4 from men); for example,

(28) Seminars to me are a way to listen to the ideas of others and then use them as a springboard. (woman).

I find this salience of the community in metaphors used by women; in fact, only women spoke of adjusting their own viewpoints:

(29) I feel that their insight is valuable to me so I may expand my own processes of understanding.

(30) I find I adjust the way I view things by having a broader perspective.

The salience of the actor who acquires skills in the game is highlighted in the metaphors used by two men:

(31) I enter seminar with the knowledge I have gained from reading, films and/or lectures and expand that knowledge using the thoughts and interpretations from other members of seminar.

(32) We're trying to hone the seminar to get the most effective communication I think. At least I'm trying it.

The speaker in example (32) first highlights the group in his use of we, but reformulates his thought by highlighting the I (*I'm trying it*). In the only metaphor referring to others, the speaker comments on the strategy of an individual (female) student:

(33) She could have expanded on that a lot.

3.4. Ideas are throwable objects

In another cluster of metaphors Reddy does mention (in this same aspect of his minor framework) that metaphors using the ground IDEAS AS THROWABLE OBJECTS[7] were used by both men and women (N = 20; 4 from women, 16 from men). Sometimes throwing ideas is not useful:

(34) And so it was like nothing got brought through to its fruition. It just kinda, you know, people were throwing things out. (woman)

One problem with throwing is captured in one woman's words (and it demonstrates the third aspect of the minor framework),

(35) I didn't really catch what he was saying.

7. Note that Lakoff's metaphor page lists this metaphor as Ideas are Projectiles (http://cogsci.berkeley.edu/lakoff/metaphors/The_Conduit_Metaphor.html)

Another problem is that ideas that can be thrown are not necessarily substantial:

(36) Someone could just throw out a statement just on something...not like any deep impression thing. (man)

(37) It seems like a lot of this is just kind of throwing out lots of information. I see why [the professor] seemed to get frustrated with this for having a lack of direction. (woman)

Finally, some found a problem in throwing statements or ideas back and forth:

(38) And statements like this kind of volley ... the goal isn't actually to learn ... but to ... put down the other person. (man)

(39) Here we're just sort of bandying about different notions and nothing ever seems to be solidified in my mind. (man)

Several men did find throwing ideas useful, however:

(40) If you constantly stick to the topic it's going to get boring after two hours, so if you throw a little bit of pizzazz in there it's going to be better, I think.

(41) Things were really difficult to put into an abstract conversational piece that we could toss around the room ... I try to make at least a couple of reflective type comments just kinda throw it in the air and see what happens.

(42) I also talk with him a lot outside of class and in a way it's like a seminar because, I mean, I throw lots of ideas at him.

If the metaphor SEMINAR IS A GAME underlies the men's metaphors, then throwing ideas as a way of playing the game should be useful sometimes.

I only found one metaphor from a woman that was similar in supporting throwing ideas. However, unlike the men, she explicitly refers to a game of footwork and the notion of testing:

(43) I was thinking that we were using that footwork kind of idea, tossing it around just to see how it would work before we presented it,

cause it's kind of a good idea to test your ideas before you present them to somebody else.

Her formulation of the IDEAS ARE THROWABLE OBJECTS metaphor contrasts with the metaphors men used where tossing or throwing ideas is a tactic that may be understood to be valuable in itself at times. Her elaboration (it's kind of a good idea …) seems to categorize this as a marked metaphor for this woman.

Because the metalanguage under investigation comes from seminar discussions in a college setting, it is important to examine speakers' alignment to the seminar discussion itself. I identified six conceptual metaphors namely, SEMINAR IS A JOURNEY, SEMINAR IS A BUILDING, SEMINAR IS A MACHINE, SEMINAR IS WAR, and, to a lesser extent, SEMINAR IS A FLOW and SEMINAR IS A CONTAINER. Although he does not mention them, these metaphors relate to Reddy's (1979) idea space. Clearly that space is structured for the students in this study. Lakoff (1993) addresses this type of metaphor with the EVENT STRUCTURE metaphor in which the target domain is events, in this case the seminar, and the source domain is space. In addition, individual students may use metaphors from two domains: they are not mutually exclusive. In other words, a student could use both the SEMINAR IS A JOURNEY (*he's on a tangent*) and SEMINAR IS A CONTAINER (*she doesn't get much out of seminar*) metaphor.

3.5. Seminar is a journey

The most common metaphor cluster used by men and women was SEMINAR IS A JOURNEY (N = 87: 51 from women, 36 from men). In one case a man personified the topic (of the seminar) and did not assign responsibility for moving away from the goal:

(44) The only problem I have is the tendency for the topic at hand to wander through a digression.

The focus is generally on others for the men:

(45) When others go off on tangents or get off the subject, then I go into my prosecutor mode.

(46) People lose sight of the goal and stray.

(47) I'm totally lost as to what's going on here cause they're all talking at the same time, you know.

(48) There didn't seem to be any real direction, kinda circular direction but that's fine that's the way I think (laughs).

Note that the lack of direction in example (48) has nothing to do with this speaker. He adds a commentary that this lack of direction is all right because it relates to the way his own mind works.

In contrast, women's metaphors emphasize the *we*:

(49) That's evident in the wandering, unfocussed seminars we have had.

(50) It's kinda interesting how we jump from subject to subject.

(51) We have this tendency to go off on this tangent.

(52) We ended up talking around it 'til we got it. We kept going back and forth with that.

In the one instance of a woman's metaphor lacking an explicit *we*, the speaker still highlights the community:

(53) Someone will kind of get off on a tangent which is ok, but then you'll kind of lose some people, at least some people's interest.

In this comment the speaker acknowledges that tangents are acceptable for herself, but she considers the negative consequences for others.

3.6. Seminar is a building

In the metaphor SEMINARS ARE BUILDINGS (N = 44; 21 from women, 23 from men), metaphors from two men highlight their own ideas. In these metaphors, the starting point is one's own ideas – it is the *I* which is salient:

(54) It is a place to build on my ideas.

(55) I build on what I already know.

For the women in this study the importance seemed to lie in the act of collaboration:

(56) We keep building on it.

(57) What we're trying to do is to get all the different viewpoints and accumulate them together – collage them into some kind of idea.

(58) We're starting at a common base.

(59) We got more and more information built on each other which was good.

The *we* these women used highlights the importance of the group rather than the individual actor, and their emphasis on collaboration fits with the notion of community which relies on the process individuals use to create and maintain the whole.

3.7. Seminar is a machine

In this metaphor (N = 10; 7 from women; 3 from men), engaging in the discussion and considering its workings is a concern. There are few metaphors in these data relating to machines, but I include them because engagement in the discussion is a key evaluative term for both faculty and students at this college and therefore part of commonly used terminology.

(60) Just the ideas were spinning so fast that day just really fast. It was really fun to watch it. (woman)

(61) I felt like I was pretty engaged in this seminar and then I definitely shift back because that exchange sort of ended and there was a shift in the conversation and I disengaged some at that point. (woman)

(62) I didn't want to be deprived of her input. (woman)

These women see the talk as separate from themselves, but they can engage with it. One metaphor from a man highlights his potential agency:

(63) I know how I would like seminar to be run.

3.8. Seminar is war

Although *conflict* may be more appropriate as a category than war, I rely on Lakoff and Johnson's (1980) discussion of rational argument for this metaphor cluster. There were a total of 54 metaphors; 39 by men, 15 by women.

(64) He took over some people's sentences. (man)

(65) Sometimes I feel like I've been just assaulted in seminar and uh, you know, it'll be for expressing a controversial opinion. (man)

(66) Sometimes I feel that there is an exclusive group of people dominating the discussion and that interrupting them might be combative. (man)

(67) I don't feel like I learn much from him because he's mostly just trying to cut people down. (man)

(68) Beth sometimes reinforces what I'm thinking and sometimes it challenges what I'm thinking and sometimes it just totally blows me away because I never thought of something from that focus. (woman)

(69) At this point it's kind of strange. Usually when we talk about topics there's like a mixed amount of people that are supporting one side or the other. (woman)

(70) There are always 4 or 5 dominant voices that control the entire discussion. I tend to be quieter because of their disrespect to give others a chance to participate. (woman)

(71) Seminar can shut down participants. (woman)

As in previous metaphors, the women's concern (examples 68–71) is with others if the metaphor is negative, or in the case of being blown away by someone's comments (a positive remark), it is an appreciation of someone else's contributions. These metaphors highlight the notion of community. The men (examples 64–67) are either critiquing the performance of others (especially men), or in the case of being reluctant to interrupt, being perceived as combative. These metaphors highlight the agency of others or the self.

3.9. Seminar is a flow

Both men and women use this metaphor which depicts the discussion as flowing, and, the discussion seems to move without human agency. Possibly because of this lack of agency or because there are fewer examples in these data (N = 13; 3 by women, 10 by men), I find few differences in alignment.

(72) I think those are really classic examples of adding on to a general idea that's already flowing through the group. (man)

(73) It's kind of interesting that the whole conversation has drifted to the power issue. (man)

(74) [Seminar] flowed pretty much all the way through. (woman)

(75) I don't want to interrupt the flow of thought so if I do it at all it'll be very subtle and quietly. (woman)

(76) I'll find a point that I want to make and … I'll make like a little speech in my mind and then usually I miss the right point to jump in. (man)

The woman's statement in example (75) indicates a concern for the movement of the discussion. The man in example (76) is also talking about the movement, but his formulation of the metaphor conforms more to the notion that, as an agent, he could jump in, he just misses the entry point. With so few examples, however, there may not be different alignments towards this idea space.

3.10. Seminar is a container

As in the case of Seminar is a Flow, the container (N = 31, 8 by women, 23 by men) presents students with an opportunity to get in and to pull ideas in or out.

(77) I wonder how much he gets out of seminar and I don't think he gets much, cause he always seems to be arguing rather than learning. (man)

(78) When it's a particularly good one, I come out and feel sort of energized intellectually. (man)

(79) I broke the ice. (man)

(80) She's not afraid to jump in. (man)

(81) I think as a whole the group got a lot out of it. (man)

(82) I don't like jumping in. (woman)

(83) I wasn't into this discussion. (woman)

(84) People are really into it. (woman)

(85) I broke in. (woman)

(86) There is no room for emotion. (woman)

(87) There's just everything in here, this is just a big huge glomeration of thought. (man)

Note that both men and women use strength to break in. Both comment on the structure of the container (*huge glomeration*; *no room*). Only men comment on individual efforts by other speakers, but there does not seem to be much difference in alignment in these data with this metaphor cluster.

The barrier for speakers using this metaphor (or the flow metaphor) to enter the discussion may seem greater than when they use the journey or building metaphors. In the container metaphor, speakers have to break something or jump. In the flow metaphor, the steady movement of the discussion topics may become more important to the students than their individual wants or needs to *get into* the discussion. These metaphors highlight different aspects of the discourse than journeys, buildings, machines, and war in the sense that collaborative work is not a significant feature of the entailments – the flow and the container exist, they do not need to be constructed or manipulated.

4. Alignment to other speakers

Turning from the language as conduit metaphor to an examination of the speakers' relationship to other speakers provides additional evidence for the underlying conceptual metaphors SEMINAR IS A GAME and SEMINAR IS A COMMUNITY in these data. It is striking how differently men and women speak of other seminar members.

(88) He joined the pieces [of the puzzle]. (man)

(89) She's not afraid to jump in. (man)

(90) That was really intelligent and she could have expanded on that a lot more and I think that she wanted to but it just like, whew, went right by her. (man)

These men comment on the individual actions of other seminar members much as one comments on the strategies of individual members on a team. Women, on the other hand, seem to speak of others within the context of the group, particularly in how they might help other members:

(91) He often will say something and then feel that it hasn't been accepted by the group and I like to reinforce him whenever I can.

(92) Seminars clarify the material to people who need help.

(93) Painfully shy people deserve a little space.

These latter two comments taken out of context may not seem to imply helping, but they refer to specific points in the discourse when these speakers either did not speak or gave clarification to a particular point. This is not to say men never commented on helping:

(94) I try to make an effort in seminar to help other people by giving my metaphors when I can and with that they would do the same thing and help me – show me your metaphor and I'll show you mine. (man)

(95) When I listen to how others think about a subject it helps me to understand just about how others feel and I can help them with other ways of looking at a subject. (man)

The helping for these two men, then, comes with the condition of reciprocity: as an individual they interact with the group. Women made many more comments about the seminar group as a whole, underscoring their grounding in the conceptual metaphor of community. For example,

(96) Everybody is connected.

(97) Most people got to get their points across.

(98) Everybody gets a chance or is forced to say something, so people like me don't hog the whole seminar and people like her get a chance to talk.

(99) I kinda wanna let people ... run over what I'm saying or to question it. I don't wanna sound too obnoxious and I'd really like it if more people got involved.

This concern for the whole, for the community to take part in the discussion, was made evident in the women's metaphors. While the men may have the same desire of group involvement and their metaphor SEMINAR IS A GAME certainly allows a focus on the group, they instead highlighted themselves as actors, the *I* rather than the *we* in their metaphors. One man's comments are particularly illustrative of this point:

(100) And also, I was really-um my role as someone in seminar has changed out of the four years at Evergreen from being someone who just totally talks off the top of my head, says whatever I want and talks very often, cuts people off, to one where now I've- I try to learn as much as I can from- from the people that are around me, and as a result I talk much less and so I need, I haven't quite struck a balance between that.

Clearly, experience in seminar discussions influenced this student's view of his interaction.

5. Conclusion

The metaphor clusters I have analyzed here, particularly IDEAS AS VALUABLE OBJECTS, IDEAS AS MALLEABLE OBJECTS, IDEAS AS THROWABLE OBJECTS, SEMINAR IS A JOURNEY, SEMINAR IS A BUILDING, SEMINAR IS A MACHINE, and SEMINAR IS WAR describe a cultural schema or model of collaborative classroom discourse. This schema shares some features with the schema of traditional classroom discourse namely, setting, participants, and time constraints. As I noted in the findings, SEMINAR IS A JOURNEY was the most used by all students. In research categorizing metaphor in lectures in the classroom, Corts (2006) notes that throughout all lectures LECTURE IS A JOURNEY occurred at least once, marking transition points. The conceptual metaphor Course is a Journey occurs very frequently in students' online chat in an experimental study examining metaphor use (Hussey 2006). Although this was a study of online chat in a controlled experiment, students were not prompted to use metaphors; they were prompted to discuss courses. It could be, then, that in college courses the notion of the Journey is exploited so often that it helps create a shared participation framework. Hussey (2006) also reports that students, whether men or women, used the same conceptual metaphors.

The question is, to what extent is this cultural schema shared by men and women in these data? Clearly one shared goal is collaborative learning, but it appears this notion of sharedness is complex. The conceptually grounded metaphors I identified – SEMINAR IS A GAME and SEMINAR IS COMMUNITY – emphasize collaborative ways of learning together, but the speakers' formulation of them highlighted different aspects of that collaboration. The men highlighted the *I* in the *I/you* relationship indicating agency in SEMINAR IS A GAME; the women highlighted the *we* indicating a collective agency using SEMINAR IS A COMMUNITY. If speakers believe they are working together using common grounding, they may expect common discourse strategies to reach those goals. Morgan (this volume) points out that these two underlying conceptual metaphors come from two different metaphor families. It could be that one reason students sometimes assess the value of seminars differently has to do with these different ways of conceiving it.

Looking back at the research on classroom discourse in the schools, researchers find the functions of language are different for boys and girls, as are the ways they draw on linguistic resources. In addition, teachers and others may interact in particular ways to underscore these differences. The finding of gendered metalanguage indicates that students not only use language in gendered ways, they also understand talk in gendered ways. Does this different alignment to the discourse matter? If the goal of collaborative learning matters, then these different alignments matter as well because they lead to different definitions of collaboration and to some extent, different understanding about what constitutes collaborative learning. The implied goals within each metaphor cluster for seminars may be the same: staying on track, for example, but the manner in which students prefer to accomplish that and, consequently, their learning are affected.

It appears that metaphors which indicate the relationship of self to other and self to discourse both reflect and reinforce different conceptualizations of each which are subtle but distinct. These differing conceptualizations may in fact evolve just as conversational style evolves in our socialization. Fiumara raises the question of maturation in cognitive styles. If we "view our thought processes as correlates of self-creation projects, we may come to perceive an inner maturational course (1995: 36)." Fiumara suggests that a central concern of infants is developing the understanding between pronouns and predicates in order to establish identity and that infants do this through metaphor. In the metaphors examined in this chapter, however, we find a particular social context for the shaping of the seminar experience as a collaborative effort. This shaping affects the ways in which the speakers talk about the discourse, and the ways they appear to conceptualize the discourse.

One intriguing way of understanding how this socialization occurs is through the concept of legitimate peripheral participation (Lave and Wenger 1991). Lave and Wenger argue that learning is situated in language through participation frameworks (somewhat like apprenticeships) in communities of practice rather than taking place individually. They further argue that this participation involves the construction of identities. The 10 metaphor clusters identified here are clear evidence of these practices. The fact that these metaphor clusters vary according to gender indicates the importance of including the social and cultural nature of talk in a consideration of cognition. It is, to a great extent, through talk that we learn metaphors, participate in cultural schemas or models, and create and perform gendered identities. Quinn (1991) argues that metaphor plays a comparatively minor role in constituting understanding; it is cultural models that are primary. If the cultural schema or model is primary, it is essential to fully describe that model and how it might be acquired.

Cognitive scientists, cognitive anthropologists, and sociolinguists may examine cognition from different perspectives and with different questions. The goal should be interrelating the multiple ways our findings interact. Clearly students can learn to interact within a cultural schema of collaborative classroom discourse in their college years even though they have been participating in a schema of traditional classroom discourse previously. The findings presented here of gendered metaphorical metalanguage suggest that socialization through language is probably just as important as the existence of metaphor and cultural models in constituting understanding, and there are certainly other variables as well.

For example, another aspect of students' alignment in seminars may be learning styles, or what Boers and Littlemore (2000) call cognitive styles. They tested these styles before asking students to analyze metaphors. These styles were analytic or holistic and imager or verbalizer. If these styles are hard-wired, genetics could also be involved in the analysis of students' alignment to the discourse.

Turning to my findings regarding Reddy's framework, I found support for the notion of a conduit because ideas were moving from individuals to the idea space. There was less evidence that the ideas moved from speaker to speaker. These ideas were malleable, throwable, and valuable. I found no evidence of a major or minor metaphor framework; in fact, the idea space received more attention than reified ideas. I believe the image of the conduit must be opened to include this idea space (rather than be thought of as a closed tube). One could argue that the conduit is transparent because some students can see the flow of ideas and want to jump in – they must see something there.

References

Balaban, Victor
1999 Self and agency in religious discourse: perceptual metaphors for knowledge at a Marian apparition site. In: Raymond W. Gibbs, Jr. and Gerard J. Steen (eds.), *Metaphor in Cognitive Linguistics*, 125–144. Amsterdam/Philadelphia: Benjamins.

Baxter, Judith
2002 Competing discourses in the classroom: a post-structuralist discourse analysis of girls' and boy's speech in public contexts. *Discourse and Society* 13 (6): 827–842.

Bergvall, Victoria L.
1996 Constructing and enacting gender through discourse: negotiating multiple roles as female engineering students. In: Victoria L. Bergvall, Janet M. Bing and Alice F. Freed (eds.), *Rethinking Language and Gender Research: Theory and Practice*, 173–201. London: Longman.

Bergvall, Victoria L. and Kathryn A. Remlinger.
1996 Reproduction, resistance and gender in educational discourse: the role of critical discourse analysis. *Discourse and Society* 7 (4): 453–479.

Bialostok, Steven
2002 Metaphors for literacy: a cultural model of white, middle-class parents. *Linguistics and Education* 13 (3): 347–371.

Boers, Frank
1999 When a bodily source domain becomes prominent: the joy of counting metaphors in the socio-economic domain. In: Raymond W. Gibbs and Gerard J. Steen (eds.), *Metaphor in Cognitive Linguistics*, 47–56. Amsterdam/Philadelphia: Benjamins.

Boers, Frank and Jeannette Littlemore
2000 Cognitive style variables in participants' explanations of conceptual metaphors. *Metaphor and Symbol* 15 (3): 177–187.

Cameron, Lynne and Alice Deignan
2003 Combining large and small corpora to investigate tuning devices around metaphor in spoken discourse. *Metaphor and Symbol* 18 (3): 149–160.

Corts, Daniel P.
2006 Factors characterizing bursts of figurative language and gesture in college lectures. *Discourse Studies* 8: 211–233.

Crisp, Peter
2002 Metaphorical propositions: a rationale. *Language and Literature* 11 (1): 7–16.

Davies, Julia
2003 Expressions of gender: an analysis of pupils' gendered discourse styles in small group classroom discussions. *Discourse and Society* 14 (2): 115–132.

D'Andrade, Roy G.
1992 Schemas and motivation. In Roy G. D'Andrade and Claudia Strauss (eds.), *Human Motives and Cultural Models,* 23–44. Cambridge/New York: Cambridge University Press.
Dirven, René and Ralf Pörings (eds.)
2003 *Metaphor and Metonymy in Comparison and Contrast.* Berlin/ New York: Mouton de Gruyter.
Eckert, Penelope and Sally McConnell-Ginet
2003 *Language and Gender.* Cambridge/New York: Cambridge University Press.
Eubanks, Philip
2001 Understanding metaphors for writing: in defense of the conduit metaphor. *College Composition and Communication* 53: 92–118.
Fiksdal, Susan
1990 *The Right Time and Pace: A Microanalysis of Cross-Cultural, Gatekeeping Interviews.* Norwood, NJ: Ablex.
1993 Getting the floor. Ms. Olympia, WA: The Evergreen State College
1999 Metaphorically speaking: gender and person. *Language Sciences* 21: 345–354.
Fiumara, Gemma C.
1995 *The Metaphoric Process.* London: Routledge.
Goffman, Erving
1981 *Forms of Talk.* Philadelphia: University of Pennsylvania Press.
Goossens, Louis
1994 Metonymy in the pipeline: another way of looking at the container metaphor. In Keith Carlon, Kristin Davidse, and Brygida Rudzka-Ostyn (eds.), *Perspectives on English. Studies in Honour of Professor Emma Vorlat,* Vol 2, 386–394. Leuven/Paris: Peeters.
Gozzi Jr., Raymond
1998 The conduit metaphor in the rhetoric of education reform: a critique of hidden assumptions. *New Jersey Journal of Communication* 6: 81–89.
Gülich, Elisabeth
2003 Conversational techniques used in transferring knowledge between medical experts and non-experts. *Discourse Studies* 5 (2): 235–263.
Gumperz, John
1976 Language, communication, and public negotiation. In: Peggy R. Sanday (ed.), *Anthropology and the Public Interest.* New York: Academic Press.
Hall, Kira and Mary Bucholtz (eds.)
1995 *Gender Articulated: Language and the Socially Constructed Self.* New York/London: Routledge.
Hussey, Karen A.
2006 Metaphor production in online conversation: gender and friendship status. *Discourse Processes* 42: 75–98.

Johnson, Sally and Ulrike Hanna Meinhof (eds.)
1997 *Language and Masculinity*. Oxford: Blackwell Publishers.

Johnson, Mark
1987 *The Body in the Mind*. Chicago: Chicago University Press.

Kramarae, Cheris and Paula A. Treichler
1990 Power relationships in the classroom. In: Susan L. Babriel and Isaiah Smithson (eds.), *Gender in the Classroom*, 41–59. Urbana, IL: University of Illinois Press.

Lakoff, George
1987 *Women, Fire, and Dangerous Things: What Categories Reveal about the Mind*. Chicago: University of Chicago Press.
1993 The contemporary theory of metaphor. In: Andrew Ortony (ed.), *Metaphor and Thought*, 2nd ed. Cambridge: Cambridge University Press.

Lakoff, George and Mark Johnson
1980 *Metaphors We Live By*. Chicago: University of Chicago Press.

Lave, Jean and Etienne Wenger
1991 *Situated Learning: Legitimate Peripheral Participation*. Cambridge: Cambridge University Press.

Mehan, H.
1979 *Learning Lessons: Social Organizations in the Classroom*. Cambridge, MA: Harvard University Press.

Quinn, Naomi
1991 The cultural basis of metaphor. In: James W. Fernandez (ed.), *Beyond Metaphor: The Theory of Tropes in Anthropology*, 56–93. Stanford, CA: Stanford University Press.
1997 Research on shared task solutions. In: Claudia Strauss and Naomi Quinn (eds.), *Cultural Models in Language and Thought*, 137–188. Cambridge/New York: Cambridge University Press.

Reddy, Michael J.
1979 The conduit metaphor – A case of frame conflict in our language about language. In: Andrew Ortony (ed.), *Metaphor and Thought*, 284–324. Cambridge/New York: Cambridge University Press.

Sadker, Myra and David Sadker
1994 *Failing at Fairness: How America's Schools Cheat Girls*. New York: Charles Scribners' Sons.

Sinclair, John and Malcolm Coulthard
1975 *Towards an Analysis of Discourse: The English Used by Teachers and Pupils*. Oxford: Oxford University Press.

Swann, Joan
1988 Talk control: an illustration from the classroom of problems in analyzing male dominance of conversation. In: Jennifer Coates and Deborah Cameron (eds.), *Women in Their Speech Communities*, 123–140. London: Longman.

Tannen, Deborah (ed.)
1993 *Gender and Conversational Interaction*. New York: Oxford University Press.

Taylor, John R.
1987 Metaphors of communication and the nature of listening and reading comprehension. *Journal of Applied Linguistics* 1: 119–134.
Zinken, Jörg.
2003 Ideological imagination: intertextual and correlational metaphors in political discourse. *Discourse and Society* 14 (4): 507–523.

The business model of the university: Sources and consequences of its construal

Nancy Urban

Abstract

The demand for "competitive" administrative salaries, the gravitation of curricular control to the administration, and the establishment of explicitly for-profit universities are just a few aspects of the ways in which higher education is becoming indistinguishable from business. In the United States higher education, once seen as a public good, with cost a secondary concern to benefit, is increasingly described as a service bought and paid for like any other, subject to the same considerations of efficiency and productivity, and restricted to those who can afford it. What are the origins of this change of construal, and what are its consequences for the breadth and quality of higher education in this country? In Section 1 below I will provide a brief examination of the metaphorical precursors to the business model. In Section 2, I will examine the mapping of the business model to the university, and provide examples. In Section 3, I will explore some of the consequences of this construal.

Keywords: metaphor, education, university, business, Lakoff.

1. Introduction

Education has been the subject of much debate, especially in recent decades. The controversy concerns the purpose of education, who should be educated, who should pay for it, how it should be accomplished, how to promote efficiency, measure success, and so on. Texts invoke different images of the university, and assume or propound different purposes of education. None of these has taken into account the underlying differences in how people understand the function of schools.

In order to understand social institutions, we must understand what has gone into the construction of the metaphors by which we understand and reason about them. The subject of this study is those metaphors which underlie higher education in our culture; it is hoped that an understanding of those metaphors will clarify the larger discussion about the state and future of education.

The dominant metaphor for education in our time is business. In this paper I will outline the ways in which education has come to be construed as a business, and I will discuss some of the consequences of this construal for higher education in the United States.

1.1. Theoretical background

A metaphor is a means of understanding one domain in terms of another; often elements and relationships from a more basic, experiential domain are used to reason about a more abstract domain. For instance, time can be seen as a kind of resource, and thus can be talked about like money; ideas can be construed as objects, and can therefore be "given" or "stolen." These construals bring with them certain entailments which influence our behavior – e.g., it becomes good to save time; the ownership of ideas is a real, legal matter. Following from the precepts first laid out in *Metaphors We Live By* (1980), Lakoff and Johnson have made comprehensive metaphorical analyses of political and philosophical domains (see Lakoff 1996; Lakoff and Johnson 1999). They have shown that systematic metaphorical structures underlie and inform major philosophical theories and political ideologies. The role of metaphorical construal has been observed in many domains: the sciences (Kuhn 1993; Leatherdale 1974; Maasen and Winterhager 2001; Maasen, Mendelsohn and Weingart 2001), psychology (Leary 1990), philosophy (Lakoff and Johnson 1999; Leddy 1995; Kuhn 1993), politics (Mio 1997), geopolitics (Rohrer 1995), economics (White 2003), and business (Boers 1997; Koller 2002, 2004).

When the university is seen as a business, and education as a product, certain conclusions follow: it must be standardized; its production must be as efficient as possible; it is impersonal; it must meet the demands of the consumer; it can be guaranteed; and so on. These conclusions and their ramifications are discussed below.

1.2. Brief history

The history of education is inseparable from social, economic, and political history. The school is a naturally conservative institution: it is slow to change, and tends to reflect other institutions familiar to us from the social and political world. Higher education in the West began as an extension of the Church in the Middle Ages. Thus, its institutional manners bore (and still bear) many aspects and customs taken from clerical tradition. The sometimes isolated and independent model of the monastery provided the image of the *ivory tower*). The schools were seen as communities unto themselves. As monastery schools banded together and formed the university, the institutional model took the form of guilds, which had become successful; guilds established interior hierarchies of members and protected their economic and social position in the larger society.

The factory model came about after the Industrial Revolution, in a time of increasing numbers of students at all levels of education. Upton Sinclair observed to students in 1923 that "You are in a great education factory, with the whirr of its machinery all around you" (Sinclair 1923: 42). Corresponding to this growth, the factory construal was motivated by and foregrounded elements such as increased production, streamlined efficiency, and uniformity of the product, which at this stage was the students. The metaphor of the school as factory introduced the economic framing of education. Veblen noted the increased focus of the university on business, efficiency, accounting, and so on: "[I]n this insistence on an efficient system [...] these corporations of learning shall set their affairs in order after the pattern of a well-conducted business concern." (Veblen 1965: 85)

With the progressive era, the university came to be seen, along with government, as a means of actively shaping society. After the postwar boom, with the immense energy poured into education to create a competitive basis for scientific advances, "research took a place along with teaching as a major function" of the university. (Hofstadter 1955: xiii)

The business model gathered real momentum under new socioeconomic forces in higher education, in a period of declining enrollments, when colleges and universities were searching for ways to attract more students, to cut costs, and in effect to survive in an increasingly competitive environment.

> A shift from a seller's to a buyer's market has spurred competition among institutions in the search for students and introduced marketing techniques and attitudes into postsecondary education. These developments [...] have helped turn institutional attentions outward – to competitor institutions, to the world of business, to government agencies concerned with regulating the education "marketplace." (Kaplin 1985: 7)

Education had become seen as a product in a market of harsh competition. The business model focuses on the school as becoming competitive within the market, on the need for advertising and other image-grooming to attract students – now the customers; and on other business concerns, such as cutting overhead and increasing production.

The business model came to influence education via a number of routes. The increasing numbers of businesspeople acting in official capacity on boards of trustees, governing positions, and administrative positions in universities has directly influenced policy and administration. The growing involvement of schools with business concerns such as holding patents, overseeing large-scale externally-funded research projects, and owning stock and investments has been an economic factor. As universities have grown increasingly dependent on public funding, the demands for "accountability," for "productivity," and for "efficiency," have grown more strident, leading administrators to look increasingly to the business domain for guidance in how to achieve these economic goals.[1]

1.3. The source domain of business and the market: the cultural model of Darwinian natural selection

Our central metaphor for understanding the domain of business and the market comes from a folk model of the Darwinian conception of the natural world and the mechanism of natural selection. Business is itself the target domain of a related set of metaphors described by Grady, Morgan and Taub, in their work on Metaphor Families (1996). It is perceived of as a game, as a sport, and as a battle or war. We will not go into the full analysis of these here; but even a cursory examination of what features they share reveals a fundamental construal of business in our culture: as competition and survival. The most common and direct source domain for construing competition and survival is the Darwinian model of natural selection.

The Darwinian model is fundamentally about resources: it rests on, and arises from, the economic understanding of the world. As Gould notes, "Darwin grafted Adam Smith upon nature to establish his theory of natural selection." (Gould 1977: 100) Smith's view of individuals in competition with one another for survival in business, and their need to adapt to the market, formed an apt framework for understanding the competition of organisms for survival in a shifting ecosystem. Economic metaphors provided a systematic set of ways of thinking about resources, the use and expense thereof, wise and unwise uses, and so on. The Dar-

1. For a further discussion of these developments, see Urban 1999, especially Part I, Sections 3 ff.

winian model places resource-users into a closed system in competition over limited resources. This metaphor draws from another, the Strict Father metaphor, which corresponds in a number of ways with the competition model: the notion of each individual as responsible for his own survival, without help from others (i.e. parents), succeeding only through individual effort, adaptiveness, preparedness. The premises of the Darwinian model "derive from Strict Father morality." (Lakoff and Johnson 1999: 561) The convergence of the two models is evident in Social Darwinism, which found particular resonance in the United States, where individual independence has been a virtue from the nation's beginnings, propounded by Franklin, Emerson, Thoreau, and others. For the Social Darwinists, if an individual does not succeed, it must be because he is not fit to compete in the system; if he is not fit to compete, he does not deserve to succeed. Spencer argued that "the weeding out of inferior specimens would produce a cumulatively better race of men." (Fleming 1970: 123)

As is typical with such models, the structure of the natural world as rendered in this cultural model is drastically simplified. To give just one counterexample, biologists have noted a great number of kinds of behavior in animals which result in an increase in the likely survival of the phenotype, and not the genotype, or of the kin set, and not the individual. The cultural model of simple individual-level competition in a dog-eat-dog struggle is a misleading representation of the processes of natural selection.

But it is clearly a compelling model, taking together as it does some major elements of our existence in the world – life, struggle, survival, success, and death – and giving them a shape and a purpose. Although Darwin called up images from Adam Smith's description of the market to impel his reader's understanding of how natural selection worked, Smith's view of the market is commonly thought of as Darwinian. When Darwin was concocting his model, the experience of the market was familiar to people, and therefore provided a basis for leading them to understand the parallels of competition and survival in his new view of the natural world. But since that time, the analogy is almost always made in the reverse direction. This reversal is motivated by the primacy of the natural in our Western dichotomy of natural and artificial.

Beside presenting a very clear format for understanding competition, the Darwinian model offers an appeal to the natural world which provides considerable further motivation for its use as a model in other domains. Business is a very social, relatively recent development in culture, and as such has little to make its processes and outcomes seem inherently necessary. To ground it in this model of the natural world is to give it a set of justifications, a connection to the essence of the world, which grant it an authenticity and motivation it would otherwise lack.

The model of business used as metaphor takes some elements from the Darwinian scheme: a business is an organism, with all its corresponding characteristics (*business is growing,* or *thriving,* or *dead*). This is a version of the metaphor by which a social institution is an organism, having the characteristics of a living organism: a life span, a state of normal health and strength, etc. We find this metaphor regularly in descriptions of e.g. nations' economies: *a strong economy, a healthy economy, Japan is suffering from a recession*, or *1776 marked the birth of the United States.* Thus, the business exists in a system; the system is a natural one with an equilibrium; the economic health of the business is physical health. Its economic fitness is physical/biological fitness, and economic competition is physical competition. Economic survival is physical survival (continued life).

The metaphor of business as an organism provides some, but not all, of the framework for the discourse of education. The domain of business itself, with its emphasis on profit motive, standardization, efficiency, and so on, provides an additional source of mappings.

2. The target domain: Education

In the application of the business metaphor to education, we use several models of that target domain. The one which applies generally to public universities has the following structure: a school, which accepts students, not of especially high or low caliber, but average, and deals in the commodities of education and credentials/degrees. The faculty and administration are a permanent part of the institution, engaged in an effort to provide education to the transient population of students. This parallels the structure in the source domain in which the employees and managers of a business are permanent parts of it, engaged in providing a product or service to the external and transient population of consumers or clients. Examples of these mappings are provided below.

2.1. General mappings

Below are the mappings of the business metaphor in education, the specific correspondences between the source domain and the target domain, with illustrations of their application. The mappings have two sources, as noted above: first are those which come from the Darwinian model and the view of business as an organism in an ecosystem; following those are the mappings from business itself; some entailments from these domains are observed below.

2.1.1. Mappings between the business domain and education which pertain to the Darwinian model

Colleges compete against one another: "It's a Darwinian world out there: some two hundred colleges have closed during the last ten years." (Traub 1997: 116) This competitive field of education is commonly referred to as a market:

> For-profit colleges and universities constitute the only sector of the higher-education industry that is growing. [...] For-profits will continue to grow in number and market share throughout the next decade. (Ruch 2001: 4)

The market is increasingly driven by competition, as the involvement of public interests declines (seen within the market as "regulation"):

> The weakening influence of traditional regulations and the emergence of new competitive forces, driven by changing societal needs, economic realities, and technology, are likely to drive a massive restructuring of the higher education enterprise. From experience with other restructured sectors of the economy, such as health care, transportation, communications, and energy, we could expect to see a significant reorganization of higher education, complete with mergers, acquisitions, new competitors, and new products and services. (Duderstadt 1999:1)

The market determines what will make a business succeed or fail, and pressures institutions to devise "new products and services." Competition fosters a healthy market, lowers prices, and benefits the consumer.

> American colleges and universities are no more or no less than vigorous competitors in an increasingly diversified and dynamic marketplace. This free-market competition drives innovation, encourages price/value decisions by both seller and buyer, and produces winners and losers. It's good for higher education and good for students; it should be nurtured, not condemned. (Freeland 1997: 1)

One entailment from the Darwinian model is that competition among schools is necessarily beneficial, as it leads to streamlined, more efficient production. Inefficient (unfit) institutions are unable to compete, and should be weeded out.

> [T]he postsecondary education market [is] very real and demanding, with the capacity to reward those who can respond to rapid change and punish those who cannot. Universities will have to learn to cope with the competitive pressures of this marketplace [...] (Duderstadt 1999: 1)

Technological developments in business correspond to genetic developments in the Darwinian model, to changes that make it more fit for competition and survival. Institutions (must) evolve:

> To be sure, most colleges and universities are responding to the challenges presented by a changing world. They are evolving to serve a new age. (Duderstadt 1999: 2)

A further entailment of the Darwinian model is that technological developments are good, and thus that failure of schools to implement every such development will put them at a disadvantage in the market. Technology boosts the efficiency and productivity of schools: more students can be educated per faculty member, services can be delivered more efficiently. Institutions that do not evolve will not survive: "Some have even suggested that in the face of rapidly evolving technology and emerging competition, the very survival of the university, at least as we know it, may be at risk." (Duderstadt 2000: 5) Traditional institutions become "dinosaurs" which will be eliminated by the climate of competition.

Some aspects of the business model are thus Darwinian. Other characteristics come directly from our experience of business.

2.1.2. Mappings from business

Aspects of the business metaphor applied to education which come directly from business, and do not originate in the Darwinian model, include cost/benefit as the sole metric of success, the emphasis on productivity, the concern with product standardization, and the tendency to look to the short term. As the President of Miami University said in his 2001 address on the State of the University, "I am often asked why more money always seems to be the solution to higher education's needs. Why can't universities become more efficient, so that our dollars stretch farther? Why can't we increase our productivity, the way American businesses have done?" (Garland 2001: Section 9, Paragraph 1)

Efficiency and streamlining internal processes such as decision-making are central concerns: "In the Internet Age, globalization and technological change are forcing organizations to do everything they can to streamline allowing faster decision making and increased efficiency." (Friedman 2001: Introduction, Paragraph 4)

The success of a business is measured in profit. Since the fundamental worth of a business, product, service, etc. is measured in money, the monetary metric becomes the overwhelming determiner of a business's health, strength, and longevity.

The notion of productivity has no direct correlate in the natural world: products are specific to business, and to the workings of the market. But productivity correlates generally with profit, and is thus a means to success for a business. Measured by a ratio of product to cost, and to business size; increased productivity is increased competitiveness. Following this model, in education, the more students the better. The goal of productivity could then influence administrative behavior:

> For example, ask yourselves whether we want to nurture institutions where Presidents and Provosts will be able to vote themselves bonuses or perks for meeting enrollment, retention, or graduation rates?
>
> (*CHE* on the Web, Colloquy, 1997)

Streamlined production is good (cf. assembly-line style production): the faster students can be educated, the better. An increase in productivity is desirable: as businesses are constantly seeking to increase output, so should schools. Efficiency is desirable: any measures which allow the business/school to produce more, with less expenditure of funds and effort, are good. Reorganizations are implemented such that "the familiar inefficiencies of the traditional college in such areas as space utilization, class size, and efficient deployment of faculty, are minimized." (Ruch 2001: 17)

Efficiency can be aided by streamlining organizational structure. The division of this structure into, e.g., departments, can be seen as a hindrance to this streamlining process:

> The bottom line is that departments often care more about themselves than students or the university as a whole. In business, this is exactly the kind of organizational structure one would come up with if one wanted to create a firm that would have no chance of succeeding. Imagine a company in which every product manager demanded resources, even if there were no demand for the product. This is essentially what we have in academe.
>
> (Friedman 2001: Conclusion, Paragraph 4)

Standardization is of increasing concern. The assembly-line style of production also increases the consistency of products, labor, and so on.

In education, this means that there should be a high ratio of students to instructors, and that pedagogic techniques should be uniform. The cutting edge of standardization is of course online education, which has served as a harbinger of developments in "brick-and-mortar" universities.

> "Over the last five years, DeVry has been a leader in online learning as measured by its quality online offerings, technology adoption rates, and enrollment growth," said Oakleigh Thorne, chairman and CEO of eCollege. "The University's standardization initiative again keeps it at the forefront of online education, in what we believe will be a major trend among universities wanting to optimize online offerings."
>
> (eCollege Press Release 2003: Paragraph 5)

Even the "chain-store" goal of business can be found in education:

> The word "campus" is understood, at the University of Phoenix, to mean "site," or even "outlet." The university is a franchise operation, with forty-seven sites all over the West and in Michigan, Florida, and Louisiana.
>
> (Traub 1997: 114)

Success in the short term is preferable to long-term planning: the goal of a business is to make money; whatever measures are necessary to do this must be taken. There is little or no conception, in the business domain, of long-term planning necessary to produce long-term return.

2.2. Versions of the model

Illustrated below are three versions of education as a business, differentiated by the three elements which correspond to the *product*: students, knowledge and education. The first two arose with the factory model: the school as a student factory, and as a knowledge factory. The view of education as a product arose later, with the business model.[2]

Further, there are two forms of the version in which the students are consumers. In one, education is a *product*, students are consumers, and so on. In the service-industry version, education is a *service* of which students are the clients. Both of these models, however, introduce the role of the student as *customer* whose requirements drive the industry: "Most of the nation's [...] colleges see themselves as market-driven institutions trying to satisfy customer demand." (Traub 1997: 116)

---

2. For a further discussion of the origins and development of these three versions of the mapping, please see Urban (1999), Part 2.

2.2.1. Students as product

As in the student factory metaphor, students are the product, with the addition of schools as competing with one another in a market for high-quality high school graduates, the raw materials in their production process.

The consumer of the product is either industry, as employers, or society at large, as the collection of employers and businesses which benefit from educated workers. Faculty are the laborers employed by the business who produce the product. Invoking this metaphor, Barzun (1993: 189) writes of

> the student fed raw and young into the machine at one gate and emerging bearded and gray at another, machine-finished, qualified in a dozen ways, and even "Inspected by No. 23" ...

As is clear in this image, education is the process by which the raw material is transformed into the finished product. Since high school students are the raw material to be made into the product of higher education, the better quality high school student the school can obtain, the higher quality its product will be. It was with the rising awareness of product quality that the practices of merit scholarships and other forms of "discounted" tuition have greatly increased in recent years.

If there are more students receiving degrees than there are positions open for them, there is a glut in the market: "I agree with you, Mr. McManus, that the production of new Ph.D.'s should be slowed down ... ." (*CHE* on the Web Colloquy 1997: 6/4)

> So many of these comments seem to blame "society" and "culture" for an anti-intellectual attitude that is somehow failing to create a market for surplus Ph.D.'s. (*CHE* on the Web Colloquy 1997: 6/4)

2.2.2. Knowledge as product

> Knowledge itself becomes a key commodity, to be produced and sold to the highest bidder, under conditions that are themselves increasingly organized on a competitive basis. Universities and research institutes compete fiercely for personnel as well as for being first in patenting new scientific discoveries. [...] Organized knowledge production has expanded remarkably over the past few decades [...]. (Harvey 1989: 159–160)

The university as a knowledge factory competes within the market. The notions of ranking and competition among institutions can be seen in the illustration below.

> Chicago is moving quickly to license its technology. Stanford and MIT, aggressive pioneers of such arrangements, are way ahead of the pack, with 259 and 257 active licenses and options on technology, respectively. Chicago has just 36 such deals, but it's catching up: in 1996, by virtue of a few big payouts, it ranked sixth in royalty income, up from 29th the year before and ahead of MIT. (Melcher 1998: 96)

The assumption here is that research in universities should result in products, and have direct profitability. "I've told the faculty they have an additional responsibility to go beyond the discovery of new knowledge," says one administrator. He "talks of a new ethic, one that requires measuring progress in commercialization and boosting collaboration" with private industry. (Ibid.)

One of the dangers of this trend is a decline in less obviously profitable research. It has been a truism in science that we cannot always see what knowledge will be of use to us. Even this article which argues for a more business-like research program in universities notes that "research universities have helped drive innovation for decades, spurring development of everything from jet engines to the Internet." (Ibid.: 94) Research geared most immediately to profitability is necessarily shortsighted. As one critic of the industrial direction of university research notes, this tendency draws efforts and funds away from "the quest for fundamental research, which is long-term and uncertain, but can result in true innovation." (Ibid.)

Noble (1998) and others have criticized the relationship between industry and universities as an exploitative one by which industry gets the fruits of government-subsidized basic research. At least in this case, however, there is still basic research. If the purely business view of the university should come to pass, even this will disappear.

2.2.3. Education as product

> In fact, the top research universities – those that are the most criticized for their lack of attention to *the "customers," the students* – are exactly those universities that *maintain artificially low prices for their products* – lower prices than the market would support.
>
> (*CHE* on the Web Colloquy)

Competition forces improvements to the product: "In recent years, many colleges and universities have concluded [...] the only way to beat the competition is to offer a better product." (Freeland 1997: Paragraph 7)

Through the metonymy between *education* and *credentials,* as the indicator or proof of having a certain education, we get from education as a product to the certification of that education as a product. This extension is seen in the common pejorative term of a *diploma mill* for a school which is seen as having low standards of credentialing. The image invokes the cookie-cutter production line in a criticism of a school which churns out degrees for a price paid. Diploma mills arise in response to the demand for certification. Some products are commodities. Sinha (2002) discusses the commodity metaphor with particular reference to theories, noting that a theory is "not just any old kind of commodity, but a special kind of commodity that can generate other scientific commodities, such as hypotheses and satisfying explanations." (Sinha 2002: 271) In the same way, education is not a simple consumed commodity, but is seen as one that generates further value: it is often described as an investment: "Looked at strictly as a financial investment, a student with an undergraduate degree will earn, on average, 75 percent more per year than someone who foregoes post secondary education. Not a bad return on investment." (Freeland 1997: Paragraph 11) "There is considerable support for the notion that the rate of return on investment in higher education is high enough to warrant the financial burden associated with pursuing a college degree." (Porter 2002: Paragraph 3)

An offshoot of education as a product and students as consumers is the development of marketing programs in college recruiting: this is advertising of the product.

> Demographic changes and cuts in important sources of student financial aid brought significant enrollment declines to higher education in the 1980s. Colleges responded by engaging in market oriented activities intended to attract students while *students became more like academic shoppers* [...]. Understanding individual enrollment behavior *can help enrollment managers tailor and target their college's marketing mix of programs, prices, and places.* (Paulsen 1990: Page 4)

2.2.4. *Education as service*

> In higher education as in other service industries, such as health care and financial services, consumer-market responsiveness is an increasingly important aspect of institutional effectiveness. (Ruch 2001: 144)

Over the course of the 20th century America became increasingly an economy based on industries of services rather than goods. The increasing pressure on educational institutions to attract previously untapped markets among the population, most notably older and returning students, has led them to modify their curricular offerings to appeal to part-time students, returning students, special program trainees, and others whose interests may not be the traditional four-year undergraduate degree. The development of "education on demand" has opened the way for the understanding of education as a service provided to the client students.

A survey of non-full-time on-campus students (Traub 1997: 116) found that what students expected from the university was a kind of service:

> [T]hey wanted the kind of relationship with a college that they had with their bank, their supermarket, and their gas company. They say, "I want terrific service, I want convenience, I want quality control."

2.2.5. *Subcase of the school as a business: The Ivy League school*

In the submodel of the Ivy League school, prestige is as important a commodity in the school as degrees or education. The school gains prestige through having renowned faculty and graduates who go on to become distinguished in their careers. It uses this prestige to attract promising students who will then become successful and continue the cycle. Students seek out the school in order to benefit from its prestigious reputation in making their careers. There is a side-business which arises in this model, which involves the school selling prestige to wealthy students.

> Why is there such a demand for [Ivy League] universities? In part it's because an active researcher often makes a better teacher. But it's also because the research itself *raises the prestige of the institution, thereby raising the value of the degree on the job market.* (*CHE* on the Web Colloquy)

It is arguable that prestige has the appearance of a commodity because it does in fact raise the value of the labor of those students who earn degrees from a prestigious institution. Marx argues that education increases the value of the individual's labor power (Tucker 1978: 340), and that different kinds of education have different values.

2.3. Entailments

Entailments of the business model include the assumption that public education constitutes a "monopoly" and is therefore bad for competition; that the institution should have one focus; that there is a single metric of success; and that the organization of power in the institution should be hierarchical. These are illustrated below.

A monopoly, in which one provider holds the majority or entirety of business in some market, is bad for competition and for the consumer.

> Pioneer [an education management business] sponsors seminars bringing together entrepreneurs selling curriculum packages, management systems and assessment and evaluation programs. Conservatives want to 'outsource' these functions as part of an effort to neutralize 'the government monopoly on education'. (Vine 1997: 14)

The business model only allows for one production goal. In education this can mean choosing between research and teaching:

> What is the primary goal of the institution? If you were absolutely forced to choose research or teaching, which would it be? Although institutions needn't choose just one or the other, *they need to be clear about which activity they value more.* If the answer is teaching, then why aren't senior faculty members doing most of it? Are 90 percent of the institution's discretionary funds (those not absolutely fully obligated) spent on programs related to teaching? (*CHE* on the Web Colloquy)

As there can only be one production goal, there can only be one metric of productivity: the output of students.

> The higher-ed management elite [...] increasingly see themselves not as educators, but as managers no different from those in the corporate world, whose mission is simply to *maximize through-put – that is, to move the greatest number of students and dollars through the system.*
> (*CHE* on the Web Colloquy)

This view removes justification for, e.g., research, mentoring, or community involvement of academics. Instead, these become frills, or wasteful expenditures of resources which could be put into increasing production or customer satisfaction.

Since business is hierarchical in structure, universities should be organized this way as well. But as Ruch (2001: 14) points out, "standing in the way of quick effective decision making is the tradition of shared governance." If the administration are managers, and the faculty are employees, then any faculty involvement in decisions regarding the direction of the university amounts to an awkward encumbrance, and introduces inefficient, counterproductive complications into the management process.

Astute designers of for-profit institutions have made some of the elements of traditional academe work to their advantage, however, as for example the appearance of shared governance. As Ruch (2001: 14) points out, "the management strategy of for-profits is to allow enough shared governance to appease regional accreditation visiting teams and keep faculty from unionizing." But at the same time managerial control is preserved: "faculty in the for-profits do not have tenure, which changes the balance of power between the faculty member (employee) and the institution (employer)." (Ruch 2001: 15)

3. Some specific ramifications of the business model for education

Assumptions from the business model about the need for productivity, competitiveness, and marketing, change the shape of the university. Some effects are growing class sizes, grade inflation, and the pressure for school voucher programs.

Further issues of serious consequence include affirmative action, the status of tenure, academic freedom, choice of curricular content, remedial education, and pressures on scholarships and tuition. These are discussed below.

3.1. Affirmative action

Affirmative action has come under fire in recent years because it appears to some critics to confound the fair competitive basis of educational admissions. The debate about affirmative action arises primarily because of differing background models held regarding the nature of society and the purpose of education. Society is held on the one hand to be a mechanistic system in which there are no internal constraints, pockets of influence, or strata, i.e. without particular privileges or disadvantages arising from one's position. On the other side of the debate is a model of society as inherently tending to inequality of privilege and opportunity. One side regards higher education as a purely merit-based system which looks only at aptitude and performance, ignoring prior conditions. The second view takes socioeconomic factors into consideration, either with an eye to redressing past or present social injustices, or in the more immediate assumption that a candidate who has performed reasonably well in a difficult situation has effectively more promise than one who has performed very well in a situation of privilege.

The educational implementation of affirmative action makes the university a tool in social reform. It takes as its foundation the assumption that "the social goal of greater minority representation justifies the admission of less or differently qualified applicants into educational programs, particularly in the professions." (Kaplin 1985: 252) The corresponding policies of minority-oriented admissions have especially in recent years become the target of discussion. Critics of affirmative action argue that it is unfair discrimination; proponents argue that it is meant to counter invisible discrimination, as well as to aid by a kind of brute force the creation of a more egalitarian society. Lucas (1996: 91) observes two American ideals in conflict with each other:

> Reduced to their essentials, one point of view holds that higher learning should be reserved for the few; the other insists that it should be for the many. The former is inspired by the ideal of individual distinction and achievement. The latter invokes the ideal of democracy, of equal rights for all.

These two ideals are also related to the two metaphorical models of the family, discussed above. The former is akin to the Strict Father model, in which each individual must succeed on his own merit in competition with others. The latter is akin to the Nurturant Parent, providing the means for a good life to all. It is thus the kind of parent that the university should be which is under debate.

Opponents of affirmative action, working from the model of society without internal barriers and advantages, hold to the Horatio Alger myth: they believe that everyone begins with equal assets and possibilities, and that the individual is solely responsible for the situation in which he or she finds himself. In the extreme case of this no social context for an action is recognized:

> When I have been asked during these last weeks who caused the riots and the killing in L.A., my answer has been direct and simple: Who is to blame for the riots? The rioters are to blame. Who is to blame for the killings? The killers are to blame.
> (Vice President J. Danforth Quayle, in an address to the Commonwealth Club of California, May 19, 1992)

Proponents argue the opposite: it is not that simple; privilege is an invisible but powerful force shaping the lives of individuals. In Moss Hart's summing-up, "Poor people know poor people and rich people know rich people. It is one of the few things La Rochefoucauld did not say, but then La Rochefoucauld never lived in the Bronx."

Supporters of affirmative action argue that people are by nature inclined to form alliances to groups based on kinship, social similarity, or other such factors, and to distribute their attention, loyalty, and so on within these groups. "One of the lessons of the *Republic* was to propose a way to counter the natural tendency of individuals to pass on to their children the gains they have acquired during their own lives, thereby establishing conditions of inequality for the next generation." (Murphy; in Froomkin 1983: 19) But this is just the beginning. Individuals pass on their gains in streams of privilege which are compounded into their class, creating disparities which over generations become generalized, institutionalized, and legalized.

If the fates of individuals are shaped by the socioeconomically defined pockets within which they live, affirmative action is seen as one solution to this problem. The role of the university has been critical to social change. Education was the means to a better life; everyone was seen as deserving access to this means; thus the university was used directly to address social inequity. Americans believe that opportunities should be made available to all. The expectation that education as an opportunity should be made generally accessible underlies public higher education. The notion of education as a public service here collides with that of customer service:

> Many in higher education recoil at the word "customer." They believe that education has a higher purpose than selling products like detergent or garage door openers. Nevertheless, we prefer and use the word ... because we believe that it is an important reminder that higher education is in business to serve others ... (Armajami et al. 1994: 2)

According to these proponents of affirmative action, education provides preparation and connections for later life, and as such, no one should be excluded from access to it. But this is changing. Across the country, affirmative action is being overturned. The discussion increasingly revolves around the competitive basis of admissions, casting affirmative action programs as discrimination. There has been an interesting development in the character of the arguments about affirmative action, however. Once the discussion was shaped as a debate about two kinds of discrimination, about social engineering versus merit and competition from even starting-points. But increasingly, the controversy is about service, with those against affirmative action arguing that education should be extended as a service equally available to all consumers, and that quotas are unfair business practices.

3.2. Tenure

Tenure originated in faculty demands for a more business-like job security: for contractual determinations of academic work, for standards of promotion, and for uniform procedures for dismissal. But this model would eventually endanger that same job security. The standard business management hierarchy assumes that directors and managers have complete administrative discretion over the employees and the production process. This means being able to hire and fire faculty as the administration sees fit, as they meet or fail to meet production standards. Administrators talk about "the bottom line," "flexibility," and "adaptability:" "Institutions are very concerned about the long-term costs of a tenured appointment and the need in an increasingly volatile environment to maintain flexibility." (Wilson 1998: A12)

The arrangement of the business model conceals entirely the question of why one might want faculty to be independent of the short-term financial strictures of the administration:

> Universities are rapidly reaching the point at which they need to ask not "Can we reform tenure?" or "Dare we?" but rather "How can we go about it?" Some educational institutions have successfully bought out or phased out unproductive faculty members. A few have talked of designing 5-year or 10-year employment contracts to replace tenure. [...] Just think about the cost of 10 or 15 years of salary and support services for unproductive people, and you will see that you can easily raise the ante in a fair manner to induce their departure and make way for new faculty appointments.
> (*CHE* on the Web Colloquy)

This passage raises the issue of who determines what counts as "productive." More critically it does not touch on or recognize the issue of tenure as a safeguard of academic freedom.

Another factor in both tenure and academic freedom is the role of the "consumer" in education. As we saw above, the student as consumer holds a new and often definitive power over curricular content.

> And if what's called tenure reform – which generally just means the abolition of tenure – is broadly enacted, professors will be yet more vulnerable to the whims of their customer-students. Teach what pulls the kids in, or walk. What about entire departments that don't deliver? If the kids say no to Latin and Greek, is it time to dissolve classics? Such questions are being entertained more and more seriously by university administrators.
> (Edmundson 1997: 45)

Of critical relevance, but too often unrecognized in the discussion about tenure, is the fact that the alternative to tenure in determining faculty positions is neverending politics, within and among departments. A great deal of institutional time and energy is saved by fixing professorial contracts in current tenure practice. Further, the basis of cooperation between faculty, departments, and universities would be completely undermined by the competition for funds and support to guarantee continued work.

Often the defense of tenure itself invokes the business model and underscores its less desirable entailment. One president of a major research university (Brand 1999: A64) has spoken up in defense of tenure by pointing out that the kind of job flexibility that corporations seek in their employees does not readily transfer to the academic domain: "Shifting an employee from one corporate department to another might make sense, but imagine trying to retrain a scholar of medieval French literature to teach astrophysics." But there are farther-reaching dangers in the abolition of tenure:

> A tenured faculty member will accept lower compensation in exchange for job security – knowing that his or her position is unlikely to be eliminated during downsizing or restructuring. If tenure were eliminated tomorrow, taking academic job security with it, faculty compensation would have to increase. Higher pay would mean increases in tuition or the student/faculty ratio. The first result would curtail access to higher education; the second would decrease its quality.
> (Ibid.)

Across the country, universities and colleges have been replacing tenure-track positions with contract positions; some new institutions have dispensed with tenure entirely.[3] What is noteworthy about this process is its comparative invisibility. As Epstein observes, the "growing number of

---

3. Among these are the for-profit University of Phoenix, and Arizona International Campus (AIC), a new experimental non-tenure campus of the University of Arizona (UA).

dismissals for financial reasons rather than on specific charges of misconduct" constitutes an "attack on freedom [that] is not direct." (Epstein 1974: 121) This leads us into the issue of academic freedom, and of the determination of curricular content.

3.3. Academic freedom

The ideal of academic freedom was in its origin closely connected to the metaphor of the community of scholars. Both the independence of the university and its role as a discoverer of new knowledge, and a pursuer of truth, are central to the background of this ideal.

> It was ... in nineteenth century Germany that the modern concept of academic freedom came to be formulated. The idea of the university as a place where scholars are to pursue truth, as well as to formulate and transmit it to students, who at the same time learn to pursue truth for themselves, came to be dominant there. (Baade 1964: 5)

This ideal of the freedom of ideas has sunk deep into our national ideology, and our Western view of ourselves as a liberal and rational people. "Our nation is deeply committed to safeguarding academic freedom, which is of transcendent value to all of us and not merely to the teachers concerned." (*United States vs. Associated Press*, 52 F. Supp. 362, 372; in Kaplin 1985: 182) But academic freedom is an early casualty to the encroachment of business principles and practices in education. As tenure disappears, professors are no longer assured of permanent positions. As their job security is lost, their inclination to bow to local pressures and interests is increased. The curriculum is increasingly shaped by consumer demand and by political forces. The interpretation of professors as employees in the business hierarchy undermines the independence of faculty from administrative directives. Business domain imagery had by 1980 permeated the view of the university enough to shape a court decision regarding the managerial status of faculty, with the Court noting that "the faculty determines within each school the product to be produced, the terms upon which it will be offered, and the customers who will be served." (*NRLB v. Yeshiva University*, 100 S. Ct. 856 (1980); in Kaplin 1985: 108) But as the dissenting justices in the Yeshiva case noted (Kaplin 1985: 110), "The notion that a faculty member's professional competence could depend on his undivided loyalty to management is antithetical to the whole concept of academic freedom."

Education has always been caught between the conflicting interests of an establishment seeking to maintain and promote, and the generation of students seeking to make their own way, forcing the institution to respond in some degree to their more unformed or different interests. It has also been caught in the tension between the academic world with its slightly dry, dusty tone and relation to the rest of society, and the hum and bustle of in-the-moment business and people's livelihoods. A consideration of these conflicts foregrounds the question of who should determine what is taught and learned in schools. There have even been attempts to defend academic freedom using the logic of the free market. The court ruling cited above continues:

> That freedom is therefore a special concern of the First Amendment, which does not tolerate laws that cast a pall of orthodoxy over the classroom ... The classroom is peculiarly the "marketplace of ideas." The nation's future depends upon leaders trained through wide exposure to that robust exchange of ideas which discovers truth "out of a multitude of tongues, [rather] than through any kind of authoritative selection."
>
> (*United States vs. Associated Press*, 52 F. Supp. 362, 372; in Kaplin 1985: 182)

In this view, the oppression of academic freedom constitutes a regulation of the marketplace which inhibits free trade and therefore harms the consumer, mapped here to the American public.

But this mapping requires the recognition of ideas themselves, the product here, as entities. In the standard mapping of the business model to the university, ideas have no place. Arguments about academic freedom are about what should be taught, who should determine what is taught, and about what research should be conducted. But the exigencies of the market, with its control in the hands of the consumer, offers no basis for the contemplation of these questions. There is no room within the business model for ideas as independent actors in the cultural drama.

The exercise of academic freedom takes two forms: freedom of teaching, and freedom of research. Historically both of these have been the object of interference by outside forces, and both have been argued to be critical to the health of a democracy: students need access to a range of ideas, and society needs the benefits of the less obviously profitable research.

The role of the consumer in determining the curriculum has already been seen: within this frame, the notion of freedom of teaching is moot. The market supersedes any understanding of a need for academic independence. The freedom of research is eroded from below by the nature of corporate funding in academia. Forty years ago, Kirk observed the influence of academia's increasing dependence on governmental and private sources of funding in the exercise of academic freedom. He (Kirk 1964: 177) points out the dangers of such dependence: "For no proverb is truer than this, that 'The man who pays the piper calls the tune.' If educational institutions become dependent for their increase of reputation, or perhaps even for their existence, upon a few sources of benefaction, ineluctably most administrators and even professors will play their pipes accordingly."

Academic freedom has for most of the history of higher education been a tenuous goal. But in the modern era, it has come to be accepted that institutions of learning and teaching must have a certain independence from political powers in order to pursue longer-term research and intellectual endeavor.

The struggle between academics and their would-be censors has traditionally been overt. But the nature of this conflict is changing: instead of explicit censorship or oppression, control of academic voices is an accidental-seeming byproduct of the business model in education. The market does not recognize ideology, it does not recognize theory, it does not recognize individual academic positions and differences: it recognizes only what is efficient, what is productive, what sells.

Discussions of academic freedom are as irrelevant as quarrels about the canon, as a result of the influence of the business model. Nobody is seeking to depose academics; it is simply that the mechanism of academia no longer accommodates views which are undesirable to the majority. The market determines in part what is taught, what is disseminated; the market is now students, mostly interested in preparing for their careers, mostly careers in the business world. And the market determines what research is conducted: corporate funders seek profitable results, and academics increasingly dependent on such funding must tailor their research to its demands.

3.4. Remedial education

The fundamental issues bringing down affirmative action, the competition model and conservative assumptions about social structure, are also the driving forces in the decline of remedial education programs around the country. The competition model has come to bear upon the issue of remedial education in two ways: the first is via the notion that public schools should be competitive with one another; the second, that students themselves should be competitive.

The assumption that public schools should be competitive rests on the claim that the system of public schools should be treated as a marketplace, with the goal of weeding out the weaker less effective institutions and leaving the strong. This may sound like a fine ideal, but in practice it raises some problems. Consider, for example, the following "story," concerning the hypothetical case of two principals for "Large City, New York." The two are discussing a recent *Large City Times* article which notes that "P.S. A rose 96 places in the citywide rankings, while P.S. F fell 78 places." (Hedges; in Callaway 1990: 205) Why, the article asks, are two schools otherwise so similar receiving such disparate rankings? The article goes on to laud the faculty, program, and leadership in School A and to criticize the faculty, program, and leadership in School F.

The principal of school A describes to the principal of F what he has done. He figured out, he explains, that if he got rid of 50 marginal students, reading averages would improve and the school would rise in the rankings. Further, he could then attract better students from elsewhere, and raise his school's ranking even further. His fellow principal points out that a good number of the 50 students expelled from school A wound up in his own, and that many of those "better students" attracted to the first school were drawn from his own. Hence the source of his own lowered ranking.

The implications of the kind of competition between schools created by a voucher system or other "incentives" are foreboding for the future of education for students whose backgrounds prepare them less for higher education. If schools are measured by standards which encourage the selection of abler students, public education as a general social opportunity will suffer.

The second assumption, that students should be competitive, assures that the only criterion for admission to schools should be performance along one set of metrics given to all applicants. Remedial education, as the provision of resources to the undeserving, is seen as educational welfare, encouraging the unworthy and discouraging those who have worked for their position. The unfitness of students for the competition, and for academia, is a matter of their own preparation, their own effort, and therefore their own fault:

> One board member, George J. Rios, said the plan sounded a "realistic warning bell" that students must be better prepared, and that "we as educators will no longer tolerate mediocrity and failed opportunity."
>
> (Healy 1998: A26)

The student's failure to be prepared is a personal failure, rather than a reflection of social stratification and restricted opportunity.

3.5. The purpose of education and the future of the curriculum

A major conflict arises between educators who believe that there are certain things all students should be taught, for reasons of general knowledge, or for citizen preparation, or of cultural cohesion, and students who see education as a service they pay for and therefore should determine the content of.

Required courses arise from two different sources. On the one hand, they represent the long-standing goal of educators to create a uniform culture through common curricular structure and content; this goal arises within the view of education as having a conservative social function and serving the larger needs of a culture for commonality and cohesion. On the other hand, an entailment of the factory model, as we have seen, is that the product meet standards of construction, quality, etc.; in the model of the student as a product, prepared for employment in the society's workforce, the goal of standardization translates to students receiving a uniform education.

Both of these models of education come into conflict with the more recent view of education as a service. The student as consumer determines what sort of service he or she shall receive; required courses represent a lack of choice, and an abnegation of the service model. It is worth noting that requirements form an increasingly minor part of many curricula. Frankel observed, for example, that universities have brought about "the progressive elimination of foreign language requirements from the curricula [and] the steady dilution even of mild distribution requirements." (Frankel 1975: 280)

One of the most striking entailments of the business model, especially the service-industry model, in education, is that the usefulness or value of education is determined by how it serves the student in the business world, either in getting a job or performing that job. Any consideration of its contribution to a person's value as a citizen, or fulfillment as an individual, or to general cultural breadth, is ignored:

> The people who are our students don't really want the education. They want what the education provides for them – better jobs, moving up in their career, the ability to speak up in meetings, that kind of stuff. They want it to *do* something for them. (Traub 1997: 114)

The particular institution described in this article has certain requirements it places on its students for admission (its targeted "market niche"): they must be at least partly college-educated, adults, and working. This is so that "the need for general education, liberal arts, and all the other stuff that takes up so much time and money at college could be dispensed with." (Traub 1997: 117)

Historically, educators professed the value of a broad liberal education in its addition to the intellectual wealth of the country and the ability of the individual to reason and to inform himself or herself in the world. These aims of education are eradicated in the simple business model.

The existence of courses required by undergraduate programs, often called distribution requirements, reflects the ingrained belief that a set of shared fundamental courses benefit the student and the larger society by promoting a sense of common culture, a preparedness for good citizenship, a common moral training, and so on. But the growing extent of such requirements has come into conflict with the opposing desire of students to pick and choose their subjects of study.

3.6. Scholarships and tuition

In the business view, need-based scholarships become a financial burden with no benefit to the producer; they run contrary to the idea of price as determined by the market. The agreement among schools on the amounts of need-based scholarships can even be seen as price-fixing, as in one court case:

> Since the late 1950s, the eight Ivy League schools and MIT had agreed to offer financial aid solely on the basis of need, as defined by a common formula. To implement their agreement, representatives of the schools met each year to compare financial aid offers and adjust for discrepancies. [...] The Justice Department brought an antitrust action against the schools, claiming the practice amounted to price-fixing. [...] While the Ivies can continue to share common principles for awarding aid, they can no longer compare individual cases. (Sandel 1997: 29)

Furthermore, a tuition deliberately maintained at a level considered affordable to the less-than-wealthiest students is also contrary to the goals of business. One important asset of a business is its reputation for putting out high-quality products, and one necessary factor to having a product of high quality is using high-quality raw materials. In education this translates to getting the cream of the crop of available high school graduates, the most successful ones, as we saw above.

> Instead of aid being a form of charity, intended for students who require and merit support, it is increasingly offered as an inducement to able students whose families need little if any help. Often, "merit aid" is a disguise for a discount that might close a deal. (Caplan 1997: 81–82)

"Increasingly, colleges and universities think of student aid as a strategic part of revenue planning," notes one college president. (Janofsky 1999: A12) If the school directs its few scholarships toward a more highly qualified enrollment, needier students are squeezed out of the running. "It used to be [that] providing aid was a charitable operation. Now, it's investment, like brand management." (Ibid.)

Two recent legal changes affect the way that schools may determine aid. These parallel the dismantling of protection for less wealthy individuals on other economic fronts in the move to make economic institutions more "competitive." The elite schools' practice of collaborating on student aid offers to reduce costly competition was considered by the Government to be price-fixing, and was abolished. And the economic factors considered in financial aid offers were changed. The year after the "price-fixing" ruling,

> Congress eliminated home equity as a family asset in determining eligibility for Federal aid. In effect, that liberalized the definition of need, allowing colleges more flexibility in aid packages. (Ibid.)

This change removed one possibly major distinction between applicants from more wealthy and less well-off families. The "liberalization" was effectively the conversion of need-based scholarships to merit-based ones. The choice of term here clearly reflects the bias toward the free-market tactics increasingly dominating education policy: the institution needs to compete, and the government support of its competitiveness is shown in the removal of protections and provisions for needier would-be students. "The term "need" is evolving in the highest reaches of academe. Increasingly, these colleges are looking out for their own needs, using financial aid as a competitive tool to enroll the best students." (Gose 1999: A42)

What is less obvious but of singular import is the effect of these shifts on admissions of less successful, meaning usually less privileged, students, and therefore on the social mobility of less privileged socioeconomic groups. Even setting aside the question of whether the current metrics of success of high school graduates are accurate predictors of their later performance (and some studies suggest they are not (Cf., e.g. Goodman

1960; 1963), this immediately poses a difficulty for those sectors of the population which are not privileged to have easy access to good elementary and secondary education: as less desirable material for admissions offices, they are at a disadvantage – a continuing disadvantage – in the larger system.

And schools which try to maintain socioeconomically sensitive admissions policies are at a disadvantage in the larger educational system. Like isolated socialist states surrounded by capitalist countries, they cannot survive for long with generous policies whose benefits are undermined by the profit-driven motives of their neighbors.

"We're not militantly egalitarian," concedes one MIT financial aid policy person. "The question is, How long can you maintain that system if you're the only one out there? It wouldn't take long for this whole thing to fall apart if we saw top students going to other places because of merit awards." (Gose 1999: A43) The pressure of the all-consuming market compels even well-meaning admissions officers to conform to the competitive standard.

4. Conclusions

The encroachment of business-domain thinking is not unique to the domain of education. As one observer notes of the changes in education, "nothing is going on here that has not already gone on in government ..." (Harvey 1989) A proponent of more businesslike education has "suggested that higher education undergo the kind of rigorous reorganization that has taken place in health care in recent years." (*Chronicle of Higher Education*; June 19, 1998: A23) This kind of approach has been seen in government for a while already. The model of business can be seen to reach into and influence the ways we talk, think, and make decisions about all of our primary social institutions. It is more advanced in government, but is increasingly visible in the domains of health care and prisons.

The unquestioned use of language from a domain founded on the principle of self-interest to describe a domain which has been seen as critically social is striking. One might say these are "just words"; that this language has no real significance for the way people think about education or make decisions that shape the future of the institution. But we have seen that linguistic images like those above are the indicators of a complicated process of reasoning about a domain which is very much influenced by the conceptual model used.

The increasingly polarized distribution of resources and opportunity which is a result of the corporate model in academia conflicts directly with the deeply held belief that education as a public good should be available to everyone. If we as a society and as a country are to hold true to our ideal of education for all providing the possibility for advancement that is understood to be the right of every citizen, we must undertake a fundamental reconsideration of the assumptions of the market system, and the effects these have had upon our educational system and our society as a whole. The kind of analysis I have described above allows us to become aware of the social consequences of formative models and metaphors in our thought. Using and remaining aware of these models at the conscious level permits us as a society to be deliberate in our decision-making regarding social structures. Specifically, policymakers must incorporate such insights when pursuing the reform of social institutions. In the larger scheme of things, such analysis provides for the understanding of systems and institutions that is of fundamental benefit to us in our continuing social endeavor.

References

Armajami, Babak, et al.
1994 *A Model for the Reinvented Higher Education System: State Policy and College Learning*. Denver, CO: Education Commission of the States.

Baade, Hans W. and Robinson O. Everett (eds.)
1964 *Academic Freedom: The Scholar's Place in Modern Society*. Law and Contemporary Problems. Dobbs Ferry, New York: Oceana Publications.

Barzun, Jacques
1993 *The American University*. Chicago: University of Chicago Press.

Boers, Frank
1997 "No Pain, No Gain" in a free market rhetoric: A test for cognitive semantics? *Metaphor and Symbol* 12: 231–241.

Brand, Myles
1999 Why tenure is indispensible. *Chronicle of Higher Education* XLV.30: A64.

Callaway, Rolland (ed.)
1990 *Satire and Humor in Education: Selected Readings*. Lanham, MD: University Press of America.

Caplan, Lincoln
1997 Contemporary calculus. *US News and World Report* September 1, 1997: 80–82.

Chronicle of Higher Education
1998. University of Washington professors decry Governor's visions for technology. *Chronicle of Higher Education* XLIV.41: A23.
Chronicle of Higher Education on the Web (CHE)
1997 Online colloquy. 1997. http://chronicle.com/colloquy; accessed 1999.
Duderstadt, James J.
1999 The future of higher education: New roles for the 21st century university. *The Millennium Project: Issues in Science and Technology Online*. Winter 1999. http://milproj.ummu.umich.edu/publications/newroles/download/newroles.pdf; accessed May 2005.
2000 The future of the research university in the digital age. *The Millennium Project: Issues in Science and Technology Online*. 1999. http://milproj.ummu.umich.edu/publications/uw_it_and_university/uw_it_and_university.pdf; accessed May 2005.
eCollege Press Release
2003 DeVry University standardizes online offerings on e-college systems. *http://www.ecollege.com/stories/press_03_18_03.learn?page=2250*; accessed May 2005.
Edmundson, Mark
1997 On the uses of a liberal education: I. as lite entertainment for bored college students. *Harper's* September 1997: 39–49.
Ehrlich, Paul
1986 *The Machinery of Nature*. New York: Simon and Schuster.
Epstein, Leon
1974 *Governing the University: The Campus and the Public Interest*. (The Jossey-Bass Series in Higher Education). San Francisco: Jossey-Bass Publishers.
Frankel, Charles
1975 Epilogue: Reflections on a worn-out model. In: Paul Seabury (ed.), *Universities in the Western World*, 279–289. New York: The Free Press.
Freeland, Richard
1997 Let the marketplace set college prices. *Boston Herald*, December 12, 1997. http://www.president.neu.edu/opeds/market971212.html; accessed May 2005.
Friedman, Hershey H.
2001 The obsolescence of academic departments. *Radical Pedagogy* 3: 2. http://radicalpedagogy.icaap.org/content/issue3_2/friedman.html; accessed May 2005.
Froomkin, Joseph, ed.
1983 *The Crisis in Higher Education*. New York: Academy of Political Science.
Garland, James
2005 Dr. Garland on higher education issues. Office of the President, Miami University.
http://www.miami.muohio.edu/president/highered.cfm; accessed May 2005.

Goodman, Paul
1960 *Growing Up Absurd: Problems of Youth in the Organized Society.* New York: Random House.
1963 Why go to school? *The New Republic* October 5, 1963: 13–14.

Gose, Ben
1999 Changes at elite colleges fuel intense competition in student aid. *Chronicle of Higher Education* XLV.22: A42–43.

Gould, Steven Jay
1977 *Ever Since Darwin.* New York: W.W. Norton and Company, Inc.

Grady, Joseph, Sarah Taub and Pamela Morgan.
1996 Primitive and compound metaphors. In A. Goldberg (ed.), *Conceptual Structure, Discourse and Language* (177–187). Stanford, CA: CSLI.

Hart, Moss
1959 *Act One: An Autobiography.* New York: Random House.

Harvey, David
1989 *The Condition of Postmodernity.* Cambridge: Basil Blackwell.

Healy, Patrick.
1998 CUNY's 4-year colleges ordered to phase out remedial education. *Chronicle of Higher Education* XLIV:39: A26.

Hedges, William D.
1990 How to raise your school's ranking by 172 places in one year without changing the curriculum or antagonizing your teachers. In Rolland Callaway (ed.), *Satire and Humor in Education: Selected Readings,* 205–209. Lanham, MD: University Press of America.

Hofstadter, Richard
1955 *Academic Freedom in the Age of the College.* New York/London: Columbia University Press.

Janofsky, Michael
1999 Financial aid bargaining drives admissions frenzy. *New York Times* April 5, 1999: A12.

Kaplin, William A.
1985 *The Law of Higher Education. The Jossey-Bass Higher Education Series.* 2nd ed. San Francisco: Jossey-Bass Publishers.

Kirk, Russell
1964 Massive subsidies and academic freedom. In: Hans Baade and Robinson O. Everett (eds.), *Academic Freedom: The Scholar's Place in Modern Society,* 177–182. Dobbs Ferry, New York: Oceana Publications.

Koller, Veronika
2002 "A shotgun wedding": Co-occurrence of war and marriage metaphors in mergers and acquisitions discourse. *Metaphor and Symbol* 17: 179–203.
2004 Businesswomen and war metaphors: "Possessive, jealous and pugnacious"? *Journal of Sociolinguistics* 8: 3–23.

Kuhn, Thomas S.
1993 Metaphor in science. In: Andrew Ortony (ed.), *Metaphor and Thought*, 533–542. Cambridge: Cambridge University Press.

Lakoff, George
1987 *Women, Fire, and Dangerous Things: What Categories Reveal about the Mind.* Chicago: University of Chicago Press.
1996 *Moral Politics: What Conservatives Know That Liberals Don't*. Chicago and London: University of Chicago Press.

Lakoff, George, and Mark Johnson
1980 *Metaphors We Live By*. Chicago and London: University of Chicago Press.
1999 *Philosophy in the Flesh*. New York: Basic Books.

Leary, David E., Mitchell G. Ash and William R. Woodward (eds.).
1990 *Metaphors in the History of Psychology*. Cambridge: Cambridge University Press.

Leatherdale, W. H.
1974 *The Role of Analogy, Model, and Metaphor in Science*. Amsterdam and New York: North-Holland Pub. Co.

Leddy, Thomas
1995 Metaphor and metaphysics. *Metaphor and Symbolic Activity* 10: 205–222.

Lucas, Christopher J.
1996 *Crisis in the Academy: Rethinking Higher Education in America*. New York: St. Martin's Press.

Maasen, Sabine and Matthias Winterhager (eds.).
2001 *Science Studies: Probing the Dynamics of Scientific Knowledge*. Bielefeld, Germany: Transcript Verlag, Roswitha Gost, Sigrid Noke.

Maasen, Sabine, Everett Mendelsohn and Peter Weingart (eds.).
2001 *Biology as Society, Society as Biology Metaphors*. (Sociology of the Sciences Yearbook 18). Dordrecht: Kluwer.

Mahoney, Richard J.
1997 "Reinventing" the university: Object lessons from big business. *The Chronicle of Higher Education on the Web* 10/17/97. http://chronicle.com/che-data/articles.dir/art-44.dir/issue-08.dir/08b00401.htm

Melcher, Richard
1998 An old university hits the high-tech road. *Business Week* August 31, 1998: 94–96.

Mio, Jeffery Scott
1997 Metaphor and politics. *Metaphor and Symbol* 12: 113–133.

Morgan, Pamela
1996 Metaphorical "families". Prospectus. University of California at Berkeley.

Noble, David
1998 Digital diploma mills: The automation of higher education. *Web publication: cf. i.a. http://communication.ucsd.edu/dl/ddm1.html;* accessed May 2005.

Paulsen, Michael B.
1990. College choice: Understanding student enrollment behavior. *ERIC Digest.* Association for the Study of Higher Education; ERIC Clearinghouse on Higher Education, Washington, D.C.; George Washington University.

Porter, Kathleen
2002 The value of a college degree. *ERIC Digest.* ERIC Clearinghouse on Higher Education Washington DC. http://www.ericdigests.org/2003-3/value.htm; accessed May 2005.

Quayle, J. Danforth
1992 Address to the Commonwealth Club of California, May 19. See http://www.commonwealthclub.org/archive/20thcentury/92-05quayle-speech.html, accessed May 2005.

Rohrer, Tim
1995 The metaphorical logic of (political) rape: The new wor(l)d order. *Metaphor and Symbolic Activity* 10: 115–137.

Ruch, Richard S.
2001 *Higher Ed, Inc.: The Rise of the For-Profit University.* Baltimore and London: Johns Hopkins University Press.

Sandel, Michael J.
1997 The hard questions. *The New Republic* May 26, 1997: 29.

Sinclair, Upton
1923 *The Goose-step :A Study of American ducation.* Girard, KS: Haldeman-Julius Publications.

Sinha, Chris
2002 The cost of renovating the property: A reply to Marina Rakova. *Cognitive Linguistics* 13: 271–276.

Taub, Sarah
1990 Moral accounting. Unpublished ms. University of California, Berkeley.

Traub, James
1997 Drive-Thru U.: Higher education for people who mean business. *The New Yorker* October 20 & 27, 1997: 115–123.

Tucker, Robert C. (ed.)
1978 *The Marx-Engels Reader.* 2nd ed. New York: W. W. Norton and Company, Inc.

Urban, Nancy
1999 The school business: Rethinking educational reform. Dissertation, University of California, Berkeley.

Veblen, Thorstein
1965 *The Higher Learning in America.* Original Ed. 1918 ed. New York: Sentry Press.

Vine, Phyllis
1997 "To market, to market ...: The school business sells kids short." *The Nation* September 8/15, 1997: 11 ff.

White, Michael
2003 Metaphor and economics: The case of growth. *English for Specific Purposes* 22: 131–151

Wilson, Bryan R.
1962 The teacher's role – A sociological analysis. *The British Journal of Sociology* 1.13: 15–32.

Competition, cooperation, and interconnection: 'Metaphor families' and social systems

Pamela S. Morgan[1]

Abstract

This paper examines the relationship of source and target domains used to characterize interactions and systems, including social systems, and concludes that social systems are conventionally characterized in one of three ways: as competitive, as cooperative, or as an interconnected system. For each of these "metaphor families" we have a schematized model and a set of core domains whose stereotypes inherently fit the schema. However, for most social domains the family characterization is not inherently determined; usually we logically can construe the domain into more than one metaphor family. Nevertheless, there are conventionalized choices: business is viewed competitively with respect to "rival" businesses, but cooperatively with respect to much of its internal structure. Politics is viewed competitively during elections, but cooperatively when forming alliances to achieve common goals. The interconnected systems view is less well developed in most domains. Despite convention, it is possible to think of these domains in terms of the other metaphor families, leading to the possibility of different entailments with respect to beliefs, reasoning, behavior, and possible changes in social landscapes.

Keywords: metaphor, metaphor families, social systems, social change, competition, cooperation, interconnection, interdependence, systems, cognitive models.

---

1. I wish to thank George Lakoff, Eve Sweetser, Chris Johnson, and Kevin Moore, and especially Joe Grady and Sarah Taub who were fellow members of an informal, cooperative working group at the time of the early stages of development of these ideas. I owe the term "metaphor families" to George Lakoff. I also wish to thank the members of the many classes to whom I have presented these ideas, for their insightful and helpful questions and comments.

1. Introduction

Relationships among individual metaphors may consist of more than a collection of metaphors that happen to share a source or target domain.[2] The structure of metaphor "families" (MFs), in which experiential domains form complex "crossover" metaphor patterns by serving as source and target domains to each other, is a common and productive structure that underlies (and often licenses) many individual and radially-grouped metaphors. In addition, there are important social consequences: many areas of our experience – for example, business, politics, love, the legal system, life itself – can be understood as belonging to one or more of the MFs. Each MF has a different set of frames, presuppositions, reasoning patterns, and entailments; the language we use indicates the MF, and the MF defines the way we think about and understand that area of our experience, highlighting some possibilities and hiding others.

The three MFs are given in Table 1.

The data used in this study were collected over a period of several years from a variety of sources – newspapers, radio, television, and occa-

2. "Target domain" (that which is being understood by means of the metaphor), "source domain" (supplies the language and frame for the metaphor), and "entailment" (a conclusion, not necessarily explicitly stated, that is logically derived from information in the frame) are terms from the conceptual metaphor theory of Lakoff and Johnson as presented in Lakoff and Johnson 1980 and succeeding work in that theory. Important points of this conceptual metaphor theory include the following: (i) conceptual metaphors are experientially-based, non-arbitrary pairings of concepts/domains; (ii) conceptual metaphors are systematic and recurring in thought, language, and image; (iii) conceptual metaphors (like other kinds of cognitive models) include reasoning patterns; (iv) expressions of conceptual metaphors are either conventionalized or novel. Conceptual metaphor theory is not the only linguistic approach of importance for metaphor families. Others include prototypes, radial categories, contested concepts/categories, frame semantics as developed by Charles Fillmore, my own work in cultural cognitive models, pragmatics, and discourse analysis. However, there will not be space to discuss these other elements in the present paper. For prototypes and radial categories, see Lakoff 1987; for essentially contested concepts, see Gallie 1956; for an introductory paper on frame semantics, see Fillmore 1982. Theoretical terms and concepts presented in this paper ("core" vs. "construal" members, or the "Principle of Prior Construal," for example) that are not otherwise attributed are part of my original work and are published here for the first time.

Table 1. Identified Metaphor Families

– COMPETITION
– COOPERATION
– INTERCONNECTION (SYSTEMS)

sionally conversation – as well as being generated in some cases from introspection and checked with other English speakers. The study began with an observation of the metaphors BUSINESS IS WAR and POLITICS ARE WAR, alongside other metaphors for both business and politics and other metaphors comparing other target domains to war. As the collection of occurrences of metaphors using war as a source domain and various aspects of social life as target domains proceeded, other metaphors were noticed that used these same domains of experience as either source or target domains.

It soon became clear that, when an alternating and iterative process of collection and analysis was used to widen, group, and classify the relevant source and target domains, there are image-schematic groupings. As the data was collected and analyzed, the patterns of cooperation, competition, and interconnection emerged. Of course, these three patterns do not exhaust all the metaphors using any of the domains as source or target domains. Business, for example, is often conceptualized as a form of art, which does not belong to these metaphor families (see Morgan 1998).

Because the data were collected primarily from American media sources, this study reflects mainstream public discourse in American English. Other varieties of English, and other languages, may or may not exhibit the same patterns, and this would be worth checking.

These three MFs may be defined as follows. COMPETITION focuses on an external struggle between two or more adversaries for a single goal that only one can have. COOPERATION focuses on the successful internal coordinated functioning within a group of two or more collaborators with the aim of achieving a shared goal. INTERCONNECTION ("SYSTEMS") or interdependence conceptualizes the comparison of one entity to another either in terms of their wholes or their internal structures – that is, "static" systems – or in terms of some aspect of their "functioning" – i.e., "dynamic" systems. In the COMPETITION metaphor family there have to be winners and losers; in the COOPERATION family everyone works together toward a common goal; in the INTERCONNECTION family, what happens to one part inescapably affects all the other parts.

Like any metaphor, there are advantages and disadvantages in using the term "metaphor families." The term (which replaces my original term of "crossover groups") is offered in the following sense: the domain "members" of each metaphor "family" have certain important common characteristics – related to their shared underlying image schema[3] that makes them a metaphor family – that non-members do not share. However, each member also retains a large degree of "individuality" related to its individual frame semantics. Members of MFs do not, therefore, share all their characteristics with each other, and, as this paper will suggest, this is important for pragmatics and social instantiation.

In addition, there is an important distinction between what I call central or "core members" and peripheral or "construal members" in MFs, analogous to that between "nuclear" and "extended" literal families. "Core members" are those domains that serve as both source and target domain for each other in a set of completely reciprocal relationships, by means of sharing an *inherent* underlying image schema. "Construal members" are those domains that do not inherently share that image schema, but can be conceptualized as if they do. (See Figure 1. The arrows indicate metaphors; the head of an arrow indicates a target domain). Core members of the COMPETITION MF, for example, are WAR, A (TEAM) SPORT, A RACE, A GAME, and PREDATION. Construal members include BUSINESS, POLITICS, LOVE, and ARGUMENT, among many others. This paper examines some of the core and construal metaphorical mappings of the three MFs, but there is not enough space to work through all of them.

Depending on the point of view that taken, many common domains of experience are in fact found as either core or construal members of

3. An image schema is an abstracted representation of a relationship, most often emphasizing spatial relationships but also applicable to abstracted motor or (as here) dynamic relationships, that reduces the complexities of the relationship to their most skeletal, removing all but the most necessary details. Spatial examples include the "container" image schema, the "center-periphery" image schema, the "up-down" image schema, the "across" image schema, and so on. (Spatial image schemas are usually encoded in languages in prepositions or their equivalent, but the exact encodings do not correspond across languages.)

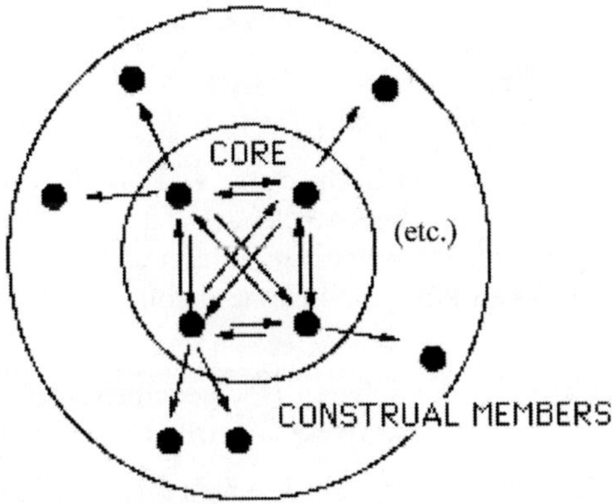

Figure 1. The core and construal structure of a Metaphor Family

more than one MF. For example, either the external or the internal situation may be the focus, and the mappings will differ accordingly. That is, if a group of entities, such as an army or a pack of dogs (core members) or a business or a nation (construal members), is seen as an undifferentiated whole in opposition to another undifferentiated group, the COMPETITION MF is being invoked. If the group is being conceptualized in terms of its internal organization, the COOPERATION MF is being invoked.

If differentiation within the group is important, any group composed of more than one participant may be viewed as part of the INTERCONNECTION family and its members as "parts" of the system. Such differentiation may focus on any of the aspects of experience that are dominant in the INTERCONNECTION family – existence, part-whole configuration, and/or functionality, usually in connection with a particular pragmatic context. It is common for groups such as armies or nations to be viewed as a smoothly-functioning machine, for example.

1.1. Definitional details of the "metaphor family" structure

Metaphor families are defined by four essential characteristics, given in Table 2. Following the table, each of the characteristics will be discussed in turn, using the COMPETITION MF for illustration.

Table 2. The defining characteristics of a Metaphor Family

(1)	There is a basic abstract frame-schema which all the core metaphors fit inherently and elaborate individually (section 2.1).
(2)	Every core member serves as both source and target domain for metaphors involving every other core member. That is, core members have complete, symmetrical, bidirectional source and target domain "crossover," barred only by (rare) experientially based frame incompatibilities (sections 2.2 and 2.3).
(3)	Construal members do not inherently or exclusively fit the basic abstract frame-schema, but can be selectively construed to fit (section 2.4).
(4)	In unmarked situations, there is unidirectionality (asymmetry) of source domain crossover between the core and construal members. That is, core members regularly serve as source domains for construal members, but construal members do not commonly serve as source domains for each other or for core source domains. When this does occur, it is very marked, for example as humorous (section 2.5).[4]

2. The COMPETITION metaphor family ("us vs. them")

2.1. Characteristic 1: The shared inherent frame-schema

The feature that makes the "crossover" structure of Characteristic 2 possible is the fact that each of the core members has the same underlying, schematized, prototypical, inherent "frame-schema" (Characteristic 1).

A frame-schema contains (1) a set of participants; (2) relationships between participants; (3) usually an ordered set of events (a "scenario"); (4) presuppositions (background assumptions) and (5) entailments (necessary conclusions). Frame-schemata are abstract, prototypical, and conventionalized. In the COMPETITION MF, for example, the underlying frame-schema is one of two entities directly struggling to get something that – importantly – only one can have (see Table 3a). The outcome is uncertain and usually depends on the relative individual efforts of the

4. Another marked example: a core-to-core metaphor across MFs, such as educational cartoons that portray the circulatory system of the human body (INTERCONNECTION: PEOPLE) as a series of tiny people all working together to transport blood (COOPERATION: WORK CREW).

Table 3a. The frame-schema of the COMPETITION MF

Frame-Schema:	"competition": "us vs. them"
	$P \rightarrow G \leftarrow P$ or $P \leftarrow G \rightarrow P$
	(P = participant, G = goal)
Some presuppositions:	prototypically 2 competitors
	prototypically 1 goal
	only one of the competitors can attain the goal
Some entailments:	one competitor will be superior to the other in some measure relevant to attaining the goal
Some source domain language:	*win, lose, victory, defeat*
Frame-Schema Real-World Prototype[6]:	hand-to-hand combat

entities. Because war, most team sports, many (although not all) games, races, and predation all can in fact by their very nature have no prototypical interpretation other than a "win-lose" scenario, they are core, not construal, members of the COMPETITION MF.[5]

The shared frame-schema itself provides a basic set of core licensing metaphors referring to HAND-TO-HAND COMBAT that result in common conventional expressions shared by all the core domains. See Table 3b (shared language is underlined).

5. Clearly, it is easier to agree on prototypes for some of these core members than for others. There are many different types of games, for example; some of them, such as board games or card games, are usually thought of as competitive, but other games, such as playing with dolls, are not. Some people may perhaps not consider playing with dolls a "game," but others would not hesitate. Furthermore, it is important to note that the prototype of a particular game may include core elements that nevertheless are not part of the COMPETITION frame-schema. (Nunberg 1978, for example, describes the core features of the game of golf, which is not just a win-lose scenario, but one which involves many other prototypical components. My thanks to the editors for pointing out this reference.)
6. In this paper, a "prototype" is understood to be the shared, abstracted, default representation of a concept. There are many kinds of prototypes used in category-based conceptualization (see, e.g., Lakoff 1987).

Table 3b. Frame-schema core licensing metaphors of the COMPETITION MF

Frame-Schema Core Licensing Metaphors:

WAR / A (TEAM) SPORT / A GAME / A RACE / PREDATION IS COMPETITION

Our army/Our baseball team/The current chess champion/The fastest horse/The tiger *won/lost*.

WAR IS HAND-TO-HAND COMBAT

The Allies *beat* the Axis powers in World War II.

A (TEAM) SPORT IS HAND-TO-HAND COMBAT

Fightin' Phillies
(newspaper headline referring to a baseball team)

A GAME IS HAND-TO-HAND COMBAT

They went *head to head* in the third round
(newspaper report on a golf tournament)

A RACE IS HAND-TO-HAND COMBAT

Citation *beat* the other horses in the backstretch

PREDATION IS HAND-TO-HAND COMBAT

The animals of the jungle engage in a constant *fight* for survival.

These expressions – "win/lose," "beat," "fight" – are so common that it takes a moment to recognize that their literal source domain is hand-to-hand combat.

2.2. Characteristic 2: The "crossover" structure of the core

Perhaps the most recognizable and easily tested of the characteristics of an MF is that of the "crossover" structure of the core members. That is, each core member is both source and target domain for conventional metaphors involving all of the other core members individually. This is schematically represented in Figure 2 with respect to the COMPETITION MF (again, the double-headed arrows indicate bidirectional metaphors, e.g., WAR IS A [TEAM] SPORT/A [TEAM] SPORT IS WAR).

The core members of the COMPETITION MF, their core "crossover" metaphors (represented by the double-headed arrows in Figure 2), and some linguistic examples of each metaphor are given in Tables 4a and 4b. Although in some cases some of these "core" metaphors (e.g., those related to PREDATION) are not as rich as others, there must be at least minimal evidence of a complete set and/or explainable frame incompatibilities in order to claim that a MF exists.

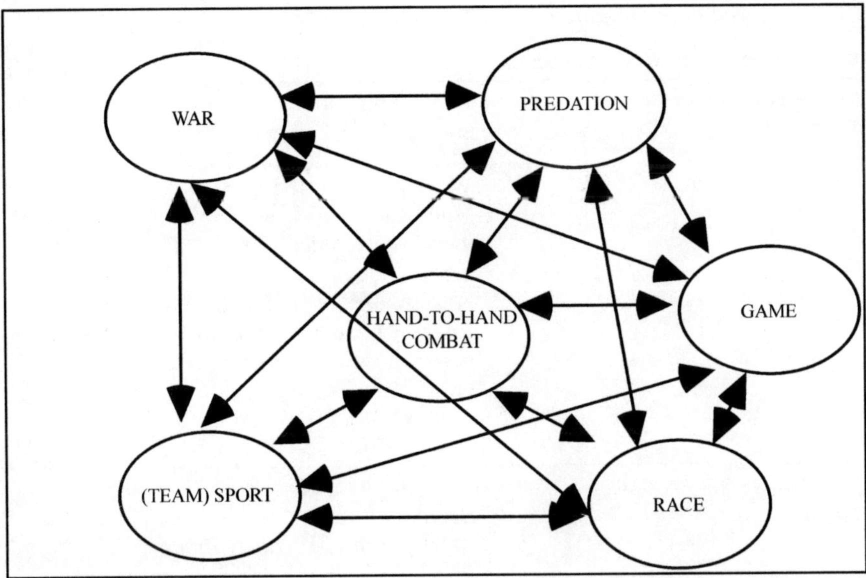

Figure 2. The core members and core metaphors of the COMPETITION MF

Table 4a. The core members of the COMPETION MF

COMPETITION MF:
Core members: HAND-TO-HAND COMBAT
(including conventional Special Cases: Fist Fights, Boxing, Duels)[7]
WAR
A (TEAM) SPORT
(including conventional U.S. Special Cases: Football, Baseball, [rare] Hockey)
A GAME
(including conventional U.S. Special Cases: Chess, Poker)
A RACE
(prototype: foot race;
including conventional Special Case: Horse Race)
PREDATION
(including conventional Special Cases: Hunting, Fishing)

7. A special case is a secondary domain (e.g., A HORSE RACE) that shares most of the frame and language of the primary frame (e.g., A RACE) but has some additional special differentiating frames and language. The set of special cases does not collectively exhaust the primary domain.

Table 4b. The core metaphors of the COMPETITION MF

COMPETITION MF: Core Metaphors:	
WAR IS A (TEAM) SPORT	– The troops made an *end run* around the enemy.[8]
?WAR IS A GAME	– The *rules* of war forbid torture.[9]
WAR IS A RACE	– We're ahead in the arms *race.*
	– "the 'Race to the Sea'" [of trench development) (*Britannica Online*, "The World Wars")[10]
WAR IS PREDATION[11]	– Richard the *Lion*-Hearted (Richard I of England); Cu Chulainn (a traditional Irish hero whose name means "Culann's [guard] Dog")
	– *shark's* "faces" painted on military aircraft
	– *hunting* down terrorists
A (TEAM) SPORT IS WAR	– the *offensive/defensive* line (football); *strategy*
	– sports teams: *Warriors*, *Raiders*
	– The Lakers *blew* the Celtics *out of the water/off* the court. (basketball)
A (TEAM) SPORT IS A GAME (American football)	– The Raiders were *dealt a bad hand* last Sunday.
A (TEAM) SPORT IS A RACE (baseball)	– The Tigers are *ahead* in the pennant *race.*
A (TEAM) SPORT IS PREDATION (hockey, American football)	– the *Sharks*, the *Lions*, the *Bears*, the *Wolverines*, the *Bengals*
(American football)	– Raiders Don't Let This *Fish* Off *Hook* (newspaper headline)

8. Cf. also the instantiation of this metaphor in the melées, or mock battles with "teams," of the European Middle Ages.
9. The source domain for this phrase may be TEAM SPORTS, since the WAR IS A GAME metaphor may be blocked by FRAME INCOMPATIBILITY; see section 2.3.
10. In order to avoid frame incompatibility based on the lack of "bloodthirstiness" in a race, examples of this metaphor seem to require first a metonymy. For example, arms production is used to stand for the purpose of the arms production, namely, the destruction of the enemy in war; or the intended goal (the sea) stands for the opposition and reaction to the opposition encountered in reaching that goal. Then the RACE metaphor is applied to emphasize the linear hierarchical ordering: capabilities are ranked according to the order of "reaching" the intended goal, that is, the larger number of or more technologically capable weapons, or the territory around the Marne.
11. In general, PREDATION examples first employ metaphors from the INTERCONNECTION MF (see section 4), e.g., PEOPLE ARE ANIMALS or MACHINES ARE ANIMALS.

Table 4b. (continued)

COMPETITION MF: Core Metaphors:	
A GAME IS WAR	– That's good *strategy* (e.g., chess, bridge).[12]
A GAME IS A (TEAM) SPORT	– *end run* (applied to a chess match)
A GAME IS A RACE	– He's not *in the running*.[13]
	– They're in a *race* to accumulate points.
A GAME IS PREDATION	– If you play him, he'll *eat you alive*.[14]
	– He's a regular pool *shark*.
A RACE IS WAR	– There's a *battle* in the backstretch for second place.
A RACE IS A (TEAM) SPORT	– The Tour de France *team* (bicycle racing); the Bridgestone *team* (auto racing)
A RACE IS A GAME	– She *gambled* everything on one last sprint.
A RACE IS PREDATION[15]	– The leader *gobbled up* the backstretch.
	– The racers *ate up* the miles.
PREDATION IS WAR	– Let us discuss this species's *strategy* for survival.
	– We witnessed a *battle* between a lion and an elephant.
PREDATION IS A (TEAM) SPORT	– *sport fishing*[16]
PREDATION IS A GAME[17]	– *game* of cat and mouse; the cat was *toying/ playing* with the mouse[18]
PREDATION IS A RACE	– FRAME INCOMPATIBILITY (see section 2.3)

2.3. Frame incompatibilities

In some cases, "frame incompatibilities" (elsewhere called "target domain overrides") block a full, rich extension of the core metaphor crossovers

12. Cf. chess itself as a literalization of this metaphor.
13. Only with respect to a multiperson game (e.g., Monopoly) or a game tournament, i.e., sets of games, because there must be at least three racers, and preferably more, for there to be an ingroup and an outgroup.
14. Also said of an individual sport, such as tennis.
15. Here the opponent is conventionally not the other racers, but rather the distance to be traveled to the finish line.
16. The use of the words like "sport," "sportsman," and related hunting terminology conceptualize PREDATION as a SPORT, although not a team sport.
17. Game Theory allows the GAME domain to be applied to many construal domains.
18. In general, with the exception of the above cat-and-mouse scenario, this metaphor is blocked by FRAME INCOMPATIBILITY (see section 2.3)

of a MF. Instances of A GAME IS PREDATION and PREDATION IS A RACE are marked, for example, because prototypical games and races are definitionally and crucially rule-governed and noninjurious to participants. People are generally shocked if these characteristics are violated (with the possible exception of a car race, which may be why a CAR RACE is not a conventional central Special Case of the RACE domain). GAMES and RACES are therefore not usually taken seriously enough to be conceived of in terms of PREDATION's "struggle for survival" – hence the humorous or disapproving tone of, for example, "He'll eat you alive." Pool "sharks" inject seriousness into a game because they play for money, which is by cultural definition serious, and they often play as their sole or primary means of earning a living. Similarly, GAMES and RACES have no trace of the bloodthirstiness found in the domains of WAR and to a lesser extent (through injuries) (TEAM) SPORTS.

Similarly, in actual predatory situations the crucial GAME element of consciously defined "rules" is missing. Since one of the main reasons to invoke the GAME source domain is precisely this element of rules (Table 5), it is less likely to be a source domain for conceptualizing PREDATION.

That is, there is in these less productive cases an incompatability between the crucial element(s) of the prototypical source-domain individual frame – i.e., those elements that distinguish the core members from each other and thereby cause a certain one of the core members to be considered appropriate for a particular situation, in order to hide or highlight something – and the (prototypical) target-domain frame, or between entailments of these frames. To put it simply, there may be elements or entailments that are at odds with the point of choosing that source domain in the first place. Non-prototypical situations within the target domain may sometimes allow these mappings, but in such cases they are necessarily marked as humorous, disapproving, or in some other way deviating from the conventional default.

Another reason to replace the name "target domain override" with "frame incompatibility" is that the incompatibility may in fact "originate" in the source domain. For example, the domain of PREDATION is not a rich and productive source domain for the other core members in large part because our accepted theory of the nature of animals bases their behavior on instinct rather than on reasoned volition. This is one of the most important aspects of what we "know" about animals, but it is incompatible with all of the other core domains. Our folk definitions of prototypical (TEAM) SPORTS, GAMES, RACES, and even WAR involve some element of rational human behavior.

Since in this view predatory animals are prototypically dangerous, ruthless, savage, random killers, it is precisely in those situations where the lack of such reason-based behavior and consequent moderation on the part of humans is being emphasized that PREDATION is the most appropriate source domain. This occurs especially in construal member situations which are by their very nature more open to alternative source domains.[19]

(1) a. They went at each other *tooth and claw.* (Target roles: business rivals, political candidates, married couples, arguers/debaters)
b. It's a *dog-eat-dog* business/presidential race/world.
c. It's a *jungle* out there. (Target domain: daily life.)

Table 5 summarizes the prototypical basic characteristics of the core members of the COMPETITION MF.

Table 5. Basic prototypical characteristics of the core members of the COMPETITION MF

	death	*physical violence*	*rules*	
Hand-to-Hand Combat	+/−	+	(−)	+2 individuals
War	+	+	+/−	+2 groups
(Team) Sport	−	+	+	+2 groups; +points
Game	−	−	+	−linear ranking; +points
Race	−	−	+	+linear ranking; −points
Predation	+	+	−	+animals; +instinct/ −rationality

(Symbols: +/− = may or may not be present in the central prototype (+)/(−) = usually present/absent in the central prototype).

2.4. Characteristic 3: The "Principle of Prior Construal"

Characteristic 2 gives rise to a third characteristic, an hypothesized "principle of prior construal":

19. The existence of the INTERCONNECTION core metaphor PEOPLE ARE ANIMALS (see section 4) licenses the inclusion of PREDATION in the core of the COMPETITION MF and AN ANIMAL GROUP in the core of COOPERATION. This "second-level" status further helps explain our intuitive sense that PREDATION and AN ANIMAL GROUP are somehow "not exactly the same" as the other core members of the COMPETITION and COOPERATION MFs.

> In order for certain entities, activities or situations to be understood as conceptually equivalent in some way(s) to one of the entities, activities, or situations included in the core of a metaphor family, the target entity/activity/situation must *first* be *construed* and understood in terms of the overall family concept. *Importantly, however, other possibilities of construal still exist, and therefore different domains may be viewed, actually or potentially, as more appropriate for different situations.*

This principle is suggested from the presence in the linguistic evidence of the presence of the same domains as construal members of two or even all three of the MFs. It would be logically impossible for this to happen if these domains were conceptualized as belonging to only one MF.

It is important that not all entities, activities, or situations belong *inherently* to a frame-schema. Such "ambiguous" entities, activities, or situations participate in a given MF only insofar as they are *first* "construed" to belong to that family at all. For example, for BUSINESS to be understood as WAR, it must first be *assumed* to be inherently competitive and based entirely on zero-sum accounting, which in fact is not always true. (I have discussed this metaphor in detail in Morgan 1998.) Sample language involving construal members includes the following:

(2) a. presidential *campaigns* (construal: POLITICS)
   cf. military *campaigns* (core: WAR)
   Metaphor: POLITICS IS WAR
 b. mayoral *races* (construal: POLITICS)
  She's not *in the running* for the nomination. (construal: POLITICS)
  This election is going right *down to the wire*. (construal: POLITICS)
   cf. Olympic 400 meter *race* (core: A RACE)
   Metaphor: POLITICS IS A RACE
 c. The new company is ahead in the *race* to bring multimedia services to the doorsteps of Californians. (construal: BUSINESS)
   cf. Olympic 400 meter *race* (core: A RACE)
   Metaphor: BUSINESS IS A RACE

See Table 6a for a list of some of the construal members of the COMPETITION MF, and Table 6b for simplified mappings of some first-level construals into the COMPETITION MF: that is, after the target domain has

Table 6a. Some construal members of the COMPETITION MF

- BUSINESS
- POLITICS
- ARGUMENT/DEBATE (important U.S. Special Cases: Legal Proceedings, Theories)
- LOVE/LUST
- MARRIAGE
- LIFE, *and so on*

Table 6b. The COMPETITION MF: Frame Semantics and mappings of two construal members

BUSINESS IS (A FORM OF) COMPETITION	
Submapping 1: External (between companies)	
Target Domain	*Source Domain*
company (or business person) 1	competitor 1
company (or business person) 2 (etc.)	competitor 2 (etc.)
most production/sales	goal
(as appropriate for the source domain)	manner of competition
Submapping 2: Internal (within a company)	
Target Domain	*Source Domain*
worker 1	competitor 1
worker 2 (etc.)	competitor 2 (etc.)
better job/pay within company	goal
(as appropriate for the source domain)	manner of competition
LOVE IS (A FORM OF) COMPETITON	
Target Domain	*Source Domain*
lover 1	competitor 1
lover 2, etc.	competitor 2, etc.
affection of 3rd person	goal
(as appropriate for the source domain)	manner of competition

been construed as COMPETITIVE but before a specific core-member source domain completes the metaphor.

Table 7 presents a partial construal-core mapping for the now-filled-out, specific metaphor AN ARGUMENT IS WAR.

Sample linguistic expressions of this metaphor are shown in example (3) (from Lakoff and Johnson 1980: 4).

(3) a. Your claims are *indefensible*.
  b. He *attacked* every weak point in my argument.

Table 7. The COMPETITON MF: The Construal Metaphor AN ARGUMENT IS WAR

ARGUMENT IS WAR	
Target Domain	*Source Domain*
argument	a battle
participants	enemies
advocating one's position	defense
challenging another's position	attack
persuading/not persuading the other(s) of the correctness of one's position	winning/losing

c. His criticisms were *right on target.*
d. You disagree? Okay, *shoot*!
e. Don't use that *strategy.*
f. He *shot down* all of my arguments.

Other examples given by Lakoff and Johnson originate in the source domain of HAND-TO-HAND combat, and are inherited by the richer frame of WAR; e.g., "I've never won an argument with him."

2.5. Characteristic 4: The "non-crossover" structure of the construal members

Unlike the core members, construal members of an MF usually do not have a "crossover" relationship as source and target domains for the core members of that MF or for other construal members, although rarely they may. If they do, the metaphor is usually marked in some way. For example, it is quite common to conceptualize BUSINESS or POLITICS as A RACE:

(4) a. IBM is *ahead in the race* to develop a new supercomputer.
b. At that moment in the American presidential primary race, Dean *was ahead of* Kerry among Democratic voters.

It is much less common to conceptualize the noneconomic aspects of A RACE as BUSINESS or POLITICS (there are always literal economic aspects, of course), or the noneconomic aspects of POLITICS as BUSINESS. In fact, it is difficult to think of noncontroversial examples, and anything that is said requires a very particular, constructed context, or sounds impossible, odd, surprising, shocking, funny, or otherwise grammatically or emotionally unusual; for example:

(5) a. *The lead runner *outspent* her opponents.
This does not mean "spent more time, e.g., in training," even with the metaphor TIME IS A RESOURCE, Special Case: the resource is MONEY.
b. ?Calling an important football player "*the chairman of the board.*"
If this is allowable, it will be humorous.

In general, then, the metaphor mappings involving the construal members are generally unidirectional, with the core members being the source domain: BUSINESS IS WAR, AN ARGUMENT IS WAR, LUST IS PREDATION, but not conventionally *WAR IS BUSINESS, *WAR IS AN ARGUMENT, *PREDATION IS LUST, *BUSINESS IS AN ARGUMENT, *AN ARGUMENT IS BUSINESS, etc.

To put it another way: core member domains appear in metaphor-family metaphors as both source and target. Construal members appear only as target domains in unmarked instances.

3. The COOPERATION MF ("working together")

The basic frame-schema of this family is that of more than one (self-willing) participant performing actions or activities in association with other such participants in order to achieve the same desired mutual or joint goal. The association must not be accidental or random if there is to be prototypical cooperation, and for there to be "cooperation" rather than "interconnection" the entities must have the possibility of opting out of the relationship.[20] (See also section 5 below.) The frame-schema of this MF is given in Table 8a and the core members are given in Table 8b.

20. In one sense the participants cannot opt out of their "FAMILIY," since it is prototypically formed by genetic relationship, but in a functional sense they can choose to leave and not be active participants. Similarly, in specific instances of a job task or a sports match or a battle, the participants cannot readily choose to leave, but in a larger sense they can. This slipperiness of opting out is one reason why COOPERATION and INTERCONNECTION are often confused; however, at a fundamental level it is a key difference.

Table 8a. The Frame-Schema of the COOPERATION MF

Frame-Schema:	"cooperation": "working together"
P → P → G	(P = participant, G = goal)
Some presuppositions:	prototypically 1 goal
	both/all of the cooperators can attain the goal
Some entailments:	the whole may be greater than the sum of the part in attaining the goal (but does not have to be)
Some source domain language: *together, cooperate, collaborate*	
(NOTE: words like "cooperate" and "collaborate" are not as basic as the COMPETIVE "win/lose," "fight," etc.)	
Frame-Schema Real-World Prototype: family	

Table 8b. The core members of the COOPERATION MF

- FAMILY
- FRIENDS
- PARTNERS
- WORK CREW
- SPORTS TEAM
- MILITARY UNIT
- A COMMUNITY
- AN ANIMAL GROUP

In every instance, these groups are presumed to be prototypically not "dysfunctional" in a psychological sense (which in effect means that they are cooperating).

Although the basic-level domains[21] are significantly different, and therefore are listed as separate core members, conceptually these domains can be grouped into four general types of human interactional groups (Table 9).

Table 9. Interactional subgroupings (people)

Human Groups Formed By: (core or construal status not indicated)[22]
- blood relationship (family)
- voluntary association (for example, friends, partners, ideologically based groups, sororities and fraternities [note the kinship language])
- occupation (for example, construction crews, musical groups, theater troupes, military units, sports teams, Robin Hood's Merry Men)
- proximity (for example, communities and neighborhoods, nations)

21. Core members of MFs are basic level categories, but the relationship of metaphorical structure and Rosch's categorization structure (e.g., Rosch et al. 1976, Mervis and Rosch 1981, etc.) is too complex to be discussed here.

Linguistic examples of core and construal members of the COOPERATION MF include the following (statement of the metaphor is given in ex. 6a as a model).

(6) a. My best friend and I are like *sisters.* (FRIENDS ARE FAMILY)
b. He *does his job* for the team. (Said with respect to a baseball player.)
c. You're the *boss.* (Said with respect to many core and construal target domains.)
d. She's a good *citizen.* (Said of, e.g., a tennis player in a core-core metaphor: A SPORTS TEAM IS A COMMUNITY; or of a person in, say, an academic department, in a core-construal metaphor.)
e. "A *Partnership* for a Better America"
f. A *queen* bee and *worker* bees (said of many core and construal target domains; source domain: ANIMAL GROUP)
g. This company is all one big happy *family.*
h. This is a "*Mom and Pop*" store.
i. "*Team* Xerox"; He's not a *team player*, so let's fire him.
j. J. P. Morgan was a *captain* of industry.

In a sense, the COOPERATION subfamily is the inverse of the COMPETITION MF, since the same organization or entity is often viewed or construed as cooperative when viewed as *in*-group, but as competitive when viewed as *out*-group. Therefore, it is not surprising that different aspects of several of the same domains (sports, the military, animals) appear as core members of both.

Once again, virtually any social group may be seen as a construal member of the MF (Table 10).

Also, although SPORTS TEAMS and MILITARY UNITS are kinds of WORK CREWS, experientially they are different basic-level categories.

22. Subject to cultural variation: in some societies, for example, proximity groups might be based on blood relations (kinship groups). The four conceptual types are not equally represented in a given language; thc bias of a culture that identifies people by what work they do rather than by, say, their family lineage, is reflected in its language as well.

Table 10. Some construal members of the COOPERATION MF

- A BUSINESS (with respect to internal organization)
- GOVERNMENT (also internally)
- MARRIAGE
- A CRIMINAL ORGANIZATION
- IDEOLOGICAL GROUPS, *and so on*

Table 11. The COOPERATION MF: Important frame-differentiating elements of the core members

FAMILY	kinship ties, (prototypically) emotional closeness
FRIENDS	emotional closeness without kin ties
PARTNERS	equality of economic/occupational standing
SPORTS TEAM	an adversarial situation (not potentially lethal, literally or metaphorically); requires skill; often roughly egalitarian members + leader
WORK CREW	occupation-related (usually specific occupations as special cases, e.g., ship's crew, theater troupe, orchestra); requires skill; roughly egalitarian "workers" + "foreman"
MILITARY UNIT	an adversarial situation (potentially lethal); a clearly defined and strictly enforced internal hierarchy
COMMUNITY	prototypically physical proximity of residence; related to a form of "political" organization; perhaps (prototypically) roughly egalitarian in, e.g., American folk ideology (NOTE: There is a frequent metaphorical extension to religious organizations.)
ANIMAL GROUP	rationality replaced by instinct, emotion, etc.

Table 11 indicates some of the most important of the prototypical frame-differentiating elements of the core members.

Frame incompatibilities again operate to block some of the symmetry-based core metaphors. It would be very unlikely, for example, to view a prototypical monastic COMMUNITY (a Special Case) as AN irrational, instinctive ANIMAL GROUP. Similarly, the discipline and rigid chain of command (with intermediate ranks) of the prototypical MILITARY UNIT are not considered appropriate for the prototypical FAMILY; hence we do not get, except marked as a cynical or humorous sense, expressions such as the following:

(7) Who's the *general* around this house?[23]

23. A word on HIERARCHY and the internal organization of groups: any group made up of individual entities has an internal structure that defines the rela-

4. The INTERCONNECTION (SYSTEMS) metaphor family ("we're all in this together")

Table 12 presents the basic frame-schema aspects of the INTERCONNECTION MF.

Table 12. The Frame-Schemata of the INTERCONNECTION MF

– One or more entities
– With:
STATIC:
– Whole-to-whole analogical comparison, triggered by salient aspect(s); and/or
– Part-whole configuration/structure of a single interdependent cluster of participants (P)
(prototypically symmetrical)
(may be same or different kinds of parts)
DYNAMIC:
– "Functioning" of the parts together to characterize the function of the system as a whole (e.g., as a machine); and/or
– Regularity and/or repetitiveness of the "functioning"

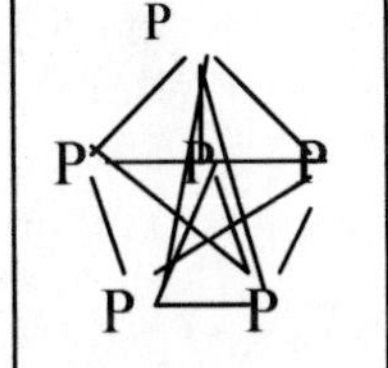

Like the relationship of COMPETITION and COOPERATION, the paired STATIC and DYNAMIC subfamilies of the INTERCONNECTION MF share many core and construal members, depending on whether the focus is on similarity to another entity or configurational structure (STATIC) or active functioning (DYNAMIC).

4.1. The STATIC INTERCONNECTION subfamily

Table 13 gives the core members of this subfamily.

---

tionships of the associated entities to each other, e.g., hierarchical, egalitarian. In a hierarchical organization the entities are ranked or ordered by control, power, dominance, and/or status. The idea of HIERARCHY is often correlated with the metaphors CONTROL IS UP and STATUS IS UP, but need not be (e.g., 'precedence' < Latin "to go before/in front of," via Old French, Middle English).

Table 13. The core members of the INTERCONNECTION/STATIC MF

– ORGANISMS (Special Cases: PEOPLE, ANIMALS, PLANTS)
– CONSTRUCTED OBJECTS (Special Cases: BUILDINGS, TEXTILES/WOVEN [including WEBS, NETS, NETWORKS], MACHINES)
– NATURAL OBJECTS (Special Cases: TOPOGRAPHICAL FEATURES, GEMS, WEATHER)

This subfamily provides many familiar conventional metaphorical expressions.

(8) Core metaphor examples (again, the metaphor is expressed only in the first example):
   a. She's a *pussycat*; his *bark* is worse than his *bite.* (PEOPLE ARE ANIMALS)
   b. She has a *blooming* complexion.
   c. The lion is the *king* of beasts.
   d. He was a *tower* of strength*;* she has bats in her *belfry.*
   e. Cows are milk *machines.*
   f. Car brands: *Pinto*, *Bronco*
   g. The *foot* of the mountain
   h. She's a *fountain* of wisdom.
   i. She's an *iceberg*; he's the *salt* of the earth.
   j. The *heart* of the ruby
   k. He's a *diamond in the rough.*
   l. You are my *sunshine.*

(9) Construal metaphorical expressions:
   a. *Head* of state/*head* of society
   b. *Mother* Russia
   c. The government was *toppled* by a military coup.
   d. The theories *agree with each other.*
   e. The *root* of that theory is …
   f. One *piece* of that theory doesn't *fit.*
   g. The *foundation* of her theory is *sound.*
   h. A *finely-woven* theory, a *patchwork* of a theory
   i. All the *machinery* of his theory was clearly visible.
   j. I got *bogged down* in that theory.

When the language reflects only a "whole : whole" relationship, it often involves a highlighted salient feature that is seen as essentially representative of the source domain entity and some folk model or proverb-like stereotype.

(10) a. Don't be such a *chicken* [cowardly]/*donkey* [stupid]/etc.
b. He's as crazy as a *fox*/brave as a *lion*/dumb as a *dodo*/etc.
c. Plant names: e.g., *pussy*willow (based on texture)

As usual, the conventional frame is a limited representation of our real-world experience. Our experience of the domain of BUILDINGS, for example, includes not only foundations and ground floors and girders, but ceilings, bedrooms, and so on, and is further differentiated by basic-level categories such as HOUSE or OFFICE BUILDING, yet these aspects of BUILDINGS do not appear in the metaphors. (See also Grady 1997a, 1997b; Grady, Taub and Morgan 1996.) As one might expect, the richest and most productive source domains are those of organisms, especially people, but many other previously identified metaphors (see, e.g., Lakoff, Espenson and Schwartz 1991) belong to this MF.

It is normally held in the approach to metaphor based on Lakoff and Johnson 1980 that the main motivation for metaphor is our need to conceptualize an abstraction in terms of something concrete with which we have had bodily experience. Leaving aside for the purposes of this paper the question of socially grounded cultural experience as a foundation for metaphorical understanding, conceptualizing one concrete entity in terms of another as in these examples seems to run counter to this tenet.

However, there is another important basic principle of this approach to metaphor: that metaphors hide and highlight certain aspects of a situation. Here the value of thinking of one entity in terms of another is immediately apparent. To speak of the "foot" of a mountain not only focuses attention on the verticality by comparing it to that most prototypical of verticalities for us, namely, the human body, it also allows other body parts to be projected onto the mountain – its "heart," for example – with all the appropriate conceptual resonances and the same physical and other relationships to the rest of the body-part system. Hearts are not saliently "vertical" but are located in a particular spatial relationship with respect to heads and feet; they are not easily accessible but they are of great importance; and so on.

As with the COMPETITION and COOPERATION MFs, anything that can be seen as or conceived of as an "entity" can be found as a construal member of the INTERCONNECTION/STATIC MF (Table 14).

Table 14. The INTERCONNECTION/STATIC MF: Some construal members

- SOCIAL ORGANIZATIONS
  - Nations/States/Society/Government
  - Business; etc.
- ABSTRACTIONS
  - Plans/Proposals
  - Theories
  - Beliefs/Ideologies
  - Argumentation
  - Discourse
  - Problems/Puzzles
  - Social and historical processes
  - Facts; etc.
- PSYCHOLOGICAL/MENTAL CONSTRUCTIONS
  - The mind
  - The psyche
  - The self; etc.
- TANGIBLE ITEMS (especially image-metaphors/saliency; see above); *and so on*

4.2. The DYNAMIC INTERCONNECTION MF

Just as there is overlap in the core and construal members of COMPETITION and COOPERATION, so there is overlap in the INTERCONNECTION MF between its STATIC and DYNAMIC subfamilies. Again, this overlap both conceptually results from, and linguistically and conceptually causes a focus on, different aspects of the same situation.

That is, just as a military situation in the real world involves both external opponents (COMPETITION) and internal cooperation (COOPERATION), so living creatures and many if not all objects have both "structure" (STATIC INTERCONNECTION) and some kind of what may be called "functionality" (DYNAMIC INTERCONNECTION). That is, they are at least either "on" (capable of action or of being used) or "off"; they "function" either "well" or "badly"; they often go through "stages" (at least of existence as a "functioning" whole versus removal from that state) or at least have duration associated with their existence or "on" state. Some entities have a sort of "external" functioning: rivers flow, clouds rain, night follows day, and summer follows spring, for example.

Examples (11) and (12) present some linguistic examples of both core and construal metaphors. The use of THEORIES as the target domain is repeated in the construal set (examples 12g–12s) with all the core source domains in order to show the operation of the full range of the MF. Again, the nuanced presuppositions, reasoning patterns, and entailments that result from the source domains are important.

(11) Core metaphorical expressions (again, a sample metaphor is given in ex. 11a):
 a. She is in the *flower* of her youth; he's a *budding* artist. (PEOPLE ARE PLANTS)
 b. *Baby* carrots
 c. His *plumbing*'s gone awry.
 d. "*Sick* building syndrome"
 e. I'm just *spinning my wheels.*
 f. He *(sky)rocketed* to the top. (+ STATUS IS UP)
 g. My computer/car *died.*
 h. He had a *breakdown.*

(12) Construal metaphorical expressions:
 a. *Birth* of a nation
 b. He has plans to *strengthen* the economy.
 c. A *well-oiled* government department
 d. To *build* a nation
 e. The nation is *breaking apart* along racial lines.
 f. The *twilight* of the USSR
 g. The theory *died* out.
 h. That theory was *dead and buried.*
 i. The theory was *weakened* by his arguments.
 j. The theory was *rooted out.*
 k. This theory *fathered* many others.
 l. This theory *spawned* many others.
 m. This theory is a natural *outgrowth* of his earlier work.
 n. Many new theories *sprang up* out of the *fertile soil* of his discoveries.
 o. The theory *broke down.*
 p. The theory *collapsed*/was *torn down brick by brick*/*was demolished*/was *buttressed* by her arguments.
 q. She was the *architect* of that theory.
 r. The theory *unravelled*/*came apart at the seams.*
 s. They laboriously *put together* a theory from the available data, but it *fell apart.*

Table 15 presents in brief the frame-schema of the DYNAMIC INTERCONNECTION MF.

Table 15. The Frame-Schema of the INTERCONNECTION/DYNAMIC MF

Collection of components seen as one entity that has:
– Functionality: on/off, vitality;
– Duration/time units, event stages;
– Construction and deconstruction processes

Not surprisingly, the core members are appropriate variants of the STATIC INTERCONNECTION core members, highlighting their "functionality" rather than their "structure" (Table 16).

Table 16. The core members of the INTERCONNECTION/DYNAMIC MF

– ORGANISMS – life stages, vitality, and kinship/procreation	
Special Cases:	PEOPLE
	ANIMALS
	PLANTS
– CONSTRUCTED OBJECTS – functionality	
Special Cases:	BUILDINGS
	TEXTILES/WOVEN (including WEBS, NETS, NETWORKS)
	MACHINES
– NATURAL OBJECTS	
– time units	
Special Cases:	DAY/NIGHT
	YEAR/SEASONS
– dynamic aspects of TOPOGRAPHICAL FEATURES	
Special Cases:	RIVERS
	WEATHER
	NOTE: GEMS are inherently nondynamic, although their long "development" period is referred to as "growth" = "life stages."

Many aspects or characteristics of the ORGANISM frame, especially those dealing with life stages (birth, old age, etc.) and vitality (alive, healthy, etc.), are common to two of the Special Cases (PEOPLE and ANIMALS) or to all three. Kinship terms, on the other hand, tend to be determined by Special Case frames: for example, "father" and "mother" (PEOPLE) vs. "sire" and "dam" (ANIMALS); "family" (PEOPLE) vs. "breed" (ANIMALS) vs. "strain" (PLANTS).

Another set of frame elements has to do with the creation or destruction of entities in the source domains. That is, organisms are "born," but also may be "foaled" or "whelped" or "spawned"; each of these carries its specialized frame of HORSE or DOG or FISH with it, and if used outside that domain is thus marked as derogatory or humorous in some fashion that depends on stereotypes and prototypes. Organisms also "die." CONSTRUCTED OBJECTS, on the other hand, are in the general case "put together" or "assembled," and "break apart" or are "disassembled." There are Special Cases: BUILDINGS are "built" or "constructed," and "topple" or "collapse" or "are demolished"; TEXTILES and other WOVEN objects can be "sewn" or "ripped apart," "knit together" or "unraveled"; MACHINES are "put together" or "assembled," including by specific means (for example, "Her head is *screwed on* right"), and "fall apart" or are "disassembled." Similar specialized frames are carried in other aspects of functionality, such as "tangled" and "disentangled" (TEXTILES/WOVEN), and "broken down" versus "well-oiled" or "greased" (MACHINES).

As one might predict, the DYNAMIC INTERCONNECTION construal members are the same as those of the STATIC INTERCONNECTION MF (see Table 14).

5. Social instantiation

Metaphors may be instantiated or literalized in social or institutional behavior within a culture. This has been pointed out with respect to, say, TIME IS A RESOURCE (cf. Lakoff and Johnson 1980: 65–68; Lakoff, Espenson and Schwartz 1991): for example, in industrialized cultures many workers are paid by the hour. By such instantiation, members of a COMMUNITY who believe that it is an alternative or substitute family (permanently or temporarily) often call each other "sister" or "brother" (e.g., communes, religious institutions such as monasteries or church congregations, fraternities and sororities, some political and social movements). Members of a COMMUNITY who believe that equality between non-kin is the political ideal may refer to each other as "friends" or "comrades." Similarly, a business deal may be concluded with only a handshake, as if between FRIENDS (although this is rarer in cultures or subcultures that conceptualize BUSINESS as a form of COMPETITION).

To review: each core member has a basic, characterizing image schema that is shared, but in our real-life experience each core member scenario also comes equipped with richer, more complex frames. Metaphor families are one way to exploit that complexity for all the variety of nuances it can yield. That is, the different core members provide a variety of potential conceptualizations that maintain the key frame-schema while providing different emphases, since one of the important fundamental effects of metaphor is to highlight certain elements of a situation and hide others.

The richness of specific core member frames is what provides the specific "knowledge" – interpretation – of the situation being labeled. Our use of one core metaphor in a MF as a source domain, and often our use of the MF itself, crucially depends either on how we conventionally are conditioned to understand a situation, or on the details of a particular situation, or on how we wish to present it or ourselves to others, or on some combination of these. All of these constrain what we perceive as the possibilities in the situation, since these frames bring with them characters, scenarios, and especially presuppositions, reasoning patterns, and entailments, all set in motion – consciously or not, conventionally or not – by the use of a metaphor. This immediately suggests that considerations of pragmatics are an integral part of how metaphors are used in our daily lives, and, conversely, that metaphor choice and use should not be ignored by pragmatics. Highlighting and hiding by implicit or explicit choice are among the issues examined by pragmatics; these are also among the things that metaphors do best. Furthermore, this situation has

Table 17. Three predictions about the construal of domains into MFs

Prediction 1:	Using the Principle of Prior Construal, any entity or situation which can be made to fit the basic (abstract) schema of a family can be metaphorically viewed as any of the core members of that family (barring frame incompatibilities). Some possibilities, however, are conventionalized.
Prediction 2:	Any reversal in the bidirectionality of mappings by using a construal member as the source domain for a core member can theoretically be made understandable (unless prevented by frame incompatibilities), but will be marked and therefore humorous, disparaging, shocking, and/or cynical.
Prediction 3:	In the elaboration of the basic frame-schema, each source domain contributes a different frame semantics; these frame differences affect which source domain in the MF is most appropriate for a particular situation, or, conversely, which presuppositions, reasoning patterns, entailments, and so on are carried into the understanding of a particular situation or a particular utterance.

especially important results when the target domain is a construal member of a MF. Table 17 presents three predictions about the effects of the construal of domains into MFs.

5.1. Social effects of domains with multiple construals

Certain domains (e.g., BUSINESS, POLITICS, A LEGAL PROCEEDING, LOVE, etc.) appear as construal members of more than one MF and as core members of none. Consequently, it is these domains that tend most often to be involved in misunderstandings between individuals or across cultures or subcultures, when a construal into one MF is unreflectively accepted by some of the parties involved as if it were a core member and therefore immutable but other parties have one or more different construals. Many of the domains of our life with which we have the most frequent and important interactions in both an individual and a social sense are construal members of MFs – and usually of more than one MF.

The real-world complexity of these domains in fact requires multiple construals. It is impossible to reduce them to only one frame-schema. The fact that we need to conceptualize them metaphorically at all also results in large part from this inherent complexity. The use of these metaphors has a range of consequences, from the trivial to the devastating, as they shape our thinking and our reactions to problems in our own lives and in the broader life of our society. These conventionalized acceptances constrain our view of what is possible either to begin or to change. By using one, many of the elements of the situation are automatically removed from consideration from the very beginning, and, because these metaphors are so conventional, often we do not even recognize that this has happened. We may not even realize that there are alternatives, let alone what those alternatives might be. If we see BUSINESS as competitive only, for example, we will be blind to ways in which "rival" businesses cooperate, and we will base our behavior on what we know about competition. If we see a SOCIETY as based on "us vs. them" or even as "working together," we miss the very real social condition of "we're all in this together."

The very fact of Prior Construal into a given family thus makes some of these choices – viewing talk, say, as a COMPETITIVE "debate" rather than a COOPERATIVE "discussion." The further choice of source domain from among the core members adds an additional, more specific, frame based on experience and therefore richer and more powerful. This increased richness provides more details for the mapping, but also offers an opportunity for additional highlighting or hiding.

BUSINESS, for example, can be viewed in terms of the recognized "Commercial Transaction" frame discussed by Fillmore (1982), but this frame carries no necessary implications of either COMPETITION or COOPERATION. It merely stipulates certain essential participants and actions: a BUYER, a SELLER, some EXCHANGED COMMODITY, and some MEDIUM OF EXCHANGE (e.g., money). Further conceptualizing BUSINESS as WAR, say, allows us to justify, even seek, the total destruction of our rivals (e.g., "*capturing* total control of the market") by a wide range of means, since folk theories, proverbs, and so on also interact with these prototypical frames, and proverbially "all is fair in love *and war.*" (See Morgan 1998.) On the other hand, if we were to conceptualize BUSINESS as a GAME, we would be highlighting the existence of rules, and thereby placing unbreakable constraints on our behavior, introducing the concept of "fair play," and making the tone "fun" and "playful" rather than "serious" and "deadly." Depending on the kind of game, we might even end up with a non-COMPETITIVE "win-win" scenario outside the COMPETITION MF entirely – a far cry from the "win-lose" scenario of WAR or PREDATION. We may not want to do this, but the point is that when we socially conceptualize BUSINESS as part of the COMPETITION MF, we have closed off these options.

Similarly, conceptualizing the relationship between, say, management and unions as COMPETITIVE rather than as INTERCONNECTED makes negotiations over issues such as worker protection, wages, and so on adversarial rather than the mutually satisfactory working out of interdependence.[24]

The possibility of multiple construals thus becomes socially significant when entailments are considered, since construal-member entities, activities, or situations receive most of their entailments from their construal. And since beliefs drive behavior, it is these construals that supply the basic foundations for our daily actions in these common situations – an outcome that becomes especially relevant when people are attempting to change social trends or institutions. Those who might wish to change the American legal system from a dominantly adversarial one to one centered in mediation, for example, must first change the highly dominant, cultur-

24. Since construals into MFs are culturally determined, they may vary cross-culturally or within subgroups of a given culture.

ally conventional construal of the LEGAL interactional domain from the COMPETITION MF to that of COOPERATION or even in some cases INTERCONNECTION.

Table 18 presents the most significant differentiating feature of the three MFs: autonomy allows for a participant to choose not to participate in the relationship, that is, to opt out.

Table 18. Comparison of Metaphor Families

	Participant autonomy?	*Opt-out possible?*
– COMPETITION	Y	Y
– COOPERATION	Y	Y
– INTERCONNECTION (SYSTEMS)	N	N

People often offer "cooperation" as a desirable alternative to "competition" – but when one is in a cooperative relationship one is still acting as an autonomous individual, and therefore one still has the opportunity to choose *not* to cooperate. In this important way "competition" and "cooperation" are opposites. Cooperation may increase the power of the cooperating participants, but at any time any one of them may decide not to continue the cooperation and to return to acting independently. When the participants are part of a "system," this kind of reversion to autonomy is simply not possible – at least not if the system is to continue to function optimally, or sometimes at all.

Cooperation is good, but if the goal is to reach a resolution that is satisfactory to all parties, optimizes their conjoined structure and/or functioning, and maximizes individual structure and/or functioning within that optimized situation, an interconnected, systems way of thinking is required. Only when voluntary removal from the system is *not* possible is interdependence truly recognized. That is, if one realizes that opting out is in fact not an option, one *must* work with the other members of the system to find solutions, instead of fighting or fleeing.

Speakers of English have been much less productive in the application of INTERCONNECTION metaphors than in COMPETITION or COOPERATION ones. That may not be immediately apparent when the list of core members of each MF is compared, but the real test is in the richness of conventionalized detail mapping and in the frequency of application of the metaphors. The increasing familiarity of the Internet (itself a SYSTEMS metaphor of "net" or "web") may change things, but to date the application of SYSTEMS metaphors has remained relatively restricted in conceptual and linguistic practice and in social institutional instantiation. That is, when we have the choice of how to conceptualize construal domains such as BUSINESS or SOCIETY or LIFE, for example, English, at least, has tended to prefer COMPETITION or COOPERATION metaphors (perhaps especially COMPETITION) to the available INTERCONNECTION ones, and to construct beliefs and practices around those choices.

However, having multiple core members in a metaphor family, and in fact having multiple families at all, is a situation that may be conventionally limiting, but is also logically very rich in possibilities. On the one hand, it gives us conventionalized options for highlighting and hiding different elements of frames, constraining our thinking and behavior in conventional ways. On the other hand, the existence of metaphor families allows a space in the case of construal members for creating new applications of a shared frame, with the possibility that these may become conventionalized and ordinary and supportive of desired change.

There has been space here only to suggest the outline of how this might occur, but the pragmatic and social implications for understanding the cultural cognitive models and metaphors through which people react to present situations, and for suggesting applications to potential societal change, are clear and important.

References*

Fillmore, Charles J.
1982 Frame semantics. In: Linguistic Society of Korea (ed.), *Linguistics in the Morning Calm*, 111–137. Seoul: Hanshin.

Gallie, William B.
1956 Essentially contested concepts. *Proceedings of the Aristotelian Society* 31: 167–198.

Grady, Joseph
1997a Foundations of meaning: Primary metaphors and primary scenes. Ph.D. dissertation, University of California, Berkeley.
1997b THEORIES ARE BUILDINGS revisited. *Cognitive Linguistics* 8 (4): 267–290.

* Note: These references are restricted to works cited in the text as the origins of the terms or concepts; much excellent subsequent work has been done that has expanded our understanding.

Grady, Joseph, Sarah Taub, and Pamela S. Morgan
1996 Primitive and compound metaphors. In: Adele Goldberg (ed.), *Conceptual Structure, Discourse and Language*, 177–187. Stanford: CSLI.

Lakoff, George
1987 *Women, Fire, and Dangerous Things: What Categories Reveal about the Mind.* Chicago: University of Chicago Press.

Lakoff, George and Mark Johnson
1980 *Metaphors We Live By.* Chicago: University of Chicago Press.

Lakoff, George, Jane Espenson, and Alan Schwartz
1991 *Master Metaphor List,* 2nd ed. Available as the Conceptual Metaphor Home Page: http://cogsci.berkeley.edu/lakoff.

Mervis, Carolyn and Eleanor Rosch
1981 Categorization of natural objects. *Annual Review of Psychology* 32: 89–115.

Morgan, Pamela S.
1998 Beyond the issues: A linguistic and conceptual study of American public discourse. Ph.D. dissertation, University of California, Berkeley.

Nunberg, Geoffrey D.
1978 *The Pragmatics of Reference.* Ph.D. dissertation. Bloomington, Indiana: Indiana University Linguistics Club.

Rosch, Eleanor, Carolyn Mervis, Wayne Gray, David Johnson and Penny Boyes-Braem
1976 Basic objects in natural categories. *Cognitive Psychology* 8: 382–439.

How cognitive linguists can help to solve political problems

Karol Janicki

Abstract

This chapter includes a brief theoretical part and an applied one. In the former, I refer to the essentialist view of meaning and definitions, that is, roughly, the view that words have essential meanings and that one correct definition of a word/concept is in principle possible. I then list the main points of my own *non-essentialist* view of meaning and definitions, in terms of which I analyze the data in the latter part.

In the second part I discuss the problem of the use of definitions as emerging in the political domain. Two hypotheses are advanced: one is that definitions of words play a significant role in political conflicts. The other is that contemporary politicians are unaware of how a non-essentialist approach to language could possibly solve some of their problems. These hypotheses are tested by analyzing press reports on three political events: the Clinton-Lewinsky scandal, the Florida vote conflict, and the stem cell research debate. Both hypotheses receive considerable support.

The chapter concludes with a list of possible future research questions; these should be geared toward disclosing how widespread in the political domain essentialism actually is, what specific forms it takes, and how, in practical terms, it could be eradicated.

Keywords: essentialism, definitions, meaning, conflict, politics.

1. Introduction

One of the salient features of cognitive linguistics (CL) is its philosophical foundations, which have been formulated relatively clearly and which make cognitive linguistics mark a new epoch in language studies (cf. Lakoff 1982, Lakoff and Johnson 1980). As might be expected, cognitive linguistics had predecessors (for instance, the Sophists in the ancient times and the General Semanticists in the twentieth century). This means that many of the claims that cognitive linguists make are not entirely new. However, what seems to be entirely new and what seems to make cognitive linguistics a milestone is the awareness that accepting CL philosophical foundations leads to treating many non-linguistic phenomena in an entirely new way. In my view, CL, as opposed to other approaches to language, is special in that it allows us to understand many social phenomena around us; CL may be seen as helping us handle these phenomena in a rewarding way.

In section 4 of this chapter I will try to show how CL can help us understand political phenomena and solve political problems. I will investigate in some detail three recent political events: the Clinton-Lewinsky affair, the Florida vote conflict, and the stem cell research debate.

2. Theoretical considerations

2.1. Introduction

The theoretical position that I adopt in this chapter is a non-essentialist view of concepts and meaning (cf. for instance Popper 1945; Hallet 1991; Janicki 1990, 2006). Essentialism (correlating with the objectivist view of the world and the classical view of categorization) refers to a set of beliefs about the world, which have a direct reflection in assumptions about language. In the philosophical tradition, Essentialism goes back to Plato and Aristotle (cf. Popper 1945; Hallet 1991; Lakoff and Johnson 1999). Aspects of Essentialism which are of interest to me in this chapter concern meaning. Aristotle claimed that all things have their essences (Aristotle 1983). For Aristotle, the term that is to be defined is the name of the essence of the thing, and the defining formula is the description of that essence. (Popper 1945)

Aristotelian essentialism has flourished for the last two thousand years. It has taken a variety of forms one of which is the common belief that words have or should have one meaning (cf. Janicki 2006 for examples from linguistics and a fuller discussion of this issue).

Essentialism may take the form of an explicit intellectual commitment, a salient practice, a covert realization, or of combinations of the three. The salient practice of Essentialism most often materializes as explicit what-is-questions (cf. Popper 1945), such as 'what is science?', 'what is sociolinguistics?', 'what is a conflict?', 'what is ethical?', 'what is an explanation?', 'what is morality?', which, it is believed, require one unambiguous answer. Answers to what-is-questions are often thought not to be readily available, but they are believed to be available in principle, independent of how hard it may be to find them. Consider the following example:

> Few problems continue to generate so much endeavor and so much conflict as the problem of style. Even conferences are called to attempt to answer the questions: '*What is style*?', how can we study it? ... Marozean began by admitting that the question of style is as open today as it was two millennia ago. Some progress was made in the nineteenth century when scholars began 'traiter de style comme une object de science', but consequently the question of *what style is* became more pressing ... *Regardless of the amount of effort, money, and time expended on the problem [of establishing what style is] results curiously fail to materialize.*
>
> (my italics. KJ) (Gray 1969: 7–8)

As the above quote clearly shows, defining words/concepts is viewed at least by some as a very serious matter.

As for example Popper (1945), Wittgenstein (1967), Hallett (1991), Lakoff (1987), and Geeraerts (1997) have shown, Essentialism is wrong. The two main reasons for that, according to Popper (1945), are:

(1) It is not at all beyond argument that intuitive definitions, extolled by Aristotle, let us in on the secret of the essence of things designated by the words defined.

(2) Defining words will always require further defining of the words in the definition. We are thus led to an infinite regression of definitions. Not only, Popper claims, do we not achieve much by proposing definitions, but we also lose much by introducing an unnecessary amount of verbosity.

Anyone adhering to the Aristotelian essentialist method of definition reads definitions 'from the left to the right'. For instance, 'A hill *is* a small mountain' whereupon 'a small mountain' is believed to tell us what 'hill' is. The danger of definitional infinite regression is easily seen, as the questions that immediately come to the fore, i.e., 'What is a mountain?' and 'What is small?', elicit answers that will bring forth an array of further questions, thereby continuing the regression. This procedure hardly leads anywhere.

It follows that 'from the left to the right definitions' should not be taken at all seriously. Contrary to common belief, they do not make things simpler, or more precise; they make things more complicated and less precise! And this is primarily because any definition entails the necessity of further definitions with a continuously growing number of terms to be further defined.

The present study combines cognitive linguistics and sociolinguistics in the following way: it adheres to the CL view that words do not have fixed and determinate meanings (cf. for instance Taylor et al. 2003), and it takes up social (socio-political) phenomena including a significant linguistic aspect. Moreover, this study can be treated as work toward *applied* cognitive sociolinguistics, where the CL view on meaning is being applied to solving sociolinguistic problems of practical socio-political significance. Such work is not entirely new of course. I myself drew attention to the connection between cognitive linguistics and applied sociolinguistics in Janicki (1991). More recent examples of elaborating such a connection are Lakoff (1996, 2004) and Morgan (2001).

2.2. A non-essentialist's view

My own non-essentialist position (which correlates with prototype theory) may be traced back to the work of the philosopher Karl Popper (e.g. Popper 1945), to that of general semanticists (e.g., Korzybski 1933; Hayakawa 1939), to that of the integrational linguists (e.g., Harris 1981, 1998) as well as to that of cognitive linguists (e.g., Lakoff 1982, 1987; Johnson 1987; Lakoff and Johnson 1980, 1999; Gibbs 1994; Ungerer and Schmid 1996). But, importantly, its details do not reflect any one single theory advanced by any one single author mentioned here.

As for definitions, following Popper (1945) I view 'from the right to the left' definitions as most rewarding. The 'from the right to the left' perspective yields, with reference to our example above, 'A small mountain is (called) a hill', and should be seen as not aiming at any essence of 'hill'. Truly, the 'from the right to the left definitions' do not explain anything (but Aristotelian definitions did not either). They only introduce one short label for a somewhat longish set of labels; "they cut a long story short" (Popper 1945: 14). Though not explaining anything, the 'from the right to the left definitions' are nevertheless very handy because they save discussion time.

The most important aspects of my theoretical position which are of relevance to my discussion below are the following:

1) Concepts expressed in natural languages are fuzzy. They are fuzzy in the sense that they allow for prototypical and non-prototypical senses and that borderline examples can be given with reference to which people will usually hesitate or be in doubt about; people will tend to

be in doubt about how to classify these examples and which concept to assign them to.

2) Meanings of words are best understood as central prototypical cases and as those that gradually move from the center to the periphery. That is, there is centrality gradience (Lakoff 1987).
3) Most concepts, expressed by words, include a borderline area, which groups examples of those concepts variably assignable to or not to a given concept. That is, there is a fuzzy area allowing to speak of membership gradience (cf. Lakoff 1987).
4) The variable assignment mentioned in 3 above is rendered inter-subjectively, that is, people who belong to identifiable groups assign examples to concepts in similar ways (cf. e.g., Sharifian 2003; Kristiansen 2003).
5) Concepts are grounded in and partly shaped by an individual's experience. Thus, meanings of words, behind which there are concepts understood as mental descriptions, reflect that individual experience, in addition to the experience which is shared with other people around us. That is, concepts are shared to a degree. They are distributed socially across groups and conditioned by individual experience (cf. e.g., Tajfel 1978, 1981; Tajfel and Turner 1979; Sharifian 2003).
6) As there is no one correct nor single meaning of a word, (cf., for instance, Lakoff 1987; Geeraerts 1997; Lakoff and Johnson 1999; Cuyckens et al. 2003; Taylor et al. 2003; Allwood 2003; Janicki 2006), it is an utterly futile task to try and give final unambiguous definitions of words; such definitions are unattainable. The existence of only one correct definition of a word may be thought of as a myth, or an impossibility.
7) Definitions should always be read 'from the right to the left' and not 'from the left to the right'. That is, for instance, 'Measles is an acute contagious viral disease, usually involving the eruption of red spots' should not be understood as saying that measles really is an acute contagious … (reading the definition from left to right), but as saying merely that an acute contagious viral disease, usually involving the eruption of red spots, may be called, or is called, measles (reading the definition from right to left). A 'from the left to the right definition' implies the essentialist view that some correct ultimate meaning can be disclosed; a 'right to the left definition', on the other hand, implies no such thing; it is to be interpreted only as proposing a short label, ('measles' in our example above) to refer to 'an acute contagious viral disease, usually involving the eruption of red spots'. No more. 'From

the right to the left' nonessentialist definitions may be treated as working definitions and they should be sought only to the extent that they may help clarify a point or solve a problem.

3. Research questions, hypotheses, and methods

In the study reported below I intend to investigate the following fundamental research questions:

a) Are politicians concerned with definitions of words?
b) Are politicians aware of how a non-essentialist view of language could possibly solve some political problems?

For question (a) the hypothesis was:

A. Definitions of words play a significant role in political conflicts.

The hypothesis connected to research question (b) was:

B. Politicians are unaware of how a non-essentialist approach to language could possibly solve some of their problems.

Both hypotheses were motivated primarily by personal observation pertaining to mass media.

The data for this chapter were collected from a variety of sources. The main ones were press reports included in the weekly magazines *Newsweek*, *TIME* and *The Economist,* and the daily newspaper The *Washington Post.* The *Newsweek* and *TIME* articles which concerned the Clinton-Lewinsky affair appeared in the second half of 1998 and the first half of 1999. The *Washington Post* issue concerned appeared on September 12, 1998. The data taken from *The Economist* covered a selection of issues between 2000 and 2002. The articles referred to were picked because they were relevant to the topic.

4. Three political conflicts

4.1. The Clinton-Lewinsky case

As is well known to the general public, in 1998 there erupted a scandal featuring the President of the United States Bill Clinton and his intern Monica Lewinsky. The President and the intern had been involved in an affair that was disclosed to the public. The President was accused of having had a sexual relationship with Lewinsky. He officially rejected the charge stating explicitly, among other things, that he had never had a sexual relationship with the intern; 'I did not have sexual relations with that woman' is a well known and often quoted statement that Clinton made during his Jones deposition. Shortly after, it became very clear that Clinton had had oral sex with Lewinsky, which, according to Clinton, did not count as having had sexual relations.

The case became rather complicated as the evidence emerged. By insisting that he had not had sexual relations with Lewinsky, Clinton was accused of having lied. The argument against Clinton was that having had oral sex (which became evident at a certain point) equals having had sexual relations, a contention fully supported by the prosecuting side and vehemently rejected by the defending one. Ultimately, the question was raised whether the President should be impeached on the charge of perjury or, possibly, other crimes and misdemeanors. A conflict around the case erupted (for details cf. also Lakoff, R. 2000; Morgan 2001; Solan 2002). It must be stressed in passing that there is little doubt that the sex case was only a pretext for the Republicans to try to oust their Democratic opponent. In other words, the conflict was part of a political fight between the Republicans and the Democrats. My own interest in the present paper is, however, only in the linguistic aspects of the conflict.

There are two significant facts for the reader of the present chapter to know about with respect to the above case. One is that the legal argument focused around the definition of 'having sexual relations', which, crucially, may be seen as an argument about language. The other is that, to the best of my knowledge, no language expert was called upon to express his or her opinion on the matter. The latter fact is significant particularly as other kinds of experts (e.g. political scientists, lawyers) were present on numerous panels (e.g. CNN panels) organized at that time.

As it became evident in course of the case, the prosecuting party wanted to come through with and impose their own definition of having sexual relations, *in*cluding oral sex. The defending party wanted to come through with and impose theirs – a definition of having sexual relations *ex*cluding the oral touching of the sexual organs. So, there ensued a fight about definitions. As the *TIME* magazine reported:

> At Clinton's deposition, Jones' legal team asked Judge Susan Webber Wright to approve a very precise, three part definition of sexual relations. Clinton's attorney, Robert Bennet objected to the whole definition, but to

the last two parts especially, as being too broad. Wright agreed to disallow parts 2 and 3, leaving only the first, narrowest definition of sex in place.
(Lacayo 1998: 16)

The three-part definition in question was the following:

DEPOSITION OF WILLIAM JEFFERSON CLINTON

Definition of Sexual Relations

For the purposes of this deposition, a person engages in 'sexual relations' when the person knowingly engages in or causes –

1. contact with the genitalia, anus, groin, breast, inner thigh, or buttocks of any person with an intent to arouse or gratify the sexual desire of any person;
2. contact between any part of the person's body or an object and the genitals or anus of another person; or
3. contact between the genitals or anus of the person and any part of another person's body.

Contact means intentional touching, either directly or through clothing.
(Lacayo 1998: 16)

As mentioned above, many concepts are best understood as prototype categories, including typically central, peripheral, and borderline examples (cf. e.g., Rosch 1977, 1978; Lakoff 1987). Central examples are those that people normally agree about. The concept of 'sexual relations' is certainly eligible to join the group of concepts which can be easily handled in terms of prototypes. Like any other concept, 'sexual relations' is a fuzzy concept; various activities have varying degrees of membership in the 'sexual relations' category. It seems reasonable to assume that many people view regular sexual intercourse as the most important and typical example of 'sexual relations'. If this is so, then had Clinton and Lewinsky had sexual intercourse, there would have most probably been agreement among lawyers and the lay public about their having had sexual relations. The case would have been typical and the example central and there would have been few if any arguments about whether we were dealing with sexual relations.

Oral sex, however, appears to be viewed as a significantly less indicative sexual relationship activity. Oral sex seems to be taken by many as either a peripheral or a borderline example of sexual relations. That is why people disagree about whether oral sex is to be judged as an example of sexual relations at all. The disagreement that often occurs around peripheral and borderline examples also occurred in the Clinton-Lewinsky case. The Clinton defense made use of this disagreement and argued for their view that oral sex was not an example of sexual relations. As the *TIME* magazine further reported:

> With that, Clinton may have been given the room to offer a technically 'true' denial to the question of whether he had sex with Lewinsky – even if she happened to perform fellatio on him. The truncated definition characterizes sex in terms of a checklist of body parts, including the genitals, breast and thigh, Oral sex would not necessarily require the President to touch anything on Lewinsky that appears on that list. Strange as it may sound, under one reading of the definition, Lewinsky could have been having sex with him (because she was 'touching the President's genitals') while at the same moment, he was not having sex with her. (At the deposition, Clinton wasn't asked if she had sexual relations with him; just if he had them with her.) There are problems with the legalistic defense. For one thing, if Clinton and Lewinsky did have oral sex, is it really likely that he did not touch any body parts mentioned in the Jones definition? (Lewinsky testified that Clinton fondled her). And because that definition says that a person engages in sex if he or she 'causes' contact with the genitals of 'any person', it could be argued that Clinton caused Lewinsky's contact with his, even if he did not otherwise touch her. He could reply that she was the cause, or at least the active partner while he was merely the passive receiver, but that makes him seem like either an implausibly shrinking violet or a very cool customer. (Lacayo 1998: 16).

Lacayo finally states: "Hiding behind the ultimate tortuous legalism could help the President get through his testimony, but it won't pass the laugh test with the American people – which is why Clinton won't be parsing the meaning of 'sexual relations' in any public statements." (Lacayo 1998: 16)

Lacayo's article is written in a derisive tone with the clear implication that while everybody knows that oral sex equals having sexual relations, Clinton manipulates language to prove otherwise. In other words, Lacayo admits that while Clinton may be scoring a point on strictly definitional-legal grounds, people ('we all') know anyway what the definition of sexual relations really is. The folk perception, according to Lacayo, is different from that of Clinton's and his supporters. Lacayo's *TIME* magazine article largely reflected the view advanced by the prosecuting party. In the Kenneth Starr report (*Washington Post* 1998), we read the following:

> In the Jones deposition on January 17, 1998, the President denied having had 'a sexual affair', 'sexual relations', or 'a sexual relationship' with Mon-

ica Lewinsky … Testifying before the Grand Jury on August 17, 1998, The President acknowledged 'inappropriate intimate contact' with Lewinsky but maintained that his January deposition testimony was accurate … The President maintained that there can be no sexual relationship without sexual intercourse, regardless of what other sexual activities may transpire. He stated that 'most ordinary Americans' would embrace this distinction … The President also maintained that none of his sexual contacts with Lewinsky constitute 'sexual relations' within a specific definition used in the Jones deposition. Under that definition:

A person engages in 'sexual relations' when the person knowingly engages in or causes – (1) contact with the genitalia, anus, groin, breast, inner thigh, or buttocks of any person with an intent to arouse or gratify the sexual desire of any person … 'Contact' means intentional touching, either directly or through clothing.

According to what the President testified was his understanding, this definition 'covers contact by the person being deposed with the enumerated areas, if the contact is done with an intent to arouse or gratify,' but it does not cover oral sex performed on the person being deposed …

In the President's view, 'any person, reasonable person' would recognize that oral sex performed on the deponent falls outside this definition. If Lewinsky performed oral sex on the President, then – under this interpretation – she engaged in sexual relations but he did not.

(*Washington Post* 1998: A29)

As can be easily seen, there was considerable awareness on the part of both the President and the prosecuting party that definitions matter. Interestingly, both parties explicitly or implicitly claimed that their definitions (which are obviously different, as mentioned above) were accepted by all or almost by all Americans.

In August 1998, a *TIME* magazine/CNN poll asked the question: 'If Clinton and Lewinsky did the following, should it be considered sex?' (*TIME* magazine 1998: 38). The poll gave the following results (Table 1).

The table shows that although for very many people (87% in this poll) oral sex defines 'sexual relations', it does not necessarily do so for others. So, even if the statistics in the table are taken very seriously (which they do not have to, be it only for the fact that the question asked was not a general question about the definition of sexual relations but a question clearly geared toward eliciting a response about the Clinton-Lewinsky affair), Clinton had the right to join the 7% of respondents stating that oral sex is not included in having sexual relations. Clinton was clearly

Table 1. What is 'sexual relations'?

	Sexual relations	Not sexual relations
Engaged in oral sex	87%	7%
Touched each other in the genital area either directly or through clothing	69%	25%
Touched each other in areas such as the breasts or buttocks either directly or through clothing	59%	35%
Kissed each other in a romantic way	40%	53%

wrong, however, in claiming that "any person, reasonable person would recognize that oral sex performed on the deponent falls outside this definition" (*Washington Post* 1998: A29).

Interestingly, as the *Newsweek* magazine reports, a Kingsley Institute study from 1991 defining sex showed that only 40% of the respondents defined oral-genital contact as sex (Cowley and Springen 1999). Also interestingly, the respondents referred to themselves as 'moderate to conservative'. Clinton may have then been part of a larger group of people sharing the same definition of sexual relations than commonly admitted.

The question of whether Clinton was or was not involved in sexual relations with Lewinsky is linked with that of perjury. If it could have been proven that Clinton used an illegitimate definition of sexual relations, he could have been charged with perjury. Accepting the definition of sexual relations that he used he could not. As might be expected, the concept of perjury generates problems as well; that is, it is fuzzy. As mentioned in the Kenneth Starr Report, in section VII A – The law of perjury:

> Perjury requires proof that a defendant, while under oath, knowingly made a false statement as to material facts … The 'knowingly' requirement is a high burden: the government must prove the defendant had a subjective awareness of the falsity of his statement at the time he provided it. It is beyond debate that false testimony provided as a result of confusion, mistake, faulty memory, carelessness, misunderstanding, mistaken conclusions, unjustified inferences testified to negligently, or even recklessness does not satisfy the 'knowingly' element. (*Washington Post* 1998: A51)

In the Kenneth Report we read further:

> The Supreme Court has made abundantly clear that it is not relevant for perjury purposes whether the witness intends his answer to mislead, or indeed intends a 'pattern' of answers to mislead, if the answers are truthful or literally truthful. (A51)

And further:

> First, answers to questions under oath that are literally true, but unresponsive to the questions asked, do not, as a matter of law, fall under the scope of the federal perjury statute ... The second clear rule is that answers to questions that are fundamentally ambiguous cannot, as a matter of law, be perjurious. (A51)

Journalists and lawyers, being partly at least conditioned by their ideology, as most ordinary lay people, have their own preferences for one definition of sexual relations or another. This is understandable. Both journalists and lawyers also seem to have a measure of awareness of the openness and ambiguity of meaning and the significance of definitions. As the *Newsweek* magazine reports:

> In any ordinary prosecutor's office, and surely in the chambers of the House Judiciary Committee, the definition of such terms as 'sexual affair', 'sexual relations' and 'sexual relationship' would be seen as vital to a determination whether some violation of law had occurred. The burden that must be met by the OIC (Office of Independent Council) extends beyond showing that the President was wrong on the semantics, it must also show that, because perjury is a specific intent crime, he *knew* he was wrong and *intended* to lie – something that the OIC could not begin to demonstrate. In fact, all the OIC has is a witness who gave narrow answers to ambiguous questions ... One example will suffice to demonstrate the inherent weakness of the OIC's claim. The OIC argues that oral sex falls within the definition of sexual relations and that the President therefore lied when he said he denied having sexual relations. It is, however, the President's good faith and reasonable interpretation that oral sex was outside the special definition of sexual relations provided to him. The OIC simply asserts that it disagrees with the President's 'linguistic parsing' and that reasonable people would not have agreed with him ... (*Newsweek* 1998: 46E)

The awareness of the openness of meaning extends to other concepts related to perjury and impeachment, for example, 'high crimes and misdemeanors'. Speculating about the grounds on which a presidential impeachment may take place, Cloud (1998) rightly states that like 'treason', 'bribery' and 'maladministration', "'high crimes and misdemeanors' sounds like it could mean anything, from murder to jaywalking ... The Constitution gives the House of Representatives sole authority to decide what constitutes grounds for impeachment". (1998: 33)

The discussion above, including the numerous quotations, shows that both journalists and lawyers were indeed aware of the problem that language and definitions did in fact create a problem in handling the concepts crucial to bringing the scandal to a conclusion. These notions include 'sex', 'sexual relations', 'perjury', 'knowingly', 'high crimes and misdemeanors' and many others. Most significantly, however, what neither the journalists nor the legal professionals seemed to able to do is to offer a solution to the problem. They each argued for their definition of the crucial concept of 'sexual relations', giving us the impression that the definition they endorsed is correct in some absolute sense. Whether they really believed that their definitions are correct in some absolute sense cannot be attested. On the surface though, they acted as if they did. Recall both the OIC's and Clinton's claim (cf. above) that people who do not share their definitions of 'sexual relations' (different as these definitions are) are unreasonable!

When the discussion above is now seen in the context of what I claimed about definitions in the theoretical part of this chapter, namely that definitions are never final and unambiguous (cf. points 6–7 above), the solution to the definitional problem in question is very simple. It may be formulated in the following way: there is no one absolute definition of 'sexual relations', 'having sex' and the related concepts against which Clinton's or anybody else's statements could be evaluated. To consider the crucial concept of 'sexual relations' of Clinton's famous 'I did not have sexual relations with that woman', the fact is that neither Clinton nor the Kenneth Starr party is right in some absolute sense. Nor is either of the parties wrong in some absolute sense. 'Sexual relations' may be legitimately defined as either *ex*cluding or *in*cluding 'oral sex'. There is no arbiter that can objectively state that either of the two definitions, or any other, for that matter, is correct and needs to be adhered to. There is no such thing as an essentialist definition of 'sexual relations'. In other words, the left to the right definition of 'sexual relations', like any left to the right definition, cannot ever be reached. There are only two other types of definitions of the concept. One is the real, or functioning, definition, that is, the definition or, rather, definitions that the lay language users (that is, non-linguists) operate with. Some of these definitions were quoted in the *TIME* and *Newsweek* magazines. They are different and they change. Some include oral sex and others do not. Social groups will have different (prototypical) meanings attached to the same term, and there will be individual differences as well (social and other variables were not considered in the newspaper surveys). The other is a right to the left working (technical) definition (cf. point 7 above). Both the Clinton party and the Kenneth Starr parties worked throughout the episode with different working definitions (one including oral sex, and the other excluding it). Neither party had the right to claim, (but they in fact did) that their definition was correct and used by reasonable people. When either definition is matched with some of the available functioning (real) definitions, it can be both accepted and rejected, as ordinary people vary significantly in what they consider to be 'sexual relations'. Even if one of the two definitions is the same or very close to the definition that most people operate with (for instance, the definition that *in*cludes oral sex), this fact does not constitute any proof that the definition shared by most people is correct in any absolute sense. A definition shared by most people is a definition shared by most people. A definition shared by the remaining people is a definition shared by the remaining people. Neither one is more correct in any absolute sense.

Recapitulating, a significant part of the Clinton-Lewinsky episode was a fight about definitions. Since neither party was able to prove the point that their definition was absolutely correct, as a non-essentialist would obviously expect, the openness of language and the principled availability of various definitions of one word or expression had to be acknowledged. What seems to be true in political cases is that in definitional disputes like the one under investigation here, the winning party is the one that manages to impose its definition on others, by whatever means.

4.2. The Florida vote conflict

The Florida vote conflict of the 2000 presidential election in the United States provides us with another example of how definitions count in politics and how they can be decisive in a political struggle. As is commonly known, the Florida vote conflict revolved largely around the concept of the *hole*. The voting ballots were supposed to be punched. Holes that appeared on the ballot as a result of the punch each counted as a valid vote. The problem was, however, that very many votes were disputed because the cards had not been punched through properly and, as a result, the hole was not clear. The reasons for the punching problems (for instance, old and malfunctioning punching machines) are irrelevant to the present discussion. As *The Economist* reports:

> Of the 462,000 votes cast, only 432,000 were found valid when the results were first counted by machine. Of the discarded 30,000 ballots (7% of the total), 19,000 were double-punched – that is, voters had picked two candidates. An additional 11,000 were not properly punched through. This introduced a new political vocabulary: if the punch leaves a flap of paper, it is called a 'hanging chad'; if it does not break the skin, it produces a 'pregnant chad' or 'dimple'. (*The Economist* 2000a: 66)

Importantly, the question that this led to was what kind of punch constituted a valid vote, or, what the definition of a valid vote was.

Non-English language newspapers have also noticed and reported on the definitional quagmire as regards the hole. For instance, on November 21, 2000, the Norwegian newspaper *Bergens Tidende* carried a reprint of the Danish *Jyllands-Posten* article entitled "Hva er et hull?", Eng. "What is a hole?", (*Bergens Tidende* 2000: 10). The paper states:

> Definisjonen av hva et hull er kan tippe kampen om Florida til enten George W. Bush eller Al Gore. Florida høesterett har tatt fatt på saken. (*Bergens Tidende* 2000: 10) Translation (KJ): The definition of what a hole is can decide about the fight in Florida either in favor of George W. Bush or Al Gore. The Florida Supreme Court sets to work on this issue.[1]

Further complications emerged as stating whether the chad is pregnant or hanging was not always easy:

> Republicans have mocked scenes of officials holding up punch cards to see how much light showed through and thus ascertain whether the chad is hanging or merely pregnant. (*The Economist* 2000a: 66)

When a chad is declared to be hanging, further doubts might be raised, namely, how firmly or 'safely' does a chad need to be hanging to be declared hanging and not pregnant any longer. Decisions about this may be taken, though they may not be easy:

> Broward County will count dimpled chads and flaps of confetti attached by three corners. Palm Beach will do the same provided that there is some

1. Note that the State and the Federal Supreme Courts Judges are nominated by the sitting Governor of the State and the President, respectively. This means that the nominations of the judges can be politically and ideologically motivated to a significant degree.

other indication of an intention to vote (such as evidence from other votes on the ballot paper). Indentation and intention are both in the eye of the beholder. The counties have settled on relatively 'permissive' counting of dimples. (*The Economist* 2000b: 72)

And finally, as the Norwegian newspaper rightly reports:

Spørsmalet har endt på høyesteretts bord. Det blir således de sju dommernes oppgave å definiere hva et hull er. Og hull-definisjonen kan tippe president-posten til enten Bush eller Gore. (*Bergens Tidende* 2000: 10) Translation (KJ): The issue has ended up on the table of the Supreme Court. In this way, the task of the six judges is to define what a hole is. And the definition can decide about whether the presidential post goes either to Bush or to Gore.

Similar to the Clinton- Lewinsky case, in the Florida vote affair there seems to have been a measure of awareness that 'what makes a hole' is a crucial question, an answer to which is of utmost political significance. Again, similar to the Clinton-Lewinsky case, the pertinent parties argued about the definitions of valid ballots, and some ridiculed the procedure of detailed checking the voting ballots for clear and unclear holes having been punched through. The various parties argued about dissimilar views of what makes a hole, and thus for what makes a valid vote. That is, some people insisted that only the central, prototypical instantiations of the category (ballots clearly punched through) count as members of the category. Others allowed for non-central, less prototypical instantiaitions (ballots not clearly, or not entirely, punched through, but still punched) to count as members of the category as well. And again like in the Clinton-Lewinsky case, the definition (of a hole) was seen as a problem a solution to which was very difficult to find.

Unlike in the Clinton-Lewinsky case, however, and not surprisingly, no recourse was taken to any common, non-specialist views of the *hole*. In other words, the general public was not consulted on the meaning of the *hole*. Also unlike in the Clinton-Lewinsky case, there were no explicit arguments for any one working definition of the hole. The fact remained, no doubt, that the idea of what kind of punch does or does not make a hole is central. What is crucial for our present discussion is the fact that nobody (to the best of my knowledge) ever said explicitly how the definitional dilemma should be solved from the linguistic point of view. And the solution was very simple, namely, one of the possible definitions (e.g. the one that required that no chad was hanging in any manner) should have been adopted as the working definition (cf. point 7 above) and adhered to in practice throughout the whole procedure of counting the votes (for a discussion of the significance of working definitions in projects, cf. Janicki 2006, especially Chapter 9). As long as several different definitions were used at the various voting stations, the results were unreliable and skewed in different directions.

The confusion over the definition of the hole was exacerbated by the practical procedure of matching a voting card (punched through completely, punched through partly, the chad hanging firmly, the chad being pregnant, etc.) with whatever definition was valid at a particular voting station. This matching was done by human beings and the differences in human perception certainly played a role. Although the matching problems in question could never be entirely eliminated, accepting one working definition of the *hole* would have made things significantly simpler and fairer. Instead, the people concerned painfully argued about what *really* makes a hole, seeking what seemed to be an essentialist/objectivist definition of the concept. Recognizing and acknowledging the fact that such an essentialist/objectivist definition is unattainable as well as accepting one working definition for the whole counting procedure would have been a simple and rewarding solution to the problem (cf. points 6 and 7 above).

4.3. The stem-cell research conflict

The stem-cell research conflict illustrates disagreements about definitions of still other terms.

As *The Economist* reports:

> George Bush has come face to face with the first policy dilemma of the new world of human genetic engineering: should the federal government finance research into stem cells derived from human embryos? Stem cells can transform themselves into the many different cell types that go to make up a body. They hold out the promise of new therapies for diseases like Parkinson's or Alzheimer's. But because such cells are derived from embryos, their extraction upsets many (though, crucially, not all) anti-abortion people. (2001a: 49)

And further:

> Critics of federal funding make three arguments. First, they say, stem-cell research is immoral. Embryos are human life. You cannot (yet) reliably

> extract stem cells from them without killing them. The fact that research into embryonic stem cells will initially be conducted on cells from embryos discarded in the course of in vitro fertility treatments is irrelevant. These are still potentially human beings, and anyway they doubt whether scientists would content themselves with 'discarded' embryos only.
> (*The Economist* 2001a: 49)

Importantly, the idea of stem-cell research being immoral is to be taken as part of the Conservatives' general notion of immorality (cf. Lakoff 1996).

The definitional quagmire involved in the stem-cell research question is to many people a conundrum equal to that involved in the abortion one. In *The Economist*, we read further:

> … the supporters differ on the moral issues. The stem-cell debate is much more complex than that hardly perennial of American ethical dispute, abortion. The abortion debate hinges solely on your attitude to the cells that make up an embryo or fetus. Supporters of abortion rights, who think embryos are not meaningfully persons, can carry the same logic forward to stem-cells effortlessly. But for anti-abortionists, the issue is harder, since it requires balancing two 'pro-life' goods: the life of the embryo against the potential lives saved from research based on its stem cells. (2001a: 50)

A hot debate bordering on the stem-cell research one concerns cloning. Here again, part of the issue pertains to the definition of the 'person'.

> … they (the pro-cloning advocates, KJ) insist that an unimplanted ball of cells is not a person. Some argue it is even less of a potential person that a stem cell derived from in-vitro fertilisation, since cloning uses unfertilised eggs. (*The Economist* 2002: 46)

As can be seen, the issues raised in connection with the stem-cell research, like those raised in connection with the question of abortion, involve definitional disagreements and revolve around the fundamental questions of (a) *what is life*, (b) *what is a human being*, or (c) *what is a person*. Consider the following statement:

> Science has not *yet* pronounced its last word as to when life begins.
> (Stawicka 1990: 4)

The reasoning implied in this statement appears to be essentialist. It can be reconstructed as follows: *When life begins* is a paraphrase of the what-is question *what is the beginning of life*. Science has not yet pronounced the final word on that question, but, in principle, it can do so. Thus, the reasoning runs further, the question of *what is the beginning of life* is ultimately answerable. It is just that scientists need to work longer and harder to find out what the beginning of life really is.

Consider also a case recently reported on in *The Economist*, pondering the question of whether a fetus is a person:

> Is a fetus a person?
>
> Regina Mcknight, a 24-year-old drug addict, has been sentenced to prison for 12 years in South Carolina. Miss McKnight smoked crack cocaine in 1999 while she was pregnant. Her unborn baby died in the eighth month. Miss McKnight, who has three other young children and is now pregnant again, has been convicted of homicide.
>
> ... So far, nearly two dozen other states have rejected the criminal prosecution of pregnant women for behavior that harms their fetuses. This includes the Florida Supreme Court which ruled five years ago that a pregnant woman who had shot herself in the stomach could not be charged under a homicide statute.
>
> The thin-end-of-the-wedge argument against the South Carolina law is, however, less compelling than the unfair way it works in practice. It is mainly applied against drug addicts. Women who drink or smoke or drive recklessly while pregnant, and then deliver a stillborn child, are not being arrested; perhaps because many of them are well-to-do and white and not, like Miss McKnight, poor and black. (*The Economist* 2001b: 54–5)

As far as the linguistic aspect of the stem-cell research conflict is concerned, definitions of the relevant concepts (e.g., life, person, killing) become central. We may posit with a fair amount of certainty that the participants explicitly or implicitly maintain that their definitions are correct while those of their opponents are wrong.

5. Discussion

An analysis of the data pertaining to the three cases described above indicates that definitions of terms play a significant role in political conflict. We may thus claim that the cases analyzed offer extensive support for hypothesis A – "Definitions of words play a significant role in political conflicts".

We may also assume that at least some of the statements made by politicians (cf. in particular the Clinton-Lewinsky case) are a reflection of their essentialist frame of mind. This is because these politicians tend to claim that only their definitions of the terms concerned are correct while those of others are not. This stance is a reflection of the left to the right essentialist view of definitions that words can be defined in some one, final, unambiguous way. Clinton is reported to have claimed that his definition of 'sexual relations' (*ex*cluding oral sex) was correct while the prosecuting politicians claimed that theirs (*in*cluding oral sex) was correct. In the essentialist logic, one can claim that his or her definition is correct (in some absolute sense) only if he or she believes that one correct and unambiguous definition is in principle possible. Of course, we may also assume that a politician may only claim, that is, only say (but not believe), that his or her definition of a word is correct in some absolute sense. In such a scenario the politician would not necessarily be an essentialist; he or she would, however, act as if he or she were one. I offer no further speculation on this point because no explicitly formulated hypothesis on politicians' philosophical beliefs (essentialist, non-essentialist, partly essentialist), as opposed to their overt behavior, was formulated and tested.

As for hypothesis B, "Contemporary politicians are unaware of how a non-essentialist approach to language could possibly solve some of their problems", the materials collected for the present study fully support this hypothesis. While we may speculate about whether politicians are or are not devout or moderate essentialists, there is very little room for speculation as to whether politicians (or their advisors) are aware of how a non-essentialist view of meaning could solve at least some of their problems. The situation is fairly clear, namely, politicians are *not* aware of how a non-essentialist view of meaning could be utilized in their activities. I have not been able to find a single record of politicians' (or political commentators' for that matter) awareness of the fact that definitions of words are never final; that it is an utterly futile task to try and give unambiguous, precise, ultimate, correct, right definitions; that the existence of only one definition of a word may be thought of as a myth, or an impossibility; and that definitions can only be treated as working definitions and that they should be sought only to the extent that they may help clarify a point or solve a problem (cf. points 6 and 7 above). With respect to hypothesis B, then, the reader is asked to believe me that no evidence is available which would indicate that politicians know how the definitional dilemmas could be solved in a non-essentialist way. Interestingly and importantly, this conclusion pertains to the three cases reported above as well as to a variety of other cases which I have studied in some detail and which, however, I do not report on in the present chapter.

6. Future research

Several questions for future research may be suggested:

a) What do politicians know about language?
b) What misconceptions do politicians have about language?
c) Do the definitional disputes reflect politicians' essentialist philosophical beliefs?
d) How wide-spread is essentialism in the political domain?
e) What specific forms does essentialism take in political discourse?
f) How, in practical terms, could essentialism among politicians be combated and possibly eradicated?

Answers to these and related questions would give masses of further substantive evidence of how linguistics can fruitfully be used in analyzing political activities and, possibly, in solving political problems. More specifically, answers to these questions could give us important information on the spread of essentialism as a belief about language. Essentialism thus understood has not been studied extensively. On the contrary, beyond intuitive knowledge we have very little knowledge about how it is reflected in various walks of life, how wide-spread it is, how influential it is, etc. The domain of politics could be a good start for a series of studies in question.

7. Conclusion

In this Chapter I have tried to show how cognitive linguists can be found useful in addressing some political phenomena. I have invoked the non-essentialist view of meaning and definitions, which I assume is shared by many cognitive linguists. By doing so I have tried to indicate that adopting one of the central tenets of cognitive linguistics – that pertaining to meaning – may prove extremely rewarding in handling, and possibly solving, political problems.

Studies of the language of politics within a sociolinguistic perspective are obviously nothing new (cf. for example, Blommaert and Bulcaen 1997 as well as the numerous publications in the journal *Discourse and Society*, published by Sage). I hope to have shown, however, that it might be rewarding to add to these studies a cognitive linguistic dimension – a philosophical one which concerns meaning and definitions. I also hope that the analysis carried out in this Chapter will encourage other researchers to engage in building a more permanent bond between cognitive linguistics and sociolinguistics so that 'cognitive sociolinguistics' can soon become a commonly used label.[2]

References

Allwood, Jens
2003 Meaning potentials and context: some consequences for the analysis of variation in meaning. In: Hubert Cuyckens, René Dirven and John R. Taylor (eds.), *Cognitive Approaches to Lexical Semantics*, 29–65. Berlin/New York: Mouton de Gruyter.

Aristotle
1983 *Metafizyka (Metaphysics)*. Translated from the original Greek by Kazimierz Leśniak. Warszawa: Polish Scientific Publishers.

Bergens Tidende
2000 Hva er et hull? November 21: 10.

Blommaert Jan and Chris Bulcaen (eds.)
1997 *Political Linguistics.* Amsterdam/Philadelphia: Benjamins.

Cloud, John
1998 What exactly are 'high crimes and misdemeanors'? *TIME* Magazine. September 21: 33.

Cowley, Geoffrey and Karen Springen
1999 A second opinion on sex. *Newsweek*, January 25:16.

Cuyckens, Hubert, René Dirven and John R. Taylor (eds.)
2003 *Cognitive Approaches to Lexical Semantics*, 1–28. Berlin/New York: Mouton de Gruyter.

The Economist
2000a Unleashing the dogs of law. November 18: 65–67.
2000b Whatever will they think of next? November 25: 71–77.
2001a The cutting blob of ethical politics. July 7: 49–50.
2001b Is a fetus a person? May 26: 54–55.
2002 Biology and politics. The great cloning debate. May 11: 45–46.

2. This chapter uses data included also in a section of Janicki 2006.

Geeraerts, Dirk
1997 *Diachronic Prototype Semantics. A Contribution to Historical Lexicology.* Oxford: Clarendon Press.

Gibbs, Raymond
1994 *The Poetics of Mind.* Cambridge: Cambridge University Press.

Gray, Bennison
1969 *Style. The Problem and its Solution.* The Hague: Mouton.

Hallet, Garth
1991 *Essentialism. A Wittgensteinian Critique.* Albany: State University of New York Press.

Harris, Roy
1981 *The Language Myth.* London: Duckworth.
1998 *Introduction to Integrational Linguistics.* Oxford: Elsevier Science Ltd.

Hayakawa, S. I.
1939 *Language in Thought and Action.* London: George Allen and Unwin Ltd.

Janicki, Karol
1990 *Toward Non-Essentialist Sociolinguistics.* Berlin/New York: Mouton de Gruyter.
1991 Applying linguistics for peace education. *International Journal of Applied Linguistic* 2: 164–173.
2006 *Language Misconceived. Arguing for Applied Cognitive Sociolinguistics.* Mahwah, New Jersey: Lawrence Erlbaum.

Johnson, Mark
1987 *The Body in the Mind: The Bodily Basis of Meaning, Imagination and Reason.* Chicago: The University of Chicago Press.

Korzybski, Alfred
1933 *Science and Sanity. An Introduction to Non-Aristotelian Systems and General Semantics.* Garden City, N.Y.: Country Life Press Corporation.

Kristiansen, Gitte
2003 How to do things with allophones: Linguistic stereotypes as cognitive reference points in social cognition. In: René Dirven, Roslyn Frank and Martin Pütz (eds.), *Cognitive Models in Language and Thought. Ideology, Metaphors and Meanings*, 69–120. Berlin/New York: Mouton de Gruyter.

Lacayo, Richard
1998 When is sex not 'sexual relations'? TIME Magazine, August 24.

Lakoff, George
1982 *Categories and cognitive models.* Essen: LAUD. Paper N° 96.
1987 *Women, Fire and Dangerous Things. What Categories Reveal about the Mind.* Chicago: The University of Chicago Press.
1996 *Moral Politics.* Chicago: Chicago University Press.
2004 Don't think of an elephant. Know your values and frame the debate. White River Junction, Vermont: Chelsea Green Publishing.

Lakoff, George and Mark Johnson
1980 *Metaphors We Live By*. Chicago: The University of Chicago Press.
1999 *Philosophy in the Flesh*. New York: Basic Books.

Lakoff, Robin T.
2000 *The Language War*. Berkeley: University of California Press.

Morgan, Pamela
2001 The semantics of impeachment: Meanings and models in a political conflict. In: René Dirven, Roslyn Frank and Cornelia Ilie (eds.), *Language and Ideology. Vol. II : Descriptive Cognitive Approaches*, 77–105. Amsterdam/Philadelphia: Benjamins.

Newsweek
1998 The White House Rebuttal. September 21: 46–47.

Popper, Karl
1945 *The Open Society and its Enemies*. Vol. 2. London: Routledge and Kegan Paul.

Rosch, Eleanor
1977 Classification of real-world objects: origins and representations in cognition. In: Philip N. Johnson-Laird and Peter C. Wason (eds.), *Thinking: Readings in Cognitive Science*, 212–222. Cambridge: Cambridge University Press.
1978 Principles of categorization. In: Eleanor Rosch and Barbara B. Lloyd (eds.), *Cognition and Categorization*, 27–48. Hillsdale, N.J.: Lawrence Erlbaum.

Sharifian, Farzad
2003 On cultural conceptualizations. *Journal of Cognition and Culture* 3 (3): 187–207.

Solan, Lawrence
2002 The Clinton Scandal: some legal lessons from linguistics. In: Janet Cotterill (ed.), *Language in the Legal Process*, 180–195. Basingstoke, England: Palgrave Macmillan.

Stawicka, Joanna
1990 With no choice. *Głos Wielkopolski 7–8*. July 4.

Tajfel, Henri
1978 The structure of our views about society. In: Henri Tajfel and Colin Fraser (eds.), *Introducing Social Psychology*, 302–321. Harmondsworth: Penguin Books.
1981 *Human Groups and Social Categories*. Cambridge: Cambridge University Press.

Tajfel, Henri and John Turner
1979 An integrative theory of intergroup conflict. In: William G. Austin and Stephen Worchel (eds.), *The Social Psychology of Intergroup Relations*, 33–53. Monterey, Cal.: Brooks/Cole Publishing Company.

Taylor, John, R., Hubert Cuyckens and René Dirven
2003 Introduction: New directions in cognitive lexical research. In: Hubert Cuyckens, René Dirven and John R. Taylor (eds.), *Cognitive*

Approaches to Lexical Semantics, 1–28. Berlin/New York: Mouton de Gruyter.

TIME Magazine
1998 What is sex. August 10: 38.

Ungerer, Friedrich and Hans-Jörg Schmid
1996 *Introduction to Cognitive Linguistics*. London: Longman.

Washington Post
1998 Special Report. Referral to the United States House of *Representatives Pursuant to Title 28, United States Code, 595 (c)*. A27–A52. September 12.

Wittgenstein, Ludwig
1967 *Philosophical Investigations* (2nd ed.). Oxford: Blackwell.

Subject index

LIBRARY, UNIVERSITY OF CHESTER